Struts 2

with Hibernate 4 Project

for Beginners

Struts 2

with Hibernate 4 Project

for Beginners

Sharanam Shah
Vaishali Shah

Published in the USA by:

Arizona Business Alliance

 SHROFF PUBLISHERS & DISTRIBUTORS PVT. LTD.
Mumbai   *Bangalore*   *Kolkata*   *New Delhi*

Struts 2 With Hibernate 4 Project for Beginners
by Sharanam Shah and Vaishali Shah

Copyright © 2014 Sharanam Shah and Vaishali Shah. All rights reserved.
ISBN 13: 978-93-5110-105-5
Originally printed in India.

Published by Shroff Publishers & Distributors Pvt. Ltd. C-103, T.T.C. Industrial Area,
M.I.D.C., Pawane, Navi Mumbai - 400 703 Tel.: (91-22) 4158 4158 Fax: (91-22) 4158 4141
E-mail: spdorders@shroffpublishers.com. Web: www.shroffpublishers.com
CIN: U22200MH1992PTC067760

Series Editor: Ivan Bayross

Printing History:
First Edition: July 2014

Reprinted in the USA by Arizona Business Alliance.
Under license from Shroff Publishers & Distributors Pvt. Ltd., India.

First USA Reprint: July 2014
ISBN 13: 978-1-61903-005-3

Published by **Arizona Business Alliance LLC** 7169 W. Ashby Drive, Peoria AZ 85383
Tel: 623 297 4448, Fax: 623 687 9524 e-mail: aba.us@hotmail.com

Preface

Welcome to **Struts 2 With Hibernate 4 Project for Beginners!** Thank you for picking up this book.

Thank you for picking up this book.

This book is dedicated to **Janya**, our little princess. Thank you for coming to this world as our daughter. You are the most precious daughter we could ever ask for. We love you more than our life.

About This Book

Day by day, developers are able to get more done in less time. With today's high level languages, development environments, tools and the rapid application development mindset, both developers and managers have become accustomed to extremely fast development cycles.

Programmers are now more inclined to jump directly into development, fearing that every hour they are not writing code will result in an hour of overtime the weekend before the deadline. The process of designing before coding is becoming outdated. Documenting designs is becoming even rarer.

Many developers have never written a design document and cringe at the idea of doing so. Many who are required to, typically generate a lot of interaction diagrams and class diagrams, which do not often express the developer's thought process during the design phase.

This book aims serving students, developers, technical leads and to some extent project managers by demonstrating a structured documented modestly sized project, which will help communicate the software requirements and the design decisions.

What You'll Learn?

Reading this book, Java application developers will get an insight into how professional Web based projects are structured, documented and executed using:

❑   **MySQL Community Server 5.5.28 / Oracle Database 10g** as the <u>data store</u>
❑   **JavaServer Pages** as the <u>view technology</u>

❑ **Struts 2** as the application development <u>framework</u>

An open source Java framework used for building Web applications based on the Servlet and Java Server Pages [JSP] technologies

❑ **Hibernate 4** as the <u>Object Relational Mapping</u> tool

A popular, powerful and a free, open source Object Relational Mapping library for the Java programming language which makes the application portable to all the SQL databases supported by Hibernate

<u>All run on Microsoft Windows.</u>

We've tried to use our extensive application development experience to produce this book that should cover most of the areas that seem to puzzle developers from time to time in their application development career.

Any developer that acquires strong documentation and development skills using this framework will always be in demand and is sure of always being able to make a good living selling these skills to the highest bidder.

This book:

❑ Is a ready reference, with several add-ons and technologies, covering modestly sized project containing a **Back-end** with **Master** and **Transaction** data entry forms and a **Front-end** with application homepage and the **shopping cart**

❑ Addresses the following needs of developers:

How to **document:**

o   Case Study

o   Software Requirement Specifications

o   Project Directory and File Structure

o   Data Dictionary And Table Definitions

o   End User Manual

o   Software Design Document

How to **implement** the following technologies:

o   Shopping Cart

o   Payment Gateway for accepting payments using Credit Cards [Google Wallet]

o   Tag Clouds

o   Session Management

o   Directory

- o Search
- o Dispatch Emails using Java Mail API
- o Using BLOB to store images and PDF files
- o Validations using Struts 2
- o JavaDoc
- o Data Access Object Design Pattern
- o Access based User Management
- o Hibernate based Pagination
- o Restricted page access protection
- o User Authentication Interceptor
- o Custom Error Pages
- o Double Form Submission Prevention
- o Database migration from MySQL to Oracle
- ❑ Is suitable for students, developers, technical leads, project managers, consultants
- ❑ Assumes the reader with a good understanding of Java fundamentals and database programming using the Java Database Connectivity [JDBC] API and some familiarity with Struts 2 and Hibernate 4

To true newcomers to Struts and/or Hibernate, we recommend that you read our earlier book called **"Struts 2 For Beginners"** before diving into project development.

Like all our earlier books, this book builds concepts using simple language, in a step by step, easy to follow manner.

The sections that follow present a rundown of what the book delivers as you work through its content.

This book contains **64** chapters held within **10** sections.

In the first section of the book we give a brief introduction to **Struts 2** and **Hibernate 4**.

The second section begins by defining the project's **Case Study** which describes the Software Development Life Cycle of the project. This section then delves deeply into the project in form of the **Software Requirement Specifications, Project Files** and the **Database Table Structure**.

Section 3 is dedicated to project's **End User Manual**. This section documents the steps [how to use/operate] of using this application/project.

After the reader is familiar with the application and its usage, this book moves towards explaining the actual processes [behind the scenes] that happen when an action is performed from the user interfaces [that are defined in the end user manual]. Section 4 takes care of the **Process Flow** for each module in the project.

The next three sections [fifth, sixth and seventh] of the book hold the **Software Design Documents**. Each module is a separate chapter, just to ensure that the reader, whilst reading, is focused on a single module.

Finally, section 8, depicts how to run the project. This is done by assembling [i.e. bringing all the files together] the project using the NetBeans IDE, followed by deploying the WAR file on a Web server.

Section 9 is for those who are curious to learn the art of migration. This section covers **migrating** the project that was built using **MySQL** as the data store to **Oracle Database 10g**. This is the power that Hibernate 4 brings to the table. Applications can be simply switched to a database of choice without changing the application code spec.

The last section of this book [Appendix] holds a single chapter. This chapter documents the implementation procedure for Google **Wallet**.

This book's accompanying CD-ROM holds downloaded executables of the following:
- Java Development Kit [JDK] 7 Update 9
- NetBeans IDE 7.2
- Struts 2.3.7
- Hibernate 4.1.9.FINAL
- MySQL Community Server 5.5.28
- MySQL Connector/J 5.1.22
- Oracle Database 10g eXpress Edition
- Oracle JDBC Driver [ojdbc6.jar]

Writing this book has been one of the most challenging endeavors we've taken on and it would not have been possible without the help and support from several people.

Acknowledgments

Our sincere thanks go to:

- ❑ Our publisher Mr. Aziz Shroff for bringing up the **X-Team** concept that has brought enormous changes in our lives
- ❑ Our family for their patience, support and love
- ❑ The many programmers who read this book. We welcome both your brickbats and bouquets
- ❑ All those who helped through their comments, feedback and suggestions

If you have any questions, comments or just feel like communicating, please contact us at **enquiries@sharanamshah.com**.

We are now also available on Facebook [http://facebook.sharanamshah.com]. You can Sign up to connect with both of us.

We hope that you will enjoy reading and working through the project in this book as much as we enjoyed documenting and developing it.

For additional information on this book visit:

- ❑ http://www.sharanamshah.com
- ❑ http://www.vaishalishahonline.com

Sharanam & Vaishali Shah

How To Read This Book

This book documents a modestly sized project: **BookShop** - A Web based online shopping cart application. This application is built using **Struts 2** as the application development framework and **Hibernate 4** as the Object Relational Mapping library with **MySQL Community Server 5.5.28** as well as **Oracle Database 10g** as the <u>data store</u>.

While Struts 2 and Hibernate 4 are incredibly powerful, they present a steep learning curve when you first encounter them. Steep learning curves are good. They impart profound insight once you have scaled them. Yet gaining that insight takes some perseverance and assistance. To help you up that learning curve, we strongly recommend that you read at least the basics prior moving on with the project. The basics can be found in one of our earlier books called **Struts 2 For Beginners** [ISBN: 81-8404-665-0, 978-81-8404-665-6].

Now about this book's road map, to make the driving easy, we recommend reading this book as follows:

1. Read through the **Section 1** called *Understanding the Framework* to gain a quick recap to Struts 2 as the application framework and Hibernate 4 as the ORM library

2. Follow Section 2. Since this is a project's book, the next section [**Section 2**] describes the project that this book helps you built. It does this by presenting a Case Study [SDLC of the project being built], followed by the Software Requirements Specification, Table Structures and the Project Files. This section, makes the requirements of the project being built, crystal clear

3. Quickly run through **Section 3**: *End User Manual*. This section helps you visualize the actual application, how it appears and functions

4. After you are done with the first three sections, we strongly recommended to:

    a. Setup the development environment by installing the NetBeans IDE and the MySQL database server and Oracle Database 10g [all are available on this book's CDROM]

    b. Run the Application using **Section 8** [use the code spec from the Book's CDROM - <CDROM Drive>:/Code/MySQL Project/BookShop]

This book's accompanying CDROM holds the project code spec [**BookShop**] in a ready to run state. It also holds a MySQL SQL script [**bms.sql**] file that can be imported to quickly bring up and start using this application. **Section 8** [in detail] explains the steps involved in running the application.

This approach will be very useful. It will let the readers have a running copy of the application, whilst going through the sections to follow.

The readers will be able to quickly correlate every activity of the application with the sections such as:

a. **Section 4:** Process Flow

b. **Section 5:** Backend [Administration] Software Design Documentation

c. **Section 6:** Frontend [Customer Facing] Software Design Documentation

d. **Section 7:** Common Files Software Design Documentation

Whilst going through these sections, you can refer the appendix, to understand the Google Wallet implementation [used in this project as the Payment Gateway].

After you go through all the above mentioned sections, you should be technically ready to understand the **Migration** section [**Section 9**]. This section describes the steps invoked in migrating the application from MySQL 5.5.28 to Oracle Database 10g.

The application developers will definitely appreciate this section.

This is the beauty of Hibernate [Portability across supported databases].

Alright, let's dive in.

Sharanam & Vaishali Shah

Table Of Contents

SECTION I: UNDERSTANDING THE FRAMEWORK

Introduction To Struts 2 Framework

The Java world is very vast. Web application development in this vast world has come a long way with several Integrated Development Environments such as NetBeans, Eclipse and so on which has made creating standard Java based Web applications quite easy.

The main Java based technologies that one commonly uses to develop Web applications are **Servlet** and Java Server Pages [JSP].

Standard Application Flow

In a standard Java EE Web application:

1. Using Web based data entry form information is submitted to the server
2. Such information is handed over to a **Java Servlet** or a **Java Server Page** for processing

3.   The Java Servlet or the JSP:

❑   Interacts with the database

❑   Produces an HTML response

As an application grows in complexity, it becomes more and more difficult to manage the relationship between the **JSP** pages, the **backend business logic** and the **forms** and **validations**. Developers start finding it increasingly difficult to maintain and add additional functionality to the applications.

Both the technologies [**Java Servlets** and **JSP**] <u>mix</u> the **application** and the **business logic** with the **presentation layer** and thus make maintenance very difficult. This is not suitable for large enterprise applications. This means there's something still missing in these technologies which create a gap.

In such scenarios, most experienced developers, split various pieces of an application's functionality into small manageable pieces of code spec. These small pieces of code spec hold a single piece of functionality and when taken together as a whole, forms the basis for an application development framework.

Framework

A framework is a collection of services that provide developers with common set of functionality, which can be reused and leveraged across multiple applications.

A framework usually comes into existence by:

❑   Making generalizations about the common tasks and workflow of a specific domain

❑   Providing a platform upon which applications of that domain can be more quickly built

A framework helps automate all the tedious tasks of the domain and provides an elegant architectural solution to the common workflow of the domain.

A framework allows developers to focus on coding the **business logic** and the **presentation layer** of the application and not the overhead jobs such as heavy code spec to capture user input or to generate drop down list boxes.

Nowadays with several frameworks available, application development projects no longer begin with the question:

Should we use a framework?

Instead, they begin with:

Which framework should we use?

Why Struts?

Struts, a Java based **framework**, allows a clean separation between the application logic that interacts with a database from the HTML pages that form the response.

It cuts time, out of the development process and makes developers more productive by giving them prebuilt components to assemble Web applications from.

Struts is not a technology, it's a framework that can be used along with Java based technologies.

Struts makes the development of enterprise Web application development easier by providing a flexible and extensible application architecture, custom tags and a technique to configure common workflows within an application.

The Struts framework is a strong implementation of the widely recognized **Model View Controller** **design pattern**. The key focus of MVC pattern is separation which is what is desired.

MVC

MVC design pattern is amongst the well developed and mature design patterns in use today and is an excellent fit for Web application development.

By using the MVC design pattern, processing is broken into three **distinct** sections:
- Model
- View
- Controller

Each component of the MVC pattern:
- Has a unique responsibility
- Is independent of the other component

Changes in one component has no or less impact on other component.

The **advantage** that the MVC pattern brings in is:

❑ The business or the model specific logic is not written within the view component

❑ The presentation logic is not written within the model and business layers

This thus allows reusing the component and changing one layer's code spec with minimal effect on the other layers. <u>This is a key point and one of the main benefits of **Struts**</u>.

Application Flow In MVC

In the MVC design pattern, the application flow is mediated by a **Controller**.

The Controller delegates **HTTP requests** to an appropriate **handler**.

A **handler** is nothing more than the set of logic that is used to process the request. In the Struts framework, the handlers are called **Actions**.

The handlers are tied to a **Model** and each handler acts as an adapter or bridge, between the **Request** and the **Model**. A handler or action may use one or more JavaBeans or EJBs to perform the actual business logic.

The Action gets any information out of the request necessary to perform the desired business logic and then passes it to the JavaBean or EJB.

Technically:

❑ Using Web based data entry form information is submitted to the server

❑ The controller receives such requests and to serve them calls the appropriate handler i.e. Action

❑ Action processes the request by interacting with the application specific model code

❑ **Model** returns a result to inform the **Controller** which output page to be sent as a response

Information is passed between Model and View in the form of special **JavaBeans**.

A powerful **Tag Library** allows reading and writing the content of these beans from the presentation layer without the need for any embedded Java code spec.

From the development point of view, Struts:

❑ Provides a **Controller**

❑ Facilitates writing **templates** to form the **View** i.e. the presentation layer [JSP]

❑   Facilitates writing the **Model** code spec

A central configuration file called **struts.xml** binds all these [Model, View and Controller] together.

What Is Struts?

Struts is an application **Framework** for building Web based applications in Java using the Java Enterprise Edition platform.

Struts [formerly located under the **Apache Jakarta Project**] was originally developed by **Craig McClanahan** and donated to the Apache Foundation in May, 2000. It was formerly known as **Jakarta Struts**. Struts is maintained as a part of Apache Jakarta project.

Struts comes with an Open Source license which means it has no cost and its users have free access to all its internal source code.

Today, the Apache Struts Project offers the two major versions of the Struts framework:

❑   **Struts 1** which was recognized as the most popular Web application framework for Java

❑   **Struts 2** originally known as **WebWork 2** is now the best choice which provides elegant solutions to complex problems

What Is Struts 2?

Struts 2 is a brand new framework. It is a completely **new release** of the older Struts 1 Framework. Struts 2 is very simple as compared to Struts 1.

It is the second generation Web application framework based on the **OpenSymphony WebWork framework** that implements the MVC [Model View Controller] design pattern. In other words, Struts 2 is the rebranding of WebWork under the Apache Struts make.

Struts 2:

❑   Uses JavaBeans instead of Action Forms

❑   Is more powerful and can use Ajax and JSF

❑   Can easily integrate with other frameworks such as Webwork and Spring

Struts 2 provides a cleaner implementation of MVC and introduces several new architectural features that make the framework cleaner and more flexible.

Struts 1 And Struts 2

Both versions of Struts provide the following three key components:

❑ A **request** handler that maps Java classes to Web application URIs

❑ A **response** handler that maps logical names to server pages or other Web resources

❑ A **tag library** that helps creating rich, responsive, form-based applications

In Struts 2, all three components have been redesigned and enhanced. Struts 2 is designed to be simpler to use and closer to how Struts was always meant to be.

For those who have used Struts 1, the following section indicates how Struts 2 is different from Struts 1:

❑ Struts 1 used a Servlet controller such as the **ActionServlet** class.

Struts 2 uses a **Filter** to perform the same task.

❑ In Struts 1, an HTML form is mapped to an **ActionForm** instance.

In Struts 2, there are no Action forms which make maintenance easier as there are fewer classes. Here, an HTML form maps directly to a POJO, which does not need a separate data transfer object to be created.

In Struts 2, user inputs can be programmatically validated by simply writing the validation logic in the action class.

❑ Struts 1 provided several tag libraries such as HTML, Bean and Logic that allow using custom tags in JSP.

Struts 2 provides a single tag library that covers all.

❑ Java 5 and Servlet 2.4 are the prerequisites for Struts 2. Java 5 is mandatory because annotations, added to Java 5, play an important role in Struts 2.

❑ Struts 1 action classes had to extend org.apache.struts.action.Action.

In Struts 2 any POJO can be an action class.

❑ In Struts 1, JSTL and the Expression Language [Servlet 2.4] were used to replace the **Bean** and **Logic** tag libraries.

In Struts 2, instead of the JSP Expression Language and JSTL, OGNL is used to display object models in JSP.

❑ Tiles that was available as a subcomponent of Struts 1, has matured to an independent Apache project. It is still available in Struts 2 as a plug-in.

Why Struts 2?

The following are a few reasons why Struts 2 is recommended for Web application development:

❑ **Action** based framework

❑ **Interceptors** for layering cross-cutting concerns away from action logic

❑ **Annotation** based configuration to reduce or eliminate XML configuration

❑ Object Graph Navigation Language [OGNL]: A powerful expression language that transverses the entire framework

❑ Simplified **Actions** which are simple POJOs. Any Java class with execute() method can be used as an Action class

❑ Spring, SiteMesh and Tiles integration

❑ MVC based **tag API** that supports modifiable and reusable UI components

❑ Multiple view options [JSP, Freemarker, Velocity and XSLT]

❑ Plugins to extend and modify framework features

❑ Classes are based on interfaces

❑ Most configuration elements have a default value that can be set and forgotten

❑ Style sheet driven markup which allow creating consistent pages with less code spec

❑ Struts 2 **checkboxes** [Stateful checkboxes] do not require special handling for false values. These checkboxes have the capability to determine if the toggling took place

❑ **Cancel** button can be made to do a different action. For example, Cancel button can be used to stop the current action

❑ **Quick start feature** i.e. many changes can be made on the fly without restarting a Web container

❑ Manual testing time is saved as built-in **debugging** tools are provided for reporting problems

❑ Themes based tag libraries and Ajax tags

❑ Struts 2 supports **AJAX** with features such as:

   o   AJAX based client side validation

   o   Remote form submission support [works with the submit tag as well]

   o   An advanced DIV template that provides dynamic reloading of partial HTML

   o   An advanced template that provides the ability to load and evaluate JavaScript remotely

   o   An AJAX only tabbed Panel implementation

- o   A rich pub-sub event model
- o   Interactive auto complete tag

History Of Struts

Struts was originally created by **Craig R. McClanahan**. It was then donated to the Jakarta project of the Apache Software Foundation [ASF] in 2000.

In June of 2001, Struts 1.0 was released. Since then, many people have contributed both source code and documentation to the project and Struts has flourished

When Craig McClanahan donated Struts to the Apache Jakarta project, it became an open source software. This means that developers can download the source for Struts and modify that code spec as desired for use in their application. The standard code spec provided by ASF remains unaltered.

However, with the growing demand of Web applications, Struts did not stand firm and needed to be changed with demand. So, the team of Apache Struts and another J2EE framework, WebWork of OpenSymphony joined hands together to develop an advanced framework with all possible developing features that will make it developer and user friendly.

The Struts communities and the WebWork team brought together several special features in WebWork 2 to make it more advance in the Open Source world. Later WebWork 2 was renamed to Struts 2 which is more developer friendly with features like Ajax, rapid development and extensibility.

Struts 2 has now reached a point where it is stable and mature enough for production applications. A lot of Web applications all over the world are running production applications based on the Struts 2 framework.

Architecture Of Struts

Before plunging into application development using Struts 2, it's essential to understand the **architecture** of **Struts 2**.

The Struts 2 framework is based on the **MVC** [Model-View-Controller] architecture.

What Is MVC?

A lot of beginners misunderstand MVC to be a Java library or an API. But that is not true.

MVC is a **Design Pattern**.

Design Patterns help define the coding pattern / style.

The MVC architecture separates an **application** into <u>three</u> different parts:
1.   The object **Model** of the application
2.   The **View** through which the user interacts with the application
3.   The **Controller** that controls all the processing done by the application

Model

In an MVC application, the Model is considered the largest and most important part.

The Model represents the enterprise information / data of the application. Anything that an application **persists** becomes a part of Model.

The Model also defines the manner of accessing such data and the business logic for data manipulation.

It is unaware of the way the data will be displayed by the application. It simply serves the data and allows modifying it.

<u>In **Struts 2**, the Model is implemented by the **Action** component</u>.

Struts 2 does not provide any constraints for developing the Model layer of the application.

Even though **Struts 2** is designed for building MVC applications, it **does not dictate** how the Model should be built.

Struts 2 gives the application the flexibility to use any desired approach or technology for building the Model code spec. It can be Enterprise Java Beans [EJB], Java Data Objects [JDO], or the **Data Access Objects** [DAO] pattern. Struts will simply have room for them.

View

The View represents the application's presentation. The View queries the Model for its content and renders it.

The View defines the manner in which the Model i.e. the data / information will be rendered.

The view is independent of the data or the Application Logic changes. It remains the same even if the Business Logic undergoes modification.

A single model can have multiple views for different purposes. For example, an application could have a **Web** interface and a **Wireless** interface. Each interface is separate but both of them use the same **Model**.

The primary purpose of having a View object is to maintain consistency in data presentation with constant Model changes.

A View does not contain:

❑ **Business Logic** such as calculating rate of interest or deleting items from a shopping cart and so on

❑ Code for persisting data to or retrieving data from a data source

Struts 2 provides an out-of-the-box support for using most common view layer technologies as **Results**.

A **View in Struts 2** can be:

❑ HTML/JSP

❑ XML/XSLT

❑ Velocity

❑ Swing

and many more.

Since HTML / JSP is the most common and typical **View** technology used for Java based Web applications, this book uses it.

Controller

All the user interaction between the View and the Model is managed by the Controller. All user requests to an MVC application flow through the Controller. The Controller **intercepts** such requests from View and passes it to the Model for appropriate action.

Based on the result of the action on data, the Controller directs the user to the subsequent view.

The controller does not include any business logic.

It **strictly** exposes only those methods that are included in the Model to the user through the View.

In **Struts 2**, the role of the **Controller** is played by the **Filter Dispatcher**. This is a **Servlet filter** that examines each incoming request to determine the **Action** that will handle the request.

In practical scenario,

A **Model** is the business object that has no user interface

A **View** either:

❑   Determines the updates by **querying** the **Model** for changes
❑   Expects the **Controller** to update the **View** when the view needs to be re-rendered

Keeping the **Model** and **View** separate from one another allows an application's interface to change **independent** of the **Model** layer and vice versa.

The Request Response Paradigm In Struts 2

To understand how the requests and responses are handled in Struts 2, let's take a practical example.

A user desires to view a list of books available to buy using the online Shopping Cart.

Example

The user achieves this by reaching:
www.sharanamshah.com/bookshop/showBooks.action

Doing so, retrieves the data from the **Model** [A database that holds book information] and displays the same as a list in a Web browser.

Technically, this happens as follows:

1.   A user using a Web browser requests for showBooks.action

2.   The **Filter Dispatcher [Controller]** of the Struts 2 framework consults the application
     configuration and determines the appropriate Action

     In this case, the action is **showBooks**

3.   After the **Action** is determined, the **Interceptors** are applied

     Interceptors help applying common functionality to the request such as workflow,
     validation, file upload handling and so on

4.   After the **Interceptors** are applied, the action method is executed

     In this case, the action method when executed retrieves the data i.e. a list of books from
     the database [**Model**]

5.   Finally, the **Result [View]** renders the output to the Web browser that requested it in the
     form of book list

The above defined process is diagrammatically represented as shown in diagram 1.1.

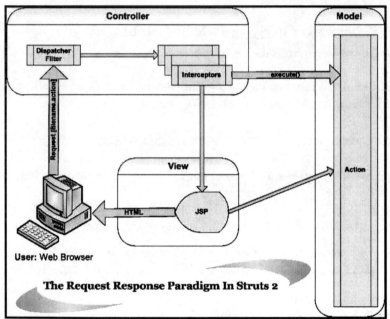

Diagram 1.1: The Request Response Paradigm In Struts 2

Model-View-Controller in **Struts 2** is recognized using with the following **CORE**
components:

1.   Filter Dispatcher

2.   Actions

3. Interceptors

4. Value stack / OGNL

5. Results and Result types [View technologies]

In **Struts 2**, the **Controller** is implemented by a dispatch **Servlet Filter** and **Interceptors**, the **Model** is implemented by **Actions** and the **View** as a combination of **Result Types** and **Results**.

The **Value Stack** and **OGNL** provide common thread, linking and enable integration between the other components.

Struts 2 Framework Architecture

Diagram 1.2 shows the core components that participate in the Request Response paradigm.

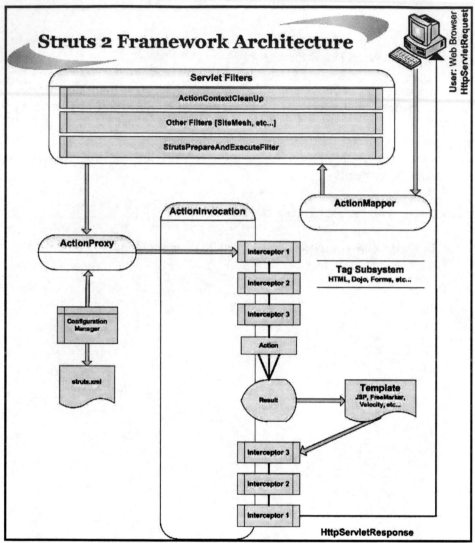

Diagram 1.2: Struts 2 Framework Architecture

Diagram 1.2 depicts the following:

Request Initiation [HttpServletRequest]

A request begins from and ends in a user's Web browser. A request is in form of a URL that represents an **Action**.

A user request is passed through a standard filter chain which makes the actual decision by invoking the required **FilterDispatcher**.

Struts 2 Servlet Filter [StrutsPrepareAndExecuteFilter]

REMINDER

 FilterDispatcher which was used instead of **StrutsPrepareAndExecuteFilter** has been deprecated, since Struts version 2.1.3.

StrutsPrepareAndExecuteFilter plays the role of the **Controller** in Struts 2. This filter handles both the preparation and execution phases of the Struts dispatching process. It is advisable to use this filter when there is no other filter that needs access to the action context information.

This filter when called consults the **ActionMapper** to determine if the request should invoke an **Action**.

The framework handles all of the controller work. The framework only needs to be informed about which request URL maps to which action. This information is passed to the framework using an XML configuration file [struts.xml].

Action Mapper

If the ActionMapper determines that an Action should be invoked, the FilterDispatcher delegates control to the **ActionProxy**.

Action Proxy

The ActionProxy consults the framework **Configuration Manager** [struts.xml] and holds the **configuration** and **context** information to process the request and the **execution** results after the request has been processed.

Action Invocation

The ActionProxy creates an **ActionInvocation**, which is responsible for the command pattern implementation.

ActionInvocation does the following:

1. Consults the configuration being used and then creates an **instance** of the **Action**
2. Invokes the **Interceptors** [if configured] and then invokes the **Action**

3. Once the Action returns, the ActionInvocation looks for a result that is associated with the Action result code spec mapped in struts.xml

4. Executes the result, which involves rendering of JSP or templates

HINT

 In Struts 2, a new action object instance is created for each and every request that is received.

REMINDER

 Interceptors provide a simple way to add processing logic around the method being called on the action.

The prime purpose of having Interceptors is to add cross-functional features in a convenient and consistent manner thus avoiding the need for adding code spec to each and every action.

Interceptors that are set to be called after the action is invoked are executed again in reverse order.

Finally the response returns [if one is generated] back to the user, which completes the current request processing cycle.

This chapter introduces Struts 2 with a brief induction to the **Struts 2 Framework Architecture** and how Struts 2 implements **MVC** with a strong understanding of the **Request–Response paradigm** that Struts 2 follows.

Prerequisites

For those who are completely new to Struts 2, please refer to our earlier book called "**Struts 2 For Beginners**", prior going through this book's project.

Chapter

2

SECTION I: UNDERSTANDING THE FRAMEWORK

Introduction To Hibernate 4

Persistence is one of the most vital piece of an application without which all the data is simply lost.

Often when choosing the persistence storage medium the following fundamental qualifiers are considered:

❑ The length of time data must be persisted

❑ The volume of data

For example,
An HTTP session can be considered when the life of a piece of data is limited to the user's session. However, persistence over several sessions or several users, requires a Database

Large amounts of data should not be stored in an HTTP session, instead a database should be considered.

The type of database that is chosen also plays an important influence on the architecture and design.

In today's object-oriented world, data is represented as OBJECTS. This is often called a DOMAIN model. However, the storage medium is based on a RELATIONAL paradigm. These objects have to be persisted to a relational database.

The inevitable mismatch between the object-oriented code spec [DOMAIN model] and the relational database requires writing a lot of code spec that maps one to the other. This code spec is often complex, tedious and costly to develop.

One of the most popular tools to address the mismatch problem is object-relational mappers.

An object-relational mapper is software used to transform an object view of the data into a relational one and provide persistence services such as CREATE, READ, UPDATE and DELETE [CRUD].

One of the most popular object-relational mappers is the open source Hibernate project. Hibernate acts as a layer between the application and the database by taking care of loading and saving of objects.

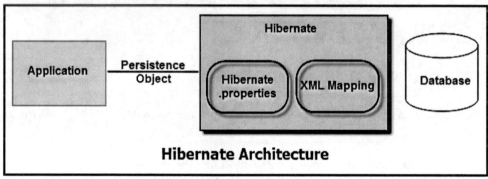

Diagram 2.1

About Hibernate

Hibernate applications are cheaper, more portable and more resilient to change.

Hibernate is a popular, powerful and a free, open source Object Relational Mapping library for the Java programming language. It can be used both in standalone Java applications and in Java EE applications using Servlets or EJB - Session Beans.

Hibernate was developed by a team of Java software developers around the world led by Gavin King, JBoss Inc. [now part of Red Hat] and later hired the lead Hibernate developers and worked with them in supporting Hibernate.

Hibernate allows the developer to focus on the objects and features of the application, without having to worry about how to store them or find them later.

Hibernate provides a framework for mapping an object oriented domain model to a traditional relational database.

Hibernate provides mapping between:

❏ The Java classes and the database tables
❏ The Java data types and SQL data types

Hibernate also provides data query and retrieval facilities. It generates the SQL calls and relieves the developer from manual result set handling and object conversion, keeping the application portable to all supported SQL databases, with database portability delivered at very little performance overhead.

When dealing with the database programming, it can significantly speed up the productivity and simplify the procedure of development.

To use Hibernate:

❏ Java bean classes [POJOs] that represents the table in the database are created
❏ The instance variables of the class are mapped to the columns in the database table

Hibernate allows performing operations SELECT, INSERT, UPDATE and DELETE on the database tables by automatically creating the required SQL query.

Architecture Of Hibernate

Hibernate is made up of the following three components:

Connection Management

Hibernate's Connection management service provides efficient management of the database connections. Database connection is the most expensive portion of an application that allows interacting with the database.

Transaction Management

Transaction management service provides the ability to execute more than one database statements at a time.

Object Relational Mapping

Object relational mapping is a technique of mapping the data representation from an object model to a relational data model. This part of Hibernate is used to SELECT, INSERT, UPDATE and DELETE records from the underlying database tables.

Usually a populated object of a POJO is passed to **Session.save()**. Hibernate reads the state of the variables of that object and executes the necessary SQL query.

A Quick Overview Of Hibernate

Hibernate makes use of persistent objects commonly called as **POJO** [Plain Old Java Object] along with XML mapping documents for persisting objects to the database layer.

HINT

 POJO refers to a simple Java object that does not serve any other special role or implement any special interfaces of any of the Java frameworks such as EJB, JDBC, DAO and so on.

Hibernate uses runtime reflection to determine the persistent properties of a class. The objects to be persisted are defined in a mapping document, which serves to describe the persistent fields and associations, as well as any subclasses or proxies of the persistent object.

The mapping documents are compiled when the application starts. These documents provide the framework with the necessary information about a class. Additionally, they are used in support operations such as generating the database schema or creating stub Java source files.

Reviewing Typical Hibernate Code Spec

The Authors Table

This table stores the author details.

Column Name	Data Type	Size	Null	Default	Constraints
AuthorNo	Integer	10	No	- -	Primary Key
Description	An identity number of the author				
FirstName	Varchar	30	No	- -	- -
Description	The first name of the author				
LastName	Varchar	30	No	- -	- -
Description	The last name of the author				

Hibernate Configuration File [hibernate.cfg.xml]

Hibernate configuration file holds information needed to connect to the persistent layer and the linked mapping documents.

Here, either the data source name or JDBC details can be specified. These details are required for hibernate to make JDBC connection to the database.

<mapping-resource> refers to the mapping document that contains mapping for domain object and database table columns:

```
1   <?xml version="1.0" encoding="UTF-8"?>
2   <!DOCTYPE hibernate-configuration PUBLIC "-//Hibernate/Hibernate Configuration DTD 3.0//EN"
    "http://hibernate.sourceforge.net/hibernate-configuration-3.0.dtd">
3   <hibernate-configuration>
4    <session-factory>
5     <property name="hibernate.dialect">org.hibernate.dialect.MySQLDialect</property>
6     <property name="hibernate.connection.driver_class">com.mysql.jdbc.Driver</property>
7     <property name="hibernate.connection.url">jdbc:mysql://localhost:3306/bms</property>
8     <property name="hibernate.connection.username">root</property>
9     <property name="hibernate.connection.password">123456</property>
10    <property name="hibernate.default_catalog">bms</property>
11    <mapping resource="Authors.hbm.xml"/>
12   </session-factory>
13  </hibernate-configuration>
```

POJO [Authors.java]

To use Hibernate, it is required to create Java classes [POJO's] that represents the table in the database and then map the instance variables of the class with the columns in the database table. After which Hibernate can be used to perform operations on the database such as SELECT, INSERT, UPDATE and DELETE.

Hibernate automatically creates the SQL query to perform these operations.

```
1   package beans;
2
3   public class Authors {
4       private int AuthorNo;
5       private String FirstName, LastName;
6       public Authors() {
7       }
8       public int getAuthorNo() {
9           return AuthorNo;
10      }
11      public void setAuthorNo(int AuthorNo) {
12          this.AuthorNo = AuthorNo;
13      }
14      public String getFirstName() {
15          return FirstName;
16      }
17      public void setFirstName(String FirstName) {
18          this.FirstName = FirstName;
19      }
20      public String getLastName() {
21          return LastName;
22      }
23      public void setLastName(String LastName) {
24          this.LastName = LastName;
25      }
26  }
```

Hibernate is not restricted in its usage of property types. All Java JDK types and primitives such as String, char, Date and so on can be mapped, including classes from the Java collections framework.

These can be mapped as values, collections of values or associations to other entities.

Mapping Document [Authors.hbm.xml]

Each persistent class [POJO] needs to be mapped with its configuration file.

The following code spec represents Hibernate mapping file for the Authors class:

```
1   <?xml version="1.0" encoding="UTF-8"?>
2   <!DOCTYPE hibernate-mapping PUBLIC "-//Hibernate/Hibernate Mapping DTD 3.0//EN"
    "http://hibernate.sourceforge.net/hibernate-mapping-3.0.dtd">
3   <hibernate-mapping>
4    <class name="beans.Authors" table="authors">
5     <id name="AuthorNo" type="integer">
6      <column name="AuthorNo"/>
7      <generator class="increment"/>
8     </id>
9     <property name="FirstName" type="string">
10     <column length="30" name="FirstName" not-null="true"/>
11    </property>
12    <property name="LastName" type="string">
13     <column length="30" name="LastName" not-null="true"/>
14    </property>
15   </class>
16  </hibernate-mapping>
```

Hibernate mapping documents are straight forward.

<class> maps a table with corresponding class.

<id> represents the primary key column and its associated attribute in the domain object. It represents the database IDENTIFER [primary key] of that class, Hibernate can use identifiers only internally.

<property> represent all other attributes available in the domain object.

Performing Database Operations

Here is how Hibernate can be used in an application.

A typical Hibernate application begins with configuration that is required for Hibernate.

Hibernate can be configured in two ways, Programmatically or using a Configuration file.

In Configuration file based mode, Hibernate looks for configuration file **hibernate.cfg.xml** in the classpath.

Based on the resource mapping provided, Hibernate creates mapping of tables and domain objects.

In the programmatic configuration method, the details such as JDBC connection details and resource mapping details are supplied in the program using Configuration API.

Prior performing database operations, a Hibernate session needs to be created.

Creating The Session Factory

Here, the application retrieves the Hibernate Session.

Hibernate **Session** is the <u>main runtime interface</u> between a Java application and Hibernate.

SessionFactory allows applications to create hibernate session by reading hibernate configurations file **hibernate.cfg.xml:**

```
1  sessionFactory = new Configuration().configure().buildSessionFactory();
2
3  Session session = sessionFactory.openSession();
```

Performing A Database Operation [Insert]

```
1   Transaction tx = session.beginTransaction();
2
3   Authors newAuthor = new Authors();
4   newAuthor.setFirstName("Sharanam");
5   newAuthor.setLastName("Shah");
6
7   session.save(newAuthor);
8
9   tx.commit();
10
11  session.close();
```

After the Hibernate session is available, to insert data in the Authors table, a transaction is required.

After specifying the transaction boundaries, application can make use of persistent Java objects and use session for persisting to the database.

Hence, an object of the Authors class is created and the required data is assigned to that object using the SETTER methods.

Finally, the Authors object is passed to the Hibernate session object's **save()** to save this as a new record in the database table.

The transaction is committed and the session is closed.

REMINDER

 AuthorNo is set to automatically increment in the Mapping document
<generator class="**increment**"/>

Hence, it's not set using the SETTER method.

Performing A Database Operation [Select]

```
1  ArrayList arrayList = null;
2
3  String SQL_STRING = "FROM Authors";
4
5  Query query = session.createQuery(SQL_STRING);
6
7  ArrayList list = (ArrayList)query.list();
8
9  for(int i=0; i<list.size();i++)
10 {
11     System.out.println(list.get(i));
12 }
13
14 session.close();
```

Here, the domain object called Authors is queried.

Hibernate automatically generates the SELECT SQL query and returns the result.

This result is retrieved and placed in an ArrayList object. This object is typically used in a JSP to display the records available in that object.

Prerequisites

Hibernate is an amazing technology. With a little experience and the power of Java 5 annotations, it's possible to build a complex database-backed application with ease.

It's often noticed that once a developer builds an application using Hibernate, the developer will never ever want to go back to the traditional method.

To true newcomers to the Hibernate API, it's recommended to gain at-least some basic knowledge before diving into this book's project.

Chapter 13 of our earlier book called **"Struts 2 For Beginners"** will definitely help the newcomers gain the required knowledge on Hibernate and its **integration** with Struts 2.

Chapter 3

SECTION II: ABOUT THE PROJECT

The Project Case Study

The Web has come a long way in the last few years. Today, visitors want more than a pretty website design. They need meaningful and efficient E-Commerce websites packed with interactive elements that let them indicate their requirements to the business houses.

Running an online business requires flexible tools that are at the cutting edge of technology.

Once such popular E-Commerce Web application is online shopping.

Online Shopping has made the life of the customers easier. Now, the customer has more variety, easier way of searching and browsing and more consistent modes of payment.

Building an online shopping cart has become possible due to enhancement of Internet technologies used to develop Web applications. These Web applications are some business supporting websites which make a product accessible to the customer in an easier and efficient manner.

A standard online shopping Web application must:

❑ Support the customers efficiently

❑ Successfully market the products

❑ Support online credit card processing

❑ Provide easy payment and checkout options

❑ Provide detailed transaction/sales reports

These features make the e-business thrive in a relentlessly competitive Web environment.

In this book, we would be developing an Online Shopping Web Application, which can be used to search and buy products online. Both the customer and the owner would be benefited by the use of this website which helps them to commence their transactions in a better, consistent and reliable manner.

This application will provide a large range of categories and products for the customers. The site will change the business domain of the client from local to international. Customers from all over world can search and browse for the available products. A customer can select the products, place order and make the payment for the selected items.

Software Requirements

This project/application will be built using the following applications and APIs:

❑ JDK 7 Update 9

❑ NetBeans 7.2

❑ Struts 2.3.7 API

❑ Hibernate 4.1.9.FINAL API

❑ MySQL 5.5.28 / Oracle Database 10g XE

❑ MySQL Connector/J 5.1.22 /Oracle JDBC 6

Software Development Life Cycle Of The Project

This project is a Web application, which will be developed using the **Struts 2** as the Web Application Framework and **Hibernate 4** as the Object-Relational Mapping [ORM] library.

Requirement Analysis

This is the first part in the life cycle of any project. Here the requirements of the end user are gathered and analyzed. This project development is based on this analysis.

Usually the client is asked the following questions:

❑   What are the requirements of the client?

❑   What requirements are expected to be fulfilled by the project?

These are the questions, which must be answered before moving on to the next stage of the project development.

Client Side Requirements

The client is a book shop owner who desires to make their products [books] accessible to the customers in an efficient manner.

This project should help them in:

❑   Maintaining a detailed record of the following:

  o   Available categories and products associated with each category

  o   Authors who have written these books

  o   Publishers who have published these books

❑   Making each book available for all customers to see, browse and buy online

❑   Adding, deleting, modifying various categories of books

❑   Adding, deleting, modifying the book details

❑   Adding, deleting, modifying various authors of books

❑   Adding, deleting, modifying various publishers of books

❑   Accepting orders and payments from customers

❑   Viewing transactions [orders placed] performed by the customers

Customer Side Requirements

The customers must be able to access the application to browse the required books. They must be able to search the available books, add them into the shopping cart, place order and make online payment using credit cards.

The requirements once analyzed help in creating a platform to design the software.

Software Design

The software designing phase can be divided into two separate phase i.e. high level and low level. In the high level phase, all the interfaces and forms are designed and the way of input and output is decided.

The formats of input and output are finalized and a framework of all the interfaces or the Web pages is designed.

This high level designing is done according to the requirement specification. All the interfaces should be designed, keeping in mind the need and convenience of the user.

Based upon the output of the high level design phase, a detailed design of the application is developed. This is called the low level design phase, which gives proper details such as functions of various modules of the application, number of classes and so on.

The Design Pattern

This application will follow the Model View Controller [MVC] design paradigm separating the application in three layers:

- **Model:** Application State
- **View:** Presentation Layer [JSP]
- **Controller:** Routing of Application Flow

Section 4: Process Flow, Section 5: Backend Software Design Documentation and *Section 6: Frontend Software Design Documentation* take care of the High Level and Low Level Software Design Phase.

The most important thing about this project is that it is developed using Struts 2 and Hibernate 4, which is becoming standard for developing well structured Java based Web applications.

This application [based on these requirements] will be bifurcated as:

- Backend [Administration - For The Client]
- Frontend [Customer Facing]

Backend [Administration - For The Client]

This includes various functionalities related to the administrator who will be the client and its employees.

A valid set of username and password from a person having appropriate privileges is required to log in to this module.

After gaining access to the system, the administrator can add, delete and update various items, categories, authors and publishers.

Customer Module

A customer is a user of the site who browses / searches the website for the products of choice. The customer can add the desired products into the shopping cart.

A customer can also place an order for the selected products and make an online payment using a credit card.

Data Flow Diagram

The Context level Data Flow Diagram [DFD], shown in diagram 3.1 can be helpful to understand the basic functioning of the project. The arrow shows the flow of data from one person to another through various processes.

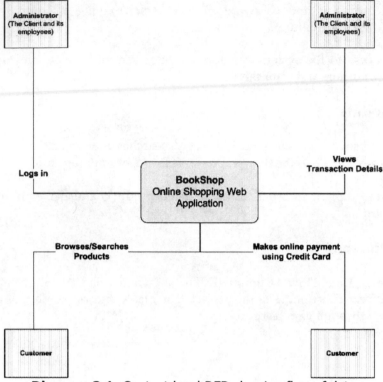

Diagram 3.1: Context level DFD showing flow of data

Development

In this phase, all the designed user interfaces and other supporting code files are written.

Various components like JSP pages, JavaBeans [POJO's] and some other classes are developed.

The code is written and compiled and all developed components are put together in a standard manner to work together.

The projects complete source code can be found on this book's accompanying CDROM.

The project folder is named **BookShop**.

The reader can copy the project folder [BookShop], update the configuration files with the appropriate database username / password, build it using an IDE like NetBeans and deploy the .WAR on a Web server of choice.

Diagram 3.2 presents the home page of this Web application.

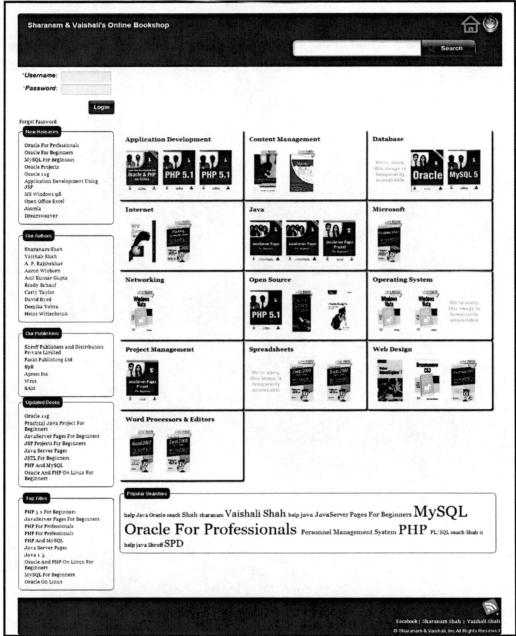

Diagram 3.2: Home page of the BookShop application

This chapter discussed the various phases of the life cycle of this project and also provided a brief description of the software requirements and what a reader should know prior to starting this project.

Every phase is critical. The development of the next phase totally depends upon the outcome of the previous one. Hence a proper requirement specification helps in a better design and a better design makes the life of developer easier.

Chapter

4

SECTION II: ABOUT THE PROJECT

Software Requirements Specification

Backend Modules

Login

Objective	To allow a system user to login to the system
Actors	Book shop employee, Book shop owner, System administrator
Pre-Condition	Person trying to log in should have the System User or the System Administrator privileges
Post-Condition	Actors successfully authenticate themselves and log in to the system

Steps

1. System User navigates to the homepage
2. System User clicks Administration

3. System displays the Administration Login Page with a data entry form to capture the following:

Form Field	Type	Unique	Required	Max Size
Username	Text box	Yes	Yes	- -
Password	Text box	Yes	Yes	- -

4. System User enters the username and the password

5. System User clicks Login [Refer A-1]

6. System authenticates the username and password. If found valid, the system displays Manage Transactions

Alternate Steps

A-1: Invalid User

System displays a message indicating that the username or password is not valid.

Data Validations

Basic form validation must be done before submitting the form:

a. Required fields

    i.   Username

    ii. Password

Manage Countries

All countries where authors, publishers or end users reside should be managed via the application.

This includes the ability to view all the countries, add a new country, edit and delete an existing country.

View Countries

Objective	To view a list of all Countries
Actors	Book shop employee, Book shop owner, System administrator
Pre-Condition	Users have sufficient privileges to view all countries At least one Country exists
Post-Condition	Actors view all the available countries

Steps

1. User navigates to the backend [site administration] login page

2. User logs in successfully

3. System displays the backend home page with Countries as one of the menu options

4. User selects the Countries option to view existing countries [Refer A-1]

5. System displays a list of all countries currently in the system

Alternate Steps

A-1: No existing countries

System displays a message indicating that there are no countries existing in the system.

Add Countries

Objective	To add a new Country
Actors	Book shop employee, Book shop owner, System administrator
Pre-Condition	Users have sufficient privileges to add countries
Post-Condition	Actors successfully add a new country

Steps

1. User navigates to the backend [site administration] login page

2. User logs in successfully

3. System displays the backend home page with Countries as one of the menu options

4. User selects the Countries option to add a new country

5. System displays a data entry form to capture the following:

Form Field	Type	Unique	Required	Max Size
Country	Text box	Yes	Yes	25

6. User enters all required information in the fields

7. User selects option to save data [Refer A-1]

8. System saves data and creates the new country

9. System refreshes the page to reflect the newly added countries

Alternate Steps

A-1: User selects Cancel

System does not save any user entered data.
System does not create a new country.

Edit Countries

Objective	To edit an existing Country
Actors	Book shop employee, Book shop owner, System administrator
Pre-Condition	Users have sufficient privileges to edit countries
Post-Condition	Actors successfully edit an existing country

Steps

1. User navigates to the backend [site administration] login page
2. User logs in successfully
3. System displays the backend home page with Countries as one of the menu options
4. User selects the Countries option to view and edit existing countries [Refer **A-1**]
5. Users clicks the desired country for editing
6. System displays a data entry form pre-populated with the existing form data
7. User edits the desired information in the fields
8. User selects option to save data [Refer A-2]
9. System saves data and updates the existing country
10. System refreshes the page to reflect the updated list of countries

Alternate Steps

A-1: No existing countries

System displays a message indicating that there are no countries existing in the system.

A-2: User selects Cancel

System does not save any user entered data.
System does not update the country.

Delete Countries

Objective	To delete an existing Country
Actors	Book shop employee, Book shop owner, System administrator
Pre-Condition	Users have sufficient privileges to delete countries
Post-Condition	Actors successfully delete an existing country

Steps

1. User navigates to the backend [site administration] login page

2. User logs in successfully

3. System displays the backend home page Manage Countries as one of the menu options

4. User selects Manage Countries option to view and delete existing countries [Refer A-1]

5. User selects the Delete link of the desired information to delete an existing country

6. System deletes the country only if that country is not referenced by a customer or an author or a publisher in the system [Refer A-2]

7. System refreshes the page to reflect the updated list of countries

Alternate Steps

A-1: No existing countries

System displays a message indicating that there are no countries existing in the system.

A-2: Country is referenced by a customer, author and publisher

System displays a message indicating that the record(s) cannot be deleted as they are associated with exiting data.
System does not delete the country.

Data Validations

Basic form validation must be done before submitting the forms:

a. Required fields

   i. Country

Manage States

All states where authors, publishers or end users reside should be managed via the application.

This includes the ability to view all states, add a new state, edit and delete an existing state.

View States

Objective	To view a list of all States
Actors	Book shop employee, Book shop owner, System administrator
Pre-Condition	Users have sufficient privileges to view all locations
	At least one State exists
Post-Condition	Actors view all the available states

Steps

1. User navigates to the backend [site administration] login page
2. User logs in successfully
3. System displays the backend home page with States as one of the menu options
4. User selects the States option to view existing states [Refer A-1]
5. System displays a list of all states currently in the system

Alternate Steps

A-1: No existing states

System displays a message indicating that there are no states existing in the system.

Add States

Objective	To add a new State
Actors	Book shop employee, Book shop owner, System administrator
Pre-Condition	Users have sufficient privileges to add states
Post-Condition	Actors successfully adds a new state

Steps

1. User navigates to the backend [site administration] login page
2. User logs in successfully
3. System displays the backend home page with States as one of the menu options
4. User selects the States option to add a new state

5. System displays a data entry form to capture the following:

Form Field	Type	Unique	Required	Max Size
State	Text box	No	Yes	25

6. User enters all required information in the fields

7. User selects option to save data [Refer A-1]

8. System saves data and creates the new state

9. System refreshes the page to reflect the newly added states

Alternate Steps

A-1: User selects Cancel

System does not save any user entered data.
System does not create a new state.

Edit States

Objective	To edit an existing State
Actors	Book shop employee, Book shop owner, System administrator
Pre-Condition	Users have sufficient privileges to edit states
Post-Condition	Actors successfully edit an existing state

Steps

1. User navigates to the backend [site administration] login page

2. User logs in successfully

3. System displays the backend home page with States as one of the menu options

4. User selects the States option to view and edit existing states [Refer A-1]

5. Users clicks the desired state for editing

6. System displays a data entry form pre-populated with the existing form data

7. User edits the desired information in the fields

8. User selects option to save data [Refer A-2]

9. System saves data and updates the existing state

10. System refreshes the page to reflect the updated list of states

Alternate Steps

A-1: No existing states

System displays a message indicating that there are no states existing in the system.

A-2: User selects Cancel

System does not save any user entered data.
System does not update the state.

Delete States

Objective	To delete an existing State
Actors	Book shop employee, Book shop owner, System administrator
Pre-Condition	Users have sufficient privileges to delete states
Post-Condition	Actors successfully delete an existing state

Steps

1.   User navigates to the backend [site administration] login page

2.   User logs in successfully

3.   System displays the backend home page with States as one of the menu options

4.   User selects the States option to view and delete existing states [Refer A-1]

5.   User selects the Delete link of the desired information to delete an existing state

6.   System deletes the state only if that state is not referenced by a customer or an author or a publisher in the system [Refer A-2]

7.   System refreshes the page to reflect the updated list of states

Alternate Steps

A-1: No existing states

System displays a message indicating that there are no states existing in the system.

A-2: State is referenced by a customer, author and publisher

System displays a message indicating that the record(s) cannot be deleted as they are associated with exiting data.
System does not delete the state.

Data Validations

Basic form validation must be done before submitting the forms:

a.   Required fields

    i.   State

Manage Authors

All author's details should be managed via the application.

This includes the ability to view all the authors, add a new author, edit and delete an existing author.

View Authors

Objective	To view a list of all Authors
Actors	Book shop employee, Book shop owner, System administrator
Pre-Condition	Users have sufficient privileges to view all authors At least one Author exists
Post-Condition	Actors view all the available authors

Steps

1.   User navigates to the backend [site administration] login page

2.   User logs in successfully

3.   System displays the backend home page with Authors as one of the menu options

4.   User selects the Authors option to view existing authors [Refer A-1]

5.   System displays a list of all authors currently in the system with the following information:

    ❑   Name of the Author

    ❑   Speciality of the Author

    ❑   Photograph of the Author

Alternate Steps

A-1: No existing authors

System displays a message indicating that there are no authors existing in the system.

Add Authors

Objective	To add a new Author
Actors	Book shop employee, Book shop owner, System administrator
Pre-Condition	Users have sufficient privileges to add authors
Post-Condition	Actors successfully add a new author

Steps

1. User navigates to the backend [site administration] login page

2. User logs in successfully

3. System displays the backend home page with Authors as one of the menu options

4. User selects the Authors option to add a new author

5. System displays a data entry form to capture the following:

Form Field	Type	Unique	Required	Max Size
First Name	Text box	No	Yes	25
Last Name	Text box	No	Yes	25
Address Line 1	Text box	No	No	50
Address Line 2	Text box	No	No	50
Country	Drop down list box	No	No	- -
State	Drop down list box	No	No	- -
City	Text box	No	No	50
Pincode	Text box	No	No	15
Birthdate	Date picker	No	No	- -
Degree	Text box	No	Yes	25
Email Address	Text box	Yes	Yes	50
Photograph	File upload	No	No	- -
Speciality	Text Area	No	Yes	60 cols 5 rows

6. User enters all required information in the fields

7. User selects option to save data [Refer A-1]

8. System saves data and creates the new author [Refer A-2]

9. System refreshes the page to reflect the newly added authors

Alternate Steps

A-1: User selects Cancel

System does not save any user entered data.

System does not create a new author.

A-2: Duplicate Email Address

User enters an email address that already exists.
System displays a message that the email address already exists.
System does not create a new author.

Edit Authors

Objective	To edit an existing Author
Actors	Book shop employee, Book shop owner, System administrator
Pre-Condition	Users have sufficient privileges to edit authors
Post-Condition	Actors successfully edit an existing author

Steps

1. User navigates to the backend [site administration] login page

2. User logs in successfully

3. System displays the backend home page with Authors as one of the menu options

4. User selects the Authors option to view and edit existing authors [Refer A-1]

5. Users clicks the desired author for editing

6. System displays a data entry form pre-populated with the existing form data

7. User edits the desired information in the fields

8. User selects option to save data [Refer A-2]

9. System saves data and updates the existing author [Refer A-3]

10. System refreshes the page to reflect the updated list of authors

Alternate Steps

A-1: No existing authors

System displays a message indicating that there are no authors existing in the system.

A-2: User selects Cancel

System does not save any user entered data.
System does not update the author.

A-3: Duplicate Email Address

User enters an email address that already exists.
System displays a message that the email address already exists.
System does not update the author.

Delete Authors

Objective	To delete an existing Author
Actors	Book shop employee, Book shop owner, System administrator
Pre-Condition	Users have sufficient privileges to delete authors
Post-Condition	Actors successfully delete an existing author

Steps

1. User navigates to the backend [site administration] login page

2. User logs in successfully

3. System displays the backend home page with Authors as one of the menu options

4. User selects the Authors option to view and delete existing authors [Refer A-1]

5. User selects the Delete link of the desired information to delete existing authors

6. System deletes the author only if that author is not referenced by a book in the system [Refer A-2]

7. System refreshes the page to reflect the updated list of authors

Alternate Steps

A-1: No existing authors

System displays a message indicating that there are no authors existing in the system.

A-2: Author is referenced by a book

System displays a message indicating that the record(s) cannot be deleted as they are associated with exiting data.
System does not delete the author.

Data Validations

Basic form validation must be done before submitting the forms:

a. Required fields

    i. First Name

    ii. Last Name

    iii. Degree

    iv. Email Address

b. Duplicate entries not allowed

    i. Email Address

c. Email Address should be well formed and valid

Manage Publishers

All publisher's details should be managed via the application.

This includes the ability to view all the publishers, add a new publisher, edit and delete an existing publisher.

View Publishers

Objective	To view a list of all Publishers
Actors	Book shop employee, Book shop owner, System administrator
Pre-Condition	Users have sufficient privileges to view all publishers At least one Publisher exists
Post-Condition	Actors view all the available publishers

Steps

1. User navigates to the backend [site administration] login page

2. User logs in successfully

3. System displays the backend home page with Publishers as one of the menu options

4. User selects the Publishers option to view existing publishers [Refer A-1]

5. System displays a list of all publishers currently in the system with the following information:

    ❑ Name of the Publisher

    ❑ Email Address of the Publisher

Alternate Steps

A-1: No existing publishers

System displays a message indicating that there are no publishers existing in the system.

Add Publishers

Objective	To add a new Publisher
Actors	Book shop employee, Book shop owner, System administrator
Pre-Condition	Users have sufficient privileges to add publishers
Post-Condition	Actors successfully add a new publisher

Steps

1. User navigates to the backend [site administration] login page

2. User logs in successfully

3. System displays the backend home page with Publishers as one of the menu options

4. User selects the Publishers option to add a new publisher

5. System displays a data entry form to capture the following:

Form Field	Type	Unique	Required	Max Size
Publisher Name	Text box	Yes	Yes	50
Email Address	Text box	Yes	Yes	50
Address Line 1	Text box	No	No	50
Address Line 2	Text box	No	No	50
Country	Drop down list box	No	No	- -
State	Drop down list box	No	No	- -
City	Text box	No	No	50
Pincode	Text box	No	No	15

6. User enters all required information in the fields

7. User selects option to save data [Refer A-1]

8. System saves data and creates the new publisher [Refer A-2]

9. System refreshes the page to reflect the newly added publishers

Alternate Steps

A-1: User selects Cancel

System does not save any user entered data.

System does not create a new publisher.

A-2: Duplicate Email Address

User enters an email address that already exists.
System displays a message that the email address already exists.
System does not create a new publisher.

Edit Publishers

Objective	To edit an existing Publisher
Actors	Book shop employee, Book shop owner, System administrator
Pre-Condition	Users have sufficient privileges to edit publishers
Post-Condition	Actors successfully edit an existing publisher

Steps

1. User navigates to the backend [site administration] login page

2. User logs in successfully

3. System displays the backend home page with Publishers as one of the menu options

4. User selects the Publishers option to view and edit existing publishers [Refer A-1]

5. Users clicks the desired publisher for editing

6. System displays a data entry form pre-populated with the existing form data

7. User edits the desired information in the fields

8. User selects option to save data [Refer A-2]

9. System saves data and updates the existing publisher [Refer A-3]

10. System refreshes the page to reflect the updated list of publishers

Alternate Steps

A-1: No existing publishers

System displays a message indicating that there are no publishers existing in the system.

A-2: User selects Cancel

System does not save any user entered data.
System does not update the publisher.

A-3: Duplicate Email Address

User enters an email address that already exists.
System displays a message that the email address already exists.
System does not update the publisher.

Delete Publishers

Objective	To delete an existing Publisher
Actors	Book shop employee, Book shop owner, System administrator
Pre-Condition	Users have sufficient privileges to delete publishers
Post-Condition	Actors successfully delete an existing publisher

Steps

1. User navigates to the backend [site administration] login page

2. User logs in successfully

3. System displays the backend home page with Publishers as one of the menu options

4. User selects the Publishers option to view and delete existing publishers [Refer A-1]

5. User selects the Delete link of the desired information to delete an existing publisher

6. System deletes the publisher only if that publisher is not referenced by a book in the system [Refer A-2]

7. System refreshes the page to reflect the updated list of publishers

Alternate Steps

A-1: No existing publishers

System displays a message indicating that there are no publishers existing in the system.

A-2: Publisher is referenced by a book

System displays a message indicating that the record(s) cannot be deleted as they are associated with exiting data.
System does not delete the publisher.

Data Validations

Basic form validation must be done before submitting the forms:

a. Required fields

    i.   Publisher Name

    ii. Email Address

b. Duplicate entries not allowed

    i.   Email Address

c. Email Address should be well formed and valid

Manage Categories

All categories of the books should be managed via the application.

This includes the ability to view all the categories, add a new category, edit and delete an existing category.

View Categories

Objective	To view a list of all Categories
Actors	Book shop employee, Book shop owner, System administrator
Pre-Condition	Users have sufficient privileges to view all categories
	At least one Category exists
Post-Condition	Actors view all the available categories

Steps

1. User navigates to the backend [site administration] login page

2. User logs in successfully

3. System displays the backend home page with Categories as one of the menu options

4. User selects the Categories option to view existing categories [Refer A-1]

5. System displays a list of all categories currently in the system

Alternate Steps

A-1: No existing categories

System displays a message indicating that there are no categories existing in the system.

Add Categories

Objective	To add a new Category
Actors	Book shop employee, Book shop owner, System administrator
Pre-Condition	Users have sufficient privileges to add categories
Post-Condition	Actors successfully add a new category

Steps

1. User navigates to the backend [site administration] login page

2. User logs in successfully

3. System displays the backend home page with Categories as one of the menu options

4. User selects the Categories option to add a new category

5. System displays a data entry form to capture the following:

Form Field	Type	Unique	Required	Max Size
Category	Text box	Yes	Yes	25
Description	Text area	No	Yes	70 cols 5 rows

6. User enters all required information in the fields

7. User selects option to save data [Refer A-1]

8. System saves data and creates the new category

9. System refreshes the page to reflect the newly added categories

Alternate Steps

A-1: User selects Cancel

System does not save any user entered data.
System does not create a new category.

Edit Categories

Objective	To edit an existing Category
Actors	Book shop employee, Book shop owner, System administrator
Pre-Condition	Users have sufficient privileges to edit categories
Post-Condition	Actors successfully edit an existing category

Steps

1. User navigates to the backend [site administration] login page

2. User logs in successfully

3. System displays the backend home page with Categories as one of the menu options

4. User selects the Categories option to view and edit existing categories [Refer A-1]

5. Users clicks the desired category for editing

6. System displays a data entry form pre-populated with the existing form data

7. User edits the desired information in the fields

8. User selects option to save data [Refer A-2]

9. System saves data and updates the existing category

10. System refreshes the page to reflect the updated list of categories

Alternate Steps

A-1: No existing categories

System displays a message indicating that there are no categories existing in the system.

A-2: User selects Cancel

System does not save any user entered data.
System does not update the category.

Delete Categories

Objective	To delete an existing Category
Actors	Book shop employee, Book shop owner, System administrator
Pre-Condition	Users have sufficient privileges to delete categories
Post-Condition	Actors successfully delete an existing category

Steps

1. User navigates to the backend [site administration] login page

2. User logs in successfully

3. System displays the backend home page with Categories as one of the menu options

4. User selects the Categories option to view and delete existing categories [Refer A-1]

5. User selects the Delete link of the desired information to delete an existing category

6. System deletes the category only if that category is not referenced by a book in the system [Refer A-2]

7. System refreshes the page to reflect the updated list of categories

Alternate Steps

A-1: No existing categories

System displays a message indicating that there are no categories existing in the system.

A-2: Category is referenced by a book

System displays a message indicating that the record(s) cannot be deleted as they are associated with exiting data.
System does not delete the category.

Data Validations

Basic form validation must be done before submitting the forms:

a. Required fields

    i.   Category

    ii. Description

Manage Users

All users of the administration department should be managed via the application.

This includes the ability to view all the users, add a new user, edit and delete an existing user.

View Users

Objective	To view a list of all Users
Actors	Book shop employee, Book shop owner, System administrator
Pre-Condition	Users have sufficient privileges to view all users
	At least one User exists
Post-Condition	Actors view all the available users

Steps

1. User navigates to the backend [site administration] login page

2. User logs in successfully

3. System displays the backend home page with Users as one of the menu options

4. User selects the Users option to view existing users [Refer A-1]

5. System displays a list of all users currently in the system with the following information:

   ❑ Name of the User

   ❑ Email Address of the User

   ❑ Username of the User

Alternate Steps

A-1: No existing users

System displays a message indicating that there are no users existing in the system.

Add Users

Objective	To add a new User
Actors	Book shop employee, Book shop owner, System administrator
Pre-Condition	Users have sufficient privileges to add users
Post-Condition	Actors successfully add a new user

Steps

1. User navigates to the backend [site administration] login page

2. User logs in successfully

3. System displays the backend home page with Users as one of the menu options

4. User selects the Users option to add a new user

5. System displays a data entry form to capture the following:

Form Field	Type	Unique	Required	Max Size
First Name	Text box	No	Yes	25
Last Name	Text box	No	Yes	25
Email Address	Text box	Yes	Yes	50
Username	Text box	Yes	Yes	25

Form Field	Type	Unique	Required	Max Size
Password	Text box	No	Yes	8
Manage Countries	Check box	No	No	- -
Manage States	Check box	No	No	- -
Manage Authors	Check box	No	No	- -
Manage Publishers	Check box	No	No	- -
Manage Categories	Check box	No	No	- -
Manage Users	Check box	No	No	- -
Manage Books	Check box	No	No	- -
Manage Customers	Check box	No	No	- -
Manage Transactions	Checkbox	No	No	- -

6.   User enters all required information in the fields

7.   User selects option to save data [Refer A-1]

8.   System saves data and creates the new user [Refer A-2]

9.   System refreshes the page to reflect the newly added users

Alternate Steps

A-1: User selects Cancel

System does not save any user entered data.
System does not create a new user.

A-2: Duplicate Email Address and/or Username

User enters an email address and/or a username that already exists.
System displays a message that the email address or the username already exists.
System does not create a new user.

Edit Users

Objective	To edit an existing User
Actors	Book shop employee, Book shop owner, System administrator
Pre-Condition	Users have sufficient privileges to edit users
Post-Condition	Actors successfully edit an existing user

Steps

1.   User navigates to the backend [site administration] login page

2.   User logs in successfully

3. System displays the backend home page with Users as one of the menu options

4. User selects the Users option to view and edit existing users [Refer A-1]

5. Users clicks the desired user for editing

6. System displays a data entry form pre-populated with the existing form data

7. User edits the desired information in the fields

8. User selects option to save data [Refer A-2]

9. System saves data and updates the existing user [Refer A-3]

10. System refreshes the page to reflect the updated list of users

Alternate Steps

A-1: No existing users

System displays a message indicating that there are no users existing in the system.

A-2: User selects Cancel

System does not save any user entered data.
System does not update the user.

A-3: Duplicate Email Address and/or Username

User enters an email address and/or a username that already exists.
System displays a message that the email address or the username already exists.
System does not update the user.

Delete Users

Objective	To delete an existing User
Actors	Book shop employee, Book shop owner, System administrator
Pre-Condition	Users have sufficient privileges to delete users
Post-Condition	Actors successfully deletes an existing user

Steps

1. User navigates to the backend [site administration] login page

2. User logs in successfully

3. System displays the backend home page with Users as one of the menu options

4.   User selects the Users option to view and delete existing users [Refer A-1]

5.   User selects the Delete link of the desired information to delete an existing user

6.   System deletes the user only if the user being deleted is not Admin [Refer A-2]

7.   System refreshes the page to reflect the updated list of users

Alternate Steps

A-1: No existing users

System displays a message indicating that there are no users existing in the system.

A-2: Admin User being Deleted

System displays a message indicating that it cannot be deleted.
System does not delete the user.

Data Validations

Basic form validation must be done before submitting the forms:

a.   Required fields

    i.   First Name

    ii.   Last Name

    iii.   Email Address

    iv.   Username

    v.   Password

b.   Duplicate entries not allowed

    i.   Email Address

    ii.   Username

c.   Email Address should be well formed and valid

Manage Books

All books authored and published should be managed via the application.

This includes the ability to view all the books, add a new book, edit and delete an existing book.

View Books

Objective	To view a list of all Books
Actors	Book shop employee, Book shop owner, System administrator
Pre-Condition	Users have sufficient privileges to view all books At least one Book exists
Post-Condition	Actors view all the available books

Steps

1. User navigates to the backend [site administration] login page

2. User logs in successfully

3. System displays the backend home page with Books as one of the menu options

4. User selects the Books option to view existing books [Refer A-1]

5. System displays a list of all books currently in the system with the following information:
   - ❑ Name of the Book
   - ❑ ISBN of the Book
   - ❑ Synopsis of the Book
   - ❑ The image of the Cover Page of the Book
   - ❑ The Download links of TOC and Sample Chapter of the Book

Alternate Steps

A-1: No existing books

System displays a message indicating that there are no books existing in the system.

Add Books

Objective	To add a new Book
Actors	Book shop employee, Book shop owner, System administrator
Pre-Condition	Users have sufficient privileges to add books
Post-Condition	Actors successfully add a new book

Steps

1. User navigates to the backend [site administration] login page

2. User logs in successfully

3. System displays the backend home page with Books as one of the menu options

4. User selects the Books option to add a new book

5. System displays a data entry form to capture the following:

Form Field	Type	Unique	Required	Max Size
Book	Text box	No	Yes	25
Publisher	Drop down list box	No	Yes	- -
Category	Drop down list box	No	Yes	- -
Cover Page Image	File upload	No	No	- -
ISBN	Text box	Yes	Yes	15
Edition	Text box	No	Yes	25
Year	Text box	No	Yes	4
Cost	Text box	No	Yes	8
First Author	Drop down list box	No	Yes	- -
Second Author	Drop down list box	No	No	- -
Third Author	Drop down list box	No	No	- -
Fourth Author	Drop down list box	No	No	- -
Synopsis	Text area	No	Yes	60 cols 5 rows
About Authors	Text area	No	Yes	60 cols 5 rows
Topics Covered	Text area	No	No	60 cols 5 rows
Contents of CDROM	Text area	No	No	60 cols 5 rows
TOC	File upload	No	No	- -
Sample Chapter	File upload	No	No	- -

6. User enters all required information in the fields

7. User selects option to save data [Refer A-1]

8. System saves data and creates the new book

9. System refreshes the page to reflect the newly added books

Alternate Steps

A-1: User selects Cancel

System does not save any user entered data.
System does not create a new book.

Edit Books

Objective	To edit an existing Book
Actors	Book shop employee, Book shop owner, System administrator
Pre-Condition	Users have sufficient privileges to edit books
Post-Condition	Actors successfully edit an existing book

Steps

1. User navigates to the backend [site administration] login page

2. User logs in successfully

3. System displays the backend home page with Manage Books as one of the menu options

4. User selects the Manage Books option to view and edit existing books [Refer A-1]

5. Users clicks the desired book for editing

6. System displays a data entry form pre-populated with the existing form data

7. User edits the desired information in the fields

8. User selects option to save data [Refer A-2]

9. System saves data and updates the existing book

10. System refreshes the page to reflect the updated list of books

Alternate Steps

A-1: No existing books

System displays a message indicating that there are no books existing in the system.

A-2: User selects Cancel

System does not save any user entered data.
System does not update the book.

Delete Books

Objective	To delete an existing Book
Actors	Book shop employee, Book shop owner, System administrator
Pre-Condition	Users have sufficient privileges to delete books
Post-Condition	Actors successfully delete an existing book

Steps

1. User navigates to the backend [site administration] login page
2. User logs in successfully
3. System displays the backend home page with Manage Books as one of the menu options
4. User selects the Manage Books option to view and delete existing books [Refer A-1]
5. User selects the Delete link of the desired information to delete an existing book
6. System deletes the book
7. System refreshes the page to reflect the updated list of books

Alternate Steps

A-1: No existing books

System displays a message indicating that there are no books existing in the system.

Data Validations

Basic form validation must be done before submitting the forms:

a. Required fields
    i. Book
    ii. Publisher
    iii. Category
    iv. ISBN
    v. Edition
    vi. Year
    vii. Cost
    viii. First Author
    ix. Synopsis
    x. About Authors

Manage Customers

All customers who have registered with the site should be managed via the application.

This includes the ability to view all the customers, edit and delete an existing customer.

View Customers

Objective	To view a list of all Customers
Actors	Book shop employee, Book shop owner, System administrator
Pre-Condition	Users have sufficient privileges to view all customers At least one Customer exists
Post-Condition	Actors view all the available customers

Steps

1. User navigates to the backend [site administration] login page

2. User logs in successfully

3. System displays the backend home page with Customers as one of the menu options

4. User selects the Customers option to view existing customers [Refer A-1]

5. System displays a list of all customers currently in the system with the following information:

   ❑ Name of the Customer

   ❑ Email Address of the Customer

   ❑ Username of the Customer

Alternate Steps

A-1: No existing customers

System displays a message indicating that there are no customers existing in the system.

Edit Customers

Objective	To edit an existing Customer
Actors	Book shop employee, Book shop owner, System administrator
Pre-Condition	Users have sufficient privileges to edit customers
Post-Condition	Actors successfully edit an existing customer

Steps

1. User navigates to the backend [site administration] login page

2. User logs in successfully

3. System displays the backend home page with Customers as one of the menu options

4. User selects the Customers option to view and edit existing customers [Refer A-1]

5. Users clicks the desired customer for editing

6. System displays a data entry form pre-populated with the existing form data

7. User edits the desired information in the fields

8. User selects option to save data [Refer A-2]

9. System saves data and updates the existing customer [Refer A-3]

10. System refreshes the page to reflect the updated list of customers

Alternate Steps

A-1: No existing customers

System displays a message indicating that there are no customers existing in the system.

A-2: User selects Cancel

System does not save any user entered data.
System does not update the customer.

A-3: Duplicate Email Address and/or Username

User enters an email address and/or a username that already exists.
System displays a message that the email address and the username already exists.
System does not update the customer.

Delete Customers

Objective	To delete an existing Customer
Actors	Book shop employee, Book shop owner, System administrator
Pre-Condition	Users have sufficient privileges to delete customers
Post-Condition	Actors successfully delete an existing customer

Steps

1. User navigates to the backend [site administration] login page

2. User logs in successfully

3. System displays the backend home page with Customers as one of the menu options

4. User selects the Customers option to view and delete existing customers [Refer A-1]

5. User selects the Delete link of the desired information to delete an existing customer

6. System deletes the customer

7. System refreshes the page to reflect the updated list of customers

Alternate Steps

A-1: No existing customers

System displays a message indicating that there are no customers existing in the system.

Data Validations

Basic form validation must be done before submitting the forms:

a. Required fields

   i. First Name

   ii. Last Name

   iii. Email Address

   iv. Username

   v. Password

b. Duplicate entries not allowed

   i. Email Address

   ii. Username

c. Email Address should be well formed and valid

Manage Transactions

All the transactions that are performed by the customers should be managed via the application.

View Transactions

Objective	To view a list of transactions on a particular date
Actors	Book shop employee, Book shop owner, System administrator
Pre-Condition	Users have sufficient privileges to view all transactions
	At least one Transaction exists
Post-Condition	Actors view the transactions for the chosen username

Steps

1. User navigates to the backend [site administration] login page

2. User logs in successfully

3. System displays the backend home page with Transactions as one of the menu options

4. User selects the Transactions option to view the transactions for a desired date

5. User selects a username for which the transaction are to be viewed and clicks Search [Refer A-1]

6. System displays a list of transactions along with the transaction details with the following information:

   ❑ Transaction Number

   ❑ Transaction Date

   ❑ Book Name

   ❑ Amount

Alternate Steps

A-1: No existing transactions

System displays a message indicating that there are no transactions for that particular username.

Logout

Objective	To allow a system user to logout
Actors	Book shop employee, Book shop owner, System administrator
Pre-Condition	System User should have logged in to the system
Post-Condition	Actors successfully logout

Steps

1. System User clicks the Logout link to logout

2. System destroys the session

3. System displays the Administration Login Page after logout

Frontend Modules

Homepage

Homepage is the customer's entry point to the application. This page should serve the customers with their requirements.

The homepage is made up of the following:

Signup

Objective	To allow a visitor to signup and become a Customer
Actors	Visitors
Pre-Condition	None
Post-Condition	Actors successfully become a customer

Steps

1. Visitor navigates to the homepage and clicks Signup

2. System displays the Signup data entry form

3. Visitor enters the information required to signup and clicks Submit [Refer A-1 and A-2]

4. System performs the necessary validations and if all fine, registers the customers details and dispatches an email to the customer

5. System displays a Thank you page

Alternate Steps

A-1: Already existing customer

System displays a message indicating that this customer [username or email address] already available in the system.

A-2: User selects Cancel

System does not save any user entered data.
System does not register the customer.

Data Validations

Basic form validation must be done before submitting the forms:

b.   Required fields

    i.   First Name

    ii.   Last Name

    iii.   Email Address

    iv.   Username

    v.   Password

c.   Duplicate entries not allowed

    i.   Email Address

    ii.   Username

d.   Email Address should be well formed and valid

Login

Objective	To allow a customer to login to the system
Actors	Customers
Pre-Condition	Person trying to log in should have signed up and thus is assumed to be a customer
Post-Condition	Actors successfully authenticate themselves and log in to the system

Steps

1.   Customer navigates to the homepage

2.   System displays a data entry form to capture the following:

Form Field	Type	Unique	Required	Max Size
Username	Text box	Yes	Yes	25
Password	Text box	Yes	Yes	8

3.   Customer enters the username and the password

4.   Customer clicks Login [Refer A-1]

5. System authenticates the username and password. If found valid, the system displays a welcome message and unlocks the shopping cart and download links for books

Alternate Steps

A-1: Invalid User

System displays a message indicating that the username or password is not valid.

Data Validations

Basic form validation must be done before submitting the forms:

b. Required fields

    i. Username

    ii. Password

Forgot Password

Objective	To allow a customer to retrieve the forgotten password
Actors	Customers
Pre-Condition	Person trying to retrieve the forgotten password should be aware of the username
	Person trying to retrieve the forgotten password should be a customer
Post-Condition	Actors successfully retrieve the forgotten password

Steps

1. Customer navigates to the homepage and clicks Forgot Password

2. System displays a data entry form to capture the following:

Form Field	Type	Unique	Required	Max Size
Username	Text box	Yes	Yes	25

3. Customer enters the required information and clicks Fetch

4. System validates the information captured and if found valid, the system fetches and dispatches the password via email [Refer A-1]

Alternate Steps

A-1: Invalid Information

System displays a message indicating that the information entered is not valid.

Data Validations

Basic form validation must be done before submitting the form:

1. Required fields
    a. Username

Search

Objective	To allow a visitor to search for the required books
Actors	Visitors
Pre-Condition	None
Post-Condition	Actors successfully retrieve the required information if it is available in the system

Steps

1. Visitor navigates to the homepage
2. System displays a data entry form to capture the following:

Form Field	Type	Unique	Required	Max Size
Search For	Text box	Yes	Yes	- -

3. Visitor enters the required information and clicks Search
4. System fetches the required information from the database based on the search term entered by the visitor and displays the same on the Search page [Refer A-1]

Alternate Steps

A-1: No Results

System displays a message indicating that the search didn't yield any results.

Directory Of Books

Objective	To allow a visitor to browse through the available books by categories
Actors	Visitors
Pre-Condition	None
Post-Condition	Actors successfully view the book details of the chosen book

Steps

1. Visitor navigates to the homepage

2. System displays a list of books under category heads

3. Visitor glances through the list of book's cover page and clicks the desired book if one exists

OR

4. Visitor clicks the category name to view a list of all the available books under that category

5. System fetches the book details of the chosen book and displays it

Popular Searches

Objective	To allow a visitor to view search tags that were used the most
Actors	Visitors
Pre-Condition	None
Post-Condition	Actors successfully view the search results based on the search tags available in this section

Steps

1. Visitor navigates to the homepage

2. System displays a list of Popular search tags

3. Visitor glances through the list and clicks the desired tag [link to search results]

4. System fetches and displays the details [search results] of the chosen tag

Alternate Steps

A-1: No Results

System displays a message indicating that the search did not yield any results.

New Releases

Objective	To allow a visitor to browse through the new books that are just released
Actors	Visitors
Pre-Condition	None
Post-Condition	Actors successfully view the book details of the chosen book

Steps

1. Visitor navigates to the homepage

2. System displays a list of new books

3. Visitor glances through the list of books and clicks the desired book name

4. System fetches the book details of the chosen book and displays it

Updated Books

Objective	To allow a visitor to browse through the books that are updated [New Edition]
Actors	Visitors
Pre-Condition	None
Post-Condition	Actors successfully view the book details of the chosen book

Steps

1. Visitor navigates to the homepage

2. System displays a list of updated books

3. Visitor glances through the list of books and clicks the desired book name

4. System fetches the book details of the chosen book and displays it

Top Titles

Objective	To allow a visitor to browse through the books that are most viewed
Actors	Visitors
Pre-Condition	None
Post-Condition	Actors successfully view the book details of the chosen book

Steps

1. Visitor navigates to the homepage

2. System displays a list of top titles books

3. Visitor glances through the list of books and clicks the desired book name

4. System fetches the book details of the chosen book and displays it

Our Authors

Objective	To allow a visitor to browse through the authors available in the system
Actors	Visitors
Pre-Condition	None
Post-Condition	Actors successfully view the author details of the chosen author

Steps

1. Visitor navigates to the homepage

2. System displays a list of available authors

3. Visitor glances through the list of authors and clicks the desired author name

4. System fetches the author and the details of the books written by that author and displays it

Our Publishers

Objective	To allow a visitor to browse through the publishers available in the system
Actors	Visitors
Pre-Condition	None
Post-Condition	Actors successfully view the publisher details of the chosen publishers

Steps

1. Visitor navigates to the homepage

2. System displays a list of available publishers

3. Visitor glances through the list of publishers and clicks the desired publisher name

4. System fetches the publisher and the details of the books published by that publisher and displays it

Add To Cart

Objective	To allow a customer to add books to the cart
Actors	Customers
Pre-Condition	Customer should have logged in to the system
Post-Condition	Actors successfully add the desired books to the cart

Steps

1. Customer navigates to the homepage

2. Customer opens the book details page by clicking a book name from one of the following sections on the home page:

    i.   New Releases

    ii. Top Titles

    iii. Updated Books

    iv. Directory of Books

    v. Popular Searches

    vi. Our Authors → List of Books

    vii. Our Publishers → List of Books

3. Customer adds the desired book by clicking Add To Cart

4. System adds the selected book to the Cart

Cart

Objective	To allow a customer to view the books available in the cart
Actors	Customers
Pre-Condition	Customer should have logged in to the system Customer must have added at least one book in the Cart
Post-Condition	Actors successfully view the books available in the cart

Steps

1. Customer navigates to the homepage

2. Customer clicks Show Cart

3. System displays a list of books that are available in the cart [Refer A-1]

4. Customer may choose to checkout by clicking Google Wallet

Alternate Steps

A-1: Empty Cart

System displays a message indicating that there are no books available in the cart.

Google Wallet

Objective	To allow a customer to checkout
Actors	Customers
Pre-Condition	Customer should have logged in to the system Customer must have added at least one book in the Cart Customer must be desirous to buy the books available in the cart Customer must have a Google account Customer must have a valid Credit Card
Post-Condition	Actors successfully checkout and make the payment

Steps

1. Customer navigates to the homepage

2. Customer clicks Show Cart

3. System displays a list of books that are available in the cart [Refer A-1]

4. Customer clicks Google Wallet

5. System sends the book details from the cart to the Google Payment gateway for processing

6. Customer is prompted to login to Google

7. Customer successfully logs in to Google

8. System prompts for the:

    i. Credit Card Number

    ii. Credit Card Expiry Date

    iii. Credit Card CVV Number

9. Customer enters the credit card information

10. Google authenticates and validates the card details and if all fine, processes the order and the payment [Refer A-2]

11. Google shows a Thank you page with a link to reach the site homepage if the customer desires

12. If the customer clicks the link, the site's home page is served

Alternate Steps

A-1: Empty Cart

System displays a message indicating that there are no books available in the cart.

A-2: Authentication Failure

System displays a message indicating that the card details are invalid.

Logout

Objective	To allow a customer to logout
Actors	Customers
Pre-Condition	Customer should have logged in to the system
Post-Condition	Actors successfully logout

Steps

1. Customer clicks the Logout link to logout
2. System destroys the session and the cart contents
3. System displays the site homepage after logout

Chapter

5

SECTION II: ABOUT THE PROJECT

Project Files

Based on the software requirements specification defined in *Chapter 04: Software Requirements Specification*, the application will be held in the following directory structure.

Directory Structure - BookShop

Diagram 5.1

Dedicated Library Directory [lib]

This project holds all its libraries [.jar files] in a dedicated directory called **lib**, as shown in diagram 5.2.

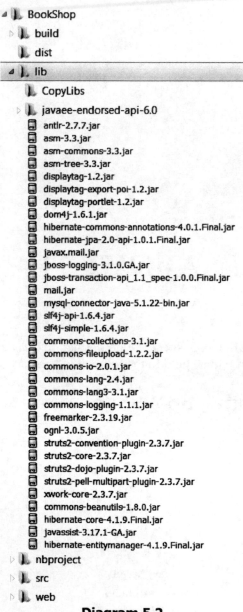

Diagram 5.2

Library File Name	Description
`antlr-2.7.7.jar`	ANTLR [**Another Tool for Language Recognition**] is a language tool that provides a framework for constructing recognizers, interpreters, compilers and translators from grammatical descriptions containing actions in a variety of target languages.

`asm-3.3.jar`
`asm-commons-3.3.jar`
`asm-tree-3.3.jar`
	ASM is an all purpose Java byte code manipulation and analysis framework. It can be used to modify existing classes or dynamically generate classes, directly in binary form.

`commons-beanutils-1.8.0.jar`	Most Java developers are used to creating Java classes that conform to the JavaBeans naming patterns for property getters and setters. It is natural to then access these methods directly, using calls to the corresponding getter and setter methods. However, there are some occasions where dynamic access to Java object properties is needed.
`commons-collections-3.1.jar`	Commons-Collections seek to build upon the JDK classes by providing new interfaces, implementations and utilities.
`commons-fileupload-1.2.2.jar`	Commons FileUpload package makes it easy to add robust, high-performance, file upload capability to the Web applications.
`commons-io-2.0.1.jar`	Commons IO is a library of utilities such as Utility classes, Filters, Comparators and Streams to assist with developing IO functionality.
`commons-lang-2.4.jar` `commons-lang3-3.1.jar`	Commons Lang provides a host of helper utilities for: ❏ java.lang ❏ Notably String manipulation methods ❏ Basic numerical methods ❏ Object reflection ❏ Concurrency ❏ Creation ❏ Serialization and System properties Note that Lang version 3.0 onwards use a different package than the previous versions, allowing it to be used at the same time as an earlier version.

Library File Name	Description
commons-logging-1.1.1.jar	Commons Logging provides a Log interface that is intended to be both light-weight and an independent abstraction of other logging toolkits. It provides the middleware/tooling developer with a simple logging abstraction that allows the developer to plug in a specific logging implementation.
displaytag-1.2.jar displaytag-export-poi-1.2.jar displaytag-portlet-1.2.jar	Display tag library is an open source suite of custom tags that provide high-level web presentation patterns which will work in an MVC model. Actually the display tag library can just display tables! Give it a list of objects and it will handle column display, sorting, paging, cropping, grouping, exporting, smart linking and decoration of a table in a customizable XHTML style.
dom4j-1.6.1.jar	dom4j is an easy to use, open source library for working with XML, XPath and XSLT on the Java platform using the Java Collections Framework and with full support for DOM, SAX and JAXP.
freemarker-2.3.19.jar	FreeMarker is a template engine i.e. a generic tool to generate text output based on templates. It's a Java package, a class library for Java programmers. It's not an application for end-users in itself, but something that programmers can embed into their products.
hibernate-commons-annotations-4.0.1.Final.jar	This package ships the Hibernate Commons Annotations classes used by annotations based Hibernate sub-projects.
hibernate-core-4.1.9.Final.jar	Hibernate is a powerful, high performance object / relational persistence and query service. Hibernate allows developing persistent classes following object-oriented idiom including association, inheritance, polymorphism, composition and collections.
hibernate-entitymanager-4.1.9.Final.jar	Hibernate EntityManager implements the standard Java Persistence: ❑ Management API ❑ Query Language ❑ Object lifecycle rules ❑ Configuration and packaging Hibernate EntityManager wraps the powerful and mature Hibernate Core.

Library File Name	Description
`hibernate-jpa-2.0-api-1.0.1.Final.jar`	This is the JAR containing the JPA 2.0 API. It provides all the interfaces and concrete classes that the specification defines as public API.
`javassist-3.17.1-GA.jar`	Javassist is a Java library providing means to manipulate the Java byte code of an application.
`javax.mail.jar`	JavaMail API provides classes that model a mail system.
`jboss-logging-3.1.0.GA.jar`	JBoss Logging acts as a logging bridge. If there are no other logging libraries added to the project, it will delegate all logging calls it handles to the logging facility built into the Java platform [commonly referred to as JDK logging].
`jboss-transaction-api_1.1_spec-1.0.0.Final.jar`	The interfaces specified by the many transaction standards tend to be too low-level for most application programmers. Therefore, Sun Microsystems created Java Transaction API [JTA], which specifies higher-level interfaces to assist in the development of distributed transactional applications.
`mail.jar`	JavaMail API provides a platform-independent and protocol-independent framework to build mail and messaging applications.
`mysql-connector-java-5.1.22-bin.jar`	MySQL Connector/J converts JDBC calls into the network protocol used by the MySQL database.
`ognl-3.0.5.jar`	OGNL, an expression language, library is used for getting and setting properties of Java objects.
`slf4j-api-1.6.4.jar` `slf4j-simple-1.6.4.jar`	Simple Logging Facade for Java [SLF4J] serves as a simple facade or abstraction for various logging frameworks. For example: java.util.logging, log4j and logback, allowing the end user to plug in the desired logging framework at deployment time.
`struts2-convention-plugin-2.3.7.jar`	Convention plugin provides the following features: ❑ Action location by package naming conventions ❑ Result [JSP, FreeMarker] location by naming conventions ❑ Class name to URL naming convention ❑ Package name to namespace convention ❑ Action name, Interceptor, Namespace and XWork package overrides using annotations

Library File Name	Description
`struts2-core-2.3.7.jar`	Struts 2 Core is an elegant, extensible framework for creating enterprise-ready Java web applications. The framework is designed to streamline the full development cycle, from building, to deploying, to maintaining applications over time.
`struts2-dojo-plugin-2.3.7.jar`	Dojo plugin is no longer officially supported by the Struts 2 team. However, Struts 2 comes with a Dojo Toolkit plugin which makes developing an AJAX application easier than ever.
`struts2-pell-multipart-plugin-2.3.7.jar`	Instructs Struts 2 to use multipart parser to process file uploads.
`xwork-core-2.3.7.jar`	XWork is a command-pattern framework that is used to power Struts[2]. XWork provides an Inversion of Control container, a powerful expression language, data type conversion, validation and pluggable configuration.

The Project Source Code Directory (src/java)

The project source code is placed under /src/java, as shown in diagram 5.3.

Diagram 5.3

Java Packages

The modules in this project are placed, as shown in diagram 5.4.

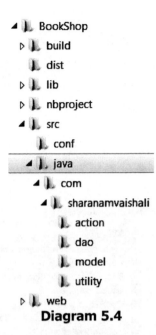

Diagram 5.4

Directory/Package Name	Description
`com.sharanamvaishali.action`	The Action classes
`com.sharanamvaishali.dao`	The **Data Access Object** classes
`com.sharanamvaishali.model`	The Model/Entity classes
`com.sharanamvaishali.utility`	The Service classes

Actions (src\java\com\sharanamvaishali\action)

The **src\java\com\sharanamvaishali\action** directory of this project holds the following files, as shown in diagram 5.5.

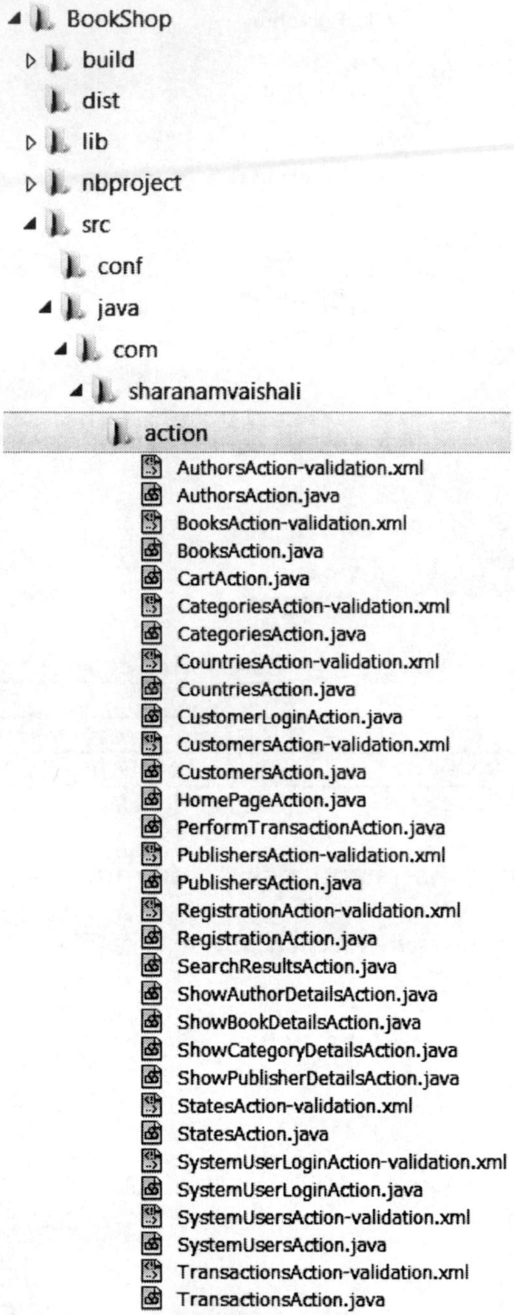

- ▲ BookShop
  - ▷ build
  - dist
  - ▷ lib
  - ▷ nbproject
  - ▲ src
    - conf
    - ▲ java
      - ▲ com
        - ▲ sharanamvaishali
          - action
            - AuthorsAction-validation.xml
            - AuthorsAction.java
            - BooksAction-validation.xml
            - BooksAction.java
            - CartAction.java
            - CategoriesAction-validation.xml
            - CategoriesAction.java
            - CountriesAction-validation.xml
            - CountriesAction.java
            - CustomerLoginAction.java
            - CustomersAction-validation.xml
            - CustomersAction.java
            - HomePageAction.java
            - PerformTransactionAction.java
            - PublishersAction-validation.xml
            - PublishersAction.java
            - RegistrationAction-validation.xml
            - RegistrationAction.java
            - SearchResultsAction.java
            - ShowAuthorDetailsAction.java
            - ShowBookDetailsAction.java
            - ShowCategoryDetailsAction.java
            - ShowPublisherDetailsAction.java
            - StatesAction-validation.xml
            - StatesAction.java
            - SystemUserLoginAction-validation.xml
            - SystemUserLoginAction.java
            - SystemUsersAction-validation.xml
            - SystemUsersAction.java
            - TransactionsAction-validation.xml
            - TransactionsAction.java

Diagram 5.5

File Name	Description
AuthorsAction.java	The action that allows performing insert, update, delete and view of the author details and download the photograph of an author.
AuthorsAction-validation.xml	The XML file that performs client side validation for authors.
BooksAction.java	The action that allows performing insert, update, delete and view of the book details and download the cover page, toc and sample chapters of the book.
BooksAction-validation.xml	The XML file that performs client side validation for books.
CartAction.java	The action that allows adding, removing and viewing cart items.
CategoriesAction.java	The action that allows performing insert, update, delete and view categories.
CatgeoriesAction-validation.xml	The XML file that performs client side validation for categories.
CountriesAction.java	The action that allows performing insert, update, delete and view countries.
CountriesAction-validation.xml	The XML file that performs client side validation for countries.
CustomerLoginAction.java	The action that allows login, logout and retrieve forgotten password for customers.
CustomersAction.java	The action that allows performing update, delete and view customers.
CustomersAction-validation.xml	The XML file that performs client side validation for customers.
HomePageAction.java	The action that allows viewing homepage data.
PerformTransactionAction.java	The action that allows creating a new transaction(s) for the items in the cart on checkout.
PublishersAction.java	The action that allows performing insert, update, delete and view publishers.
PublishersAction-validation.xml	The XML file that performs client side validation for publishers.
RegistrationAction.java	The action that allows performing customer registration.
RegistrationAction-validation.xml	The XML file that performs client side validation for customers.
SearchResultsAction.java	The action that allows performing search and viewing the search results.

File Name	Description
ShowAuthorDetailsAction.java	The action that allows viewing author details of a particular author.
ShowBookDetailsAction.java	The action that allows viewing book details of a particular book.
ShowCategoryDetailsAction.java	The action that allows viewing books under a category.
ShowPublisherDetailsAction.java	The action that allows viewing publisher details of a particular publisher.
StatesAction.java	The action that allows performing insert, update, delete and view states.
StatesAction-validation.xml	The XML file that performs client side validation for states.
SystemUsersLoginAction.java	The action that allows login and logout for the admin users.
SystemUsersLoginAction-validation.xml	The XML file that performs client side validation for admin user's login.
SystemUsersAction.java	The action that allows performing insert, update, delete and view system users.
SystemUsersAction-validation.xml	The XML file that performs client side validation for system users.
TransactionsAction.java	The action that allows performing updates and view transactions.
TransactionsAction-validation.xml	The XML file that performs client side validation for transactions.

DAO Classes (src\java\com\sharanamvaishali\ dao)

The **src\java\com\sharanamvaishali\dao** directory of this project holds the following files, as shown in diagram 5.6.

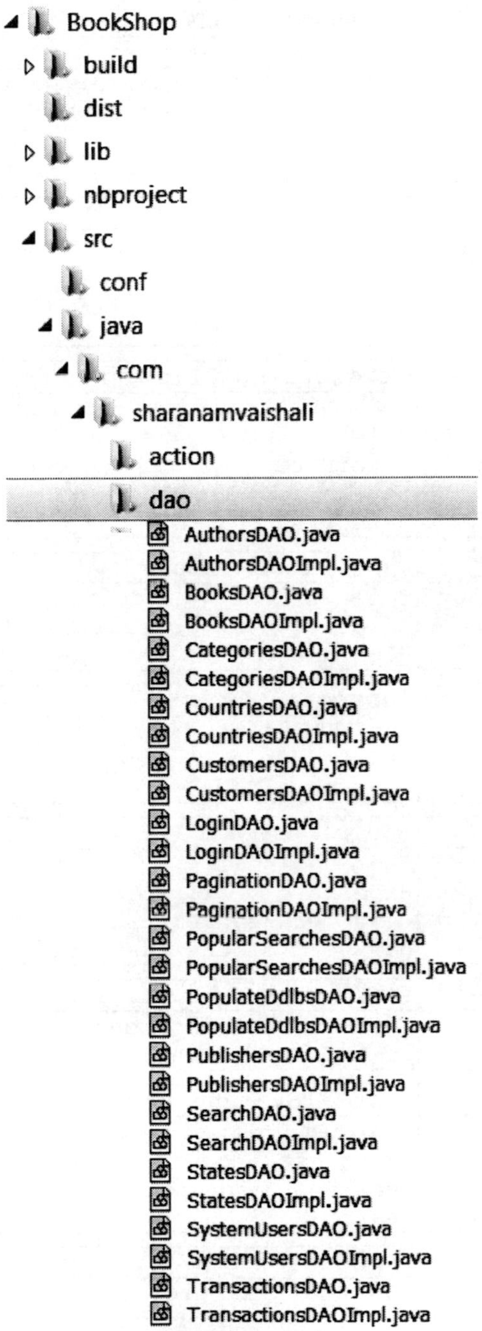

- BookShop
  - build
  - dist
  - lib
  - nbproject
  - src
    - conf
    - java
      - com
        - sharanamvaishali
          - action
          - dao
            - AuthorsDAO.java
            - AuthorsDAOImpl.java
            - BooksDAO.java
            - BooksDAOImpl.java
            - CategoriesDAO.java
            - CategoriesDAOImpl.java
            - CountriesDAO.java
            - CountriesDAOImpl.java
            - CustomersDAO.java
            - CustomersDAOImpl.java
            - LoginDAO.java
            - LoginDAOImpl.java
            - PaginationDAO.java
            - PaginationDAOImpl.java
            - PopularSearchesDAO.java
            - PopularSearchesDAOImpl.java
            - PopulateDdlbsDAO.java
            - PopulateDdlbsDAOImpl.java
            - PublishersDAO.java
            - PublishersDAOImpl.java
            - SearchDAO.java
            - SearchDAOImpl.java
            - StatesDAO.java
            - StatesDAOImpl.java
            - SystemUsersDAO.java
            - SystemUsersDAOImpl.java
            - TransactionsDAO.java
            - TransactionsDAOImpl.java

Diagram 5.6

Interface Name	Implementation Name
AuthorsDAO.java	AuthorsDAOImpl.java
Description	The DAO that performs actual insert, update, delete, view operation for authors using Hibernate. It also retrieves the list of authors and the books written by that author.
BooksDAO.java	BooksDAOImpl.java
Description	The DAO that performs actual insert, update, delete, view operation for books using Hibernate. It also retrieves the list of new releases, updated books and top titles.
CategoriesDAO.java	CategoriesDAOImpl.java
Description	The DAO that performs actual insert, update, delete, view operation for categories using Hibernate. It also retrieves the list of categories and the books available under that category.
CountriesDAO.java	CountriesDAOImpl.java
Description	The DAO that performs actual insert, update, delete, view operation for countries using Hibernate.
CustomersDAO.java	CustomersDAOImpl.java
Description	The DAO that performs actual insert, update, delete, view operation for customers using Hibernate.
LoginDAO.java	LoginDAOImpl.java
Description	The DAO that fires the actual query using Hibernate on login to authenticate customers/system users or to retrieve forgotten password of the customers.
PaginationDAO.java	PaginationDAOImpl.java
Description	The DAO that provides the pagination support to the admin section.
PopularSearchesDAO.java	PopularSearchesDAOImpl.java
Description	The DAO that fires the actual query using Hibernate to retrieve the list of popular searches and delete the records of popular searches.
PopulateDdlbsDAO.java	PopulateDdlbsDAOImpl.java
Description	The DAO that provides data to pre-populate the drop down list boxes.

PublishersDAO.java	PublishersDAOImpl.java
Description	The DAO that performs actual insert, update, delete, view operation for publishers using Hibernate. It also retrieves the list of publishers and the books published by that publisher.

SearchDAO.java	SearchDAOImpl.java
Description	The DAO that fires the actual query using Hibernate to perform the search operation.

StatesDAO.java	StatesDAOImpl.java
Description	The DAO that performs actual insert, update, delete, view operation for states using Hibernate.

SystemUsersDAO.java	SystemUsersDAOImpl.java
Description	The DAO that performs actual insert, update, delete, view operation for system users using Hibernate.

TransactionsDAO.java	TransactionsDAOImpl.java
Description	The DAO that performs actual view operation for transactions using Hibernate.

Bean Classes (src\java\com\sharanamvaishali\model)

The **src\java\com\sharanamvaishali\model** directory of this project holds the following files, as shown in diagram 5.7.

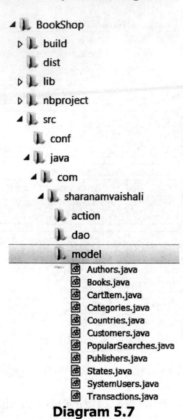

Diagram 5.7

File Name	Table Name
Authors.java	Authors
Books.java	Books
CartItem.java	- -
Categories.java	Categories
Countries.java	Countries
Customers.java	Customers
PopularSearches.java	PopularSearches
Publishers.java	Publishers
States.java	States
SystemUsers.java	SystemUsers
Transactions.java	Transactions

Common Classes (src\java\utility)

The **src\java\com\sharanamvaishali\utility** directory of this project holds the following files, as shown in diagram 5.8.

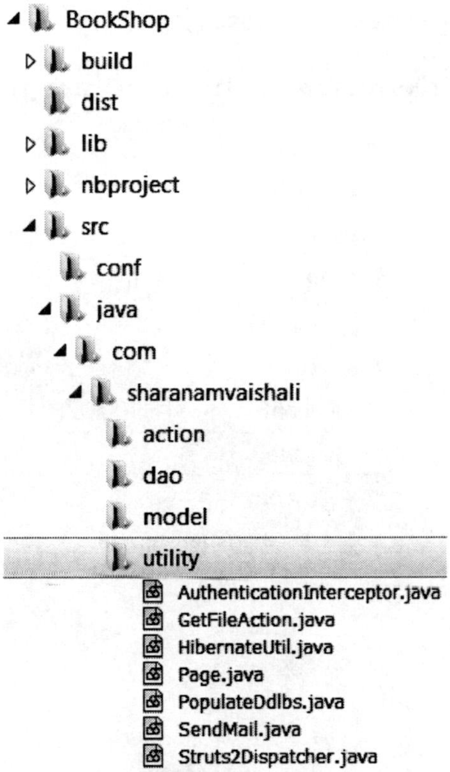

▲ 📁 BookShop
  ▷ 📁 build
  📁 dist
  ▷ 📁 lib
  ▷ 📁 nbproject
  ▲ 📁 src
    📁 conf
    ▲ 📁 java
      ▲ 📁 com
        ▲ 📁 sharanamvaishali
          📁 action
          📁 dao
          📁 model
          📁 utility
            📄 AuthenticationInterceptor.java
            📄 GetFileAction.java
            📄 HibernateUtil.java
            📄 Page.java
            📄 PopulateDdlbs.java
            📄 SendMail.java
            📄 Struts2Dispatcher.java

Diagram 5.8

File Name	Description
AuthenticationInterceptor.java	An interceptor that invokes the login form.
GetFileAction.java	The action that allows retrieving a file that is stored in a BLOB column of the database.
HibernateUtil.java	The Hibernate Session Factory.
Page.java	The pagination logic.
PopulateDdlbs.java	The JavaBean class that provides data to pre-populate the drop down list boxes.
SendMail.java	A Java class that allows dispatching emails using the Gmail SMTP service.
Struts2Dispatcher.java	A customer Struts2Dispatcher that invokes Hibernate.

Configuration and Properties Files (src\java*)

The configuration and properties files are available under **src\java**, as shown in diagram 5.9.

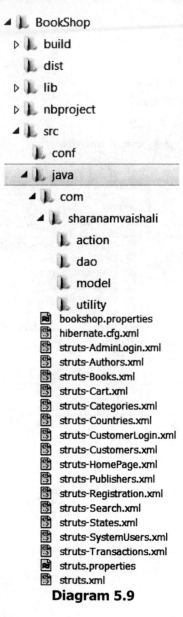

Diagram 5.9

File Name	Description
`bookshop.properties`	The properties [Resource Bundle] file that holds: googleMerchantID emailFrom emailUser emailFromPasswd
`hibernate.cfg.xml`	The Hibernate configuration file that holds references to the mappings between the model classes and the database tables.
`struts.properties`	The Struts properties file that holds mappings to the Resource Bundle to allow data retrieval using the Struts 2 i18n tags.

`struts.xml`
`struts-AdminLogin.xml`
`struts-Authors.xml`
`struts-Books.xml`
`struts-Cart.xml`
`struts-Categories.xml`
`struts-Countries.xml`
`struts-CustomerLogin.xml`
`struts-Customers.xml`
`struts-HomePage.xml`
`struts-Publishers.xml`
`struts-Registration.xml`
`struts-Search.xml`
`struts-States.xml`
`struts-SystemUsers.xml`
`Struts-Transactions.xml`
	Module wise struts configuration [Action → Result mappings] file.

The Web Directory (web)

The web pages in this project are placed under **web**, as shown in diagram 5.10.

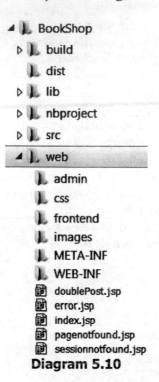

Diagram 5.10

The following table displays the details of the directory names under the **web**:

Directory Name	Description
admin	The admin section web based data entry forms.
css	The cascading style sheet.
frontend	The customer facing web pages.
images	The images used by all the web pages.

The following table displays the details of the file names under the **web**:

File Name	Description
doublePost.jsp	The custom double form submission Error page [configured in struts.xml]
error.jsp	The custom Error page [configured in web.xml]
index.jsp	The index page of the project.
Pagenotfound.jsp	The custom Page not found Error page [configured in web.xml]
Sessionnotfound.jsp	The custom Session not found Error page [configured in struts.xml]

Backend [Administration] Web Pages (web\admin)

The **web\admin** directory in this project holds the following files, as shown in diagram 5.11.

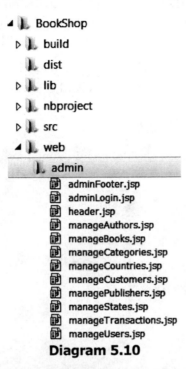

Diagram 5.10

File Name	Description
adminFooter.jsp	The Backend [Administration] footer that appears on all the administrative web pages.
adminLogin.jsp	The Backend [Administration] Login form.
header.jsp	The Backend [Administration] header file that provides the menu bar.
manageAuthors.jsp	The Backend [Administration] – Manage Authors data entry form that allows Add, View, Update and Delete.
manageBooks.jsp	The Backend [Administration] – Manage Books data entry form that allows Add, View, Update and Delete.
manageCategories.jsp	The Backend [Administration] – Manage Categories data entry form that allows Add, View, Update and Delete.
manageCountries.jsp	The Backend [Administration] – Manage Countries data entry form that allows Add, View, Update and Delete.
manageCustomers.jsp	The Backend [Administration] – Manage Customers data entry form that allows View, Update and Delete.

File Name	Description
managePublishers.jsp	The Backend [Administration] – Manage Publishers data entry form that allows Add, View, Update and Delete.
manageStates.jsp	The Backend [Administration] – Manage States data entry form that allows Add, View, Update and Delete.
manageTransactions.jsp	The Backend [Administration] – Manage Transactions data entry form that allows View.
manageUsers.jsp	The Backend [Administration] – Manage Users data entry form that allows Add, View, Update and Delete.

Cascading Style Sheet (web\css)

The **web\css** directory in this project holds the following files, as shown in diagram 5.12.

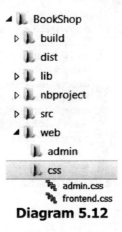

Diagram 5.12

File Name	Description
admin.css	The cascading style sheet that is applied to the administrative web pages.
frontend.css	The cascading style sheet that is applied to the frontend [customer facing] web pages.

Frontend [Customer Facing] Web Pages (web\frontend)

The **web\frontend** directory in this project holds the following files, as shown in diagram 5.13.

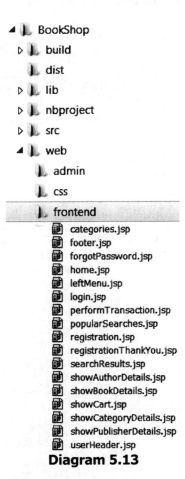

Diagram 5.13

File Name	Description
categories.jsp	The directory of books according to the category wise page.
footer.jsp	The Frontend [Customer Facing] footer that appears on all the frontend web pages.
forgotPassword.jsp	The Forgot Password data entry form.
home.jsp	The home page.
leftMenu.jsp	The list of New Releases, Updated Books, Top Titles, Our Authors and Our Publishers shown in home page.
login.jsp	The Frontend [Customer Facing] Login form.
performTransaction.jsp	The page that takes the customer to Google Checkout.
popularSearches.jsp	The list of popular searches shown in the home page.
registration.jsp	The Customer Registration data entry form.
registrationThankYou.jsp	The page that appears after a successful registration.

File Name	Description
searchResults.jsp	The page that allows searching and displays the search results.
showAuthorDetails.jsp	The page that displays author details for a particular author.
showBookDetails.jsp	The page that displays book details for a particular book.
showCart.jsp	The page that shows the cart contents and allows deleting cart items and checking out via Google Wallet.
showCategoryDetails.jsp	The page that displays books and its details for a particular category.
showPublisherDetails.jsp	The page that displays publisher details for a particular publisher.
userHeader.jsp	The Frontend [Customer Facing] header file that provides the menu and the search bar.

Chapter

6

SECTION II: ABOUT THE PROJECT

Data Dictionary

This chapter documents:

❑ The **Entity Relationship Diagram** that helps understand the relationship between the tables used in this project

❑ **Table Definitions** that provides the column attributes:

- o Constraints
- o Default Values
- o Data Type
- o Size
- o Null / Not Null
- o Description

<u>HINT</u>

 The Book's accompanying CDROM holds a .sql file that is a dump [export] of the entire database [all tables] with sample data that will be useful to begin using this project.

Entity Relationship Diagram

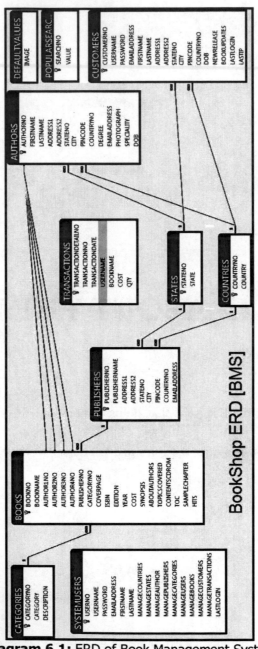

Diagram 6.1: ERD of Book Management System

Table Definitions

Countries

This table stores the country name captured using the Manage Countries d/e form.

Column Name	Data Type	Size	Null	Default	Constraints
CountryNo	Integer	10	No	NULL	Primary key
Description	An identity number of the country				
Country	Varchar	50	No	- -	Unique key
Description	The name of the country				

States

This table stores the state names captured using the Manage States d/e form.

Column Name	Data Type	Size	Null	Default	Constraints
StateNo	Integer	10	No	- -	Primary key
Description	An identity number of the state				
State	Varchar	50	No	- -	Unique Key
Description	The name of the state				

DefaultValues

This table stores the default image for all the not available images.

Column Name	Data Type	Size	Null	Default	Constraints
Image	Blob	- -	Yes	- -	- -
Description	The image displayed in case the author or book image is not uploaded while adding or updating.				

Authors

This table stores the author details captured using the Manage Authors d/e form.

Column Name	Data Type	Size	Null	Default	Constraints
AuthorNo	Integer	10	No	- -	Primary Key
Description	An identity number of the author				
FirstName	Varchar	30	No	- -	- -
Description	The first name of the author				
LastName	Varchar	30	No	- -	- -
Description	The last name of the author				
Address1	Varchar	50	Yes	NULL	- -
Description	The street address where the author resides				
Address2	Varchar	50	Yes	NULL	- -
Description	The street address where the author resides				
StateNo	Integer	10	Yes	NULL	States(StateNo)
Description	An identity number of the State				
Pincode	Varchar	20	Yes	NULL	- -
Description	The pincode of the city where the author resides				
City	Varchar	50	Yes	NULL	- -
Description	The name of the city where the author resides				
CountryNo	Integer	10	Yes	NULL	Country(CountryNo)
Description	An identity number of the country				
Degree	Varchar	30	No	- -	- -
Description	The qualifications of the author				
EmailAddress	Varchar	50	No	- -	Unique key
Description	The email address of the author				
Photograph	LongBlob	- -	Yes	NULL	- -
Description	The photograph of the author				
Speciality	Varchar	4000	Yes	NULL	- -
Description	The speciality of the author				
DOB	Varchar	15	Yes	NULL	- -
Description	The date of birth of the author				

Publishers

This table stores the publisher details captured using the Manage Publishers d/e form.

Column Name	Data Type	Size	Null	Default	Constraints
PublisherNo	Integer	10	No	- -	Primary Key
Description	An identity number of the publisher				
PublisherName	Varchar	50	No	- -	Unique key
Description	The name of the publisher				
Address1	Varchar	50	Yes	NULL	- -
Description	The street address where the publisher resides				
Address2	Varchar	50	Yes	NULL	- -
Description	The street address where the publisher resides				
StateNo	Integer	10	Yes	NULL	States(StateNo)
Description	An identity number of the State				
Pincode	Varchar	20	Yes	NULL	- -
Description	The pincode of the city where the publisher resides				
City	Varchar	50	Yes	NULL	- -
Description	The name of the city where the publisher resides				
CountryNo	Integer	10	Yes	NULL	Country(CountryNo)
Description	An identity number of the country				
EmailAddress	Varchar	50	No	- -	Unique key
Description	The email address of the publisher				

Categories

This table stores the category details captured using the Manage Categories d/e form.

Column Name	Data Type	Size	Null	Default	Constraints
CategoryNo	Integer	10	No	- -	Primary key
Description	An identity number of the category				
Category	Varchar	30	No	- -	Unique key
Description	The name of the category				
Description	Varchar	4000	No	- -	- -
Description	The description of the category				

Books

This table stores the book details captured using the Manage Books d/e form.

Column Name	Data Type	Size	Null	Default	Constraints
BookNo	Integer	10	No	- -	Primary Key
Description	An identity number of the book				
BookName	Varchar	255	No	- -	- -
Description	The name of the book				
Author1No	Integer	10	No	- -	Authors(AuthorNo)
Description	An identity number of the first author				
Author2No	Integer	10	Yes	NULL	Authors(AuthorNo)
Description	An identity number of the second author				
Author3No	Integer	10	Yes	NULL	Authors(AuthorNo)
Description	An identity number of the third author				
Author4No	Integer	10	Yes	NULL	Authors(AuthorNo)
Description	An identity number of the fourth author				
PublisherNo	Integer	10	No	- -	Publishers(PublisherNo)
Description	An identity number of the publisher				
CategoryNo	Integer	10	No	- -	Categories(CategoryNo)
Description	An identity number of the category				
CoverPage	LongBlob	- -	Yes	NULL	- -
Description	The cover page image of the book				
ISBN	Varchar	20	No	- -	Unique key
Description	The ISBN of the book				
Edition	Varchar	20	No	- -	- -
Description	The edition of the book				
Year	Integer	4	No	- -	- -
Description	The year when the book was published				
Cost	Integer	12	No	- -	- -
Description	The cost of the book				
Synopsis	Varchar	4000	No	- -	- -
Description	The synopsis of the book				
AboutAuthors	Varchar	4000	No	- -	- -
Description	The information about the book authors				

Column Name	Data Type	Size	Null	Default	Constraints
TopicsCovered	Varchar	4000	Yes	NULL	- -
Description	The topics covered in the book				
ContentsCDROM	Varchar	4000	Yes	NULL	- -
Description	The contents of the CDROM of the book				
TOC	LongBlob	- -	Yes	NULL	- -
Description	The TOC of the book in PDF format				
SampleChapter	LongBlob	- -	Yes	NULL	- -
Description	The sample chapter of the book in PDF format				
Hits	Integer	- -	Yes	0 [Zero]	- -
Description	The number of times the book was viewed				

Customers

This table stores the customer details captured while registering.

Column Name	Data Type	Size	Null	Default	Constraints
CustomerNo	Integer	10	No	- -	Primary key
Description	An identity number of the customer				
Username	Varchar	30	No	- -	Unique key
Description	The username of the customer				
Password	Varchar	30	No	- -	- -
Description	The password of the customer				
EmailAddress	Varchar	50	No	- -	Unique key
Description	The email address of the customer				
FirstName	Varchar	30	No	- -	- -
Description	The first name of the customer				
LastName	Varchar	30	No	- -	- -
Description	The last name of the customer				
Address1	Varchar	50	Yes	NULL	- -
Description	The street address where the customer resides				
Address2	Varchar	50	Yes	NULL	- -
Description	The street address where the customer resides				
StateNo	Integer	10	Yes	NULL	States(StateNo)
Description	An identity number of the State				
Pincode	Varchar	20	Yes	NULL	- -
Description	The pincode of the city where the customer resides				

Column Name	Data Type	Size	Null	Default	Constraints
City	Varchar	50	Yes	NULL	- -
Description	The name of the city where the customer resides				
CountryNo	Integer	10	Yes	NULL	Country(CountryNo)
Description	An identity number of the country				
DOB	Varchar	15	Yes	NULL	- -
Description	The date of birth of the customer				
NewRelease	Varchar	30	Yes	NULL	- -
Description	A flag to indicate if the customer has subscribed to New Releases				
BookUpdates	Varchar	30	Yes	NULL	- -
Description	A flag to indicate if the customer has subscribed to Book Updates				
LastLogin	Varchar	50	Yes	NULL	- -
Description	The last login date of the customer				
LastIP	Varchar	25	Yes	NULL	- -
Description	The last IP address from where the customer had logged in				

PopularSearches

This table stores the search criteria and the associated value of all the searches attempted by the user using the Search d/e form. These values are used to represent tag clouds under popular searches.

Column Name	Data Type	Size	Null	Default	Constraints
SearchNo	Integer	10	No	- -	Primary key
Description	An identity number of the search				
Value	Varchar	100	Yes	NULL	- -
Description	The value of the search				

SystemUsers

This table stores the system user details captured using the Manage Users d/e form.

Column Name	Data Type	Size	Null	Default	Constraints
UserNo	Integer	10	No	- -	Primary key
Description	An identity number of the system user				

Column Name	Data Type	Size	Null	Default	Constraints
Username	Varchar	30	No	- -	Unique key
Description	The username of the system user					
Password	Varchar	30	No	- -	- -
Description	The password of the system user					
EmailAddress	Varchar	50	No	- -	Unique key
Description	The email address of the system user					
FirstName	Varchar	30	No	- -	- -
Description	The first name of the system user					
LastName	Varchar	30	No	- -	- -
Description	The last name of the system user					
ManageCountries	Varchar	10	Yes	NULL	- -
Description	A flag to indicate if the system user has permissions to Countries d/e form					
ManageStates	Varchar	10	Yes	NULL	- -
Description	A flag to indicate if the system user has permissions to State d/e form					
ManageAuthors	Varchar	10	Yes	NULL	- -
Description	A flag to indicate if the system user has permissions to Authors d/e form					
ManagePublishers	Varchar	10	Yes	NULL	- -
Description	A flag to indicate if the system user has permissions to Publishers d/e form					
ManageCategories	Varchar	10	Yes	NULL	- -
Description	A flag to indicate if the system user has permissions to Categories d/e form					
ManageUsers	Varchar	10	Yes	NULL	- -
Description	A flag to indicate if the system user has permissions to System Users d/e form					
ManageBooks	Varchar	10	Yes	NULL	- -
Description	A flag to indicate if the system user has permissions to Books d/e form					
ManageCustomers	Varchar	10	Yes	NULL	- -
Description	A flag to indicate if the system user has permissions to Customers d/e form					
ManageTransactions	Varchar	10	Yes	NULL	- -
Description	A flag to indicate if the system user has permissions to Transactions d/e form					

Column Name	Data Type	Size	Null	Default	Constraints
LastLogin	Varchar	25	Yes	NULL	- -
Description	The last login date of the system user				

Transactions

This table stores the entries of the transactions [purchases] performed by the users.

Column Name	Data Type	Size	Null	Default	Constraints
TransactionDetailNo	Integer	15	No	- -	Primary key
Description	An identity number of the transaction details				
TransactionNo	Integer	10	No	- -	- -
Description	An identity number of the transaction				
TransactionDate	Date	- -	No	- -	- -
Description	The date on which transaction is made				
Username	Varchar	25	No	- -	Customers(Username)
Description	The username of the customer who made any purchases				
BookName	Varchar	255	No	- -	- -
Description	The name of the book				
Cost	Integer	12	No	- -	- -
Description	The cost of the book				
Qty	Integer	5	No	- -	- -
Description	The quantity of the book				

Chapter

7

SECTION III: END USER MANUAL

Backend [Administration]

The backend consists of the following:

❑ Login
❑ Manage
   o Countries
   o States
   o Authors
   o Publishers
   o Categories
   o Users
   o Books
   o Customers
   o Transactions

To be able to use the backend [site administration], system users can be created using the Manage Users data entry form. By default, a super user called **admin** is pre-created with the password set to **admin**. This user can always login to the system and <u>no other system users can delete this user</u>.

The Application's Homepage

To begin using this application, invoke it. The application's homepage appears, as shown in diagram 7.1, which holds a link to the **Administration** section.

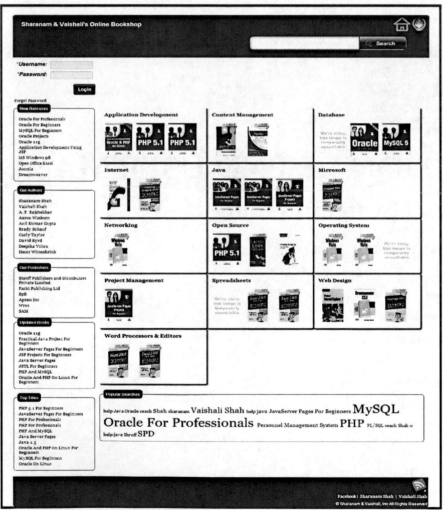

Diagram 7.1: The Application's Homepage

Backend [Administration] Login Page

Click  from the application's homepage. This delivers the login page, as shown in diagram 7.2.

Login

Username:
Password:

Login

Facebook | Sharanam Shah | Vaishali Shah
© Sharanam & Vaishali, Inc All Rights Reserved

Diagram 7.2: The Backend Login page

Enter the username as **admin** and password as **admin**. Click  Login.
This is a super admin account which is pre-created.

HINT

Since this login was attempted using a super admin, all the menu options are available. However, this application allows restricting certain modules to certain system users using the Manage Users data entry form [explained later].

The system displays the Manage Transactions page after a successful login.

Manage Countries

Click  Countries. This delivers the Manage Countries data entry form, as shown in diagram 7.3.1.

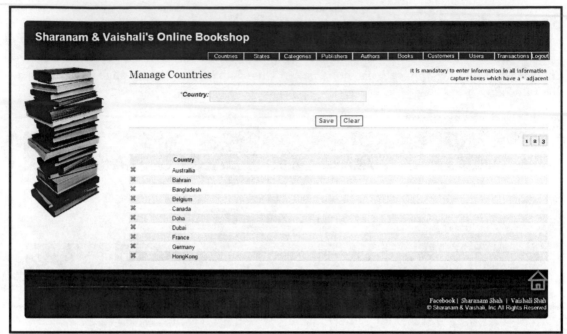

Diagram 7.3.1: Manage Countries

REMINDER

  It is mandatory to enter information in all information capture boxes which have a * adjacent indicates entering values for all the form field labels that are marked * is mandatory.

| 1 | 2 | 3 | 4 | 5 | can be used to navigate across additional records that are paginated to save space.

Data entered in this form is used to populate Country drop down list boxes in the following pages:

❑ Manage Authors

❑ Manage Publishers

❑ Manage Customers

❑ Signup

Adding New Record

As soon as the data entry form loads in the web browser, it's ready to capture new records.

To add a new country, key in the required form field(s) and click **Save**.

Clicking **Save**, performs the following client side validations:

❑   Country name cannot be left blank

If any one of the above mentioned validations fails, an appropriate error message is displayed, as shown in diagram 7.3.2.

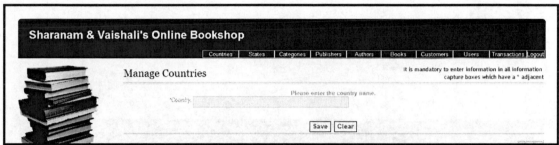

Diagram 7.3.2: Manage Countries [Error Message]

Correct the error. After doing so, click **Save** to save the entered data in the database.

If all the validations mentioned above go through without any errors, the data is saved in the database and the page is reloaded to reflect the newly added data.

Modifying Existing Record

To modify an already existing record, click the desired record from the GRID, as shown in diagram 7.3.3.

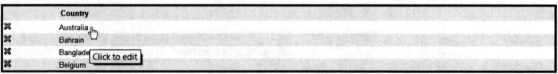

Diagram 7.3.3: Manage Countries [GRID for modification]

Doing so populates the record data in the data entry form, as shown in diagram 7.3.4.

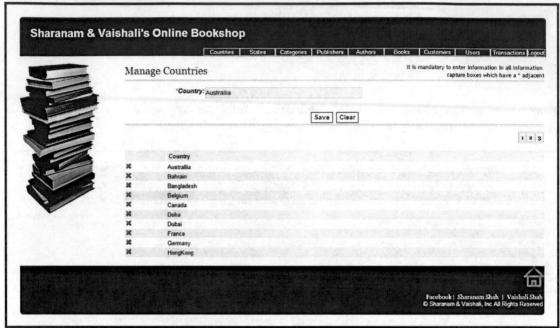

Diagram 7.3.4: Manage Countries [Data Populated]

Make the desired changes and click **Save**.

Clicking **Save**, performs the following client side validations:

❑   Country name cannot be left blank

If any one of the above mentioned validation fail, an appropriate error message is displayed, as shown in diagram 7.3.5.

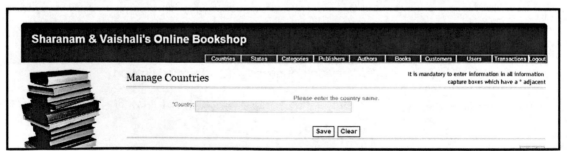

Diagram 7.3.5: Manage Countries [Error Message]

Correct the error. After doing so, click **Save** to save the entered data in the database.

If all the validations mentioned above go through without any errors, the data is updated in the database and the page is reloaded to reflect the modified data.

Deleting Existing Record

To delete already existing record, click ✖ adjacent to the desired record from the GRID, as shown in diagram 7.3.6.

	Country
✖	Australlia
✖	Bahrain
✖	Bangladesh
✖	Belgium

Diagram 7.3.6: Manage Countries [GRID for deletion]

Clicking ✖, performs the delete operation and reloads the page to reflect the deleted records.

If the user attempts to delete record that is associated with the existing data an error message appears indicating the same, as shown in diagram 7.3.7.

Deleting a master record that has been associated with detail records in this case Authors, Publishers, Customers and Signup cannot be deleted.

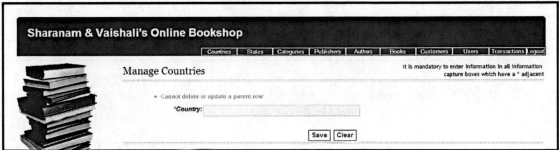

Diagram 7.3.7: Manage Countries [Error Message]

Manage States

Click **States** . This delivers the Manage States data entry form, as shown in diagram 7.4.1.

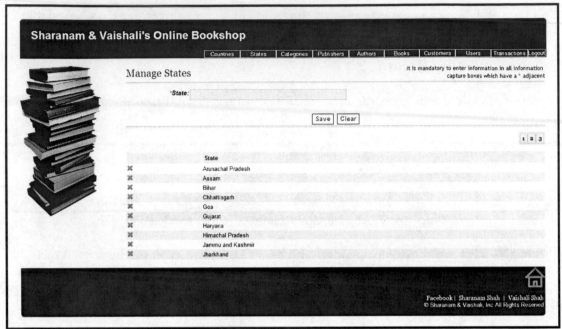

Diagram 7.4.1: Manage States

REMINDER

It is mandatory to enter information in all information
capture boxes which have a * adjacent indicates entering values for all the form
field labels that are marked * is mandatory.

 can be used to navigate across additional records that are paginated to save space.

Data entered in this form is used to populate State drop down list boxes in the following pages:

❑ Manage Authors
❑ Manage Publishers
❑ Manage Customers
❑ Signup

Adding New Record

As soon as the data entry form loads in the web browser, it's ready to capture new records.

To add a new state, key in the required form field(s) and click Save .

Clicking Save , performs the following client side validations:

❏   State name cannot be left blank

If any one of the above mentioned validation fail, an appropriate error message is displayed, as shown in diagram 7.4.2.

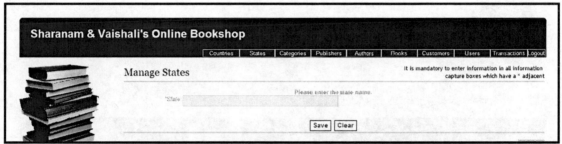

Diagram 7.4.2: Manage States [Error Message]

Correct the error. After doing so, click Save to save the entered data in the database.

If all the validations mentioned above go through without any errors, the data is saved in the database and the page is reloaded to reflect the newly added data.

Modifying Existing Record

To modify an already existing record, click the desired record from the GRID, as shown in diagram 7.4.3.

Diagram 7.4.3: Manage States [GRID for modification]

Doing so populates the record data in the data entry form, as shown in diagram 7.4.4.

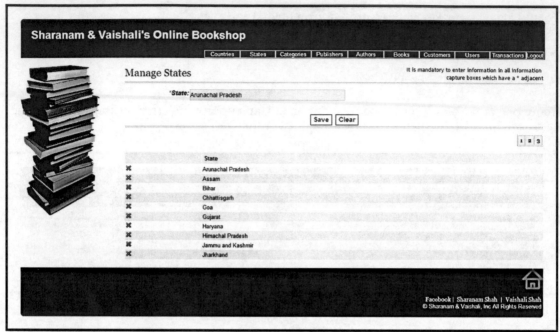

Diagram 7.4.4: Manage States [Data Populated]

Make the desired changes and click Save .

Clicking Save , performs the following client side validations:

❑   State name cannot be left blank

If any one of the above mentioned validation fail, an appropriate error message is displayed, as shown in diagram 7.4.5.

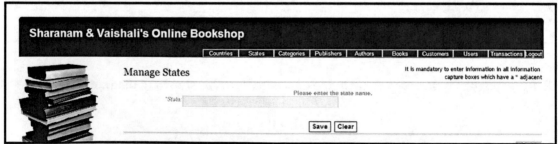

Diagram 7.4.5: Manage States [Error Message]

Correct the error. After doing so, click Save to save the entered data in the database.

If all the validations mentioned above go through without any errors, the data is updated in the database and the page is reloaded to reflect the modified data.

Deleting Existing Record

To delete already existing record, click ✖ adjacent to the desired record from the GRID, as shown in diagram 7.4.6.

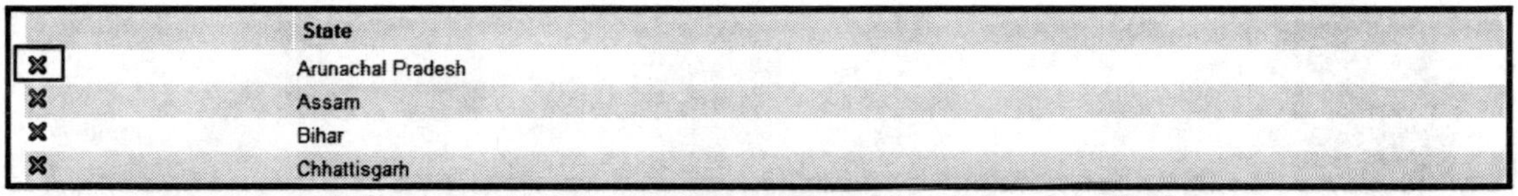

	State
✖	Arunachal Pradesh
✖	Assam
✖	Bihar
✖	Chhattisgarh

Diagram 7.4.6: Manage States [GRID for deletion]

Clicking ✖, performs the delete operation and reloads the page to reflect the deleted records.

If the user attempts to delete record that is associated with the existing data an error message appears indicating the same, as shown in diagram 7.4.7.

Deleting a master record that has been associated with detail records in this case Authors, Publishers, Customers and Signup cannot be deleted.

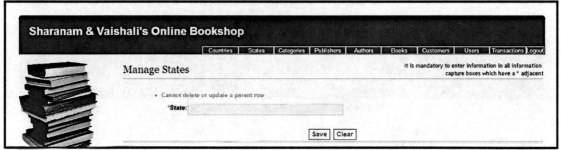

Diagram 7.4.7: Manage States [Error Message]

Manage Categories

Click **Categories**. This delivers the Manage Categories data entry form, as shown in diagram 7.5.1.

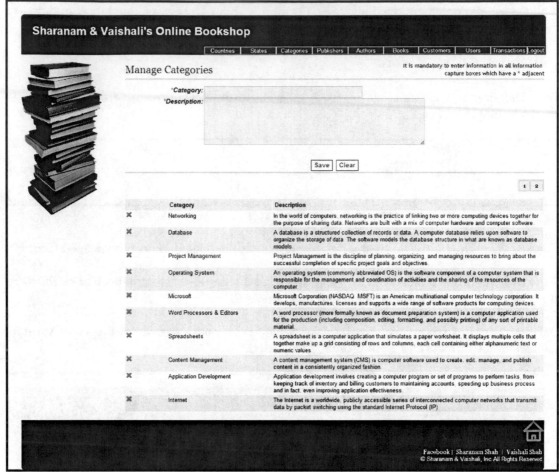

Diagram 7.5.1: Manage Categories

REMINDER

It is mandatory to enter information in all information capture boxes which have a * adjacent indicates entering values for all the form field labels that are marked * is mandatory.

1 2 3 4 5 can be used to navigate across additional records that are paginated to save space.

Data entered in this form is used to populate Category drop down list boxes in the Manage Books page.

Adding New Record

As soon as the data entry form loads in the web browser, it's ready to capture new records.

To add a new category, key in the required form field(s) and click **Save**.

Clicking **Save**, performs the following client side validations:

❑ Category name cannot be left blank
❑ Description cannot be left blank

If any one of the above mentioned validations fails, an appropriate error message is displayed, as shown in diagram 7.5.2.

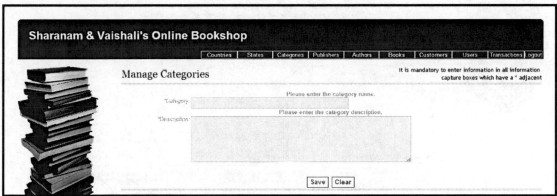

Diagram 7.5.2: Manage Categories [Error Message]

Correct the errors. After doing so, click **Save** to save the entered data in the database.

If all the validations mentioned above go through without any errors, the data is saved in the database and the page is reloaded to reflect the newly added data.

Modifying Existing Record

To modify an already existing record, click the desired record from the GRID, as shown in diagram 7.5.3.

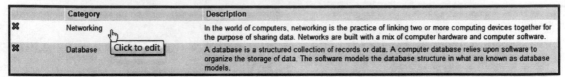

Diagram 7.5.3: Manage Categories [GRID for modification]

Doing so populates the record data in the data entry form, as shown in diagram 7.5.4.

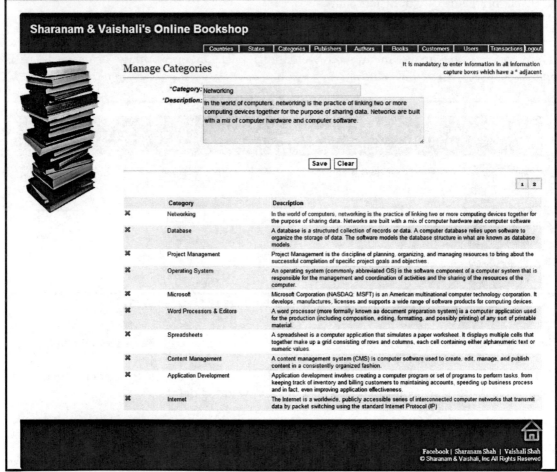

Diagram 7.5.4: Manage Categories [Data Populated]

Make the desired changes and click **Save**.

Clicking **Save**, performs the following client side validations:

❑ Category name cannot be left blank

❑ Description cannot be left blank

If any one of the above mentioned validations fails, an appropriate error message is displayed, as shown in diagram 7.5.5.

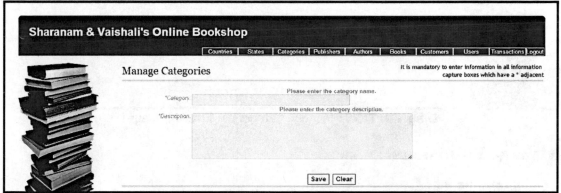

Diagram 7.5.5: Manage Categories [Error Message]

Correct the errors. After doing so, click **Save** to save the entered data in the database.

If all the validations mentioned above go through without any errors, the data is updated in the database and the page is reloaded to reflect the modified data.

Deleting Existing Record

To delete already existing record, click ✖ adjacent to the desired record from the GRID, as shown in diagram 7.5.6.

	Category	Description
✖	Networking	In the world of computers, networking is the practice of linking two or more computing devices together for the purpose of sharing data. Networks are built with a mix of computer hardware and computer software.
✖	Database	A database is a structured collection of records or data. A computer database relies upon software to organize the storage of data. The software models the database structure in what are known as database models.

Diagram 7.5.6: Manage Categories [GRID for deletion]

Clicking ✖, performs the delete operation and reloads the page to reflect the deleted records.

If the user attempts to delete record(s) that are associated with the existing data an error message appears indicating the same, as shown in diagram 7.5.7.

Deleting a master record that has been associated with detail records in this case Books cannot be deleted.

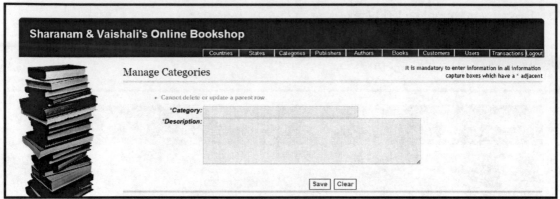

Diagram 7.5.7: Manage Categories [Error Message]

Manage Publishers

Click **Publishers**. This delivers the Manage Publishers data entry form, as shown in diagram 7.6.1.

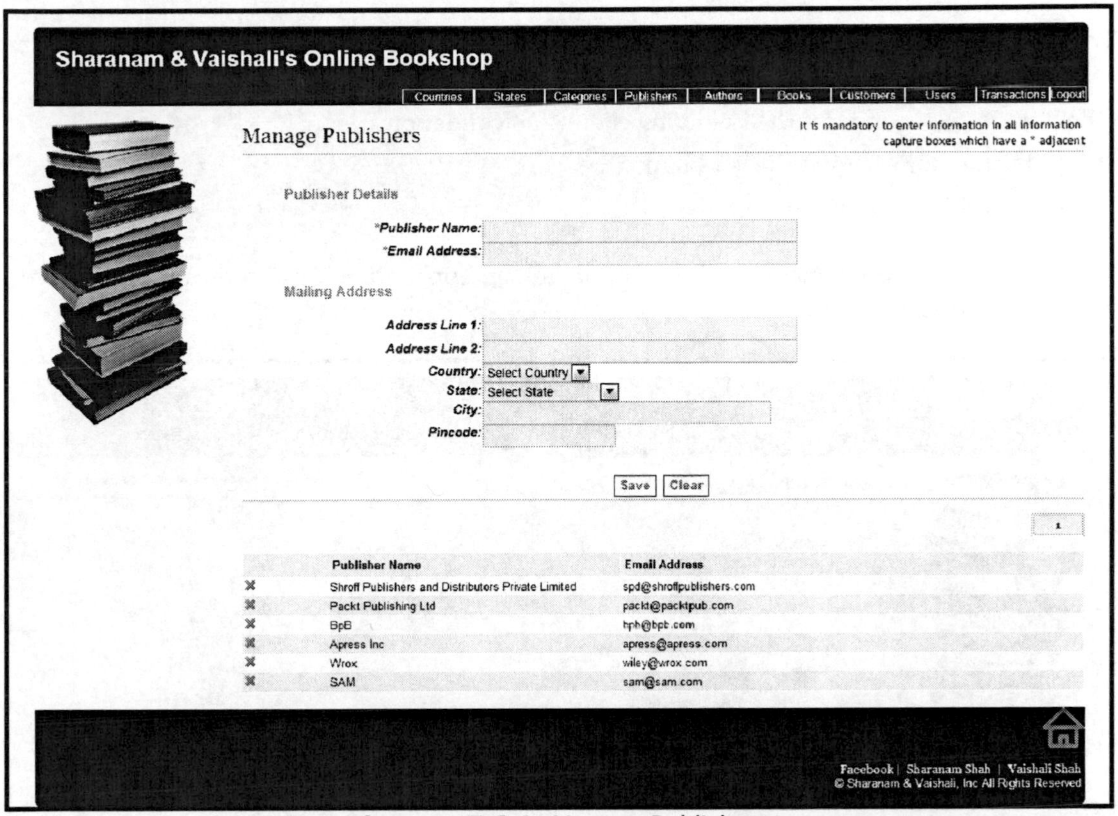

Diagram 7.6.1: Manage Publishers

REMINDER

It is mandatory to enter information in all information capture boxes which have a * adjacent indicates entering values for all the form field labels that are marked * is mandatory.

1 2 3 4 5 can be used to navigate across additional records that are paginated to save space.

Data entered in this form is used to populate Publisher drop down list boxes in the Manage Books page.

Adding New Record

As soon as the data entry form loads in the web browser, it's ready to capture new records.

To add a new publisher, key in the required form field(s) and click **Save**.

Clicking **Save**, performs the following client side validations:

❑ Publisher name cannot be left blank

❑ Email address cannot be left blank

If any one of the above mentioned validation fail, an appropriate error message is displayed as shown in diagram 7.6.2.

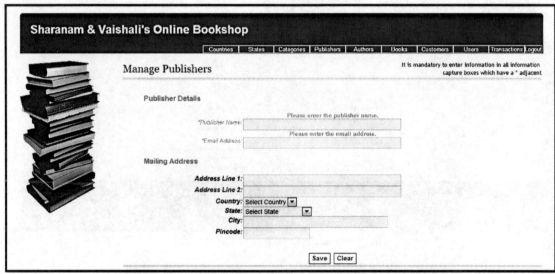

Diagram 7.6.2: Manage Publishers [Error Message]

Correct the errors. After doing so, click **Save** to save the entered data in the database.

If all the validations mentioned above go through without any errors, the data is saved in the database and the page is reloaded to reflect the newly added data.

Modifying Existing Record

To modify an already existing record, click the desired record from the GRID, as shown in diagram 7.6.3.

	Publisher Name	Email Address
✖	Shroff Publishers and Distributors Private Limited	spd@shroffpublishers.com
✖	Packt Publishing Ltd	packt@packtpub.com
✖	BpB	Click to edit b.com

Diagram 7.6.3: Manage Publishers [GRID for modification]

Doing so populates the record data in the data entry form, as shown in diagram 7.6.4.

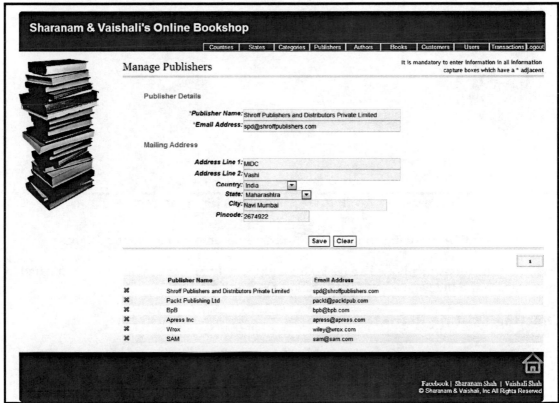

Diagram 7.6.4: Manage Publishers [Data Populated]

Make the desired changes and click Save .

Clicking Save , performs the following client side validations:

❑ Publisher name cannot be left blank

❑ Email address cannot be left blank

If any one of the above mentioned validations fails, an appropriate error message is displayed, as shown in diagram 7.6.5.

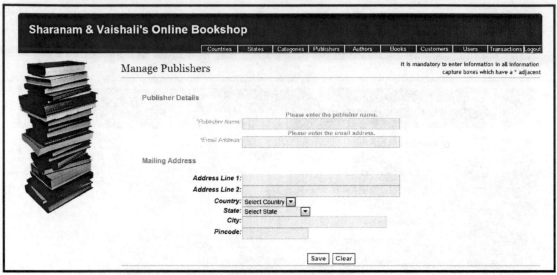

Diagram 7.6.5: Manage Publishers [Error Message]

Correct the error. After doing so, click **Save** to save the entered data in the database.

If all the validations mentioned above go through without any errors, the data is updated in the database and the page is reloaded to reflect the modified data.

Deleting Existing Record

To delete already existing record, click ✖ adjacent to the desired record from the GRID, as shown in diagram 7.6.6.

	Publisher Name	Email Address
✖	Shroff Publishers and Distributors Private Limited	spd@shroffpublishers.com
✖	Packt Publishing Ltd	packt@packtpub.com
✖	BpB	bpb@bpb.com

Diagram 7.6.6: Manage Publishers [GRID for deletion]

Clicking ✖, performs the delete operation and reloads the page to reflect the deleted records.

If the user attempts to delete record(s) that are associated with the existing data an error message appears indicating the same, as shown in diagram 7.6.7.

Deleting a master record that has been associated with detail records in this case Books cannot be deleted.

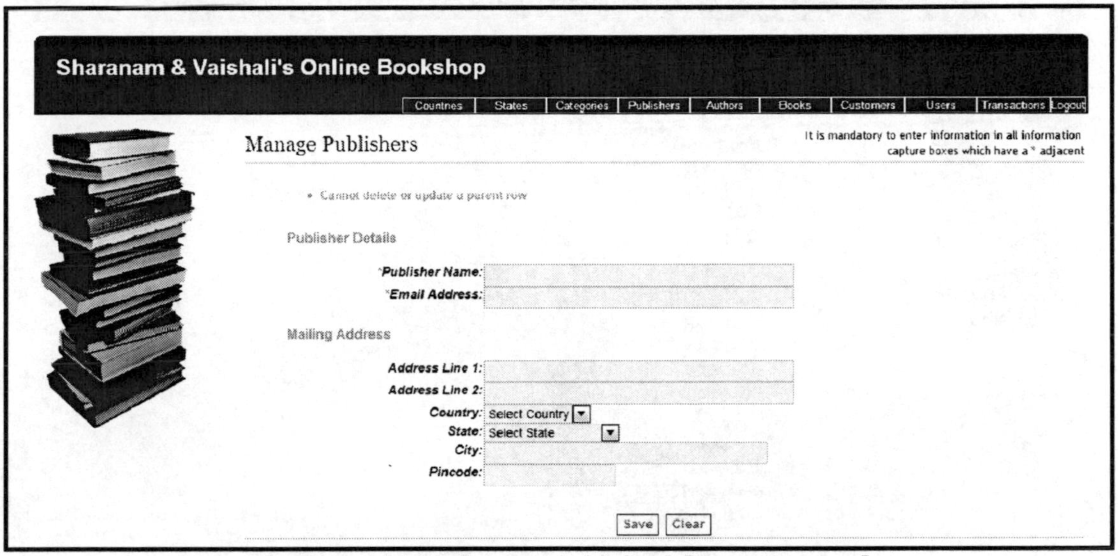

Diagram 7.6.7: Manage Publishers [Error Message]

Manage Authors

Click **Authors** . This delivers the Manage Authors data entry form, as shown in diagram 7.7.1.

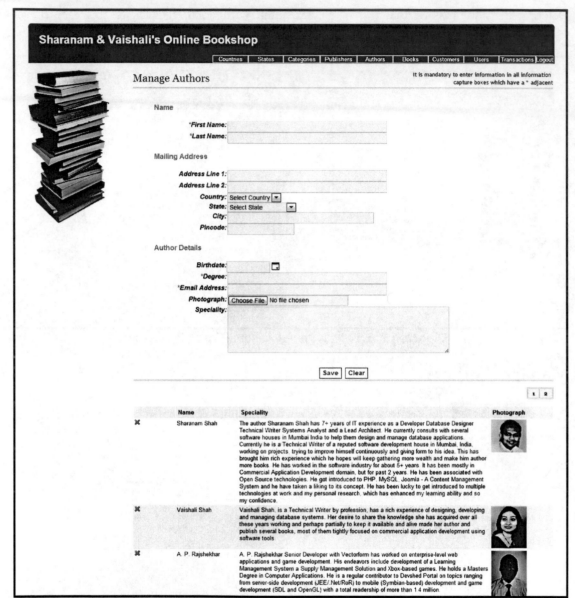

Diagram 7.7.1: Manage Authors

REMINDER

It is mandatory to enter information in all information capture boxes which have a * adjacent indicates entering values for all the form field labels that are marked * is mandatory.

1 2 3 4 5 can be used to navigate across additional records that are paginated to save space.

Data entered in this form is used to populate Author drop down list boxes in the Manage Books page.

Adding New Record

As soon as the data entry form loads in the web browser, it's ready to capture new records.

To add a new author, key in the required form field(s) and click **Save** .

To upload the author photograph, click **Choose File**. Clicking **Choose File** opens **Open** dialog box, as shown in diagram 7.7.1.1.

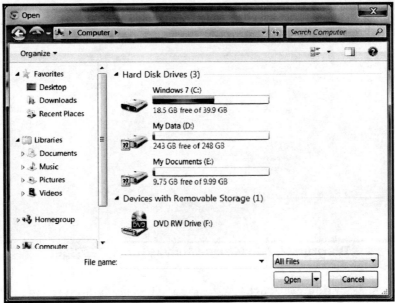

Diagram 7.7.1.1: Manage Authors [Upload Photograph]

Choose the desired image file and click **Open** .

Clicking **Save** , performs the following client side validations:
- First name cannot be left blank
- Last name cannot be left blank

❑ Degree cannot be left blank

❑ Email address cannot be left blank

If any one of the above mentioned validation fail, an appropriate error message is displayed, as shown in diagram 7.7.2.

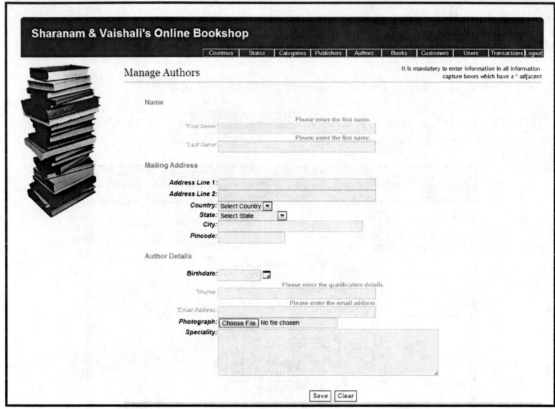

Diagram 7.7.2: Manage Authors [Error Message]

Correct the errors. After doing so, click **Save** to save the entered data in the database.

If all the validations mentioned above go through without any errors, the data is saved in the database and the page is reloaded to reflect the newly added data.

Modifying Existing Record

To modify an already existing record click the desired record from the GRID, as shown in diagram 7.7.3.

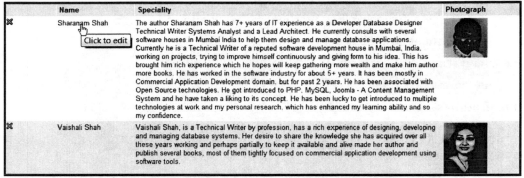

Name	Speciality	Photograph
Sharanam Shah	The author Sharanam Shah has 7+ years of IT experience as a Developer Database Designer Technical Writer Systems Analyst and a Lead Architect. He currently consults with several software houses in Mumbai India to help them design and manage database applications. Currently he is a Technical Writer of a reputed software development house in Mumbai, India, working on projects, trying to improve himself continuously and giving form to his idea. This has brought him rich experience which he hopes will keep gathering more wealth and make him author more books. He has worked in the software industry for about 5+ years. It has been mostly in Commercial Application Development domain, but for past 2 years. He has been associated with Open Source technologies. He got introduced to PHP, MySQL, Joomla - A Content Management System and he have taken a liking to its concept. He has been lucky to get introduced to multiple technologies at work and my personal research, which has enhanced my learning ability and so my confidence.	
Vaishali Shah	Vaishali Shah, is a Technical Writer by profession, has a rich experience of designing, developing and managing database systems. Her desire to share the knowledge she has acquired over all these years working and perhaps partially to keep it available and alive made her author and publish several books, most of them tightly focused on commercial application development using software tools.	

Diagram 7.7.3: Manage Authors [GRID for modification]

Doing so populates the record data in the data entry form, as shown in diagram 7.7.4.

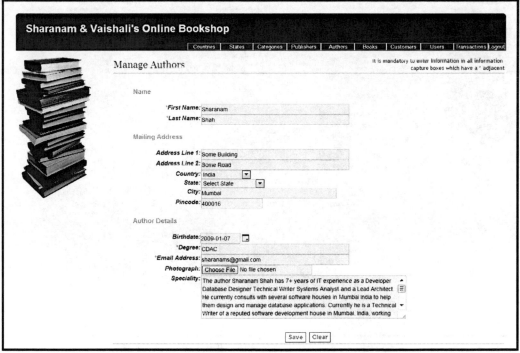

Diagram 7.7.4: Manage Authors [Data Populated]

Make the desired changes and click Save.

Clicking **Save** , performs the following client side validations:

❑ First name cannot be left blank

❑ Last name cannot be left blank

❑ Degree cannot be left blank

❑ Email address cannot be left blank

If any one of the above mentioned validation fail, an appropriate error message is displayed, as shown in diagram 7.7.5.

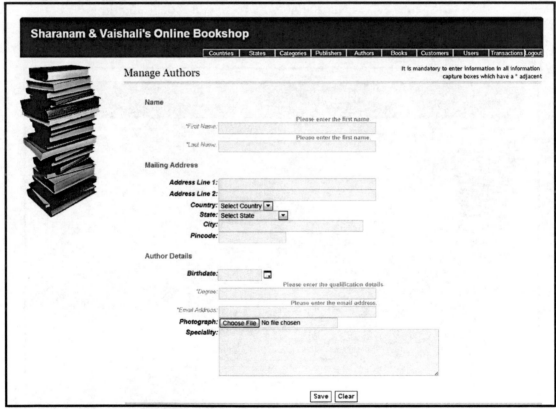

Diagram 7.7.5: Manage Authors [Error Message]

Correct the errors. After doing so, click **Save** to save the entered data in the database.

If all the validations mentioned above go through without any errors, the data is updated in the database and the page is reloaded to reflect the modified data.

Deleting Existing Record

To delete already existing record, click ✖ adjacent to the desired record from the GRID, as shown in diagram 7.7.6.

	Name	Speciality	Photograph
✖	Sharanam Shah	The author Sharanam Shah has 7+ years of IT experience as a Developer Database Designer Technical Writer Systems Analyst and a Lead Architect. He currently consults with several software houses in Mumbai India to help them design and manage database applications. Currently he is a Technical Writer of a reputed software development house in Mumbai, India, working on projects, trying to improve himself continuously and giving form to his idea. This has brought him rich experience which he hopes will keep gathering more wealth and make him author more books. He has worked in the software industry for about 5+ years. It has been mostly in Commercial Application Development domain, but for past 2 years. He has been associated with Open Source technologies. He got introduced to PHP, MySQL, Joomla - A Content Management System and he have taken a liking to its concept. He has been lucky to get introduced to multiple technologies at work and my personal research, which has enhanced my learning ability and so my confidence.	
✖	Vaishali Shah	Vaishali Shah, is a Technical Writer by profession, has a rich experience of designing, developing and managing database systems. Her desire to share the knowledge she has acquired over all these years working and perhaps partially to keep it available and alive made her author and publish several books, most of them tightly focused on commercial application development using software tools.	

Diagram 7.7.6: Manage Authors [GRID for deletion]

Clicking ✖, performs the delete operation and reloads the page to reflect the deleted records.

If the user attempts to delete record that is associated with the existing data an error message appears indicating the same, as shown in diagram 7.7.7.

Deleting a master record that has been associated with detail records in this case Books cannot be deleted.

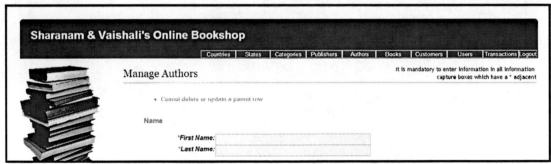

Diagram 7.7.7: Manage Authors [Error Message]

Manage Books

Click **Books**. This delivers the Manage Books data entry form, as shown in diagram 7.8.1.

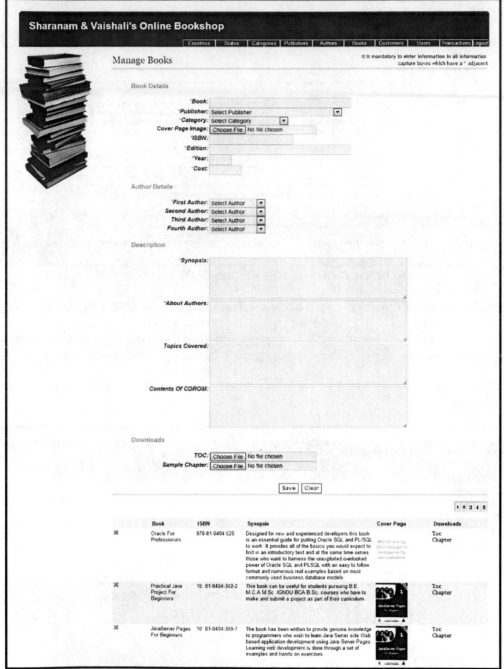

Diagram 7.8.1: Manage Books

REMINDER

It is mandatory to enter information in all information capture boxes which have a * adjacent indicates entering values for all the form field labels that are marked * is mandatory.

1 2 3 4 5 can be used to navigate across additional records that are paginated to save space.

Adding New Record

As soon as the data entry form loads in the web browser, it's ready to capture new records.

To add a new book, key in the required form field(s) for the book being added and click **Save**.

To upload the book's cover page, click Choose File. Clicking Choose File opens Open dialog box, as shown in diagram 7.8.1.1.

Diagram 7.8.1.1: Manage Books [Upload Cover Page]

Choose the desired image file and click Open. Similarly, TOC and Sample Chapter files can be uploaded.

Clicking **Save**, performs the following client side validations:

❑ Book name cannot be left blank

❑ Publisher name cannot be left blank

❑ Category name cannot be left blank

❑ ISBN cannot be left blank

❑ Edition cannot be left blank

❑ Year cannot be left blank

❑ Cost cannot be left blank

❑ First author cannot be left blank

❑ Synopsis cannot be left blank

❑ About authors cannot be left blank

If any one of the above mentioned validations fails, an appropriate error message is displayed, as shown in diagram 7.8.2.

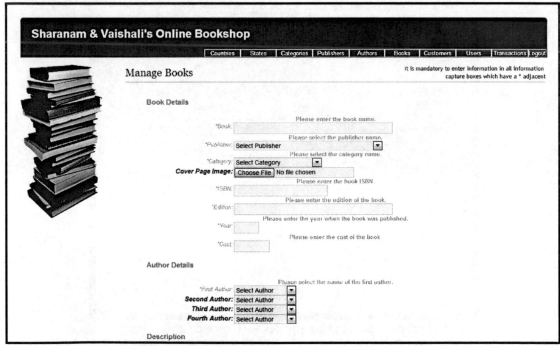

Diagram 7.8.2: Manage Books [Error Message]

Correct the errors. After doing so, click **Save** to save the entered data in the database.

If all the validations mentioned above go through without any errors, the data is saved in the database and the page is reloaded to reflect the newly added data.

After the book is added, an email, as shown in diagram 7.8.3, is dispatched to all those customers who had subscribed for **New Releases** whilst signing up.

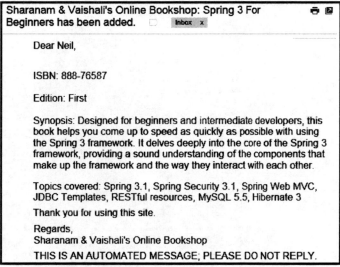

Diagram 7.8.3: Email for New Releases

Modifying Existing Record

To modify an already existing record click the desired record from the GRID, as shown in diagram 7.8.4.

	Book	ISBN	Synopsis	Cover Page	Downloads
✖	Oracle For Professionals Click to edit	978-81-8404-526	Designed for new and experienced developers this book is an essential guide for putting Oracle SQL and PL/SQL to work. It provides all of the basics you would expect to find in an introductory text and at the same time serves those who want to harness the unexploited overlooked power of Oracle SQL and PLSQL with an easy to follow format and numerous real examples based on most commonly used business database models.	We're sorry, this image is temporarily unavailable	Toc Chapter
✖	Practical Java Project For Beginners	10: 81-8404-342-2	This book can be useful for students pursuing B.E. M.C.A M.Sc. IGNOU BCA B.Sc. courses who have to make and submit a project as part of their curriculum.		Toc Chapter
✖	JavaServer Pages For Beginners	10: 81-8404-359-7	The book has been written to provide genuine knowledge to programmers who wish to learn Java Server side Web based application development using Java Server Pages. Learning web development is done through a set of examples and hands on exercises		Toc Chapter

Diagram 7.8.4: Manage Books [GRID for modification]

Doing so populates the record data in the data entry form, as shown in diagram 7.8.5.

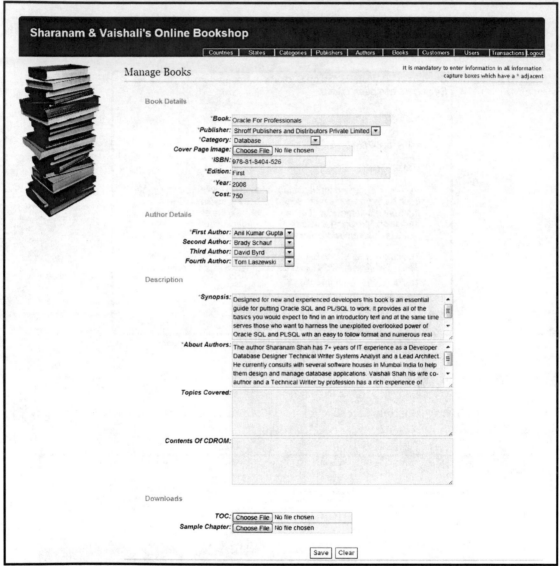

Diagram 7.8.5: Manage Books [Data Populated]

Make the desired changes and click **Save**.

If the TOC or Sample Chapter is not re-uploaded whilst editing the record, then the previous ones are deleted.

Clicking **Save**, performs the following client side validations:

❏   Book name cannot be left blank

❏   Publisher name cannot be left blank

❏   Category name cannot be left blank

❏   ISBN cannot be left blank

❏   Edition cannot be left blank

❏   Year cannot be left blank

❏   Cost cannot be left blank

❏   First author cannot be left blank

❏   Synopsis cannot be left blank

❏   About authors cannot be left blank

If any one of the above mentioned validations fails, an appropriate error message is displayed, as shown in diagram 7.8.6.

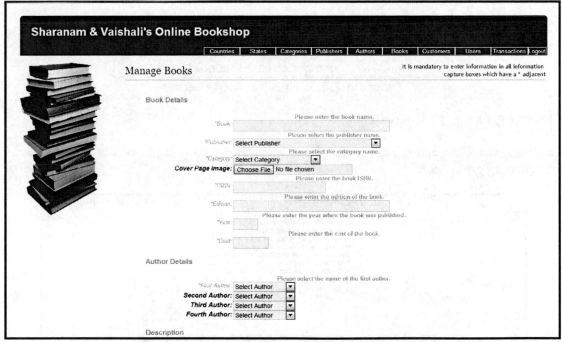

Diagram 7.8.6: Manage Books [Error Message]

Correct the errors. After doing so, click **Save** to save the entered data in the database.

If all the validations mentioned above go through without any errors, the data is updated in the database and the page is reloaded to reflect the modified data.

After the book is updated, an email, as shown in diagram 7.8.7, is dispatched to all those customers who had subscribed for **Book Updates** whilst signing up.

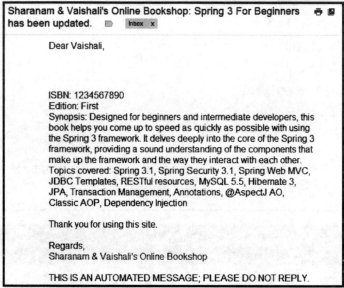

Diagram 7.8.7: Email for Book Updates

Deleting Existing Record

To delete already existing record, click ✖ adjacent to the desired record from the GRID, as shown in diagram 7.8.8.

	Book	ISBN	Synopsis	Cover Page	Downloads
✖	Oracle For Professionals	978-81-8404-526	Designed for new and experienced developers this book is an essential guide for putting Oracle SQL and PL/SQL to work. It provides all of the basics you would expect to find in an introductory text and at the same time serves those who want to harness the unexploited overlooked power of Oracle SQL and PLSQL with an easy to follow format and numerous real examples based on most commonly used business database models.	We're sorry, this image is temporarily unavailable	Toc Chapter
✖	Practical Java Project For Beginners	10: 81-8404-342-2	This book can be useful for students pursuing B.E. M.C.A M.Sc. IGNOU BCA B.Sc. courses who have to make and submit a project as part of their curriculum.		Toc Chapter
✖	JavaServer Pages For Beginners	10: 81-8404-359-7	The book has been written to provide genuine knowledge to programmers who wish to learn Java Server side Web based application development using Java Server Pages. Learning web development is done through a set of examples and hands on exercises		Toc Chapter

Diagram 7.8.8: Manage Books [GRID for deletion]

Clicking ✖, performs the delete operation and reloads the page to reflect the deleted records.

Manage Customers

After the customer registers/signs up using the signup data entry form, the system user from the backend can modify, delete or view the customer details.

Click Customers . This delivers the Manage Customers data entry form, as shown in diagram 7.9.1.

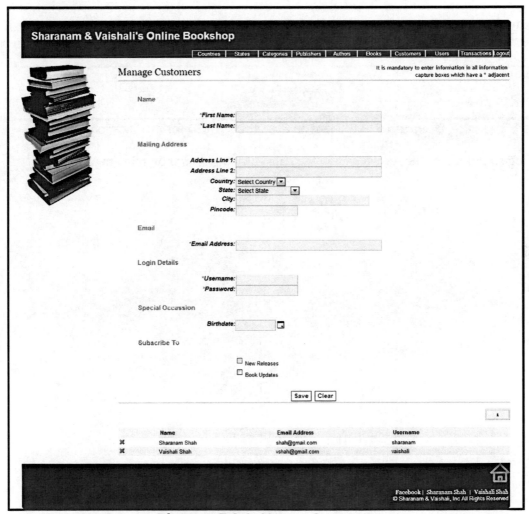

Diagram 7.9.1: Manage Customers

REMINDER

It is mandatory to enter information in all information capture boxes which have a * adjacent indicates entering values for all the form field labels that are marked * is mandatory.

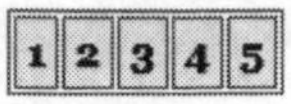

 can be used to navigate across additional records that are paginated to save space.

Modifying Existing Record

To modify an already existing record click the desired record from the GRID, as shown in diagram 7.9.2.

	Name	Email Address	Username
✖	Sharanam Shah	shah@gmail.com	sharanam
✖	Vaishali Shah	vshah@gmail.com	vaishali

Click to edit

Diagram 7.9.2: Manage Customers [GRID for modification]

Doing so populates the record data in the data entry form, as shown in diagram 7.9.3.

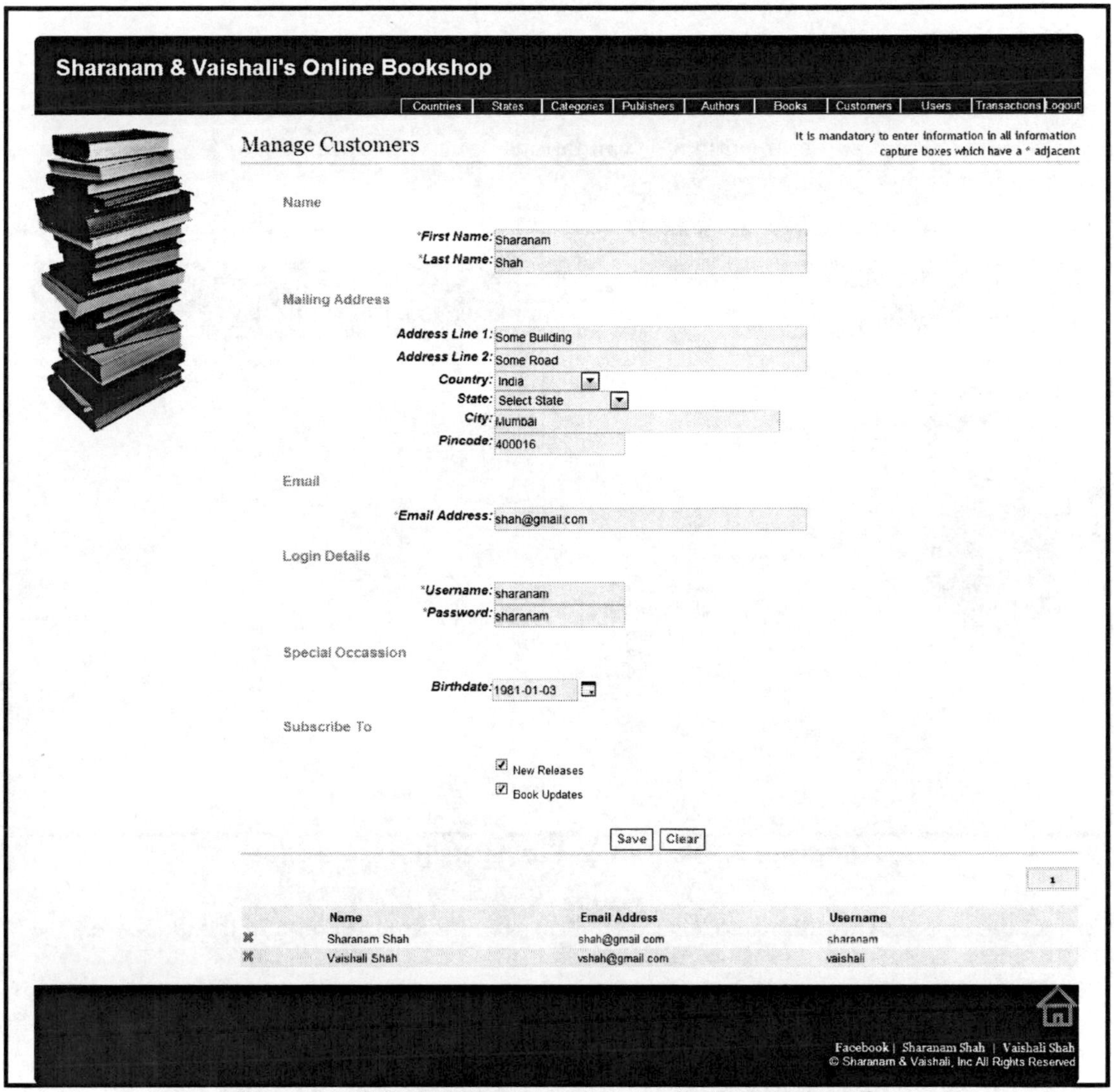

Diagram 7.9.3: Manage Customers [Data Populated]

Make the desired changes and click **Save**.

Clicking **Save**, performs the following client side validations:

❑ First name cannot be left blank

❑ Last name cannot be left blank

❑ Email address cannot be left blank

❑ Username cannot be left blank
❑ Password cannot be left blank

If any one of the above mentioned validations fails, an appropriate error message is displayed, as shown in diagram 7.9.4.

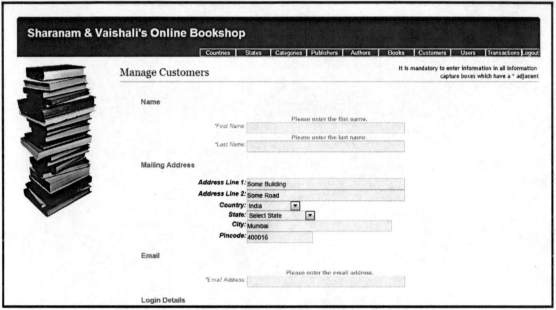

Diagram 7.9.4: Manage Customers [Error Message]

Correct the errors. After doing so, click **Save** to save the entered data in the database.

If all the validations mentioned above go through without any errors, the data is updated in the database and the page is reloaded to reflect the modified data.

Deleting Existing Record

To delete already existing record, click ✖ adjacent to the desired record from the GRID, as shown in diagram 7.9.5.

	Name	Email Address	Username
✖	Sharanam Shah	shah@gmail.com	sharanam
✖	Vaishali Shah	vshah@gmail.com	vaishali

Diagram 7.9.5: Manage Customers [GRID for deletion]

Clicking ✖, performs the delete operation and reloads the page to reflect the deleted records.

Manage Users

Click [Users]. This delivers the Manage Users data entry form, as shown in diagram 7.10.1.

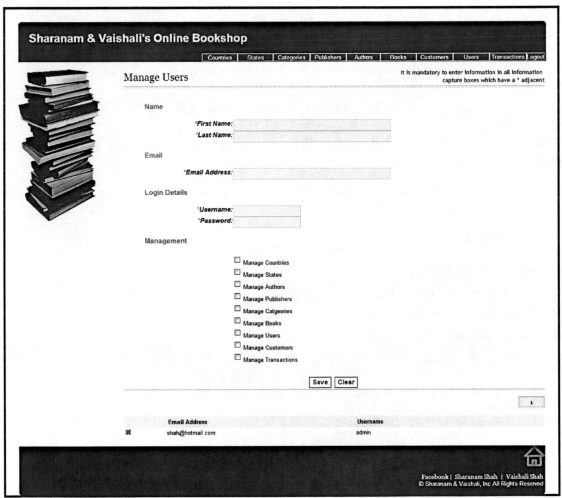

Diagram 7.10.1: Manage Users

REMINDER

 It is mandatory to enter information in all information
capture boxes which have a * adjacent indicates entering values for all the form
field labels that are marked * is mandatory.

1 2 3 4 5 can be used to navigate across additional records that are paginated to save space.

Adding New Record

As soon as the data entry form loads in the web browser, it's ready to capture new records.

To add a new user, key in the required form field(s) and click **Save**.

In this form, the **Management** section allows assigning rights to the user based on which access to appropriate data entry forms will be granted to that user on login.

The options under the Management section that are not chosen will simply not be visible as menu options when that user logs into the system.

Clicking **Save**, performs the following client side validations:
- First name cannot be left blank
- Last name cannot be left blank
- Email address cannot be left blank
- Username cannot be left blank
- Password cannot be left blank

If any one of the above mentioned validations fails, an appropriate error message is displayed, as shown in diagram 7.10.2.

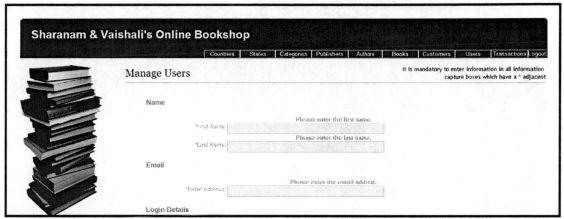

Diagram 7.10.2: Manage Users [Error Message]

Correct the errors. After doing so, click **Save** to save the entered data in the database.

If all the validations mentioned above go through without any errors, the data is saved in the database and the page is reloaded to reflect the newly added data.

Modifying Existing Record

To modify an already existing record click the desired record from the GRID, as shown in diagram 7.10.3.

Diagram 7.10.3: Manage Users [GRID for modification]

Doing so populates the record data in the data entry form, as shown in diagram 7.10.4.

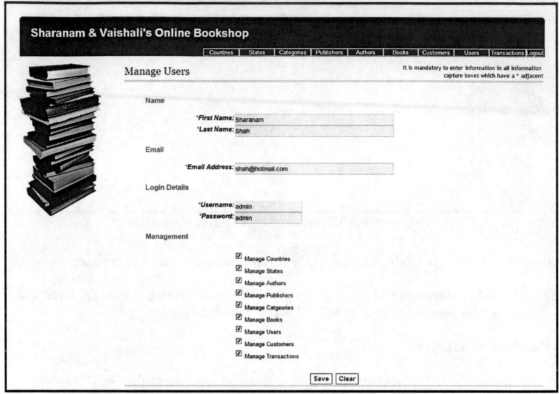

Diagram 7.10.4: Manage Users [Data Populated]

Make the desired changes and click **Save**.

Clicking **Save**, performs the following client side validations:

❑   First name cannot be left blank

❑   Last name cannot be left blank

❑   Email address cannot be left blank

❑   Username cannot be left blank

❑   Password cannot be left blank

If any one of the above mentioned validations fails, an appropriate error message is displayed, as shown in diagram 7.10.5.

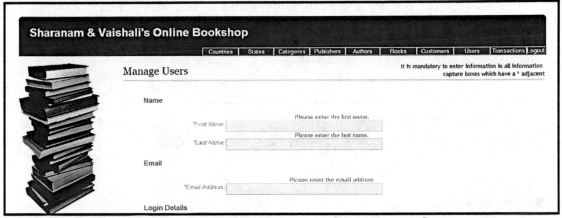

Diagram 7.10.5: Manage Users [Error Message]

Correct the error. After doing so, click **Save** to save the entered data in the database.

If all the validations mentioned above go through without any errors, the data is updated in the database and the page is reloaded to reflect the modified data.

Deleting Existing Record

To delete already existing record, click ✖ adjacent to the desired record from the GRID, as shown in diagram 7.10.6.

Diagram 7.10.6: Manage Users [GRID for deletion]

Clicking ✖, performs the delete operation and reloads the page to reflect the deleted records.

Manage Transactions

After the order is placed and an email is received, the seller [site owner] ensures that the payment is received/credited to the bank account. If this is true then the seller arranges to deliver the said books to the buyer [customer].

Every transaction that takes place is logged by the application and is displayed under Site Administration [Backend] → Manage Transactions.

The site owner or the employee logs in to the backend and views such transactions, if desired.

To manage transactions, click Transactions . This delivers the Manage Transactions data entry form, as shown in diagram 7.11.1.

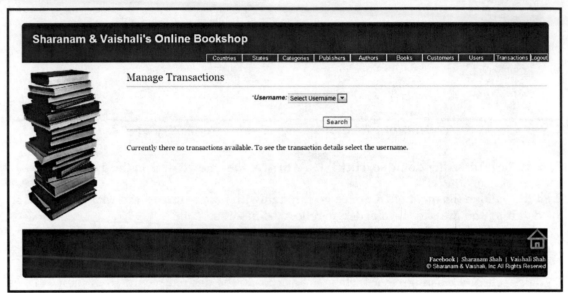

Diagram 7.11.1: Manage Transactions

Viewing The Transaction Reports

To view transactions for a user, choose a username from the drop down list box and click Search .

This displays all the transactions details that were performed by that user, as shown in diagram 7.11.2.

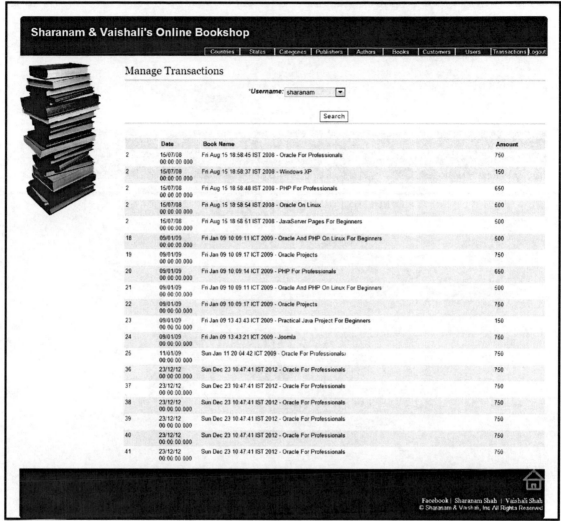

Diagram 7.11.2: Manage Transactions

Logout

Logout when clicked, destroys the user session and delivers the backend Login page, as shown in diagram 7.12.

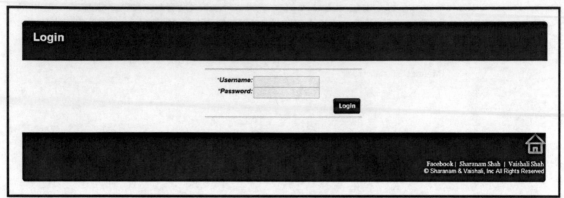

Diagram 7.12: The Backend Login page

Chapter

8

SECTION III: END USER MANUAL

Frontend [Customer Facing]

The frontend consists of the following:

- Login
  - Forgot Password
- Signup
- New Releases

  Ability to display a list of book names that were recently released
- Updated Books

  Ability to display a list of book names that were recently updated
- Top Titles

  Ability to display a list of book names that were most viewed
- Our Authors

  Ability to display a list of available author names
- Our Publishers

  Ability to display a list of available publisher names

❑ Search

  Using any keywords such as book name, author name, ISBN, cost of the book, synopsis, about authors

❑ Directory of available books [Category Wise]

  Ability to view book names segregated under category heads

❑ Payment Gateway using Google Wallet

  Ability to buy books using the shopping cart and transferring the information [individual book details: Book Name, Price] to Google Wallet for payment processing using Credit Card

To be able to use the Frontend, Master records need to be added to the database using the following data entry forms. The book's CDROM holds a .sql file which can be imported to have some sample data to work with:

❑ Manage

  o Countries

  o States

  o Authors

  o Publishers

  o Categories

  o Books

Frontend Home Page

The frontend homepage, as shown in diagram 8.1 can be reached by invoking the application.

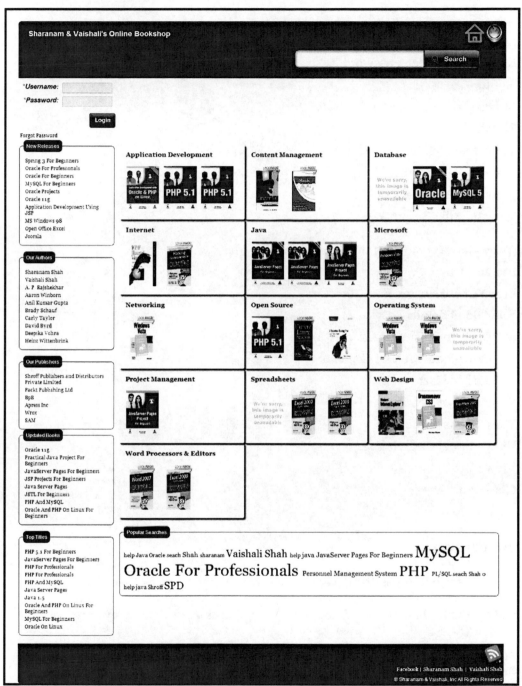

Diagram 8.1: The Frontend Homepage

This page allows visitors [who have not logged in] to:

❑ Login
❑ Retrieve Forgotten Password
❑ Signup
❑ Browse books using the Books directory
❑ Search
❑ View Book details
❑ View Author details
❑ View Publisher details
❑ View Popular Search Tags

This page allows customers [who have logged in] to:

❑ Search
❑ Browse books using Book directory
❑ View Book details
   o Download Sample Chapter
   o Download Table of Contents
   o Add to Cart
❑ View Author details
❑ View Publisher details
❑ View Popular Search Tags
❑ View Cart
❑ Checkout
❑ Logout

Forgot Password

To retrieve a forgotten password, click Forgot Password.

Forgot Password when clicked delivers the forgot password data entry form, as shown in diagram 8.2.1.

REMINDER

It is mandatory to enter information in all information
capture boxes which have a * adjacent indicates entering values for all the form
field labels that are marked * is mandatory.

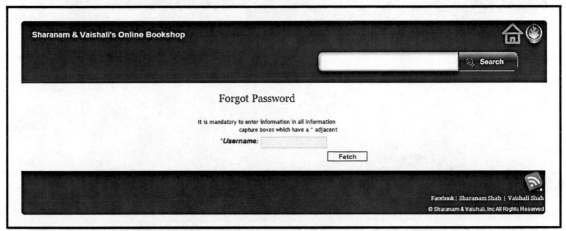

Diagram 8.2.1: The Forgot Password data entry form

Enter the username and click **Fetch**. Clicking **Fetch**, validates the captured details and if all fine, an email is send with the registration details such as username and password, as shown in diagram 8.2.2.

Diagram 8.2.2: The Forgot Password Email [Password retrieved]

Signup

Visitors can signup to the site using on the homepage.

when clicked delivers the Signup page, as shown in diagram 8.3.1.

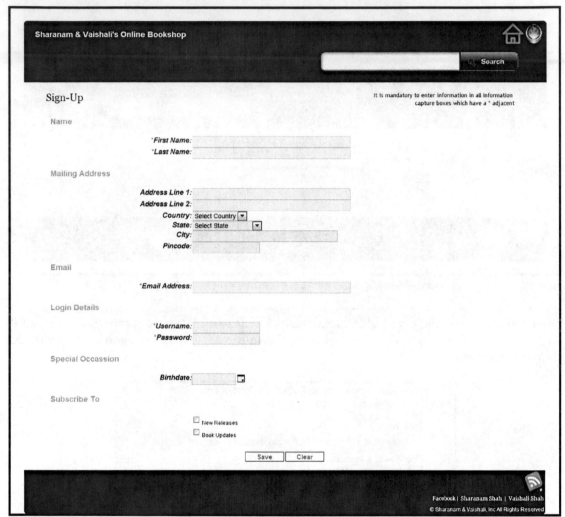

Diagram 8.3.1: The Signup page

REMINDER

    It is mandatory to enter information in all information capture boxes which have a * adjacent indicates entering values for all the form field labels that are marked * is mandatory.

Enter the required details as indicated in the data entry form and click Save.

Clicking Save , performs the following client side validations:

❑ First name cannot be left blank

❑ Last name cannot be left blank

❑ Email address cannot be left blank

❑ Username cannot be left blank

❑ Username should be unique

❑ Password cannot be left blank

If any one of the above mentioned client side validations fail, an appropriate error message is displayed, as shown in diagram 8.3.2.

Diagram 8.3.2: Signup [Error Message]

Correct the errors. After doing so, click **Save** to save the entered data in the database.

If all the validations mentioned above go through without any errors, the data is saved in the database and the thank you page appears, as shown in diagram 8.3.3.

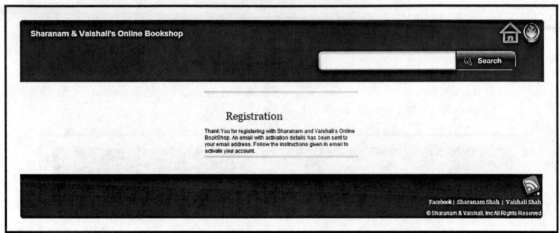

Diagram 8.3.3: Thank you page after registration

After successful registration, an email, as shown in diagram 8.3.4, is dispatched to the user.

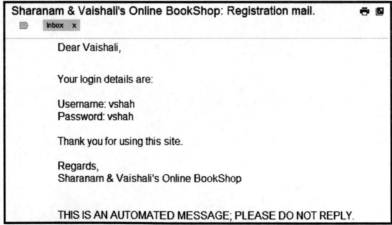

Diagram 8.3.4: Email on successful registration

Login

After a visitor registers and becomes a customer, the customer can login using the Login section in the homepage, as shown in diagram 8.4.1.

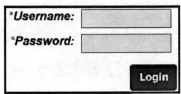

Diagram 8.4.1: The Frontend Homepage [Login]

Enter the appropriate username and password. Click [Login].

Homepage After Logging In

Clicking [Login], authenticates the username and password and if found valid,

❑ Creates a user session

❑ Unlocks the download links to Sample Chapter and TOC under book details

❑ Unlocks the Add to Cart links under book details

❑ Unlocks the Cart link in the homepage to view the cart contents [if any]

❑ Displays the Logout option

❑ Delivers the homepage with a welcome message, as shown in diagram 8.4.2

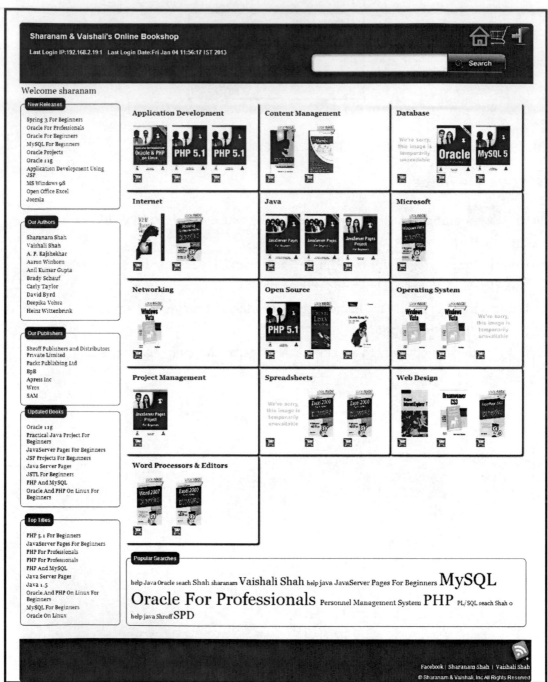

Diagram 8.4.2: The Homepage after logging in

Book Details

A visitor can view the book details of a book selected from one of the following sections:

Directory Listing

Diagram 8.5.1: Directory Listing

New Releases

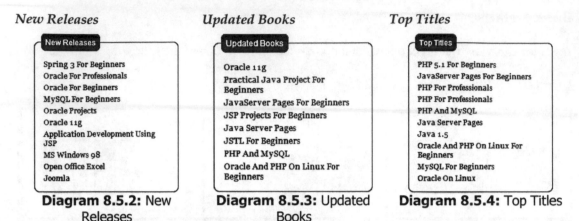

New Releases
Spring 3 For Beginners
Oracle For Professionals
Oracle For Beginners
MySQL For Beginners
Oracle Projects
Oracle 11g
Application Development Using JSP
MS Windows 98
Open Office Excel
Joomla

Diagram 8.5.2: New Releases

Updated Books

Updated Books
Oracle 11g
Practical Java Project For Beginners
JavaServer Pages For Beginners
JSP Projects For Beginners
Java Server Pages
JSTL For Beginners
PHP And MySQL
Oracle And PHP On Linux For Beginners

Diagram 8.5.3: Updated Books

Top Titles

Top Titles
PHP 5.1 For Beginners
JavaServer Pages For Beginners
PHP For Professionals
PHP For Professionals
PHP And MySQL
Java Server Pages
Java 1.5
Oracle And PHP On Linux For Beginners
MySQL For Beginners
Oracle On Linux

Diagram 8.5.4: Top Titles

Book Details Without Logging In

A link identified by a book name in one of these sections when clicked, displays book details of the selected book, as shown in diagram 8.5.5.

Sharanam & Vaishali's Online Bookshop
Search
Oracle Projects
Oracle
Designed for new and experienced developers this book is an essential guide for putting Oracle SQL and PL/SQL to work. It provides all of the basics you would expect to find in an introductory text and at the same time serves those who want to harness the unexploited overlooked power of Oracle SQL and PLSQL with an easy to follow format and numerous real examples based on most commonly used business database models.
ISBN: 978-681-8404-526
Edition: First
About Author(s)
The author Sharanam Shah has 7+ years of IT experience as a Developer Database Designer Technical Writer Systems Analyst and a Lead Architect. He currently consults with several software houses in Mumbai India to help them design and manage database applications. Vaishali Shah his wife co-author and a Technical Writer by profession has a rich experience of designing developing and managing database systems.
Topics Covered
Oracle, SQL, PLSQL, Java, PHP
Contents Of The CDROM
Source Code, Oracle XE 10g
Facebook | Sharanam Shah | Vaishali Shah
© Sharanam & Vaishali, Inc All Rights Reserved

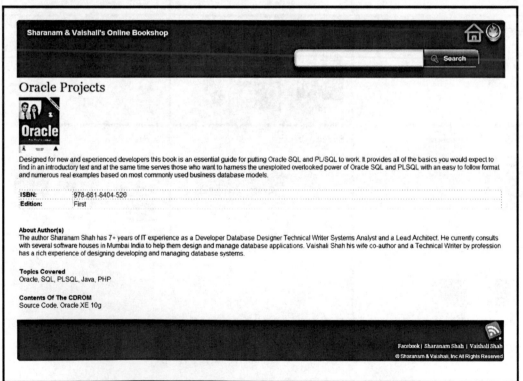

Diagram 8.5.5: Book Details page [without logged in]

Book Details After Logging In

If the customer has logged in and is viewing the book details page, then the page appears with additional options that allow adding the book to the cart, downloading sample chapters and TOC, as shown in diagram 8.5.6.

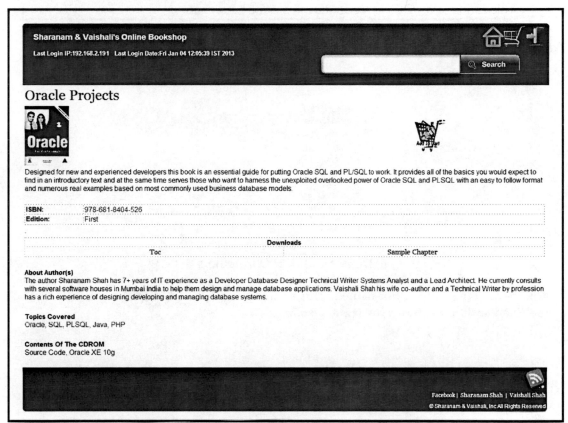

Diagram 8.5.6: Book Details page [after logging in]

Downloading Sample Chapter

Clicking Sample Chapter downloads the PDF file.

WARNING

 This requires a PDF file reader such as Adobe Acrobat.

Downloading TOC

Clicking TOC downloads the PDF file.

WARNING

 This requires a PDF file reader such as Adobe Acrobat.

Author Details

A visitor can view the author details from the following section on the homepage.

Diagram 8.6.1: Our Authors

A link identified by an author name in this section when clicked, displays author details of the selected author, as shown in diagram 8.6.2.

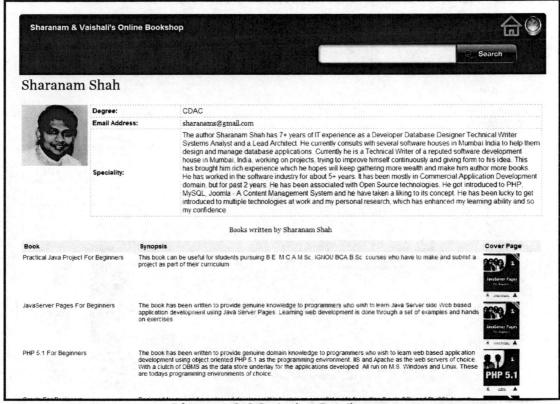

Diagram 8.6.2: Author Details page

This page shows **Add to cart** link, as shown in diagram 8.6.3, for logged in users.

Diagram 8.6.3: Author Details page [Logged in user]

This page also displays a list of the books written by that author.

Clicking an entry from the list displays that book's details, as shown in diagram 8.6.4. **Add To Cart** link appears for logged in users only.

Diagram 8.6.4: Book Details page [after logging in]

Category Details

A visitor can view the books available under a category from the following section on the homepage.

Diagram 8.7.1: Category wise books

A link identified by a category name in this section when clicked, displays books under that category, as shown in diagram 8.7.2.

Diagram 8.7.2: Category Details page

Clicking an entry from the list displays that book's details, as shown in diagram 8.7.3. **Add To Cart** link appears for logged in users only.

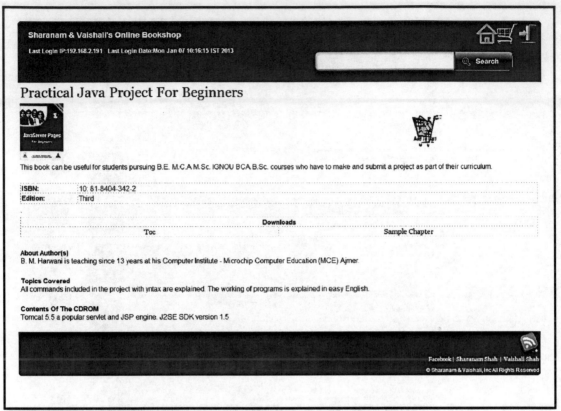

Diagram 8.7.3: Book Details page [after logging in]

Publisher Details

A visitor can view the publisher details from the following section on the homepage.

Diagram 8.8.1: Our Publishers

A link identified by a publisher name in this section when clicked, displays publisher details of the selected publisher, as shown in diagram 8.8.2.

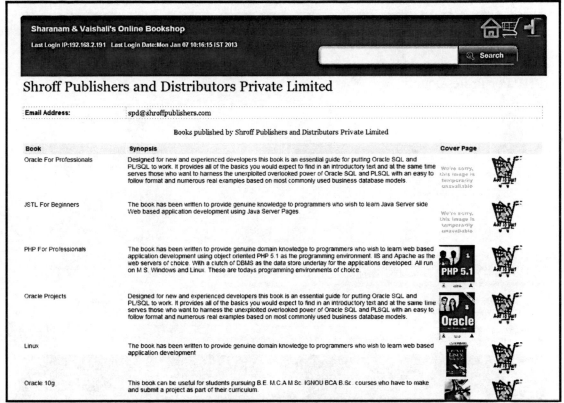

Diagram 8.8.2: Publisher Details page

This page also displays a list of the books published by that publisher.

Clicking an entry from the list displays that book's details, as shown in diagram 8.8.3. **Add To Cart** link appears for logged in users only.

Diagram 8.8.3: Book Details page [after logging in]

Search

A visitor can search for the desired book, author or publisher by keyword using the search section available in the homepage, as shown in diagram 8.9.1.

Diagram 8.9.1: Search section

Enter a keyword of choice and click Search.

Clicking Search, delivers the Search results, as shown in diagram 8.9.2.

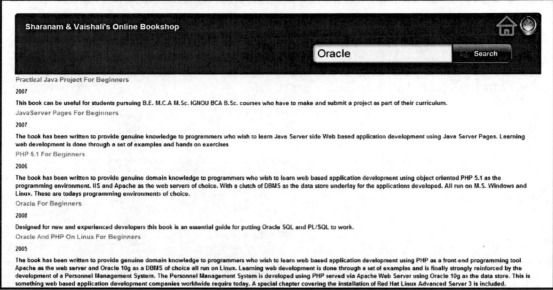

Diagram 8.9.2: The Search Results

Cart

A customer after logging in can click 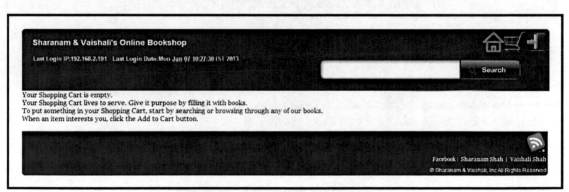 to view the content of the cart. If the customer has not added any books to the cart it will be empty, as shown in diagram 8.10.1.

Diagram 8.10.1: The Empty Cart

To add a book to the cart the customer needs to log in and click the book name link of the book of choice from the homepage. This delivers the book details page, as shown in diagram 8.10.2.

Diagram 8.10.2: Book Details page [after logging in]

Click 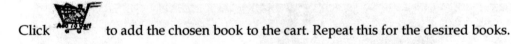 to add the chosen book to the cart. Repeat this for the desired books.

Now if the user clicks [cart icon], it will be populated with the books selected, as shown in diagram 8.10.3.

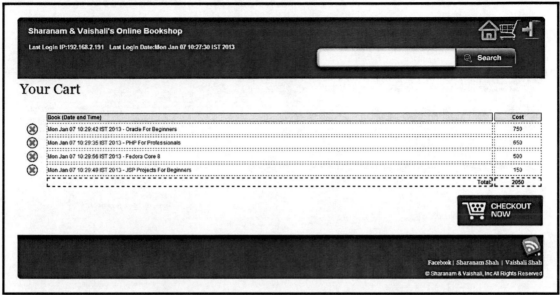

Diagram 8.10.3: The Cart with books added

 when clicked removes the book from the cart.

Checkout

WARNING

 For demonstration purpose, this application uses Google Wallet in sandbox mode, hence actual orders and payments do not take place. In a production environment, the sandbox mode should be disabled and actual mode should be enabled via code spec.

After the cart holds the desired books, the user can choose to checkout. This application uses Google Wallet.

Click ![CHECKOUT NOW]. This sends the cart details to Google for further processing and payment, as shown in diagram 8.11.1.

WARNING

If the Google Merchant ID is not set in the properties file, then the Google Wallet's Checkout option will not be available.

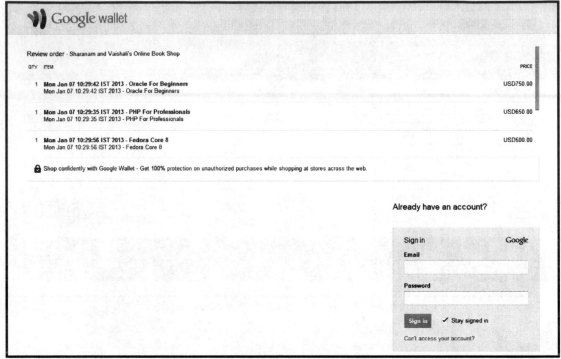

Diagram 8.11.1: Google Wallet

HINT

 This requires having a Google Account. If it does not exist, then create one using the "Create a Google Account to complete this purchase" section. Refer to *Appendix A: Understanding Google Wallet* for more information on Google Wallet.

Login using the Google account or create a new account, if one does not exist. Enter the credit card details.

Since this is a dummy [Sandbox] checkout, the following credit card details can be used:

❑ Credit card number: 4111-1111-1111-1111

❑ CVV number: Any three digits

❑ Card Expiry: Any month and year beyond the current date

Doing this delivers the page, as shown in diagram 8.11.2.

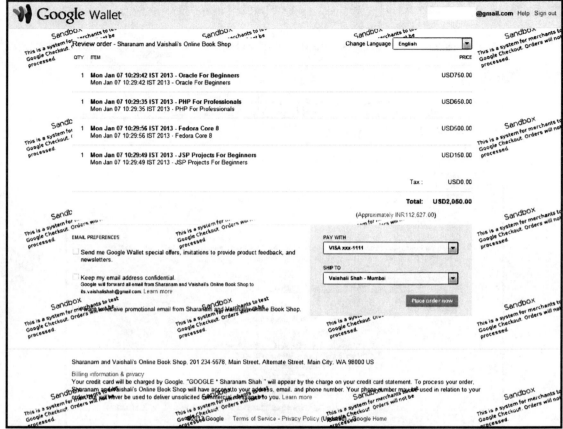

Diagram 8.11.2: Google Wallet - Place your order

Click [Place order now] to place the order and make the payment.

This delivers the Thank you page, as shown in diagram 8.11.3.

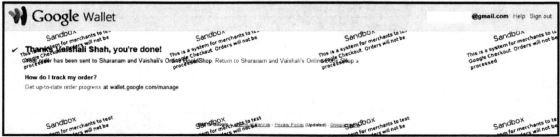

Diagram 8.11.3: Google Wallet – Thank you page

Click Return to Sharanam & Vaishali's Online Bookshop » to return to the site home page.

After the order is placed, Google checkout delivers an email to the buyer as well as seller.

Buyer's Email

Diagram 8.11.4: Email received by the buyer

Seller's Email

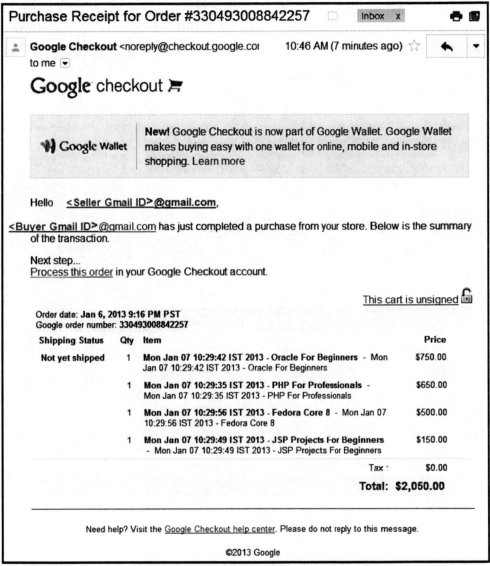

Diagram 8.11.5: Email received by the seller

After Placing The Order

After the order is placed and an email is received, the seller [site owner] ensures that the payment is received/credited to the bank account. If this is true, then the seller arranges to deliver the said books to the buyer [customer].

Every transaction that takes place is logged by the application and is displayed under Site Administration [Backend] → Manage Transactions.

The site owner or the employee can log in to the backend and view the transactions made by the customers.

Chapter

9

SECTION IV: PROCESS FLOW

The Index Page [index.jsp]

The application when invoked begins with **index.jsp**, as shown in diagram 9.1.

This file displays the application initialization progress and automatically redirects to the action called **showHomePage.action**.

showHomePage.action is the application's homepage, the customer facing page.

web.xml holds the appropriate configuration to invoke **index.jsp**.

Code Spec [web.xml]

```
1  <?xml version="1.0" encoding="UTF-8"?>
2  <web-app version="2.5" xmlns="http://java.sun.com/xml/ns/javaee"
   xmlns:xsi="http://www.w3.org/2001/XMLSchema-instance"
   xsi:schemaLocation="http://java.sun.com/xml/ns/javaee
   http://java.sun.com/xml/ns/javaee/web-app_2_5.xsd">
3      <filter>
4          <filter-name>struts2</filter-name>
5          <filter-class>com.sharanamvaishali.utility.Struts2Dispatcher</filter-class>
6      </filter>
7      <filter-mapping>
8          <filter-name>struts2</filter-name>
9          <url-pattern>/*</url-pattern>
10     </filter-mapping>
11
12     <session-config>
13         <session-timeout>
14             30
15         </session-timeout>
16     </session-config>
17     <welcome-file-list>
18         <welcome-file>index.jsp</welcome-file>
19     </welcome-file-list>
20     <error-page>
21         <error-code>404</error-code>
22         <location>/pagenotfound.jsp</location>
23     </error-page>
24     <error-page>
25         <exception-type>java.lang.Exception</exception-type>
26         <location>/error.jsp</location>
27     </error-page>
28 </web-app>
```

Code Spec [index.jsp]

```
1  <!DOCTYPE HTML PUBLIC "-//W3C//DTD HTML 4.01 Transitional//EN"
2  "http://www.w3.org/TR/html4/loose.dtd">
3  <html>
4      <head>
5          <meta http-equiv="Refresh" content="2;URL=showHomePage.action">
6          <title>BookShop [Sharanam & Vaishali Shah]</title>
7      </head>
8      <body>
9          <table height="500" border="0" cellpadding="25" align="center">
10             <tr>
11                 <td valign="top">
12                     <img src="/BookShop/images/BookShop.jpg" height="250"/>
13                     <br/><br/>
14                     <font color="#6b8e23" size="4">Loading Application</font>
15                     <img id="WaitImage" src="/BookShop/images/progressbar_box.gif">
16                 </td>
17             </tr>
```

```
18          </table>
19      </body>
20  </html>
```

User Interface

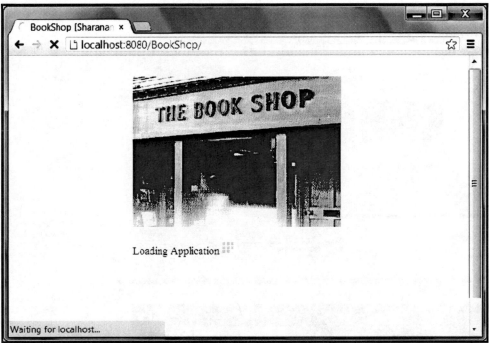

Diagram 9.1

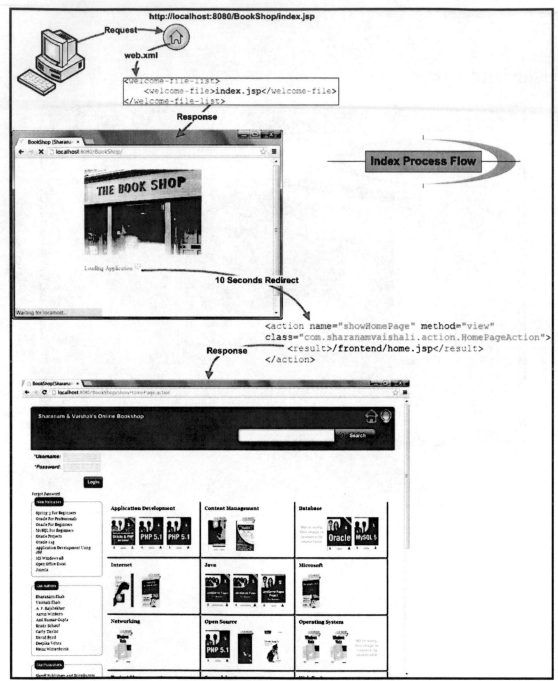

Diagram 9.2: Index Process Flow

Chapter

10

SECTION IV: PROCESS FLOW

The Application's Home Page [home.jsp]

Just after the loading completes, the application's home page is served, as shown in diagram 10.1.

User Interface [showHomePage.action → home.jsp]

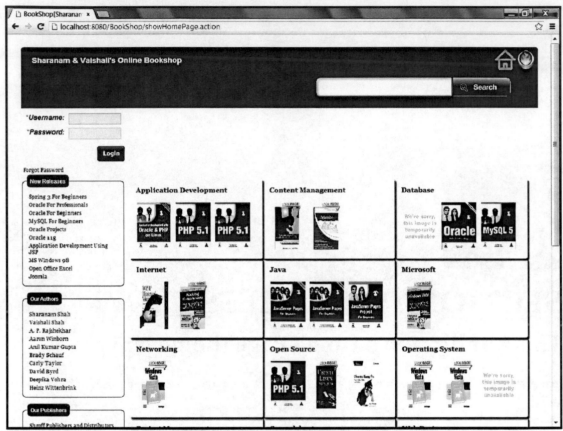

Diagram 10.1

struts.xml holds a mapping to help the redirection:

```
<action name="showHomePage" method="view"
class="com.sharanamvaishali.action.HomePageAction">
    <result>/frontend/home.jsp</result>
</action>
```

Using this mapping the control shifts to the home.jsp page and the home page is served, as shown in diagram 10.1.

Process Flow

As soon as the application loading completes, home.jsp is served based on:

☐ **showHomePage.action** → **HomePageAction** → **view()**

☐ **showBooksForThisCategory.action** → **HomePageAction** → **viewBooksByCategory()**

Here,

☐ **showHomePage.action** is the action configured in **struts.xml**, which invokes **view()** of **HomePageAction**

☐ **showBooksForThisCategory.action** is the action configured in **struts-HomePage.xml**, which invokes **viewBooksByCategory()** of **HomePageAction**

☐ **HomePageAction** is the action, which displays the home page contents

☐ **view()** and **viewBooksByCategory()** are the methods available in the action, which populates the List objects with the appropriate data. These List objects are made available to home.jsp

view() and viewBooksByCatgeory() invokes the following methods of the DAO layer:

DAO	Method	Description
BooksDAO	listNewReleases()	Does the actual retrieval of the available newly released books.
	listUpdatedBooks()	Does the actual retrieval of the available updated books.
	listTopTitles()	Does the actual retrieval of the available top titled books.
AuthorsDAO	listOurAuthors()	Does the actual retrieval of the available authors.
PublishersDAO	listOurPublishers()	Does the actual retrieval of the available publishers.
CategoriesDAO	listCategories()	Does the actual retrieval of the available categories.
	listBooksByCategory()	Does the actual retrieval of the available books under a particular category.
PopularSearchesDAO	listPopularSearches()	Does the actual retrieval of the available popular searches.

Diagram 10.2 depicts the use of these **List objects** to populate several sections of home.jsp.

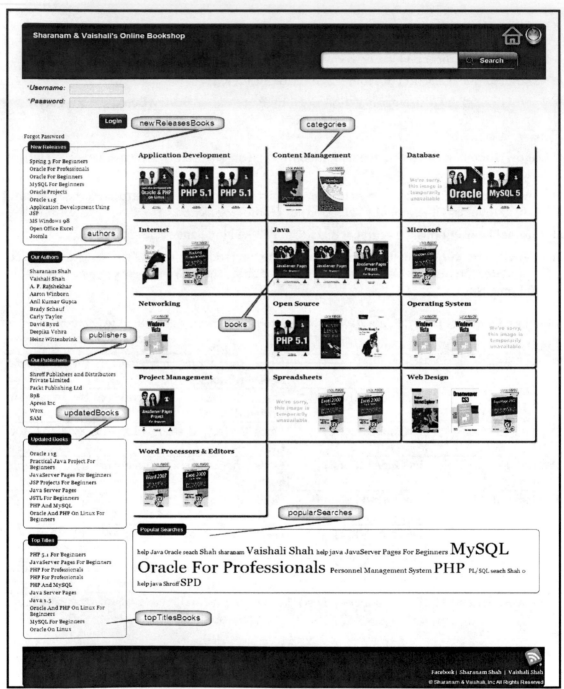

Diagram 10.2

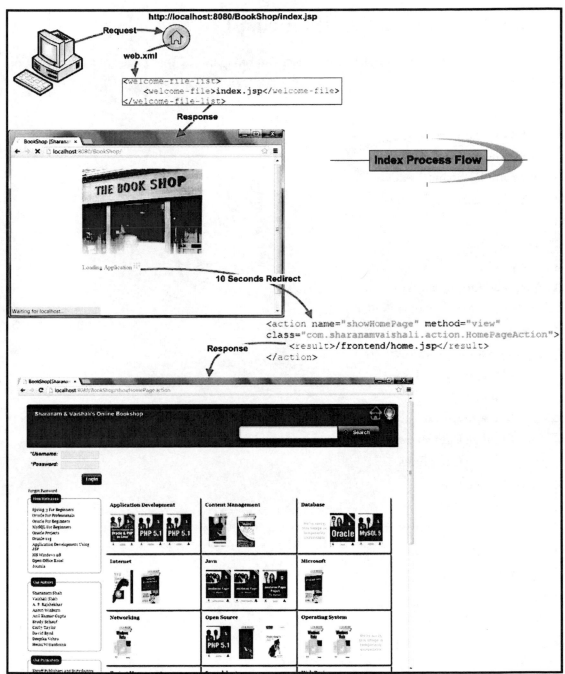

Diagram 10.3: Index and Home Page Process Flow

Home Page Navigation [home.jsp]

After the home page loads completely, the user can navigate to other pages of the application using the hyper links.

The home page allows:
- Viewing Book Details
- Viewing Author Details
- Viewing Publisher Details
- Viewing Category Details
- Search
- Popular Searches
- Signup
- Login & Forgot Password
- Viewing Cart & Google Wallet
- Logout
- Administration [BackOffice]
  - Manage Countries
  - Manage States
  - Manage Authors
  - Manage Publishers
  - Manage Categories
  - Manage Users
  - Manage Books
  - Manage Customers
  - Manage Transactions
  - Logout

Chapter

11

SECTION IV: PROCESS FLOW
Book Details [showBookDetails.jsp]

To view details of a book, the home page provides hyper links in the following sections:

New Releases

Spring 3 For Beginners
Oracle For Professionals
Oracle For Beginners
MySQL For Beginners
Oracle Projects
Oracle 11g
Application Development Using JSP
MS Windows 98
Open Office Excel
Joomla

Updated Books

Oracle 11g
Practical Java Project For Beginners
JavaServer Pages For Beginners
JSP Projects For Beginners
Java Server Pages
JSTL For Beginners
PHP And MySQL
Oracle And PHP On Linux For Beginners

Top Titles

PHP 5.1 For Beginners
JavaServer Pages For Beginners
PHP For Professionals
PHP For Professionals
PHP And MySQL
Java Server Pages
Java 1.5
Oracle And PHP On Linux For Beginners
MySQL For Beginners
Oracle On Linux

Application Development

Content Management

Database

We're sorry, this image is temporarily unavailable

Every hyper link under the above mentioned sections invoke an action:

```
<a href='<s:url action='showBookDetails'><s:param name='book.BookNo'
value='BookNo' /></s:url>'>
    <s:property value="BookName"/>
</a>
```

To view the details of a particular book, **BookNo** is passed as a parameter [using Strut's <s:param>] to the action. This helps the action determine the method to be invoked [based on struts.xml], which returns the appropriate book's details.

To locate the action, struts-HomePage.xml holds:

```
<action name="showBookDetails" method="viewBooks"
class="com.sharanamvaishali.action.ShowBookDetailsAction">
    <result name="success">/frontend/showBookDetails.jsp</result>
</action>
```

When the user clicks the hyper link, showBookDetails.jsp is served, as shown in diagram 11.1.

User Interface [showBookDetails.action → showBookDetails.jsp]

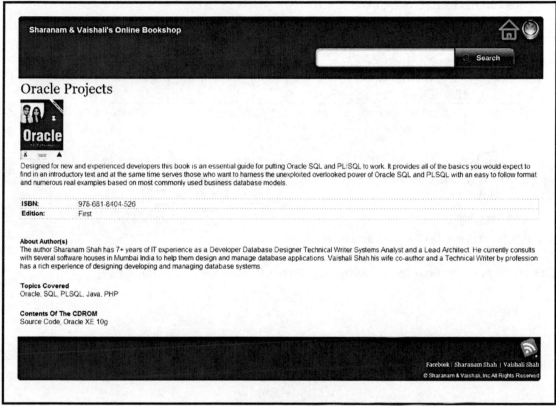

Diagram 11.1

Process Flow

Show Book Details displays the details of the book.

The book details in Show Book details is populated by **showBookDetails.action → ShowBookDetailsAction → viewBooks() → BooksDAO**.

Here,

❑ **showBookDetails.action** is the action configured in **struts-HomePage.xml**, which invokes **viewBooks()** of **ShowBookDetailsAction**

❑ **ShowBookDetailsAction** is the action

❑ **viewBooks()** is the method available in the action, which retrieves the book details via **BooksDAO**

❑ **BooksDAO** is the Data Access Object Layer [DAO], which does the actual retrieval of the book details from the database

viewBooks() invokes the following methods of **BooksDAO:**

Methods	Description
getBookById()	Returns the appropriate book's object from the Books database table using **BookNo** as the reference.
updateHits()	Updates the Hits column of the appropriate Book's object using BookNo as the reference.

Whilst populating these details in Show Book Details, the system checks if the user has logged in. Only if the user has logged in, additional links such as the following are displayed in Show Book Details:

❑ Add To Cart

❑ TOC and Sample Chapter download

This check is performed by accessing the username from the SESSION object.

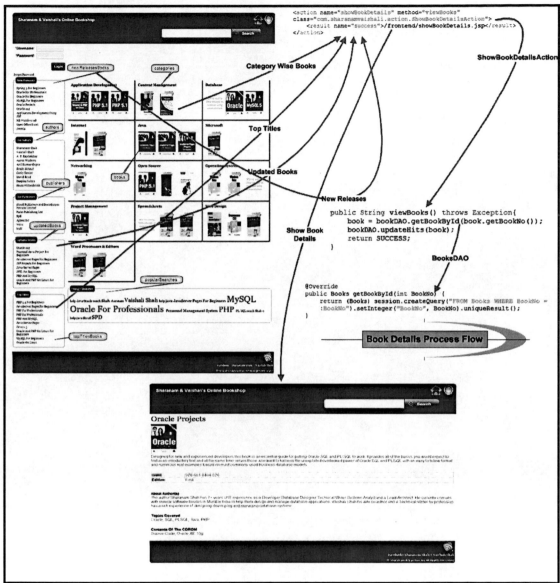

Diagram 11.2: Book Details Process Flow

Chapter

12

SECTION IV: PROCESS FLOW
Author Details [showAuthorDetails.jsp]

To view details of an author, the home page provides hyper links in the following section:

Our Authors

Sharanam Shah
Vaishali Shah
A. P. Rajshekhar
Aaron Winborn
Anil Kumar Gupta
Brady Schauf
Carly Taylor
David Byrd
Deepika Vohra
Heinz Wittenbrink

Every hyper link under the above mentioned section invokes an action:

```
<a href='<s:url action='showAuthorDetails'><s:param name='author.AuthorNo'
value='AuthorNo' /></s:url>'>
    <s:property value="FirstName"/> <s:property value="LastName"/>
</a>
```

To view the details of a particular author, **AuthorNo** is passed as a parameter [using Struts's <s:param>] to the action. This helps the action determine the method to be invoked [based on struts.xml] which returns the appropriate author's details.

To locate the action, struts-HomePage.xml holds:

```
<action name="showAuthorDetails" method="viewAuthorBooks"
class="com.sharanamvaishali.action.ShowAuthorDetailsAction">
    <result name="success">/frontend/showAuthorDetails.jsp</result>
</action>
```

When the user clicks the hyper link, showAuthorDetails.jsp is served, as shown in diagram 12.1.

User Interface [showAuthorDetails.action → showAuthorDetails.jsp]

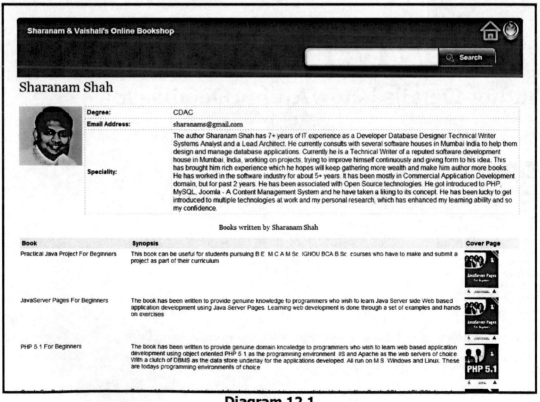

Diagram 12.1

Process Flow

Show Author Details displays the details of the author.

The author details in Show Author details is populated by **showAuthorDetails** →
ShowAuthorDetailsAction → **viewAuthorBooks()** → **AuthorsDAO**.

Here,

- ❑ **showAuthorDetails** is the action configured in **struts-HomePage.xml**, which invokes **viewAuthorBooks()** of **ShowAuthorDetailsAction**
- ❑ **showAuthorDetailsAction** is the action
- ❑ **viewAuthorBooks()** is the method available in the action, which retrieves the author details along with the list of books written by that particular author
- ❑ AuthorsDAO is the Data Access Object Layer [DAO], which does the actual retrieval of the author details along with the list of books written by that particular author from the database

viewAuthorBooks() invokes the following methods of AuthorsDAO:

Methods	Description
getAuthorById()	Returns the appropriate author's object from the Authors database table using **AuthorNo** as the reference.
getBooksByAuthor()	Returns the appropriate books List object from the Books database table using **AuthorNo** as the reference.

Whilst populating these details in Show Author Details, the system checks if the user has logged in. Only if the user has logged in, the additional link **Add To Cart** is displayed in Show Author Details.

This check is performed by accessing the username from the SESSION object.

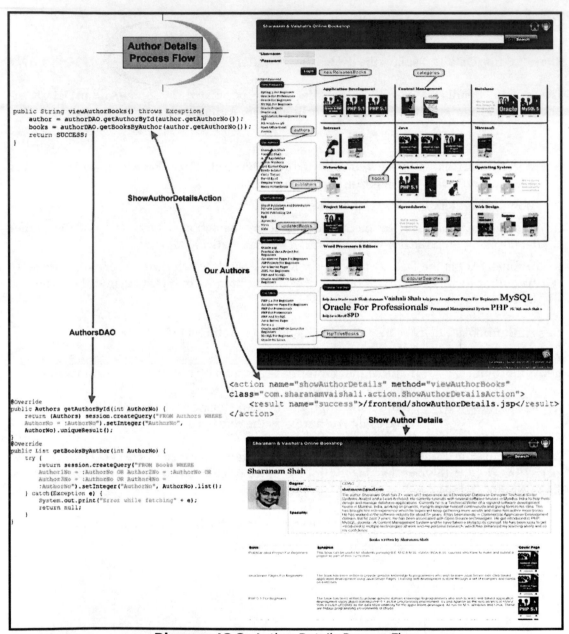

```
public String viewAuthorBooks() throws Exception{
    author = authorDAO.getAuthorById(author.getAuthorNo());
    books = authorDAO.getBooksByAuthor(author.getAuthorNo());
    return SUCCESS;
}
```

```
@Override
public Authors getAuthorById(int AuthorNo) {
    return (Authors) session.createQuery("FROM Authors WHERE
    AuthorNo = :AuthorNo").setInteger("AuthorNo",
    AuthorNo).uniqueResult();
}
@Override
public List getBooksByAuthor(int AuthorNo) {
    try {
        return session.createQuery("FROM Books WHERE
        Author1No = :AuthorNo OR Author2No = :AuthorNo OR
        Author3No = :AuthorNo OR Author4No =
        :AuthorNo").setInteger("AuthorNo", AuthorNo).list();
    } catch (Exception e) {
        System.out.print("Error while fetching" + e);
        return null;
    }
}
```

```
<action name="showAuthorDetails" method="viewAuthorBooks"
class="com.sharanamvaishali.action.ShowAuthorDetailsAction">
    <result name="success">/frontend/showAuthorDetails.jsp</result>
</action>
```

Diagram 12.2: Author Details Process Flow

SECTION IV: PROCESS FLOW

Publisher Details [showPublisherDetails.jsp]

To view details of a publisher, the home page provides hyper links in the following section:

Every hyper link under the above mentioned section invokes an action:

```
<a href='<s:url action='showPublisherDetails'><s:param
name='publisher.PublisherNo' value='PublisherNo' /></s:url>'>
    <s:property value="PublisherName"/>
</a>
```

To view the details of a particular publisher, **PublisherNo** is passed as a parameter [using Struts's <s:param>] to the action. This helps the action determine the method to be invoked [based on struts.xml] which returns the appropriate publisher's details.

To locate the action, struts-HomePage.xml holds:

```
<action name="showPublisherDetails" method="viewPublisherBooks"
class="com.sharanamvaishali.action.ShowPublisherDetailsAction">
    <result name="success">/frontend/showPublisherDetails.jsp</result>
</action>
```

When the user clicks the hyper link, showPublisherDetails.jsp is served, as shown in diagram 13.1.

User Interface [showPublisherDetails.action → showPublisherDetails.jsp]

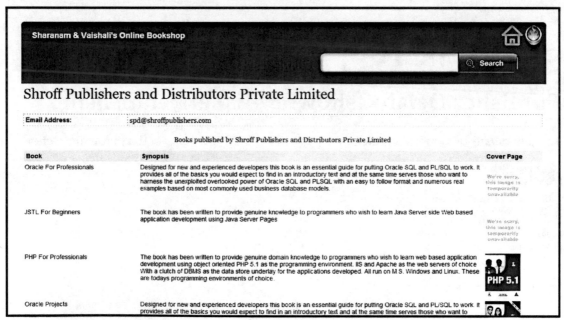

Diagram 13.1

Process Flow

Show Publisher Details displays the details of the publisher.

The publisher details in Show Publisher details is populated by **showPublisherDetails** →
ShowPublisherDetailsAction → **viewPublisherBooks()** → PublishersDAO.

Here,

❑ **showPublisherDetails** is the action configured in **struts-HomePage.xml**, which invokes
viewPublisherBooks() of **ShowPublisherDetailsAction**

❑ **showPublisherDetailsAction** is the action

❑ **viewPublisherBooks()** is the method available in the action, which retrieves the
publisher details along with the list of books published by that particular publisher

❑ PublishersDAO is the Data Access Object Layer [DAO], which does the actual retrieval of
the publisher details along with the list of books published by that particular publisher
from the database

viewPublisherBooks() invokes the following methods of PublishersDAO:

Methods	Description
getPublisherById()	Returns the appropriate publisher's object from the Publishers database table using **PublisherNo** as the reference.
getBooksByPublisher()	Returns the appropriate books List object from the Books database table using **PublisherNo** as the reference.

Whilst populating these details in Show Publisher Details, the system checks if the user has
logged in. Only if the user has logged in, the additional link **Add To Cart** is displayed in
Show Publisher Details.

This check is performed by accessing the username from the SESSION object.

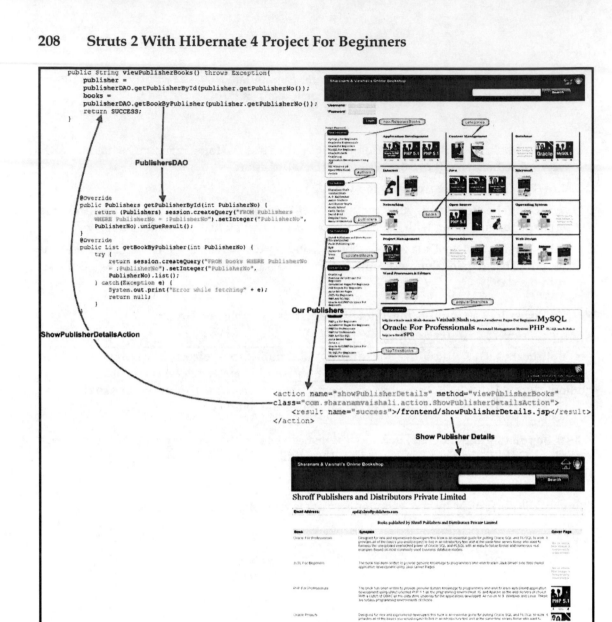

Diagram 13.2: Publisher Details Process Flow

SECTION IV: PROCESS FLOW

Category Details [showCategoryDetails.jsp]

To view details of a category, the home page provides hyper links in the following section:

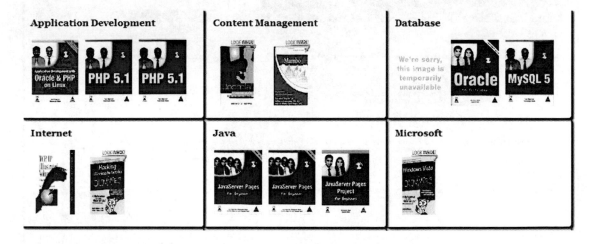

Every hyper link [Category Name] under the above mentioned section invokes an action:

```
<a href='<s:url action='showCategoryDetails'><s:param name='category.CategoryNo'
value='CategoryNo' /></s:url>'>
   <s:property value="Category"/>
</a>
```

To view the details of a particular category, **CategoryNo** is passed as a parameter [using Struts'S <s:param>] to the action. This helps the action determine the method to be invoked [based on struts.xml] which will return the appropriate category details.

To locate the action, struts-HomePage.xml holds:

```
<action name="showCategoryDetails" method="viewCategoryBooks"
class="com.sharanamvaishali.action.ShowCategoryDetailsAction">
   <result name="success">/frontend/showCategoryDetails.jsp</result>
</action>
```

When the user clicks the hyper link, showCategoryDetails.jsp is served, as shown in diagram 14.1.

User Interface [showCategoryDetails.action → showCategoryDetails.jsp]

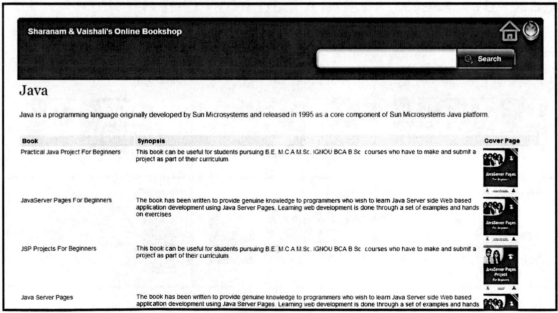

Diagram 14.1

Process Flow

Show Category Details displays the details of the category.

The category details in Show Category details is populated by **showCategoryDetails** → **ShowCategoryDetailsAction** → **viewCategoryBooks()** → **CategoriesDAO**.

Here,

- ❑ **showCategoryDetails** is the action configured in **struts-HomePage.xml**, which invokes **viewCategoryBooks()** of **ShowCategoryDetailsAction**
- ❑ **showCategoryDetailsAction** is the action
- ❑ **viewCategoryBooks()** is the method available in the action, which retrieves the category details along with the list of books under that particular category
- ❑ **CategoriesDAO** is the Data Access Object Layer [DAO], which does the actual retrieval of the category details along with the list of books under that particular category from the database

viewCategoryBooks() invokes the following methods of CategoriesDAO:

Methods	Description
getCategoryById()	Returns the appropriate category's object from the Categories database table using **CategoryNo** as the reference.
getAllBooksByCategory()	Returns the appropriate books List object from the Books database table using **CategoryNo** as the reference.

Whilst populating these details in Show Category Details, the system checks if the user has logged in. Only if the user has logged in, the additional link **Add To Cart** is displayed in Show Category Details.

This check is performed by accessing the username from the SESSION object.

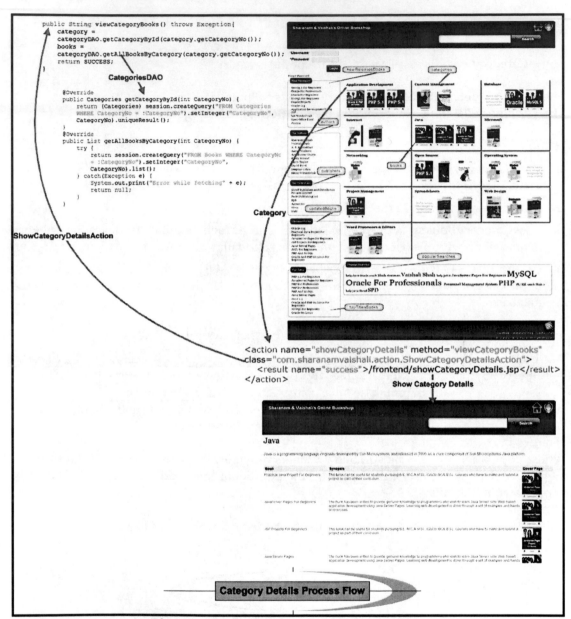

Diagram 14.2: Category Details Process Flow

SECTION IV: PROCESS FLOW

Search [searchResults.jsp]

The header of the Frontend [customer facing] holds a Search data entry form.

The user can key in the desired search criteria and click ▮ Search ▮.

Clicking ▮ Search ▮, invokes an action:

```
<s:submit action="performSearch" theme="simple" cssClass="search-button"
name="Search" id="Search" value="" />
```

To view the search results, **SearchCriteria** is passed as a parameter to the action. This helps the action determine the method to be invoked [based on struts.xml] which returns the appropriate search results.

To locate the action, struts-Search.xml holds:

```
<action name="performSearch" method="performSearch"
class="com.sharanamvaishali.action.SearchResultsAction">
    <result name="success">/frontend/searchResults.jsp</result>
</action>
```

When the user clicks [Search], searchResults.jsp is served, as shown in diagram 15.1.

User Interface [performSearch.action → searchResults.jsp]

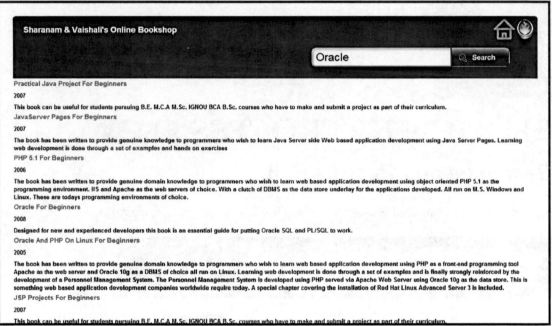

Diagram 15.1

Process Flow

When the customer keys in the search criteria and clicks [Search], the search results are displayed in searchResults.jsp by **performSearch.action** → **SearchResultsAction** → **performSearch()** → **SearchDAO**.

Here,

❑ **performSearch** is the action configured in **struts-Search.xml**, which invokes **performSearch()** of **SearchResultsAction**

❑ **SearchResultsAction** is the action

❑ **performSearch()** is the method available in action, which first checks whether the search criteria has been entered by the user and accordingly displays the search results

❑ **SearchDAO** is the Data Access Object Layer [DAO], which does the actual retrieval of the search criteria details from the database

performSearch() invokes the following methods of SearchDAO:

Methods	Description
searchResults()	Returns the appropriate search results from the database tables using **SearchCriteria** as the reference.
searchAllResults()	Returns all the search results from the database tables.
savePopularSearch()	Does the actual saving of the SearchCriteria in the PopularSearches database table.

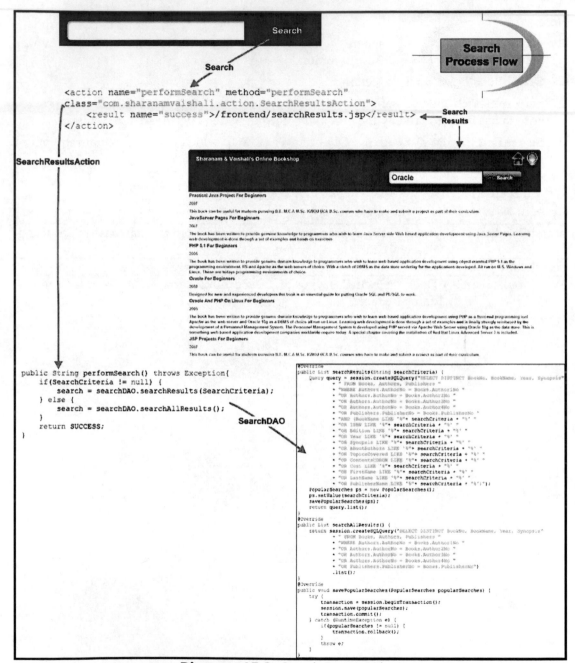

Diagram 15.2: Search Process Flow

Chapter

16

SECTION IV: PROCESS FLOW

Popular Searches

The home page holds a Popular Searches section.

```
Popular Searches
```

o help java JavaServer Pages For Beginners MySQL Oracle Oracle For Professionals Personnel Management System PHP PL/SQL seach Shah sharanam Shroff SPD Vaishali Shah

The user can click a desired search keyword to view the search results.

Every search keyword that is listed under the Popular Searches is hyper linked to an action:

```
<a href="<s:url action='performSearch'><s:param name='SearchCriteria'
value='#popularSearches[0]' /></s:url>" style="font-size:13px; cursor:pointer;"
title="Click to search for <s:property value='#popularSearches[0]'/>">
    <s:property value="#popularSearches[0]"/>
</a>
```

To view the search results for a particular popular search keyword, **SearchCriteria** is passed as a parameter to the action. This helps the action determine the method to be invoked [based on struts.xml] which returns the appropriate search results.

To locate the action, struts-Search.xml holds:

```
<action name="performSearch" method="performSearch"
class="com.sharanamvaishali.action.SearchResultsAction">
    <result name="success">/frontend/searchResults.jsp</result>
</action>
```

When the user clicks the desired hyper link an appropriate searchResults.jsp is served, as shown in diagram 15.1 in *Chapter 15: Search [searchResults.jsp]*.

Process Flow

When the user clicks the desired hyperlink, the search results of that search criteria are displayed in searchResults.jsp by **performSearch.action** → **SearchResultsAction** → **performSearch()** → **SearchDAO**.

Here,

❑ **performSearch** is the action configured in **struts-Search.xml**, which invokes **performSearch()** of **SearchResultsAction**

❑ **SearchResultsAction** is the action

❑ **performSearch()** is the method available in action, which first checks whether the search criteria has been entered by the user and accordingly displays the search results

❑ **SearchDAO** is the Data Access Object Layer [DAO], which does the actual retrieval of the search criteria details from the database

performSearch() invokes the following methods of SearchDAO:

Methods	Description
searchResults()	Returns the appropriate search results from the database tables using **SearchCriteria** as the reference.
searchAllResults()	Returns all the search results from the database tables.
savePopularSearch()	Does the actual saving of the SearchCriteria in the PopularSearches database table.

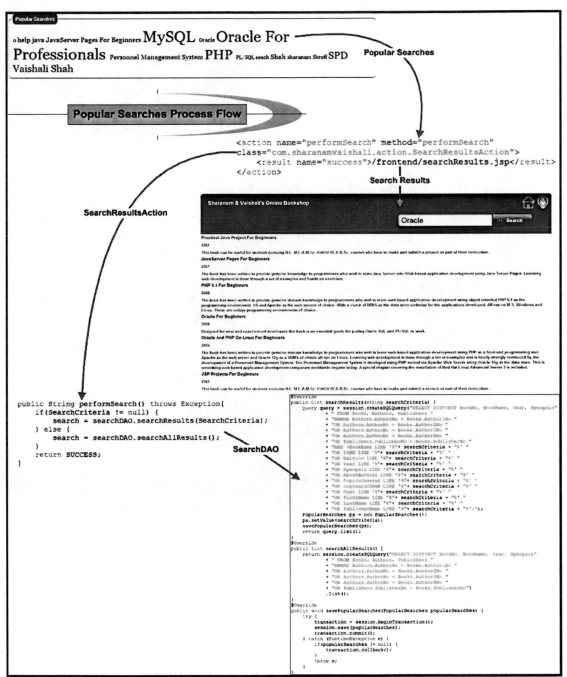

Diagram 16.1: Popular Searches Process Flow

Chapter 17

SECTION IV: PROCESS FLOW

Sign Up

Show Sign Up Page

The home page holds a hyper link to the **Signup** page.

Sharanam & Vaishali's Online Bookshop

When the user clicks this link the sign up page appears:

```
<td>
    <s:a href="showRegistrationPage.action">
        <img src="/BookShop/images/signup.png" title="Sign Up"/>
    </s:a>
</td>
```

To locate the action, struts-Registration.xml holds:

```
<action name="showRegistrationPage"
class="com.sharanamvaishali.action.RegistrationAction">
    <result>/frontend/registration.jsp</result>
</action>
```

When the user clicks 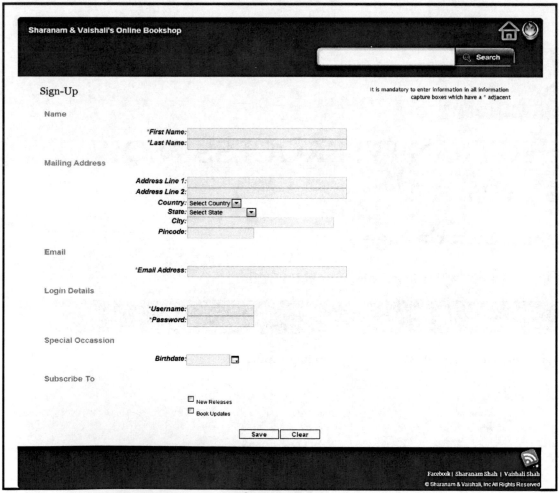, registration.jsp is served, as shown in diagram 17.1.

User Interface [showRegistrationPage.action → registration.jsp]

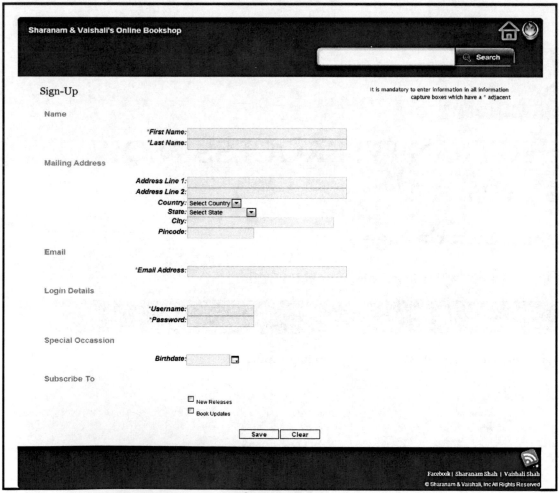

Diagram 17.1

Process Flow

After the user clicks 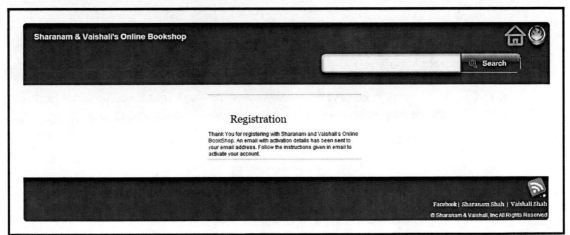, Sign Up is served by **showRegistrationPage.action** →
RegistrationAction → **execute()**.

Here,

☐ **showRegistrationPage.action** is the action configured in struts-Registration.xml, which
invokes **execute()** of **RegistrationAction**

☐ **RegistrationAction** is the controller

☐ **execute()** is the method available in action, which displays the sign up form for the user
to sign up

Adding New Customer

After the user keys in the sign up data and clicks $\boxed{\textbf{Save}}$, registrationThankYou.jsp is served,
as shown in diagram 17.2.

User Interface [doInsertCustomer.action →
showRegistrationThankYouPage.action →
registrationThankYou.jsp]

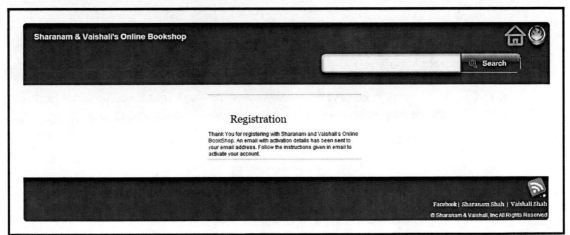

Diagram 17.2

To locate the action, struts-Registration.xml holds:

```
<action name="showRegistrationThankYouPage">
    <result>/frontend/registrationThankYou.jsp</result>
</action>
```

Process Flow

This is a standard data entry form. By default, when the form loads, it's in the **INSERT** mode.

After SignUp loads, the user can simply key in the required data and click $\boxed{\textbf{Save}}$.

After the user keys in the required inputs and clicks $\boxed{\textbf{Save}}$, the FORM is submitted and the save operation is performed by **doInsertCustomer.action** → **RegistrationAction** → saveCustomer() → CustomersDAO → saveCustomer().

Here,

❑ **doInsertCustomer.action** is the action configured in **struts-Registration.xml**, which invokes **saveCustomer()** of **RegistrationAction**

❑ **RegistrationAction** is the action

❑ **saveCustomer()** is the method available in the action, which does the saving of the captured data and in turn calls **registrationThankYou()** of **RegistrationAction**

❑ **registrationThankYou()** is the method available in the action, which sends an email to the registered customer

❑ **CustomersDAO** is the Data Access Object Layer [DAO]

❑ **saveCustomer()** is the method available in the DAO, which does the actual saving of the captured data in the database

If the captured data is found to be invalid while saving the captured data, then the Sign Up Page is re-served with the appropriate error messages, as shown in diagram 17.3.

User Interface For Validation Errors [doInsertCustomer.action → registration.jsp]

Diagram 17.3

To locate the action, struts-Registration.xml holds:

```
<action name="doInsertCustomer" method="saveCustomer"
class="com.sharanamvaishali.action.RegistrationAction">
    <result name="success"
    type="redirectAction">showRegistrationThankYouPage</result>
    <result name="input">/frontend/registration.jsp</result>
    <result name="error">/frontend/registration.jsp</result>
</action>
```

Process Flow

If the captured data is found to be invalid, then Sign Up with appropriate error messages is served by **doInsertCustomer** → **RegistrationAction [saveCustomer()]**.

Here,

❑ **doInsertCustomer.action** is the action configured in **struts-Registration.xml**, which invokes **saveCustomer()** of **RegistrationAction**

❑ **RegistrationAction** is the action

❑ **saveCustomer()** is the method available in the action, which traps the errors and forwards it to the Sign Up page

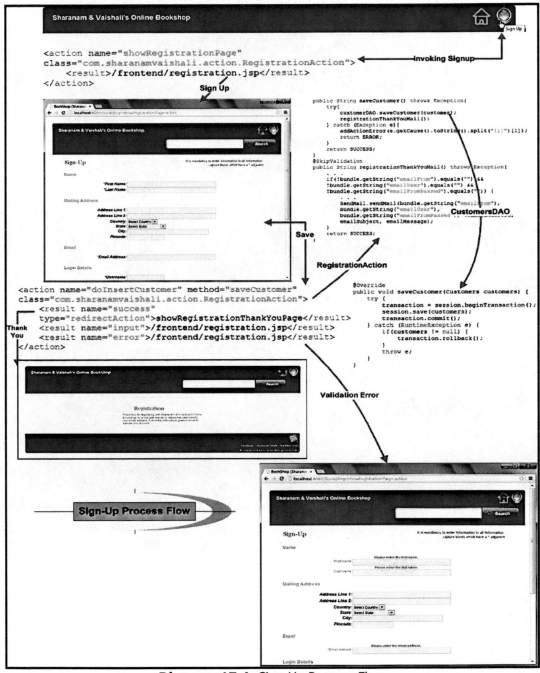

Diagram 17.4: Sign-Up Process Flow

SECTION IV: PROCESS FLOW

Customer Login And Logout

Customer Login

The home page holds a Login data entry form.

*Username:	
*Password:	
	Login

When the user keys in the login details and clicks **Login** the user is authenticated and if the user is found valid, home.jsp is served again with a welcome message.

When the user clicks **Login**, the Login form in home.jsp is submitted to the action called **doCustomerLogin**.

To locate the action, struts-CustomerLogin.xml holds:

```
<action name="doCustomerLogin" method="loginCustomer"
class="com.sharanamvaishali.action.CustomerLoginAction">
    <result name="success" type="redirectAction">showHomePage</result>
    <result name="error">/frontend/home.jsp</result>
    <result name="input">/frontend/home.jsp</result>
</action>
```

If the login attempted is successful then home.jsp is served again with a welcome message and the login form disappears, as shown in diagram 18.1.

Successful Login

User Interface [doCustomerLogin.action → showHomePage → home.jsp]

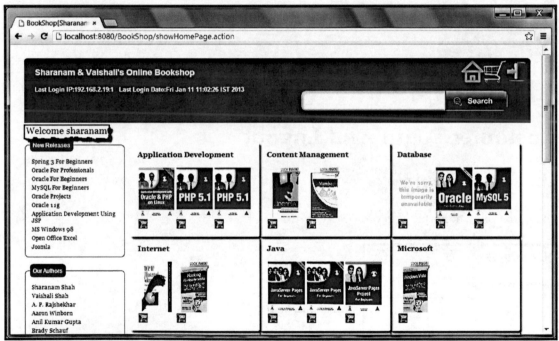

Diagram 18.1

Process Flow

When the user keys in the username and password and clicks **Login**, the user is authenticated and then on successful authentication, the application renders the home page, which is the startup page.

When the user keys in the username and password and clicks [Login], the login details are authenticated by **doCustomerLogin** → **CustomerLoginAction** → **loginCustomer()** → **LoginDAO [validateCustomerLogin() and updateCustomerLastLoginDetails()]**.

Here,

☐ **doCustomerLogin** is the action configured in struts-CustomerLogin.xml, which invokes **loginCustomer()** of **CustomerLoginAction**

☐ **CustomerLoginAction** is the action

☐ **loginCustomer()** is the method available in the action, which validates the customer and upon successful validation adds the customer details in a session

☐ **LoginDAO** is the Data Access Object Layer [DAO]

☐ **validateCustomerLogin()** is the method available in the DAO, which does the actual validation of customer and retrieves the customer details from the database

☐ **updateCustomerLastLoginDetails()** is the method available in the DAO, which does the actual update of the customer's IP address of the customer and the date when the customer logged in

Since the login details are available in the Session, some application features such as [Add To Cart, Show Cart, Downloads of TOC and Sample Chapter] are switched on using the values available in the session to determine a valid authenticated user.

Login Failed

When the user clicks [Login], the Login form in home.jsp is submitted to the action called **doCustomerLogin**.

To locate the action, struts-CustomerLogin.xml holds:

```
<action name="doCustomerLogin" method="loginCustomer"
class="com.sharanamvaishali.action.CustomerLoginAction">
    <result name="success" type="redirectAction">showHomePage</result>
    <result name="error">/frontend/home.jsp</result>
    <result name="input">/frontend/home.jsp</result>
</action>
```

If the login attempted is un-successful then home.jsp is served again with an error message, as shown in diagram 18.2.

User Interface [doCustomerLogin.action → home.jsp]

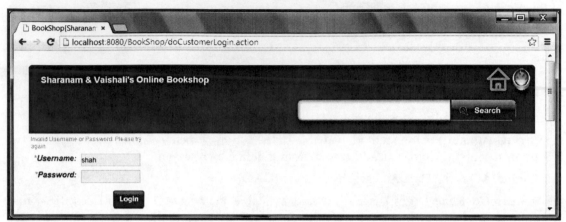

Diagram 18.2

Process Flow

When the login credentials are found invalid, the login form is reserved along with the appropriate error messages by **doCustomerLogin** → **CustomerLoginAction** → **loginCustomer()**.

Here,

❑   **doCustomerLogin** is the action configured in struts-CustomerLogin.xml, which invokes **loginCustomer()** of **CustomerLoginAction**

❑   **CustomerLoginAction** is the action

❑   **loginCustomer()** is the method available in the action, which displays Home page along with the appropriate error messages

Logout

The home page holds a hyper-link to logout only if the customer has logged in.

The user can choose to logout of the application by clicking ![] .

When the user clicks ▣, the user details [stored in the session whilst logging in] is removed and the session is destroyed. After which the user is redirected to the application's home page.

When the user clicks ▣ the action named **doCustomerLogout** is invoked which shows the application's home page.

To locate the action, struts-CustomerLogin.xml holds:

```
<action name="doCustomerLogout" method="logoffCustomer"
class="com.sharanamvaishali.action.CustomerLoginAction">
    <result name="success" type="redirectAction">showHomePage</result>
</action>
```

Process Flow

▣ when clicked destroys the session and redirects the user to the home page with the login form included using **doCustomerLogout → CustomerLoginAction → logoffCustomer()**.

Here,

❑ **doCustomerLogout** is the action configured in struts-CustomerLogin.xml, which invokes **logoffCustomer()** of **CustomerLoginAction**

❑ **CustomerLoginAction** is the action

❑ **logoffCustomer()** is the method available in the action, which returns the user to Home page along with the login form included

Since logout destroys the session, some of the application features such as Add To Cart, Show Cart, Downloads of TOC and Sample Chapter are switched off.

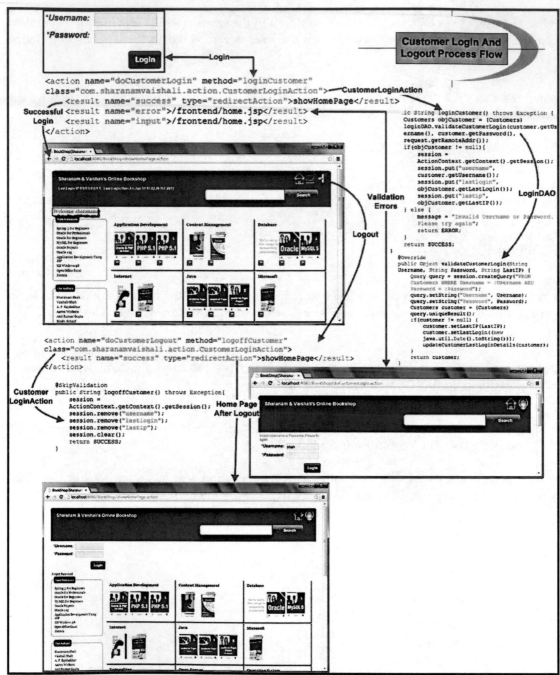

Diagram 18.3: Customer Login And Logout Process Flow

SECTION IV: PROCESS FLOW

Forgot Password

Displaying Forgot Password Page

The Forgot password data entry form retrieves the password for the customers who have forgotten it.

The home page holds a link to the Forgot Password data entry form.

When the user clicks Forgot Password, the action named **CustomerLoginAction.java** is invoked.

To locate the action, struts-CustomerLogin.xml holds:

```
<action name="showForgotPassword">
    <result>/frontend/forgotPassword.jsp</result>
</action>
```

When the user clicks Forgot Password, forgotPassword.jsp is served, as shown in diagram 19.1.

User Interface [showForgotPassword.action → forgotPassword.jsp]

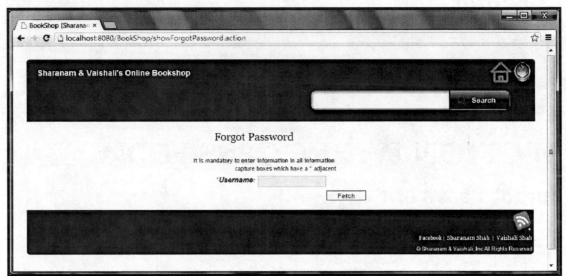

Diagram 19.1

Retrieving Password

The user needs to key in the Username and click **Fetch**.

When the user clicks **Fetch**, the data entry form is submitted to **doRetrievePassword.action** and **home.jsp** is served again.

To locate the action, struts-CustomerLogin.xml holds:

```
<action name="doRetrievePassword" method="retrieveCustomerPassword"
class="com.sharanamvaishali.action.CustomerLoginAction">
    <result name="success" type="redirectAction">showHomePage</result>
    <result name="error">/frontend/forgotPassword.jsp</result>
</action>
```

Process Flow

When the user keys in the username and clicks **Fetch**, the captured username is authenticated by **doRetrievePassword** → **CustomerLoginAction** → **retrieveCustomerPassword()**.

Here,

❑ **doRetrievePassword** is the action configured in struts-CustomerLogin.xml, which invokes **retrieveCustomerPassword()** of **CustomerLoginAction**

❑ **CustomerLoginAction** is the action

❑ **retrieveCustomerPassword()** is the method available in action, which sends the password via an email on successful authentication of the captured data

retrieveCustomerPassword() invokes the following methods:

File Name	Method	Description
LoginDAO	getCustomerPassword()	Returns the appropriate user's details from the Customers database table using **Username** as the reference.
SendMail	sendMail()	Holds the business logic to send an email.

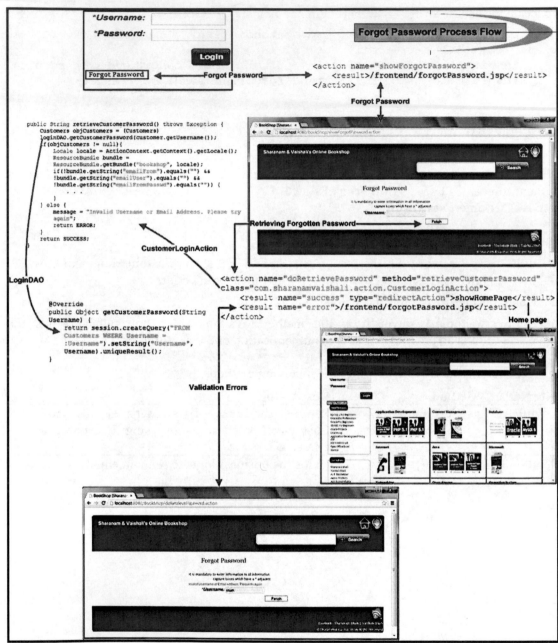

Diagram 19.2: Forgot Password Process Flow

SECTION IV: PROCESS FLOW

Cart [showCart.jsp]

Add To Cart

When the user logs in:

appears in the home page, as shown in diagram 20.1

appears in the Show Book Details, ShowAuthor Details, Show Publisher Details and Show Category Details, as shown in diagram 20.2

User Interface [addToCart.action]

Diagram 20.1

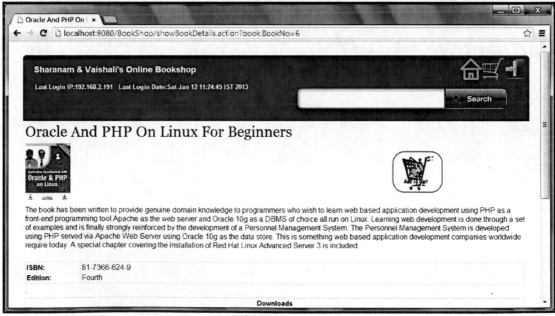

Diagram 20.2

Every hyperlink under the above mentioned section invokes an action:

```
<a href="<s:url action="addToCart"><s:param name="BookNo"><s:property
value="BookNo"/></s:param><s:param name="BookName"><s:property
value="BookName"/></s:param><s:param name="Cost"><s:property
value="Cost"/></s:param></s:url>">
    <img src="/BookShop/images/cart.jpg" style="cursor:pointer;" border="0"/>
</a>
```

To locate the action, struts-Cart.xml holds:

```
<action name="addToCart" method="addBook"
class="com.sharanamvaishali.action.CartAction">
    <result type="redirect">
        <param name="location">
            ${#context.get(@org.apache.struts2.StrutsStatics
            @HTTP_REQUEST).getHeader("Referer")}
        </param>
    </result>
</action>
```

Process Flow

When a user clicks  or , the book details are added to the cart by **addToCart** →
CartAction → **addBook()**.

Here,

❑ **addToCart** is the action configured in struts-Cart.xml, which invokes **addBook()** of
CartAction

❑ **CartAction** is the action

❑ **addBook()** is the method available in the action, which adds the book details such as the
book name and cost to the session

Show Cart

The home page holds a link to the Shopping Cart. The link appears only if the user has
logged in.

Sharanam & Vaishali's Online Bookshop

Last Login IP:192.168.2.191   Last Login Date:Sat Jan 12 11:24:45 IST 2013

Search

After the books are added by **Add To Cart** link, the details about the books purchased are
displayed in the **Show Cart** page.

When the user clicks 🛒, the action class named **CartAction.java** is invoked.

To locate the action, struts-Cart.xml holds:

```
<action name="showCart" method="showCart"
class="com.sharanamvaishali.action.CartAction">
    <result>/frontend/showCart.jsp</result>
</action>
```

When the user clicks 🛒, showCart.jsp is served, as shown in diagram 20.3.

User Interface [showCart.action → showCart.jsp]

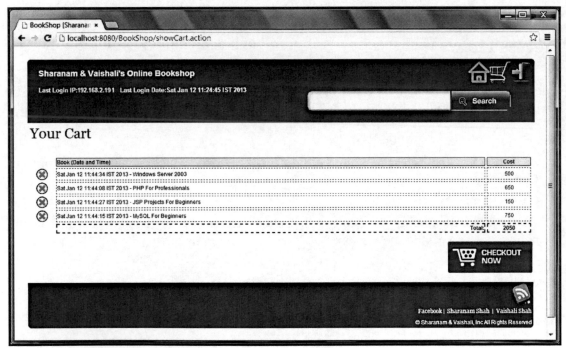

Diagram 20.3

Process Flow

Show Cart displays the details of the books added to the cart by the customer.

The book details in the JSP are populated by **showCart → CartAction → showCart()**.

Here,

- ❑ **showCart** is the action configured in struts-Cart.xml, which invokes **showCart()** of **CartAction**
- ❑ **CartAction** is the action
- ❑ **showCart()** is the method available in the action, which displays the list of books added to the cart by the customer

Removing The Cart Items [Books]

Every item [book] that is listed in showCart.jsp has ⊗ adjacent to it.

⊗ is hyperlinked to an action removeFromCart.action:

```
<a href="<s:url action="removeFromCart"><s:param name="BookName"><s:property
value="BookName"/></s:param></s:url>">
    <img src="/BookShop/images/delete.png" border="0" width="25px" alt="Click
    to remove the Book from the cart">
</a>
```

To locate the action, struts-Cart.xml holds:

```
<action name="removeFromCart" method="removeBook"
class="com.sharanamvaishali.action.CartAction">
    <result type="redirectAction">showCart</result>
</action>
```

⊗ when clicked removes the selected item and re-serves showCart.jsp.

Process Flow

Show Cart allows the user to delete/remove a book from the cart using ⊗. The deletion is done by **removeFromCart** → **CartAction** → **removeBook()**.

Here,

- ❑ **removeFromCart** is the action configured in struts-Cart.xml, which invokes **removeBook()** of **CartAction**
- ❑ **CartAction** is the action
- ❑ **removeBook()** is the method available in the action, which deletes/removes the book from session based on the parameter received from showCart.jsp

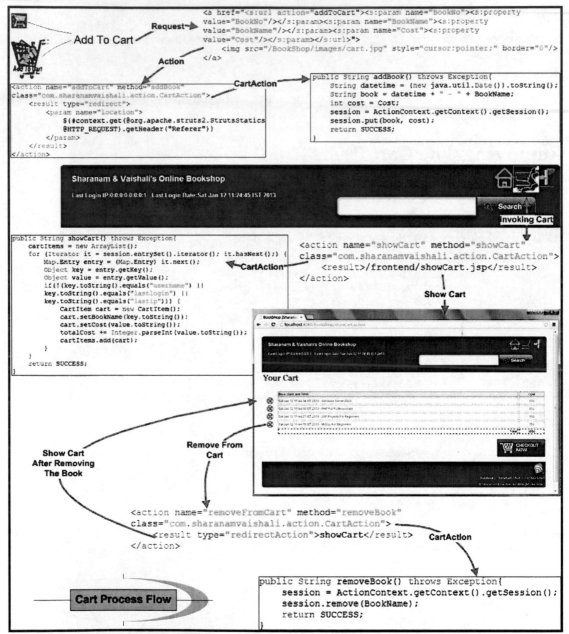

Diagram 20.4: Cart Process Flow

Chapter 21

SECTION IV: PROCESS FLOW

Checkout

The Shopping Cart [showCart.jsp] holds a link to checkout.

When the user clicks this link, the action named **performTransactionAction.java** is invoked.

To locate the action, struts-Cart.xml holds:

```
<action name="performTransaction" method="addTransactions"
class="com.sharanamvaishali.action.PerformTransactionAction">
    <result>/frontend/performTransaction.jsp</result>
</action>
```

When the user clicks this link, the Google Wallet is served, as shown in diagram 21.1.

User Interface [performTransaction.action → Google Wallet]

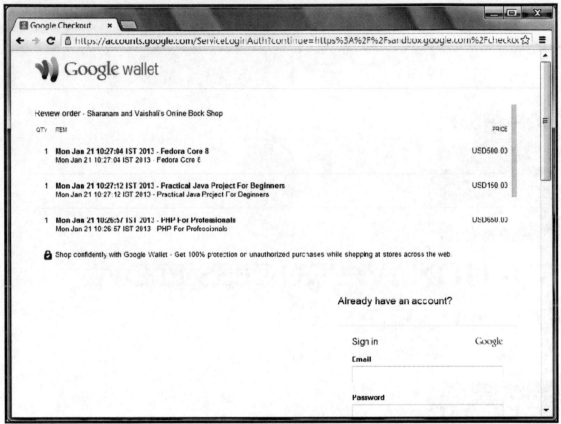

Diagram 21.1

Process Flow

When the user clicks the CheckOut link, the cart details are added to the database by **performTransaction** → **PerformTransactionAction** → **addTransactions()** → **TransactionsDAO**.

Here,

❑ **performTransaction** is the action configured in struts-Cart.xml, which invokes **addTransactions()** of PerformTransactionAction

❑ **PerformTransactionAction** is the action

- **addTransactions()** is the method available in the action, which adds the book details such as the book name, cost, quantity to the Transactions database table via **TransactionsDAO**

- **TransactionsDAO** is the Data Access Object Layer [DAO]

- **saveTransaction()** is the method available in the DAO, which does the actual saving of the transaction [CartItem] in the Transactions database table

- **PerformTransactionAction's** **addTransactions()** also invokes **TransactionsDAO's** **getNextTransactionNo()**, which retrieves the next TransactionNo from the underlying Transactions database table

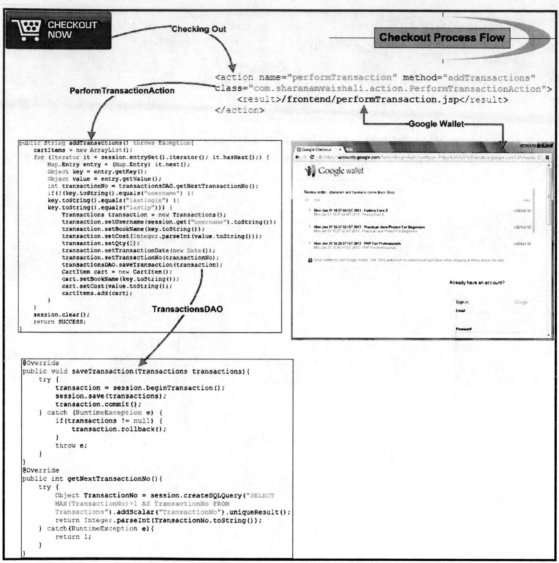

Diagram 21.2: Checkout Process Flow

Chapter

22

SECTION IV: PROCESS FLOW
Administration Login And Logout

Administration Login

The home page holds a link to the application's back office [administration].

When the user clicks [icon], the action **admin.action** is invoked.

To locate the action, struts-AdminLogin.xml holds:

```
<action name="admin">
    <result>/admin/adminLogin.jsp</result>
</action>
```

When the user clicks [icon], **adminLogin.jsp** is served, as shown in diagram 22.1.

User Interface [admin.action → adminLogin.jsp]

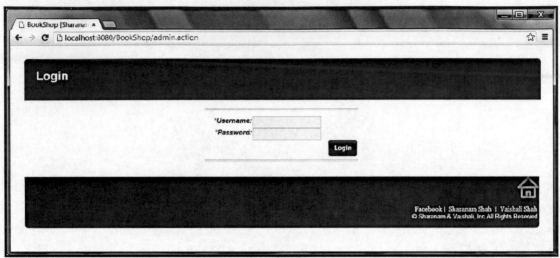

Diagram 22.1

Successful Login

After the user keys in the login details and clicks **Login**, the user is authenticated and if the user is found valid, manageTransactions.jsp is served, otherwise an error message is shown.

Clicking **Login**, invokes the action named **SystemUserLoginAction.java**.

To locate the action, struts-AdminLogin.xml holds:

```
<action name="doLogin" method="loginSystemUser"
class="com.sharanamvaishali.action.SystemUserLoginAction">
    <result name="success"
    type="redirectAction">showManageTransactions</result>
    <result name="error">/admin/adminLogin.jsp</result>
    <result name="input">/admin/adminLogin.jsp</result>
</action>
```

When the user clicks **Login**, the Login FORM is submitted to the action called **doLogin**.

If the login attempted is successful, manageTransactions.jsp is served, as shown in diagram 22.2.

User Interface [doLogin.action → showManageTransactions → manageTransactions.jsp]

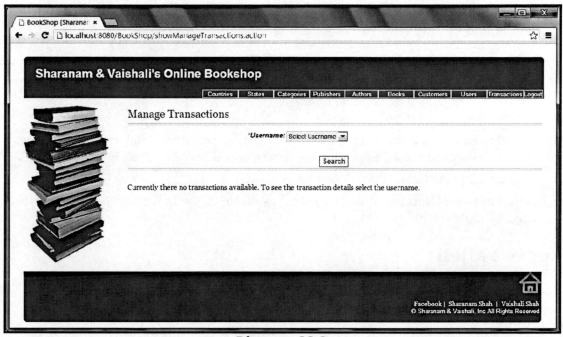

Diagram 22.2

The login data entry form allows the registered administration users to login to the backend application.

After an administration user logs in to the backend application, the user is allowed to manage:

❑ Countries

❑ States

❑ Categories

❑ Publishers

❑ Authors

❑ Books

❑ Customers

❑ Users

❑ Transactions

Process Flow

When the user keys in the username and password and clicks **Login**, the login details are authenticated by **doLogin** → **SystemUserLoginAction** → **loginSystemUser()** → **LoginDAO** → **validateSystemUserLogin()**.

Here,

- **doLogin** is the action configured in struts-AdminLogin.xml, which invokes **loginSystemUser()** of **SystemUserLoginAction**
- **SystemUserLoginAction** is the action
- **loginSystemUser()** is the method available in the action, which validates the system user and upon successful validation adds the system user details in a session
- **LoginDAO** is the Data Access Object Layer [DAO]
- **validateSystemUserLogin()** is the method available in the DAO, which does the actual validation of system user

Login Failed

If the login attempted is un-successful, adminLogin.jsp is served again with an error message, as shown in diagram 22.3.

User Interface [doLogin.action → adminLogin.jsp]

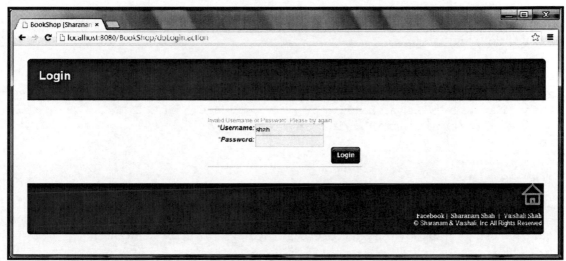

Diagram 22.3

Process Flow

When the login credentials are found invalid, the login form is reserved along with the appropriate error messages by **doLogin → SystemUserLoginAction → loginSystemUser()**.

Here,

❑ **doLogin** is the action configured in struts-AdminLogin.xml, which invokes **loginSystemUser()** of **SystemUserLoginAction**

❑ **SystemUserLoginAction** is the action

❑ **loginSystemUser()** is the method available in the action, which displays administration login page along with the appropriate error messages

Logout

The user can choose to logout of the administration section by clicking **Logout**.

When the user clicks **Logout**, the user details [stored in the session whilst logging in] is removed and the session is destroyed. After which the user is redirected to the Administration Login page.

Clicking [Logout], invokes the action class named **SystemUserLoginAction.java**.

When the user clicks [Logout], the action named **doLogout** is invoked which shows the administration login page.

To locate the action, struts-AdminLogin.xml holds:

```
<action name="doLogout" method="logoffSystemUser"
class="com.sharanamvaishali.action.SystemUserLoginAction">
    <result>/admin/adminLogin.jsp</result>
</action>
```

Process Flow

[Logout] when clicked destroys the session and redirects the user to the administration login page using **doLogout → SystemUserLoginAction → logoffSystemUser()**.

Here,

❑ **doLogout** is the action configured in struts-AdminLogin.xml, which invokes **logoffSystemUser()** of **SystemUserLoginAction**

❑ **SystemUserLoginAction** is the action

❑ **logoffSystemUser()** is the method available in the action, which returns the user to the administration login page

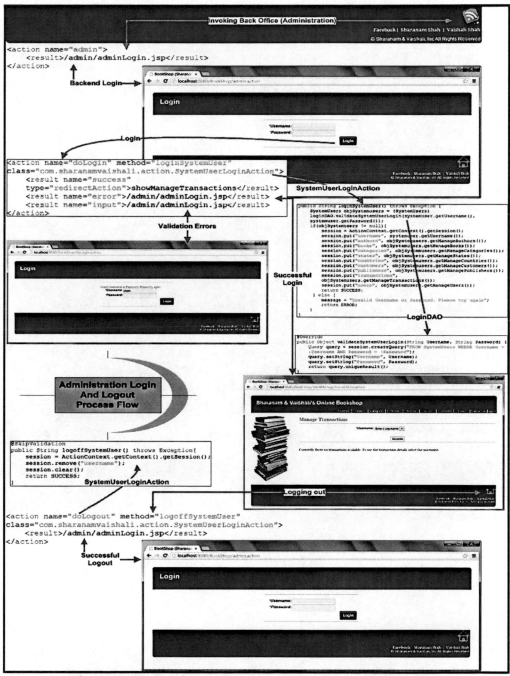

Diagram 22.4: Administration Login And Logout Process Flow

Chapter

23

SECTION IV: PROCESS FLOW

Manage Countries [manageCountries.jsp]

Manage Countries is the page that is served when `Countries` is clicked in the
Administration section after successful administration login.

It displays:

❑ A data entry form to capture the country details

❑ List of countries available

❑ Delete link to delete a particular country record

❑ Edit link to edit a particular country record

Viewing Existing Country Details

When the user clicks `Countries`, manageCountries.jsp is served, as shown in diagram
23.1.

`Countries` when clicked invokes the action class named CountriesAction.java.

To locate the action, struts-Countries.xml holds:

```
<action name="showManageCountries" method="view"
class="com.sharanamvaishali.action.CountriesAction">
    <result>/admin/manageCountries.jsp</result>
</action>
```

User Interface [showManageCountries.action → manageCountries.jsp]

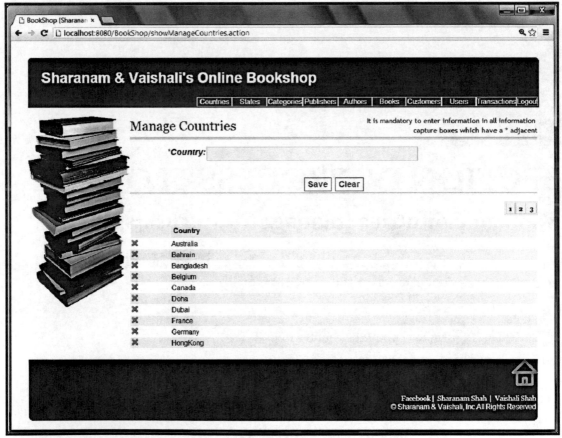

Diagram 23.1

This is a standard data entry form. By default when the form loads, it's in the **INSERT** and **VIEW** mode.

Process Flow

Manage Countries holds a data grid with a list of available records. This data grid serves the purpose of viewing.

The data grid is populated by **doViewCountries** → **CountriesAction** → **view()**.

Here,

- **doViewCountries** is the action configured in **struts-Countries.xml**
- **CountriesAction** is the action
- **view()** is the method available in the action, which displays the existing records from the Countries database table

Navigating Across Existing Country Details

By default when JSP loads **view()** always displays the first page i.e. the <u>first ten records</u>.

To navigate across other pages, the user can use the navigation links .

These links are created based on a page count [calculated as total number of records / 10] received by **doViewCountries** → **CountriesAction** → **view()**.

Every page number is hyperlinked to the action named **iterateManageCountriesPage:**

```
<a href="<s:url action="iterateManageCountriesPage"><s:param
name="pageNo"><s:property /></s:param></s:url>"><s:property /></a>
```

The user can click the desired page number to navigate to that page.

Process Flow

The page navigation is done by **iterateManageCountriesPage** → **CountriesAction** → **getPage()** → **PaginationDAO [getTotalPages() and getPage()]**.

Here,

- **iterateManageCountriesPage** is the action configured in **struts-Countries.xml**
- **CountriesAction** is the action
- **getPage()** is the method available in the action, which retrieves the required page's records via **PaginationDAO**

❑ **PaginationDAO** is the Data Access Object [DAO] Layer

❑ **getTotalPages()** is the method available in DAO, which actually does the calculation of total number of pages for pagination purpose and stores the same

❑ **getPage()** is the method available in the DAO, which actually returns the records belonging to the appropriate page number

Adding New Country Details

After manageCountries.jsp loads, the user can key in the required data and click **Save**.

On clicking **Save**, the **FORM** is submitted to doInsertCountry.action and manageCountries.jsp is re-served.

To locate the action, struts-Countries.xml holds:

```
<action name="doInsertCountry" method="saveCountry"
class="com.sharanamvaishali.action.CountriesAction">
    <interceptor-ref name="defaultStack"/>
    <interceptor-ref name="token"/>
    <result name="success" type="redirectAction">doViewCountries</result>
    <result name="input">/admin/manageCountries.jsp</result>
</action>
```

Process Flow

After the user keys in the required inputs and clicks **Save**, the FORM is submitted and the **save** operation is performed by **doInsertCountry** → **CountriesAction** → **saveCountry()** → **CountriesDAO** → **saveCountry()**.

Here,

❑ **doInsertCountry** is the action configured in **struts-Countries.xml**

❑ **CountriesAction** is the action

❑ **saveCountry()** is the method available in the action, which saves the data captured via **CountriesDAO**

❑ **CountriesDAO** is the Data Access Object [DAO] layer

❑ **saveCountry()** is the method available in DAO, which does the actual saving of the captured data in the Countries database table

If there are any errors such as country name left blank, manageCountries.jsp is re-served along with the error messages, as shown in diagram 23.2.

User Interface For Validation Errors [doInsertCountry → manageCountries.jsp]

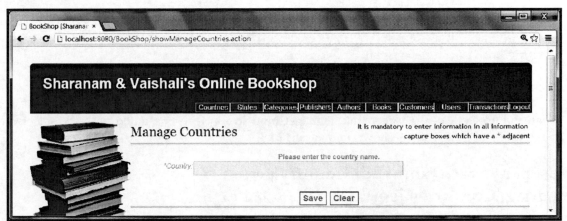

Diagram 23.2: Error messages [manageCountries.jsp]

Process Flow

If the captured data is found to be invalid, then Manage Countries with appropriate error messages is served by **doInsertCountry → CountriesAction-validation.xml**.

Here,

❏ **doInsertCountry** is the action configured in **struts-Countries.xml**

❏ **CountriesAction-validation.xml** is the validation file, which takes care of the validations and traps them and forwards it to Manage Countries

Editing Existing Country Details

To switch to the **EDIT** mode, the user needs to click a desired record from the data grid. Doing so populates the data entry form.

Every record listed in the data grid is hyperlinked to the action named **showEditCountry**:

```
<td class="manageList" onclick="javascript:location.href='<s:url
action='showEditCountry'><s:param name='country.CountryNo' value='CountryNo'
/></s:url>'">
    <s:property value="Country"/>
</td>
```

To locate the action, struts-Countries.xml holds:

```
<action name="showEditCountry" method="editCountry"
class="com.sharanamvaishali.action.CountriesAction">
    <result name="success">/admin/manageCountries.jsp</result>
</action>
```

When the user clicks the hyper link, manageCountries.jsp [pre-populated with the selected country's data] is served, as shown in diagram 23.3.

User Interface [showEditCountry.action → manageCountries.jsp]

Diagram 23.3

Process Flow

The data population of the selected record for editing is done by **showEditCountry →** **CountriesAction → editCountry() → CountriesDAO → getCountryById()**.

Here,

❑ **showEditCountry** is the action configured in **struts-Countries.xml**

❑ **CountriesAction** is the action

❑ **editCountry()** is the method available in the action, which retrieves the country details based on CountryNo as reference via CountriesDAO and re-serves Manage Countries with the required data

❑ **editCountry()** also invokes **view()** of **CountriesAction**, which takes care of the data grid population

❑ **CountriesDAO** is the Data Access Object Layer [DAO]

❑ **getCountryById()** is the method available in DAO, which returns the appropriate country's object from the Countries database table using **CountryNo** as the reference

After the user makes the desired changes and clicks **Save** , the **FORM** is submitted to doInsertCountry.action and manageCountries.jsp is re-served.

To locate the action, struts-Countries.xml holds:

```
<action name="doInsertCountry" method="saveCountry"
class="com.sharanamvaishali.action.CountriesAction">
    <interceptor-ref name="defaultStack"/>
    <interceptor-ref name="token"/>
    <result name="success" type="redirectAction">doViewCountries</result>
    <result name="input">/admin/manageCountries.jsp</result>
</action>
```

Process Flow

After the user keys in the required inputs and clicks **Save** , the FORM is submitted and the **update** operation is performed by **doInsertCountry** → **CountriesAction** → **saveCountry()** → **CountriesDAO** → **updateCountry()**.

Here,

❑ **doInsertCountry** is the action configured in **struts-Countries.xml**

❑ **CountriesAction** is the action

❑ **saveCountry()** is the method available in the action, which saves the data captured via **CountriesDAO**

❑ **CountriesDAO** is the Data Access Object [DAO] layer

❑ **updateCountry()** is the method available in DAO, which does the actual updating of the captured data in the Countries database table

Deleting Existing Country Details

Every record that is listed in manageCountries.jsp holds ✖ which is hyper linked to an action called doDeleteCountry:

```
<a href="<s:url action="doDeleteCountry"><s:param name="country.CountryNo"
value="CountryNo" /></s:url>">
    <img src="/BookShop/images/TrashIcon.png" border="0" alt="Delete"
    style="cursor:pointer;"/>
</a>
```

To locate the action, struts-Countries.xml holds:

```
<action name="doDeleteCountry" method="removeCountry"
class="com.sharanamvaishali.action.CountriesAction">
    <result name="success" type="redirectAction">doViewCountries</result>
    <result name="error">/admin/manageCountries.jsp</result>
</action>
```

When the user clicks ✖, the selected record is deleted and manageCountries.jsp is re-served.

Process Flow

The record deletion is done by **doDeleteCountry** → **CountriesAction** → **removeCountry()** → **CountriesDAO** → **deleteCountry()**.

Here,

❑ **doDeleteCountry** is the action configured in **struts-Countries.xml**

❑ **CountriesAction** is the action

❑ **removeCountry()** is the method available in the action, which deletes the country record based on CountryNo as reference via CountriesDAO and re-serves Manage Countries with the available records

❑ **CountriesDAO** is the Data Access Object Layer [DAO]

❑ **deleteCountry()** is the method available in DAO, which deletes the appropriate country from the Countries database table based on **CountryNo** received as a reference

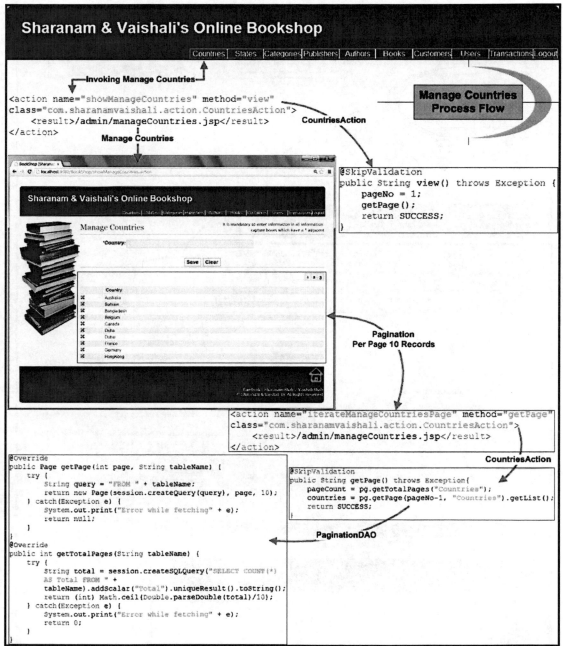

Diagram 23.4: Manage Countries Process Flow

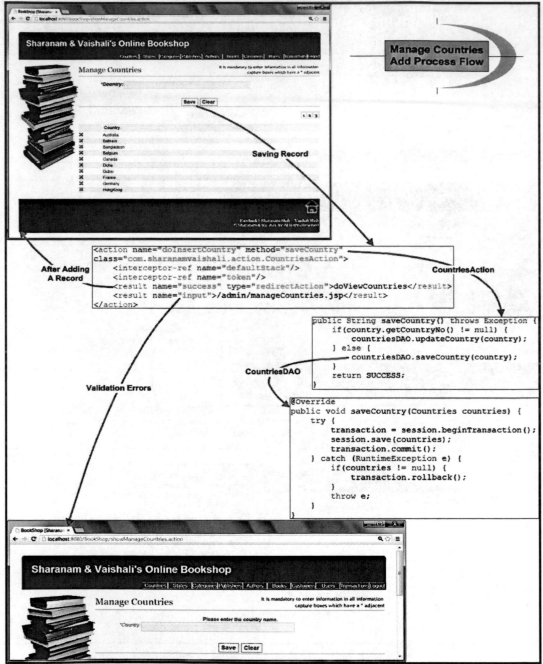

Diagram 23.5: Manage Countries - Add Process Flow

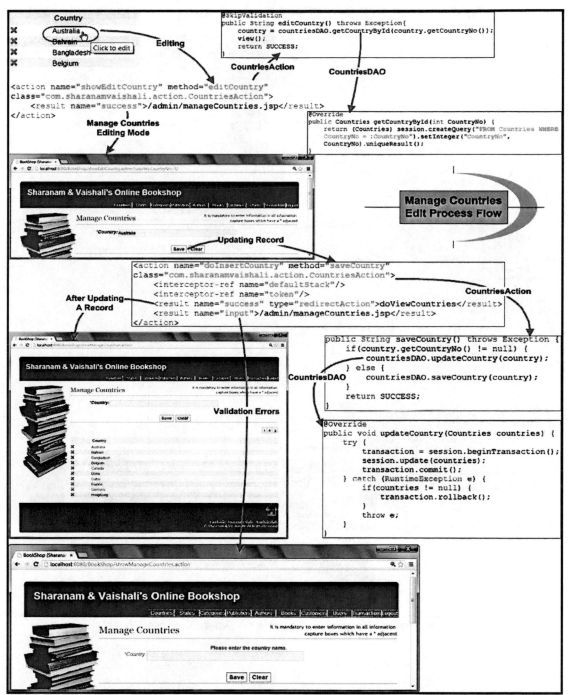

Diagram 23.6: Manage Countries - Edit Process Flow

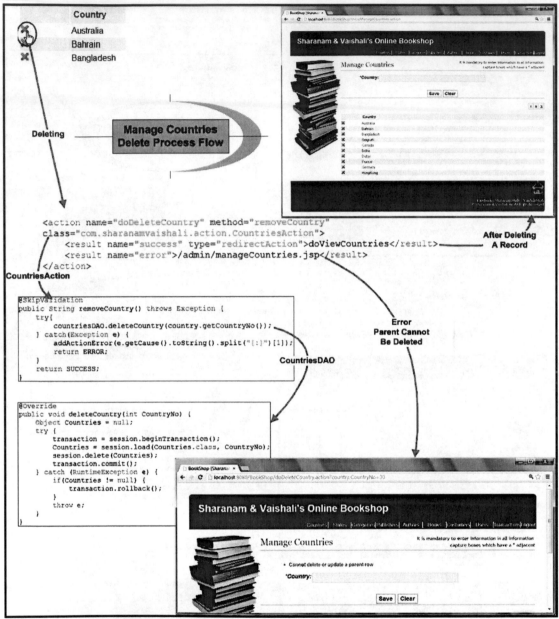

Diagram 23.7: Manage Countries - Delete Process Flow

SECTION IV: PROCESS FLOW

Manage States [manageStates.jsp]

Manage States is the page that is served when █ States █ is clicked in the Administration section after successful administration login.

It displays:

❏ A data entry form to capture the state details

❏ List of states available

❏ Delete link to delete a particular state record

❏ Edit link to edit a particular state record

Viewing Existing State Details

When the user clicks █ States █, manageStates.jsp is served, as shown in diagram 24.1.

█ States █ when clicked invokes the action class named StatesAction.java.

To locate the action, struts-States.xml holds:

```
<action name="showManageStates" method="view"
class="com.sharanamvaishali.action.StatesAction">
    <result>/admin/manageStates.jsp</result>
</action>
```

User Interface [showManageStates.action → manageStates.jsp]

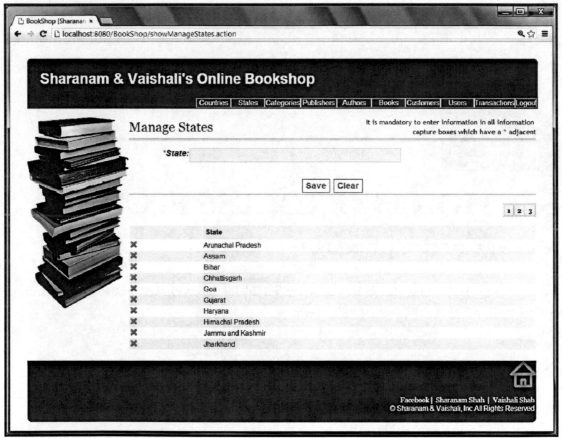

Diagram 24.1

This is a standard data entry form. By default when the form loads, it's in the **INSERT** and **VIEW** mode.

Process Flow

Manage States holds a data grid with a list of available records. This data grid serves the purpose of viewing.

The data grid is populated by **doViewStates** → **StatesAction** → **view()**.

Here,

❑ **doViewStates** is the action configured in **struts-States.xml**

❑ **StatesAction** is the action

❑ **view()** is the method available in the action, which displays the existing records from the States database table

Navigating Across Existing State Details

By default when JSP loads **view()** always displays the first page i.e. the <u>first ten records</u>.

To navigate across other pages, the user can use the navigation links 1 2 3.

These links are created based on a page count [calculated as total number of records / 10] received by **doViewStates** → **StatesAction** → **view()**.

Every page number is hyperlinked to the action named **iterateManageStatesPage:**

```
<a href="<s:url action="iterateManageStatesPage"><s:param
name="pageNo"><s:property /></s:param></s:url>"><s:property /></a>
```

The user can click the desired page number to navigate to that page.

Process Flow

The page navigation is done by **iterateManageStatesPage** → **StatesAction** → **getPage()** → **PaginationDAO [getTotalPages() and getPage()]**.

Here,

❑ **iterateManageStatesPage** is the action configured in **struts-States.xml**

❑ **StatesAction** is the action

❑ **getPage()** is the method available in the action, which retrieves the required page's records via **PaginationDAO**

❑ **PaginationDAO** is the Data Access Object [DAO] Layer

❑ **getTotalPages()** is the method available in DAO, which actually does the calculation of total number of pages for pagination purpose and stores the same

❑ **getPage()** is the method available in the DAO, which actually returns the records belonging to the appropriate page number

Adding New State Details

After manageStates.jsp loads, the user can key in the required data and click **Save** .

On clicking **Save** , the **FORM** is submitted to doInsertState.action and manageStates.jsp is re-served.

To locate the action, struts-States.xml holds:

```
<action name="doInsertState" method="saveState"
class="com.sharanamvaishali.action.StatesAction">
    <interceptor-ref name="defaultStack"/>
    <interceptor-ref name="token"/>
    <result name="success" type="redirectAction">doViewStates</result>
    <result name="input">/admin/manageStates.jsp</result>
</action>
```

Process Flow

After the user keys in the required inputs and clicks **Save** , the FORM is submitted and the **save** operation is performed by **doInsertState** → **StatesAction** → **saveState()** → **StatesDAO** → **saveState()**.

Here,

❑ **doInsertState** is the action configured in **struts-States.xml**

❑ **StatesAction** is the action

❑ **saveState()** is the method available in the action, which saves the data captured via **StatesDAO**

❑ **StatesDAO** is the Data Access Object [DAO] layer

❑ **saveState()** is the method available in DAO, which does the actual saving of the captured data in the States database table

If there are any errors such as state name left blank, manageStates.jsp is re-served along with the error messages, as shown in diagram 24.2.

User Interface For Validation Errors [doInsertState → manageStates.jsp]

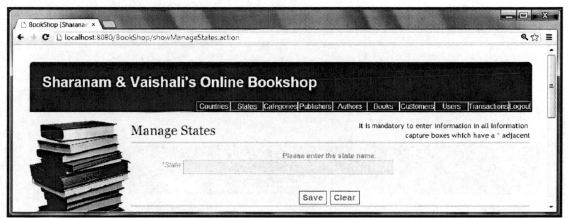

Diagram 24.2: Error messages [manageStates.jsp]

Process Flow

If the captured data is found to be invalid, then Manage States with appropriate error messages is served by **doInsertState → StatesAction-validation.xml**.

Here,

❑ **doInsertState** is the action configured in **struts-States.xml**

❑ **StatesAction-validation.xml** is the validation file, which takes care of the validations and traps them and forwards it to Manage States

Editing Existing State Details

To switch to the **EDIT** mode, the user needs to click a desired record from the data grid. Doing so populates the data entry form.

Every record listed in the data grid is hyperlinked to the action named **showEditState:**

```
<td width="45%" class="manageList" onclick="javascript:location.href='<s:url
action='showEditState'><s:param name='state.StateNo' value='StateNo' /></s:url>'">
    <s:property value="State"/>
</td>
```

To locate the action, struts-States.xml holds:

```
<action name="showEditState" method="editState"
class="com.sharanamvaishali.action.StatesAction">
    <result name="success">/admin/manageStates.jsp</result>
</action>
```

When the user clicks the hyper link, manageStates.jsp [pre-populated with the selected state's data] is served, as shown in diagram 24.3.

User Interface [showEditState.action → manageStates.jsp]

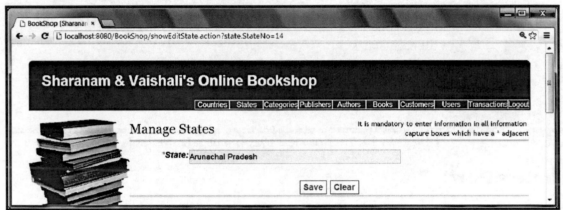

Diagram 24.3

Process Flow

The data population of the selected record for editing is done by **showEditState →
StatesAction → editState() → StatesDAO → getStateById()**.

Here,

❑ **showEditState** is the action configured in **struts-States.xml**

❑ **StatesAction** is the action

❑ **editState()** is the method available in the action, which retrieves the state details based on StateNo as reference via StatesDAO and re-serves Manage States with the required data

❑ **editState()** also invokes **view()** of **StatesAction**, which takes care of the data grid population

❑ **StatesDAO** is the Data Access Object Layer [DAO]

❑ **getStateById()** is the method available in DAO, which returns the appropriate state's object from the States database table using **StateNo** as the reference

After the user makes the desired changes and clicks **Save**, the **FORM** is submitted to doInsertState.action and manageStates.jsp is re-served.

To locate the action, struts-States.xml holds:

```
<action name="doInsertState" method="saveState"
class="com.sharanamvaishali.action.StatesAction">
    <interceptor-ref name="defaultStack"/>
    <interceptor-ref name="token"/>
    <result name="success" type="redirectAction">doViewStates</result>
    <result name="input">/admin/manageStates.jsp</result>
</action>
```

Process Flow

After the user keys in the required inputs and clicks **Save**, the FORM is submitted and the **update** operation is performed by **doInsertState** → **StatesAction** → **saveState()** → **StatesDAO** → **updateState()**.

Here,

❑ **doInsertState** is the action configured in **struts-States.xml**

❑ **StatesAction** is the action

❑ **saveState()** is the method available in the action, which saves the data captured via **StatesDAO**

❑ **StatesDAO** is the Data Access Object [DAO] layer

❑ **updateState()** is the method available in DAO, which does the actual updating of the captured data in the States database table

Deleting Existing State Details

Every record that is listed in manageStates.jsp holds ❌ which is hyper linked to an action called doDeleteState:

```
<a href="<s:url action="doDeleteState"><s:param name="state.StateNo"
value="StateNo" /></s:url>">
    <img src="/BookShop/images/TrashIcon.png" border="0" alt="Delete"
    style="cursor:pointer;"/>
</a>
```

To locate the action, struts-States.xml holds:

```
<action name="doDeleteState" method="removeState"
class="com.sharanamvaishali.action.StatesAction">
    <result name="success" type="redirectAction">doViewStates</result>
    <result name="error">/admin/manageStates.jsp</result>
</action>
```

When the user clicks ✖, the selected record is deleted and manageStates.jsp is re-served.

Process Flow

The record deletion is done by **doDeleteState** → **StatesAction** → **removeState()** → **StatesDAO** → **deleteState()**.

Here,

❑ **doDeleteState** is the action configured in **struts-States.xml**

❑ **StatesAction** is the action

❑ **removeState()** is the method available in the action, which deletes the state record based on StateNo as reference via StatesDAO and re-serves Manage States with the available records

❑ **StatesDAO** is the Data Access Object Layer [DAO]

❑ **deleteState()** is the method available in DAO, which deletes the appropriate state from the States database table based on **StateNo** received as a reference

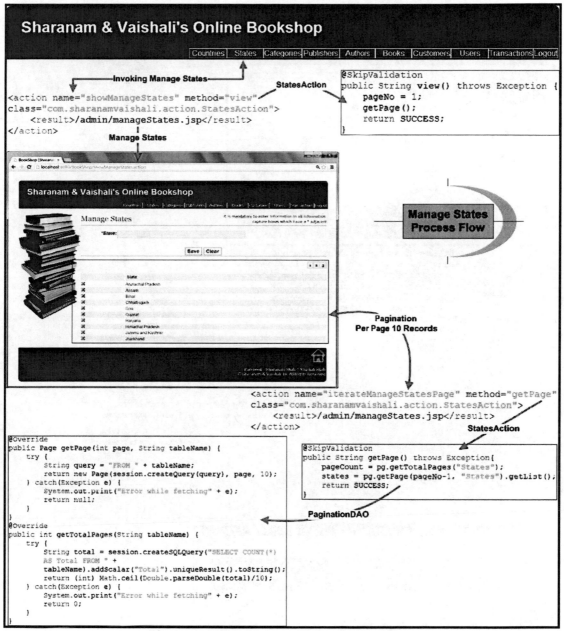

Diagram 24.4: Manage States Process Flow

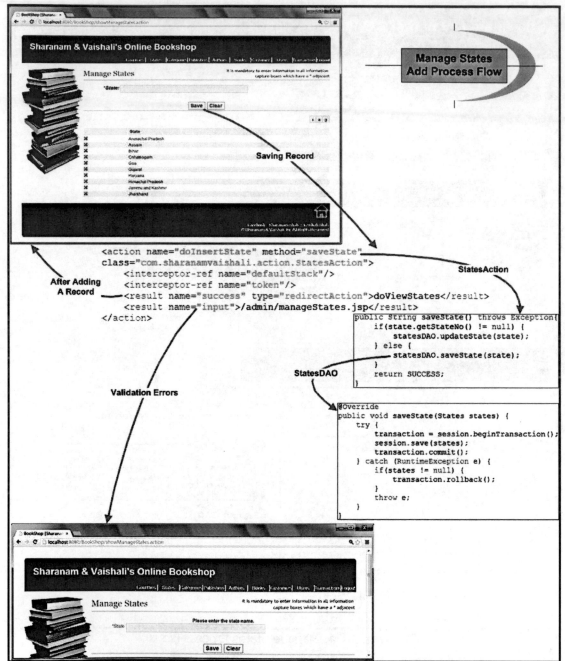

Diagram 24.5: Manage States - Add Process Flow

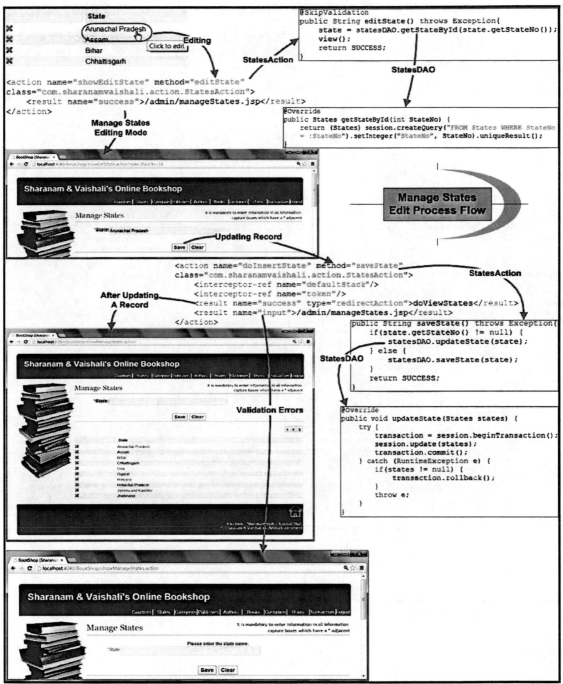

Diagram 24.6: Manage States - Edit Process Flow

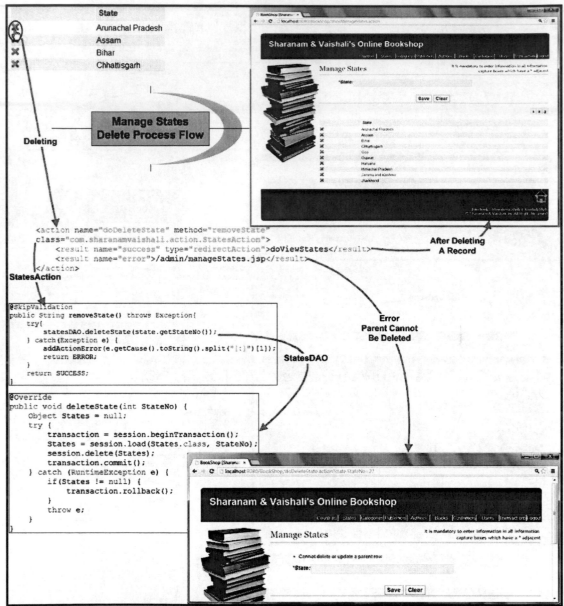

Diagram 24.7: Manage States - Delete Process Flow

Chapter

25

SECTION IV: PROCESS FLOW

Manage Categories [manageCategories.jsp]

Manage Categories is the page that is served when Categories is clicked in the Administration section after successful administration login.

It displays:

❑ A data entry form to capture the category details

❑ List of categories available

❑ Delete link to delete a particular category record

❑ Edit link to edit a particular category record

Viewing Existing Category Details

When the user clicks Categories, manageCategories.jsp is served, as shown in diagram 25.1.

Categories when clicked invokes the action class named CategoriesAction.java.

To locate the action, struts-Categories.xml holds:

```
<action name="showManageCategories" method="view"
class="com.sharanamvaishali.action.CategoriesAction">
    <result>/admin/manageCategories.jsp</result>
</action>
```

User Interface [showManageCategories.action → manageCategories.jsp]

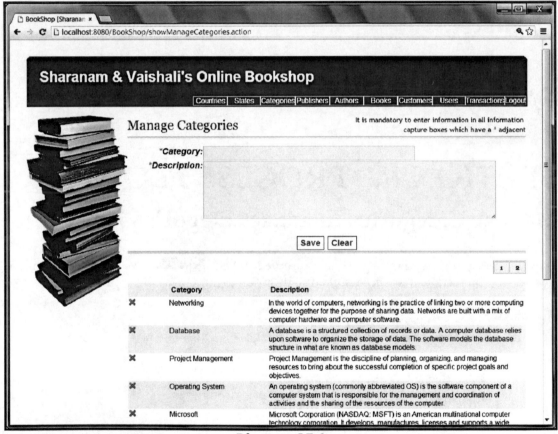

Diagram 25.1

This is a standard data entry form. By default when the form loads, it's in the **INSERT** and **VIEW** mode.

Process Flow

Manage Categories holds a data grid with a list of available records. This data grid serves the purpose of viewing.

The data grid is populated by **doViewCategories** → **CategoriesAction** → **view()**.

Here,

- **doViewCategories** is the action configured in **struts-Categories.xml**
- **CategoriesAction** is the action
- **view()** is the method available in the action, which displays the existing records from the Categories database table

Navigating Across Existing Category Details

By default when JSP loads **view()** always displays the first page i.e. the <u>first ten records</u>.

To navigate across other pages, the user can use the navigation links [1] [2] [3].

These links are created based on a page count [calculated as total number of records / 10] received by **doViewCategories** → **CategoriesAction** → **view()**.

Every page number is hyperlinked to the action named **iterateManageCategoriesPage**:

```
<a href="<s:url action="iterateManageCategoriesPage"><s:param
name="pageNo"><s:property /></s:param></s:url>"><s:property /></a>
```

The user can click the desired page number to navigate to that page.

Process Flow

The page navigation is done by **iterateManageCategoriesPage** → **CategoriesAction** → **getPage()** → **PaginationDAO [getTotalPages() and getPage()]**.

Here,

- **iterateManageCategoriesPage** is the action configured in **struts-Categories.xml**
- **CategoriesAction** is the action
- **getPage()** is the method available in the action, which retrieves the required page's records via **PaginationDAO**

❑ **PaginationDAO** is the Data Access Object [DAO] Layer

❑ **getTotalPages()** is the method available in DAO, which actually does the calculation of total number of pages for pagination purpose and stores the same

❑ **getPage()** is the method available in the DAO, which actually returns the records belonging to the appropriate page number

Adding New Category Details

After manageCategories.jsp loads, the user can key in the required data and click Save .

On clicking Save , the **FORM** is submitted to doInsertCategory.action and manageCategories.jsp is re-served.

To locate the action, struts-Categories.xml holds:

```
<action name="doInsertCategory" method="saveCategory"
class="com.sharanamvaishali.action.CategoriesAction">
    <interceptor-ref name="defaultStack"/>
    <interceptor-ref name="token"/>
    <result name="success" type="redirectAction">doViewCategories</result>
    <result name="input">/admin/manageCategories.jsp</result>
</action>
```

Process Flow

After the user keys in the required inputs and clicks Save , the FORM is submitted and the **save** operation is performed by **doInsertCategory → CategoriesAction → saveCategory() → CategoriesDAO → saveCategory()**.

Here,

❑ **doInsertCategory** is the action configured in **struts-Categories.xml**

❑ **CategoriesAction** is the action

❑ **saveCategory()** is the method available in the action, which saves the data captured via **CategoriesDAO**

❑ **CategoriesDAO** is the Data Access Object [DAO] layer

❑ **saveCategory()** is the method available in DAO, which does the actual saving of the captured data in the Categories database table

If there are any errors such as category name left blank, manageCategories.jsp is re-served along with the error messages, as shown in diagram 25.2.

User Interface For Validation Errors [doInsertCategory → manageCategories.jsp]

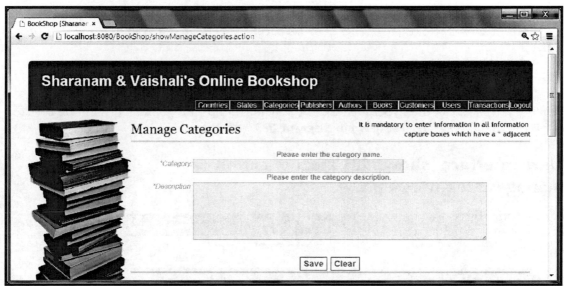

Diagram 25.2: Error messages [manageCategories.jsp]

Process Flow

If the captured data is found to be invalid, then Manage Categories with appropriate error messages is served by **doInsertCategory → CategoriesAction-validation.xml**.

Here,

❏ **doInsertCategory** is the action configured in **struts-Categories.xml**

❏ **CategoriesAction-validation.xml** is the validation file, which takes care of the validations and traps them and forwards it to Manage Categories

Editing Existing Category Details

To switch to the **EDIT** mode, the user needs to click a desired record from the data grid. Doing so populates the data entry form.

Every record listed in the data grid is hyperlinked to the action named **showEditCategory**:

```
<td width="25%" class="manageList" onclick="javascript:location.href='<s:url
action='showEditCategory'><s:param name='category.CategoryNo' value='CategoryNo'
/></s:url>'">
    <s:property value="Category"/>
</td>
```

To locate the action, struts-Categories.xml holds:

```
<action name="showEditCategory" method="editCategory"
class="com.sharanamvaishali.action.CategoriesAction">
    <result name="success">admin/manageCategories.jsp</result>
</action>
```

When the user clicks the hyper link, manageCategories.jsp [pre-populated with the selected category's data] is served, as shown in diagram 25.3.

User Interface [showEditCategory.action → manageCategories.jsp]

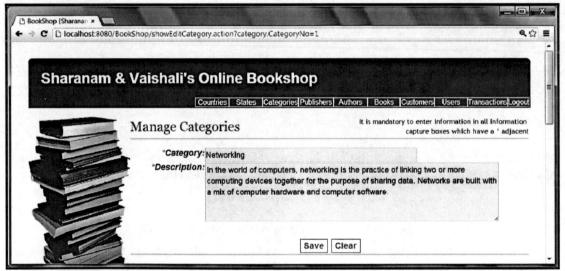

Diagram 25.3

Process Flow

The data population of the selected record for editing is done by **showEditCategory → CategoriesAction → editCategory() → CategoriesDAO → getCategoryById()**.

Here,

☐ **showEditCategory** is the action configured in **struts-Categories.xml**

☐ **CategoriesAction** is the action

☐ **editCategory()** is the method available in the action, which retrieves the category details based on CategoryNo as reference via CategoriesDAO and re-serves Manage Categories with the required data

☐ **editCategory()** also invokes **view()** of **CategoriesAction**, which takes care of the data grid population

☐ **CategoriesDAO** is the Data Access Object Layer [DAO]

☐ **getCategoryById()** is the method available in DAO, which returns the appropriate category's object from the Categories database table using **CategoryNo** as the reference

After the user makes the desired changes and clicks �[**Save**], the **FORM** is submitted to doInsertCategory.action and manageCategories.jsp is re-served.

To locate the action, struts-Categories.xml holds:

```
<action name="doInsertCategory" method="saveCategory"
class="com.sharanamvaishali.action.CategoriesAction">
    <interceptor-ref name="defaultStack"/>
    <interceptor-ref name="token"/>
    <result name="success" type="redirectAction">doViewCategories</result>
    <result name="input">/admin/manageCategories.jsp</result>
</action>
```

Process Flow

After the user keys in the required inputs and clicks [**Save**], the FORM is submitted and the **update** operation is performed by **doInsertCategory → CategoriesAction → saveCategory() → CategoriesDAO → updateCategory()**.

Here,

☐ **doInsertCategory** is the action configured in **struts-Categories.xml**

☐ **CategoriesAction** is the action

☐ **saveCategory()** is the method available in the action, which saves the data captured via **CategoriesDAO**

☐ **CategoriesDAO** is the Data Access Object [DAO] layer

☐ **updateCategory()** is the method available in DAO, which does the actual updating of the captured data in the Categories database table

Deleting Existing Category Details

Every record that is listed in manageCategories.jsp holds ✖ which is hyper linked to an action called doDeleteCategory:

```
<a href="<s:url action="doDeleteCategory"><s:param name="category.CategoryNo"
value="CategoryNo" /></s:url>">
    <img src="/BookShop/images/TrashIcon.png" border="0" alt="Delete"
    style="cursor:pointer;"/>
</a>
```

To locate the action, struts-Categories.xml holds:

```
<action name="doDeleteCategory" method="removeCategory"
class="com.sharanamvaishali.action.CategoriesAction">
    <result name="success" type="redirectAction">doViewCategories</result>
    <result name="error">/admin/manageCategories.jsp</result>
</action>
```

When the user clicks ✖, the selected record is deleted and manageCategories.jsp is re-served.

Process Flow

The record deletion is done by **doDeleteCategory** ➜ **CategoriesAction** ➜ **removeCategory()** ➜ **CategoriesDAO** ➜ **deleteCategory()**.

Here,

❑ **doDeleteCategory** is the action configured in **struts-Categories.xml**

❑ **CategoriesAction** is the action

❑ **removeCategory()** is the method available in the action, which deletes the category record based on CategoryNo as reference via CategoriesDAO and re-serves Manage Categories with the available records

❑ **CategoriesDAO** is the Data Access Object Layer [DAO]

❑ **deleteCategory()** is the method available in DAO, which deletes the appropriate category from the Categories database table based on **CategoryNo** received as a reference

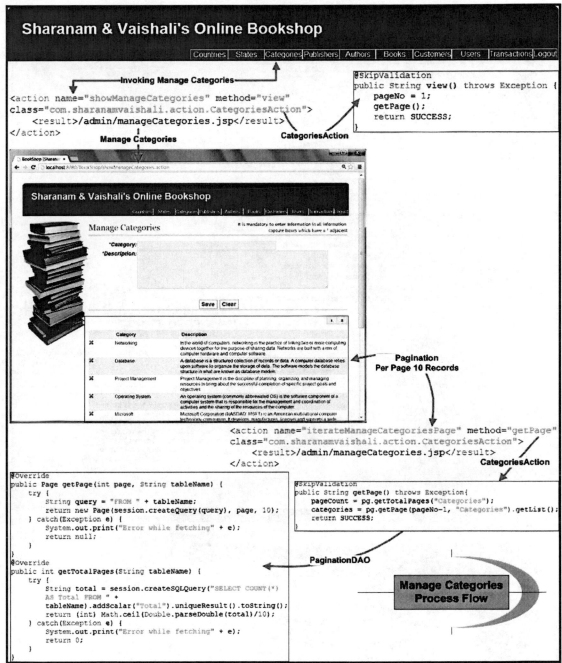

Diagram 25.4: Manage Categories Process Flow

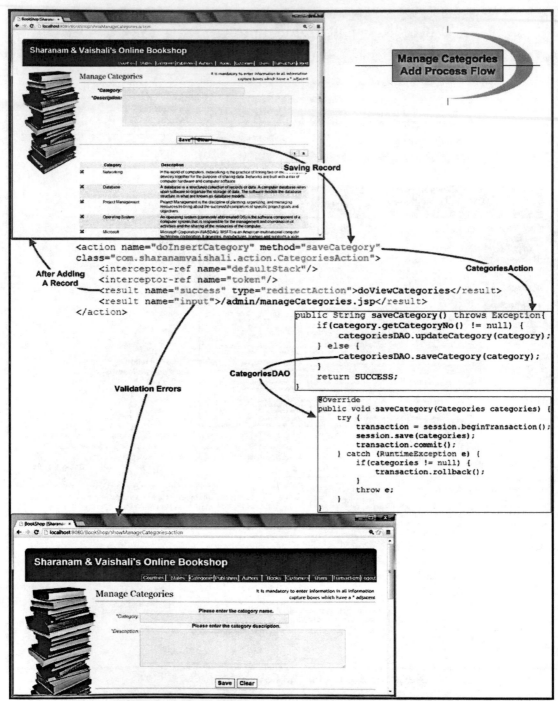

Diagram 25.5: Manage Categories - Add Process Flow

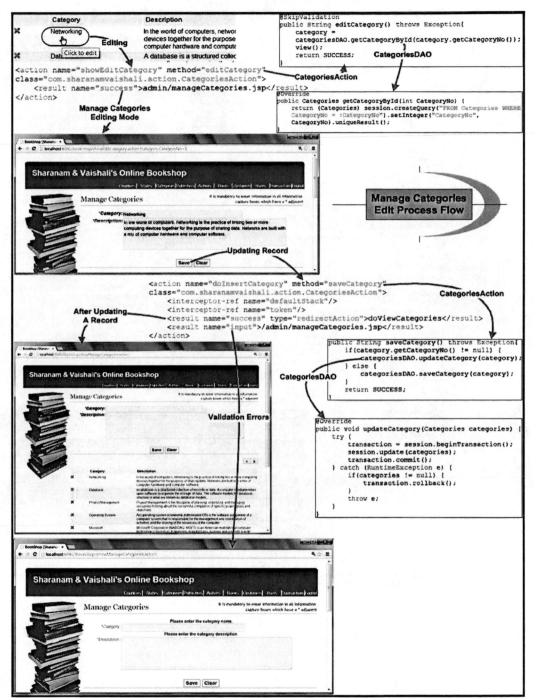

Diagram 25.6: Manage Categories - Edit Process Flow

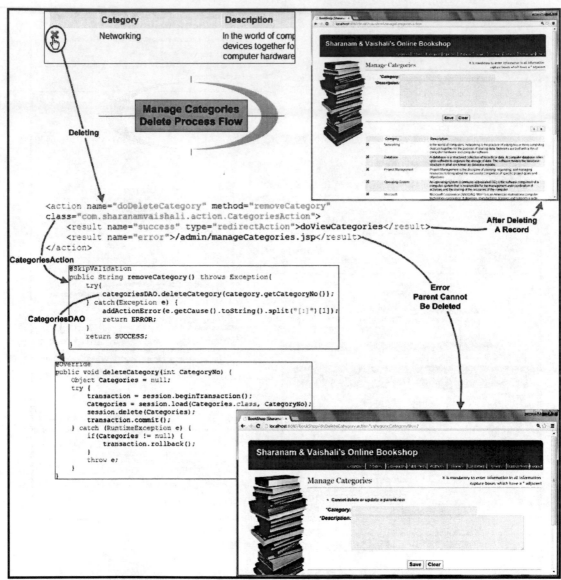

Diagram 25.7: Manage Categories - Delete Process Flow

Chapter

26

SECTION IV: PROCESS FLOW

Manage Publishers [managePublishers.jsp]

Manage Publishers is the page that is served when **Publishers** is clicked in the Administration section after successful administration login.

It displays:

❑ A data entry form to capture the publisher details

❑ List of publishers available

❑ Delete link to delete a particular publisher record

❑ Edit link to edit a particular publisher record

Viewing Existing Publisher Details

When the user clicks **Publishers**, managePublishers.jsp is served, as shown in diagram 26.1.

Publishers when clicked invokes the action class named PublishersAction.java.

To locate the action, struts-Publishers.xml holds:

```
<action name="showManagePublishers" method="view"
class="com.sharanamvaishali.action.PublishersAction">
    <result>/admin/managePublishers.jsp</result>
</action>
```

User Interface [showManagePublishers.action →
managePublishers.jsp]

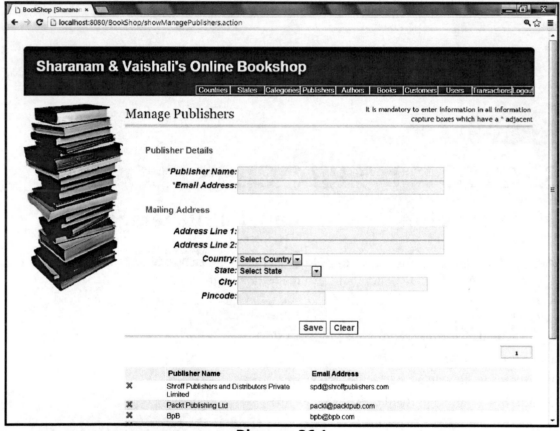

Diagram 26.1

This is a standard data entry form. By default when the form loads, it's in the **INSERT** and **VIEW** mode.

Process Flow

Manage Publishers holds a data grid with a list of available records. This data grid serves the purpose of viewing.

The data grid is populated by **doViewPublishers** → **PublishersAction** → **view()**.

Here,

❑ **doViewPublishers** is the action configured in **struts-Publishers.xml**

❑ **PublishersAction** is the action

❑ **view()** is the method available in the action, which displays the existing records from the Publishers database table

Navigating Across Existing Publisher Details

By default when JSP loads **view()** always displays the first page i.e. the <u>first ten records</u>.

To navigate across other pages, the user can use the navigation links ⬚ 1 .

These links are created based on a page count [calculated as total number of records / 10] received by **doViewPublishers** → **PublishersAction** → **view()**.

Every page number is hyperlinked to the action named **iterateManagePublishersPage**:

```
<a href="<s:url action="iterateManagePublishersPage"><s:param
name="pageNo"><s:property /></s:param></s:url>"><s:property /></a>
```

The user can click the desired page number to navigate to that page.

Process Flow

The page navigation is done by **iterateManagePublishersPage** → **PublishersAction** → **getPage()** → **PaginationDAO [getTotalPages() and getPage()]**.

Here,

❑ **iterateManagePublishersPage** is the action configured in **struts-Publishers.xml**

❑ **PublishersAction** is the action

❑ **getPage()** is the method available in the action, which retrieves the required page's records via **PaginationDAO**

- ❑ **PaginationDAO** is the Data Access Object [DAO] Layer
- ❑ **getTotalPages()** is the method available in DAO, which actually does the calculation of total number of pages for pagination purpose and stores the same
- ❑ **getPage()** is the method available in the DAO, which actually returns the records belonging to the appropriate page number

Adding New Publisher Details

After managePublishers.jsp loads, the user can key in the required data and click **Save**.

On clicking **Save**, the **FORM** is submitted to doInsertPublisher.action and managePublishers.jsp is re-served.

To locate the action, struts-Publishers.xml holds:

```
<action name="doInsertPublisher" method="savePublisher"
class="com.sharanamvaishali.action.PublishersAction">
    <interceptor-ref name="defaultStack"/>
    <interceptor-ref name="token"/>
    <result name="success"
    type="redirectAction">doViewPublishers</result>
    <result name="input">/admin/managePublishers.jsp</result>
</action>
```

Process Flow

After the user keys in the required inputs and clicks **Save**, the FORM is submitted and the **save** operation is performed by **doInsertPublisher** → **PublishersAction** → **savePublisher()** → **PublishersDAO** → **savePublisher()**.

Here,

- ❑ **doInsertPublisher** is the action configured in **struts-Publishers.xml**
- ❑ **PublishersAction** is the action
- ❑ **savePublisher()** is the method available in the action, which saves the data captured via **PublishersDAO**
- ❑ **PublishersDAO** is the Data Access Object [DAO] layer
- ❑ **savePublisher()** is the method available in DAO, which does the actual saving of the captured data in the Publishers database table

If there are any errors such as publisher name left blank, managePublishers.jsp is re-served along with the error messages, as shown in diagram 26.2.

User Interface For Validation Errors [doInsertPublisher → managePublishers.jsp]

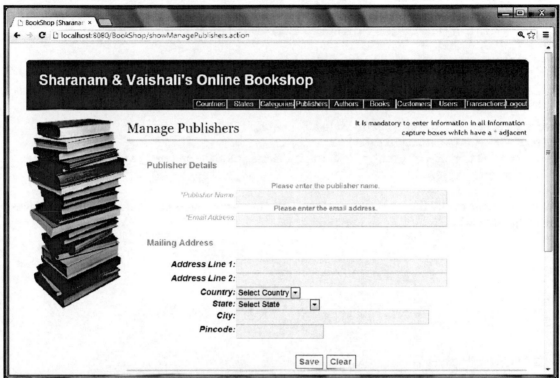

Diagram 26.2: Error messages [managePublishers.jsp]

Process Flow

If the captured data is found to be invalid, then Manage Publishers with appropriate error messages is served by **doInsertPublisher → PublishersAction-validation.xml**.

Here,

❑ **doInsertPublisher** is the action configured in **struts-Publishers.xml**

❑ **PublishersAction-validation.xml** is the validation file, which takes care of the validations and traps them and forwards it to Manage Publishers

Editing Existing Publisher Details

To switch to the **EDIT** mode, the user needs to click a desired record from the data grid. Doing so populates the data entry form.

Every record listed in the data grid is hyperlinked to the action named **showEditPublisher:**

```
<td width="35%" class="manageList" onclick="javascript:location.href='<s:url
action='showEditPublisher'><s:param name='publisher.PublisherNo'
value='PublisherNo' /></s:url>'">
    <s:property value="PublisherName"/>
</td>
```

To locate the action, struts-Publishers.xml holds:

```
<action name="showEditPublisher" method="editPublisher"
class="com.sharanamvaishali.action.PublishersAction">
    <result name="success">/admin/managePublishers.jsp</result>
</action>
```

When the user clicks the hyper link, managePublishers.jsp [pre-populated with the selected publisher's data] is served, as shown in diagram 26.3.

User Interface [showEditPublisher.action → managePublishers.jsp]

Diagram 26.3

Process Flow

The data population of the selected record for editing is done by **showEditPublisher** → **PublishersAction** → **editPublisher()** → **PublishersDAO** → **getPublisherById()**.

Here,

❑ **showEditPublisher** is the action configured in **struts-Publishers.xml**

❑ **PublishersAction** is the action

❑ **editPublisher()** is the method available in the action, which retrieves the publisher details based on PublisherNo as reference via PublishersDAO and re-serves Manage Publishers with the required data

❑ **editPublisher()** also invokes **view()** of **PublishersAction**, which takes care of the data grid population

❑ **PublishersDAO** is the Data Access Object Layer [DAO]

❑ **getPublisherById()** is the method available in DAO, which returns the appropriate publisher's object from the Publishers database table using **PublisherNo** as the reference

After the user makes the desired changes and clicks **Save** , the **FORM** is submitted to doInsertPublisher.action and managePublishers.jsp is re-served.

To locate the action, struts-Publishers.xml holds:

```
<action name="doInsertPublisher" method="savePublisher"
class="com.sharanamvaishali.action.PublishersAction">
    <interceptor-ref name="defaultStack"/>
    <interceptor-ref name="token"/>
    <result name="success"
type="redirectAction">doViewPublishers</result>
    <result name="input">/admin/managePublishers.jsp</result>
</action>
```

Process Flow

After the user keys in the required inputs and clicks **Save** , the FORM is submitted and the **update** operation is performed by **doInsertPublisher → PublishersAction → savePublisher() → PublishersDAO → updatePublisher()**.

Here,

❑ **doInsertPublisher** is the action configured in **struts-Publishers.xml**

❑ **PublishersAction** is the action

❑ **savePublisher()** is the method available in the action, which saves the data captured via **PublishersDAO**

❑ **PublishersDAO** is the Data Access Object [DAO] layer

❑ **updatePublisher()** is the method available in DAO, which does the actual updating of the captured data in the Publishers database table

Deleting Existing Publisher Details

Every record that is listed in managePublishers.jsp holds ✖ which is hyper linked to an action called doDeletePublisher:

```
<a href="<s:url action="doDeletePublisher"><s:param name="publisher.PublisherNo"
value="PublisherNo" /></s:url>">
    <img src="/BookShop/images/TrashIcon.png" border="0" alt="Delete"
    style="cursor:pointer;"/>
</a>
```

To locate the action, struts-Publishers.xml holds:

```
<action name="doDeletePublisher" method="removePublisher"
class="com.sharanamvaishali.action.PublishersAction">
    <result name="success"
    type="redirectAction">doViewPublishers</result>
    <result name="error">/admin/managePublishers.jsp</result>
</action>
```

When the user clicks ✖, the selected record is deleted and managePublishers.jsp is re-served.

Process Flow

The record deletion is done by **doDeletePublisher** → **PublishersAction** → **removePublisher()** → **PublishersDAO** → **deletePublisher()**.

Here,

❑ **doDeletePublisher** is the action configured in **struts-Publishers.xml**

❑ **PublishersAction** is the action

❑ **removePublisher()** is the method available in the action, which deletes the publisher record based on PublisherNo as reference via PublishersDAO and re-serves Manage Publishers with the available records

❑ **PublishersDAO** is the Data Access Object Layer [DAO]

❑ **deletePublisher()** is the method available in DAO, which deletes the appropriate publisher from the Publishers database table based on **PublisherNo** received as a reference

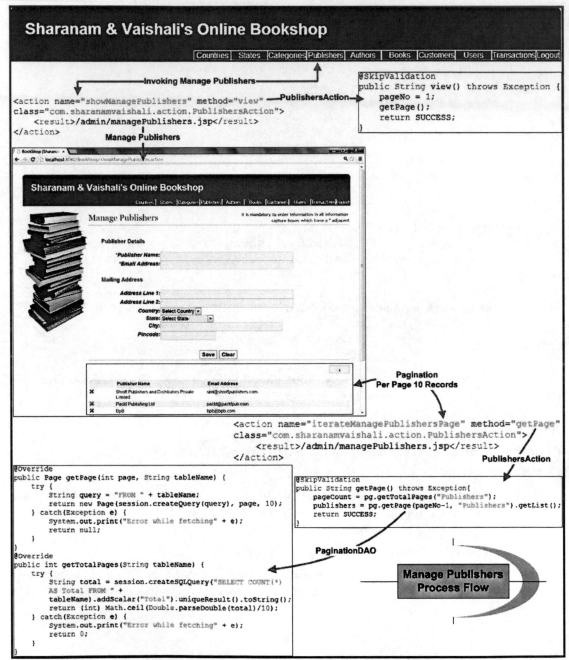

Diagram 26.4: Manage Publishers Process Flow

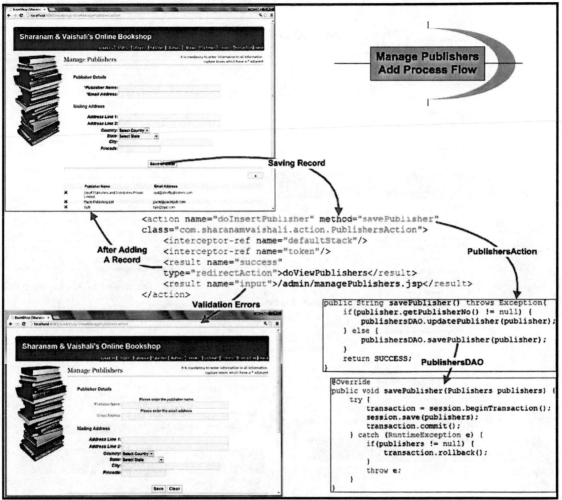

Diagram 26.5: Manage Publishers - Add Process Flow

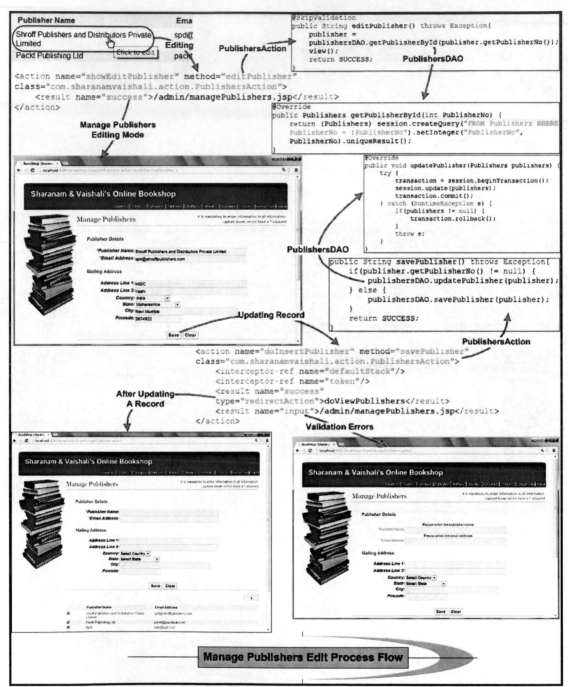

Diagram 26.6: Manage Publishers - Edit Process Flow

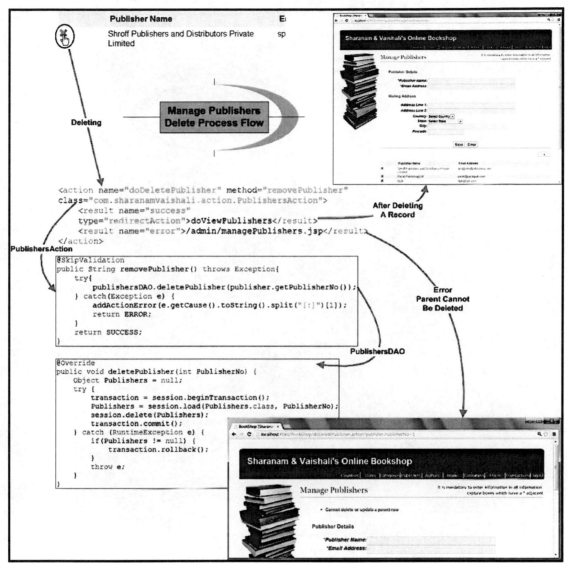

Diagram 26.7: Manage Publishers - Delete Process Flow

SECTION IV: PROCESS FLOW

Manage Authors [manageAuthors.jsp]

Manage Authors is the page that is served when ███ Authors ███ is clicked in the Administration section after successful administration login.

It displays:

- ❑ A data entry form to capture the author details
- ❑ List of authors available
- ❑ Delete link to delete a particular author record
- ❑ Edit link to edit a particular author record

Viewing Existing Author Details

When the user clicks ███ Authors ███, manageAuthors.jsp is served, as shown in diagram 27.1.

███ Authors ███ when clicked invokes the action class named AuthorsAction.java.

To locate the action, struts-Authors.xml holds:

```
<action name="showManageAuthors" method="view"
class="com.sharanamvaishali.action.AuthorsAction">
    <result>/admin/manageAuthors.jsp</result>
</action>
```

User Interface [showManageAuthors.action → manageAuthors.jsp]

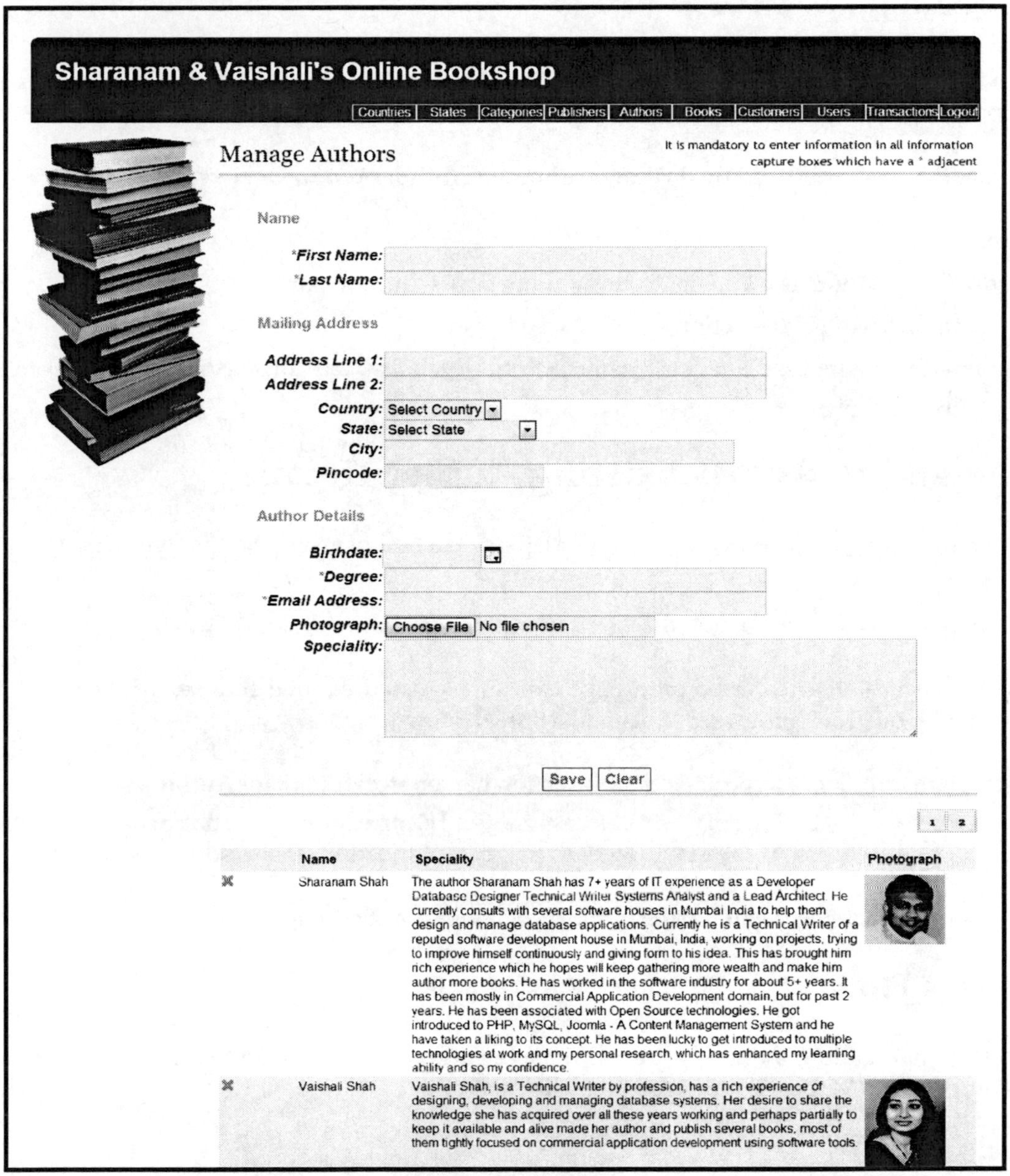

Diagram 27.1

This is a standard data entry form. By default when the form loads, it's in the **INSERT** and **VIEW** mode.

Process Flow

Manage Authors holds a data grid with a list of available records. This data grid serves the purpose of viewing.

The data grid is populated by **doViewAuthors** → **AuthorsAction** → **view()**.

Here,

❑ **doViewAuthors** is the action configured in **struts-Authors.xml**

❑ **AuthorsAction** is the action

❑ **view()** is the method available in the action, which displays the existing records from the Authors database table

Navigating Across Existing Author Details

By default when JSP loads **view()** always displays the first page i.e. the <u>first ten records</u>.

To navigate across other pages, the user can use the navigation links | 1 | 2 |.

These links are created based on a page count [calculated as total number of records / 10] received by **doViewAuthors** → **AuthorsAction** → **view()**.

Every page number is hyperlinked to the action named **iterateManageAuthorsPage**:

```
<a href="<s:url action="iterateManageAuthorsPage"><s:param
name="pageNo"><s:property /></s:param></s:url>"><s:property /></a>
```

The user can click the desired page number to navigate to that page.

Process Flow

The page navigation is done by **iterateManageAuthorsPage** → **AuthorsAction** → **getPage()** → **PaginationDAO** [**getTotalPages()** and **getPage()**].

Here,

❑ **iterateManageAuthorsPage** is the action configured in **struts-Authors.xml**

❑ **AuthorsAction** is the action

❑ **getPage()** is the method available in the action, which retrieves the required page's records via **PaginationDAO**

❑ **PaginationDAO** is the Data Access Object [DAO] Layer

❑ **getTotalPages()** is the method available in DAO, which actually does the calculation of total number of pages for pagination purpose and stores the same

❑ **getPage()** is the method available in the DAO, which actually returns the records belonging to the appropriate page number

Adding New Author Details

After manageAuthors.jsp loads, the user can key in the required data and click **Save**.

On clicking **Save**, the FORM is submitted to doInsertAuthor.action and manageAuthors.jsp is re-served.

To locate the action, struts-Authors.xml holds:

```
<action name="doInsertAuthor" method="saveAuthor"
class="com.sharanamvaishali.action.AuthorsAction">
    <interceptor-ref name="defaultStack"/>
    <interceptor-ref name="token"/>
    <result name="success"
    type="redirectAction">doViewAuthors</result>
    <result name="input">/admin/manageAuthors.jsp</result>
</action>
```

Process Flow

After the user keys in the required inputs and clicks **Save**, the FORM is submitted and the save operation is performed by **doInsertAuthor** → **AuthorsAction** → **saveAuthor()** → **AuthorsDAO** → **saveAuthor()**.

Here,

❑ **doInsertAuthor** is the action configured in **struts-Authors.xml**

❑ **AuthorsAction** is the action

❑ **saveAuthor()** is the method available in the action, which saves the data captured via **AuthorsDAO**

❑ **AuthorsDAO** is the Data Access Object [DAO] layer

❑   **saveAuthor()** is the method available in DAO, which does the actual saving of the captured data in the Authors database table

If there are any errors such as duplicate email address, manageAuthors.jsp is re-served along with the error messages, as shown in diagram 27.2.

User Interface For Validation Errors [doInsertAuthor → manageAuthors.jsp]

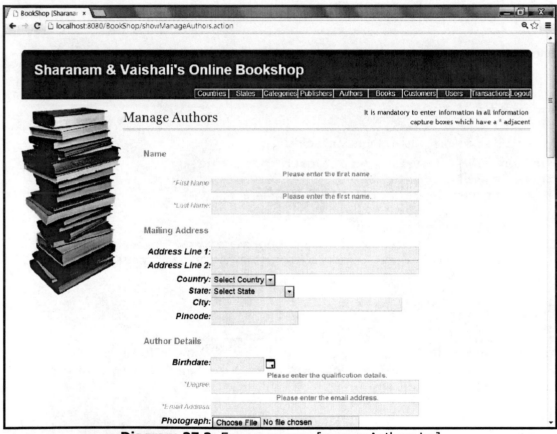

Diagram 27.2: Error messages [manageAuthors.jsp]

Process Flow

If the captured data is found to be invalid, then Manage Authors with appropriate error messages is served by **doInsertAuthor → AuthorsAction-validation.xml**.

Here,

❑ **doInsertAuthor** is the action configured in **struts-Authors.xml**

❑ **AuthorsAction-validation.xml** is the validation file, which takes care of the validations and traps them and forwards it to Manage Authors

If the photographs are uploaded by the user, then the photographs are converted to Blob and saved in the Authors database table.

Editing Existing Author Details

To switch to the **EDIT** mode, the user needs to click a desired record from the data grid. Doing so populates the data entry form.

Every record listed in the data grid is hyperlinked to the action named **showEditAuthor:**

```
<td width="15%" class="manageList" onclick="javascript:location.href='<s:url
action='showEditAuthor'><s:param name='author.AuthorNo' value='AuthorNo'
/></s:url>'">
    <s:property value="FirstName"/> <s:property value="LastName" />
</td>
```

To locate the action, struts-Authors.xml holds:

```
<action name="showEditAuthor" method="editAuthor"
class="com.sharanamvaishali.action.AuthorsAction">
    <result name="success">/admin/manageAuthors.jsp</result>
</action>
```

When the user clicks the hyper link, manageAuthors.jsp [pre-populated with the selected author's data] is served, as shown in diagram 27.3.

User Interface [showEditAuthor.action → manageAuthors.jsp]

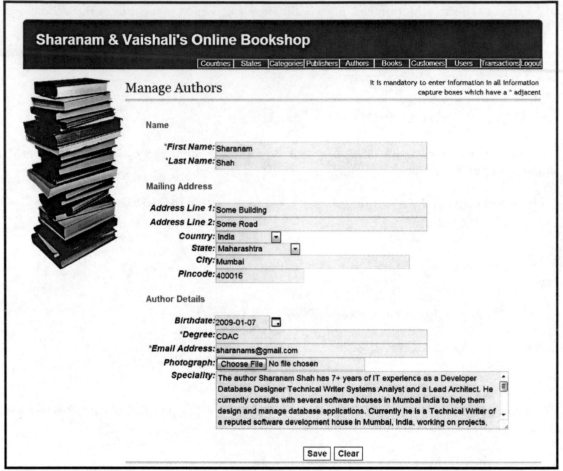

Diagram 27.3

Process Flow

The data population of the selected record for editing is done by **showEditAuthor** → **AuthorsAction** → **editAuthor()** → **AuthorsDAO** → **getAuthorById()**.

Here,

❑ **showEditAuthor** is the action configured in **struts-Authors.xml**

❑ **AuthorsAction** is the action

❑ **editAuthor()** is the method available in the action, which retrieves the author details based on AuthorNo as reference via AuthorsDAO and re-serves Manage Authors with the required data

❑ **editAuthor()** also invokes **view()** of **AuthorsAction**, which takes care of the data grid population

❑ **AuthorsDAO** is the Data Access Object Layer [DAO]

❑ **getAuthorById()** is the method available in DAO, which returns the appropriate author's object from the Authors database table using **AuthorNo** as the reference

After the user makes the desired changes and clicks Save , the **FORM** is submitted to doInsertAuthor.action and manageAuthors.jsp is re-served.

To locate the action, struts-Authors.xml holds:

```
<action name="doInsertAuthor" method="saveAuthor"
class="com.sharanamvaishali.action.AuthorsAction">
    <interceptor-ref name="defaultStack"/>
    <interceptor-ref name="token"/>
    <result name="success"
    type="redirectAction">doViewAuthors</result>
    <result name="input">/admin/manageAuthors.jsp</result>
</action>
```

Process Flow

After the user keys in the required inputs and clicks Save , the FORM is submitted and the **update** operation is performed by **doInsertAuthor** → **AuthorsAction** → **saveAuthor()** → **AuthorsDAO** → **updateAuthor()**.

Here,

❑ **doInsertAuthor** is the action configured in **struts-Authors.xml**

❑ **AuthorsAction** is the action

❑ **saveAuthor()** is the method available in the action, which saves the data captured via **AuthorsDAO**

❑ **AuthorsDAO** is the Data Access Object [DAO] layer

❑ **updateAuthor()** is the method available in DAO, which does the actual updating of the captured data in the Authors database table

Deleting Existing Author Details

Every record that is listed in manageAuthors.jsp holds ✖ which is hyper linked to an action called doDeleteAuthor:

```
<a href="<s:url action="doDeleteAuthor"><s:param name="author.AuthorNo"
value="AuthorNo" /></s:url>">
    <img src="/BookShop/images/TrashIcon.png" border="0" alt="Delete"
    style="cursor:pointer;"/>
</a>
```

To locate the action, struts-Authors.xml holds:

```
<action name="doDeletePublisher" method="removePublisher"
class="com.sharanamvaishali.action.PublishersAction">
    <result name="success"
    type="redirectAction">doViewPublishers</result>
    <result name="error">/admin/managePublishers.jsp</result>
</action>
```

When the user clicks ✖, the selected record is deleted and manageAuthors.jsp is re-served.

Process Flow

The record deletion is done by **doDeleteAuthor** ➔ **AuthorsAction** ➔ **removeAuthor()** ➔ **AuthorsDAO** ➔ **deleteAuthor()**.

Here,

❑ **doDeleteAuthor** is the action configured in **struts-Authors.xml**

❑ **AuthorsAction** is the action

❑ **removeAuthor()** is the method available in the action, which deletes the author record based on AuthorNo as reference via AuthorsDAO and re-serves Manage Authors with the available records

❑ **AuthorsDAO** is the Data Access Object Layer [DAO]

❑ **deleteAuthor()** is the method available in DAO, which deletes the appropriate author from the Authors database table based on **AuthorNo** received as a reference

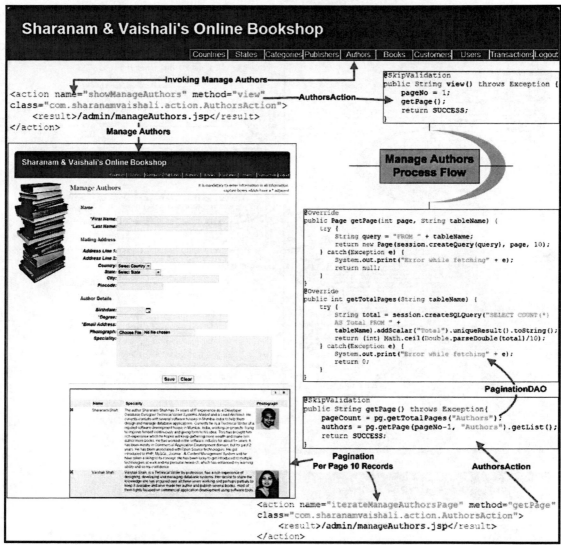

Diagram 27.4: Manage Authors Process Flow

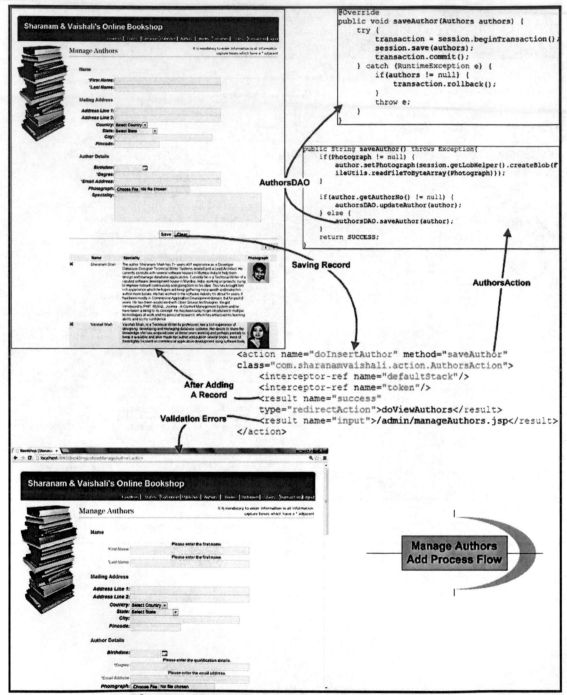

Diagram 27.5: Manage Authors - Add Process Flow

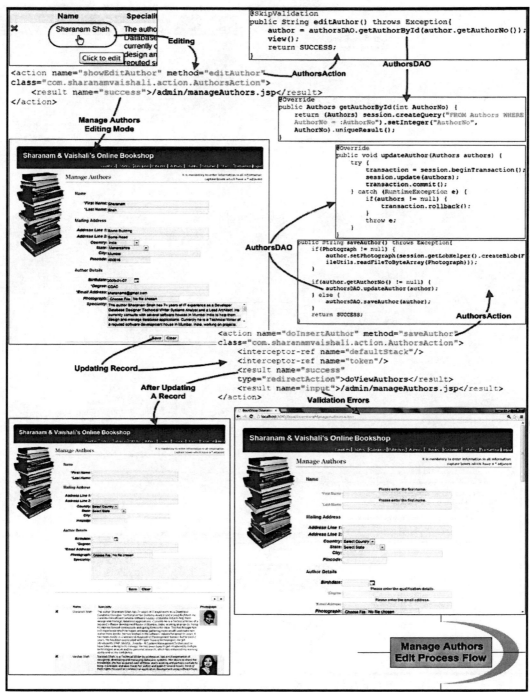

Diagram 27.6: Manage Authors - Edit Process Flow

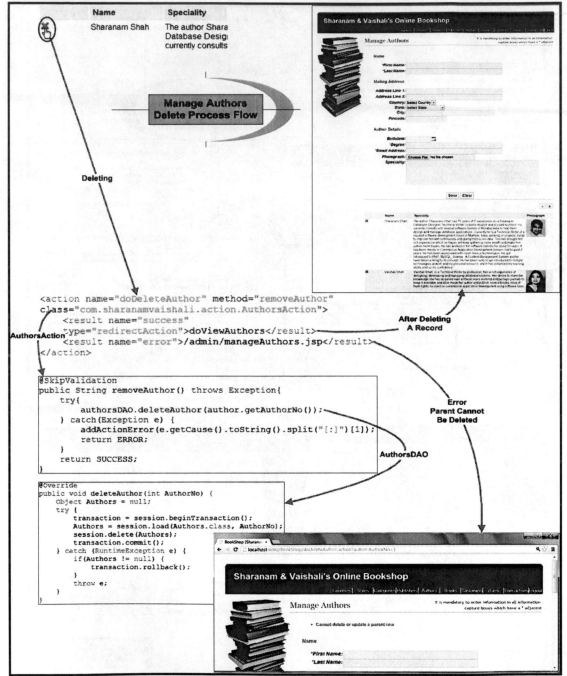

Diagram 27.7: Manage Authors - Delete Process Flow

SECTION IV: PROCESS FLOW

Manage Books [manageBooks.jsp]

Manage Books is the page that is served when **Books** is clicked in the Administration section after successful administration login.

It displays:

❑ A data entry form to capture the book details

❑ List of books available

❑ Delete link to delete a particular book record

❑ Edit link to edit a particular book record

Viewing Existing Book Details

When the user clicks **Books**, manageBooks.jsp is served, as shown in diagram 28.1.

Books when clicked invokes the action class named BooksAction.java.

To locate the action, struts-Books.xml holds:

```
<action name="showManageBooks" method="view"
class="com.sharanamvaishali.action.BooksAction">
    <result>/admin/manageBooks.jsp</result>
</action>
```

User Interface [showManageBooks.action → manageBooks.jsp]

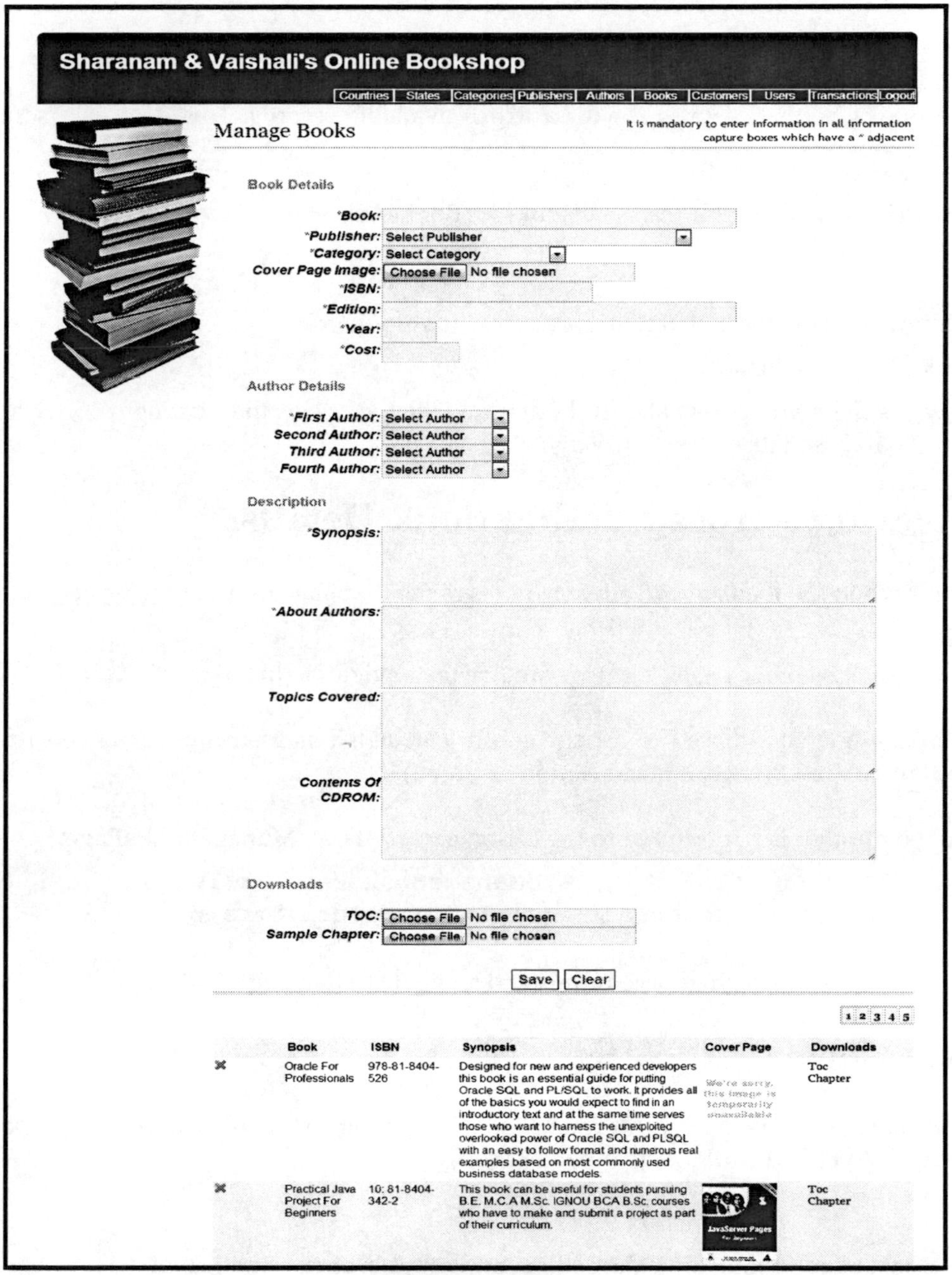

Diagram 28.1

This is a standard data entry form. By default when the form loads, it's in the **INSERT** and **VIEW** mode.

Process Flow

Manage Books holds a data grid with a list of available records. This data grid serves the purpose of viewing.

The data grid is populated by **doViewBooks → BooksAction → view()**.

Here,

❑ **doViewBooks** is the action configured in **struts-Books.xml**

❑ **BooksAction** is the action

❑ **view()** is the method available in the action, which displays the existing records from the Books database table

Navigating Across Existing Book Details

By default when JSP loads **view()** always displays the first page i.e. the <u>first ten records</u>.

To navigate across other pages, the user can use the navigation links [1] [2] [3] [4] [5].

These links are created based on a page count [calculated as total number of records / 10] received by **doViewBooks → BooksAction → view()**.

Every page number is hyperlinked to the action named **iterateManageBooksPage:**

```
<a href="<s:url action="iterateManageBooksPage"><s:param
name="pageNo"><s:property /></s:param></s:url>"><s:property /></a>
```

The user can click the desired page number to navigate to that page.

Process Flow

The page navigation is done by **iterateManageBooksPage → BooksAction → getPage() → PaginationDAO [getTotalPages() and getPage()]**.

Here,

❑ **iterateManageBooksPage** is the action configured in **struts-Books.xml**

❑   **BooksAction** is the action

❑   **getPage()** is the method available in the action, which retrieves the required page's records via **PaginationDAO**

❑   **PaginationDAO** is the Data Access Object [DAO] Layer

❑   **getTotalPages()** is the method available in DAO, which actually does the calculation of total number of pages for pagination purpose and stores the same

❑   **getPage()** is the method available in the DAO, which actually returns the records belonging to the appropriate page number

Adding New Book Details

After manageBooks.jsp loads, the user can key in the required data and click `Save`.

On clicking `Save`, the **FORM** is submitted to doInsertBook.action and manageBooks.jsp is re-served.

To locate the action, struts-Books.xml holds:

```
<action name="doInsertBook" method="saveBook"
class="com.sharanamvaishali.action.BooksAction">
    <interceptor-ref name="defaultStack"/>
    <interceptor-ref name="token"/>
    <result name="success" type="redirectAction">doViewBooks</result>
    <result name="input">/admin/manageBooks.jsp</result>
</action>
```

Process Flow

After the user keys in the required inputs and clicks `Save`, the FORM is submitted and the **save** operation is performed by **doInsertBook → BooksAction → saveBook() → BooksDAO → saveBook()**.

Here,

❑   **doInsertBook** is the action configured in **struts-Books.xml**

❑   **BooksAction** is the action

❑   **saveBook()** is the method available in the action, which saves the data captured via **BooksDAO**

❑   **BooksDAO** is the Data Access Object [DAO] layer

❑ **saveBook()** is the method available in DAO, which does the actual saving of the captured data in the Books database table

If there are any errors such as book name left blank, manageBooks.jsp is re-served along with the error messages, as shown in diagram 28.2.

User Interface For Validation Errors [doInsertBook → manageBooks.jsp]

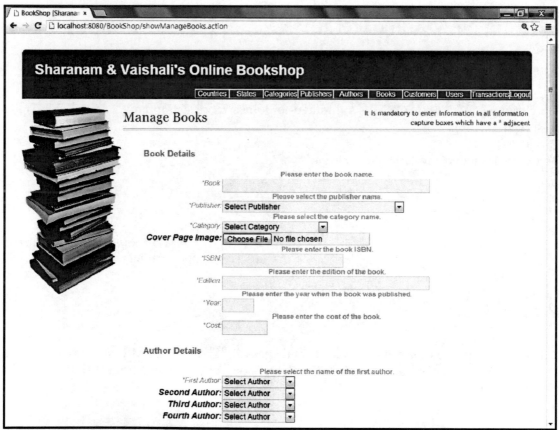

Diagram 28.2: Error messages [manageBooks.jsp]

Process Flow

If the captured data is found to be invalid, then Manage Books with appropriate error messages is served by **doInsertBook → BooksAction-validation.xml**.

Here,

❑ **doInsertBook** is the action configured in **struts-Books.xml**

❑ **BooksAction-validation.xml** is the validation file, which takes care of the validations and traps them and forwards it to Manage Books

If the cover page, sample chapter and TOC are uploaded by the user, then the cover page, sample chapter and TOC are converted to Blob and saved in the Books database table.

Editing Existing Book Details

To switch to the **EDIT** mode, the user needs to click a desired record from the data grid. Doing so populates the data entry form.

Every record listed in the data grid is hyperlinked to the action named **showEditBook:**

```
<td width="12%" class="manageList" onclick="javascript:location.href='<s:url
action='showEditBook'><s:param name='book.BookNo' value='BookNo' /></s:url>'">
    <s:property value="BookName"/>
</td>
```

To locate the action, struts-Books.xml holds:

```
<action name="showEditBook" method="editBook"
class="com.sharanamvaishali.action.BooksAction">
    <result name="success">/admin/manageBooks.jsp</result>
</action>
```

When the user clicks the hyper link, manageBooks.jsp [pre-populated with the selected book's data] is served, as shown in diagram 28.3.

User Interface [showEditBook.action → manageBooks.jsp]

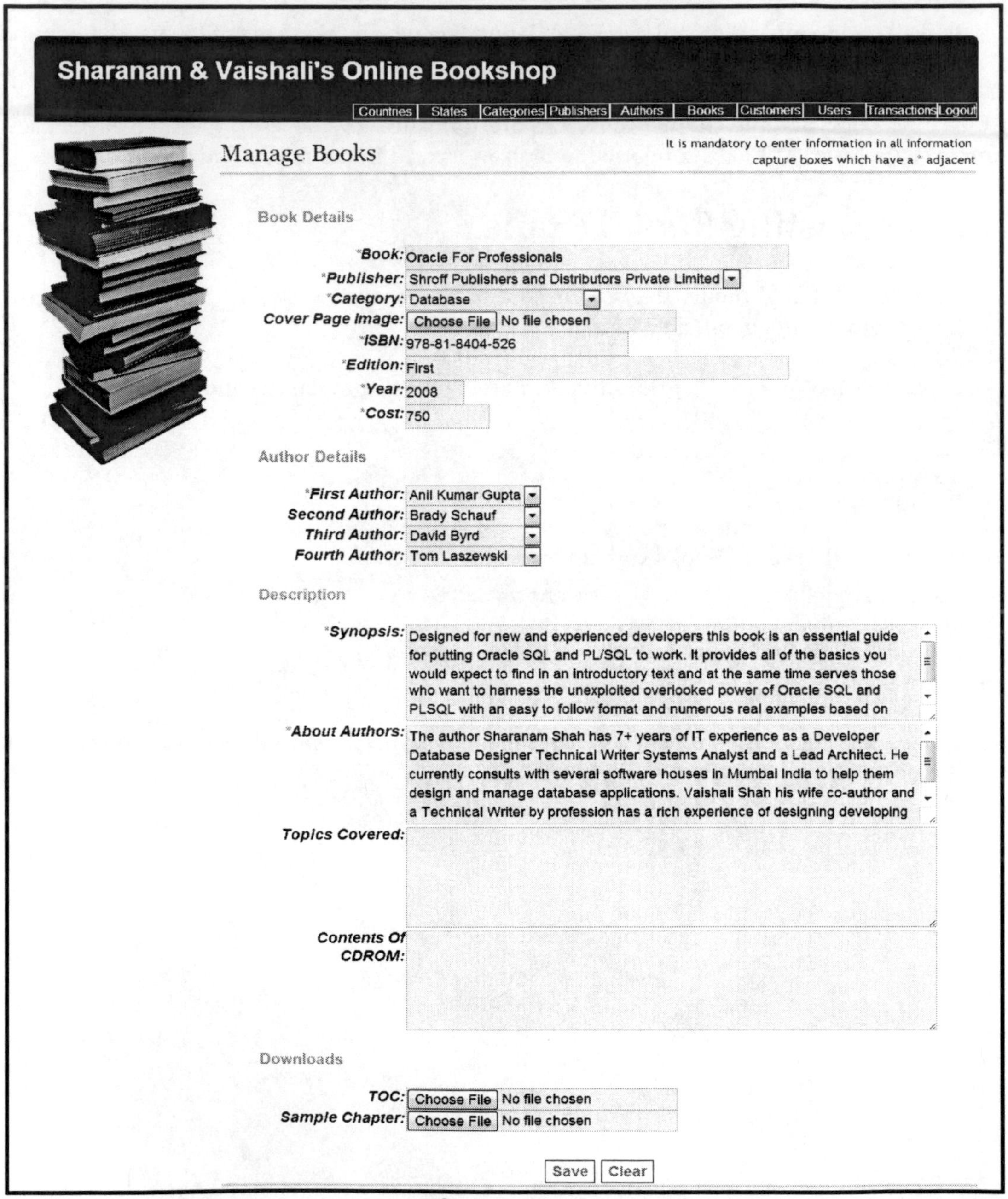

Diagram 28.3

Process Flow

The data population of the selected record for editing is done by **showEditBook** →
BooksAction → **editBook()** → **BooksDAO** → **getBookById()**.

Here,

❑ **showEditBook** is the action configured in **struts-Books.xml**

❑ **BooksAction** is the action

❑ **editBook()** is the method available in the action, which retrieves the book details based on BookNo as reference via BooksDAO and re-serves Manage Books with the required data

❑ **editBook()** also invokes **view()** of **BooksAction**, which takes care of the data grid population

❑ **BooksDAO** is the Data Access Object Layer [DAO]

❑ **getBookById()** is the method available in DAO, which returns the appropriate book's object from the Books database table using **BookNo** as the reference

After the user makes the desired changes and clicks **Save**, the **FORM** is submitted to doInsertBook.action and manageBooks.jsp is re-served.

To locate the action, struts-Books.xml holds:

```
<action name="doInsertBook" method="saveBook"
class="com.sharanamvaishali.action.BooksAction">
    <interceptor-ref name="defaultStack"/>
    <interceptor-ref name="token"/>
    <result name="success" type="redirectAction">doViewBooks</result>
    <result name="input">/admin/manageBooks.jsp</result>
</action>
```

Process Flow

After the user keys in the required inputs and clicks **Save**, the FORM is submitted and the **update** operation is performed by **doInsertBook** → **BooksAction** → **saveBook()** → **BooksDAO** → **updateBook()**.

Here,

❑ **doInsertBook** is the action configured in **struts-Books.xml**

❑ **BooksAction** is the action

❑ **saveBook()** is the method available in the action, which saves the data captured via **BooksDAO**

❑ **BooksDAO** is the Data Access Object [DAO] layer

❑ **updateBook()** is the method available in DAO, which does the actual updating of the captured data in the Books database table

Deleting Existing Book Details

Every record that is listed in manageBooks.jsp holds ✖ which is hyper linked to an action called doDeleteBook:

```
<a href="<s:url action="doDeleteBook"><s:param name="book.BookNo"
value="BookNo" /></s:url>">
    <img src="/BookShop/images/TrashIcon.png" border="0" alt="Delete"
    style="cursor:pointer;"/>
</a>
```

To locate the action, struts-Books.xml holds:

```
<action name="doDeleteBook" method="removeBook"
class="com.sharanamvaishali.action.BooksAction">
    <result name="success" type="redirectAction">doViewBooks</result>
</action>
```

When the user clicks ✖, the selected record is deleted and manageBooks.jsp is re-served.

Process Flow

The record deletion is done by **doDeleteBook** ➔ **BooksAction** ➔ **removeBook()** ➔ **BooksDAO** ➔ **deleteBook()**.

Here,

❑ **doDeleteBook** is the action configured in **struts-Books.xml**

❑ **BooksAction** is the action

❑ **removeBook()** is the method available in the action, which deletes the book record based on BookNo as reference via BooksDAO and re-serves Manage Books with the available records

❑ **BooksDAO** is the Data Access Object Layer [DAO]

❑ **deleteBook()** is the method available in DAO, which deletes the appropriate book from the Books database table based on **BookNo** received as a reference

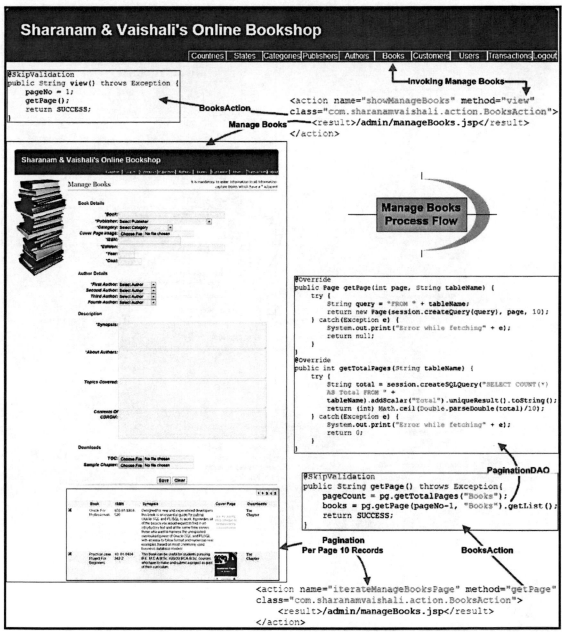

Diagram 28.4: Manage Books Process Flow

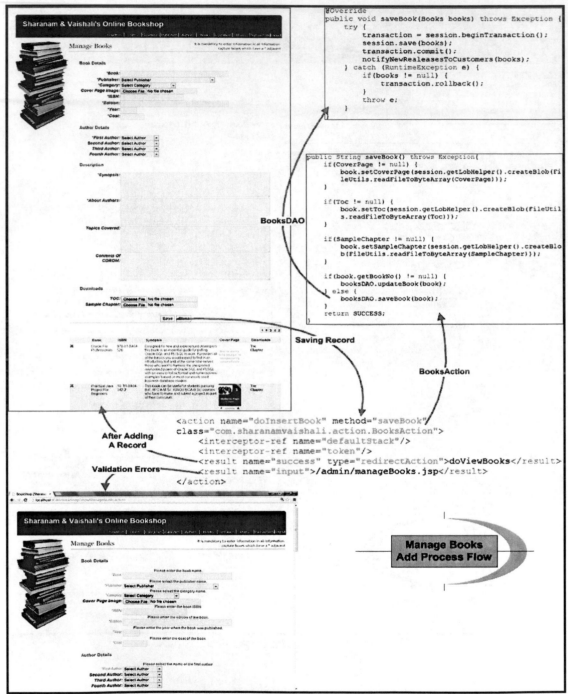

Diagram 28.5: Manage Books - Add Process Flow

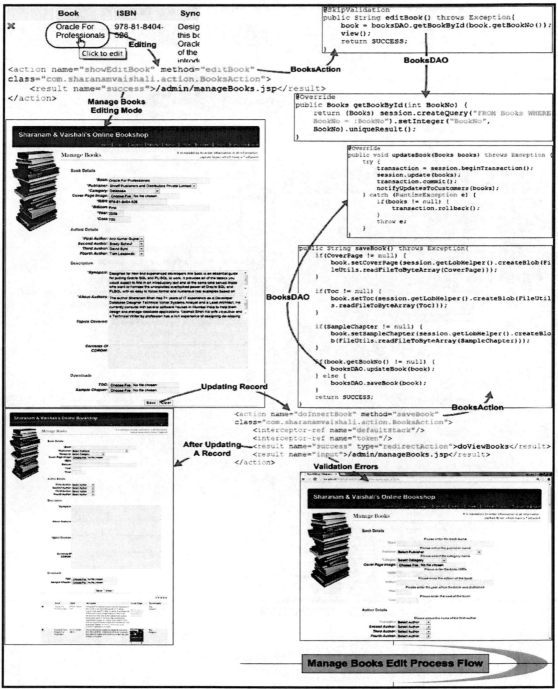

Diagram 28.6: Manage Books - Edit Process Flow

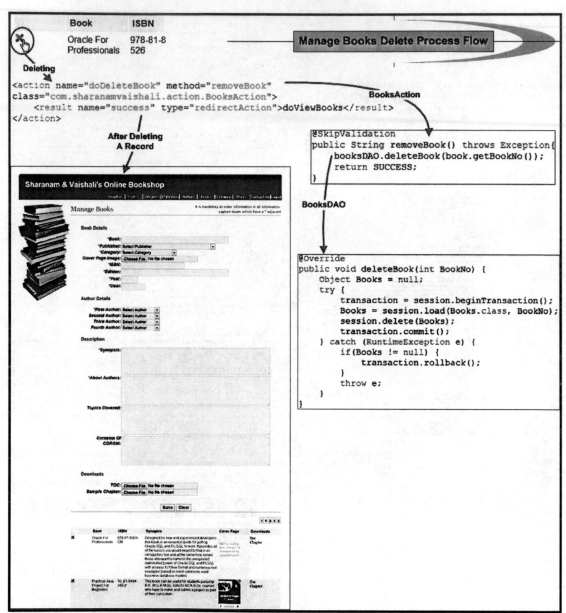

Diagram 28.7: Manage Books - Delete Process Flow

Chapter

29

SECTION IV: PROCESS FLOW

Manage Customers [manageCustomers.jsp]

Manage Customers is the page that is served when **Customers** is clicked in the Administration section after successful administration login.

It displays:

❑ List of customers available

❑ Delete link to delete a particular customer record

❑ Edit link to edit a particular customer record

Viewing Existing Customer Details

When the user clicks **Customers** , manageCustomers.jsp is served, as shown in diagram 29.1.

Customers when clicked invokes the action class named CustomersAction.java.

To locate the action, struts-Customers.xml holds:

```
<action name="showManageCustomers" method="view"
class="com.sharanamvaishali.action.CustomersAction">
    <result>/admin/manageCustomers.jsp</result>
</action>
```

User Interface [showManageCustomers.action → manageCustomers.jsp]

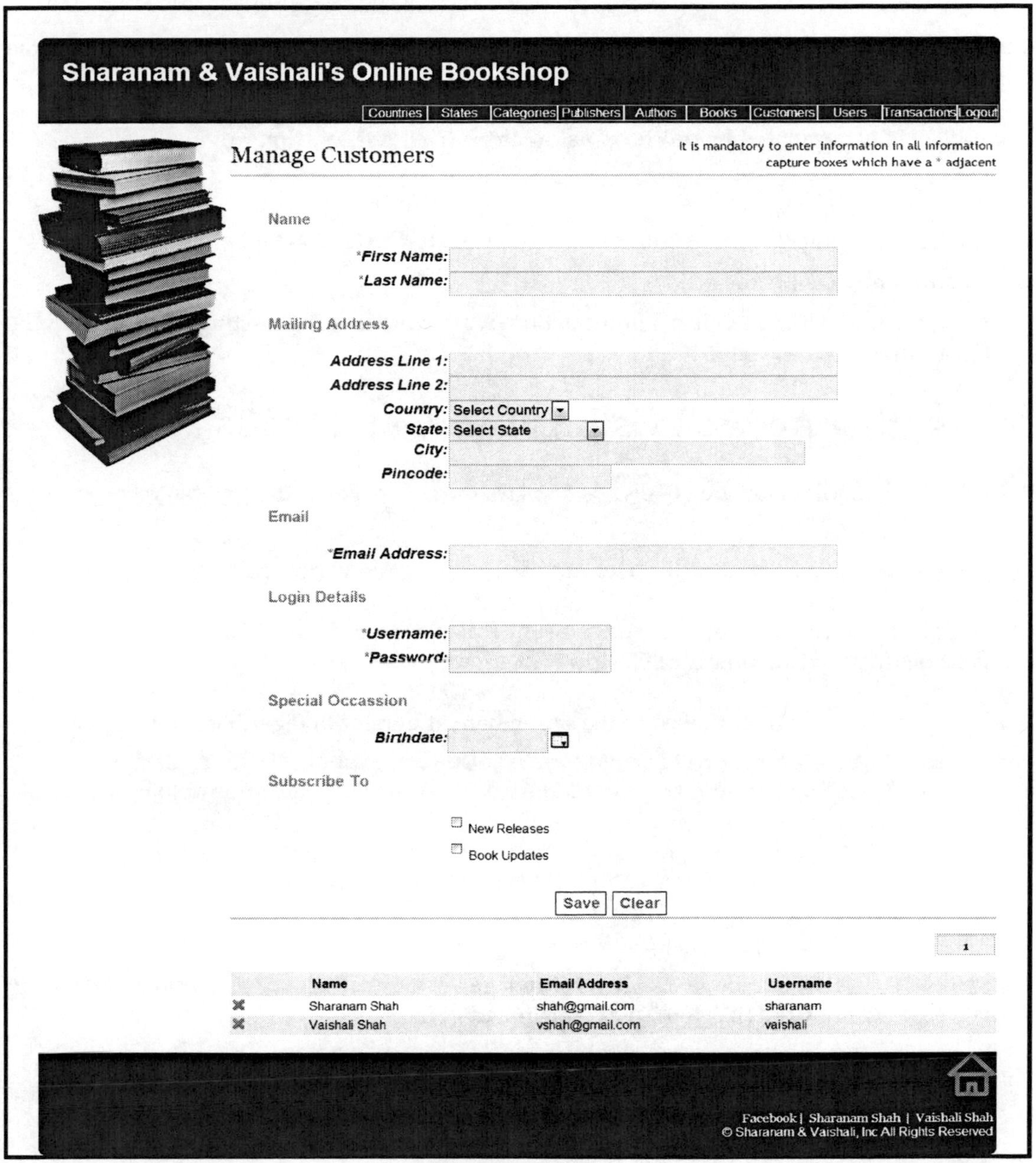

Sharanam & Vaishali's Online Bookshop

| Countries | States | Categories | Publishers | Authors | Books | Customers | Users | Transactions | Logout |

Manage Customers

It is mandatory to enter information in all information capture boxes which have a * adjacent

Name

First Name:
Last Name:

Mailing Address

Address Line 1:
Address Line 2:
Country: Select Country
State: Select State
City:
Pincode:

Email

Email Address:

Login Details

Username:
Password:

Special Occassion

Birthdate:

Subscribe To

☐ New Releases

☐ Book Updates

Save   Clear

1

	Name	Email Address	Username
✖	Sharanam Shah	shah@gmail.com	sharanam
✖	Vaishali Shah	vshah@gmail.com	vaishali

Diagram 29.1

This is a standard data entry form. By default when the form loads, it's in the **VIEW** mode.

Process Flow

Manage Customers holds a data grid with a list of available records. This data grid serves the purpose of viewing.

The data grid is populated by **doViewCustomers → CustomersAction → view()**.

Here,

❑ **doViewCustomers** is the action configured in **struts-Customers.xml**

❑ **CustomersAction** is the action

❑ **view()** is the method available in the action, which displays the existing records from the Customers database table

Navigating Across Existing Customer Details

By default when JSP loads **view()** always displays the first page i.e. the <u>first ten records</u>.

To navigate across other pages, the user can use the navigation links [**1**].

These links are created based on a page count [calculated as total number of records / 10] received by **doViewCustomers → CustomersAction → view()**.

Every page number is hyperlinked to the action named **iterateManageCustomersPage**:

```
<a href="<s:url action="iterateManageCustomersPage"><s:param
name="pageNo"><s:property /></s:param></s:url>"><s:property /></a>
```

The user can click the desired page number to navigate to that page.

Process Flow

The page navigation is done by **iterateManageCustomersPage → CustomersAction → getPage() → PaginationDAO [getTotalPages() and getPage()]**.

Here,

❑ **iterateManageCustomersPage** is the action configured in **struts-Customers.xml**

❑ **CustomersAction** is the action

- ❑ **getPage()** is the method available in the action, which retrieves the required page's records via **PaginationDAO**

- ❑ **PaginationDAO** is the Data Access Object [DAO] Layer

- ❑ **getTotalPages()** is the method available in DAO, which actually does the calculation of total number of pages for pagination purpose and stores the same

- ❑ **getPage()** is the method available in the DAO, which actually returns the records belonging to the appropriate page number

Editing Existing Customer Details

To switch to the **EDIT** mode, the user needs to click a desired record from the data grid. Doing so populates the data entry form.

Every record listed in the data grid is hyperlinked to the action named **showEditCustomer**:

```
<td width="30%" class="manageList" onclick="javascript:location.href='<s:url
action='showEditCustomer'><s:param name='customer.CustomerNo'
value='CustomerNo' /></s:url>'">
    <s:property value="FirstName"/> <s:property value="LastName" />
</td>
```

To locate the action, struts-Customers.xml holds:

```
<action name="showEditCustomer" method="editCustomer"
class="com.sharanamvaishali.action.CustomersAction">
    <result name="success">/admin/manageCustomers.jsp</result>
</action>
```

When the user clicks the hyper link, manageCustomers.jsp [pre-populated with the selected customer's data] is served, as shown in diagram 29.2.

User Interface [showEditCustomer.action → manageCustomers.jsp]

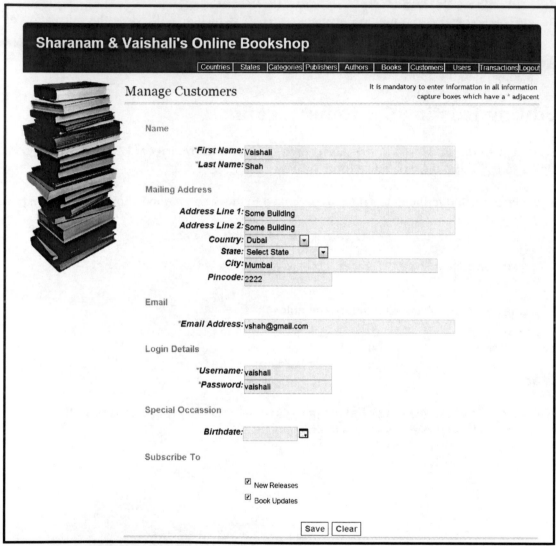

Diagram 29.2

Process Flow

The data population of the selected record for editing is done by **showEditCustomer** → **CustomersAction** → **editCustomer()** → **CustomersDAO** → **getCustomerById()**.

Here,

❑ **showEditCustomer** is the action configured in **struts-Customers.xml**

❑ **CustomersAction** is the action

❑ **editCustomer()** is the method available in the action, which retrieves the customer details based on CustomerNo as reference via CustomersDAO and re-serves Manage Customers with the required data

❑ **editCustomer()** also invokes **view()** of **CustomersAction**, which takes care of the data grid population

❑ **CustomersDAO** is the Data Access Object Layer [DAO]

❑ **getCustomerById()** is the method available in DAO, which returns the appropriate customer's object from the Customers database table using **CustomerNo** as the reference

After the user makes the desired changes and clicks **Save**, the **FORM** is submitted to doUpdateCustomer.action and manageCustomers.jsp is re-served.

To locate the action, struts-Customers.xml holds:

```
<action name="doUpdateCustomer" method="updateCustomer"
class="com.sharanamvaishali.action.CustomersAction">
    <interceptor-ref name="defaultStack"/>
    <interceptor-ref name="token"/>
    <result name="success"
    type="redirectAction">doViewCustomers</result>
    <result name="input">/admin/manageCustomers.jsp</result>
    <result name="error">/admin/manageCustomers.jsp</result>
</action>
```

Process Flow

After the user keys in the required inputs and clicks **Save**, the FORM is submitted and the **update** operation is performed by **doUpdateCustomer** → **CustomersAction** → **updateCustomer()** → **CustomersDAO** → **updateCustomer()**.

Here,

❑ **doUpdateCustomer** is the action configured in **struts-Customers.xml**

❑ **CustomersAction** is the action

❑ **updateCustomer()** is the method available in the action, which updates the data captured via **CustomersDAO**

❑ **CustomersDAO** is the Data Access Object [DAO] layer

❑ **updateCustomer()** is the method available in DAO, which does the actual updating of the captured data in the Customers database table

If there are any errors such as duplicate email address, manageCustomers.jsp is re-served along with the error messages, as shown in diagram 29.3.

User Interface For Validation Errors [doUpdateCustomer → manageCustomers.jsp]

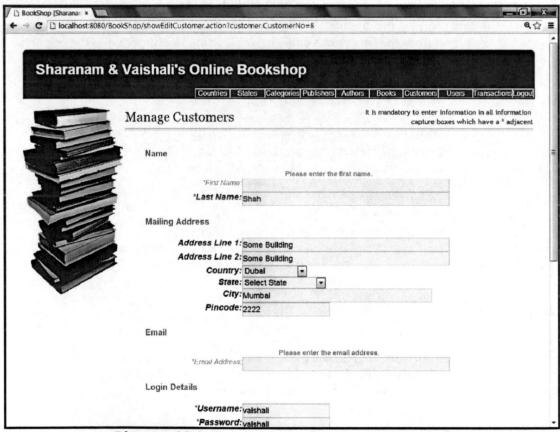

Diagram 29.3: Error messages [manageCustomers.jsp]

Process Flow

If the captured data is found to be invalid, then Manage Customers with appropriate error messages is served by **doUpdateCustomer → CustomersAction-validation.xml**.

Here,

- ❑ **doUpdateCustomer** is the action configured in **struts-Customers.xml**

- ❑ **CustomersAction-validation.xml** is the validation file, which takes care of the validations and traps them and forwards it to Manage Customers

Deleting Existing Customer Details

Every record that is listed in manageCustomers.jsp holds ✖ which is hyper linked to an action called doDeleteCustomer:

```
<a href="<s:url action="doDeleteCustomer"><s:param name="customer.CustomerNo"
value="CustomerNo" /></s:url>">
    <img src="/BookShop/images/TrashIcon.png" border="0" alt="Delete"
    style="cursor:pointer;"/>
</a>
```

To locate the action, struts-Customers.xml holds:

```
<action name="doDeleteCustomer" method="removeCustomer"
class="com.sharanamvaishali.action.CustomersAction">
    <result name="success"
    type="redirectAction">doViewCustomers</result>
</action>
```

When the user clicks ✖, the selected record is deleted and manageCustomers.jsp is re-served.

Process Flow

The record deletion is done by **doDeleteCustomer** → **CustomersAction** → **removeCustomer()** → **CustomersDAO** → **deleteCustomer()**.

Here,

- ❑ **doDeleteCustomer** is the action configured in **struts-Customers.xml**

- ❑ **CustomersAction** is the action

- ❑ **removeCustomer()** is the method available in the action, which deletes the customer record based on CustomerNo as reference via CustomersDAO and re-serves Manage Customers with the available records

- ❑ **CustomersDAO** is the Data Access Object Layer [DAO]

- ❑ **deleteCustomer()** is the method available in DAO, which deletes the appropriate customer from the Customers database table based on **CustomerNo** received as a reference

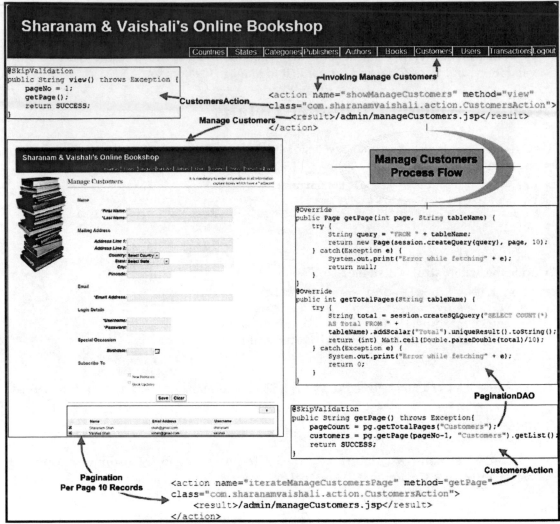

Diagram 29.4: Manage Customers Process Flow

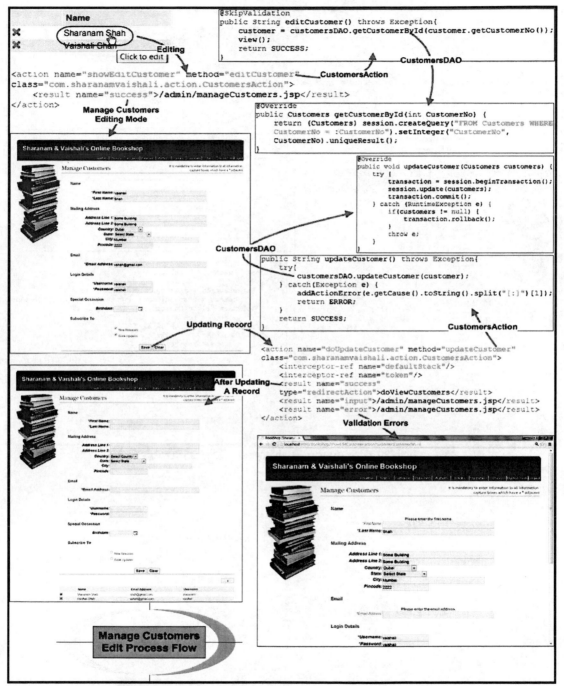

Diagram 29.5: Manage Customers - Edit Process Flow

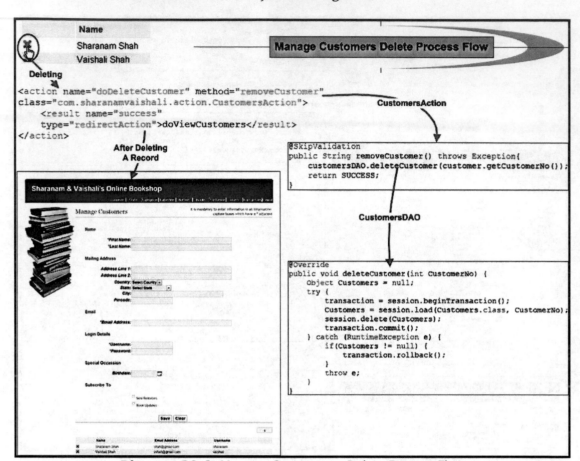

Diagram 29.6: Manage Customers - Delete Process Flow

Chapter

30

SECTION IV: PROCESS FLOW

Manage Users [manageUsers.jsp]

Manage Users is the page that is served when **Users** is clicked in the Administration section after successful administration login.

It displays:

❑ A data entry form to capture the system user details

❑ List of system users available

❑ Delete link to delete a particular system user record

❑ Edit link to edit a particular system user record

Viewing Existing System User Details

When the user clicks **Users**, manageUsers.jsp is served, as shown in diagram 30.1.

Users when clicked invokes the action class named SystemUsersAction.java.

To locate the action, struts-SystemUsers.xml holds:

```
<action name="showManageUsers" method="view"
class="com.sharanamvaishali.action.SystemUsersAction">
    <result>/admin/manageUsers.jsp</result>
</action>
```

User Interface [showManageUsers.action → manageUsers.jsp]

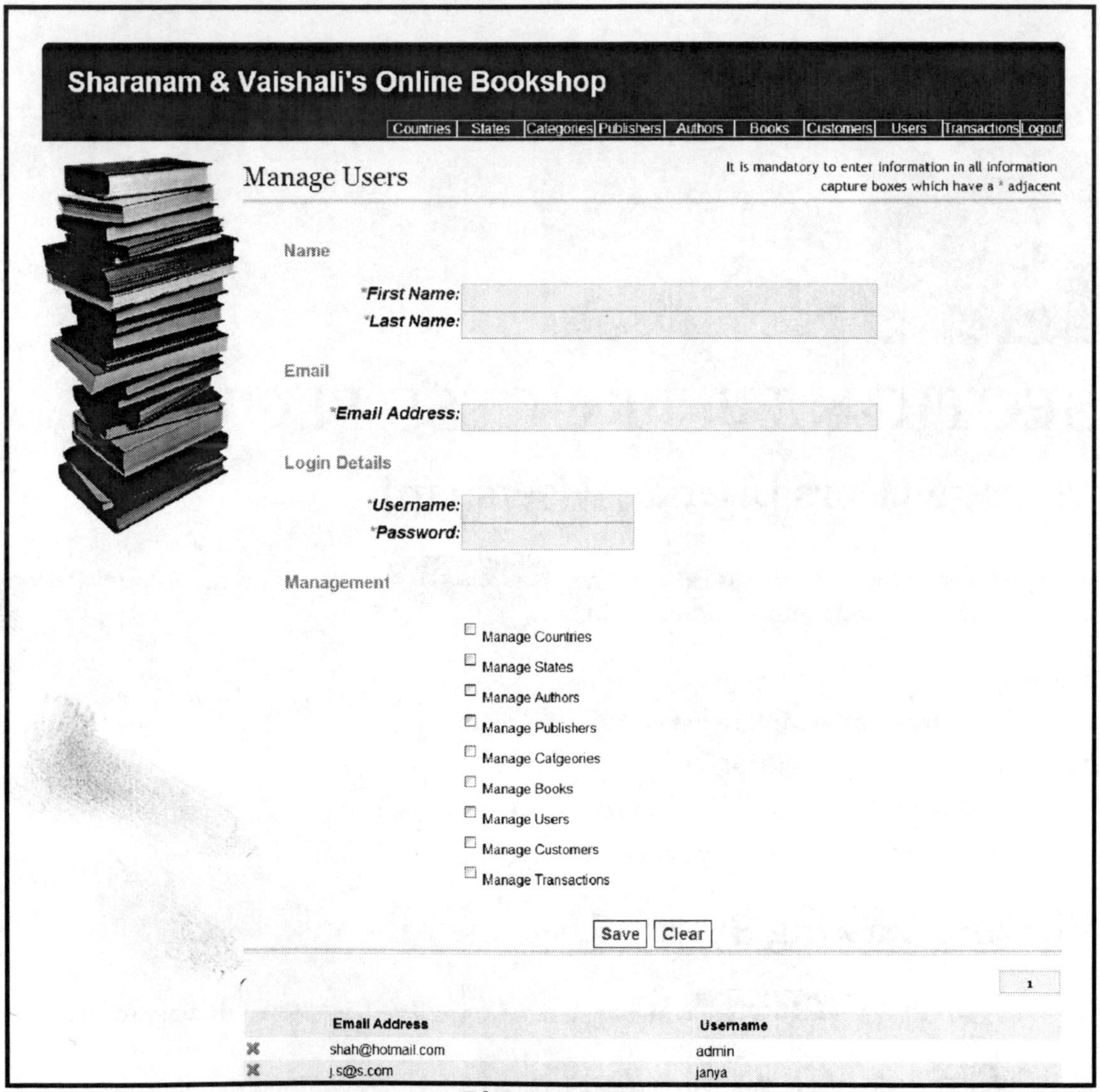

Diagram 30.1

This is a standard data entry form. By default when the form loads, it's in the **INSERT** and **VIEW** mode.

Process Flow

Manage Users holds a data grid with a list of available records. This data grid serves the purpose of viewing.

The data grid is populated by **doViewUsers** → **SystemUsersAction** → **view()**.

Here,

❑ **doViewUsers** is the action configured in **struts-SystemUsers.xml**

❑ **SystemUsersAction** is the action

❑ **view()** is the method available in the action, which displays the existing records from the SystemUsers database table

Navigating Across Existing System User Details

By default when JSP loads **view()** always displays the first page i.e. the <u>first ten records</u>.

To navigate across other pages, the user can use the navigation links ⬚ **1** ⬚.

These links are created based on a page count [calculated as total number of records / 10] received by **doViewUsers** → **SystemUsersAction** → **view()**.

Every page number is hyperlinked to the action named **iterateManageUsersPage:**

```
<a href="<s:url action="iterateManageUsersPage"><s:param
name="pageNo"><s:property /></s:param></s:url>"><s:property /></a>
```

The user can click the desired page number to navigate to that page.

Process Flow

The page navigation is done by **iterateManageUsersPage** → **SystemUsersAction** → **getPage()** → **PaginationDAO [getTotalPages() and getPage()]**.

Here,

❑ **iterateManageUsersPage** is the action configured in **struts-SystemUsers.xml**

❑ **SystemUsersAction** is the action

❑ **getPage()** is the method available in the action, which retrieves the required page's records via **PaginationDAO**

❑ **PaginationDAO** is the Data Access Object [DAO] Layer

❑ **getTotalPages()** is the method available in DAO, which actually does the calculation of total number of pages for pagination purpose and stores the same

❑ **getPage()** is the method available in the DAO, which actually returns the records belonging to the appropriate page number

Adding New System User Details

After manageUsers.jsp loads, the user can key in the required data and click Save .

On clicking Save , the **FORM** is submitted to doInsertUser.action and manageUsers.jsp is re-served.

To locate the action, struts-SystemUsers.xml holds:

```
<action name="doInsertUser" method="saveSystemUser"
class="com.sharanamvaishali.action.SystemUsersAction">
    <interceptor-ref name="defaultStack"/>
    <interceptor-ref name="token"/>
    <result name="success" type="redirectAction">doViewUsers</result>
    <result name="input">/admin/manageUsers.jsp</result>
    <result name="error">/admin/manageUsers.jsp</result>
</action>
```

Process Flow

After the user keys in the required inputs and clicks Save , the **FORM** is submitted and the save operation is performed by **doInsertUser → SystemUsersAction → saveSystemUser() → SystemUsersDAO → saveSystemUser()**.

Here,

❑ **doInsertUser** is the action configured in **struts-SystemUsers.xml**

❑ **SystemUsersAction** is the action

❑ **saveSystemUser()** is the method available in the action, which saves the data captured via **SystemUsersDAO**

❑ **SystemUsersDAO** is the Data Access Object [DAO] layer

❑ **saveSystemUser()** is the method available in DAO, which does the actual saving of the captured data in the SystemUsers database table

If there are any errors such as duplicate email address, manageUsers.jsp is re-served along with the error messages, as shown in diagram 30.2.

User Interface For Validation Errors [doInsertUser → manageUsers.jsp]

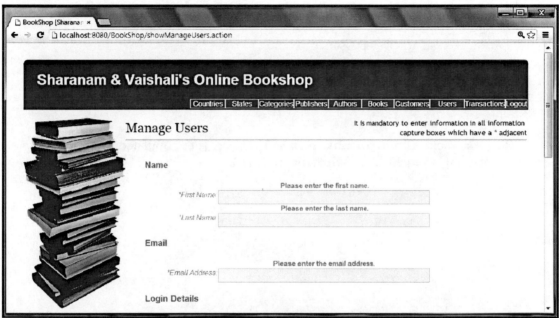

Diagram 30.2: Error messages [manageUsers.jsp]

Process Flow

If the captured data is found to be invalid, then Manage Users with appropriate error messages is served by **doInsertUser → SystemUsersAction-validation.xml**.

Here,

❑ **doInsertUser** is the action configured in **struts-SystemUsers.xml**

❑ **SystemUsersAction-validation.xml** is the validation file, which takes care of the validations and traps them and forwards it to Manage Users

Editing Existing System User Details

To switch to the **EDIT** mode, the user needs to click a desired record from the data grid. Doing so populates the data entry form.

Every record listed in the data grid is hyperlinked to the action named **showEditUser:**

```
<td width="45%" class="manageList" onclick="javascript:location.href='<s:url
action='showEditUser'><s:param name='systemuser.UserNo' value='UserNo'
/></s:url>'">
    <s:property value="EmailAddress"/>
</td>
```

To locate the action, struts-SystemUsers.xml holds:

```
<action name="showEditUser" method="editSystemUser"
class="com.sharanamvaishali.action.SystemUsersAction">
    <result name="success">/admin/manageUsers.jsp</result>
</action>
```

When the user clicks the hyper link, manageUsers.jsp [pre-populated with the selected system user's data] is served, as shown in diagram 30.3.

User Interface [showEditUser.action → manageUsers.jsp]

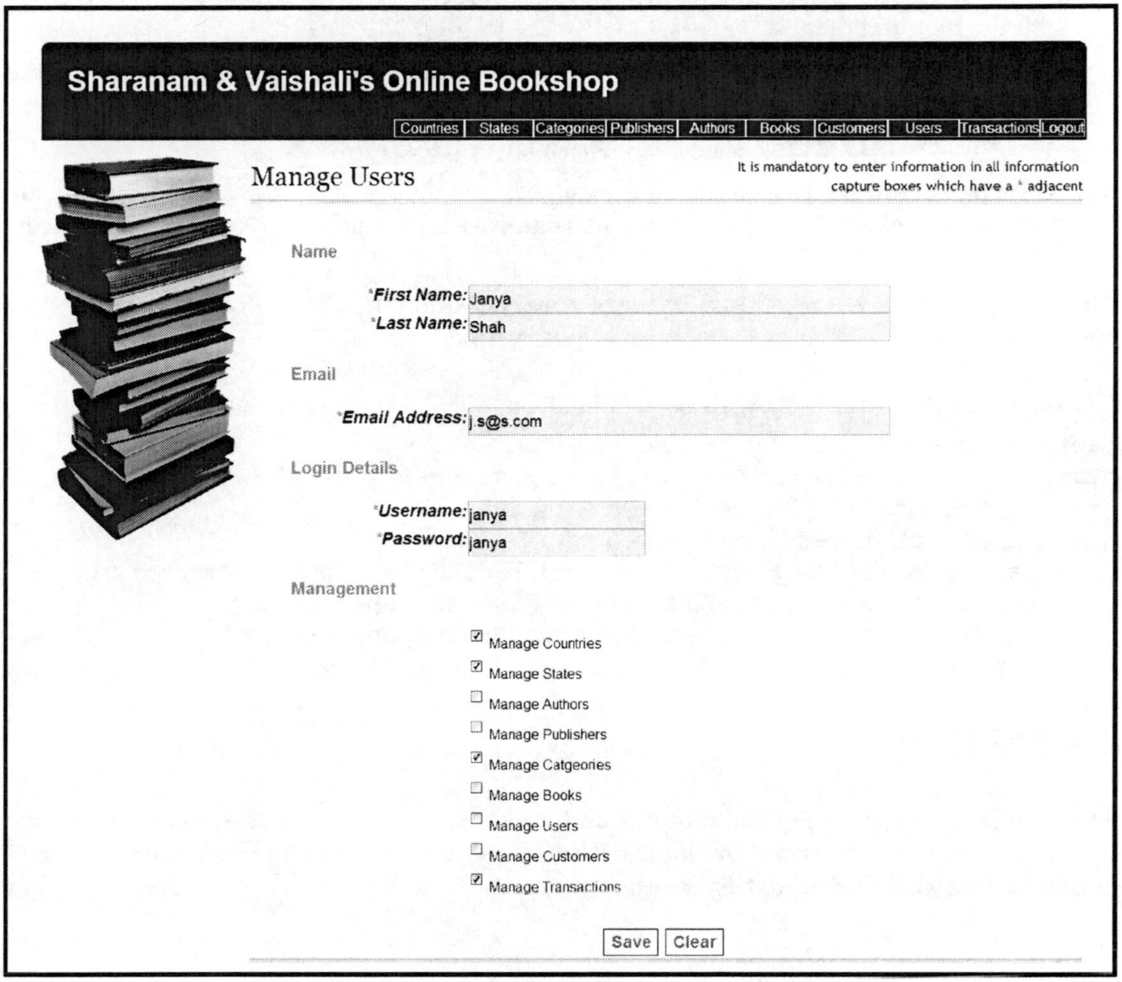

Diagram 30.3

Process Flow

The data population of the selected record for editing is done by **showEditUser** → **SystemUsersAction** → **editSystemUser()** → **SystemUsersDAO** → **getSystemUserById()**.

Here,

❑ **showEditUser** is the action configured in **struts-SystemUsers.xml**

❑ **SystemUsersAction** is the action

❏   **editSystemUser()** is the method available in the action, which retrieves the system user details based on UserNo as reference via SystemUsersDAO and re-serves Manage Users with the required data

❏   **editSystemUser()** also invokes **view()** of **SystemUsersAction**, which takes care of the data grid population

❏   **SystemUsersDAO** is the Data Access Object Layer [DAO]

❏   **getSystemUserById()** is the method available in DAO, which returns the appropriate system user's object from the SystemUsers database table using **UserNo** as the reference

After the user makes the desired changes and clicks **Save**, the **FORM** is submitted to doInsertUser.action and manageUsers.jsp is re-served.

To locate the action, struts-SystemUsers.xml holds:

```
<action name="doInsertUser" method="saveSystemUser"
class="com.sharanamvaishali.action.SystemUsersAction">
    <interceptor-ref name="defaultStack"/>
    <interceptor-ref name="token"/>
    <result name="success" type="redirectAction">doViewUsers</result>
    <result name="input">/admin/manageUsers.jsp</result>
    <result name="error">/admin/manageUsers.jsp</result>
</action>
```

Process Flow

After the user keys in the required inputs and clicks **Save**, the FORM is submitted and the **update** operation is performed by **doInsertUser → SystemUsersAction → saveSystemUser() → SystemUsersDAO → updateSystemUser()**.

Here,

❏   **doInsertUser** is the action configured in **struts-SystemUsers.xml**

❏   **SystemUsersAction** is the action

❏   **saveSystemUser()** is the method available in the action, which saves the data captured via **SystemUsersDAO**

❏   **SystemUsersDAO** is the Data Access Object [DAO] layer

❏   **updateSystemUser()** is the method available in DAO, which does the actual updating of the captured data in the SystemUsers database table

Deleting Existing System User Details

Every record that is listed in manageUsers.jsp holds ✖ which is hyper linked to an action called doDeleteUser:

```
<a href="<s:url action="doDeleteUser"><s:param name="systemuser.UserNo"
value="UserNo" /></s:url>">
    <img src="/BookShop/images/TrashIcon.png" border="0" alt="Delete"
    style="cursor:pointer;"/>
</a>
```

To locate the action, struts-SystemUsers.xml holds:

```
<action name="doDeleteUser" method="removeSystemUser"
class="com.sharanamvaishali.action.SystemUsersAction">
    <result name="success" type="redirectAction">doViewUsers</result>
</action>
```

When the user clicks ✖, the selected record is deleted and manageUsers.jsp is re-served.

Process Flow

The record deletion is done by **doDeleteUser** → **SystemUsersAction** → **removeSystemUser()** → **SystemUsersDAO** → **deleteSystemUser()**.

Here,

❑ **doDeleteUser** is the action configured in **struts-SystemUsers.xml**

❑ **SystemUsersAction** is the action

❑ **removeSystemUser()** is the method available in the action, which deletes the system user record based on UserNo as reference via SystemUsersDAO and re-serves Manage Users with the available records

❑ **SystemUsersDAO** is the Data Access Object Layer [DAO]

❑ **deleteSystemUser()** is the method available in DAO, which deletes the appropriate system user from the SystemUsers database table based on **UserNo** received as a reference

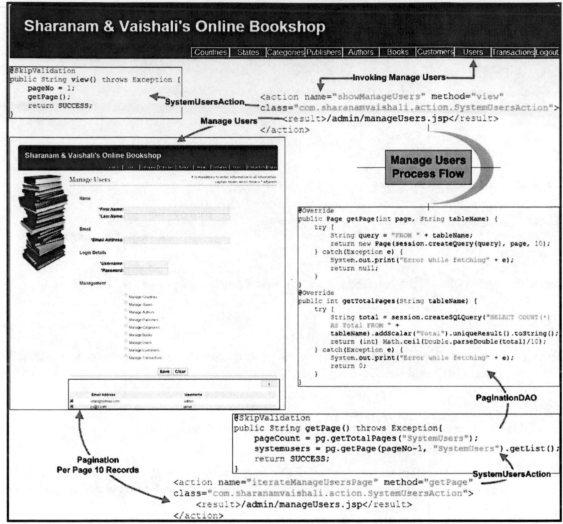

Diagram 30.4: Manage Users Process Flow

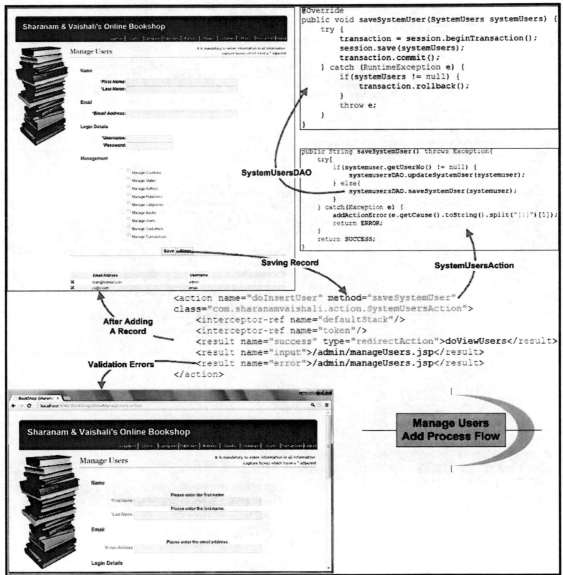

Diagram 30.5: Manage Users - Add Process Flow

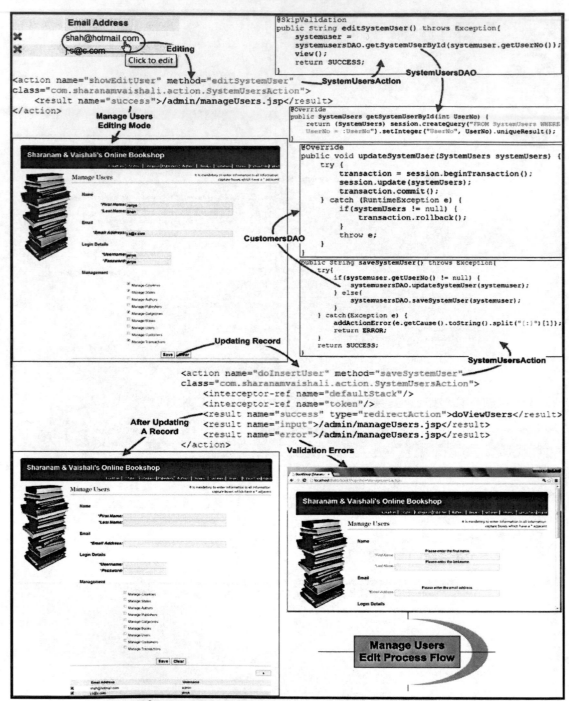

Diagram 30.6: Manage Users - Edit Process Flow

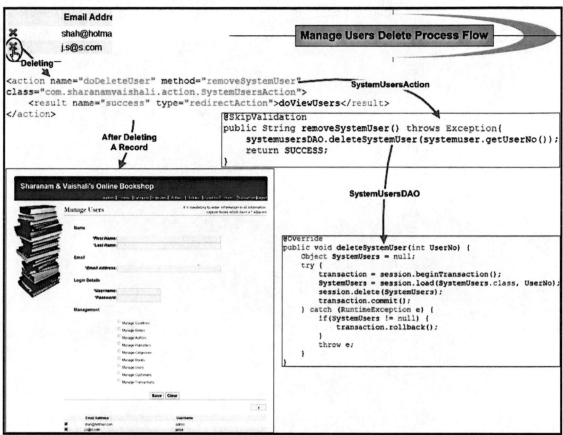

Diagram 30.7: Manage Users - Delete Process Flow

SECTION IV: PROCESS FLOW

Manage Transactions [manageTransactions.jsp]

Manage Transactions is the page that is served when Transactions is clicked in the Administration section after successful administration login.

Manage Transactions accepts the username and accordingly displays the transactions for that particular user

Displaying The Manage Transactions Page

When the user clicks Transactions , manageTransactions.jsp is served, as shown in diagram 31.1.

To locate the action, struts-Transactions.xml holds:

```
<action name="showManageTransactions" method="populateUsernames"
class="com.sharanamvaishali.action.TransactionsAction">
    <result>/admin/manageTransactions.jsp</result>
</action>
```

User Interface [showManageTransactions.action → manageTransactions.jsp]

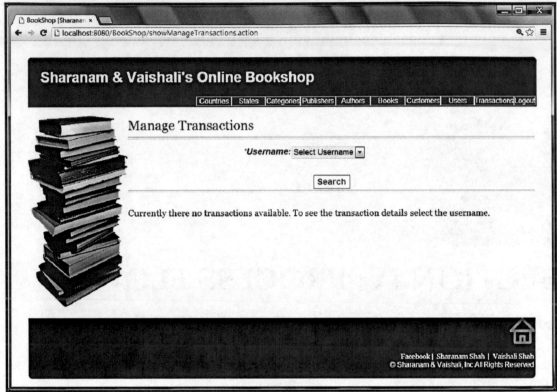

Diagram 31.1

Process Flow

Manage Transactions holds a data entry form which accepts the username.

The data entry form is displayed by **showManageTransactions → TransactionsAction → populateUsername() → TransactionsDAO → getUsernames()**.

Here,

❑ **showManageTransactions** is the action configured in **struts-Transactions.xml**

❑ **TransactionsAction** is the action

❑ **populateUsername()** is the method available in the action, which retrieves all the usernames of the customers registered with the Online BookShop via **TransactionsDAO**

❑ **TransactionsDAO** is the Data Access Object [DAO] layer

❑ **getUsernames()** is the method available in DAO, which does the actual retrieval of all the usernames of the customers registered with the Online BookShop from the Customers database table

Viewing The Transaction Reports

After manageTransactions.jsp loads, the user can key in the required username and click **Search**.

On clicking **Search**, the **FORM** is submitted to doViewTransactions.action and manageTransactions.jsp is re-served.

To locate the action, struts-Transactions.xml holds:

```
<action name="doViewTransactions" method="view"
class="com.sharanamvaishali.action.TransactionsAction">
    <interceptor-ref name="defaultStack"/>
    <interceptor-ref name="token"/>
    <result name="success">/admin/manageTransactions.jsp</result>
    <result name="error"
    type="redirectAction">showManageTransactions</result>
</action>
```

User Interface [doViewTransactions.action → manageTransactions.jsp]

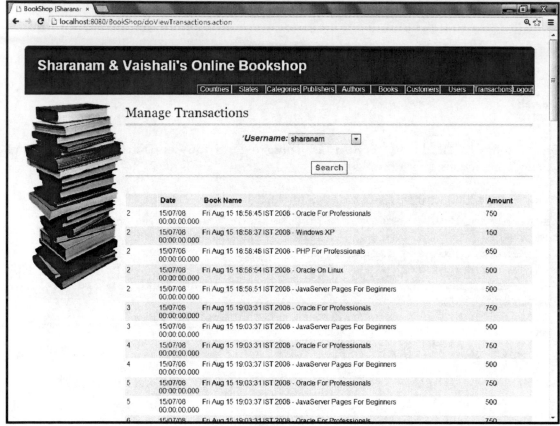

Diagram 31.2

This is a standard data entry form. By default when the form loads, it's in the **INSERT** mode.

Process Flow

After the user keys in the required inputs and clicks **Search**, the FORM is submitted and the **search** operation is performed by **doViewTransactions → TransactionsAction → view() → TransactionsDAO → getTransactions()**.

Here,

❑   **doViewTransactions** is the action configured in **struts-Transactions.xml**

- **TransactionsAction** is the action
- **view()** is the method available in the action, which retrieves all the transactions of a particular customer via TransactionsDAO and displays the same in Manage Transactions
- **TransactionsDAO** is the Data Access Object [DAO] layer
- **getTransactions()** is the method available in DAO, which does the actual retrieval of all the transactions of a particular customer from the Transactions database table using **Username** as the reference

If there are any errors such as no username selected, manageTransactions.jsp is re-served along with the error messages, as shown in diagram 31.3.

User Interface For Validation Errors [doViewTransactions → manageTransactions.jsp]

Diagram 31.3: Error messages [manageTransactions.jsp]

Process Flow

If the data is not selected, then Manage Transactions with appropriate error messages is served by **doViewTransactions → TransactionsAction-validation.xml**.

Here,

- **doViewTransactions** is the action configured in **struts-Transactions.xml**
- **TransactionsAction-validation.xml** is the validation file, which takes care of the validations and traps them and forwards it to Manage Transactions

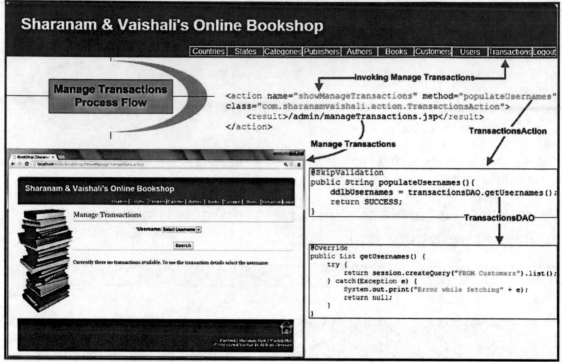

Diagram 31.4: Manage Transactions Process Flow

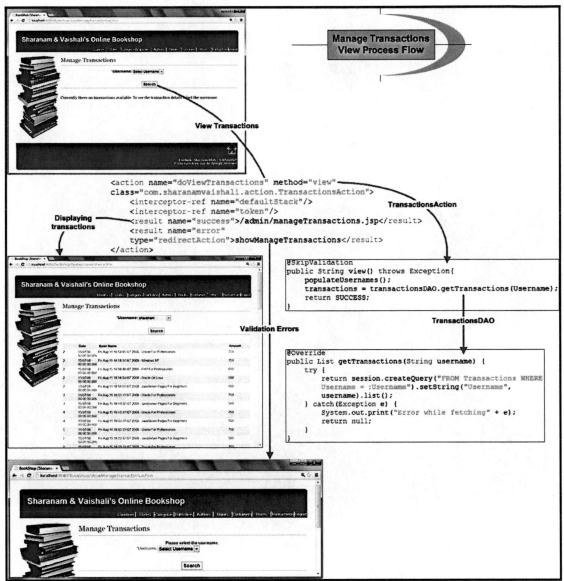

Diagram 31.5: Manage Transactions - View Process Flow

SECTION V: BACKEND [ADMINISTRATION] SOFTWARE DESIGN DOCUMENTATION

Administration Login And Logout

Administration Login is a Login data entry form which allows the administration users to login to the backend section to add, update or delete the master records.

This module uses the bms.SystemUsers table to perform the above operations.

This module is made up of the following:

Type	Name	Description
JSP	adminLogin.jsp	The data entry form.
Struts 2		
Action	SystemUserLoginAction.java	The action class that facilitates data operation.
DAO	LoginDAO.java	The interface for the DAO layer.
	LoginDAOImpl.java	The implementation class that perform the actual data operations.

Struts 2		
Validation	SystemUserLoginAction-validation.xml	The XML based validation file.
Struts Configuration	Struts-AdminLogin.xml	Struts configuration file.

JSP [adminLogin.jsp]

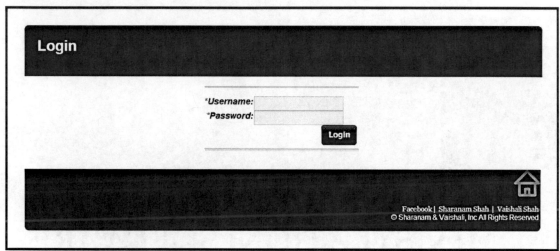

Diagram 32.1: Administration Login

This is a JSP which holds a data entry form, as shown in diagram 32.1. This form appears when the user clicks available on the footer of the frontend section of the application.

Form Specifications

File Name	adminLogin.jsp
Title	BookShop [Sharanam & Vaishali Shah] - Admin Login
Bound To Table	bms.SystemUsers
Form Name	frmAdminLogin
Action	doLogin
Method	POST

Data Fields

Label	Name	Bound To	Validation Rules
Username	systemuser.Username	SystemUsers.Username	Cannot be left blank
Password	systemuser.Password	SystemUsers.Password	Cannot be left blank

Data Controls

Object	Label	Name
submit	Login	submit

Code Spec

```
1   <%@page contentType="text/html" pageEncoding="UTF-8"%>
2   <%@ taglib prefix="s" uri="/struts-tags" %>
3   <!DOCTYPE HTML PUBLIC "-//W3C//DTD HTML 4.01 Transitional//EN"
4       "http://www.w3.org/TR/html4/loose.dtd">
5   <html xmlns="http://www.w3.org/1999/xhtml">
6       <head>
7           <title>BookShop [Sharanam & Vaishali Shah] - Admin Login</title>
8           <meta http-equiv="content-type" content="text/html; charset=iso-8859-1">
9           <link href="/BookShop/css/admin.css" type="text/css" rel="stylesheet">
10          <s:head/>
11      </head>
12      <body>
13          <div id="headerDiv">
14              <table class="headerTable" border="0" width="100%">
15                  <tr><td><h1>Login</h1></td></tr>
16              </table>
17          </div>
18          <s:form name="frmAdminLogin" id="frmAdminLogin" method="post"
            action="doLogin" validate="true">
19              <table align="center" cellspacing="0" cellpadding="0" border="0"
                width="30%">
20                  <tr><td width="100%" colspan="2"> </td></tr>
21                  <tr><td class="hrLine" width="100%" colspan="2"> </td></tr>
22                  <tr>
23                      <td colspan="2" class="error">
24                          <s:property value="message" />
25                      </td>
26                  </tr>
27                  <tr>
28                      <td width="30%" valign="middle">
29                          <s:textfield required="true" requiredposition="left"
                            maxLength="25" label="Username"
                            name="systemuser.Username" title="Enter Username"/>
30                          <s:password required="true" requiredposition="left"
                            maxLength="8" label="Password" name="systemuser.Password"
                            title="Enter Password"/>
31                      </td>
```

```
32                    </tr>
33                    <tr>
34                        <td class="loginButtonAlign">
35                            <s:submit cssClass="loginButton" name="login" value="" />
36                        </td>
37                    </tr>
38                    <tr><td class="hrLine" width="100%" colspan="2"> </td></tr>
39                </table>
40            </s:form>
41            <s:include value="adminFooter.jsp" />
42        </body>
43 </html>
```

Explanation:

Administration Login is served when the user clicks , which is available in the footer of the application's home page.

This is a simple JSP page which holds a form to capture the login credentials. These credentials are passed to the action class which takes care of authenticating the user credentials and if found valid takes the user in.

The login data entry form allows the registered administration users to login to the backend application.

After an administration user logs in to the backend application, the user is allowed to:

❑   Manage Countries

❑   Manage States

❑   Manage Categories

❑   Manage Publishers

❑   Manage Authors

❑   Mange Books

❑   Manage Customers

❑   Manage Users

❑   Manage Transactions

Action [SystemUserLoginAction.java]

This is an action class with the following specifications:

Class Name	SystemUserLoginAction
Package	com.sharanamvaishali.action

Extends	ActionSupport
Implements	SessionAware

Objects		
Object Name	**Class Name**	**Object Type**
loginDAO	LoginDao	Data Access Object
systemuser	SystemUsers	Model

Properties			
Property Name	**Property Type**	**Methods**	
For the data entry form fields			
systemuser	SystemUsers	getSystemuser()	setSystemuser()
For verification			
message	String	getMessage()	- -
session	Map	getSession()	setSession()

Methods	
Method Name	**Return Values**
loginSystemUser()	SUCCESS ERROR
logOffSystemUser()	SUCCESS - -

Code Spec

```
1  package com.sharanamvaishali.action;
2
3  import com.opensymphony.xwork2.ActionContext;
4  import com.opensymphony.xwork2.ActionSupport;
5  import com.sharanamvaishali.dao.LoginDAO;
6  import com.sharanamvaishali.dao.LoginDAOImpl;
7  import com.sharanamvaishali.model.SystemUsers;
8  import java.util.*;
9  import org.apache.struts2.interceptor.SessionAware;
10 import org.apache.struts2.interceptor.validation.SkipValidation;
11
12 public class SystemUserLoginAction extends ActionSupport implements
   SessionAware{
13     private LoginDAO loginDAO = new LoginDAOImpl();
14
15     private SystemUsers systemuser;
16
17     private String message;
18
19     private Map session;
20
21     public Map getSession() {
22         return session;
23     }
24     @Override
25     public void setSession(Map session) {
26         this.session = session;
```

```
27        }
28
29        public String getMessage() {
30            return message;
31        }
32
33        public SystemUsers getSystemuser() {
34            return systemuser;
35        }
36        public void setSystemuser(SystemUsers systemuser) {
37            this.systemuser = systemuser;
38        }
39
40        public String loginSystemUser() throws Exception {
41            SystemUsers objSystemusers = (SystemUsers)
                loginDAO.validateSystemUserLogin(systemuser.getUsername(),
                systemuser.getPassword());
42            if(objSystemusers != null){
43                session = ActionContext.getContext().getSession();
44                session.put("username", systemuser.getUsername());
45                session.put("authors", objSystemusers.getManageAuthors());
46                session.put("books", objSystemusers.getManageBooks());
47                session.put("categories", objSystemusers.getManageCategories());
48                session.put("states", objSystemusers.getManageStates());
49                session.put("countries", objSystemusers.getManageCountries());
50                session.put("customers", objSystemusers.getManageCustomers());
51                session.put("publishers", objSystemusers.getManagePublishers());
52                session.put("transactions", objSystemusers.getManageTransactions());
53                session.put("users", objSystemusers.getManageUsers());
54                return SUCCESS;
55            } else {
56                message = "Invalid Username or Password. Please try again";
57                return ERROR;
58            }
59        }
60
61    @SkipValidation
62    public String logoffSystemUser() throws Exception{
63            session = ActionContext.getContext().getSession();
64            session.remove("username");
65            session.clear();
66            return SUCCESS;
67        }
68    }
```

Explanation:

The following section describes the above code spec.

loginSystemUser()

loginSystemUser() is invoked when the system user keys in the username and password and clicks **Login** .

This method passes the captured login information to LoginDAO's **validateSystemUserLogin()**, which validates and returns an object with the authenticated user's data.

If the object holds user data then the same is added to the **SESSION**.

The following information is added to the SESSION:
- Username
- Manage Countries
- Manage States
- Manage Categories
- Manage Publishers
- Manage Authors
- Mange Books
- Manage Customers
- Manage Users
- Manage Transactions

This information is displayed in the backend application's header.

Sharanam & Vaishali's Online Bookshop

Countries | States | Categories | Publishers | Authors | Books | Customers | Users | Transactions | Logout

If the object does not hold user data then an appropriate error message is send to adminLogin.jsp.

Diagram 32.2: Error message

logOffSystemUser()

logoffSystemUser() is invoked when the system user clicks Logout.

This method destroys the session.

DAO Class

Interface [LoginDAO.java]

This is a Data Access Object interface with the following specifications:

Class Name	Package
LoginDAO	com.sharanamvaishali.dao

Code Spec

```
1  package com.sharanamvaishali.dao;
2
3  import com.sharanamvaishali.model.Customers;
4
5  public interface LoginDAO {
6      public Object validateSystemUserLogin(String Username, String Password);
7  }
```

Implementation Class [LoginDAOImpl.java]

This is a **Data Access Object** class with the following specifications:

Class Name	Package	Implements
LoginDAOImpl	com.sharanamvaishali.dao	LoginDAO

Objects	
Object Name	**Class Name**
session	Session
transaction	Transaction

Methods		
Method Name	**Arguments**	**Return Values**
validateSystemUserLogin()	String Username String Password	Username Password

Code Spec

```
1  package com.sharanamvaishali.dao;
2
3  import com.sharanamvaishali.model.Customers;
4  import com.sharanamvaishali.utility.HibernateUtil;
5  import org.hibernate.Query;
6  import org.hibernate.Session;
7  import org.hibernate.Transaction;
8
9  public class LoginDAOImpl implements LoginDAO {
10     Session session = HibernateUtil.getSession();
11     Transaction transaction = null;
12
13     @Override
14     public Object validateSystemUserLogin(String Username, String Password) {
15         Query query = session.createQuery("FROM SystemUsers WHERE Username =
           :Username AND Password = :Password");
16         query.setString("Username", Username);
17         query.setString("Password", Password);
18         return query.uniqueResult();
19     }
20  }
```

Explanation:

The following section describes the above code spec.

validateSystemUserLogin()

validateSystemUserLogin() is invoked by **loginSystemUser()** of the Action class to authenticate System Users.

This method receives Username and Password which is used as the WHERE clause criteria. It queries the underlying tables using Hibernate Session object's **createQuery()** to retrieve the chosen record's data to return to loginSystemUser():

```
FROM SystemUsers WHERE Username = :Username AND Password = :Password
```

Validations [SystemUserLoginAction-validation.xml]

If the required **input** fields are kept empty whilst submitting the form, the SystemUserLoginAction-validation.xml file takes care of the validations.

Code Spec

```
1  <?xml version="1.0" encoding="UTF-8"?>
2  <!DOCTYPE validators PUBLIC '-//OpenSymphony Group//XWork Validator 1.0.2//EN'
   'http://www.opensymphony.com/xwork/xwork-validator-1.0.2.dtd'>
3  <validators>
4      <field name="systemuser.Username">
5          <field-validator type="requiredstring">
6              <message>Please enter the username.</message>
7          </field-validator>
8      </field>
9
10     <field name="systemuser.Password">
11         <field-validator type="requiredstring">
12             <message>Please enter the password.</message>
13         </field-validator>
14     </field>
15 </validators>
```

If any errors are detected the data entry form is re-served with appropriate error messages, as shown in diagram 32.3.

struts-AdminLogin.xml holds a mapping to serve the data entry form.

```
<action name="doLogin" method="loginSystemUser"
class="com.sharanamvaishali.action.SystemUserLoginAction">
    <result name="success"
    type="redirectAction">showManageTransactions</result>
    <result name="error">/admin/adminLogin.jsp</result>
    <result name="input">/admin/adminLogin.jsp</result>
</action>
```

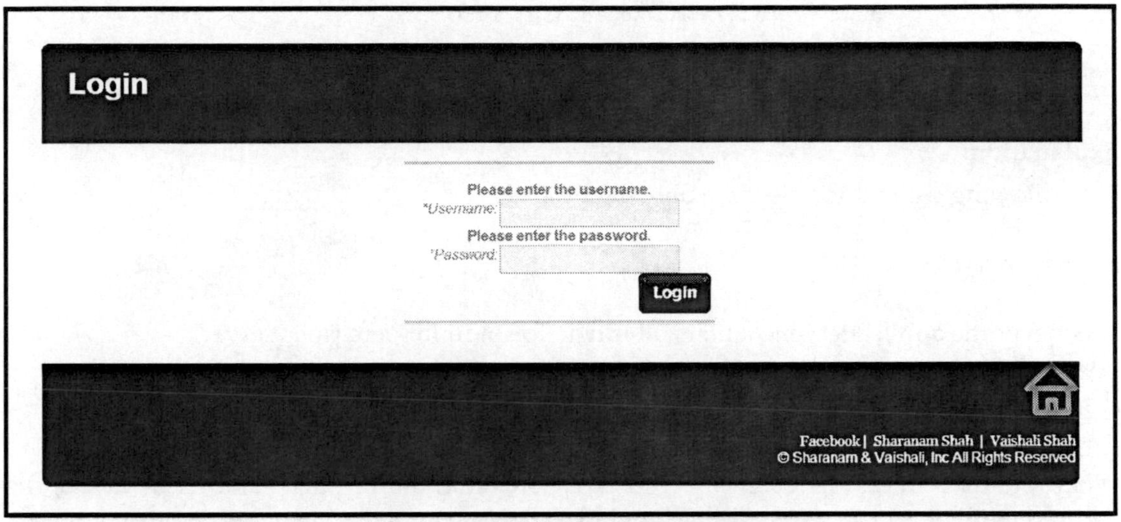

Diagram 32.3: Error messages

Struts Configuration [struts-AdminLogin.xml]

Struts-AdminLogin.xml contains the configuration information. All the actions such as the displaying the Administration Login page, validating the login credentials and logging off are defined in this file.

Code Spec

```
1   <?xml version="1.0" encoding="UTF-8"?>
2   <!DOCTYPE struts PUBLIC
3   "-//Apache Software Foundation//DTD Struts Configuration 2.0//EN"
4   "http://struts.apache.org/dtds/struts-2.0.dtd">
5   <struts>
6       <package name="adminLogin" extends="default">
7           <action name="admin">
8               <result>/admin/adminLogin.jsp</result>
9           </action>
10
11          <action name="doLogin" method="loginSystemUser"
            class="com.sharanamvaishali.action.SystemUserLoginAction">
12              <result name="success"
                type="redirectAction">showManageTransactions</result>
13              <result name="error">/admin/adminLogin.jsp</result>
14              <result name="input">/admin/adminLogin.jsp</result>
15          </action>
16
17          <action name="doLogout" method="logoffSystemUser"
            class="com.sharanamvaishali.action.SystemUserLoginAction">
```

```
18              <result>/admin/adminLogin.jsp</result>
19          </action>
20      </package>
21  </struts>
```

Explanation:

The following section describes the above code spec.

admin.action

Whenever the application encounters **admin.action**, adminLogin.jsp is served.

doLogin.action

When the user enters the username and password in adminLogin.jsp and clicks [Login], the login credentials are passed to loginSystemUser() of SystemUserLoginAction via **doLogout.action** for verification.

If verification is successful, doLogin.action displays the Manage Transactions page.

If the login credentials are invalid, doLogin.action returns to adminLogin.jsp with appropriate error messages.

doLogout.action

When the user clicks [Logout], **doLogout.action** logs off the user by calling logOffSystemUser() of SystemUserLoginAction.

Chapter 33

SECTION V: BACKEND [ADMINISTRATION] SOFTWARE DESIGN DOCUMENTATION

Manage Countries

This module allows performing the following operations:

- ❑ Adding new countries
- ❑ Editing existing countries
- ❑ Viewing existing countries
- ❑ Deleting existing countries

This module uses the bms.Countries table to perform the above operations.

This module is made up of the following:

Type	Name	Description
JSP	manageCountries.jsp	The data entry form
Struts 2		
Action	CountriesAction.java	The action class that facilitates data operations.
Validation	CountriesAction-validation.xml	The XML based validation file.
DAO Class	CountriesDAO.java	The interfaces for the DAO layer.
	PaginationDAO.java	
	CountriesDAOImpl.java	The implementation classes that performs the actual data operations.
	PaginationDAOImpl.java	
Struts Configuration	struts-Countries.xml	Struts configuration file.
Hibernate		
Mapping	hibernate.cfg.xml	The mapping file that holds Model class mapping.
Model Class	Countries.java	The model class.

JSP [manageCountries.jsp]

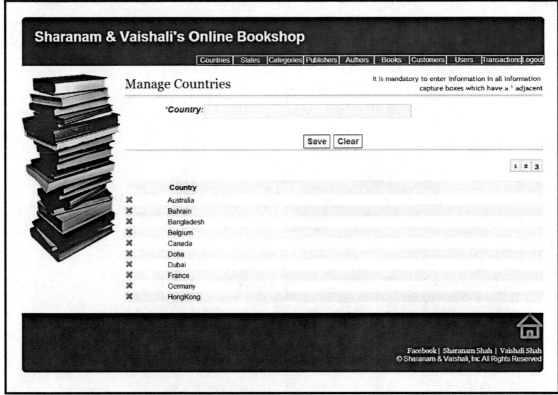

Diagram 33.1: Manage Countries [Data entry form]

This is a JSP which holds a data entry form, as shown in diagram 33.1. This form appears when the user clicks Countries .

Form Specifications

File Name	manageCountries.jsp
Title	BookShop[Sharanam & Vaishali Shah] - Manage Countries
Bound To Table	bms.Countries
Form Name	frmCountries
Action	doInsertCountry
Method	POST

Data Fields

Label	Name	Bound To	Validation Rules
Country	country.Country	Countries.Country	Cannot be left blank

Micro-Help For Form Fields

Form Field	Micro Help Statement
country.Country	Enter the country name

Data Controls

Object	Label	Name
s:submit	Save	btnSubmit
s:reset	Clear	btnReset

Code Spec

```
1   <%@page contentType="text/html" pageEncoding="UTF-8"%>
2   <%@ taglib prefix="s" uri="/struts-tags" %>
3   <!DOCTYPE HTML PUBLIC "-//W3C//DTD HTML 4.01 Transitional//EN"
4     "http://www.w3.org/TR/html4/loose.dtd">
5   <html xmlns="http://www.w3.org/1999/xhtml">
6     <head>
7       <title>BookShop [Sharanam & Vaishali Shah] - Manage Countries</title>
8       <meta http-equiv="content-type" content="text/html; charset=iso-8859-1">
9       <link href="/BookShop/css/admin.css" type="text/css" rel="stylesheet">
10      <s:head/>
11    </head>
12    <body>
13      <s:include value="header.jsp" />
14      <br>
15      <s:form action="doInsertCountry" method="post" name="frmCountries"
        id="frmCountries" validate="true">
16        <s:token/>
17        <s:hidden name="country.CountryNo" id="CountryNo"/>
18        <table width="100%" border="0" align="center" cellpadding="0" cellspacing="0">
19          <tr>
20            <td valign="top" width="20%">
21              <img src="/BookShop/images/leftImg.jpg" height="350"/>
22            </td>
23            <td valign="top">
24              <table width="100%" border="0" align="center" cellpadding="0"
              cellspacing="0">
25                <tr>
26                  <td>
27                    <table border="0" cellpadding="0" cellspacing="0"
                    width="100%">
```

```
28                              <tr>
29                                  <td class="manageForms">Manage Countries</td>
30                                  <td class="information">
31                                      It is mandatory to enter information in all information
                                        <br>capture boxes which have a <span
                                        class="mandatory">*</span> adjacent
32                                  </td>
33                              </tr>
34                          </table>
35                      </td>
36                  </tr>
37                  <tr><td class="hrLine"> </td></tr>
38                  <tr align="left" valign="top">
39                      <td>
40                          <table width="90%" border="0" align="center" cellpadding="0"
                            cellspacing="0">
41                              <tr>
42                                  <td>
43                                      <table width="100%" border="0" cellpadding="0"
                                        cellspacing="0">
44                                          <s:textfield required="true" requiredposition="left"
                                            id="Country" label="Country" name="country.Country"
                                            title="Enter the country name" maxLength="25"
                                            size="55"/>
45                                          <s:actionerror/>
46                                      </table>
47                                  </td>
48                              </tr>
49                              <tr>
50                                  <td style="text-align: center;">
51                                      <br /><br />
52                                      <s:submit theme="simple" cssClass="groovybutton"
                                        name="btnSubmit" id="btnSubmit" value="Save" />
53                                      <s:reset theme="simple" cssClass="groovybutton"
                                        name="btnReset" id="btnReset" value="Clear"
                                        onclick="javascript:document.location.href='showManageC
                                        ountries.action" />
54                                  </td>
55                              </tr>
56                          </table>
57                      </td>
58                  </tr>
59                  <tr><td class="hrLine"> </td></tr>
60                  <tr>
61                      <td align="center">
62                          <table width="60px" border="0" align="right" cellpadding="3"
                            cellspacing="1" style="border:#c3bca4 1px solid">
63                              <tr>
64                                  <s:bean name="org.apache.struts2.util.Counter"
                                    id="counter">
65                                      <s:param name="last" value="%{pageCount}" />
66                                  </s:bean>
67                                  <s:iterator value="#counter">
```

```
68                              <td align="center" width="2px" style="border:#c3bca4
                                 1px solid; background:#efebde; font-family:sans-serif;
                                 font-size:12px; font-weight:bolder; text-align:center;
                                 vertical-align:middle;">
69                                  <a href="<s:url
                                    action="iterateManageCountriesPage"><s:param
                                    name="pageNo"><s:property
                                    /></s:param></s:url>"><s:property /></a>
70                                  </td>
71                              </s:iterator>
72                          </tr>
73                      </table>
74                  </td>
75              </tr>
76              <tr>
77                  <td>
78                      <br>
79                      <table class="view" align="center" cellspacing="0" cellpadding="0"
                         width="100%">
80                          <tr>
81                              <th width="10%" align="center"> </th>
82                              <th class="Arial13BrownB" align="left">Country</th>
83                          </tr>
84                          <s:iterator value="countries" id="countries" status="stat">
85                              <tr title="Click to edit" class="<s:if test="#stat.odd ==
                                 true">odd</s:if><s:else>even</s:else>">
86                                  <td width="10%" valign="top">
87                                      <a href="<s:url action="doDeleteCountry"><s:param
                                        name="country.CountryNo" value="CountryNo"
                                        /></s:url>">
88                                          <img src="/BookShop/images/TrashIcon.png"
                                            border="0" alt="Delete" style="cursor:pointer;"/>
89                                      </a>
90                                  </td>
91                                  <td class="manageList"
                                    onclick="javascript:location.href='<s:url
                                    action='showEditCountry'><s:param
                                    name='country.CountryNo' value='CountryNo'
                                    /></s:url>'">
92                                      <s:property value="Country"/>
93                                  </td>
94                              </tr>
95                          </s:iterator>
96                          <s:if test="#countries==null">
97                              <span class="emptyMessage">Currently there exists no
                                 countries in the database. Please add a few countries to begin
                                 managing them.</span>
98                          </s:if>
99                      </table>
100                 </td>
101             </tr>
102         </table>
103     </td>
104 </tr>
105 </table>
```

```
106        </s:form>
107        <s:include value="adminFooter.jsp" />
108     </body>
109  </html>
```

Explanation:

This is a standard data entry form, which captures the country details. By default, when the form loads, it is in the **INSERT** and **VIEW** mode. The form also has Delete and Edit options to delete and edit a particular country record.

To use the form tags, import the Struts's tag library:

<%@ taglib prefix="s" uri="/struts-tags" %>

<s:head>

<s:head> renders required JavaScript code to configure Dojo and is required in order to use any of the tags included in the Dojo plugin.

<s:head>:

❑ Debugs the JavaScript errors

❑ Debugs Dojo and Struts widgets and displays their warning and error messages at the bottom of the page

❑ By default compresses the Core Dojo files, to improve loading time, which makes them very hard to read

<s:include>

<s:include> includes a Servlet's output i.e. result of Servlet or a JSP page.

<s:form>

<s:form> renders a HTML FORM tag. All the other tags in this library are nested tags of <s:form>.

The HTTP POST method is used to submit the form:

<s:form action="doInsertCountry" method="post" name="frmCountries" id="frmCountries" validate="true">

Where:

❑ **action** is the action name to submit to, without .action suffix. Here, the action points to doInsertCountry action

❑   **method** is the HTML FORM method attribute

❑   **name** is the name of the form

❑   **id** is the HTML id attribute

❑   **validate** checks whether client side or remote validation should be performed

<s:token>

<s:token> is used to stop double-submission of forms i.e. is used to help with the **double click** submission problem.

<s:token> merely places a hidden element that contains the unique token.

<s:hidden>

<s:hidden> renders an HTML input element of type hidden, populated by the specified property from the ValueStack:

<s:hidden name="country.CountryNo" id="CountryNo"/>

Where:

❑   **name** is the name of the hidden field. Here, CountryNo is an hidden attribute to check the data entered by the user is in INSERT mode or UPDATE mode

❑   **id** is the HTML id attribute

<s:textfield>

<s:textfield> renders a HTML INPUT field of type text:

<s:textfield required="true" requiredposition="left"
id="Country" label="Country" name="country.Country"
title="Enter the country name" maxLength="25"
size="55"/>

Where:

❑   **required** indicates that the input is required

❑   **requiredposition** defines the required position of the required form element [left or right]

❑   **id** is the HTML id attribute

❑   **label** is the label expression used for rendering Country's label

❑ **name** is the name of the text field. Here, **country** is the domain object set in the action class for **Countries** model:

private **Countries country;**

and Country is the JavaBean property set in the Countries model:

private String **Country;**

❑ **title** is the micro help for the form fields

❑ **maxLength** is the maximum length of characters hold by a particular field

❑ **size** is the size of characters a field can hold

\<s:actionerror\>

\<s:actionerror\> render action errors if they exists in the JSP pages.

In this JSP page \<s:actionerror\> displays errors [if there are any] for the field Country.

\<s:submit\>

\<s:submit\> renders a submit button:

\<s:submit theme="simple" **cssClass**="groovybutton" name="btnSubmit" id="btnSubmit" value="Save" />

Where:

❑ **theme** is the theme used for rendering the submit button. Here, the simple theme is used, which means a minimal theme with no "bells and whistles". For example, \<s:textfield\> renders the HTML \<input/\> without a label, validation, error reporting or any other formatting or functionality

❑ **cssClass** is the CSS used for the submit button

❑ **name** is the name of the submit button

❑ **id** is the HTML id attribute

❑ **value** is preset the value of the submit button

\<s:submit\> is used together with \<s:form\> to provide asynchronous form submissions.

\<s:reset\>

\<s:reset\> renders a reset button:

\<s:reset theme="simple" **cssClass**="groovybutton"

```
name="btnReset" id="btnReset" value="Clear"
onclick="javascript:document.location.href='showManageC
ountries.action'" />
```

Where:

❑ **theme** is the theme used for rendering the reset button

❑ **cssClass** is the CSS used for the reset button

❑ **name** is the name of the reset button

❑ **id** is the HTML id attribute

❑ **value** is preset the value of the reset button

❑ **onclick** is a JavaScript code spec, which clears all the form fields

<s:reset> is used together with <s:form> to provide form resetting.

<s:bean>

<s:bean> instantiates a class that conforms to the JavaBeans specification. <s:bean> has a body which can contain a number of <s:param> to set any mutator methods on that class.

In the above code spec, a bean named **Counter** is instantiated. The **id** is given a value named **counter**, which means that Counter bean will be placed into the stack's context.

<s:param>

<s:param> can be used to parameterize other tags.

<s:param> has the following two attributes:

❑ **name** is the name of the parameter

❑ **value** is the value of the parameter

In the above code spec, <s:param> is used to parameterize <s:bean>. So, <s:param> sets the **last** property i.e. setLast('%{pageCount}').

<s:iterator>

<s:iterator> iterates over a value. An iterable value can be either of java.util.Collection or java.util.Iterator.

In the above code spec, <s:bean> is used to instantiate Counter and place the same into ActionContext. <s:iterator> retrieves the object from ActionContext and then calls its getCounter() on the ValueStack and uses it to iterate over.

<s:property>

<s:property> is used to get the property of a value, which will default to the top of the stack if none is specified.

In the above code spec:

```
<s:property />
```

Prints out the current value of the iterator.

```
<s:property value="Country"/>
```

<s:iterator> uses the status attribute, using countries [declared as **List<Countries>** in action class]. <s:property> prints the result of **Countries's getCountry()**.

<s:url>

<s:url> is used to create a URL:

```
<a href="<s:url action="doDeleteCountry"><s:param
name="country.CountryNo" value="CountryNo"
/></s:url>">
```

Where:

❏   **action** is the action to generate the URL for.

In the above code spec, <s:param> is used inside <s:url> to provide additional request parameters. Here, when the user clicks **Delete** button, an action **doDeleteCountry.action** is triggered and is passed **CountryNo**.

<s:if>

<s:if> performs basic condition flow:

```
<s:if test="#countries==null">
    <span class="emptyMessage">Currently there exists no
    countries in the database. Please add a few countries to begin
    managing them.</span>
</s:if>
```

Where:

❏   **test** is the expression to determine if the body of the tag is to be displayed

In the above code spec, it is determined whether the Countries hold records, if not then display a message indicating that the database holds no records.

Action [CountriesAction.java]

This is an action class with the following specifications:

Class Name	CountriesAction
Package	com.sharanamvaishali.action
Extends	ActionSupport
Implements	- -

Objects		
Object Name	**Class Name**	**Object Type**
countriesDAO	CountriesDAO	Data Access Layer
pg	PaginationDAO	Data Access Layer
country	Countries	Model

Properties			
Property Name	**Property Type**	**Methods**	
For the data entry form fields			
country	Countries	getCountry()	setCountry()
For the data grid population			
countries	List<Countries>	getCountries()	setCountries()
For pagination			
pageNo	int	getPageNo()	setPageNo()
pageCount	int	getPageCount()	setPageCount()

Methods	
Method Name	**Return Values**
saveCountry()	SUCCESS
view()	SUCCESS
removeCountry()	SUCCESS
	ERROR
editCountry()	SUCCESS
getPage()	SUCCESS

Code Spec

```
1  package com.sharanamvaishali.action;
2
3  import com.opensymphony.xwork2.ActionSupport;
4  import com.sharanamvaishali.dao.CountriesDAO;
5  import com.sharanamvaishali.dao.CountriesDAOImpl;
6  import com.sharanamvaishali.dao.PaginationDAO;
7  import com.sharanamvaishali.dao.PaginationDAOImpl;
```

```
 8  import com.sharanamvaishali.model.Countries;
 9  import java.util.List;
10  import org.apache.struts2.interceptor.validation.SkipValidation;
11
12  public class CountriesAction extends ActionSupport{
13      private CountriesDAO countriesDAO = new CountriesDAOImpl();
14
15      private PaginationDAO pg = new PaginationDAOImpl();
16
17      private Countries country;
18
19      private List<Countries> countries;
20
21      private int pageNo, pageCount;
22
23      public int getPageNo() {
24          return pageNo;
25      }
26      public void setPageNo(int pageNo) {
27          this.pageNo = pageNo;
28      }
29
30      public int getPageCount() {
31          return pageCount;
32      }
33      public void setPageCount(int pageCount) {
34          this.pageCount = pageCount;
35      }
36
37      public Countries getCountry() {
38          return country;
39      }
40      public void setCountry(Countries country) {
41          this.country = country;
42      }
43
44      public List<Countries> getCountries() {
45          return countries;
46      }
47      public void setCountries(List<Countries> countries) {
48          this.countries = countries;
49      }
50
51      public String saveCountry() throws Exception {
52          if(country.getCountryNo() != null) {
53              countriesDAO.updateCountry(country);
54          } else {
55              countriesDAO.saveCountry(country);
```

```
56          }
57          return SUCCESS;
58      }
59
60      @SkipValidation
61      public String view() throws Exception {
62          pageNo = 1;
63          getPage();
64          return SUCCESS;
65      }
66
67      @SkipValidation
68      public String removeCountry() throws Exception {
69          try{
70              countriesDAO.deleteCountry(country.getCountryNo());
71          } catch(Exception e) {
72              addActionError(e.getCause().toString().split("[:]")[1]);
73              return ERROR;
74          }
75          return SUCCESS;
76      }
77
78      @SkipValidation
79      public String editCountry() throws Exception{
80          country = countriesDAO.getCountryById(country.getCountryNo());
81          view();
82          return SUCCESS;
83      }
84
85      @SkipValidation
86      public String getPage() throws Exception{
87          pageCount = pg.getTotalPages("Countries");
88          countries = pg.getPage(pageNo-1, "Countries").getList();
89          return SUCCESS;
90      }
91  }
```

Explanation:

The following section describes the above code spec.

saveCountry()

saveCountry() is invoked when the user keys in the desired data and clicks **Save** .

saveCountry():

❑ Performs an update operation [using CountriesDAO's updateCountry()] if **country.getCountryNo()** returns a valid CountryNo

❑ Performs an insert operation [using CountriesDAO's saveCountry()] if **country.getCountryNo()** returns empty

view()

view() is invoked every time Manage Countries is served.

It invokes **getPage()** to populate the List object [countries] which is used in the JSP page's **<s:iterator>** to populate the data grid. This data grid displays existing records from the **Countries** database table.

@SkipValidation is used to skip validation for this method.

removeCountry()

removeCountry() is invoked when the user clicks ✖ adjacent to the desired record [in the data grid] for deletion.

The delete operation is performed by invoking CountriesDAO's **deleteCountry()**.

deleteCountry() is passed **CountryNo** which is made available by JSP using **<s:param>** on click of ✖.

@SkipValidation is used to skip validation for this method.

editCountry()

editCountry() is invoked when the user clicks a desired record from the data grid in Manage Countries for updating it.

It populates the bean class object [country] with the chosen record's data. The data is retrieved using CountriesDAO's **getCountryById()** which is passed CountryNo which is made available by JSP's <s:param> on click of the record.

Struts 2 framework automatically transfers the values from the bean class object to the FORM fields thus making it available to the user for editing the same.

@SkipValidation is used to skip validation for this method.

getPage()

getPage() is invoked every time Manage Countries is served or the user clicks a page number link from Manage Countries using pagination.

It calculates the total number of pages for pagination purpose and stores the same in the property named **pageCount**.

It populates the List object [countries] which is used in the JSP page's <s:iterator> to form the data grid. This data grid displays existing records from the Countries database table.

The data to be populated in the List object is retrieved using PaginationDAO's **getPage()** which returns the records belonging to the appropriate page number.

@SkipValidation is used to skip validation for this method.

DAO Class

Interface [CountriesDAO.java]

This is a Data Access Object interface with the following specifications:

Class Name	Package
CountriesDAO	com.sharanamvaishali.dao

Code Spec

```
1  package com.sharanamvaishali.dao;
2
3  import com.sharanamvaishali.model.Countries;
4
5  public interface CountriesDAO {
6      public void saveCountry(Countries countries);
7      public void updateCountry(Countries countries);
8      public void deleteCountry(int CountryNo);
9      public Countries getCountryById(int CountryNo);
10 }
```

REMINDER

PaginationDAO.java is explained later in the *Section V: Backend [Administration] Software Design Documentation* under the *Chapter 42: Common Files.*

Implementation Class [CountriesDAOImpl.java]

This is a **Data Access Object** class with the following specifications:

Class Name	CountriesDAOImpl
Package	com.sharanamvaishali.dao
Implements	CountriesDAO

Objects	
Object Name	**Class Name**
session	Session
transaction	Transaction

Methods		
Method Name	**Arguments**	**Return Values**
saveCountry()	Countries countries	void
updateCountry()	Countries countries	void
deleteCountry()	Integer CountryNo	void
getCountryById()	Integer CountryNo	Countries

Code Spec

```
1    package com.sharanamvaishali.dao;
2
3    import com.sharanamvaishali.model.Countries;
4    import com.sharanamvaishali.utility.HibernateUtil;
5    import org.hibernate.Session;
6    import org.hibernate.Transaction;
7
8    public class CountriesDAOImpl implements CountriesDAO {
9        Session session = HibernateUtil.getSession();
10       Transaction transaction;
11
12       @Override
13       public void saveCountry(Countries countries) {
14           try {
15               transaction = session.beginTransaction();
16               session.save(countries);
17               transaction.commit();
18           } catch (RuntimeException e) {
19           if(countries != null) {
20               transaction.rollback();
21           }
22           throw e;
23           }
24       }
25
```

```
26      @Override
27      public void updateCountry(Countries countries) {
28          try {
29              transaction = session.beginTransaction();
30              session.update(countries);
31              transaction.commit();
32          } catch (RuntimeException e) {
33              if(countries != null) {
34                  transaction.rollback();
35              }
36              throw e;
37          }
38      }
39
40      @Override
41      public void deleteCountry(int CountryNo) {
42          Object Countries = null;
43          try {
44              transaction = session.beginTransaction();
45              Countries = session.load(Countries.class, CountryNo);
46              session.delete(Countries);
47              transaction.commit();
48          } catch (RuntimeException e) {
49              if(Countries != null) {
50                  transaction.rollback();
51              }
52              throw e;
53          }
54      }
55
56      @Override
57      public Countries getCountryById(int CountryNo) {
58          return (Countries) session.createQuery("FROM Countries WHERE CountryNo
            = :CountryNo").setInteger("CountryNo", CountryNo).uniqueResult();
59      }
60  }
```

Explanation:

The following section describes the above code spec.

saveCountry()

saveCountry() does the actual saving of the country in the Countries database table.

saveCountry() uses **save()** of Session, which takes care of adding new country details when the user has entered all the country details and clicked **Save**.

After the save operation is performed, the transaction is committed to make the changes permanent.

Whilst performing the save operation, if a runtime exception occurs, than the transaction is **rolled back**.

updateCountry()

updateCountry() does the actual updation of the existing country in the Countries database table.

updateCountry() uses **update()** of Session, which takes care of updating an existing country details when the user has made changes to the existing country details and clicked **Save**.

After the update operation is performed, the transaction is committed to make the changes permanent.

Whilst performing the update operation, if a runtime exception occurs, than the transaction is **rolled back**.

deleteCountry()

deleteCountry() deletes the appropriate country based on **CountryNo** received as a reference.

This method uses:

- ❑ **load()** of Session, which retrieves the appropriate Country to be deleted using CountryNo as a reference
- ❑ **delete()** of Session, which deletes the country from the Countries database table

After the delete operation is performed, the transaction is committed to make the changes permanent.

Whilst performing the delete operation, if a runtime exception occurs, than the transaction is **rolled back**.

getCountryById()

getCountryById() returns the appropriate country's object from the Countries database table using **CountryNo** as the reference.

This method uses:

❑ **createQuery()** of Session, which creates a new instance of Query to retrieve the Country details using CountryNo as reference

❑ **setInteger()** of Query, which states the parameter to be used as the WHERE clause criteria when querying the Countries database table

❑ **uniqueResult()** of Query, which ensures that only unique record is retrieved from the Countries database table and prevents any kinds of errors

REMINDER

PaginationDAOImpl.java is explained later in the *Section V: Backend [Administration] Software Design Documentation* under the *Chapter 42: Common Files*.

Validations [CountriesAction-validation.xml]

If the required **input** fields are kept empty whilst submitting the form, CountriesAction-validation.xml takes care of the validations.

Code Spec

```
1   <?xml version="1.0" encoding="UTF-8"?>
2   <!DOCTYPE validators PUBLIC '-//OpenSymphony Group//XWork Validator
    1.0.2//EN' 'http://www.opensymphony.com/xwork/xwork-validator-1.0.2.dtd'>
3   <validators>
4     <field name="country.Country">
5       <field-validator type="requiredstring">
6         <message>Please enter the country name.</message>
7       </field-validator>
8     </field>
9   </validators>
```

If any errors are detected the data entry form is re-served with appropriate error messages, as shown in diagram 33.2.

struts-Countries.xml file holds a mapping to serve the data entry form:

```
17      <action name="doInsertCountry" method="saveCountry"
        class="com.sharanamvaishali.action.CountriesAction">
18        <interceptor-ref name="defaultStack"/>
19        <interceptor-ref name="token"/>
20        <result name="success"
          type="redirectAction">doViewCountries</result>
21        <result name="input">/admin/manageCountries.jsp</result>
22      </action>
```

Diagram 33.2: Error messages

Struts Configuration [struts-Countries.xml]

This is the struts configuration file with the following specifications:

File Name	Package Name	Extends
Countries	manageCountries	default

Actions	
Action Name	**Results**
showManageCountries	SUCCESS - manageCountries.jsp
iterateManageCountriesPage	SUCCESS - manageCountries.jsp
doInsertCountry	SUCCESS - doViewCountries
	INPUT - manageCountries.jsp
doViewCountries	SUCCESS - manageCountries.jsp
	ERROR - showManageCountries
doDeleteCountry	SUCCESS - doViewCountries
	ERROR - manageCountries.jsp
showEditCountry	SUCCESS - manageCountries.jsp

Code Spec

```
1   <?xml version="1.0" encoding="UTF-8"?>
2   <!DOCTYPE struts PUBLIC
3   "-//Apache Software Foundation//DTD Struts Configuration 2.0//EN"
4   "http://struts.apache.org/dtds/struts-2.0.dtd">
5   <struts>
6      <package name="manageCountries" extends="default">
7         <default-interceptor-ref name="chkSession"/>
8
9         <action name="showManageCountries" method="view"
           class="com.sharanamvaishali.action.CountriesAction">
```

```
10            <result>/admin/manageCountries.jsp</result>
11        </action>
12
13        <action name="iterateManageCountriesPage" method="getPage"
          class="com.sharanamvaishali.action.CountriesAction">
14            <result>/admin/manageCountries.jsp</result>
15        </action>
16
17        <action name="doInsertCountry" method="saveCountry"
          class="com.sharanamvaishali.action.CountriesAction">
18            <interceptor-ref name="defaultStack"/>
19            <interceptor-ref name="token"/>
20            <result name="success"
              type="redirectAction">doViewCountries</result>
21            <result name="input">/admin/manageCountries.jsp</result>
22        </action>
23
24        <action name="doViewCountries" method="view"
          class="com.sharanamvaishali.action.CountriesAction">
25            <result name="success">/admin/manageCountries.jsp</result>
26            <result name="error"
              type="redirectAction">showManageCountries</result>
27        </action>
28
29        <action name="doDeleteCountry" method="removeCountry"
          class="com.sharanamvaishali.action.CountriesAction">
30            <result name="success"
              type="redirectAction">doViewCountries</result>
31            <result name="error">/admin/manageCountries.jsp</result>
32        </action>
33
34        <action name="showEditCountry" method="editCountry"
          class="com.sharanamvaishali.action.CountriesAction">
35            <result name="success">/admin/manageCountries.jsp</result>
36        </action>
37    </package>
38 </struts>
```

Explanation:

The following section describes the above code spec.

showManageCountries.action

showManageCountries is an action to help viewing.

This means the data entry form and the list of country details are displayed.

The list of country details are retrieved by **CountriesAction**'s **view()**.

iterateManageCountriesPage.action

iterateManageCountriesPage is an action to help iterate.

This means displaying 10 records of country details per page in the form of data grid.

This iterated data is retrieved by **CountriesAction**'s **getPage()**.

doInsertCountry.action

doInsertCountry is an action to help adding new country details or updating existing country details.

defaultStack interceptor is referenced, which a complete stack with all the common interceptors in place.

token interceptor is referenced, which checks for valid token presence in Action and prevents duplicate form submission.

doInsertCountry.action:

❑ Calls **CountriesAction**'s **saveCountry()** to add new country details or update the existing country details

❑ Ensures that the captured data is valid

❑ If the validation is successful then the data is saved and the result is redirected to **doViewCountries.action**

❑ If the validation fails then the Manage Countries page along with error messages is displayed

doViewCountries.action

doViewCountries is an action to help viewing.

This means the list of country details is displayed.

The list of country details are retrieved by **CountriesAction**'s **view()**.

If there are no data available in the database then the error message is displayed in the Manage Countries page by redirecting the page to **showManageCountries.action**.

doDeleteCountry.action

In case, the user chooses to delete a country and clicks ✖, **doDeleteCountry.action** is the action to help delete a country record from Manage Countries.

doDeleteCountry.action:

❑   Calls **CountriesAction's removeCountry()** to delete a country record

❑   If the country record is deleted successfully then the result is redirected to **doViewCountries.action**

❑   If the record being deleted is referenced by a record in another database table then the Manage Countries page displays the error message indicating that this record cannot be deleted

showEditCountry.action

showEditCountry is an action to help the editing of existing countries.

In case, the user chooses to edit a country and clicks that particular record, **showEditCountry.action** helps fill up the Manage Countries form with country details.

showEditCountry.action:

❑   Calls **CountriesAction's editCountry()** to retrieve the country details

❑   Returns to the Manage Countries page along with the data to be populated in the form

Domain Class [Countries.java]

This is a domain class with the following specifications:

Class Name	Package	Implements
Countries	com.sharanamvaishali.model	java.io.Serializable

Properties			
Property Name	**Property Type**	**Methods**	
CountryNo	Integer	getCountryNo()	setCountryNo()
Country	String	getCountry()	setCountry()

Code Spec

```
1  package com.sharanamvaishali.model;
2
3  import javax.persistence.Column;
4  import javax.persistence.Entity;
```

```
 5  import javax.persistence.GeneratedValue;
 6  import javax.persistence.Id;
 7  import javax.persistence.Table;
 8
 9  @Entity
10  @Table(name="COUNTRIES")
11  public class Countries implements java.io.Serializable {
12      @Id
13      @GeneratedValue
14      @Column(name="COUNTRYNO")
15      private Integer CountryNo;
16      @Column(name="COUNTRY")
17      private String Country;
18
19      public Countries() {
20      }
21
22      public String getCountry() {
23          return Country;
24      }
25      public void setCountry(String Country) {
26          this.Country = Country;
27      }
28
29      public Integer getCountryNo() {
30          return CountryNo;
31      }
32      public void setCountryNo(Integer CountryNo) {
33          this.CountryNo = CountryNo;
34      }
35  }
```

Chapter

34

SECTION V: BACKEND [ADMINISTRATION] SOFTWARE DESIGN DOCUMENTATION

Manage States

This module allows performing the following operations:

- Adding new states
- Editing existing states
- Viewing existing states
- Deleting existing states

This module uses the bms.States table to perform the above operations.

This module is made up of the following:

Type	Name	Description
JSP	manageStates.jsp	The data entry form
Struts 2		
Action	StatesAction.java	The action class that facilitates data operations.
Validation	StatesAction-validation.xml	The XML based validation file.
DAO Class	StatesDAO.java	The interfaces for the DAO layer.
	PaginationDAO.java	
	StatesDAOImpl.java	The implementation classes that performs the actual data operations.
	PaginationDAOImpl.java	
Struts Configuration	struts-States.xml	Struts configuration file.
Hibernate		
Mapping	hibernate.cfg.xml	The mapping file that holds Model class mapping.
Model Class	States.java	The model class.

JSP [manageStates.jsp]

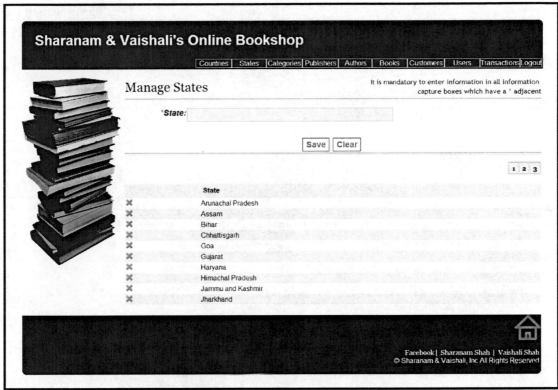

Diagram 34.1: Manage States [Data entry form]

This is a JSP which holds a data entry form, as shown in diagram 34.1. This form appears when the user clicks **States** .

Form Specifications

File Name	manageStates.jsp
Title	BookShop[Sharanam & Vaishali Shah] - Manage States
Bound To Table	bms.States
Form Name	frmStates
Action	doInsertState
Method	POST

Data Fields

Label	Name	Bound To	Validation Rules
State	state.State	States.State	Cannot be left blank

Micro-Help For Form Fields

Form Field	Micro Help Statement
state.State	Enter the state name

Data Controls

Object	Label	Name
s:submit	Save	btnSubmit
s:reset	Clear	btnReset

Code Spec

```
1   <%@page contentType="text/html" pageEncoding="UTF-8"%>
2   <%@ taglib prefix="s" uri="/struts-tags" %>
3   <!DOCTYPE HTML PUBLIC "-//W3C//DTD HTML 4.01 Transitional//EN"
4     "http://www.w3.org/TR/html4/loose.dtd">
5   <html xmlns="http://www.w3.org/1999/xhtml">
6     <head>
7       <title>BookShop [Sharanam & Vaishali Shah] - Manage States</title>
8       <meta http-equiv="content-type" content="text/html; charset=iso-8859-1">
9       <link href="/BookShop/css/admin.css" type="text/css" rel="stylesheet">
10      <s:head/>
11    </head>
12    <body>
13      <s:include value="header.jsp" />
14      <br>
15      <s:form action="doInsertState" method="post" name="frmState" id="frmState"
        validate="true">
16        <s:token/>
17        <s:hidden name="state.StateNo" id="StateNo"/>
18        <table width="100%" border="0" align="center" cellpadding="0"
          cellspacing="0">
19          <tr>
20            <td valign="top" width="20%">
21              <img src="/BookShop/images/leftImg.jpg" height="350"/>
22            </td>
23            <td valign="top">
24              <table width="100%" border="0" align="center" cellpadding="0"
                cellspacing="0">
25                <tr>
26                  <td>
```

```
27          <table border="0" cellpadding="0" cellspacing="0"
            width="100%">
28              <tr>
29                  <td class="manageForms">Manage States</td>
30                  <td class="information">
31                      It is mandatory to enter information in all information
                        <br>capture boxes which have a <span
                        class="mandatory">*</span> adjacent
32                  </td>
33              </tr>
34          </table>
35      </td>
36  </tr>
37  <tr><td class="hrLine"> </td></tr>
38  <tr align="left" valign="top">
39      <td>
40          <table width="90%" border="0" align="center" cellpadding="0"
            cellspacing="0">
41              <tr>
42                  <td>
43                      <table width="100%" border="0" cellpadding="0"
                        cellspacing="0">
44                          <s:textfield required="true" requiredposition="left"
                            id="State" label="State" name="state.State"
                            title="Enter the state name" maxLength="25"
                            size="55"/>
45                          <s:actionerror/>
46                      </table>
47                  </td>
48              </tr>
49              <tr>
50                  <td style="text-align: center;">
51                      <br /><br />
52                      <s:submit theme="simple" cssClass="groovybutton"
                        name="btnSubmit" id="btnSubmit" value="Save" />
53                      <s:reset theme="simple" cssClass="groovybutton"
                        name="btnReset" id="btnReset" value="Clear"
                        onclick="javascript:document.location.href='showManag
                        eStates.action'"/>
54                  </td>
55              </tr>
56          </table>
57      </td>
58  </tr>
59  <tr><td class="hrLine"> </td></tr>
60  <tr>
61      <td align="center">
62          <table width="60px" border="0" align="right" cellpadding="3"
            cellspacing="1" style="border:#c3bca4 1px solid">
63              <tr>
64                  <s:bean name="org.apache.struts2.util.Counter"
                    id="counter">
65                      <s:param name="last" value="%{pageCount}" />
66                  </s:bean>
```

```
67                                    <s:iterator value="#counter">
68                                        <td align="center" width="2px" style="border:#c3bca4
                                         1px solid; background:#efebde; font-family:sans-serif;
                                         font-size:12px; font-weight:bolder; text-align:center;
                                         vertical-align:middle;">
69                                            <a href="<s:url
                                             action="iterateManageStatesPage"><s:param
                                             name="pageNo"><s:property
                                             /></s:param></s:url>"><s:property /></a>
70                                        </td>
71                                    </s:iterator>
72                                </tr>
73                            </table>
74                        </td>
75                    </tr>
76                    <tr>
77                        <td>
78                            <br>
79                            <table class="view" align="center" cellspacing="0"
                             cellpadding="0" width="100%">
80                                <tr>
81                                    <th width="10%" align="center"> </th>
82                                    <th width="45%" class="Arial13BrownB"
                                     align="left">State</th>
83                                </tr>
84                                <s:iterator value="states" id="states" status="stat">
85                                    <tr title="Click to edit" class="<s:if test="#stat.odd ==
                                     true">odd</s:if><s:else>even</s:else>">
86                                        <td width="10%" valign="top">
87                                            <a href="<s:url action="doDeleteState"><s:param
                                             name="state.StateNo" value="StateNo" /></s:url>">
88                                                <img src="/BookShop/images/TrashIcon.png"
                                                 border="0" alt="Delete" style="cursor:pointer;"/>
89                                            </a>
90                                        </td>
91                                        <td width="45%" class="manageList"
                                         onclick="javascript:location.href='<s:url
                                         action='showEditState'><s:param name='state.StateNo'
                                         value='StateNo' /></s:url>'">
92                                            <s:property value="State"/>
93                                        </td>
94                                    </tr>
95                                </s:iterator>
96                            </table>
97                            <s:if test="#states==null">
98                                <span class="emptyMessage">Currently there exists no
                                 states in the database. Please add a few states to begin
                                 managing them.</span>
99                            </s:if>
100                       </td>
101                   </tr>
102               </table>
103           </td>
104       </tr>
```

```
105          </table>
106          </s:form>
107          <s:include value="adminFooter.jsp" />
108       </body>
109   </html>
```

Explanation:

This is a standard data entry form, which captures the state details. By default, when the form loads, it is in the **INSERT** and **VIEW** mode. The form also has Delete and Edit options to delete and edit a particular state record.

Action [StatesAction.java]

This is an action class with the following specifications:

Class Name	StatesAction
Package	com.sharanamvaishali.action
Extends	ActionSupport
Implements	- -

Objects		
Object Name	**Class Name**	**Object Type**
statesDAO	StatesDAO	Data Access Layer
pg	PaginationDAO	Data Access Layer
state	States	Model

Properties			
Property Name	**Property Type**	**Methods**	
For the data entry form fields			
state	States	getState()	setState()
For the data grid population			
states	List<States>	getStates()	setStates()
For pagination			
pageNo	int	getPageNo()	setPageNo()
pageCount	int	getPageCount()	setPageCount()

Methods	
Method Name	**Return Values**
saveState()	SUCCESS
view()	SUCCESS
removeState()	SUCCESS
	ERROR
editState()	SUCCESS
getPage()	SUCCESS

Code Spec

```
1   package com.sharanamvaishali.action;
2
3   import com.opensymphony.xwork2.ActionSupport;
4   import com.sharanamvaishali.dao.PaginationDAO;
5   import com.sharanamvaishali.dao.PaginationDAOImpl;
6   import com.sharanamvaishali.dao.StatesDAO;
7   import com.sharanamvaishali.dao.StatesDAOImpl;
8   import com.sharanamvaishali.model.States;
9   import java.util.List;
10  import org.apache.struts2.interceptor.validation.SkipValidation;
11
12  public class StatesAction extends ActionSupport{
13      private StatesDAO statesDAO = new StatesDAOImpl();
14
15      private PaginationDAO pg = new PaginationDAOImpl();
16
17      private States state;
18
19      private List<States> states;
20
21      private int pageNo, pageCount;
22
23      public int getPageNo() {
24          return pageNo;
25      }
26      public void setPageNo(int pageNo) {
27          this.pageNo = pageNo;
28      }
29
30      public int getPageCount() {
31          return pageCount;
32      }
33      public void setPageCount(int pageCount) {
34          this.pageCount = pageCount;
35      }
36
37      public States getState() {
38          return state;
39      }
40      public void setState(States state) {
41          this.state = state;
42      }
43
44      public List<States> getStates() {
45          return states;
46      }
47      public void setStates(List<States> states) {
```

```
48        this.states = states;
49      }
50
51      public String saveState() throws Exception{
52         if(state.getStateNo() != null) {
53            statesDAO.updateState(state);
54         } else {
55            statesDAO.saveState(state);
56         }
57         return SUCCESS;
58      }
59
60      @SkipValidation
61      public String view() throws Exception{
62         pageNo = 1;
63         getPage();
64         return SUCCESS;
65      }
66
67      @SkipValidation
68      public String removeState() throws Exception{
69         try{
70            statesDAO.deleteState(state.getStateNo());
71         } catch(Exception e) {
72            addActionError(e.getCause().toString().split("[:]")[1]);
73            return ERROR;
74         }
75         return SUCCESS;
76      }
77
78      @SkipValidation
79      public String editState() throws Exception{
80         state = statesDAO.getStateById(state.getStateNo());
81         view();
82         return SUCCESS;
83      }
84
85      @SkipValidation
86      public String getPage() throws Exception{
87         pageCount = pg.getTotalPages("States");
88         states = pg.getPage(pageNo-1, "States").getList();
89         return SUCCESS;
90      }
91  }
```

Explanation:

The following section describes the above code spec.

saveState()

saveState() is invoked when the user keys in the desired data and clicks [Save].

saveState():

❑ Performs an update operation [using StatesDAO's updateState()] if **state.getStateNo()** returns a valid StateNo

❑ Performs an insert operation [using StatesDAO's saveState()] if **state.getStateNo()** returns empty

view()

view() is invoked every time Manage States is served.

It invokes **getPage()** to populate the List object [states] which is used in the JSP page's **<s:iterator>** to populate the data grid. This data grid displays existing records from the **States** database table.

@SkipValidation is used to skip validation for this method.

removeState()

removeState() is invoked when the user clicks ✖ adjacent to the desired record [in the data grid] for deletion.

The delete operation is performed by invoking StatesDAO's **deleteState()**.

deleteState() is passed **StateNo** which is made available by JSP using **<s:param>** on click of ✖.

@SkipValidation is used to skip validation for this method.

editState()

editState() is invoked when the user clicks a desired record from the data grid in Manage States for updating it.

It populates the bean class object [state] with the chosen record's data. The data is retrieved using StatesDAO's **getStateById()** which is passed StateNo which is made available by JSP's <s:param> on click of the record.

Struts 2 framework automatically transfers the values from the bean class object to the FORM fields thus making it available to the user for editing the same.

@SkipValidation is used to skip validation for this method.

getPage()

getPage() is invoked every time Manage States is served or the user clicks a page number link from Manage States using pagination.

It calculates the total number of pages for pagination purpose and stores the same in the property named **pageCount**.

It populates the List object [states] which is used in the JSP page's <s:iterator> to form the data grid. This data grid displays existing records from the States database table.

The data to be populated in the List object is retrieved using PaginationDAO's **getPage()** which returns the records belonging to the appropriate page number.

@SkipValidation is used to skip validation for this method.

DAO Class

Interface [StatesDAO.java]

This is a Data Access Object interface with the following specifications:

Class Name	Package
StatesDAO	com.sharanamvaishali.dao

Code Spec

```
1  package com.sharanamvaishali.dao;
2
3  import com.sharanamvaishali.model.States;
4
5  public interface StatesDAO {
6     public void saveState(States states);
7     public void updateState(States states);
8     public void deleteState(int StateNo);
9     public States getStateById(int StateNo);
10 }
```

REMINDER

 PaginationDAO.java is explained later in the *Section V: Backend [Administration] Software Design Documentation* under the *Chapter 42: Common Files.*

Implementation Class [StatesDAOImpl.java]

This is a **Data Access Object** class with the following specifications:

Class Name	StatesDAOImpl
Package	com.sharanamvaishali.dao
Implements	StatesDAO

Objects	
Object Name	**Class Name**
session	Session
transaction	Transaction

Methods		
Method Name	**Arguments**	**Return Values**
saveState()	States states	void
updateState()	States states	void
deleteState()	Integer StateNo	void
getStateById()	Integer StateNo	States

Code Spec

```
1   package com.sharanamvaishali.dao;
2
3   import com.sharanamvaishali.model.States;
4   import com.sharanamvaishali.utility.HibernateUtil;
5   import org.hibernate.Session;
6   import org.hibernate.Transaction;
7
8   public class StatesDAOImpl implements StatesDAO {
9      Session session = HibernateUtil.getSession();
10     Transaction transaction;
11
12     @Override
13     public void saveState(States states) {
14        try {
15           transaction = session.beginTransaction();
16           session.save(states);
17           transaction.commit();
18        } catch (RuntimeException e) {
19           if(states != null) {
20              transaction.rollback();
```

```
21          }
22              throw e;
23          }
24      }
25
26      @Override
27      public void updateState(States states) {
28          try {
29              transaction = session.beginTransaction();
30              session.update(states);
31              transaction.commit();
32          } catch (RuntimeException e) {
33              if(states != null) {
34                  transaction.rollback();
35              }
36              throw e;
37          }
38      }
39
40      @Override
41      public void deleteState(int StateNo) {
42          Object States = null;
43          try {
44              transaction = session.beginTransaction();
45              States = session.load(States.class, StateNo);
46              session.delete(States);
47              transaction.commit();
48          } catch (RuntimeException e) {
49              If(States != null) {
50                  transaction.rollback();
51              }
52              throw e;
53          }
54      }
55
56      @Override
57      public States getStateById(int StateNo) {
58          return (States) session.createQuery("FROM States WHERE StateNo =
            :StateNo").setInteger("StateNo", StateNo).uniqueResult();
59      }
60  }
```

Explanation:

The following section describes the above code spec.

saveState()

saveState() does the actual saving of the state in the States database table.

saveState() uses **save()** of Session, which takes care of adding new state details when the user has entered all the state details and clicked `Save`.

After the save operation is performed, the transaction is committed to make the changes permanent.

Whilst performing the save operation, if a runtime exception occurs, than the transaction is **rolled back**.

updateState()

updateState() does the actual updation of the existing state in the States database table.

updateState() uses **update()** of Session, which takes care of updating an existing state details when the user has made changes to the existing state details and clicked `Save`.

After the update operation is performed, the transaction is committed to make the changes permanent.

Whilst performing the update operation, if a runtime exception occurs, than the transaction is **rolled back**.

deleteState()

deleteState() deletes the appropriate state based on **StateNo** received as a reference.

This method uses:
❑   **load()** of Session, which retrieves the appropriate State to be deleted using StateNo as a reference
❑   **delete()** of Session, which deletes the state from the States database table

After the delete operation is performed, the transaction is committed to make the changes permanent.

Whilst performing the delete operation, if a runtime exception occurs, than the transaction is **rolled back**.

getStateById()

getStateById() returns the appropriate state's object from the States database table using **StateNo** as the reference.

This method uses:

❑ **createQuery()** of Session, which creates a new instance of Query to retrieve the State details using StateNo as reference

❑ **setInteger()** of Query, which states the parameter to be used as the WHERE clause criteria when querying the States database table

❑ **uniqueResult()** of Query, which ensures that only unique record is retrieved from the States database table and prevents any kinds of errors

REMINDER

PaginationDAOImpl.java is explained later in the *Section V: Backend [Administration] Software Design Documentation* under the *Chapter 42: Common Files*.

Validations [StatesAction-validation.xml]

If the required **input** fields are kept empty whilst submitting the form, StatesAction-validation.xml takes care of the validations.

Code Spec

```
1  <?xml version="1.0" encoding="UTF-8"?>
2  <!DOCTYPE validators PUBLIC '-//OpenSymphony Group//XWork Validator
   1.0.2//EN' 'http://www.opensymphony.com/xwork/xwork-validator-1.0.2.dtd'>
3  <validators>
4    <field name="state.State">
5      <field-validator type="requiredstring">
6        <message>Please enter the state name.</message>
7      </field-validator>
8    </field>
9  </validators>
```

If any Errors are detected the data entry form is re-served with appropriate error messages, as shown in diagram 34.2.

struts-States.xml file holds a mapping to serve the data entry form:

```
17        <action name="doInsertState" method="saveState"
          class="com.sharanamvaishali.action.StatesAction">
18            <interceptor-ref name="defaultStack"/>
19            <interceptor-ref name="token"/>
20            <result name="success" type="redirectAction">doViewStates</result>
21            <result name="input">/admin/manageStates.jsp</result>
22        </action>
```

Diagram 34.2: Error messages

Struts Configuration [struts-States.xml]

This is the struts configuration file with the following specifications:

File Name	Package Name	Extends
States	manageStates	default

Actions	
Action Name	**Results**
showManageStates	SUCCESS - manageStates.jsp
iterateManageStatesPage	SUCCESS - manageStates.jsp
doInsertState	SUCCESS - doViewStates
	INPUT - manageStates.jsp
doViewStates	SUCCESS - manageStates.jsp
	ERROR - showManageStates
doDeleteState	SUCCESS - doViewStates
	ERROR - manageStates.jsp
showEditState	SUCCESS - manageStates.jsp

Code Spec

```
1  <?xml version="1.0" encoding="UTF-8"?>
2  <!DOCTYPE struts PUBLIC
3  "-//Apache Software Foundation//DTD Struts Configuration 2.0//EN"
4  "http://struts.apache.org/dtds/struts-2.0.dtd">
5  <struts>
6     <package name="manageStates" extends="default">
7        <default-interceptor-ref name="chkSession"/>
8
9        <action name="showManageStates" method="view"
          class="com.sharanamvaishali.action.StatesAction">
10          <result>/admin/manageStates.jsp</result>
11       </action>
12
13       <action name="iterateManageStatesPage" method="getPage"
          class="com.sharanamvaishali.action.StatesAction">
14          <result>/admin/manageStates.jsp</result>
15       </action>
16
17       <action name="doInsertState" method="saveState"
          class="com.sharanamvaishali.action.StatesAction">
18          <interceptor-ref name="defaultStack"/>
19          <interceptor-ref name="token"/>
20          <result name="success" type="redirectAction">doViewStates</result>
21          <result name="input">/admin/manageStates.jsp</result>
22       </action>
23
24       <action name="doViewStates" method="view"
          class="com.sharanamvaishali.action.StatesAction">
25          <result name="success">/admin/manageStates.jsp</result>
26          <result name="error" type="redirectAction">showManageStates</result>
27       </action>
28
29       <action name="doDeleteState" method="removeState"
          class="com.sharanamvaishali.action.StatesAction">
30          <result name="success" type="redirectAction">doViewStates</result>
31          <result name="error">/admin/manageStates.jsp</result>
32       </action>
33
34       <action name="showEditState" method="editState"
          class="com.sharanamvaishali.action.StatesAction">
35          <result name="success">/admin/manageStates.jsp</result>
36       </action>
37    </package>
38  </struts>
```

Explanation:

The following section describes the above code spec.

showManageStates.action

showManageStates is an action to help viewing.

This means the data entry form and the list of state details are displayed.

The list of state details are retrieved by **StatesAction's view()**.

iterateManageStatesPage.action

iterateManageStatesPage is an action to help iterate.

This means displaying 10 records of state details per page in the form of data grid.

This iterated data is retrieved by **StatesAction's getPage()**.

doInsertState.action

doInsertState is an action to help adding new state details or updating existing state details.

defaultStack interceptor is referenced, which a complete stack with all the common interceptors in place.

token interceptor is referenced, which checks for valid token presence in Action and prevents duplicate form submission.

doInsertState.action:

- ❑ Calls **StatesAction's saveState()** to add new state details or update the existing state details
- ❑ Ensures that the captured data is valid
- ❑ If the validation is successful then the data is saved and the result is redirected to **doViewStates.action**
- ❑ If the validation fails then the Manage States page along with error messages is displayed

doViewStates.action

doViewStates is an action to help viewing.

This means the list of state details is displayed.

The list of state details are retrieved by **StatesAction**'s **view()**.

If there are no data available in the database then the error message is displayed in the Manage States page by redirecting the page to **showManageStates.action**.

doDeleteState.action

In case, the user chooses to delete a state and clicks ✖, **doDeleteState.action** is the action to help delete a state record from Manage States.

doDeleteState.action:

❏ Calls **StatesAction**'s **removeState()** to delete a state record

❏ If the state record is deleted successfully then the result is redirected to **doViewStates.action**

❏ If the record being deleted is referenced by a record in another database table then the Manage States page displays the error message indicating that this record cannot be deleted

showEditState.action

showEditState is an action to help the editing of existing states.

In case, the user chooses to edit a state and clicks that particular record, **showEditState.action** helps fill up the Manage States form with state details.

showEditState.action:

❏ Calls **StatesAction**'s **editState()** to retrieve the state details

❏ Returns to the Manage States page along with the data to be populated in the form

Domain Class [States.java]

This is a domain class with the following specifications:

Class Name	Package	Implements
States	com.sharanamvaishali.model	java.io.Serializable

Properties			
Property Name	Property Type	Methods	
StateNo	Integer	getStateNo()	setStateNo()
State	String	getState()	setState()

Code Spec

```
1   package com.sharanamvaishali.model;
2
3   import javax.persistence.Column;
4   import javax.persistence.Entity;
5   import javax.persistence.GeneratedValue;
6   import javax.persistence.Id;
7   import javax.persistence.Table;
8
9   @Entity
10  @Table(name="STATES")
11  public class States implements java.io.Serializable {
12      @Id
13      @GeneratedValue
14      @Column(name="STATENO")
15      private Integer StateNo;
16      @Column(name="STATE")
17      private String State;
18
19      public States() {
20      }
21
22      public Integer getStateNo() {
23          return StateNo;
24      }
25      public void setStateNo(Integer StateNo) {
26          this.StateNo = StateNo;
27      }
28
29      public String getState() {
30          return State;
31      }
32      public void setState(String State) {
33          this.State = State;
34      }
35  }
```

Chapter

35

SECTION V: BACKEND [ADMINISTRATION] SOFTWARE DESIGN DOCUMENTATION

Manage Categories

This module allows performing the following operations:

❑ Adding new categories

❑ Editing existing categories

❑ Viewing existing categories

❑ Deleting existing categories

This module uses the bms.Categories table to perform the above operations.

This module is made up of the following:

Type	Name	Description
JSP	manageCategories.jsp	The data entry form
Struts 2		
Action	CategoriesAction.java	The action class that facilitates data operations.
Validation	CategoriesAction-validation.xml	The XML based validation file.
DAO Class	CategoriesDAO.java	The interfaces for the DAO layer.
	PaginationDAO.java	
	CategoriesDAOImpl.java	The implementation classes that performs the actual data operations.
	PaginationDAOImpl.java	
Struts Configuration	struts-Categories.xml	Struts configuration file.
Hibernate		
Mapping	hibernate.cfg.xml	The mapping file that holds Model class mapping.
Model Class	Categories.java	The model class.

JSP [manageCategories.jsp]

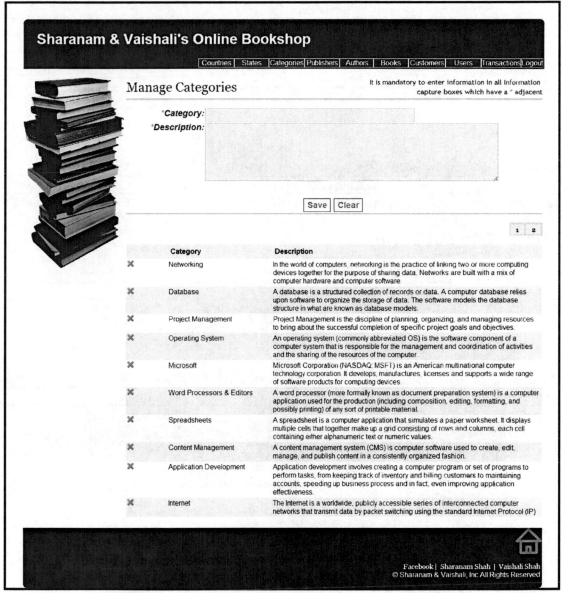

Diagram 35.1: Manage Categories [Data entry form]

This is a JSP which holds a data entry form, as shown in diagram 35.1. This form appears when the user clicks **Categories**.

Form Specifications

File Name	manageCategories.jsp
Title	BookShop[Sharanam & Vaishali Shah] - Manage Categories
Bound To Table	bms.Categories
Form Name	frmCategories
Action	doInsertCategory
Method	POST

Data Fields

Label	Name	Bound To	Validation Rules
Category	category.Category	Categories.Category	Cannot be left blank
Description	category.Description	Categories.Description	Cannot be left blank

Micro-Help For Form Fields

Form Field	Micro Help Statement
category.Category	Enter the category name
category.Description	Enter the description of the category

Data Controls

Object	Label	Name
s:submit	Save	btnSubmit
s:reset	Clear	btnReset

Code Spec

```
1   <%@page contentType="text/html" pageEncoding="UTF-8"%>
2   <%@ taglib prefix="s" uri="/struts-tags" %>
3   <!DOCTYPE HTML PUBLIC "-//W3C//DTD HTML 4.01 Transitional//EN"
4     "http://www.w3.org/TR/html4/loose.dtd">
5   <html xmlns="http://www.w3.org/1999/xhtml">
6     <head>
7       <title>BookShop [Sharanam & Vaishali Shah] - Manage Categories</title>
8       <meta http-equiv="content-type" content="text/html; charset=iso-8859-1">
9       <link href="/BookShop/css/admin.css" type="text/css" rel="stylesheet">
10      <s:head/>
11    </head>
12    <body>
13      <s:include value="header.jsp" />
14      <br>
15      <s:form action="doInsertCategory" method="post" name="frmCategories"
```

```
            id="frmCategories" validate="true">
16          <s:token/>
17          <s:hidden name="category.CategoryNo" id="CategoryNo"/>
18          <table width="100%" border="0" align="center" cellpadding="0" cellspacing="0">
19              <tr>
20                  <td valign="top" width="20%">
21                      <img src="/BookShop/images/leftImg.jpg" height="350"/>
22                  </td>
23                  <td valign="top">
24                      <table width="100%" border="0" align="center" cellpadding="0"
                        cellspacing="0">
25                          <tr>
26                              <td>
27                                  <table border="0" cellpadding="0" cellspacing="0"
                                    width="100%">
28                                      <tr>
29                                          <td class="manageForms">Manage Categories</td>
30                                          <td class="information">
31                                              It is mandatory to enter information in all information
                                            <br>capture boxes which have a <span
                                            class="mandatory">*</span> adjacent
32                                          </td>
33                                      </tr>
34                                  </table>
35                              </td>
36                          </tr>
37                          <tr><td class="hrLine"> </td></tr>
38                          <tr align="left" valign="top">
39                              <td>
40                                  <table width="90%" border="0" align="center" cellpadding="0"
                                    cellspacing="0">
41                                      <tr>
42                                          <td>
43                                              <table width="100%" border="0" cellpadding="0"
                                            cellspacing="0">
44                                                  <s:textfield required="true" requiredposition="left"
                                                id="Category" label="Category"
                                                name="category.Category" title="Enter the category
                                                name" maxLength="25" size="55"/>
45                                                  <s:textarea required="true" requiredposition="left"
                                                id="Description" label="Description"
                                                name="category.Description" title="Enter the description
                                                of the category" cols="80" rows="5"></s:textarea>
46                                                  <s:actionerror/>
47                                              </table>
48                                          </td>
49                                      </tr>
50                                      <tr>
51                                          <td style="text-align: center;">
52                                              <br /><br />
53                                              <s:submit theme="simple" cssClass="groovybutton"
                                                name="btnSubmit" id="btnSubmit" value="Save" />
54                                              <s:reset theme="simple" cssClass="groovybutton"
                                                name="btnReset" id="btnReset" value="Clear"
                                                onclick="javascript:document.location.href='showManageCa
```

```
                                                tegories.action'"/>
55                                          </td>
56                                      </tr>
57                                  </table>
58                              </td>
59                          </tr>
60                          <tr><td class="hrLine"> </td></tr>
61                          <tr>
62                              <td align="center">
63                                  <table width="60px" border="0" align="right" cellpadding="3"
                                    cellspacing="1" style="border:#c3bca4 1px solid">
64                                      <tr>
65                                          <s:bean name="org.apache.struts2.util.Counter"
                                            id="counter">
66                                              <s:param name="last" value="%{pageCount}" />
67                                          </s:bean>
68                                          <s:iterator value="#counter">
69                                              <td align="center" width="2px" style="border:#c3bca4
                                                1px solid; background:#efebde; font-family:sans-serif;
                                                font-size:12px; font-weight:bolder; text-align:center;
                                                vertical-align:middle;">
70                                                  <a href="<s:url
                                                    action="iterateManageCategoriesPage"><s:param
                                                    name="pageNo"><s:property
                                                    /></s:param></s:url>"><s:property /></a>
71                                              </td>
72                                          </s:iterator>
73                                      </tr>
74                                  </table>
75                              </td>
76                          </tr>
77                          <tr>
78                              <td>
79                                  <br>
80                                  <table class="view" align="center" cellspacing="0" cellpadding="0"
                                    width="100%">
81                                      <tr>
82                                          <th width="10%" align="center"> </th>
83                                          <th width="25%" class="Arial13BrownB"
                                            align="left">Category</th>
84                                          <th width="65%" class="Arial13BrownB"
                                            align="left">Description</th>
85                                      </tr>
86                                      <s:iterator value="categories" id="categories" status="stat">
87                                          <tr title="Click to edit" class="<s:if test="#stat.odd ==
                                            true">odd</s:if><s:else>even</s:else>">
88                                              <td width="10%" valign="top">
89                                                  <a href="<s:url action="doDeleteCategory"><s:param
                                                    name="category.CategoryNo" value="CategoryNo"
                                                    /></s:url>">
90                                                      <img src="/BookShop/images/TrashIcon.png"
                                                        border="0" alt="Delete" style="cursor:pointer;"/>
91                                                  </a>
92                                              </td>
93                                              <td width="25%" class="manageList"
```

```
              onclick="javascript:location.href='<s:url
              action='showEditCategory'><s:param
              name='category.CategoryNo' value='CategoryNo'
              /></s:url>'">
94                <s:property value="Category"/>
95              </td>
96              <td width="65%" class="manageList"
              onclick="javascript:location.href='<s:url
              action='showEditCategory'><s:param
              name='category.CategoryNo' value='CategoryNo'
              /></s:url>'">
97                <s:property value="Description"/>
98              </td>
99            </tr>
100          </s:iterator>
101          <s:if test="#categories==null">
102            <span class="emptyMessage">Currently there exists no
              categories in the database. Please add a few categories to
              begin managing them.</span>
103          </s:if>
104        </table>
105      </td>
106    </tr>
107    </table>
108    </td>
109    </tr>
110    </table>
111    </s:form>
112    <s:include value="adminFooter.jsp" />
113    </body>
114  </html>
```

Explanation:

This is a standard data entry form, which captures the category details. By default, when the form loads, it is in the **INSERT** and **VIEW** mode. The form also has Delete and Edit options to delete and edit a particular category record.

<s:textarea>

<s:textfield> renders a HTML TEXTAREA field:

```
<s:textarea required="true" requiredposition="left"
id="Description" label="Description"
name="category.Description" title="Enter the description
of the category" cols="80" rows="5"></s:textarea>
```

Where:

❑ **required** indicates that the input is required

❑ **requiredposition** defines the required position of the required form element [left or right]

❑   **id** is the HTML id attribute

❑   **label** is the label expression used for rendering Description's label

❑   **name** is the name of the text field. Here, **category** is the domain object set in the action class for **Categories** model and Description is the JavaBean property set in the Categories model

❑   **title** is the micro help for the form fields

❑   **cols** is the number of columns

❑   **rows** is the number of rows

Action [CategoriesAction.java]

This is an action class with the following specifications:

Class Name	CategoriesAction
Package	com.sharanamvaishali.action
Extends	ActionSupport
Implements	- -

Objects		
Object Name	**Class Name**	**Object Type**
categoriesDAO	CategoriesDAO	Data Access Layer
pg	PaginationDAO	Data Access Layer
category	Categories	Model

Properties		
Property Name	**Property Type**	**Methods**
For the data entry form fields		
category	Categories	getCategory() setCategory()
For the data grid population		
categories	List<Categories>	getCategories() setCategories()
For pagination		
pageNo	int	getPageNo() setPageNo()
pageCount	int	getPageCount() setPageCount()

Methods	
Method Name	**Return Values**
saveCategory()	SUCCESS
view()	SUCCESS
removeCategory()	SUCCESS ERROR
editCategory()	SUCCESS
getPage()	SUCCESS

Code Spec

```
1   package com.sharanamvaishali.action;
2
3   import com.opensymphony.xwork2.ActionSupport;
4   import com.sharanamvaishali.dao.CategoriesDAO;
5   import com.sharanamvaishali.dao.CategoriesDAOImpl;
6   import com.sharanamvaishali.dao.PaginationDAO;
7   import com.sharanamvaishali.dao.PaginationDAOImpl;
8   import com.sharanamvaishali.model.Categories;
9   import java.util.List;
10  import org.apache.struts2.interceptor.validation.SkipValidation;
11
12  public class CategoriesAction extends ActionSupport{
13      private CategoriesDAO categoriesDAO = new CategoriesDAOImpl();
14
15      private PaginationDAO pg = new PaginationDAOImpl();
16
17      private Categories category;
18
19      private List<Categories> categories;
20
21      private int pageNo, pageCount;
22
23      public int getPageNo() {
24          return pageNo;
25      }
26      public void setPageNo(int pageNo) {
27          this.pageNo = pageNo;
28      }
29
30      public int getPageCount() {
31          return pageCount;
32      }
33      public void setPageCount(int pageCount) {
34          this.pageCount = pageCount;
35      }
36
37      public Categories getCategory() {
38          return category;
39      }
40      public void setCategory(Categories category) {
41          this.category = category;
42      }
43
44      public List<Categories> getCategories() {
45          return categories;
46      }
```

```
47      public void setCategories(List<Categories> categories) {
48          this.categories = categories;
49      }
50
51      public String saveCategory() throws Exception{
52          if(category.getCategoryNo() != null) {
53              categoriesDAO.updateCategory(category);
54          } else {
55              categoriesDAO.saveCategory(category);
56          }
57          return SUCCESS;
58      }
59
60      @SkipValidation
61      public String view() throws Exception{
62          pageNo = 1;
63          getPage();
64          return SUCCESS;
65      }
66
67      @SkipValidation
68      public String removeCategory() throws Exception{
69          try{
70              categoriesDAO.deleteCategory(category.getCategoryNo());
71          } catch(Exception e) {
72              addActionError(e.getCause().toString().split("[:]")[1]);
73              return ERROR;
74          }
75          return SUCCESS;
76      }
77
78      @SkipValidation
79      public String editCategory() throws Exception{
80          category = categoriesDAO.getCategoryById(category.getCategoryNo());
81          view();
82          return SUCCESS;
83      }
84
85      @SkipValidation
86      public String getPage() throws Exception{
87          pageCount = pg.getTotalPages("Categories");
88          categories = pg.getPage(pageNo-1, "Categories").getList();
89          return SUCCESS;
90      }
91  }
```

Explanation:

The following section describes the above code spec.

saveCategory()

saveCategory() is invoked when the user keys in the desired data and clicks **Save** .

saveCategory():

❑ Performs an update operation [using CategoriesDAO's updateCategory()] if **category.getCategoryNo()** returns a valid CategoryNo

❑ Performs an insert operation [using CategoriesDAO's saveCategory()] if **category.getCategoryNo()** returns empty

view()

view() is invoked every time Manage Categories is served.

It invokes **getPage()** to populate the List object [categories] which is used in the JSP page's **<s:iterator>** to populate the data grid. This data grid displays existing records from the **Categories** database table.

@SkipValidation is used to skip validation for this method.

removeCategory()

removeCategory() is invoked when the user clicks ✖ adjacent to the desired record [in the data grid] for deletion.

The delete operation is performed by invoking CategoriesDAO's **deleteCategory()**.

deleteCategory() is passed **CategoryNo** which is made available by JSP using **<s:param>** on click of ✖.

@SkipValidation is used to skip validation for this method.

editCategory()

editCategory() is invoked when the user clicks a desired record from the data grid in Manage Categories for updating it.

It populates the bean class object [category] with the chosen record's data. The data is retrieved using CategoriesDAO's **getCategoryById()** which is passed CategoryNo which is made available by JSP's <s:param> on click of the record.

Struts 2 framework automatically transfers the values from the bean class object to the FORM fields thus making it available to the user for editing the same.

@SkipValidation is used to skip validation for this method.

getPage()

getPage() is invoked every time Manage Categories is served or the user clicks a page number link from Manage Categories using pagination.

It calculates the total number of pages for pagination purpose and stores the same in the property named **pageCount**.

It populates the List object [categories] which is used in the JSP page's <s:iterator> to form the data grid. This data grid displays existing records from the Categories database table.

The data to be populated in the List object is retrieved using PaginationDAO's **getPage()** which returns the records belonging to the appropriate page number.

@SkipValidation is used to skip validation for this method.

DAO Class

Interface [CategoriesDAO.java]

This is a Data Access Object interface with the following specifications:

Class Name	Package
CategoriesDAO	com.sharanamvaishali.dao

Code Spec

```
1   package com.sharanamvaishali.dao;
2
3   import com.sharanamvaishali.model.Categories;
4
5   public interface CategoriesDAO {
6       public void saveCategory(Categories categories);
7       public void updateCategory(Categories categories);
8       public void deleteCategory(int CategoryNo);
9       public Categories getCategoryById(int CategoryNo);
10  }
```

Implementation Class [CategoriesDAOImpl.java]

This is a **Data Access Object** class with the following specifications:

Class Name	CategoriesDAOImpl
Package	com.sharanamvaishali.dao
Implements	CategoriesDAO

Objects	
Object Name	**Class Name**
session	Session
transaction	Transaction

Methods		
Method Name	**Arguments**	**Return Values**
saveCategory()	Categories categories	void
updateCategory()	Categories categories	void
deleteCategory()	Integer CategoryNo	void
getCategoryById()	Integer CategoryNo	Categories

Code Spec

```
1   package com.sharanamvaishali.dao;
2
3   import com.sharanamvaishali.model.Categories;
4   import com.sharanamvaishali.utility.HibernateUtil;
5   import org.hibernate.Session;
6   import org.hibernate.Transaction;
7
8   public class CategoriesDAOImpl implements CategoriesDAO {
9       Session session = HibernateUtil.getSession();
10      Transaction transaction;
11
12      @Override
13      public void saveCategory(Categories categories) {
14          try {
15              transaction = session.beginTransaction();
16              session.save(categories);
17              transaction.commit();
18          } catch (RuntimeException e) {
19              if(categories != null) {
20                  transaction.rollback();
```

```
21              }
22              throw e;
23          }
24      }
25
26      @Override
27      public void updateCategory(Categories categories) {
28          try {
29              transaction = session.beginTransaction();
30              session.update(categories);
31              transaction.commit();
32          } catch (RuntimeException e) {
33              if(categories != null) {
34                  transaction.rollback();
35              }
36              throw e;
37          }
38      }
39
40      @Override
41      public void deleteCategory(int CategoryNo) {
42          Object Categories = null;
43          try {
44              transaction = session.beginTransaction();
45              Categories = session.load(Categories.class, CategoryNo);
46              session.delete(Categories);
47              transaction.commit();
48          } catch (RuntimeException e) {
49              if(Categories != null) {
50                  transaction.rollback();
51              }
52              throw e;
53          }
54      }
55
56      @Override
57      public Categories getCategoryById(int CategoryNo) {
58          return (Categories) session.createQuery("FROM Categories WHERE
            CategoryNo = :CategoryNo").setInteger("CategoryNo",
            CategoryNo).uniqueResult();
59      }
60  }
```

Explanation:

The following section describes the above code spec.

saveCategory()

saveCategory() does the actual saving of the category in the Categories database table.

saveCategory() uses **save()** of Session, which takes care of adding new category details when the user has entered all the category details and clicked **Save**.

After the save operation is performed, the transaction is committed to make the changes permanent.

Whilst performing the save operation, if a runtime exception occurs, than the transaction is **rolled back**.

updateCategory()

updateCategory() does the actual updation of the existing category in the Categories database table.

updateCategory() uses **update()** of Session, which takes care of updating an existing category details when the user has made changes to the existing category details and clicked **Save**.

After the update operation is performed, the transaction is committed to make the changes permanent.

Whilst performing the update operation, if a runtime exception occurs, than the transaction is **rolled back**.

deleteCategory()

deleteCategory() deletes the appropriate category based on **CategoryNo** received as a reference.

This method uses:

❑ **load()** of Session, which retrieves the appropriate Category to be deleted using CategoryNo as a reference

❑ **delete()** of Session, which deletes the category from the Categories database table

After the delete operation is performed, the transaction is committed to make the changes permanent.

Whilst performing the delete operation, if a runtime exception occurs, than the transaction is rolled back.

getCategoryById()

getCategoryById() returns the appropriate category's object from the Categories database table using **CategoryNo** as the reference.

This method uses:

- **createQuery()** of Session, which creates a new instance of Query to retrieve the Category details using CategoryNo as reference
- **setInteger()** of Query, which states the parameter to be used as the WHERE clause criteria when querying the Categories database table
- **uniqueResult()** of Query, which ensures that only unique record is retrieved from the Categories database table and prevents any kinds of errors

REMINDER

PaginationDAOImpl.java is explained later in the *Section V: Backend [Administration] Software Design Documentation* under the *Chapter 42: Common Files*.

Validations [CategoriesAction-validation.xml]

If the required **input** fields are kept empty whilst submitting the form, CategoriesAction-validation.xml takes care of the validations.

Code Spec

```
1   <?xml version="1.0" encoding="UTF-8"?>
2   <!DOCTYPE validators PUBLIC '-//OpenSymphony Group//XWork Validator
    1.0.2//EN' 'http://www.opensymphony.com/xwork/xwork-validator-1.0.2.dtd'>
3   <validators>
4     <field name="category.Category">
5       <field-validator type="requiredstring">
6         <message>Please enter the category name.</message>
7       </field-validator>
8     </field>
9
10    <field name="category.Description">
11      <field-validator type="requiredstring">
12        <message>Please enter the category description.</message>
13      </field-validator>
```

```
14     </field>
15   </validators>
```

If any Errors are detected the data entry form is re-served with appropriate error messages, as shown in diagram 35.2.

struts-Categories.xml file holds a mapping to serve the data entry form:

```
17       <action name="doInsertCategory" method="saveCategory"
         class="com.sharanamvaishali.action.CategoriesAction">
18          <interceptor-ref name="defaultStack"/>
19          <interceptor-ref name="token"/>
20          <result name="success"
            type="redirectAction">doViewCategories</result>
21          <result name="input">/admin/manageCategories.jsp</result>
22       </action>
```

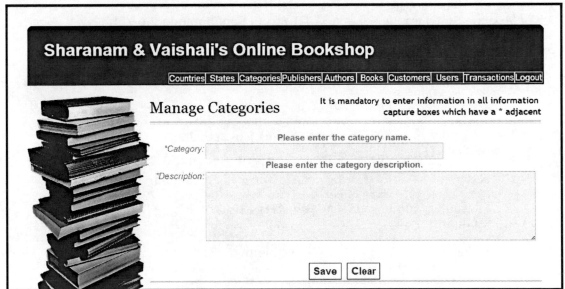

Diagram 35.2: Error messages

Struts Configuration [struts-Categories.xml]

This is the struts configuration file with the following specifications:

File Name	Package Name	Extends
Categories	manageCategories	default

Actions	
Action Name	**Results**
showManageCategories	SUCCESS - manageCategories.jsp
iterateManageCategoriesPage	SUCCESS - manageCategories.jsp
doInsertCategory	SUCCESS - doViewCategories
	INPUT - manageCategories.jsp
doViewCategories	SUCCESS - manageCategories.jsp
	ERROR - showManageCategories
doDeleteCategory	SUCCESS - doViewCategories
	ERROR - manageCategories.jsp
showEditCategory	SUCCESS - manageCategories.jsp

Code Spec

```
1   <?xml version="1.0" encoding="UTF-8"?>
2   <!DOCTYPE struts PUBLIC
3   "-//Apache Software Foundation//DTD Struts Configuration 2.0//EN"
4   "http://struts.apache.org/dtds/struts-2.0.dtd">
5   <struts>
6     <package name="manageCategories" extends="default">
7       <default-interceptor-ref name="chkSession"/>
8
9       <action name="showManageCategories" method="view"
        class="com.sharanamvaishali.action.CategoriesAction">
10        <result>/admin/manageCategories.jsp</result>
11      </action>
12
13      <action name="iterateManageCategoriesPage" method="getPage"
        class="com.sharanamvaishali.action.CategoriesAction">
14        <result>/admin/manageCategories.jsp</result>
15      </action>
16
17      <action name="doInsertCategory" method="saveCategory"
        class="com.sharanamvaishali.action.CategoriesAction">
18        <interceptor-ref name="defaultStack"/>
19        <interceptor-ref name="token"/>
20        <result name="success"
          type="redirectAction">doViewCategories</result>
21        <result name="input">/admin/manageCategories.jsp</result>
22      </action>
23
24      <action name="doViewCategories" method="view"
        class="com.sharanamvaishali.action.CategoriesAction">
25        <result name="success">/admin/manageCategories.jsp</result>
26        <result name="error"
          type="redirectAction">showManageCategories</result>
```

```
27        </action>
28
29        <action name="doDeleteCategory" method="removeCategory"
          class="com.sharanamvaishali.action.CategoriesAction">
30           <result name="success"
             type="redirectAction">doViewCategories</result>
31           <result name="error">/admin/manageCategories.jsp</result>
32        </action>
33
34        <action name="showEditCategory" method="editCategory"
          class="com.sharanamvaishali.action.CategoriesAction">
35           <result name="success">admin/manageCategories.jsp</result>
36        </action>
37     </package>
38  </struts>
```

Explanation:

The following section describes the above code spec.

showManageCategories.action

showManageCategories is an action to help viewing.

This means the data entry form and the list of category details are displayed.

The list of category details are retrieved by **CategoriesAction's view()**.

iterateManageCategoriesPage.action

iterateManageCategoriesPage is an action to help iterate.

This means displaying 10 records of category details per page in the form of data grid.

This iterated data is retrieved by **CategoriesAction's getPage()**.

doInsertCategory.action

doInsertCategory is an action to help adding new category details or updating existing category details.

defaultStack interceptor is referenced, which a complete stack with all the common interceptors in place.

token interceptor is referenced, which checks for valid token presence in Action and prevents duplicate form submission.

doInsertCategory.action:

❑ Calls **CategoriesAction's saveCategory()** to add new category details or update the existing category details

❑ Ensures that the captured data is valid

❑ If the validation is successful then the data is saved and the result is redirected to **doViewCategories.action**

❑ If the validation fails then the Manage Categories page along with error messages is displayed

doViewCategories.action

doViewCategories is an action to help viewing.

This means the list of category details is displayed.

The list of category details are retrieved by **CategoriesAction's view()**.

If there are no data available in the database then the error message is displayed in the Manage Categories page by redirecting the page to **showManageCategories.action**.

doDeleteCategory.action

In case, the user chooses to delete a category and clicks ✖, **doDeleteCategory.action** is the action to help delete a category record from Manage Categories.

doDeleteCategory.action:

❑ Calls **CategoriesAction's removeCategory()** to delete a category record

❑ If the category record is deleted successfully then the result is redirected to **doViewCategories.action**

❑ If the record being deleted is referenced by a record in another database table then the Manage Categories page displays the error message indicating that this record cannot be deleted

showEditCategory.action

showEditCategory is an action to help the editing of existing categories.

In case, the user chooses to edit a category and clicks that particular record, **showEditCategory.action** helps fill up the Manage Categories form with category details.

showEditCategory.action:

❑ Calls **CategoriesAction's editCategory()** to retrieve the category details

❑ Returns to the Manage Categories page along with the data to be populated in the form

Domain Class [Categories.java]

This is a domain class with the following specifications:

Class Name	Package	Implements
Categories	com.sharanamvaishali.model	java.io.Serializable

Properties			
Property Name	**Property Type**	**Methods**	
CategoryNo	Integer	getCategoryNo()	setCategoryNo()
Category	String	getCategory()	setCategory()
Description	String	getDescription()	setDescription()

Code Spec

```
1   package com.sharanamvaishali.model;
2
3   import javax.persistence.Column;
4   import javax.persistence.Entity;
5   import javax.persistence.GeneratedValue;
6   import javax.persistence.Id;
7   import javax.persistence.Table;
8
9   @Entity
10  @Table(name="CATEGORIES")
11  public class Categories implements java.io.Serializable {
12      @Id
13      @GeneratedValue
14      @Column(name="CATEGORYNO")
15      private Integer CategoryNo;
16      @Column(name="CATEGORY")
17      private String Category;
18      @Column(name="DESCRIPTION")
19      private String Description;
20
21      public Categories() {
22      }
23
```

```
24      public Integer getCategoryNo() {
25          return CategoryNo;
26      }
27      public void setCategoryNo(Integer CategoryNo) {
28          this.CategoryNo = CategoryNo;
29      }
30
31      public String getCategory() {
32          return Category;
33      }
34      public void setCategory(String Category) {
35          this.Category = Category;
36      }
37
38      public String getDescription() {
39          return Description;
40      }
41      public void setDescription(String Description) {
42          this.Description = Description;
43      }
44  }
```

Chapter

36

SECTION V: BACKEND [ADMINISTRATION] SOFTWARE DESIGN DOCUMENTATION

Manage Publishers

This module allows performing the following operations:

❑ Adding new publishers

❑ Editing existing publishers

❑ Viewing existing publishers

❑ Deleting existing publishers

This module uses the bms.Publishers table to perform the above operations.

This module is made up of the following:

Type	Name	Description
JSP	managePublishers.jsp	The data entry form
Struts 2		
Action	PublishersAction.java	The action class that facilitates data operations.
Validation	PublishersAction-validation.xml	The XML based validation file.
DAO Class	PublishersDAO.java	The interfaces for the DAO layer.
	PaginationDAO.java	
	PopulateDdlbsDAO.java	
	PublishersDAOImpl.java	The implementation classes that performs the actual data operations.
	PaginationDAOImpl.java	
	PopulateDdlbsDAOImpl.java	
Utility Class	PopulateDdlbs.java	The class that populates the list objects.
Struts Configuration	struts-Publishers.xml	Struts configuration file.
Hibernate		
Mapping	hibernate.cfg.xml	The mapping file that holds Model class mapping.
Model Class	Publishers.java	The model class.

JSP [managePublishers.jsp]

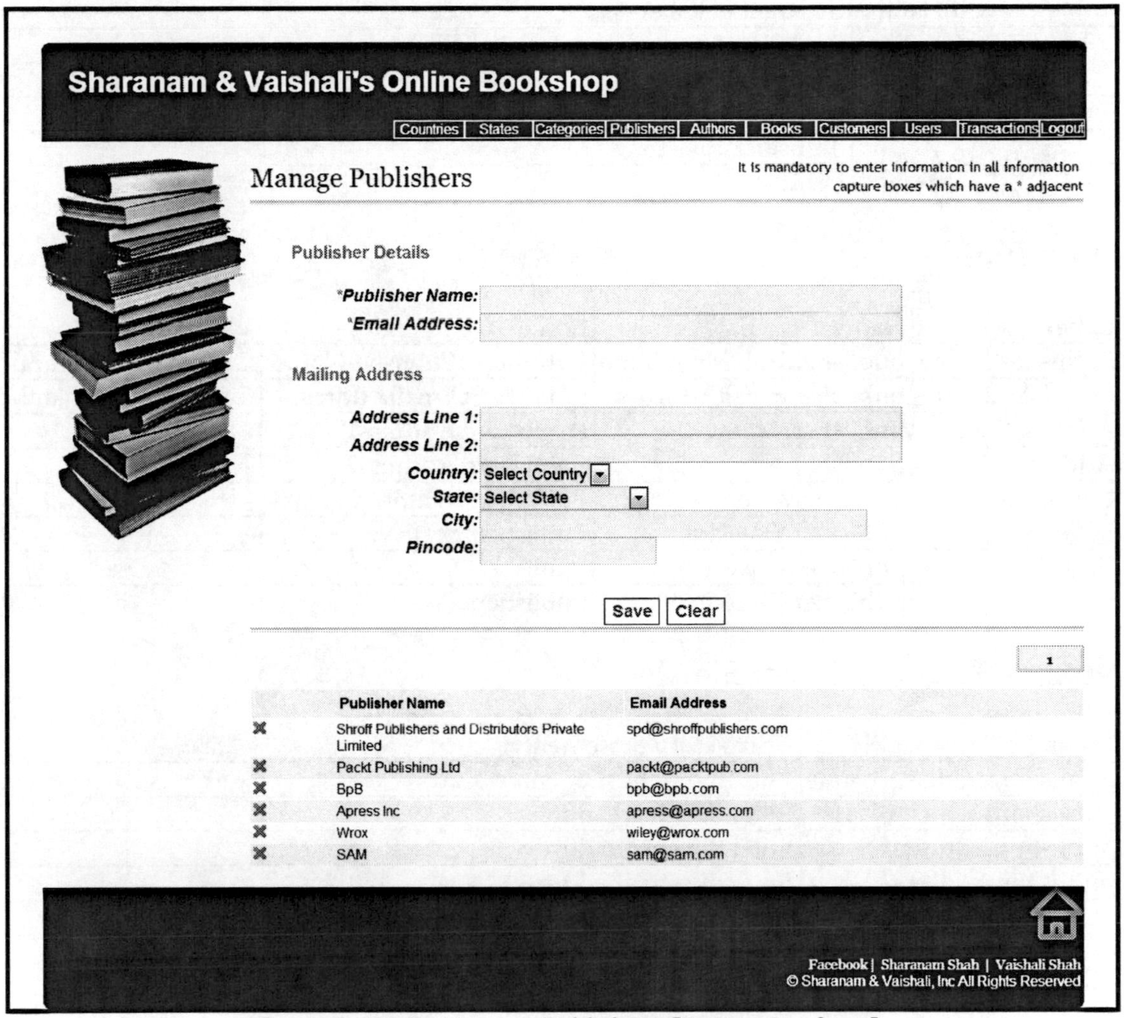

Diagram 36.1: Manage Publishers [Data entry form]

This is a JSP which holds a data entry form, as shown in diagram 36.1. This form appears when the user clicks **Publishers**.

Form Specifications

File Name	managePublishers.jsp
Title	BookShop[Sharanam & Vaishali Shah] - Manage Publishers
Bound To Table	bms.Publishers
Form Name	frmPublishers
Action	doInsertPublisher
Method	POST

Data Fields

Label	Name	Bound To	Validation Rules
Publisher Name	publisher.PublisherName	Publishers.PublisherName	Cannot be left blank
Email Address	publisher.EmailAddress	Publishers.EmailAddress	Cannot be left blank
Address Line 1	publisher.Address1	Publishers.Address1	- -
Address Line 2	publisher.Address2	Publishers.Address2	- -
Country	publisher.CountryNo	Publishers.CountryNo	- -
State	publisher.StateNo	Publishers.StateNo	- -
City	publisher.City	Publishers.City	- -
Pincode	publisher.Pincode	Publishers.Pincode	- -

Micro-Help For Form Fields

Form Field	Micro Help Statement
publisher.PublisherName	Enter the publisher name
publisher.EmailAddress	Enter the email address
publisher.Address1	Enter the street address
publisher.Address2	Enter the street address
publisher.CountryNo	Select country
publisher.StateNo	Select state
publisher.City	Enter the city name
publisher.Pincode	Enter the pincode

Data Controls

Object	Label	Name
s:submit	Save	btnSubmit
s:reset	Clear	btnReset

Code Spec

```
1   <%@page contentType="text/html" pageEncoding="UTF-8"%>
2   <%@ taglib prefix="s" uri="/struts-tags" %>
3   <!DOCTYPE HTML PUBLIC "-//W3C//DTD HTML 4.01 Transitional//EN"
4     "http://www.w3.org/TR/html4/loose.dtd">
5   <html xmlns="http://www.w3.org/1999/xhtml">
6     <head>
7       <title>BookShop [Sharanam & Vaishali Shah] - Manage Publishers</title>
8       <meta http-equiv="content-type" content="text/html; charset=iso-8859-1">
9       <link href="/BookShop/css/admin.css" type="text/css" rel="stylesheet">
10      <s:head/>
11    </head>
12    <body>
13      <s:include value="header.jsp" />
14      <br>
15      <s:form action="doInsertPublisher" method="post" name="frmPublishers"
        id="frmPublishers" validate="true">
16        <s:token/>
17        <s:hidden name="publisher.PublisherNo" id="PublisherNo"/>
18        <table width="100%" border="0" align="center" cellpadding="0" cellspacing="0">
19          <tr>
20            <td valign="top" width="20%">
21              <img src="/BookShop/images/leftImg.jpg" height="350"/>
22            </td>
23            <td valign="top">
24              <table width="100%" border="0" align="center" cellpadding="0"
              cellspacing="0">
25                <tr>
26                  <td>
27                    <table border="0" cellpadding="0" cellspacing="0"
                    width="100%">
28                      <tr>
29                        <td class="manageForms">Manage Publishers</td>
30                        <td class="information" valign="top" align="right">
31                          It is mandatory to enter information in all information
                          <br>capture boxes which have a <span
                          class="mandatory">*</span> adjacent
32                        </td>
33                      </tr>
34                    </table>
35                  </td>
36                </tr>
37                <tr><td class="hrLine"> </td></tr>
38                <tr align="left" valign="top">
39                  <td>
40                    <table width="90%" border="0" align="center" cellpadding="0"
                    cellspacing="0">
41                      <tr>
42                        <td>
43                          <table width="100%" border="0" cellpadding="0"
                          cellspacing="0">
44                            <tr>
```

```
45                                    <td class="Arial16BlueB">
46                                       <br />Publisher Details<br /><br />
47                                    </td>
48                                 </tr>
49                                 <s:actionerror/>
50                                 <s:textfield required="true" requiredposition="left"
                                 id="PublisherName" label="Publisher Name"
                                 name="publisher.PublisherName" title="Enter the
                                 publisher name" maxLength="50" size="55"/>
51                                 <s:textfield required="true" requiredposition="left"
                                 id="EmailAddress" label="Email Address"
                                 name="publisher.EmailAddress" title="Enter the email
                                 address" maxLength="50" size="55"/>
52                                 <tr>
53                                    <td class="Arial16BlueB">
54                                       <br />Mailing Address<br /><br />
55                                    </td>
56                                 </tr>
57                                 <s:textfield id="Address1" label="Address Line 1"
                                 name="publisher.Address1" title="Enter the street
                                 address" maxLength="50" size="55"/>
58                                 <s:textfield id="Address2" label="Address Line 2"
                                 name="publisher.Address2" title="Enter the street
                                 address" maxLength="50" size="55"/>
59                                 <s:select list="ddlb.ddlbCountries" listKey="CountryNo"
                                 listValue="Country" headerKey="" headerValue="Select
                                 country" id="CountryNo" name="publisher.CountryNo"
                                 label="Country" title="Select the country"></s:select>
60                                 <s:select list="ddlb.ddlbStates" listKey="StateNo"
                                 listValue="State" headerKey="" headerValue="Select
                                 state" id="StateNo" name="publisher.StateNo"
                                 label="State" title="Select the state"></s:select>
61                                 <s:textfield id="City" label="City"
                                 name="publisher.City" title="Enter the city name"
                                 maxLength="50" size="50"/>
62                                 <s:textfield id="Pincode" label="Pincode"
                                 name="publisher.Pincode" title="Enter the pincode"
                                 maxLength="15" size="20"/>
63                                 </table>
64                              </td>
65                           </tr>
66                           <tr>
67                              <td style="text-align: center;">
68                                 <br /><br />
69                                 <s:submit theme="simple" cssClass="groovybutton"
                                 name="btnSubmit" id="btnSubmit" value="Save" />
70                                 <s:reset theme="simple" cssClass="groovybutton"
                                 name="btnReset" id="btnReset" value="Clear"
                                 onclick="javascript:document.location.href='showManageP
                                 ublishers.action'"/>
71                              </td>
72                           </tr>
73                        </table>
74                     </td>
```

```
75                     </tr>
76                     <tr><td class="hrLine"> </td></tr>
77                     <tr>
78                        <td align="center">
79                          <table width="60px" border="0" align="right" cellpadding="3"
                             cellspacing="1" style="border:#c3bca4 1px solid">
80                            <tr>
81                              <s:bean name="org.apache.struts2.util.Counter"
                                 id="counter">
82                                 <s:param name="last" value="%{pageCount}" />
83                              </s:bean>
84                              <s:iterator value="#counter">
85                                 <td align="center" width="2px" style="border:#c3bca4
                                    1px solid; background:#efebde; font-family:sans-serif;
                                    font-size:12px; font-weight:bolder; text-align:center;
                                    vertical-align:middle;">
86                                    <a href="<s:url
                                       action="iterateManagePublishersPage"><s:param
                                       name="pageNo"><s:property
                                       /></s:param></s:url>"><s:property /></a>
87                                 </td>
88                              </s:iterator>
89                            </tr>
90                          </table>
91                        </td>
92                     </tr>
93                     <tr>
94                        <td>
95                          <br>
96                          <table class="view" align="center" cellspacing="0"
                             cellpadding="0" width="100%">
97                            <tr>
98                              <th width="10%" align="center"> </th>
99                              <th width="35%" class="Arial13BrownB"
                                 align="left">Publisher Name</th>
100                             <th width="55%" class="Arial13BrownB" align="left">Email
                                 Address</th>
101                            </tr>
102                            <s:iterator value="publishers" id="publishers" status="stat">
103                              <tr title="Click to edit" class="<s:if test="#stat.odd ==
                                 true">odd</s:if><s:else>even</s:else>">
104                                 <td width="10%" valign="top">
105                                    <a href="<s:url action="doDeletePublisher"><s:param
                                       name="publisher.PublisherNo" value="PublisherNo"
                                       /></s:url>">
106                                       <img src="/BookShop/images/TrashIcon.png"
                                          border="0" alt="Delete" style="cursor:pointer;"/>
107                                    </a>
108                                 </td>
109                                 <td width="35%" class="manageList"
                                    onclick="javascript:location.href='<s:url
                                    action='showEditPublisher'><s:param
                                    name='publisher.PublisherNo' value='PublisherNo'
                                    /></s:url>'">
110                                    <s:property value="PublisherName"/>
```

```
111                                        </td>
112                                        <td width="55%" class="manageList"
                                           onclick="javascript:location.href='<s:url
                                           action='showEditPublisher'><s:param
                                           name='publisher.PublisherNo' value='PublisherNo'
                                           /></s:url>'">
113                                            <s:property value="EmailAddress"/>
114                                        </td>
115                                    </tr>
116                                </s:iterator>
117                                <s:if test="#publishers==null">
118                                    <span class="emptyMessage">Currently there exists no
                                       publishers in the database. Please add a few publishers to
                                       begin managing them.</span>
119                                </s:if>
120                            </table>
121                        </td>
122                    </tr>
123                </table>
124            </td>
125        </tr>
126    </table>
127    </s:form>
128    <s:include value="adminFooter.jsp" />
129    </body>
130 </html>
```

Explanation:

This is a standard data entry form, which captures the publisher details. By default, when the form loads, it is in the **INSERT** and **VIEW** mode. The form also has Delete and Edit options to delete and edit a particular publisher record.

<s:select>

<s:select> renders a HTML INPUT field of type select:

```
<s:select list="ddlb.ddlbCountries" listKey="CountryNo"
listValue="Country" headerKey="" headerValue="Select
country" id="CountryNo" name="publisher.CountryNo"
label="Country" title="Select the country"></s:select>
```

Where:

❑   **list** is the Iterable source to populate from. Here, PopulateDdlbs's contructor is called, where ddlbCountries List object is set. This List object is set by calling PopulateDdlbDAO's getAllCountries()

ddlbCountries = populateDdlbsDAO.getAllCountries();

❑   **listKey** is the property of List object's [ddlbCountries] to get the field value from. Here, the field value is CountryNo

- **listValue** is the property of List object's [ddlbCountries] to get the field content from. Here, the field content is **Country**
- **headerKey** is the key for first item in list. Here, the key for the item is **blank**
- **headerValue** is the value expression for first item in list. Here, the value for first item is **Select country**
- **id** is the HTML id attribute
- **name** is the name of the select field. Here, **publisher** is the domain object set in the action class for **Publishers** model and **CountryNo** is the JavaBean property set in the **Publishers** model
- **label** is the label expression used for rendering Country's label
- **title** is the micro help for the form fields

Action [PublishersAction.java]

This is an action class with the following specifications:

Class Name	PublishersAction
Package	com.sharanamvaishali.action
Extends	ActionSupport
Implements	- -

Objects		
Object Name	**Class Name**	**Object Type**
publishersDAO	PublishersDAO	Data Access Layer
ddlb	PopulateDdlbs	Java Class
pg	PaginationDAO	Data Access Layer
publisher	Publishers	Model

Properties			
Property Name	**Property Type**	**Methods**	
For the data entry form fields			
publisher	Publishers	getPublisher()	setPublisher()
ddlb	PopulateDdlbs	getDdlb()	setDdlb()
For the data grid population			
publishers	List<Publishers>	getPublishers()	setPublishers()
For pagination			
pageNo	int	getPageNo()	setPageNo()
pageCount	int	getPageCount()	setPageCount()

Methods	
Method Name	Return Values
savePublisher()	SUCCESS
view()	SUCCESS
removePublisher()	SUCCESS
	ERROR
editPublisher()	SUCCESS
getPage()	SUCCESS

Code Spec

```
1   package com.sharanamvaishali.action;
2
3   import com.opensymphony.xwork2.ActionSupport;
4   import com.sharanamvaishali.dao.PaginationDAO;
5   import com.sharanamvaishali.dao.PaginationDAOImpl;
6   import com.sharanamvaishali.dao.PublishersDAO;
7   import com.sharanamvaishali.dao.PublishersDAOImpl;
8   import com.sharanamvaishali.model.Publishers;
9   import com.sharanamvaishali.utility.PopulateDdlbs;
10  import java.util.List;
11  import org.apache.struts2.interceptor.validation.SkipValidation;
12
13  public class PublishersAction extends ActionSupport{
14      private PublishersDAO publishersDAO = new PublishersDAOImpl();
15
16      private PopulateDdlbs ddlb = new PopulateDdlbs();
17
18      private PaginationDAO pg = new PaginationDAOImpl();
19
20      private Publishers publisher;
21
22      private List<Publishers> publishers;
23
24      private int pageNo, pageCount;
25
26      public PopulateDdlbs getDdlb() {
27          return ddlb;
28      }
29      public void setDdlb(PopulateDdlbs ddlb) {
30          this.ddlb = ddlb;
31      }
32
33      public int getPageNo() {
34          return pageNo;
35      }
36      public void setPageNo(int pageNo) {
```

```
34          return pageNo;
35      }
36      public void setPageNo(int pageNo) {
37          this.pageNo = pageNo;
38      }
39
40      public int getPageCount() {
41          return pageCount;
42      }
43      public void setPageCount(int pageCount) {
44          this.pageCount = pageCount;
45      }
46      public Publishers getPublisher() {
47          return publisher;
48      }
49      public void setPublisher(Publishers publisher) {
50          this.publisher = publisher;
51      }
52
53      public List<Publishers> getPublishers() {
54          return publishers;
55      }
56      public void setPublishers(List<Publishers> publishers) {
57          this.publishers = publishers;
58      }
59
60      public String savePublisher() throws Exception{
61          if(publisher.getPublisherNo() != null) {
62              publishersDAO.updatePublisher(publisher);
63          } else {
64              publishersDAO.savePublisher(publisher);
65          }
66          return SUCCESS;
67      }
68
69      @SkipValidation
70      public String view() throws Exception{
71          pageNo = 1;
72          getPage();
73          return SUCCESS;
74      }
75
76      @SkipValidation
77      public String removePublisher() throws Exception{
78          try{
79              publishersDAO.deletePublisher(publisher.getPublisherNo());
80          } catch(Exception e) {
81              addActionError(e.getCause().toString().split("[:]")[1]);
82              return ERROR;
83          }
```

```
84        return SUCCESS;
85      }
86
87      @SkipValidation
88      public String editPublisher() throws Exception{
89         publisher = publishersDAO.getPublisherById(publisher.getPublisherNo());
90         view();
91         return SUCCESS;
92      }
93
94      @SkipValidation
95      public String getPage() throws Exception{
96         pageCount = pg.getTotalPages("Publishers");
97         publishers = pg.getPage(pageNo-1, "Publishers").getList();
98         return SUCCESS;
99      }
100  }
```

Explanation:

The following section describes the above code spec.

savePublisher()

savePublisher() is invoked when the user keys in the desired data and clicks **Save**.

savePublisher():

❑ Performs an update operation [using PublishersDAO's updatePublisher()] if **publisher.getPublisherNo()** returns a valid PublisherNo

❑ Performs an insert operation [using PublishersDAO's savePublisher()] if **publisher.getPublisherNo()** returns empty

view()

view() is invoked every time Manage Publishers is served.

It invokes **getPage()** to populate the List object [publishers] which is used in the JSP page's **<s:iterator>** to populate the data grid. This data grid displays existing records from the **Publishers** database table.

@SkipValidation is used to skip validation for this method.

removePublisher()

removePublisher() is invoked when the user clicks ✖ adjacent to the desired record [in the data grid] for deletion.

The delete operation is performed by invoking PublishersDAO's **deletePublisher()**.

deletePublisher() is passed **PublisherNo** which is made available by JSP using **<s:param>** on click of ✖.

@SkipValidation is used to skip validation for this method.

editPublisher()

editPublisher() is invoked when the user clicks a desired record from the data grid in Manage Publishers for updating it.

It populates the bean class object [publisher] with the chosen record's data. The data is retrieved using PublishersDAO's **getPublisherById()** which is passed PublisherNo which is made available by JSP's <s:param> on click of the record.

Struts 2 framework automatically transfers the values from the bean class object to the FORM fields thus making it available to the user for editing the same.

@SkipValidation is used to skip validation for this method.

getPage()

getPage() is invoked every time Manage Publishers is served or the user clicks a page number link from Manage Publishers using pagination.

It calculates the total number of pages for pagination purpose and stores the same in the property named **pageCount**.

It populates the List object [publishers] which is used in the JSP page's <s:iterator> to form the data grid. This data grid displays existing records from the Publishers database table.

The data to be populated in the List object is retrieved using PaginationDAO's **getPage()** which returns the records belonging to the appropriate page number.

@SkipValidation is used to skip validation for this method.

DAO Class

Interface [PublishersDAO.java]

This is a Data Access Object interface with the following specifications:

Class Name	Package
PublishersDAO	com.sharanamvaishali.dao

Code Spec

```
1  package com.sharanamvaishali.dao;
2
3  import com.sharanamvaishali.model.Publishers;
4
5  public interface PublishersDAO {
6      public void savePublisher(Publishers publishers);
7      public void updatePublisher(Publishers publishers);
8      public void deletePublisher(int PublisherNo);
9      public Publishers getPublisherById(int PublisherNo);
10 }
```

REMINDER

PopulateDdlbsDAO.java is explained later in the *Section VII: Common Files Software Design Documentation* under the *Chapter 59: Populating Drop Down List Boxes.*

PaginationDAO.java is explained later in the *Section V: Backend [Administration] Software Design Documentation* under the *Chapter 42: Common Files.*

Implementation Class [PublishersDAOImpl.java]

This is a Data Access Object class with the following specifications:

Class Name	PublishersDAOImpl
Package	com.sharanamvaishali.dao
Implements	PublishersDAO

Objects	
Object Name	Class Name
session	Session
transaction	Transaction

Methods		
Method Name	**Arguments**	**Return Values**
savePublisher()	Publishers publishers	void
updatePublisher()	Publishers publishers	void
deletePublisher()	Integer PublisherNo	void
getPublisherById()	Integer PublisherNo	Publishers

Code Spec

```
1   package com.sharanamvaishali.dao;
2
3   import com.sharanamvaishali.model.Publishers;
4   import com.sharanamvaishali.utility.HibernateUtil;
5   import org.hibernate.Session;
6   import org.hibernate.Transaction;
7
8   public class PublishersDAOImpl implements PublishersDAO {
9       Session session = HibernateUtil.getSession();
10      Transaction transaction;
11
12      @Override
13      public void savePublisher(Publishers publishers) {
14         try {
15            transaction = session.beginTransaction();
16            session.save(publishers);
17            transaction.commit();
18         } catch (RuntimeException e) {
19            if(publishers != null) {
20               transaction.rollback();
21            }
22            throw e;
23         }
24      }
25
26      @Override
27      public void updatePublisher(Publishers publishers) {
28         try {
29            transaction = session.beginTransaction();
30            session.update(publishers);
31            transaction.commit();
32         } catch (RuntimeException e) {
33            if(publishers != null) {
34               transaction.rollback();
35            }
36            throw e;
37         }
38      }
```

```
39
40    @Override
41    public void deletePublisher(int PublisherNo) {
42       Object Publishers = null;
43       try {
44          transaction = session.beginTransaction();
45          Publishers = session.load(Publishers.class, PublisherNo);
46          session.delete(Publishers);
47          transaction.commit();
48       } catch (RuntimeException e) {
49          if(Publishers != null) {
50             transaction.rollback();
51          }
52          throw e;
53       }
54    }
55
56    @Override
57    public Publishers getPublisherById(int PublisherNo) {
58       return (Publishers) session.createQuery("FROM Publishers WHERE
          PublisherNo = :PublisherNo").setInteger("PublisherNo",
          PublisherNo).uniqueResult();
59    }
60 }
```

Explanation:

The following section describes the above code spec.

savePublisher()

savePublisher() does the actual saving of the publisher in the Publishers database table.

savePublisher() uses **save()** of Session, which takes care of adding new publisher details when the user has entered all the publisher details and clicked Save .

After the save operation is performed, the transaction is committed to make the changes permanent.

Whilst performing the save operation, if a runtime exception occurs, than the transaction is **rolled back**.

updatePublisher()

updatePublisher() does the actual updation of the existing publisher in the Publishers database table.

updatePublisher() uses **update()** of Session, which takes care of updating an existing publisher details when the user has made changes to the existing publisher details and clicked [**Save**].

After the update operation is performed, the transaction is committed to make the changes permanent.

Whilst performing the update operation, if a runtime exception occurs, than the transaction is **rolled back**.

deletePublisher()

deletePublisher() deletes the appropriate publisher based on **PublisherNo** received as a reference.

This method uses:
- ❑ **load()** of Session, which retrieves the appropriate Publisher to be deleted using PublisherNo as a reference
- ❑ **delete()** of Session, which deletes the publisher from the Publishers database table

After the delete operation is performed, the transaction is committed to make the changes permanent.

Whilst performing the delete operation, if a runtime exception occurs, than the transaction is **rolled back**.

getPublisherById()

getPublisherById() returns the appropriate publisher's object from the Publishers database table using **PublisherNo** as the reference.

This method uses:
- ❑ **createQuery()** of Session, which creates a new instance of Query to retrieve the Publisher details using PublisherNo as reference
- ❑ **setInteger()** of Query, which states the parameter to be used as the WHERE clause criteria when querying the Publishers database table
- ❑ **uniqueResult()** of Query, which ensures that only unique record is retrieved from the Publishers database table and prevents any kinds of errors

REMINDER

PopulateDdlbsDAOImpl.java is explained later in the *Section VII: Common Files Software Design Documentation* under the *Chapter 59: Populating Drop Down List Boxes.*

PaginationDAOImpl.java is explained later in the *Section V: Backend [Administration] Software Design Documentation* under the *Chapter 42: Common Files.*

Validations [PublishersAction-validation.xml]

If the required **input** fields are kept empty whilst submitting the form, PublishersAction-validation.xml takes care of the validations.

Code Spec

```
1  <?xml version="1.0" encoding="UTF-8"?>
2  <!DOCTYPE validators PUBLIC '-//OpenSymphony Group//XWork Validator
   1.0.2//EN' 'http://www.opensymphony.com/xwork/xwork-validator-1.0.2.dtd'>
3  <validators>
4     <field name="publisher.PublisherName">
5        <field-validator type="requiredstring">
6           <message>Please enter the publisher name.</message>
7        </field-validator>
8     </field>
9
10    <field name="publisher.EmailAddress">
11       <field-validator type="requiredstring" short-circuit="true">
12          <message>Please enter the email address.</message>
13       </field-validator>
14       <field-validator type="email" short-circuit="true">
15          <message>Invalid email address.</message>
16       </field-validator>
17    </field>
18 </validators>
```

If any errors are detected the data entry form is re-served with appropriate error messages, as shown in diagram 36.2.

struts-Publishers.xml file holds a mapping to serve the data entry form:

```
17        <action name="doInsertPublisher" method="savePublisher"
          class="com.sharanamvaishali.action.PublishersAction">
18          <interceptor-ref name="defaultStack"/>
19          <interceptor-ref name="token"/>
20          <result name="success"
            type="redirectAction">doViewPublishers</result>
21          <result name="input">/admin/managePublishers.jsp</result>
22        </action>
```

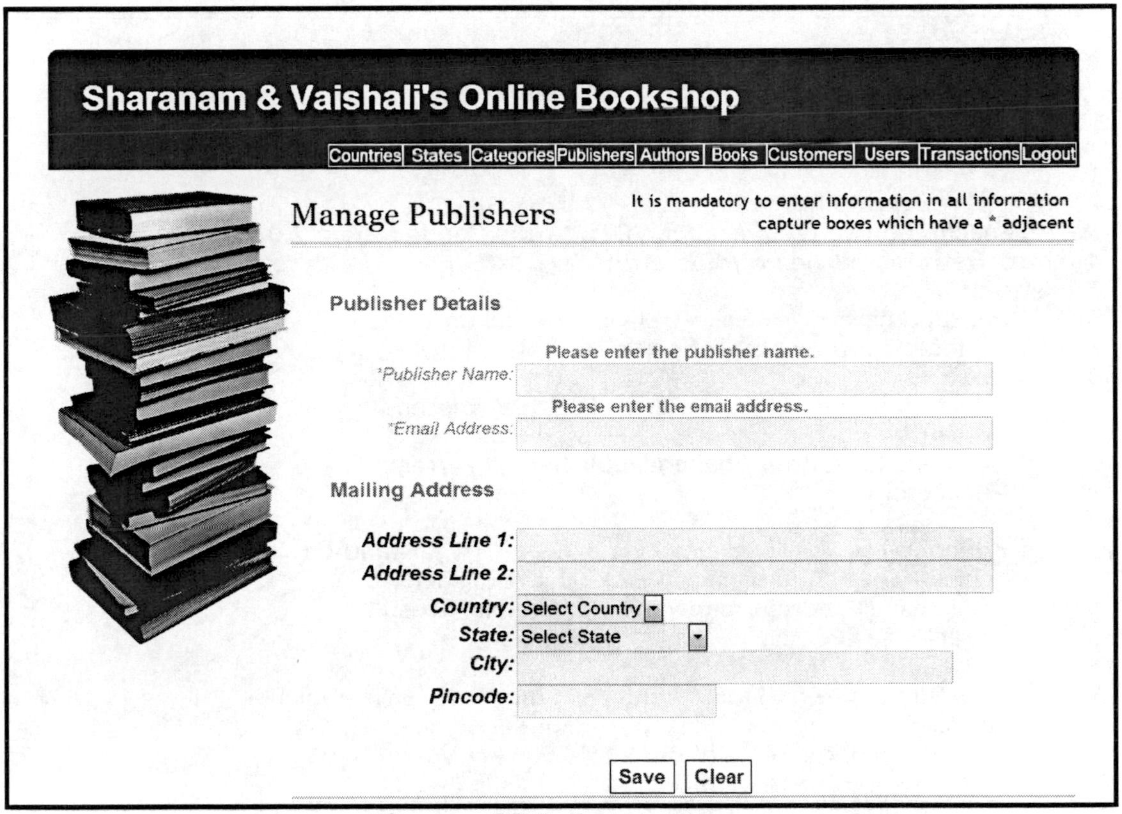

Diagram 36.2: Error messages

Struts Configuration [struts-Publishers.xml]

This is the struts configuration file with the following specifications:

File Name	Package Name	Extends
Publishers	managePublishers	default

Actions	
Action Name	**Results**
showManagePublishers	SUCCESS - managePublishers.jsp
iterateManagePublishersPage	SUCCESS - managePublishers.jsp
doInsertPublisher	SUCCESS - doViewPublishers
	INPUT - managePublishers.jsp
doViewPublishers	SUCCESS - managePublishers.jsp
	ERROR - showManagePublishers
doDeletePublisher	SUCCESS - doViewPublishers
	ERROR - managePublishers.jsp
showEditPublisher	SUCCESS - managePublishers.jsp

Code Spec

```
1   <?xml version="1.0" encoding="UTF-8"?>
2   <!DOCTYPE struts PUBLIC
3   "-//Apache Software Foundation//DTD Struts Configuration 2.0//EN"
4   "http://struts.apache.org/dtds/struts-2.0.dtd">
5   <struts>
6     <package name="managePublishers" extends="default">
7       <default-interceptor-ref name="chkSession"/>
8
9       <action name="showManagePublishers" method="view"
        class="com.sharanamvaishali.action.PublishersAction">
10        <result>/admin/managePublishers.jsp</result>
11      </action>
12
13      <action name="iterateManagePublishersPage" method="getPage"
        class="com.sharanamvaishali.action.PublishersAction">
14        <result>/admin/managePublishers.jsp</result>
15      </action>
16
17      <action name="doInsertPublisher" method="savePublisher"
        class="com.sharanamvaishali.action.PublishersAction">
18        <interceptor-ref name="defaultStack"/>
19        <interceptor-ref name="token"/>
20        <result name="success"
        type="redirectAction">doViewPublishers</result>
21        <result name="input">/admin/managePublishers.jsp</result>
22      </action>
23
24      <action name="doViewPublishers" method="view"
        class="com.sharanamvaishali.action.PublishersAction">
25        <result name="success">/admin/managePublishers.jsp</result>
26        <result name="error"
        type="redirectAction">showManagePublishers</result>
```

```
27        </action>
28
29        <action name="doDeletePublisher" method="removePublisher"
          class="com.sharanamvaishali.action.PublishersAction">
30          <result name="success"
            type="redirectAction">doViewPublishers</result>
31          <result name="error">/admin/managePublishers.jsp</result>
32        </action>
33
34        <action name="showEditPublisher" method="editPublisher"
          class="com.sharanamvaishali.action.PublishersAction">
35          <result name="success">/admin/managePublishers.jsp</result>
36        </action>
37      </package>
38  </struts>
```

Explanation:

The following section describes the above code spec.

showManagePublishers.action

showManagePublishers is an action to help viewing.

This means the data entry form and the list of publisher details are displayed.

The list of publisher details are retrieved by **PublishersAction's view()**.

iterateManagePublishersPage.action

iterateManagePublishersPage is an action to help iterate.

This means displaying 10 records of publisher details per page in the form of data grid.

This iterated data is retrieved by **PublishersAction's getPage()**.

doInsertPublisher.action

doInsertPublisher is an action to help adding new publisher details or updating existing publisher details.

defaultStack interceptor is referenced, which is a complete stack with all the common interceptors in place.

token interceptor is referenced, which checks for valid token presence in Action and prevents duplicate form submission.

doInsertPublisher.action:

❑ Calls **PublishersAction**'s **savePublisher()** to add new publisher details or update the existing publisher details

❑ Ensures that the captured data is valid

❑ If the validation is successful then the data is saved and the result is redirected to **doViewPublishers.action**

❑ If the validation fails then the Manage Publishers page along with error messages is displayed

doViewPublishers.action

doViewPublishers is an action to help viewing.

This means the list of publisher details is displayed.

The list of publisher details are retrieved by **PublishersAction**'s **view()**.

If there is no data available in the database then the error message is displayed in the Manage Publishers page by redirecting the page to **showManagePublishers.action**.

doDeletePublisher.action

In case, the user chooses to delete a publisher and clicks ✖, **doDeletePublisher.action** is the action to help delete a publisher record from Manage Publishers.

doDeletePublisher.action:

❑ Calls **PublishersAction**'s **removePublisher()** to delete a publisher record

❑ If the publisher record is deleted successfully then the result is redirected to **doViewPublishers.action**

❑ If the record being deleted is referenced by a record in another database table then the Manage Publishers page displays the error message indicating that this record cannot be deleted

showEditPublisher.action

showEditPublisher is an action to help the editing of existing publishers.

In case, the user chooses to edit a publisher and clicks that particular record, **showEditPublisher.action** helps fill up the Manage Publishers form with publisher details.

showEditPublisher.action:

❑ Calls **PublishersAction's editPublisher()** to retrieve the publisher details

❑ Returns to the Manage Publishers page along with the data to be populated in the form

Domain Class [Publishers.java]

This is a domain class with the following specifications:

Class Name	Package	Implements
Publishers	com.sharanamvaishali.model	java.io.Serializable

Properties			
Property Name	**Property Type**	**Methods**	
PublisherNo	Integer	getPublisherNo()	setPublisherNo()
StateNo	Integer	getStateNo()	setStateNo()
CountryNo	Integer	getCountryNo()	setCountryNo()
PublisherName	String	getPublisherName()	setPublisherName()
EmailAddress	String	getEmailAddress()	setEmailAddress()
Address1	String	getAddress1()	setAddress1()
Address2	String	getAddress2()	setAddress2()
City	String	getCity()	setCity()
Pincode	String	getPincode()	setPincode()

Code Spec

```
1   package com.sharanamvaishali.model;
2
3   import javax.persistence.Column;
4   import javax.persistence.Entity;
5   import javax.persistence.GeneratedValue;
6   import javax.persistence.Id;
7   import javax.persistence.Table;
8
9   @Entity
10  @Table(name="PUBLISHERS")
11  public class Publishers implements java.io.Serializable {
12      @Id
13      @GeneratedValue
14      @Column(name="PUBLISHERNO")
15      private Integer PublisherNo;
16      @Column(name="STATENO")
17      private Integer StateNo;
```

```
18      @Column(name="COUNTRYNO")
19      private Integer CountryNo;
20      @Column(name="PUBLISHERNAME")
21      private String PublisherName;
22      @Column(name="EMAILADDRESS")
23      private String EmailAddress;
24      @Column(name="ADDRESS1")
25      private String Address1;
26      @Column(name="ADDRESS2")
27      private String Address2;
28      @Column(name="CITY")
29      private String City;
30      @Column(name="PINCODE")
31      private String Pincode;
32
33      public Publishers() {
34      }
35
36      public Integer getStateNo() {
37          return StateNo;
38      }
39      public void setStateNo(Integer StateNo) {
40          this.StateNo = StateNo;
41      }
42
43      public Integer getCountryNo() {
44          return CountryNo;
45      }
46      public void setCountryNo(Integer CountryNo) {
47          this.CountryNo = CountryNo;
48      }
49
50      public String getCity() {
51          return City;
52      }
53      public void setCity(String City) {
54          this.City = City;
55      }
56
57      public String getAddress1() {
58          return Address1;
59      }
60      public void setAddress1(String Address1) {
61          this.Address1 = Address1;
62      }
63
64      public String getAddress2() {
65          return Address2;
```

```
66      }
67      public void setAddress2(String Address2) {
68          this.Address2 = Address2;
69      }
70
71      public String getEmailAddress() {
72          return EmailAddress;
73      }
74      public void setEmailAddress(String EmailAddress) {
75          this.EmailAddress = EmailAddress;
76      }
77
78      public String getPincode() {
79          return Pincode;
80      }
81      public void setPincode(String Pincode) {
82          this.Pincode = Pincode;
83      }
84
85      public String getPublisherName() {
86          return PublisherName;
87      }
88      public void setPublisherName(String PublisherName) {
89          this.PublisherName = PublisherName;
90      }
91
92      public Integer getPublisherNo() {
93          return PublisherNo;
94      }
95      public void setPublisherNo(Integer PublisherNo) {
96          this.PublisherNo = PublisherNo;
97      }
98  }
```

Chapter

37

SECTION V: BACKEND [ADMINISTRATION] SOFTWARE DESIGN DOCUMENTATION

Manage Authors

This module allows performing the following operations:

- ❑ Adding new authors
- ❑ Editing existing authors
- ❑ Viewing existing authors
- ❑ Deleting existing authors

This module uses the bms.Authors table to perform the above operations.

This module is made up of the following:

Type	Name	Description
JSP	manageAuthors.jsp	The data entry form
Struts 2		
Action	AuthorsAction.java	The action class that facilitates data operations.
	GetFileAction.java	
Validation	AuthorsAction-validation.xml	The XML based validation file.
DAO Class	AuthorsDAO.java	The interfaces for the DAO layer.
	PaginationDAO.java	
	PopulateDdlbsDAO.java	
	AuthorsDAOImpl.java	The implementation classes that performs the actual data operations.
	PaginationDAOImpl.java	
	PopulateDdlbsDAOImpl.java	
Utility Class	PopulateDdlbs.java	The class that populates the list objects.
Struts Configuration	struts-Authors.xml	Struts configuration file.
Hibernate		
Mapping	hibernate.cfg.xml	The mapping file that holds Model class mapping.
Model Class	Authors.java	The model class.

JSP [manageAuthors.jsp]

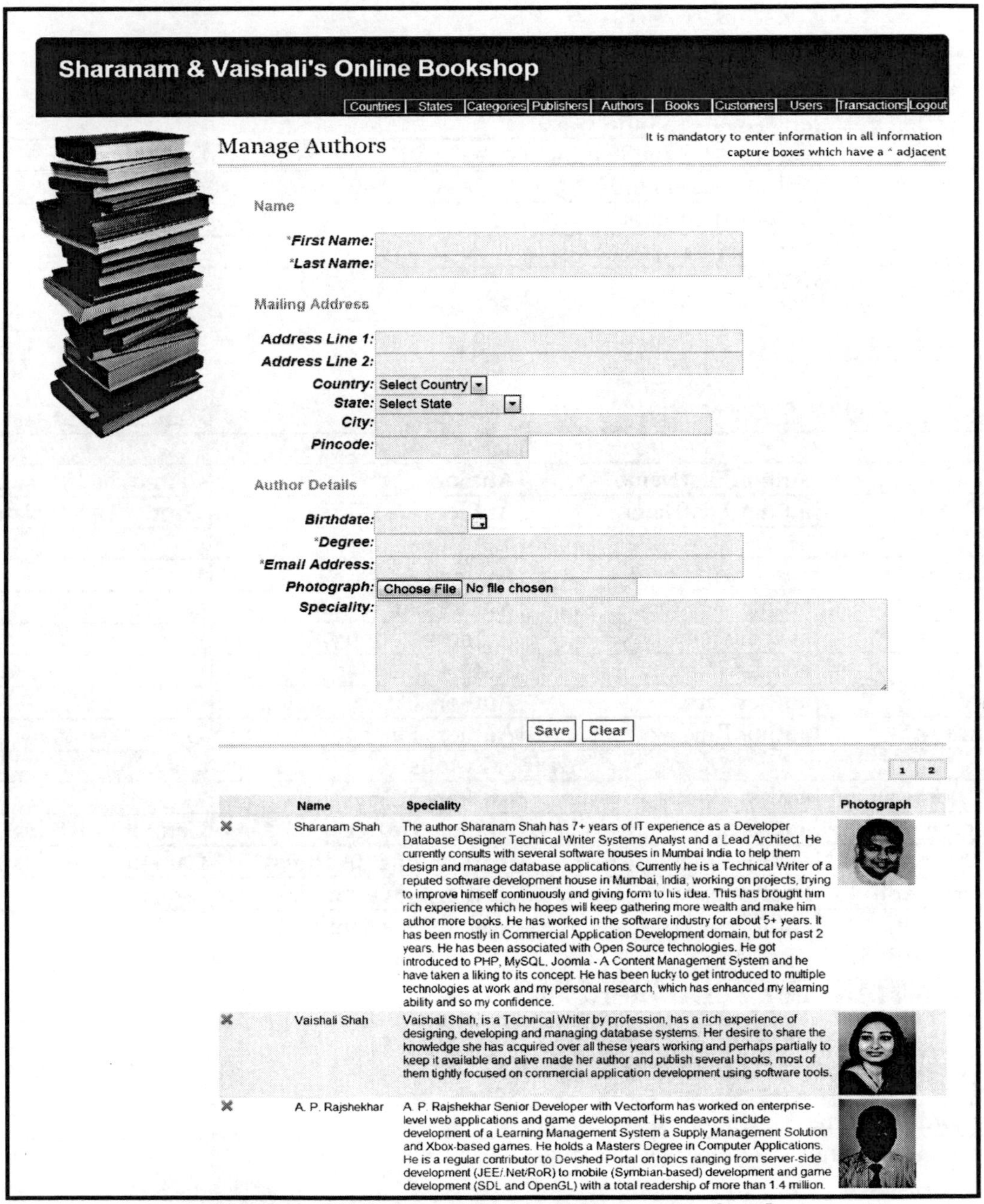

Diagram 37.1: Manage Authors [Data entry form]

This is a JSP which holds a data entry form, as shown in diagram 37.1. This form appears when the user clicks **Authors** .

Form Specifications

File Name	manageAuthors.jsp
Title	BookShop[Sharanam & Vaishali Shah] - Manage Authors
Bound To Table	bms.Authors
Form Name	frmAuthors
Action	doInsertAuthor
Method	POST

Data Fields

Label	Name	Bound To	Validation Rules
		Name	
First Name	author.FirstName	Authors.FirstName	Cannot be left blank
Last Name	author.LastName	Authors.LastName	Cannot be left blank
		Mailing Address	
Address Line 1	author.Address1	Authors.Address1	- -
Address Line 2	author.Address2	Authors.Address2	- -
Country	author.CountryNo	Authors.CountryNo	- -
State	author.StateNo	Authors.StateNo	- -
City	author.City	Authors.City	- -
Pincode	author.Pincode	Authors.Pincode	- -
		Author Details	
Birthdate	author.Dob	Authors.DOB	- -
Degree	author.Degree	Authors.Degree	Cannot be left blank
Email Address	author.EmailAddress	Authors.EmailAddress	Cannot be left blank
Photograph	Photograph	Authors.Photograph	- -
Speciality	author.Speciality	Authors.Speciality	- -

Micro-Help For Form Fields

Form Field	Micro Help Statement
	Name
author.FirstName	Enter the first name
author.LastName	Enter the last name

Form Field	Micro Help Statement
	Mailing Address
author.Address1	Enter the street address
author.Address2	Enter the street address
author.CountryNo	Select country
author.StateNo	Select state
author.City	Enter the city name
author.Pincode	Enter the pincode
	Author Details
author.Dob	--
author.Degree	Enter the degree
author.EmailAddress	Enter the email address
Photograph	Choose the image file
author.Speciality	Enter the speciality

Data Controls

Object	Label	Name
s:submit	Save	btnSubmit
s:reset	Clear	btnReset

Code Spec

```
1  <%@page contentType="text/html" pageEncoding="UTF-8"%>
2  <%@ taglib prefix="s" uri="/struts-tags" %>
3  <%@ taglib prefix="sx" uri="/struts-dojo-tags" %>
4  <!DOCTYPE HTML PUBLIC "-//W3C//DTD HTML 4.01 Transitional//EN"
5    "http://www.w3.org/TR/html4/loose.dtd">
6  <html xmlns="http://www.w3.org/1999/xhtml">
7    <head>
8      <title>BookShop [Sharanam & Vaishali Shah] - Manage Authors</title>
9      <meta http-equiv="content-type" content="text/html; charset=iso-8859-1">
10     <link href="/BookShop/css/admin.css" type="text/css" rel="stylesheet">
11     <sx:head parseContent="true"/>
12   </head>
13   <body>
14     <s:include value="header.jsp" />
15     <br>
16     <s:form action="doInsertAuthor" method="post" name="frmAuthors" id="frmAuthors"
       enctype="multipart/form-data" validate="true">
17       <s:token/>
18       <s:hidden name="author.AuthorNo" id="AuthorNo"/>
19       <table width="100%" border="0" align="center" cellpadding="0" cellspacing="0">
20         <tr>
21           <td valign="top" width="20%">
22             <img src="/BookShop/images/leftImg.jpg" height="350"/>
```

```
23                    </td>
24                <td valign="top">
25                  <table width="100%" border="0" align="center" cellpadding="0"
                     cellspacing="0">
26                    <tr>
27                      <td>
28                        <table border="0" cellpadding="0" cellspacing="0"
                         width="100%">
29                          <tr>
30                            <td class="manageForms">Manage Authors</td>
31                            <td class="information" valign="top" align="right">
32                              It is mandatory to enter information in all information
                             <br>capture boxes which have a <span
                             class="mandatory">*</span> adjacent
33                            </td>
34                          </tr>
35                        </table>
36                      </td>
37                    </tr>
38                <tr><td class="hrLine"> </td></tr>
39                <tr align="left" valign="top">
40                      <td>
41                        <table width="90%" border="0" align="center" cellpadding="0"
                         cellspacing="0">
42                          <tr>
43                            <td>
44                              <table width="100%" border="0" cellpadding="0"
                             cellspacing="0">
45                                <tr>
46                                  <td class="Arial16BlueB">
47                                    <br />Name<br /><br />
48                                  </td>
49                                </tr>
50                                <s:actionerror/>
51                                <s:textfield required="true" requiredposition="left"
                                 id="FirstName" label="First Name"
                                 name="author.FirstName" title="Enter the first name"
                                 maxLength="25" size="55"/>
52                                <s:textfield required="true" requiredposition="left"
                                 id="LastName" label="Last Name"
                                 name="author.LastName" title="Enter the last name"
                                 maxLength="25" size="55"/>
53                                <tr>
54                                  <td class="Arial16BlueB">
55                                    <br />Mailing Address<br /><br />
56                                  </td>
57                                </tr>
58                                <s:textfield id="Address1" label="Address Line 1"
                                 name="author.Address1" title="Enter the street
                                 address" maxLength="50" size="55"/>
59                                <s:textfield id="Address2" label="Address Line 2"
                                 name="author.Address2" title="Enter the street
                                 address" maxLength="50" size="55"/>
60                                <s:select list="ddlb.ddlbCountries" listKey="CountryNo"
                                 listValue="Country" headerKey="" headerValue="Select
```

```
        Country" id="CountryNo" name="author.CountryNo"
        label="Country" title="Select the country"></s:select>
61      <s:select list="ddlb.ddlbStates" listKey="StateNo"
        listValue="State" headerKey="" headerValue="Select
        State" id="StateNo" name="author.StateNo"
        label="State" title="Select the state"></s:select>
62      <s:textfield id="City" label="City" name="author.City"
        title="Enter the city name" maxLength="50"
        size="50"/>
63      <s:textfield id="Pincode" label="Pincode"
        name="author.Pincode" title="Enter the pincode"
        maxLength="15" size="20"/>
64      <tr>
65          <td class="Arial16BlueB">
66              <br />Author Details<br /><br />
67          </td>
68      </tr>
69      <sx:datetimepicker name="author.Dob"
        label="Birthdate" displayFormat="yyyy-MM-dd"/>
70      <s:textfield required="true" requiredposition="left"
        id="Degree" label="Degree" name="author.Degree"
        title="Enter the degree" maxLength="25" size="55"/>
71      <s:textfield required="true" requiredposition="left"
        id="EmailAddress" label="Email Address"
        name="author.EmailAddress" title="Enter the email
        address" maxLength="50" size="55"/>
72      <s:file id="Photograph" title="Choose the image file"
        name="Photograph" label="Photograph" />
73      <s:textarea id="Speciality" label="Speciality"
        name="author.Speciality" title="Enter the speciality"
        cols="80" rows="5"></s:textarea>
74              </table>
75          </td>
76      </tr>
77      <tr>
78          <td style="text-align: center;">
79              <br /><br />
80              <s:submit theme="simple" cssClass="groovybutton"
        name="btnSubmit" id="btnSubmit" value="Save" />
81              <s:reset theme="simple" cssClass="groovybutton"
        name="btnReset" id="htnReset" value="Clear"
        onclick="javascript:document.location.href='showManageA
        uthors.action'"/>
82          </td>
83      </tr>
84      </table>
85      </td>
86  </tr>
87  <tr><td class="hrLine"> </td></tr>
88  <tr>
89      <td align="center">
90          <table width="60px" border="0" align="right" cellpadding="3"
        cellspacing="1" style="border:#c3bca4 1px solid">
91              <tr>
92                  <s:bean name="org.apache.struts2.util.Counter"
```

```
                                    id="counter">
93                                      <s:param name="last" value="%{pageCount}" />
94                                  </s:bean>
95                              <s:iterator value="#counter">
96                                  <td align="center" width="2px" style="border:#c3bca4
                                    1px solid; background:#efebde; font-family:sans-serif;
                                    font-size:12px; font-weight:bolder; text-align:center;
                                    vertical-align:middle;">
97                                      <a href="<s:url
                                    action="iterateManageAuthorsPage"><s:param
                                    name="pageNo"><s:property
                                    /></s:param></s:url>"><s:property /></a>
98                                  </td>
99                              </s:iterator>
100                         </tr>
101                     </table>
102                 </td>
103             </tr>
104             <tr>
105                 <td>
106                     <br>
107                     <table class="view" align="center" cellspacing="0"
                        cellpadding="0" width="100%">
108                         <tr>
109                             <th width="10%" align="center"> </th>
110                             <th width="15%" class="Arial13BrownB"
                                align="left">Name</th>
111                             <th width="60%" class="Arial13BrownB"
                                align="left">Speciality</th>
112                             <th width="15%" class="Arial13BrownB"
                                align="left">Photograph</th>
113                         </tr>
114                     <s:iterator value="authors" id="authors" status="stat">
115                         <tr title="Click to edit" class="<s:if test="#stat.odd ==
                            true">odd</s:if><s:else>even</s:else>">
116                             <td width="10%" valign="top">
117                                 <a href="<s:url action="doDeleteAuthor"><s:param
                                    name="author.AuthorNo" value="AuthorNo"
                                    /></s:url>">
118                                     <img src="/BookShop/images/TrashIcon.png"
                                    border="0" alt="Delete" style="cursor:pointer;"/>
119                                 </a>
120                             </td>
121                             <td width="15%" class="manageList"
                                onclick="javascript:location.href='<s:url
                                action='showEditAuthor'><s:param
                                name='author.AuthorNo' value='AuthorNo' /></s:url>'">
122                                 <s:property value="FirstName"/> <s:property
                                    value="LastName" />
123                             </td>
124                             <td width="60%" class="manageList"
                                onclick="javascript:location.href='<s:url
                                action='showEditAuthor'><s:param
                                name='author.AuthorNo' value='AuthorNo' /></s:url>'">
125                                 <s:property value="Speciality"/>
```

```
126                                    </td>
127                                    <td width="15%" class="manageList"
                                       onclick="javascript:location.href='<s:url
                                       action='showEditAuthor'><s:param
                                       name='author.AuthorNo' value='AuthorNo' /></s:url>'">
128                                        <img
                                           src="getFile.action?columnName=Photograph&tableNam
                                           e=Authors&whereClause=AuthorNo&whereClauseValue=
                                           <s:property value="AuthorNo" />" width="80px"/>
129                                    </td>
130                                </tr>
131                            </s:iterator>
132                            <s:if test="#authors==null">
133                                <span class="emptyMessage">Currently there exists no
                                   authors in the database. Please add a few authors to begin
                                   managing them.</span>
134                            </s:if>
135                        </table>
136                    </td>
137                </tr>
138            </table>
139        </td>
140    </tr>
141    </table>
142    </s:form>
143    <s:include value="adminFooter.jsp" />
144    </body>
145 </html>
```

Explanation:

This is a standard data entry form, which captures the author details. By default, when the form loads, it is in the **INSERT** and **VIEW** mode. The form also has Delete and Edit options to delete and edit a particular author record.

Dojo Plugin

Struts 2 uses DOJO framework for Ajax implementation.

To use Ajax the following Dojo Plugin distributed with Struts 2 needs to be included in the JSP:

```
<%@ taglib prefix="sx" uri="/struts-dojo-tags" %>
```

<sx:head>

<sx:head> is configured for performance or debugging purposes:

<sx:head> initializes the Dojo framework and makes it ready for all Ajax invocations within the page.

WARNING

 The initialization of Dojo framework is important as all Ajax calls will not work without <sx:head> being initialized.

<sx:head> renders required JavaScript code to configure Dojo and is required in order to use any of the tags included in the Dojo plugin:

```
<sx:head parseContent="true"/>
```

Where, **parseContent** when set to true, Dojo will parse the response into an XHTML Document Object and traverse the nodes searching for Dojo Widget markup.

The parse and traversal is performed prior to inserting the nodes into the DOM.

parseContent attribute must be enabled to nest Dojo widgets [tags] within responses.

WARNING

 There's significant processing involved creating and parsing the document so switch off parseContent attribute when not required. Note also that the response must be valid XHTML for cross-browser support and widgets must have unique IDs.

<sx:datetimepicker>

<sx:datetimepicker> renders a date/time picker in a drop down container.

<sx:datetimepicker> creates an input field with a button next to it. When the button is pressed, a popup date time picker is displayed. When the user selects a date, the date is filled into the input text in the format that is specified in the **displayFormat** attribute.

```
<sx:datetimepicker name="author.Dob"
label="Birthdate" displayFormat="yyyy-MM-dd"/>
```

In the above code spec, the specified date format for the date is yyyy-MM-dd.

<s:file>

<s:file> is used to create a HTML file upload component to allow users select file from the local disk and upload it to the server.

```
<s:file id="Photograph" title="Choose the image file"
name="Photograph" label="Photograph" />
```

Where:

❑ **id** is the HTML id attribute

❑ **title** is the micro help for the form fields

❑ **name** is the name of the file input field. Here, **Photograph** is the JavaBean property set in the **Authors** model

❑ **label** is the label expression used for rendering Photograph's label

When <s:file> is used to render a file upload component, the **encoding type** of <s:form> has to be set as **multipart/form-data**:

```
<s:form action="doInsertAuthor" method="post" name="frmAuthors" id="frmAuthors"
enctype="multipart/form-data" validate="true">
```

Action [AuthorsAction.java]

This is an action class with the following specifications:

Class Name	AuthorsAction
Package	com.sharanamvaishali.action
Extends	ActionSupport
Implements	- -

Objects		
Object Name	**Class Name**	**Object Type**
session	Session	Hibernate Utility Class
authorsDAO	AuthorsDAO	Data Access Layer
ddlb	PopulateDdlbs	Java Class
pg	PaginationDAO	Data Access Layer
author	Authors	Model

Properties			
Property Name	**Property Type**	**Methods**	
For the data entry form fields			
author	Authors	getAuthor()	setAuthor()
ddlb	PopulateDdlbs	getDdlb()	setDdlb()
Photograph	File	getPhotograph()	setPhotograph()
For the data grid population			
authors	List<Authors>	getAuthors()	setAuthors()
For pagination			
pageNo	int	getPageNo()	setPageNo()
pageCount	int	getPageCount()	setPageCount()

Methods	
Method Name	**Return Values**
saveAuthor()	SUCCESS
view()	SUCCESS
removeAuthor()	SUCCESS
	ERROR
editAuthor()	SUCCESS
getPage()	SUCCESS

Code Spec

```
1   package com.sharanamvaishali.action;
2
3   import com.opensymphony.xwork2.ActionSupport;
4   import com.sharanamvaishali.dao.AuthorsDAO;
5   import com.sharanamvaishali.dao.AuthorsDAOImpl;
6   import com.sharanamvaishali.dao.PaginationDAO;
7   import com.sharanamvaishali.dao.PaginationDAOImpl;
8   import com.sharanamvaishali.model.Authors;
9   import com.sharanamvaishali.utility.HibernateUtil;
10  import com.sharanamvaishali.utility.PopulateDdlbs;
11  import java.io.File;
12  import java.util.List;
13  import org.apache.commons.io.FileUtils;
14  import org.apache.struts2.interceptor.validation.SkipValidation;
15  import org.hibernate.Session;
16
17  public class AuthorsAction extends ActionSupport{
18      Session session = HibernateUtil.getSession();
19
20      private AuthorsDAO authorsDAO = new AuthorsDAOImpl();
21
22      private PopulateDdlbs ddlb = new PopulateDdlbs();
23
24      private PaginationDAO pg = new PaginationDAOImpl();
25
26      private Authors author;
27
28      private List<Authors> authors;
29
30      private File Photograph;
31
32      private int pageNo, pageCount;
33
34      public PopulateDdlbs getDdlb() {
35          return ddlb;
36      }
```

```
37      public void setDdlb(PopulateDdlbs ddlb) {
38          this.ddlb = ddlb;
39      }
40
41      public int getPageNo() {
42          return pageNo;
43      }
44      public void setPageNo(int pageNo) {
45          this.pageNo = pageNo;
46      }
47
48      public int getPageCount() {
49          return pageCount;
50      }
51      public void setPageCount(int pageCount) {
52          this.pageCount = pageCount;
53      }
54
55      public Authors getAuthor() {
56          return author;
57      }
58      public void setAuthor(Authors author) {
59          this.author = author;
60      }
61
62      public List<Authors> getAuthors() {
63          return authors;
64      }
65      public void setAuthors(List<Authors> authors) {
66          this.authors = authors;
67      }
68
69      public File getPhotograph() {
70          return Photograph;
71      }
72      public void setPhotograph(File Photograph) {
73          this.Photograph = Photograph;
74      }
75
76
77      public String saveAuthor() throws Exception{
78          if(Photograph != null) {
79              author.setPhotograph(session.getLobHelper().createBlob(FileUtils.readFile
                ToByteArray(Photograph)));
80          }
81
82          if(author.getAuthorNo() != null) {
83              authorsDAO.updateAuthor(author);
84          } else {
```

```
85              authorsDAO.saveAuthor(author);
86          }
87          return SUCCESS;
88      }
89
90      @SkipValidation
91      public String view() throws Exception{
92          pageNo = 1;
93          getPage();
94          return SUCCESS;
95      }
96
97      @SkipValidation
98      public String removeAuthor() throws Exception{
99          try{
100             authorsDAO.deleteAuthor(author.getAuthorNo());
101         } catch(Exception e) {
102             addActionError(e.getCause().toString().split("[:]")[1]);
103             return ERROR;
104         }
105         return SUCCESS;
106     }
107
108     @SkipValidation
109     public String editAuthor() throws Exception{
110         author = authorsDAO.getAuthorById(author.getAuthorNo());
111         view();
112         return SUCCESS;
113     }
114
115     @SkipValidation
116     public String getPage() throws Exception{
117         pageCount = pg.getTotalPages("Authors");
118         authors = pg.getPage(pageNo-1, "Authors").getList();
119         return SUCCESS;
120     }
121 }
```

Explanation:

The following section describes the above code spec.

saveAuthor()

saveAuthor() is invoked when the user keys in the desired data and clicks Save .

saveAuthor():

❑ Checks whether the Photograph is uploaded. If the photograph is uploaded, then the photograph is set using **setPhotograph()** of the **Authors** model

　o Uses getLobHelper() of Session, which is a session's helper for creating LOB data

　o Uses createBlob() of LobHelper, which creates a new BOLB from bytes

　o Uses FileUtils, which is a general file manipulation utility

　o Uses readFileToByteArray() of FileUtils, which reads the contents of a file into a byte array

❑ Performs an update operation [using AuthorsDAO's updateAuthor()] if **author.getAuthorNo()** returns a valid AuthorNo

❑ Performs an insert operation [using AuthorsDAO's saveAuthor()] if **author.getAuthorNo()** returns empty

view()

view() is invoked every time Manage Authors is served.

It invokes **getPage()** to populate the List object [authors] which is used in the JSP page's **<s:iterator>** to populate the data grid. This data grid displays existing records from the **Authors** database table.

@SkipValidation is used to skip validation for this method.

removeAuthor()

removeAuthor() is invoked when the user clicks ✖ adjacent to the desired record [in the data grid] for deletion.

The delete operation is performed by invoking AuthorsDAO's **deleteAuthor()**.

deleteAuthor() is passed **AuthorNo** which is made available by JSP using **<s:param>** on click of ✖.

@SkipValidation is used to skip validation for this method.

editAuthor()

editAuthor() is invoked when the user clicks a desired record from the data grid in Manage Authors for updating it.

It populates the bean class object [author] with the chosen record's data. The data is retrieved using AuthorsDAO's **getAuthorById()** which is passed AuthorNo which is made available by JSP's <s:param> on click of the record.

Struts 2 framework automatically transfers the values from the bean class object to the FORM fields thus making it available to the user for editing the same.

@SkipValidation is used to skip validation for this method.

getPage()

getPage() is invoked every time Manage Authors is served or the user clicks a page number link from Manage Authors using pagination.

It calculates the total number of pages for pagination purpose and stores the same in the property named **pageCount**.

It populates the List object [authors] which is used in the JSP page's <s:iterator> to form the data grid. This data grid displays existing records from the Authors database table.

The data to be populated in the List object is retrieved using PaginationDAO's **getPage()** which returns the records belonging to the appropriate page number.

@SkipValidation is used to skip validation for this method.

REMINDER

GetFileAction.java is explained later in the *Section VII: Common Files Software Design Documentation* under the *Chapter 58: Retrieving Blob Values*.

DAO Class

Interface [AuthorsDAO.java]

This is a Data Access Object interface with the following specifications:

Class Name	Package
AuthorsDAO	com.sharanamvaishali.dao

Code Spec

```
1   package com.sharanamvaishali.dao;
```

```
2
3  import com.sharanamvaishali.model.Authors;
4
5  public interface AuthorsDAO {
6      public void saveAuthor(Authors authors);
7      public void updateAuthor(Authors authors);
8      public void deleteAuthor(int AuthorNo);
9      public Authors getAuthorById(int AuthorNo);
10 }
```

REMINDER

PopulateDdlbsDAO.java is explained later in the *Section VII: Common Files*
Software Design Documentation under the *Chapter 59: Populating Drop Down*
List Boxes.

PaginationDAO.java is explained later in the *Section V: Backend [Administration]*
Software Design Documentation under the *Chapter 42: Common Files*.

Implementation Class [AuthorsDAOImpl.java]

This is a **Data Access Object** class with the following specifications:

Class Name	AuthorsDAOImpl
Package	com.sharanamvaishali.dao
Implements	AuthorsDAO

Objects	
Object Name	**Class Name**
session	Session
transaction	Transaction

Methods		
Method Name	**Arguments**	**Return Values**
saveAuthor()	Authors authors	void
updateAuthor()	Authors authors	void
deleteAuthor()	Integer AuthorNo	void
getAuthorById()	Integer AuthorNo	Authors

Code Spec

```
1  package com.sharanamvaishali.dao;
2
3  import com.sharanamvaishali.model.Authors;
4  import com.sharanamvaishali.utility.HibernateUtil;
5  import org.hibernate.Session;
6  import org.hibernate.Transaction;
7
```

```java
 8   public class AuthorsDAOImpl implements AuthorsDAO {
 9       Session session = HibernateUtil.getSession();
10       Transaction transaction;
11
12       @Override
13       public void saveAuthor(Authors authors) {
14           try {
15               transaction = session.beginTransaction();
16               session.save(authors);
17               transaction.commit();
18           } catch (RuntimeException e) {
19               if(authors != null) {
20                   transaction.rollback();
21               }
22               throw e;
23           }
24       }
25
26       @Override
27       public void updateAuthor(Authors authors) {
28           try {
29               transaction = session.beginTransaction();
30               session.update(authors);
31               transaction.commit();
32           } catch (RuntimeException e) {
33               if(authors != null) {
34                   transaction.rollback();
35               }
36               throw e;
37           }
38       }
39
40       @Override
41       public void deleteAuthor(int AuthorNo) {
42           Object Authors = null;
43           try {
44               transaction = session.beginTransaction();
45               Authors = session.load(Authors.class, AuthorNo);
46               session.delete(Authors);
47               transaction.commit();
48           } catch (RuntimeException e) {
49               if(Authors != null) {
50                   transaction.rollback();
51               }
52               throw e;
53           }
54       }
55
```

```
56      @Override
57      public Authors getAuthorById(int AuthorNo) {
58          return (Authors) session.createQuery("FROM Authors WHERE AuthorNo =
            :AuthorNo").setInteger("AuthorNo", AuthorNo).uniqueResult();
59      }
60  }
```

Explanation:

The following section describes the above code spec.

saveAuthor()

saveAuthor() does the actual saving of the author in the Authors database table.

saveAuthor() uses **save()** of Session, which takes care of adding new author details when the user has entered all the author details and clicked **Save** .

After the save operation is performed, the transaction is committed to make the changes permanent.

Whilst performing the save operation, if a runtime exception occurs, than the transaction is **rolled back.**

updateAuthor()

updateAuthor() does the actual updation of the existing author in the Authors database table.

updateAuthor() uses **update()** of Session, which takes care of updating an existing author details when the user has made changes to the existing author details and clicked **Save** .

After the update operation is performed, the transaction is committed to make the changes permanent.

Whilst performing the update operation, if a runtime exception occurs, than the transaction is **rolled back.**

deleteAuthor()

deleteAuthor() deletes the appropriate author based on **AuthorNo** received as a reference.

This method uses:

❑   **load()** of Session, which retrieves the appropriate Author to be deleted using AuthorNo as a reference

❑   **delete()** of Session, which deletes the author from the Authors database table

After the delete operation is performed, the transaction is committed to make the changes permanent.

Whilst performing the delete operation, if a runtime exception occurs, than the transaction is **rolled back**.

getAuthorById()

getAuthorById() returns the appropriate author's object from the Authors database table using **AuthorNo** as the reference.

This method uses:

❑   **createQuery()** of Session, which creates a new instance of Query to retrieve the Author details using AuthorNo as reference

❑   **setInteger()** of Query, which states the parameter to be used as the WHERE clause criteria when querying the Authors database table

❑   **uniqueResult()** of Query, which ensures that only unique record is retrieved from the Authors database table and prevents any kinds of errors

REMINDER

PopulateDdlbsDAOImpl.java is explained later in the *Section VII: Common Files Software Design Documentation* under the *Chapter 59: Populating Drop Down List Boxes*.

PaginationDAOImpl.java is explained later in the *Section V: Backend [Administration] Software Design Documentation* under the *Chapter 42: Common Files*.

Validations [AuthorsAction-validation.xml]

If the required **input** fields are kept empty whilst submitting the form, AuthorsAction-validation.xml takes care of the validations.

Code Spec

```xml
1  <?xml version="1.0" encoding="UTF-8"?>
2  <!DOCTYPE validators PUBLIC '-//OpenSymphony Group//XWork Validator
   1.0.2//EN' 'http://www.opensymphony.com/xwork/xwork-validator-1.0.2.dtd'>
3  <validators>
4    <field name="author.FirstName">
5      <field-validator type="requiredstring">
6        <message>Please enter the first name.</message>
7      </field-validator>
8    </field>
9
10   <field name="author.LastName">
11     <field-validator type="requiredstring">
12       <message>Please enter the first name.</message>
13     </field-validator>
14   </field>
15
16   <field name="author.Degree">
17     <field-validator type="requiredstring">
18       <message>Please enter the qualification details.</message>
19     </field-validator>
20   </field>
21
22   <field name="author.EmailAddress">
23     <field-validator type="requiredstring" short-circuit="true">
24       <message>Please enter the email address.</message>
25     </field-validator>
26     <field-validator type="email" short-circuit="true">
27       <message>Invalid email address.</message>
28     </field-validator>
29   </field>
30 </validators>
```

If any errors are detected the data entry form is re-served with appropriate error messages, as shown in diagram 37.2.

struts-Authors.xml file holds a mapping to serve the data entry form:

```xml
17      <action name="doInsertAuthor" method="saveAuthor"
        class="com.sharanamvaishali.action.AuthorsAction">
18        <interceptor-ref name="defaultStack"/>
19        <interceptor-ref name="token"/>
20        <result name="success" type="redirectAction">doViewAuthors</result>
21        <result name="input">/admin/manageAuthors.jsp</result>
22      </action>
```

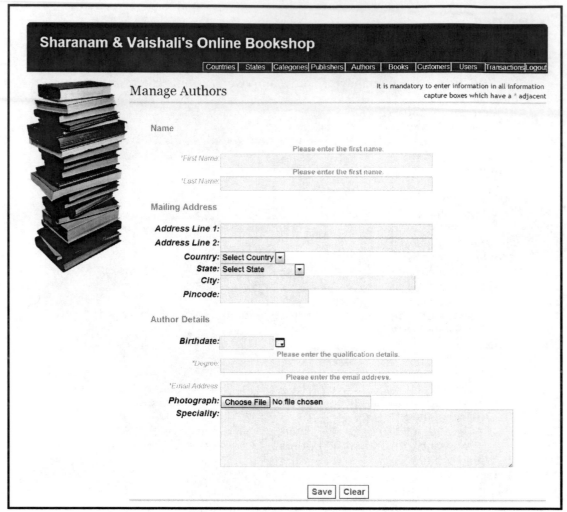

Diagram 37.2: Error messages

Struts Configuration [struts-Authors.xml]

This is the struts configuration file with the following specifications:

File Name	Package Name	Extends
Authors	manageAuthors	default

Actions	
Action Name	**Results**
showManageAuthors	SUCCESS - manageAuthors.jsp
iterateManageAuthorsPage	SUCCESS - manageAuthors.jsp

Actions [continued]	
Action Name	**Results**
doInsertAuthor	SUCCESS - doViewAuthors
	INPUT - manageAuthors.jsp
doViewAuthors	SUCCESS - manageAuthors.jsp
	ERROR - showManageAuthors
doDeleteAuthor	SUCCESS - doViewAuthors
	ERROR - manageAuthors.jsp
showEditAuthor	SUCCESS - manageAuthors.jsp

Code Spec

```
1   <?xml version="1.0" encoding="UTF-8"?>
2   <!DOCTYPE struts PUBLIC
3   "-//Apache Software Foundation//DTD Struts Configuration 2.0//EN"
4   "http://struts.apache.org/dtds/struts-2.0.dtd">
5   <struts>
6      <package name="manageAuthors" extends="default">
7         <default-interceptor-ref name="chkSession"/>
8
9         <action name="showManageAuthors" method="view"
           class="com.sharanamvaishali.action.AuthorsAction">
10           <result>/admin/manageAuthors.jsp</result>
11        </action>
12
13        <action name="iterateManageAuthorsPage" method="getPage"
           class="com.sharanamvaishali.action.AuthorsAction">
14           <result>/admin/manageAuthors.jsp</result>
15        </action>
16
17        <action name="doInsertAuthor" method="saveAuthor"
           class="com.sharanamvaishali.action.AuthorsAction">
18           <interceptor-ref name="defaultStack"/>
19           <interceptor-ref name="token"/>
20           <result name="success" type="redirectAction">doViewAuthors</result>
21           <result name="input">/admin/manageAuthors.jsp</result>
22        </action>
23
24        <action name="doViewAuthors" method="view"
           class="com.sharanamvaishali.action.AuthorsAction">
25           <result name="success">/admin/manageAuthors.jsp</result>
26           <result name="error"
             type="redirectAction">showManageAuthors</result>
27        </action>
28
29        <action name="doDeleteAuthor" method="removeAuthor"
           class="com.sharanamvaishali.action.AuthorsAction">
```

```
30              <result name="success" type="redirectAction">doViewAuthors</result>
31              <result name="error">/admin/manageAuthors.jsp</result>
32          </action>
33
34          <action name="showEditAuthor" method="editAuthor"
            class="com.sharanamvaishali.action.AuthorsAction">
35              <result name="success">/admin/manageAuthors.jsp</result>
36          </action>
37      </package>
38  </struts>
```

Explanation:

The following section describes the above code spec.

showManageAuthors.action

showManageAuthors is an action to help viewing.

This means the data entry form and the list of author details are displayed.

The list of author details are retrieved by **AuthorsAction's view()**.

iterateManageAuthorsPage.action

iterateManageAuthorsPage is an action to help iterate.

This means displaying 10 records of author details per page in the form of data grid.

This iterated data is retrieved by **AuthorsAction's getPage()**.

doInsertAuthor.action

doInsertAuthor is an action to help adding new author details or updating existing author details.

defaultStack interceptor is referenced, which a complete stack with all the common interceptors in place.

token interceptor is referenced, which checks for valid token presence in Action and prevents duplicate form submission.

doInsertAuthor.action:

❑ Calls **AuthorsAction's saveAuthor()** to add new author details or update the existing author details

❑ Ensures that the captured data is valid

❑ If the validation is successful then the data is saved and the result is redirected to **doViewAuthors.action**

❑ If the validation fails then the Manage Authors page along with error messages is displayed

doViewAuthors.action

doViewAuthors is an action to help viewing.

This means the list of author details is displayed.

The list of author details are retrieved by **AuthorsAction's view()**.

If there are no data available in the database then the error message is displayed in the Manage Authors page by redirecting the page to **showManageAuthors.action**.

doDeleteAuthor.action

In case, the user chooses to delete a author and clicks ✖, **doDeleteAuthor.action** is the action to help delete a author record from Manage Authors.

doDeleteAuthor.action:

❑ Calls **AuthorsAction's removeAuthor()** to delete a author record

❑ If the author record is deleted successfully then the result is redirected to **doViewAuthors.action**

❑ If the record being deleted is referenced by a record in another database table then the Manage Authors page displays the error message indicating that this record cannot be deleted

showEditAuthor.action

showEditAuthor is an action to help the editing of existing authors.

In case, the user chooses to edit an author and clicks that particular record, **showEditAuthor.action** helps fill up the Manage Authors form with author details.

showEditAuthor.action:

❑   Calls **AuthorsAction's editAuthor()** to retrieve the author details

❑   Returns to the Manage Authors page along with the data to be populated in the form

Domain Class [Authors.java]

This is a domain class with the following specifications:

Class Name	Package	Implements
Authors	com.sharanamvaishali.model	java.io.Serializable

Properties			
Property Name	**Property Type**	**Methods**	
AuthorNo	Integer	getAuthorNo()	setAuthorNo()
FirstName	String	getFirstName()	setFirstName()
LastName	String	getLastName()	setLastName()
Address1	String	getAddress1()	setAddress1()
Address2	String	getAddress2()	setAddress2()
City	String	getCity()	setCity()
StateNo	Integer	getStateNo()	setStateNo()
Pincode	String	getPincode(0	setPincode()
CountryNo	Integer	getCountryNo()	setCountryNo()
Degree	String	getDegree()	setDegree()
EmailAddress	String	getEmailAddress()	setEmailAddress()
Photograph	Blob	getPhotograph()	setPhotograph()
Speciality	String	getSpeciality()	setSpeciality()
Dob	String	getDob()	setDob()

Code Spec

```
1   package com.sharanamvaishali.model;
2
3   import java.sql.Blob;
4   import javax.persistence.*;
5
6   @Entity
7   @Table(name="AUTHORS")
8   public class Authors implements java.io.Serializable {
9       @Id
10      @GeneratedValue
11      @Column(name="AUTHORNO")
12      private Integer AuthorNo;
13      @Column(name="STATENO")
14      private Integer StateNo;
15      @Column(name="CITY")
```

```
16      private String City;
17      @Column(name="COUNTRYNO")
18      private Integer CountryNo;
19      @Column(name="FIRSTNAME")
20      private String FirstName;
21      @Column(name="LASTNAME")
22      private String LastName;
23      @Column(name="ADDRESS1")
24      private String Address1;
25      @Column(name="ADDRESS2")
26      private String Address2;
27      @Column(name="PINCODE")
28      private String Pincode;
29      @Column(name="DEGREE")
30      private String Degree;
31      @Column(name="EMAILADDRESS")
32      private String EmailAddress;
33      @Column(name="SPECIALITY")
34      private String Speciality;
35      @Column(name="DOB")
36      private String Dob;
37      @Column(name="PHOTOGRAPH")
38      private Blob Photograph;
39
40      public Authors() {
41      }
42
43      public String getAddress1() {
44          return Address1;
45      }
46      public void setAddress1(String Address1) {
47          this.Address1 = Address1;
48      }
49
50      public String getAddress2() {
51          return Address2;
52      }
53      public void setAddress2(String Address2) {
54          this.Address2 = Address2;
55      }
56
57      public Integer getAuthorNo() {
58          return AuthorNo;
59      }
60      public void setAuthorNo(Integer AuthorNo) {
61          this.AuthorNo = AuthorNo;
62      }
63
64      public Integer getStateNo() {
```

```
65          return StateNo;
66      }
67      public void setStateNo(Integer StateNo) {
68          this.StateNo = StateNo;
69      }
70
71      public String getCity() {
72          return City;
73      }
74      public void setCity(String City) {
75          this.City = City;
76      }
77
78      public Integer getCountryNo() {
79          return CountryNo;
80      }
81      public void setCountryNo(Integer CountryNo) {
82          this.CountryNo = CountryNo;
83      }
84
85      public String getDob() {
86          return Dob;
87      }
88      public void setDob(String Dob) {
89          this.Dob = Dob;
90      }
91
92      public String getDegree() {
93          return Degree;
94      }
95      public void setDegree(String Degree) {
96          this.Degree = Degree;
97      }
98
99      public String getEmailAddress() {
100         return EmailAddress;
101     }
102     public void setEmailAddress(String EmailAddress) {
103         this.EmailAddress = EmailAddress;
104     }
105
106     public String getFirstName() {
107         return FirstName;
108     }
109     public void setFirstName(String FirstName) {
110         this.FirstName = FirstName;
111     }
112
113     public String getLastName() {
```

```
114         return LastName;
115      }
116      public void setLastName(String LastName) {
117         this.LastName = LastName;
118      }
119
120      public Blob getPhotograph() {
121         return Photograph;
122      }
123      public void setPhotograph(Blob Photograph) {
124         this.Photograph = Photograph;
125      }
126
127      public String getPincode() {
128         return Pincode;
129      }
130      public void setPincode(String Pincode) {
131         this.Pincode = Pincode;
132      }
133
134      public String getSpeciality() {
135         return Speciality;
136      }
137      public void setSpeciality(String Speciality) {
138         this.Speciality = Speciality;
139      }
140   }
```

Chapter

38

SECTION V: BACKEND [ADMINISTRATION] SOFTWARE DESIGN DOCUMENTATION

Manage Books

This module allows performing the following operations:

- ❑ Adding new books
- ❑ Editing existing books
- ❑ Viewing existing books
- ❑ Deleting existing books

This module uses the bms.Books table to perform the above operations.

This module is made up of the following:

Type	Name	Description
JSP	manageBooks.jsp	The data entry form
Struts 2		
Action	BooksAction.java	The action class that facilitates data operations.
	GetFileAction.java	
Validation	BooksAction-validation.xml	The XML based validation file.
DAO Class	BooksDAO.java	The interfaces for the DAO layer.
	PaginationDAO.java	
	PopulateDdlbsDAO.java	
	BooksDAOImpl.java	The implementation classes that performs the actual data operations.
	PaginationDAOImpl.java	
	PopulateDdlbsDAOImpl.java	
Utility Class	PopulateDdlbs.java	The class that populates the list objects.
	SendMail.java	The class that sends mail.
Struts Configuration	struts-Books.xml	Struts configuration file.
Hibernate		
Mapping	hibernate.cfg.xml	The mapping file that holds Model class mapping.
Model Class	Books.java	The model class.
	Customers.java	

JSP [manageBooks.jsp]

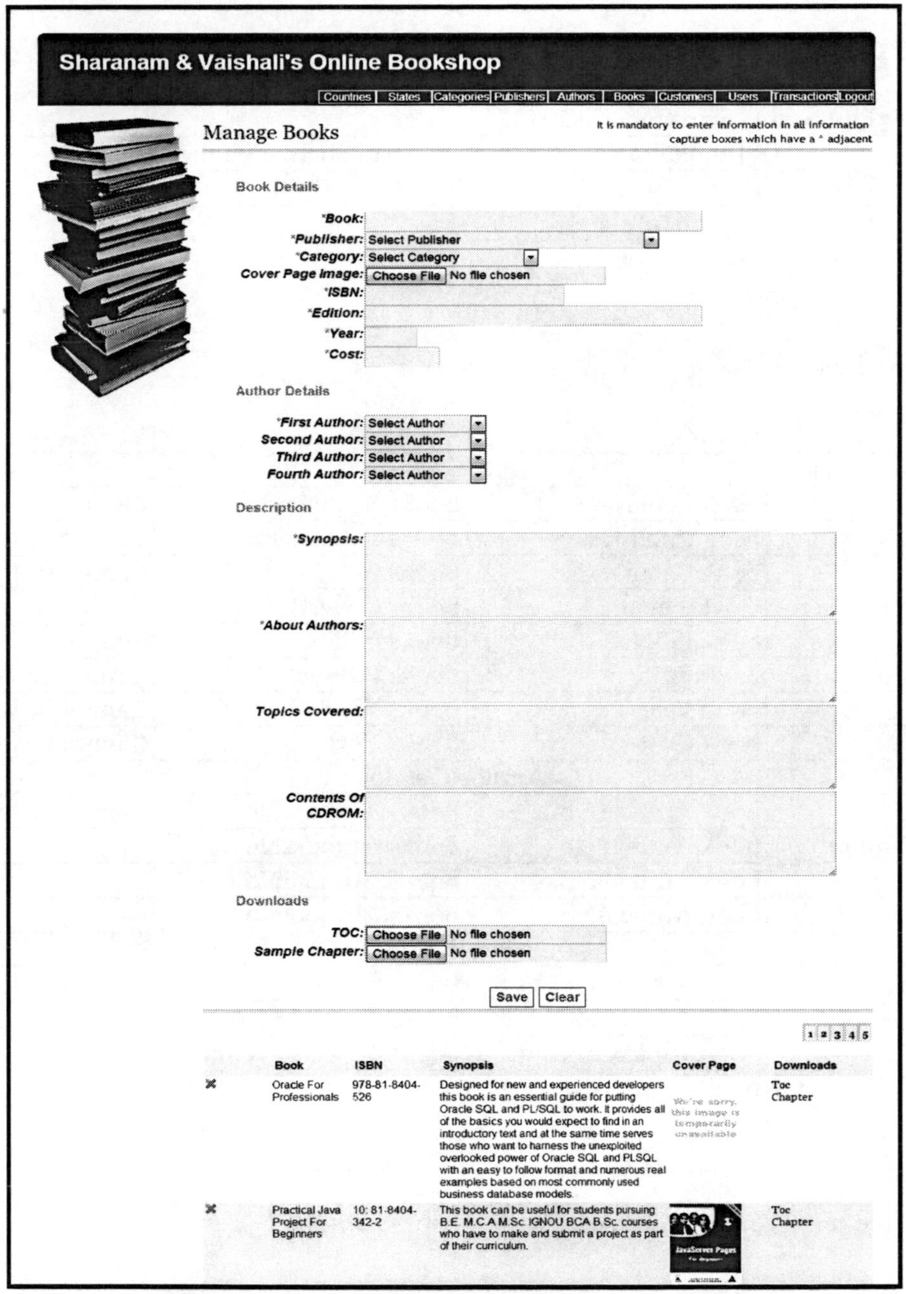

Diagram 38.1: Manage Books [Data entry form]

This is a JSP which holds a data entry form, as shown in diagram 38.1. This form appears when the user clicks ▐ Books ▐ .

Form Specifications

File Name	manageBooks.jsp
Title	BookShop[Sharanam & Vaishali Shah] - Manage Books
Bound To Table	bms.Books
Form Name	frmBooks
Action	doInsertBook
Method	POST

Data Fields

Label	Name	Bound To	Validation Rules
Book Details			
Book	book.BookName	Books.BookName	Cannot be left blank
Publisher	book.PublisherNo	Books.PublisherNo	Cannot be left blank
Category	book.CategoryNo	Books.CategoryNo	Cannot be left blank
Cover Page Image	CoverPage	Books.CoverPage	- -
ISBN	book.ISBN	Books.ISBN	Cannot be left blank
Edition	book.Edition	Books.Edition	Cannot be left blank
Year	book.Year	Books.Year	Cannot be left blank
Cost	book.Cost	Books.Cost	Cannot be left blank
Author Details			
First Author	book.Author1No	Books.Author1No	Cannot be left blank
Second Author	book.Author2No	Books.Author2No	- -
Third Author	book.Author3No	Books.Author3No	- -
Fourth Author	book.Author4No	Books.Author4No	- -
Description			
Synopsis	book.Synopsis	Books.Synopsis	Cannot be left blank
About Authors	book.AboutAuthors	Books.AboutAuthors	Cannot be left blank
Topics Covered	book.TopicsCovered	Books.TopicsCovered	- -
Contents Of CDROM	book.ContentsCDROM	Books.ContentsCDROM	- -
Downloads			
TOC	Toc	Books.TOC	- -
Sample Chapter	SampleChapter	Books.SampleChapter	- -

Micro-Help For Form Fields

Form Field	Micro Help Statement
Book Details	
book.BookName	Enter the book name
book.PublisherNo	Select the publisher name
book.CategoryNo	Select the category name
CoverPage	Enter the path of the cover page image
book.ISBN	Enter the ISBN
book.Edition	Enter the edition of the book
book.Year	Enter the year
book.Cost	Enter the cost of the book
Author Details	
book.Author1No	Select the name of the author
book.Author2No	Select the name of the author
book.Author3No	Select the name of the author
book.Author4No	Select the name of the author
Description	
book.Synopsis	Enter the synopsis
book.AboutAuthors	Enter the about author details
book.TopicsCovered	Enter the topics covered in the book
book.ContentsCDROM	Enter the contents of CDROM
Downloads	
Toc	Enter the path of the TOC
SampleChapter	Enter the path of the sample chapter

Data Controls

Object	Label	Name
s:submit	Save	btnSubmit
s:reset	Clear	btnReset

Code Spec

```
1   <%@page contentType="text/html" pageEncoding="UTF-8"%>
2   <%@ taglib prefix="s" uri="/struts-tags" %>
3   <!DOCTYPE HTML PUBLIC "-//W3C//DTD HTML 4.01 Transitional//EN"
4     "http://www.w3.org/TR/html4/loose.dtd">
5   <html xmlns="http://www.w3.org/1999/xhtml">
6     <head>
7       <title>BookShop [Sharanam & Vaishali Shah] - Manage Books</title>
8       <meta http-equiv="content-type" content="text/html; charset=iso-8859-1">
```

```
9      <link href="/BookShop/css/admin.css" type="text/css" rel="stylesheet">
10     <s:head/>
11    </head>
12    <body>
13     <s:include value="header.jsp" />
14     <br>
15     <s:form action="doInsertBook" method="post" name="frmBooks" id="frmBooks"
       enctype="multipart/form-data" validate="true">
16        <s:token/>
17        <s:hidden name="book.BookNo" id="BookNo"/>
18        <table width="100%" border="0" align="center" cellpadding="0" cellspacing="0">
19           <tr>
20              <td valign="top" width="20%">
21                 <img src="/BookShop/images/leftImg.jpg" height="350"/>
22              </td>
23              <td valign="top">
24                 <table width="100%" border="0" align="center" cellpadding="0"
                    cellspacing="0">
25                    <tr>
26                       <td>
27                          <table border="0" cellpadding="0" cellspacing="0"
                            width="100%">
28                             <tr>
29                                <td class="manageForms">Manage Books</td>
30                                <td class="information" valign="top" align="right">
31                                   It is mandatory to enter information in all information
                                   <br>capture boxes which have a <span
                                   class="mandatory">*</span> adjacent
32                                </td>
33                             </tr>
34                          </table>
35                       </td>
36                    </tr>
37                    <tr><td class="hrLine"> </td></tr>
38                    <tr align="left" valign="top">
39                       <td>
40                          <table width="90%" border="0" align="center" cellpadding="0"
                            cellspacing="0">
41                             <tr>
42                                <td>
43                                   <table width="100%" border="0" cellpadding="0"
                                      cellspacing="0">
44                                      <tr>
45                                         <td class="Arial16BlueB">
46                                            <br />Book Details<br /><br />
47                                         </td>
48                                      </tr>
49                                      <s:textfield required="true" requiredposition="left"
                                         id="BookName" label="Book" name="book.BookName"
                                         title="Enter the book name" maxLength="25"
                                         size="55"/>
50                                      <s:select list="ddlb.ddlbPublishers"
                                         listKey="PublisherNo" listValue="PublisherName"
                                         headerKey="" headerValue="Select Publisher"
```

```
     required="true" requiredposition="left"
     id="PublisherName" label="Publisher"
     name="book.PublisherNo" title="Select the publisher
     name"></s:select>
51   <s:select list="ddlb.ddlbCategories"
     listKey="CategoryNo" listValue="Category"
     headerKey="" headerValue="Select Category"
     required="true" requiredposition="left" id="Category"
     label="Category" name="book.CategoryNo" title="Select
     the category name"></s:select>
52   <s:file id="CoverPage" name="CoverPage" label="Cover
     Page Image" title="Enter the path of the cover page
     image"></s:file>
53   <s:textfield required="true" requiredposition="left"
     id="ISBN" label="ISBN" name="book.ISBN" title="Enter
     the ISBN" maxLength="15" size="30"/>
54   <s:textfield required="true" requiredposition="left"
     id="Edition" label="Edition" name="book.Edition"
     title="Enter the edition of the book" maxLength="25"
     size="55"/>
55   <s:textfield required="true" requiredposition="left"
     id="Year" label="Year" name="book.Year" title="Enter
     the year" maxLength="4" size="4"/>
56   <s:textfield required="true" requiredposition="left"
     id="Cost" label="Cost" name="book.Cost" title="Enter
     the cost of the book" maxLength="8" size="8"/>
57   <tr>
58      <td class="Arial16BlueB">
59         <br />Author Details<br /><br />
60      </td>
61   </tr>
62   <s:select list="ddlb.ddlbAuthors" listKey="AuthorNo"
     listValue="FirstName + ' ' + LastName" headerKey=""
     headerValue="Select Author" required="true"
     requiredposition="left" id="FirstAuthor" label="First
     Author" name="book.Author1No" title="Select the name
     of the author"></s:select>
63   <s:select list="ddlb.ddlbAuthors" listKey="AuthorNo"
     listValue="FirstName + ' ' + LastName" headerKey=""
     headerValue="Select Author" id="SecondAuthor"
     label="Second Author" name="book.Author2No"
     title="Select the name of the author"></s:select>
64   <s:select list="ddlb.ddlbAuthors" listKey="AuthorNo"
     listValue="FirstName + ' ' + LastName" headerKey=""
     headerValue="Select Author" id="ThirdAuthor"
     label="Third Author" name="book.Author3No"
     title="Select the name of the author"></s:select>
65   <s:select list="ddlb.ddlbAuthors" listKey="AuthorNo"
     listValue="FirstName + ' ' + LastName" headerKey=""
     headerValue="Select Author" id="FourthAuthor"
     label="Fourth Author" name="book.Author4No"
     title="Select the name of the author"></s:select>
66   <tr>
67      <td class="Arial16BlueB">
```

```
68                                    <br />Description<br /><br />
69                                </td>
70                            </tr>
71                            <s:textarea required="true" requiredposition="left"
                              id="Synopsis" label="Synopsis" name="book.Synopsis"
                              title="Enter the synopsis" cols="80"
                              rows="5"></s:textarea>
72                            <s:textarea required="true" requiredposition="left"
                              id="AboutAuthors" label="About Authors"
                              name="book.AboutAuthors" title="Enter the about
                              author details" cols="80" rows="5"></s:textarea>
73                            <s:textarea id="TopicsCovered" label="Topics Covered"
                              name="book.TopicsCovered" title="Enter the topics
                              covered in the book" cols="80" rows="5"></s:textarea>
74                            <s:textarea id="ContentsCDROM" label="Contents Of
                              CDROM" name="book.ContentsCDROM" title="Enter the
                              contents of CDROM" cols="80" rows="5"></s:textarea>
75                            <tr>
76                              <td class="Arial16BlueB">
77                                  <br />Downloads<br /><br />
78                              </td>
79                            </tr>
80                            <s:file id="Toc" name="Toc" label="TOC" title="Enter
                              the path of the TOC"></s:file>
81                            <s:file id="Sample Chapter" name="SampleChapter"
                              label="Sample Chapter" title="Enter the path of the
                              sample chapter"></s:file>
82                            <s:actionerror/>
83                          </table>
84                        </td>
85                    </tr>
86                    <tr>
87                      <td style="text-align: center;">
88                        <br /><br />
89                        <s:submit theme="simple" cssClass="groovybutton"
                          name="btnSubmit" id="btnSubmit" value="Save" />
90                        <s:reset theme="simple" cssClass="groovybutton"
                          name="btnReset" id="btnReset" value="Clear"
                          onclick="javascript:document.location.href='showManageB
                          ooks.action'"/>
91                      </td>
92                    </tr>
93                  </table>
94                </td>
95              </tr>
96              <tr><td class="hrLine"> </td></tr>
97              <tr>
98                <td align="center">
99                  <table width="60px" border="0" align="right" cellpadding="3"
                     cellspacing="1" style="border:#c3bca4 1px solid">
100                   <tr>
101                     <s:bean name="org.apache.struts2.util.Counter"
                         id="counter">
102                       <s:param name="last" value="%{pageCount}" />
```

```
103                          </s:bean>
104                          <s:iterator value="#counter">
105                            <td align="center" width="2px" style="border:#c3bca4
                             1px solid; background:#efebde; font-family:sans-serif;
                             font-size:12px; font-weight:bolder; text-align:center;
                             vertical-align:middle;">
106                              <a href="<s:url
                             action="iterateManageBooksPage"><s:param
                             name="pageNo"><s:property
                             /></s:param></s:url>"><s:property /></a>
107                            </td>
108                          </s:iterator>
109                        </tr>
110                      </table>
111                    </td>
112                  </tr>
113                  <tr>
114                    <td>
115                      <br>
116                      <table class="view" align="center" cellspacing="0"
                       cellpadding="0" width="100%">
117                        <tr>
118                          <th width="10%" align="center"> </th>
119                          <th width="12%" class="Arial13BrownB"
                           align="left">Book</th>
120                          <th width="13%" class="Arial13BrownB"
                           align="left">ISBN</th>
121                          <th width="35%" class="Arial13BrownB"
                           align="left">Synopsis</th>
122                          <th width="15%" class="Arial13BrownB" align="left">Cover
                           Page</th>
123                          <th width="15%" class="Arial13BrownB"
                           align="left">Downloads</th>
124                        </tr>
125                        <s:iterator value="books" id="books" status="stat">
126                          <tr title="Click to edit" class="<s:if test="#stat.odd ==
                           true">odd</s:if><s:else>even</s:else>">
127                            <td width="10%" valign="top">
128                              <a href="<s:url action="doDeleteBook"><s:param
                               name="book.BookNo" value="BookNo" /></s:url>">
129                                <img src="/BookShop/images/TrashIcon.png"
                                 border="0" alt="Delete" style="cursor:pointer;"/>
130                              </a>
131                            </td>
132                            <td width="12%" class="manageList"
                             onclick="javascript:location.href='<s:url
                             action='showEditBook'><s:param name='book.BookNo'
                             value='BookNo' /></s:url>'">
133                              <s:property value="BookName"/>
134                            </td>
135                            <td width="13%" class="manageList"
                             onclick="javascript:location.href='<s:url
                             action='showEditBook'><s:param name='book.BookNo'
                             value='BookNo' /></s:url>'">
```

```
136                                        <s:property value="ISBN"/>
137                                    </td>
138                                    <td width="35%" class="manageList"
                                       onclick="javascript:location.href='<s:url
                                       action='showEditBook'><s:param name='book.BookNo'
                                       value='BookNo' /></s:url>'">
139                                        <s:property value="Synopsis"/>
140                                    </td>
141                                    <td width="15%" class="manageList"
                                       onclick="javascript:location.href='<s:url
                                       action='showEditBook'><s:param name='book.BookNo'
                                       value='BookNo' /></s:url>'">
142                                        <s:if test="CoverPage==''">
143                                            <img src="/BookShop/images/imgNA.jpg"
                                            width="80px"/>
144                                        </s:if>
145                                        <s:else>
146                                            <img
                                            src="getFile.action?columnName=CoverPage&tableNa
                                            me=Books&whereClause=BookNo&whereClauseValue
                                            =<s:property value="BookNo" />" width="80px"/>
147                                        </s:else>
148                                    </td>
149                                    <td width="15%" class="manageList"
                                       onclick="javascript:location.href='<s:url
                                       action='showEditBook'><s:param name='book.BookNo'
                                       value='BookNo' /></s:url>'">
150                                        <a
                                            href="getPDF.action?columnName=Toc&tableName=Boo
                                            ks&whereClause=BookNo&whereClauseValue=<s:propert
                                            y value="BookNo" />">Toc</a>
151                                        <br/>
152                                        <a
                                            href="getPDF.action?columnName=SampleChapter&tabl
                                            eName=Books&whereClause=BookNo&whereClauseValue
                                            =<s:property value="BookNo" />">Chapter</a>
153                                    </td>
154                                </tr>
155                            </s:iterator>
156                            <s:if test="#books==null">
157                                <span class="emptyMessage">Currently there exists no books
                                   in the database. Please add a few books to begin managing
                                   them.</span>
158                            </s:if>
159                        </table>
160                    </td>
161                </tr>
162            </table>
163        </td>
164    </tr>
165    </table>
166    </s:form>
167    <s:include value="adminFooter.jsp" />
168    </body>
169 </html>
```

Explanation:

This is a standard data entry form, which captures the book details. By default, when the form loads, it is in the **INSERT** and **VIEW** mode. The form also has Delete and Edit options to delete and edit a particular book record.

Action [BooksAction.java]

This is an action class with the following specifications:

Class Name	BooksAction
Package	com.sharanamvaishali.action
Extends	ActionSupport
Implements	- -

Objects		
Object Name	**Class Name**	**Object Type**
session	Session	Hibernate Utility Class
booksDAO	BooksDAO	Data Access Layer
ddlb	PopulateDdlbs	Java Class
pg	PaginationDAO	Data Access Layer
book	Books	Model

Properties			
Property Name	**Property Type**	**Methods**	
For the data entry form fields			
book	Books	getBook()	setBook()
ddlb	PopulateDdlbs	getDdlb()	setDdlb()
CoverPage	File	getCoverPage()	setCoverPage()
Toc	File	getToc()	setToc()
SampleChapter	File	getSampleChapter()	setSampleChapter()
For the data grid population			
books	List<Books>	getBooks()	setBooks()
For pagination			
pageNo	int	getPageNo()	setPageNo()
pageCount	int	getPageCount()	setPageCount()

Methods	
Method Name	**Return Values**
saveBook()	SUCCESS
view()	SUCCESS
removeBook()	SUCCESS
	ERROR
editBook()	SUCCESS
getPage()	SUCCESS

Code Spec

```
1  package com.sharanamvaishali.action;
2
3  import com.opensymphony.xwork2.ActionSupport;
4  import com.sharanamvaishali.dao.BooksDAO;
5  import com.sharanamvaishali.dao.BooksDAOImpl;
6  import com.sharanamvaishali.dao.PaginationDAO;
7  import com.sharanamvaishali.dao.PaginationDAOImpl;
8  import com.sharanamvaishali.model.Books;
9  import com.sharanamvaishali.utility.HibernateUtil;
10 import com.sharanamvaishali.utility.PopulateDdlbs;
11 import java.io.File;
12 import java.util.List;
13 import org.apache.commons.io.FileUtils;
14 import org.apache.struts2.interceptor.validation.SkipValidation;
15 import org.hibernate.Session;
16
17 public class BooksAction extends ActionSupport{
18     Session session = HibernateUtil.getSession();
19
20     private BooksDAO booksDAO = new BooksDAOImpl();
21
22     private PopulateDdlbs ddlb = new PopulateDdlbs();
23
24     private PaginationDAO pg = new PaginationDAOImpl();
25
26     private Books book;
27
28     private List<Books> books;
29
30     private File CoverPage, Toc, SampleChapter;
31
32     private int pageNo, pageCount;
33
34     public PopulateDdlbs getDdlb() {
35         return ddlb;
36     }
37     public void setDdlb(PopulateDdlbs ddlb) {
38         this.ddlb = ddlb;
39     }
40
41     public int getPageNo() {
42         return pageNo;
43     }
44     public void setPageNo(int pageNo) {
45         this.pageNo = pageNo;
46     }
```

```
47
48      public int getPageCount() {
49          return pageCount;
50      }
51      public void setPageCount(int pageCount) {
52          this.pageCount = pageCount;
53      }
54
55      public Books getBook() {
56          return book;
57      }
58      public void setBook(Books book) {
59          this.book = book;
60      }
61
62      public List<Books> getBooks() {
63          return books;
64      }
65      public void setBooks(List<Books> books) {
66          this.books = books;
67      }
68
69      public File getSampleChapter() {
70          return SampleChapter;
71      }
72      public void setSampleChapter(File SampleChapter) {
73          this.SampleChapter = SampleChapter;
74      }
75
76      public File getToc() {
77          return Toc;
78      }
79      public void setToc(File Toc) {
80          this.Toc = Toc;
81      }
82
83      public File getCoverPage() {
84          return CoverPage;
85      }
86      public void setCoverPage(File CoverPage) {
87          this.CoverPage = CoverPage;
88      }
89
90      public String saveBook() throws Exception{
91          if(CoverPage != null) {
92             book.setCoverPage(session.getLobHelper().createBlob(FileUtils.readFileTo
               ByteArray(CoverPage)));
93          }
94
```

```
95        if(Toc != null) {
96            book.setToc(session.getLobHelper().createBlob(FileUtils.readFileToByteArr
             ay(Toc)));
97        }
98
99        if(SampleChapter != null) {
100           book.setSampleChapter(session.getLobHelper().createBlob(FileUtils.readFi
             leToByteArray(SampleChapter)));
101       }
102
103       if(book.getBookNo() != null) {
104           booksDAO.updateBook(book);
105       } else {
106           booksDAO.saveBook(book);
107       }
108       return SUCCESS;
109   }
110
111   @SkipValidation
112   public String view() throws Exception{
113       pageNo = 1;
114       getPage();
115       return SUCCESS;
116   }
117
118   @SkipValidation
119   public String removeBook() throws Exception{
120       booksDAO.deleteBook(book.getBookNo());
121       return SUCCESS;
122   }
123
124   @SkipValidation
125   public String editBook() throws Exception{
126       book = booksDAO.getBookById(book.getBookNo());
127       view();
128       return SUCCESS;
129   }
130
131   @SkipValidation
132   public String getPage() throws Exception{
133       pageCount = pg.getTotalPages("Books");
134       books = pg.getPage(pageNo-1, "Books").getList();
135       return SUCCESS;
136   }
137 }
```

Explanation:

The following section describes the above code spec.

saveBook()

saveBook() is invoked when the user keys in the desired data and clicks **Save**.

saveBook():

❑ Checks whether the Cover page, TOC and Sample chapter are uploaded. If they are uploaded, they are set using **setter methods** of the **Books** model

   o Uses getLobHelper() of Session, which is a session's helper for creating LOB data

   o Uses createBlob() of LobHelper, which creates a new BOLB from bytes

   o Uses FileUtils, which is a general file manipulation utility

   o Uses readFileToByteArray() of FileUtils, which reads the contents of a file into a byte array

❑ Performs an update operation [using BooksDAO's updateBook()] if **book.getBookNo()** returns a valid BookNo

❑ Performs an insert operation [using BooksDAO's saveBook()] if **book.getBookNo()** returns empty

view()

view() is invoked every time Manage Books is served.

It invokes **getPage()** to populate the List object [books] which is used in the JSP page's **<s:iterator>** to populate the data grid. This data grid displays existing records from the **Books** database table.

@SkipValidation is used to skip validation for this method.

removeBook()

removeBook() is invoked when the user clicks ✖ adjacent to the desired record [in the data grid] for deletion.

The delete operation is performed by invoking BooksDAO's **deleteBook()**.

deleteBook() is passed **BookNo** which is made available by JSP using **<s:param>** on click of ✖.

@SkipValidation is used to skip validation for this method.

editBook()

editBook() is invoked when the user clicks a desired record from the data grid in Manage Books for updating it.

It populates the bean class object [book] with the chosen record's data. The data is retrieved using BooksDAO's **getBookById()** which is passed BookNo which is made available by JSP's <s:param> on click of the record.

Struts 2 framework automatically transfers the values from the bean class object to the FORM fields thus making it available to the user for editing the same.

@SkipValidation is used to skip validation for this method.

getPage()

getPage() is invoked every time Manage Books is served or the user clicks a page number link from Manage Books using pagination.

It calculates the total number of pages for pagination purpose and stores the same in the property named **pageCount**.

It populates the List object [books] which is used in the JSP page's <s:iterator> to form the data grid. This data grid displays existing records from the Books database table.

The data to be populated in the List object is retrieved using PaginationDAO's **getPage()** which returns the records belonging to the appropriate page number.

@SkipValidation is used to skip validation for this method.

REMINDER

GetFileAction.java is explained later in the *Section VII: Common Files Software Design Documentation* under the *Chapter 58: Retrieving Blob Values*.

DAO Class

Interface [BooksDAO.java]

This is a Data Access Object interface with the following specifications:

Class Name	Package
BooksDAO	com.sharanamvaishali.dao

Code Spec

```
1   package com.sharanamvaishali.dao;
2
3   import com.sharanamvaishali.model.Books;
4
5   public interface BooksDAO {
6       public void saveBook(Books books) throws Exception;
7       public void updateBook(Books books) throws Exception;
8       public void deleteBook(int BookNo);
9       public Books getBookById(int BookNo);
10      public void notifyNewRealeasesToCustomers(Books books) throws Exception;
11      public void notifyUpdatesToCustomers(Books books) throws Exception;
12  }
```

REMINDER

PopulateDdlbsDAO.java is explained later in the *Section VII: Common Files Software Design Documentation* under the *Chapter 59: Populating Drop Down List Boxes*.

PaginationDAO.java is explained later in the *Section V: Backend [Administration] Software Design Documentation* under the *Chapter 42: Common Files*.

Implementation Class [BooksDAOImpl.java]

This is a Data Access Object class with the following specifications:

Class Name	BooksDAOImpl
Package	com.sharanamvaishali.dao
Implements	BooksDAO

Objects	
Object Name	**Class Name**
session	Session
transaction	Transaction

Methods		
Method Name	Arguments	Return Values
saveBook()	Books books	void
updateBook()	Books books	void
deleteBook()	Integer BookNo	void
getBookById()	Integer BookNo	Books
notifyNewReleasesToCustomers()	Books books	void
notifyUpdatesToCustomers()	Books books	void

Code Spec

```
1    package com.sharanamvaishali.dao;
2
3    import com.opensymphony.xwork2.ActionContext;
4    import com.sharanamvaishali.model.Books;
5    import com.sharanamvaishali.model.Customers;
6    import com.sharanamvaishali.utility.HibernateUtil;
7    import com.sharanamvaishali.utility.SendMail;
8    import java.util.Iterator;
9    import java.util.List;
10   import java.util.Locale;
11   import java.util.ResourceBundle;
12   import org.hibernate.Session;
13   import org.hibernate.Transaction;
14
15   public class BooksDAOImpl implements BooksDAO {
16       Session session = HibernateUtil.getSession();
17       Transaction transaction;
18
19       @Override
20       public void saveBook(Books books) throws Exception {
21           try {
22               transaction = session.beginTransaction();
23               session.save(books);
24               transaction.commit();
25               notifyNewRealeasesToCustomers(books);
26           } catch (RuntimeException e) {
27               if(books != null) {
28                   transaction.rollback();
29               }
30               throw e;
31           }
32       }
33
34       @Override
35       public void updateBook(Books books) throws Exception {
36           try {
```

```
37              transaction = session.beginTransaction();
38              session.update(books);
39              transaction.commit();
40              notifyUpdatesToCustomers(books);
41          } catch (RuntimeException e) {
42              if(books != null) {
43                  transaction.rollback();
44              }
45              throw e;
46          }
47      }
48
49      @Override
50      public void deleteBook(int BookNo) {
51          Object Books = null;
52          try {
53              transaction = session.beginTransaction();
54              Books = session.load(Books.class, BookNo);
55              session.delete(Books);
56              transaction.commit();
57          } catch (RuntimeException e) {
58              if(Books != null) {
59                  transaction.rollback();
60              }
61              throw e;
62          }
63      }
64
65      @Override
66      public Books getBookById(int BookNo) {
67          return (Books) session.createQuery("FROM Books WHERE BookNo =
                :BookNo").setInteger("BookNo", BookNo).uniqueResult();
68      }
69
70      @Override
71      public void notifyNewRealeasesToCustomers(Books books) throws Exception {
72          Locale locale = ActionContext.getContext().getLocale();
73          ResourceBundle bundle = ResourceBundle.getBundle("bookshop", locale);
74          if(!bundle.getString("emailFrom").equals("") &&
                !bundle.getString("emailUser").equals("") &&
                !bundle.getString("emailFromPasswd").equals("")) {
75              session.beginTransaction();
76              List<Customers> customers = session.createQuery("FROM Customers
                    WHERE NewRelease = 'true'").list();
77              for (Iterator i = customers.iterator(); i.hasNext(); ) {
78                  Customers objCustomer = (Customers) i.next();
79                  String toEmailAddress = objCustomer.getEmailAddress();
80                  String emailSubject = "Sharanam & Vaishali's Online BookShop: " +
                        books.getBookName() + " has been added.";
```

```
81          String emailMessage = "<html><head><meta
            http-equiv='Content-Type' content='text/html;
            charset=iso-8859-1'/><title>" + books.getBookName() + " has been
            added.</title></head><body><table width='500' border='0'
            align='center' cellpadding='15' cellspacing='0' style='font-family:
            Verdana, Arial, Helvetica, sans-serif; font-size: 12pt;
            color:#5a5a5a;'><tr><td align='left'>Dear " +
            objCustomer.getFirstName() + ",</td></tr><tr><td
            align='left'><br/><br/>ISBN: " + books.getISBN() + "<br />Edition:
            " + books.getEdition() + "<br />Synopsis: " + books.getSynopsis() +
            "<br />Topics covered: " + books.getTopicsCovered() + "<br
            /><br/>Thank you for using  this site.<br/><br/>Regards,<br
            />Sharanam & Vaishali's Online Bookshop<br /><br /><br />THIS IS
            AN AUTOMATED MESSAGE; PLEASE DO NOT
            REPLY.</td></tr></table></body></html>";
82          SendMail.sendMail(bundle.getString("emailFrom"),
            bundle.getString("emailUser"), bundle.getString("emailFromPasswd"),
            toEmailAddress, emailSubject, emailMessage);
83        }
84      }
85    }
86
87    @Override
88    public void notifyUpdatesToCustomers(Books books) throws Exception {
89      Locale locale = ActionContext.getContext().getLocale();
90      ResourceBundle bundle = ResourceBundle.getBundle("bookshop", locale);
91      if(!bundle.getString("emailFrom").equals("") &&
         !bundle.getString("emailUser").equals("") &&
         !bundle.getString("emailFromPasswd").equals("")) {
92        session.beginTransaction();
93        List<Customers> customers = session.createQuery("FROM Customers
          WHERE BookUpdates = 'true'").list();
94        for (Iterator i = customers.iterator(); i.hasNext(); ) {
95          Customers objCustomer = (Customers) i.next();
96          String toEmailAddress = objCustomer.getEmailAddress();
97          String emailSubject = "Sharanam & Vaishali's Online Bookshop: " +
            books.getBookName() + " has been updated.";
98          String emailMessage = "<html><head><meta
            http-equiv='Content-Type' content='text/html;
            charset=iso-8859-1'/><title>" + books.getBookName() + " has been
            updated.</title></head><body><table width='500' border='0'
            align='center' cellpadding='15' cellspacing='0' style='font-family:
            Verdana, Arial, Helvetica, sans-serif; font-size:12pt; color:
            #5a5a5a;'><tr><td align='left'>Dear " + objCustomer.getFirstName()
            + ",</td></tr><tr><td align='left'><br/><br/>ISBN: " +
            books.getISBN() + "<br />Edition: " + books.getEdition() + "<br
            />Synopsis: " + books.getSynopsis() + "<br />Topics covered: " +
            books.getTopicsCovered() + "<br /><br/>Thank you for using  this
            site.<br /><br/>Regards,<br />Sharanam & Vaishali's Online
```

```
        Bookshop<br /><br />THIS IS AN AUTOMATED MESSAGE; PLEASE DO
        NOT REPLY.</td></tr></table></body></html>";
99      SendMail.sendMail(bundle.getString("emailFrom"),
        bundle.getString("emailUser"), bundle.getString("emailFromPasswd"),
        toEmailAddress, emailSubject, emailMessage);
100        }
101      }
102    }
103 }
```

Explanation:

The following section describes the above code spec.

saveBook()

saveBook() does the actual saving of the book in the Books database table.

saveBook() uses **save()** of Session, which takes care of adding new book details when the user has entered all the book details and clicked **Save**.

After the save operation is performed, the transaction is committed to make the changes permanent.

saveBook() also calls **notifyNewReleasesToCustomers()** to notify the customers about the newly released book.

Whilst performing the save operation, if a runtime exception occurs, than the transaction is **rolled back**.

updateBook()

updateBook() does the actual updation of the existing book in the Books database table.

updateBook() uses **update()** of Session, which takes care of updating an existing book details when the user has made changes to the existing book details and clicked **Save**.

After the update operation is performed, the transaction is committed to make the changes permanent.

updateBook() also calls **notifyUpdatesToCustomers()** to notify the customers about the updated book.

Whilst performing the update operation, if a runtime exception occurs, than the transaction is **rolled back**.

deleteBook()

deleteBook() deletes the appropriate book based on **BookNo** received as a reference.

This method uses:

❑ **load()** of Session, which retrieves the appropriate Book to be deleted using BookNo as a reference

❑ **delete()** of Session, which deletes the book from the Books database table

After the delete operation is performed, the transaction is committed to make the changes permanent.

Whilst performing the delete operation, if a runtime exception occurs, than the transaction is **rolled back**.

getBookById()

getBookById() returns the appropriate book's object from the Books database table using **BookNo** as the reference.

This method uses:

❑ **createQuery()** of Session, which creates a new instance of Query to retrieve the Book details using BookNo as reference

❑ **setInteger()** of Query, which states the parameter to be used as the WHERE clause criteria when querying the Books database table

❑ **uniqueResult()** of Query, which ensures that only unique record is retrieved from the Books database table and prevents any kinds of errors

notifyNewReleasesToCustomers()

notifyNewReleasesToCustomers() is called by saveBook(). This method sends an email to the registered customers regarding the newly released books.

notifyNewReleasesToCustomer():

❑ Retrieves the current Locale of the current Action

❑ Retrieves a resource bundle [bookshop.properties] using the base name as bookshop and the current Locale

❑ A check is made whether the resource bundle holds all the properties such as email address, username and password for sending the mail

  o Retrieves the registered customers details of the customers who had chosen New Releases facility while registering

  o For each user:

    ▪ A message is created regarding the book details

    ▪ The mail is send for the newly released books

notifyUpdatesToCustomers()

notifyUpdatesToCustomers() is called by updateBook(). This method sends an email to the registered customers regarding the updated books.

notifyUpdatesToCustomer():

❑ Retrieves the current Locale of the current Action

❑ Retrieves a resource bundle [bookshop.properties] using the base name as bookshop and the current Locale

❑ A check is made whether the resource bundle holds all the properties such as email address, username and password for sending the mail

  o Retrieves the registered customers details of the customers who had chosen Book Updates facility while registering

  o For each user:

    ▪ A message is created regarding the book details

    ▪ The mail is send for the updated books

REMINDER

PopulateDdlbsDAOImpl.java is explained later in the *Section VII: Common Files Software Design Documentation* under the *Chapter 59: Populating Drop Down List Boxes*.

PaginationDAOImpl.java is explained later in the *Section V: Backend [Administration] Software Design Documentation* under the *Chapter 42: Common Files*.

REMINDER

SendMail.java is explained later in the *Section V: Backend [Administration] Software Design Documentation* under the *Chapter 60: Sending Mails*.

Validations [BooksAction-validation.xml]

If the required **input** fields are kept empty whilst submitting the form, BooksAction-validation.xml takes care of the validations.

Code Spec

```
1   <?xml version="1.0" encoding="UTF-8"?>
2   <!DOCTYPE validators PUBLIC '-//OpenSymphony Group//XWork Validator
    1.0.2//EN' 'http://www.opensymphony.com/xwork/xwork-validator-1.0.2.dtd'>
3   <validators>
4     <field name="book.BookName">
5       <field-validator type="requiredstring">
6         <message>Please enter the book name.</message>
7       </field-validator>
8     </field>
9
10    <field name="book.PublisherNo">
11      <field-validator type="required">
12        <message>Please select the publisher name.</message>
13      </field-validator>
14    </field>
15
16    <field name="book.CategoryNo">
17      <field-validator type="required">
18        <message>Please select the category name.</message>
19      </field-validator>
20    </field>
21
22    <field name="book.ISBN">
23      <field-validator type="requiredstring">
24        <message>Please enter the book ISBN.</message>
25      </field-validator>
26    </field>
27
28    <field name="book.Edition">
29      <field-validator type="requiredstring">
30        <message>Please enter the edition of the book.</message>
31      </field-validator>
32    </field>
33
34    <field name="book.Year">
35      <field-validator type="required" short-circuit="true">
36        <message>Please enter the year when the book was
          published.</message>
37      </field-validator>
38      <field-validator type="int" short-circuit="true">
```

```
39          <message>Enter a numeric value</message>
40        </field-validator>
41      </field>
42
43      <field name="book.Cost">
44        <field-validator type="required" short-circuit="true">
45          <message>Please enter the cost of the book.</message>
46        </field-validator>
47        <field-validator type="int" short-circuit="true">
48          <message>Enter a numeric value</message>
49        </field-validator>
50      </field>
51
52      <field name="book.Author1No">
53        <field-validator type="required">
54          <message>Please select the name of the first author.</message>
55        </field-validator>
56      </field>
57
58      <field name="book.Synopsis">
59        <field-validator type="requiredstring">
60          <message>Please enter the synopsis of the book.</message>
61        </field-validator>
62      </field>
63
64      <field name="book.AboutAuthors">
65        <field-validator type="requiredstring">
66          <message>Please enter the about the author details.</message>
67        </field-validator>
68      </field>
69    </validators>
```

If any errors are detected the data entry form is re-served with appropriate error messages, as shown in diagram 38.2.

struts-Books.xml file holds a mapping to serve the data entry form:

```
17        <action name="doInsertBook" method="saveBook"
          class="com.sharanamvaishali.action.BooksAction">
18          <interceptor-ref name="defaultStack"/>
19          <interceptor-ref name="token"/>
20          <result name="success" type="redirectAction">doViewBooks</result>
21          <result name="input">/admin/manageBooks.jsp</result>
22        </action>
```

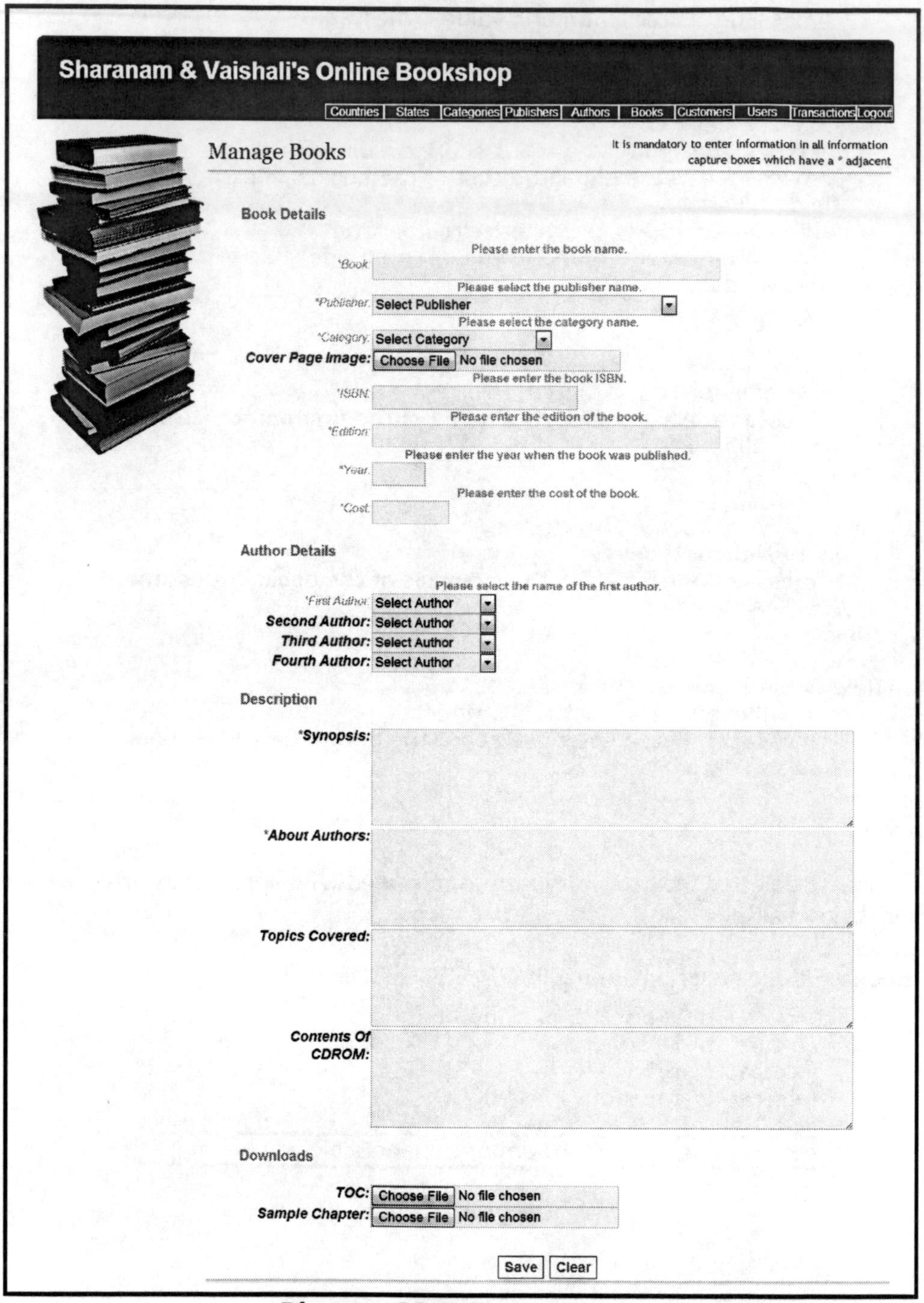

Sharanam & Vaishali's Online Bookshop

Countries | States | Categories | Publishers | Authors | Books | Customers | Users | Transactions | Logout

Manage Books

It is mandatory to enter information in all information capture boxes which have a * adjacent

Book Details

Please enter the book name.
*Book

Please select the publisher name.
*Publisher: Select Publisher

Please select the category name.
*Category: Select Category

Cover Page Image: Choose File No file chosen

Please enter the book ISBN.
*ISBN:

Please enter the edition of the book.
*Edition

Please enter the year when the book was published.
*Year:

Please enter the cost of the book.
*Cost:

Author Details

Please select the name of the first author.
*First Author: Select Author
Second Author: Select Author
Third Author: Select Author
Fourth Author: Select Author

Description

*Synopsis:

*About Authors:

Topics Covered:

Contents Of CDROM:

Downloads

TOC: Choose File No file chosen
Sample Chapter: Choose File No file chosen

Save | Clear

Diagram 38.2: Error messages

REMINDER

 In the diagram 38.2, the error message for Synopsis and About Authors are not displayed even though they are mandatory. The reason being that the previous validators such as Year and Cost are marked as short-circuit. The validators marked as short-circuit will prevent the evaluation of subsequent validators i.e. the validators of Synopsis and About Authors.

Struts Configuration [struts-Books.xml]

This is the struts configuration file with the following specifications:

File Name	Package Name	Extends
Books	manageBooks	default

Actions	
Action Name	**Results**
showManageBooks	SUCCESS - manageBooks.jsp
iterateManageBooksPage	SUCCESS - manageBooks.jsp
doInsertBook	SUCCESS - doViewBooks
	INPUT - manageBooks.jsp
doViewBooks	SUCCESS - manageBooks.jsp
	ERROR - showManageBooks
doDeleteBook	SUCCESS - doViewBooks
	ERROR - manageBooks.jsp
showEditBook	SUCCESS - manageBooks.jsp

Code Spec

```
1   <?xml version="1.0" encoding="UTF-8"?>
2   <!DOCTYPE struts PUBLIC
3   "-//Apache Software Foundation//DTD Struts Configuration 2.0//EN"
4   "http://struts.apache.org/dtds/struts-2.0.dtd">
5   <struts>
6       <package name="manageBooks" extends="default">
7           <default-interceptor-ref name="chkSession"/>
8
9           <action name="showManageBooks" method="view"
            class="com.sharanamvaishali.action.BooksAction">
10              <result>/admin/manageBooks.jsp</result>
11          </action>
12
13          <action name="iterateManageBooksPage" method="getPage"
            class="com.sharanamvaishali.action.BooksAction">
14              <result>/admin/manageBooks.jsp</result>
15          </action>
```

```
16
17        <action name="doInsertBook" method="saveBook"
          class="com.sharanamvaishali.action.BooksAction">
18          <interceptor-ref name="defaultStack"/>
19          <interceptor-ref name="token"/>
20          <result name="success" type="redirectAction">doViewBooks</result>
21          <result name="input">/admin/manageBooks.jsp</result>
22        </action>
23
24        <action name="doViewBooks" method="view"
          class="com.sharanamvaishali.action.BooksAction">
25          <result name="success">/admin/manageBooks.jsp</result>
26          <result name="error" type="redirectAction">showManageBooks</result>
27        </action>
28
29        <action name="doDeleteBook" method="removeBook"
          class="com.sharanamvaishali.action.BooksAction">
30          <result name="success" type="redirectAction">doViewBooks</result>
31        </action>
32
33        <action name="showEditBook" method="editBook"
          class="com.sharanamvaishali.action.BooksAction">
34          <result name="success">/admin/manageBooks.jsp</result>
35        </action>
36      </package>
37   </struts>
```

Explanation:

The following section describes the above code spec.

showManageBooks.action

showManageBooks is an action to help viewing.

This means the data entry form and the list of book details are displayed.

The list of book details are retrieved by **BooksAction's view()**.

iterateManageBooksPage.action

iterateManageBooksPage is an action to help iterate.

This means displaying 10 records of book details per page in the form of data grid.

This iterated data is retrieved by **BooksAction's getPage()**.

doInsertBook.action

doInsertBook is an action to help adding new book details or updating existing book details.

defaultStack interceptor is referenced, which a complete stack with all the common interceptors in place.

token interceptor is referenced, which checks for valid token presence in Action and prevents duplicate form submission.

doInsertBook.action:

❑ Calls **BooksAction's saveBook()** to add new book details or update the existing book details

❑ Ensures that the captured data is valid

❑ If the validation is successful then the data is saved and the result is redirected to **doViewBooks.action**

❑ If the validation fails then the Manage Books page along with error messages is displayed

doViewBooks.action

doViewBooks is an action to help viewing.

This means the list of book details is displayed.

The list of book details are retrieved by **BooksAction's view()**.

If there are no data available in the database then the error message is displayed in the Manage Books page by redirecting the page to **showManageBooks.action**.

doDeleteBook.action

In case, the user chooses to delete a book and clicks ✖, **doDeleteBook.action** is the action to help delete a book record from Manage Books.

doDeleteBook.action:

❑ Calls **BooksAction's removeBook()** to delete a book record

❑ The book record is deleted successfully and the result is redirected to **doViewBooks.action**

showEditBook.action

showEditBook is an action to help the editing of existing books.

In case, the user chooses to edit a book and clicks that particular record, **showEditBook.action** helps fill up the Manage Books form with book details.

showEditBook.action:

❑ Calls **BooksAction's editBook()** to retrieve the book details

❑ Returns to the Manage Books page along with the data to be populated in the form

Domain Class [Books.java]

This is a domain class with the following specifications:

Class Name	Package	Implements
Books	com.sharanamvaishali.model	java.io.Serializable

Properties		
Property Name	**Property Type**	**Methods**
BookNo	Integer	getBookNo()	setBookNo()
Year	Integer	getYear()	setYear()
Cost	Integer	getCost()	setCost()
Hits	Integer	getHits()	setHits()
Author1No	Integer	getAuthor1No()	setAuthor1No()
Author2No	Integer	getAuthor2No()	setAuthor2No()
Author3No	Integer	getAuthor3No()	setAuthor3No()
Author4No	Integer	getAuthor4No(0	setAuthor4No()
PublisherNo	Integer	getPublisherNo()	setPublisherNo()
CategoryNo	Integer	getCategoryNo()	setCategoryNo()
BookName	String	getBookName()	setBookName()
ISBN	String	getISBN()	setISBN()
Edition	String	getEdition()	setEdition()
Synopsis	String	getSynopsis()	setSynopsis()
AboutAuthors	String	getAboutAuthors()	setAboutAuthors()
TopicsCovered	String	getTopicsCovered()	setTopicsCovered()
ContentsCDROM	String	getContentsCDROM()	setContentsCDROM()
CoverPage	Blob	getCoverPage()	setCoverPage()
SampleChapter	Blob	getSampleChapter()	setSampleChapter()

Code Spec

```
1   package com.sharanamvaishali.model;
2
```

```
 3   import java.sql.Blob;
 4   import javax.persistence.Column;
 5   import javax.persistence.Entity;
 6   import javax.persistence.GeneratedValue;
 7   import javax.persistence.Id;
 8   import javax.persistence.Table;
 9
10   @Entity
11   @Table(name="BOOKS")
12   public class Books implements java.io.Serializable {
13       @Id
14       @GeneratedValue
15       @Column(name="BOOKNO")
16       private Integer BookNo;
17       @Column(name="YEAR")
18       private Integer Year;
19       @Column(name="COST")
20       private Integer Cost;
21       @Column(name="HITS")
22       private Integer Hits;
23       @Column(name="AUTHOR1NO")
24       private Integer Author1No;
25       @Column(name="AUTHOR2NO")
26       private Integer Author2No;
27       @Column(name="AUTHOR3NO")
28       private Integer Author3No;
29       @Column(name="AUTHOR4NO")
30       private Integer Author4No;
31       @Column(name="PUBLISHERNO")
32       private Integer PublisherNo;
33       @Column(name="CATEGORYNO")
34       private Integer CategoryNo;
35       @Column(name="BOOKNAME")
36       private String BookName;
37       @Column(name="ISBN")
38       private String ISBN;
39       @Column(name="EDITION")
40       private String Edition;
41       @Column(name="SYNOPSIS")
42       private String Synopsis;
43       @Column(name="ABOUTAUTHORS")
44       private String AboutAuthors;
45       @Column(name="TOPICSCOVERED")
46       private String TopicsCovered;
47       @Column(name="CONTENTSCDROM")
48       private String ContentsCDROM;
49       @Column(name="COVERPAGE")
50       private Blob CoverPage;
51       @Column(name="TOC")
```

```
52      private Blob Toc;
53      @Column(name="SAMPLECHAPTER")
54      private Blob SampleChapter;
55
56      public Books() {
57      }
58
59      public Integer getHits() {
60          return Hits;
61      }
62      public void setHits(Integer Hits) {
63          this.Hits = Hits;
64      }
65
66      public String getAboutAuthors() {
67          return AboutAuthors;
68      }
69      public void setAboutAuthors(String AboutAuthors) {
70          this.AboutAuthors = AboutAuthors;
71      }
72
73      public Integer getAuthor1No() {
74          return Author1No;
75      }
76      public void setAuthor1No(Integer Author1No) {
77          this.Author1No = Author1No;
78      }
79
80      public Integer getAuthor2No() {
81          return Author2No;
82      }
83      public void setAuthor2No(Integer Author2No) {
84          this.Author2No = Author2No;
85      }
86
87      public Integer getAuthor3No() {
88          return Author3No;
89      }
90      public void setAuthor3No(Integer Author3No) {
91          this.Author3No = Author3No;
92      }
93
94      public Integer getAuthor4No() {
95          return Author4No;
96      }
97      public void setAuthor4No(Integer Author4No) {
98          this.Author4No = Author4No;
99      }
100
```

```
101     public String getBookName() {
102         return BookName;
103     }
104     public void setBookName(String BookName) {
105         this.BookName = BookName;
106     }
107
108     public Integer getBookNo() {
109         return BookNo;
110     }
111     public void setBookNo(Integer BookNo) {
112         this.BookNo = BookNo;
113     }
114
115     public Integer getCategoryNo() {
116         return CategoryNo;
117     }
118     public void setCategoryNo(Integer CategoryNo) {
119         this.CategoryNo = CategoryNo;
120     }
121
122     public String getContentsCDROM() {
123         return ContentsCDROM;
124     }
125     public void setContentsCDROM(String ContentsCDROM) {
126         this.ContentsCDROM = ContentsCDROM;
127     }
128
129     public Integer getCost() {
130         return Cost;
131     }
132     public void setCost(Integer Cost) {
133         this.Cost = Cost;
134     }
135
136     public Blob getCoverPage() {
137         return CoverPage;
138     }
139     public void setCoverPage(Blob CoverPage) {
140         this.CoverPage = CoverPage;
141     }
142
143     public String getEdition() {
144         return Edition;
145     }
146     public void setEdition(String Edition) {
147         this.Edition = Edition;
148     }
149
```

```java
150    public String getISBN() {
151        return ISBN;
152    }
153    public void setISBN(String ISBN) {
154        this.ISBN = ISBN;
155    }
156
157    public Integer getPublisherNo() {
158        return PublisherNo;
159    }
160    public void setPublisherNo(Integer PublisherNo) {
161        this.PublisherNo = PublisherNo;
162    }
163
164    public Blob getSampleChapter() {
165        return SampleChapter;
166    }
167    public void setSampleChapter(Blob SampleChapter) {
168        this.SampleChapter = SampleChapter;
169    }
170
171    public String getSynopsis() {
172        return Synopsis;
173    }
174    public void setSynopsis(String Synopsis) {
175        this.Synopsis = Synopsis;
176    }
177
178    public Blob getToc() {
179        return Toc;
180    }
181    public void setToc(Blob Toc) {
182        this.Toc = Toc;
183    }
184
185    public String getTopicsCovered() {
186        return TopicsCovered;
187    }
188    public void setTopicsCovered(String TopicsCovered) {
189        this.TopicsCovered = TopicsCovered;
190    }
191
192    public Integer getYear() {
193        return Year;
194    }
195    public void setYear(Integer Year) {
196        this.Year = Year;
197    }
198 }
```

REMINDER

 Customers.java is explained later in the *Section V: Backend [Administration] Software Design Documentation* under the *Chapter 39: Manage Customers.*

Chapter

39

SECTION V: BACKEND [ADMINISTRATION] SOFTWARE DESIGN DOCUMENTATION

Manage Customers

This module allows performing the following operations:

- ❏ Editing existing customers
- ❏ Viewing existing customers
- ❏ Deleting existing customers

This module uses the bms.Customers table to perform the above operations.

This module is made up of the following:

Type	Name	Description
JSP	manageCustomers.jsp	The data entry form
Struts 2		
Action	CustomersAction.java	The action class that facilitates data operations.
Validation	CustomersAction-validation.xml	The XML based validation file.
DAO Class	CustomersDAO.java	The interfaces for the DAO layer.
	PaginationDAO.java	
	PopulateDdlbsDAO.java	
	CustomersDAOImpl.java	The implementation classes that performs the actual data operations.
	PaginationDAOImpl.java	
	PopulateDdlbsDAOImpl.java	
Utility Class	PopulateDdlbs.java	The class that populates the list objects.
Struts Configuration	struts-Customers.xml	Struts configuration file.
Hibernate		
Mapping	hibernate.cfg.xml	The mapping file that holds Model class mapping.
Model Class	Customers.java	The model class.

JSP [manageCustomers.jsp]

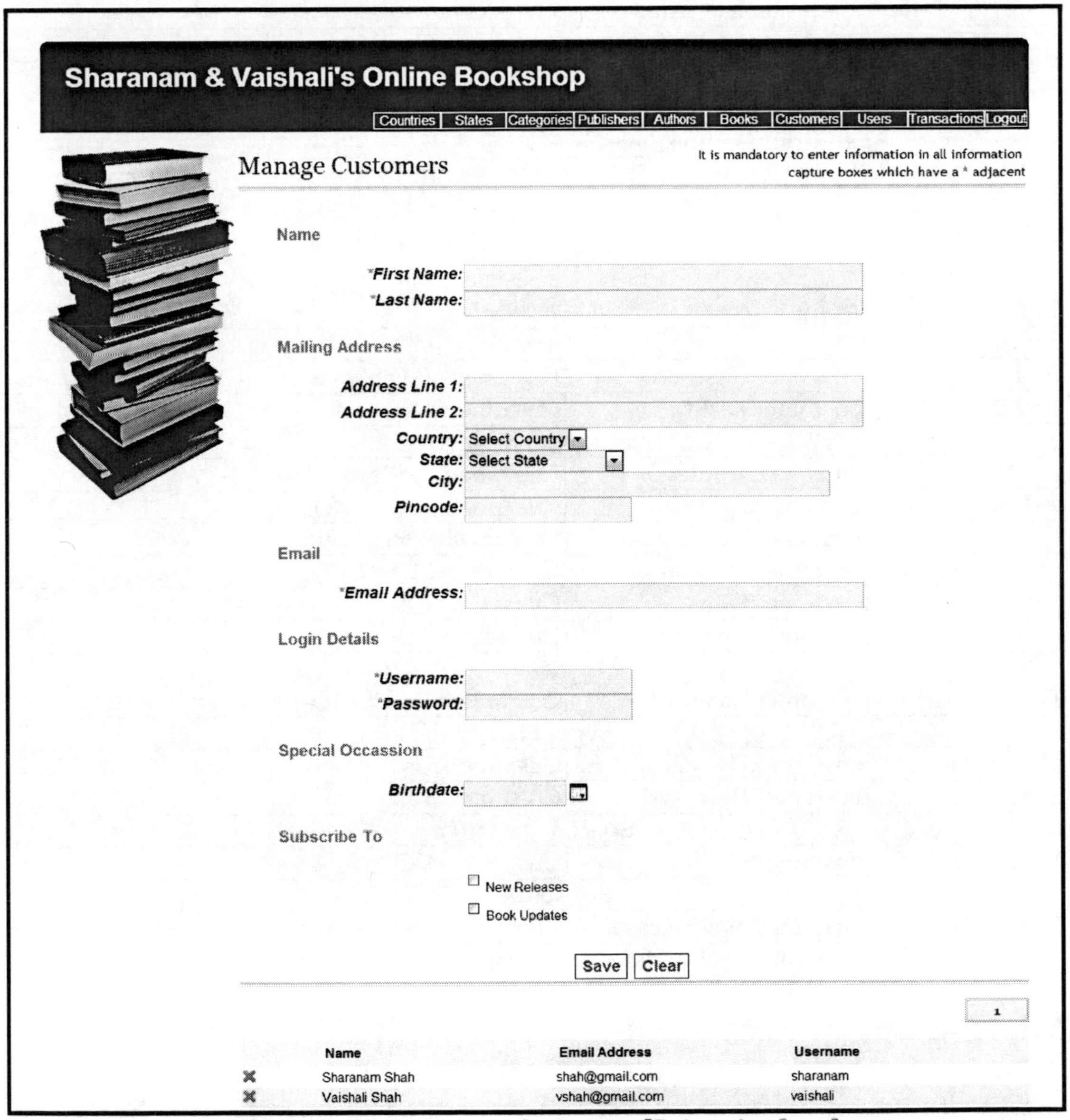

Sharanam & Vaishali's Online Bookshop

| Countries | States | Categories | Publishers | Authors | Books | Customers | Users | Transactions | Logout |

Manage Customers

It is mandatory to enter information in all information capture boxes which have a * adjacent

Name

       First Name:

       Last Name:

Mailing Address

       Address Line 1:

       Address Line 2:

       Country: Select Country

       State: Select State

       City:

       Pincode:

Email

       Email Address:

Login Details

       Username:

       Password:

Special Occassion

       Birthdate:

Subscribe To

☐ New Releases

☐ Book Updates

[Save] [Clear]

1

	Name	Email Address	Username
✖	Sharanam Shah	shah@gmail.com	sharanam
✖	Vaishali Shah	vshah@gmail.com	vaishali

Diagram 39.1: Manage Customers [Data entry form]

This is a JSP which holds a data entry form, as shown in diagram 39.1. This form appears when the user clicks `Customers`.

Form Specifications

File Name	manageCustomers.jsp
Title	BookShop[Sharanam & Vaishali Shah] - Manage Customers
Bound To Table	bms.Customers
Form Name	frmCustomers
Action	doInsertCustomer
Method	POST

Data Fields

Label	Name	Bound To	Validation Rules
		Name	
First Name	customer.FirstName	Customers.FirstName	Cannot be left blank
Last Name	customer.LastName	Customers.LastName	Cannot be left blank
		Mailing Address	
Address Line 1	customer.Address1	Customers.Address1	- -
Address Line 2	customer.Address2	Customers.Address2	- -
Country	customer.CountryNo	Customers.CountryNo	- -
State	customer.StateNo	Customers.StateNo	- -
City	customer.City	Customers.City	- -
Pincode	customer.Pincode	Customers.Pincode	- -
		Email	
Email Address	customer.EmailAddress	Customers.EmailAddress	Cannot be left blank
		Login Details	
Username	customer.Username	Customers.Username	Cannot be left blank
Password	customer.Password	Customers.Password	Cannot be left blank
		Special Occasion	
Birthdate	customer.Dob	Customers.DOB	- -
		Subscribe To	
New Releases	customer.NewRelease	Customers.NewRelease	- -
Book Updates	customer.BookUpdates	Customers.BookUpdates	- -

Micro-Help For Form Fields

Form Field	Micro Help Statement
	Name
customer.FirstName	Enter the first name
customer.LastName	Enter the last name

Form Field	Micro Help Statement
Mailing Address	
customer.Address1	Enter the street address
customer.Address2	Enter the street address
customer.CountryNo	Select country
customer.StateNo	Select state
customer.City	Enter the city name
customer.Pincode	Enter the pincode
Email	
customer.EmailAddress	Enter the email address
Login Details	
customer.Username	Enter the username
customer.Password	Enter the password
Special Occassion	
customer.Dob	- -
Subscribe To	
customer.NewRelease	Select the new releases option
customer.BookUpdates	Select the book updates option

Data Controls

Object	Label	Name
s:submit	Save	btnSubmit
s:reset	Clear	btnReset

Code Spec

```
1  <%@page contentType="text/html" pageEncoding="UTF-8"%>
2  <%@ taglib prefix="s" uri="/struts-tags" %>
3  <%@ taglib prefix="sx" uri="/struts-dojo-tags" %>
4  <!DOCTYPE HTML PUBLIC "-//W3C//DTD HTML 4.01 Transitional//EN"
5    "http://www.w3.org/TR/html4/loose.dtd">
6  <html xmlns="http://www.w3.org/1999/xhtml">
7    <head>
8      <title>BookShop [Sharanam & Vaishali Shah] - Manage Customers</title>
9      <meta http-equiv="content-type" content="text/html; charset=iso-8859-1">
10     <link href="/BookShop/css/admin.css" type="text/css" rel="stylesheet">
11     <sx:head parseContent="true"/>
12   </head>
13   <body>
14     <s:include value="header.jsp" />
15     <br>
16     <s:form action="doUpdateCustomer" method="post" name="frmCustomers"
       id="frmCustomers" validate="true">
17       <s:token/>
```

```
18        <s:hidden name="customer.CustomerNo" id="CustomerNo"/>
19        <table width="100%" border="0" align="center" cellpadding="0" cellspacing="0">
20           <tr>
21              <td valign="top" width="20%">
22                 <img src="/BookShop/images/leftImg.jpg" height="350"/>
23              </td>
24              <td valign="top">
25                 <table width="100%" border="0" align="center" cellpadding="0"
                   cellspacing="0">
26                    <tr>
27                       <td>
28                          <table border="0" cellpadding="0" cellspacing="0"
                            width="100%">
29                             <tr>
30                                <td class="manageForms">Manage Customers</td>
31                                <td class="information" valign="top" align="right">
32                                   It is mandatory to enter information in all information
                                   <br>capture boxes which have a <span
                                   class="mandatory">*</span> adjacent
33                                </td>
34                             </tr>
35                          </table>
36                       </td>
37                    </tr>
38                    <tr><td class="hrLine"> </td></tr>
39                    <tr align="left" valign="top">
40                       <td>
41                          <table width="90%" border="0" align="center" cellpadding="0"
                            cellspacing="0">
42                             <tr>
43                                <td>
44                                   <table width="100%" border="0" cellpadding="0"
                                   cellspacing="0">
45                                      <tr>
46                                         <td class="Arial16BlueB">
47                                            <br />Name<br /><br />
48                                         </td>
49                                      </tr>
50                                      <s:textfield required="true" requiredposition="left"
                                      id="FirstName" label="First Name"
                                      name="customer.FirstName" title="Enter the first name"
                                      maxLength="25" size="55"/>
51                                      <s:textfield required="true" requiredposition="left"
                                      id="LastName" label="Last Name"
                                      name="customer.LastName" title="Enter the last name"
                                      maxLength="25" size="55"/>
52                                      <tr>
53                                         <td class="Arial16BlueB">
54                                            <br />Mailing Address<br /><br />
55                                         </td>
56                                      </tr>
57                                      <s:textfield id="Address1" label="Address Line 1"
                                      name="customer.Address1" title="Enter the street
                                      address" maxLength="50" size="55"/>
```

```
58        <s:textfield id="Address2" label="Address Line 2"
          name="customer.Address2" title="Enter the street
          address" maxLength="50" size="55"/>
59        <s:select list="ddlb.ddlbCountries" listKey="CountryNo"
          listValue="Country" headerKey="" headerValue="Select
          Country" id="CountryNo" name="customer.CountryNo"
          label="Country" title="Select the country"></s:select>
60        <s:select list="ddlb.ddlbStates" listKey="StateNo"
          listValue="State" headerKey="" headerValue="Select
          State" id="StateNo" name="customer.StateNo"
          label="State" title="Select the state"></s:select>
61        <s:textfield id="City" label="City"
          name="customer.City" title="Enter the city name"
          maxLength="50" size="50"/>
62        <s:textfield id="Pincode" label="Pincode"
          name="customer.Pincode" title="Enter the pincode"
          maxLength="15" size="20"/>
63        <s:actionerror/>
64        <tr>
65           <td class="Arial16BlueB">
66              <br />Email<br /><br />
67           </td>
68        </tr>
69        <s:textfield required="true" requiredposition="left"
          id="EmailAddress" label="Email Address"
          name="customer.EmailAddress" title="Enter the email
          address" maxLength="50" size="55"/>
70        <tr>
71           <td class="Arial16BlueB">
72              <br />Login Details<br /><br />
73           </td>
74        </tr>
75        <s:textfield required="true" requiredposition="left"
          maxLength="25" label="Username"
          name="customer.Username" title="Enter the username"
          />
76        <s:textfield required="true" requiredposition="left"
          maxLength="8" label="Password"
          name="customer.Password" title="Enter the password"
          />
77        <tr>
78           <td class="Arial16BlueB">
79              <br />Special Occassion<br /><br />
80           </td>
81        </tr>
82        <sx:datetimepicker name="customer.Dob"
          label="Birthdate" displayFormat="yyyy-MM-dd"/>
83        <tr>
84           <td class="Arial16BlueB">
85              <br />Subscribe To<br /><br />
86           </td>
87        </tr>
88        <s:checkbox label="New Releases" id="NewRelease"
          name="customer.NewRelease" title="Select the new
```

```
        releases option"/>
89          <s:checkbox label="Book Updates" id="BookUpdates"
        name="customer.BookUpdates" title="Select the book
        updates option"/>
90          </table>
91        </td>
92      </tr>
93      <tr>
94        <td style="text-align: center;">
95          <br /><br />
96          <s:submit theme="simple" cssClass="groovybutton"
        name="btnSubmit" id="btnSubmit" value="Save" />
97          <s:reset theme="simple" cssClass="groovybutton"
        name="btnReset" id="btnReset" value="Clear"
        onclick="javascript:document.location.href='showManageC
        ustomers.action"/>
98        </td>
99      </tr>
100     </table>
101       </td>
102   </tr>
103   <tr><td class="hrLine"> </td></tr>
104   <tr>
105     <td align="center">
106       <table width="60px" border="0" align="right" cellpadding="3"
        cellspacing="1" style="border:#c3bca4 1px solid">
107         <tr>
108           <s:bean name="org.apache.struts2.util.Counter"
        id="counter">
109             <s:param name="last" value="%{pageCount}" />
110           </s:bean>
111           <s:iterator value="#counter">
112             <td align="center" width="2px" style="border:#c3bca4
        1px solid; background:#efebde; font-family:sans-serif;
        font-size:12px; font-weight:bolder; text-align:center;
        vertical-align:middle;">
113               <a href="<s:url
        action="iterateManageCustomersPage"><s:param
        name="pageNo"><s:property
        /></s:param></s:url>"><s:property /></a>
114             </td>
115           </s:iterator>
116         </tr>
117       </table>
118     </td>
119   </tr>
120   <tr>
121     <td>
122       <br>
123       <table class="view" align="center" cellspacing="0"
        cellpadding="0" width="100%">
124         <tr>
125           <th width="10%" align="center"> </th>
126           <th width="30%" class="Arial13BrownB"
        align="left">Name</th>
```

```
127                              <th width="30%" class="Arial13BrownB" align="left">Email
                                 Address</th>
128                              <th width="30%" class="Arial13BrownB"
                                 align="left">Username</th>
129                          </tr>
130                          <s:iterator value="customers" id="customers" status="stat">
131                              <tr title="Click to edit" class="<s:if test="#stat.odd ==
                                 true">odd</s:if><s:else>even</s:else>">
132                                  <td width="10%" valign="top">
133                                      <a href="<s:url action="doDeleteCustomer"><s:param
                                         name="customer.CustomerNo" value="CustomerNo"
                                         /></s:url>">
134                                          <img src="/BookShop/images/TrashIcon.png"
                                             border="0" alt="Delete" style="cursor:pointer;"/>
135                                      </a>
136                                  </td>
137                                  <td width="30%" class="manageList"
                                     onclick="javascript:location.href='<s:url
                                     action='showEditCustomer'><s:param
                                     name='customer.CustomerNo' value='CustomerNo'
                                     /></s:url>'">
138                                      <s:property value="FirstName"/> <s:property
                                         value="LastName" />
139                                  </td>
140                                  <td width="30%" class="manageList"
                                     onclick="javascript:location.href='<s:url
                                     action='showEditCustomer'><s:param
                                     name='customer.CustomerNo' value='CustomerNo'
                                     /></s:url>'">
141                                      <s:property value="EmailAddress"/>
142                                  </td>
143                                  <td width="30%" class="manageList"
                                     onclick="javascript:location.href='<s:url
                                     action='showEditCustomer'><s:param
                                     name='customer.CustomerNo' value='CustomerNo'
                                     /></s:url>'">
144                                      <s:property value="Username"/>
145                                  </td>
146                              </tr>
147                          </s:iterator>
148                          <s:if test="#customers==null">
149                              <span class="emptyMessage">Currently there exists no
                                 customers in the database.</span>
150                          </s:if>
151                      </table>
152                  </td>
153              </tr>
154          </table>
155      </td>
156  </tr>
157  </table>
158  </s:form>
159  <s:include value="adminFooter.jsp" />
160  </body>
161  </html>
```

Explanation:

This is a standard data entry form, which captures the customer details. By default, when the form loads, it is in the **INSERT** and **VIEW** mode. The form also has Delete and Edit options to delete and edit a particular customer record.

<s:checkbox>

<s:checkbox> renders an HTML INPUT of type CHECKBOX, which is populated by the specified property from the ValueStack:

```
<s:checkbox label="New Releases" id="NewRelease"
name="customer.NewRelease" title="Select the new
releases option"/>
```

Where:

❑ **label** is the label expression used for rendering New Releases's label

❑ **id** is the HTML id attribute

❑ **name** is the name of the checkbox input field. Here, **NewRelease** is the JavaBean property set in the **Customers** model

❑ **title** is the micro help for the form fields

Action [CustomersAction.java]

This is an action class with the following specifications:

Class Name	CustomersAction
Package	com.sharanamvaishali.action
Extends	ActionSupport
Implements	- -

Objects		
Object Name	**Class Name**	**Object Type**
customersDAO	CustomersDAO	Data Access Layer
ddlb	PopulateDdlbs	Java Class
pg	PaginationDAO	Data Access Layer
customer	Customers	Model

Properties			
Property Name	**Property Type**	**Methods**	
For the data entry form fields			
customer	Customers	getCustomer()	setCustomer()
ddlb	PopulateDdlbs	getDdlb()	setDdlb()
For the data grid population			
customers	List<Customers>	getCustomers()	setCustomers()

Properties [Continued]			
Property Name	**Property Type**	**Methods**	
For pagination			
pageNo	int	getPageNo()	setPageNo()
pageCount	int	getPageCount()	setPageCount()
Methods			
Method Name		**Return Values**	
updateCustomer()		SUCCESS ERROR	
view()		SUCCESS	
removeCustomer()		SUCCESS	
editCustomer()		SUCCESS	
getPage()		SUCCESS	

Code Spec

```
1   package com.sharanamvaishali.action;
2
3   import com.opensymphony.xwork2.ActionSupport;
4   import com.sharanamvaishali.dao.CustomersDAO;
5   import com.sharanamvaishali.dao.CustomersDAOImpl;
6   import com.sharanamvaishali.dao.PaginationDAO;
7   import com.sharanamvaishali.dao.PaginationDAOImpl;
8   import com.sharanamvaishali.model.Customers;
9   import com.sharanamvaishali.utility.PopulateDdlbs;
10  import java.util.List;
11  import org.apache.struts2.interceptor.validation.SkipValidation;
12
13  public class CustomersAction extends ActionSupport{
14      private CustomersDAO customersDAO = new CustomersDAOImpl();
15
16      private PopulateDdlbs ddlb = new PopulateDdlbs();
17
18      private PaginationDAO pg = new PaginationDAOImpl();
19
20      private Customers customer;
21
22      private List<Customers> customers;
23
24      private int pageNo, pageCount;
25
26      public PopulateDdlbs getDdlb() {
27          return ddlb;
28      }
29      public void setDdlb(PopulateDdlbs ddlb) {
30          this.ddlb = ddlb;
```

```
31     }
32
33     public int getPageNo() {
34        return pageNo;
35     }
36     public void setPageNo(int pageNo) {
37        this.pageNo = pageNo;
38     }
39
40     public int getPageCount() {
41        return pageCount;
42     }
43     public void setPageCount(int pageCount) {
44        this.pageCount = pageCount;
45     }
46
47     public Customers getCustomer() {
48        return customer;
49     }
50     public void setCustomer(Customers customer) {
51        this.customer = customer;
52     }
53
54     public List<Customers> getCustomers() {
55        return customers;
56     }
57     public void setCustomers(List<Customers> customers) {
58        this.customers = customers;
59     }
60
61     public String updateCustomer() throws Exception{
62        try{
63           customersDAO.updateCustomer(customer);
64        } catch(Exception e) {
65           addActionError(e.getCause().toString().split("[:]")[1]);
66           return ERROR;
67        }
68        return SUCCESS;
69     }
70
71     @SkipValidation
72     public String view() throws Exception{
73        pageNo = 1;
74        getPage();
75        return SUCCESS;
76     }
77
78     @SkipValidation
```

```
79     public String removeCustomer() throws Exception{
80         customersDAO.deleteCustomer(customer.getCustomerNo());
81         return SUCCESS;
82     }
83
84     @SkipValidation
85     public String editCustomer() throws Exception{
86         customer = customersDAO.getCustomerById(customer.getCustomerNo());
87         view();
88         return SUCCESS;
89     }
90
91     @SkipValidation
92     public String getPage() throws Exception{
93         pageCount = pg.getTotalPages("Customers");
94         customers = pg.getPage(pageNo-1, "Customers").getList();
95         return SUCCESS;
96     }
97 }
```

Explanation:

The following section describes the above code spec.

updateCustomer()

updateCustomer() is invoked when the user keys in the desired data and clicks **Save**.

saveCustomer() performs an update operation [using CustomersDAO's updateCustomer()] if **customer.getCustomerNo()** returns a valid CustomerNo.

view()

view() is invoked every time Manage Customers is served.

It invokes **getPage()** to populate the List object [customers] which is used in the JSP page's **<s:iterator>** to populate the data grid. This data grid displays existing records from the **Customers** database table.

@SkipValidation is used to skip validation for this method.

removeCustomer()

removeCustomer() is invoked when the user clicks ✖ adjacent to the desired record [in the data grid] for deletion.

The delete operation is performed by invoking CustomersDAO's **deleteCustomer()**.

deleteCustomer() is passed **CustomerNo** which is made available by JSP using **<s:param>** on click of ✖.

@SkipValidation is used to skip validation for this method.

editCustomer()

editCustomer() is invoked when the user clicks a desired record from the data grid in Manage Customers for updating it.

It populates the bean class object [customer] with the chosen record's data. The data is retrieved using CustomersDAO's **getCustomerById()** which is passed CustomerNo which is made available by JSP's <s:param> on click of the record.

Struts 2 framework automatically transfers the values from the bean class object to the FORM fields thus making it available to the user for editing the same.

@SkipValidation is used to skip validation for this method.

getPage()

getPage() is invoked every time Manage Customers is served or the user clicks a page number link from Manage Customers using pagination.

It calculates the total number of pages for pagination purpose and stores the same in the property named **pageCount**.

It populates the List object [customers] which is used in the JSP page's <s:iterator> to form the data grid. This data grid displays existing records from the Customers database table.

The data to be populated in the List object is retrieved using PaginationDAO's **getPage()** which returns the records belonging to the appropriate page number.

@SkipValidation is used to skip validation for this method.

DAO Class

Interface [CustomersDAO.java]

This is a Data Access Object interface with the following specifications:

Class Name	Package
CustomersDAO	com.sharanamvaishali.dao

Code Spec

```
1   package com.sharanamvaishali.dao;
2
3   import com.sharanamvaishali.model.Customers;
4
5   public interface CustomersDAO {
6       public void updateCustomer(Customers customers);
7       public void deleteCustomer(int CustomerNo);
8       public Customers getCustomerById(int CustomerNo);
9   }
```

REMINDER

PopulateDdlbsDAO.java is explained later in the *Section VII: Common Files Software Design Documentation* under the *Chapter 59: Populating Drop Down List Boxes.*

PaginationDAO.java is explained later in the *Section V: Backend [Administration] Software Design Documentation* under the *Chapter 42: Common Files.*

Implementation Class [CustomersDAOImpl.java]

This is a Data Access Object class with the following specifications:

Class Name	CustomersDAOImpl
Package	com.sharanamvaishali.dao
Implements	CustomersDAO

Objects	
Object Name	Class Name
session	Session
transaction	Transaction

Methods		
Method Name	Arguments	Return Values
updateCustomer()	Customers customers	void
deleteCustomer()	Integer CustomerNo	void
getCustomerById()	Integer CustomerNo	Customers

Code Spec

```
1   package com.sharanamvaishali.dao;
2
3   import com.sharanamvaishali.model.Customers;
4   import com.sharanamvaishali.utility.HibernateUtil;
5   import org.hibernate.Session;
6   import org.hibernate.Transaction;
7
8   public class CustomersDAOImpl implements CustomersDAO {
9       Session session = HibernateUtil.getSession();
10      Transaction transaction;
11
12      @Override
13      public void updateCustomer(Customers customers) {
14          try {
15              transaction = session.beginTransaction();
16              session.update(customers);
17              transaction.commit();
18          } catch (RuntimeException e) {
19              if(customers != null) {
20                  transaction.rollback();
21              }
22              throw e;
23          }
24      }
25
26      @Override
27      public void deleteCustomer(int CustomerNo) {
28          Object Customers = null;
29          try {
30              transaction = session.beginTransaction();
31              Customers = session.load(Customers.class, CustomerNo);
32              session.delete(Customers);
33              transaction.commit();
34          } catch (RuntimeException e) {
35              if(Customers != null) {
36                  transaction.rollback();
37              }
38              throw e;
39          }
```

```
40     }
41
42     @Override
43     public Customers getCustomerById(int CustomerNo) {
44         return (Customers) session.createQuery("FROM Customers WHERE
           CustomerNo = :CustomerNo").setInteger("CustomerNo",
           CustomerNo).uniqueResult();
45     }
46 }
```

Explanation:

The following section describes the above code spec.

updateCustomer()

updateCustomer() does the actual updation of the existing customer in the Customers database table.

updateCustomer() uses **update()** of Session, which takes care of updating an existing customer details when the user has made changes to the existing customer details and clicked **Save**.

After the update operation is performed, the transaction is committed to make the changes permanent.

Whilst performing the update operation, if a runtime exception occurs, than the transaction is **rolled back.**

deleteCustomer()

deleteCustomer() deletes the appropriate customer based on **CustomerNo** received as a reference.

This method uses:

❑ **load()** of Session, which retrieves the appropriate Customer to be deleted using CustomerNo as a reference

❑ **delete()** of Session, which deletes the customer from the Customers database table

After the delete operation is performed, the transaction is committed to make the changes permanent.

Whilst performing the delete operation, if a runtime exception occurs, than the transaction is **rolled back.**

getCustomerById()

getCustomerById() returns the appropriate customer's object from the Customers database table using **CustomerNo** as the reference.

This method uses:

❑ **createQuery()** of Session, which creates a new instance of Query to retrieve the Customer details using CustomerNo as reference

❑ **setInteger()** of Query, which states the parameter to be used as the WHERE clause criteria when querying the Customers database table

❑ **uniqueResult()** of Query, which ensures that only unique record is retrieved from the Customers database table and prevents any kinds of errors

REMINDER

PopulateDdlbsDAOImpl.java is explained later in the *Section VII: Common Files Software Design Documentation* under the *Chapter 59: Populating Drop Down List Boxes.*

PaginationDAOImpl.java is explained later in the *Section V: Backend [Administration] Software Design Documentation* under the *Chapter 42: Common Files.*

Validations [CustomersAction-validation.xml]

If the required **input** fields are kept empty whilst submitting the form, CustomersAction-validation.xml takes care of the validations.

Code Spec

```
1  <?xml version="1.0" encoding="UTF-8"?>
2  <!DOCTYPE validators PUBLIC '-//OpenSymphony Group//XWork Validator
   1.0.2//EN' 'http://www.opensymphony.com/xwork/xwork-validator-1.0.2.dtd'>
3  <validators>
4     <field name="customer.FirstName">
5        <field-validator type="requiredstring">
6           <message>Please enter the first name.</message>
7        </field-validator>
8     </field>
9
```

```
10      <field name="customer.LastName">
11        <field-validator type="requiredstring">
12          <message>Please enter the last name.</message>
13        </field-validator>
14      </field>
15
16      <field name="customer.EmailAddress">
17        <field-validator type="requiredstring" short-circuit="true">
18          <message>Please enter the email address.</message>
19        </field-validator>
20        <field-validator type="email" short-circuit="true">
21          <message>Invalid email address.</message>
22        </field-validator>
23      </field>
24
25      <field name="customer.Username">
26        <field-validator type="requiredstring">
27          <message>Please enter the username.</message>
28        </field-validator>
29      </field>
30
31      <field name="customer.Password">
32        <field-validator type="requiredstring">
33          <message>Please enter the password.</message>
34        </field-validator>
35      </field>
36   </validators>
```

If any errors are detected the data entry form is re-served with appropriate error messages, as shown in diagram 39.2.

struts-Customers.xml file holds a mapping to serve the data entry form:

```
17       <action name="doUpdateCustomer" method="updateCustomer"
         class="com.sharanamvaishali.action.CustomersAction">
18         <interceptor-ref name="defaultStack"/>
19         <interceptor-ref name="token"/>
20         <result name="success"
           type="redirectAction">doViewCustomers</result>
21         <result name="input">/admin/manageCustomers.jsp</result>
22         <result name="error">/admin/manageCustomers.jsp</result>
23       </action>
```

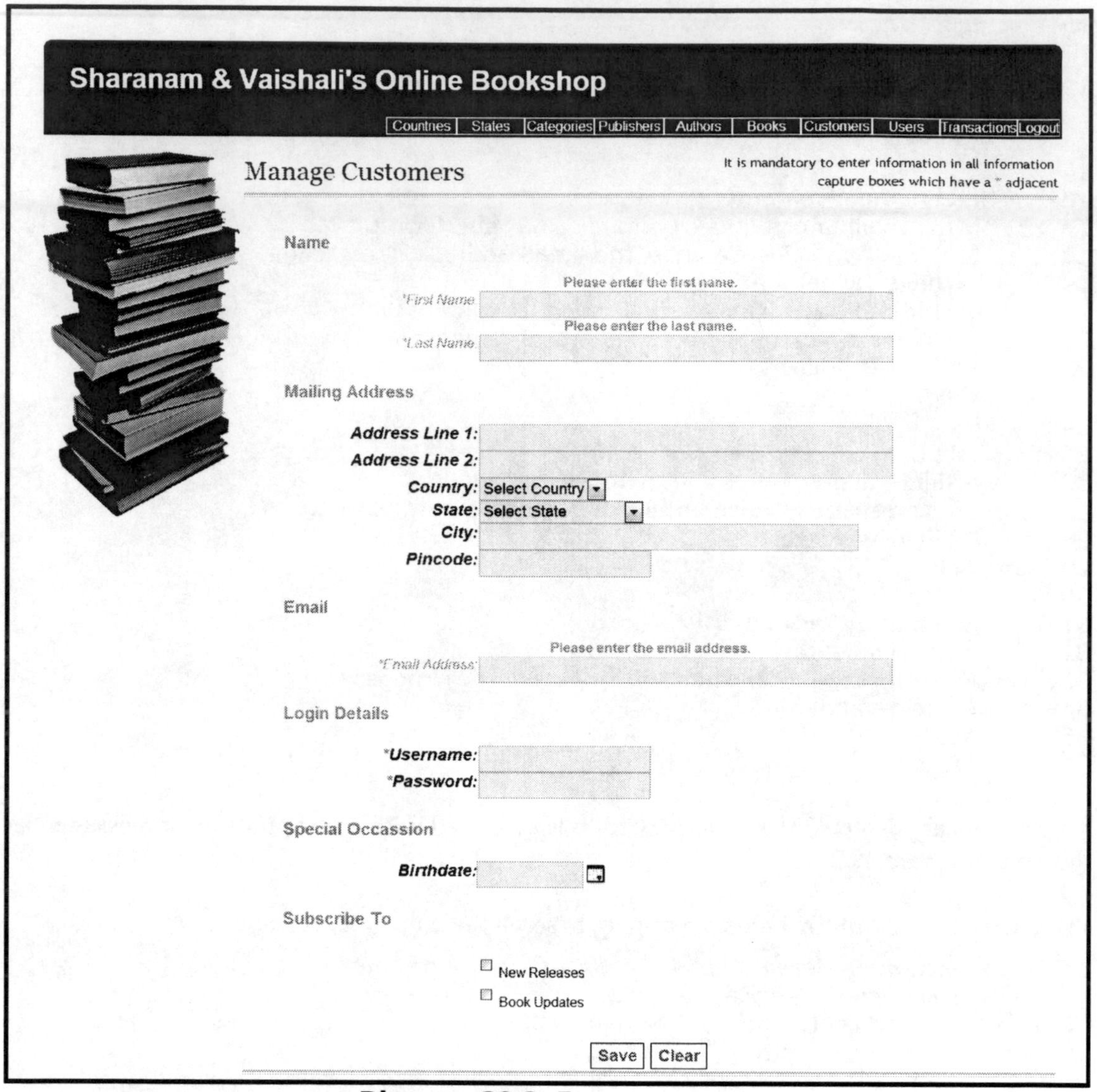

Sharanam & Vaishali's Online Bookshop

| Countries | States | Categories | Publishers | Authors | Books | Customers | Users | Transactions | Logout |

Manage Customers

It is mandatory to enter information in all information capture boxes which have a " adjacent

Name

Please enter the first name.
*First Name:

Please enter the last name.
*Last Name:

Mailing Address

Address Line 1:
Address Line 2:
Country: Select Country
State: Select State
City:
Pincode:

Email

Please enter the email address.
*Email Address:

Login Details

Username:
Password:

Special Occassion

Birthdate:

Subscribe To

☐ New Releases
☐ Book Updates

Save   Clear

Diagram 39.2: Error messages

REMINDER

In the diagram 39.2, the error message for Username and Password are not displayed even though they are mandatory. The reason being that the previous validator i.e. Email Address is marked as short-circuit. The validators marked as short-circuit will prevent the evaluation of subsequent validators i.e. the validators of Username and Password.

Struts Configuration [struts-Customers.xml]

This is the struts configuration file with the following specifications:

File Name	Package Name	Extends
Customers	manageCustomers	default

Actions	
Action Name	**Results**
showManageCustomers	SUCCESS - manageCustomers.jsp
iterateManageCustomersPage	SUCCESS - manageCustomers.jsp
doUpdateCustomer	SUCCESS - doViewCustomers
	INPUT - manageCustomers.jsp
	ERROR - manageCustomers.jsp
doViewCustomers	SUCCESS - manageCustomers.jsp
	ERROR - showManageCustomers
doDeleteCustomer	SUCCESS - doViewCustomers
showEditCustomer	SUCCESS - manageCustomers.jsp

Code Spec

```
1  <?xml version="1.0" encoding="UTF-8"?>
2  <!DOCTYPE struts PUBLIC
3  "-//Apache Software Foundation//DTD Struts Configuration 2.0//EN"
4  "http://struts.apache.org/dtds/struts-2.0.dtd">
5  <struts>
6    <package name="manageCustomers" extends="default">
7      <default-interceptor-ref name="chkSession"/>
8
9      <action name="showManageCustomers" method="view"
       class="com.sharanamvaishali.action.CustomersAction">
10        <result>/admin/manageCustomers.jsp</result>
11     </action>
12
13     <action name="iterateManageCustomersPage" method="getPage"
       class="com.sharanamvaishali.action.CustomersAction">
14        <result>/admin/manageCustomers.jsp</result>
15     </action>
16
17     <action name="doUpdateCustomer" method="updateCustomer"
       class="com.sharanamvaishali.action.CustomersAction">
18        <interceptor-ref name="defaultStack"/>
19        <interceptor-ref name="token"/>
20        <result name="success"
       type="redirectAction">doViewCustomers</result>
21        <result name="input">/admin/manageCustomers.jsp</result>
22        <result name="error">/admin/manageCustomers.jsp</result>
```

```
23        </action>
24
25        <action name="doViewCustomers" method="view"
          class="com.sharanamvaishali.action.CustomersAction">
26          <result name="success">/admin/manageCustomers.jsp</result>
27          <result name="error"
            type="redirectAction">showManageCustomers</result>
28        </action>
29
30        <action name="doDeleteCustomer" method="removeCustomer"
          class="com.sharanamvaishali.action.CustomersAction">
31          <result name="success"
            type="redirectAction">doViewCustomers</result>
32        </action>
33
34        <action name="showEditCustomer" method="editCustomer"
          class="com.sharanamvaishali.action.CustomersAction">
35          <result name="success">/admin/manageCustomers.jsp</result>
36        </action>
37     </package>
38  </struts>
```

Explanation:

The following section describes the above code spec.

showManageCustomers.action

showManageCustomers is an action to help viewing.

This means the data entry form and the list of customer details are displayed.

The list of customer details are retrieved by **CustomersAction's view()**.

iterateManageCustomersPage.action

iterateManageCustomersPage is an action to help iterate.

This means displaying 10 records of customer details per page in the form of data grid.

This iterated data is retrieved by **CustomersAction's getPage()**.

doUpdateCustomer.action

doUpdateCustomer is an action to help updating existing customer details.

defaultStack interceptor is referenced, which a complete stack with all the common interceptors in place.

token interceptor is referenced, which checks for valid token presence in Action and prevents duplicate form submission.

doInsertCustomer.action:

❏ Calls **CustomersAction's updateCustomer()** to update the existing customer details

❏ Ensures that the captured data is valid

❏ If the validation is successful then the data is saved and the result is redirected to **doViewCustomers.action**

❏ If the validation fails then the Manage Customers page along with error messages is displayed

doViewCustomers.action

doViewCustomers is an action to help viewing.

This means the list of customer details is displayed.

The list of customer details are retrieved by **CustomersAction's view()**.

If there are no data available in the database then the error message is displayed in the Manage Customers page by redirecting the page to **showManageCustomers.action**.

doDeleteCustomer.action

In case, the user chooses to delete a customer and clicks ✖, **doDeleteCustomer.action** is the action to help delete a customer record from Manage Customers.

doDeleteCustomer.action:

❏ Calls **CustomersAction's removeCustomer()** to delete a customer record

❏ If the customer record is deleted successfully then the result is redirected to **doViewCustomers.action**

showEditCustomer.action

showEditCustomer is an action to help the editing of existing customers.

In case, the user chooses to edit a customer and clicks that particular record, **showEditCustomer.action** helps fill up the Manage Customers form with customer details.

showEditCustomer.action:

❑ Calls **CustomersAction**'s **editCustomer()** to retrieve the customer details

❑ Returns to the Manage Customers page along with the data to be populated in the form

Domain Class [Customers.java]

This is a domain class with the following specifications:

Class Name	Package	Implements
Customers	com.sharanamvaishali.model	java.io.Serializable

Properties			
Property Name	**Property Type**	**Methods**	
CustomerNo	Integer	getCustomerNo()	setCustomerNo()
FirstName	String	getFirstName()	setFirstName()
LastName	String	getLastName()	setLastName()
Address1	String	getAddress1()	setAddress1()
Address2	String	getAddress2()	setAddress2()
City	String	getCity()	setCity()
StateNo	Integer	getStateNo()	setStateNo()
Pincode	String	getPincode(0	setPincode()
CountryNo	Integer	getCountryNo()	setCountryNo()
EmailAddress	String	getEmailAddress()	setEmailAddress()
Username	String	getUsername()	setUsername()
Password	String	getPassword()	setPassword()
Dob	String	getDob()	setDob()
NewRelease	String	getNewRelease()	setNewRelease()
BookUpdates	String	getBookUpdates()	setBookUpdates()
LastLogin	String	getLastLogin()	setLastLogin()
LastIP	String	getLastIP()	setLastIP()

Code Spec

```
1  package com.sharanamvaishali.model;
2
3  import javax.persistence.Column;
4  import javax.persistence.Entity;
5  import javax.persistence.GeneratedValue;
6  import javax.persistence.Id;
7  import javax.persistence.Table;
8
```

```
 9   @Entity
10   @Table(name="CUSTOMERS")
11   public class Customers implements java.io.Serializable {
12       @Id
13       @GeneratedValue
14       @Column(name="CUSTOMERNO")
15       private Integer CustomerNo;
16       @Column(name="STATENO")
17       private Integer StateNo;
18       @Column(name="COUNTRYNO")
19       private Integer CountryNo;
20       @Column(name="City")
21       private String City;
22       @Column(name="USERNAME")
23       private String Username;
24       @Column(name="PASSWORD")
25       private String Password;
26       @Column(name="EMAILADDRESS")
27       private String EmailAddress;
28       @Column(name="FIRSTNAME")
29       private String FirstName;
30       @Column(name="LASTNAME")
31       private String LastName;
32       @Column(name="ADDRESS1")
33       private String Address1;
34       @Column(name="ADDRESS2")
35       private String Address2;
36       @Column(name="PINCODE")
37       private String Pincode;
38       @Column(name="DOB")
39       private String Dob;
40       @Column(name="NEWRELEASE")
41       private String NewRelease;
42       @Column(name="BOOKUPDATES")
43       private String BookUpdates;
44       @Column(name="LASTLOGIN")
45       private String LastLogin;
46       @Column(name="LASTIP")
47       private String LastIP;
48
49       public Customers() {
50       }
51
52       public String getAddress1() {
53           return Address1;
54       }
55       public void setAddress1(String Address1) {
56           this.Address1 = Address1;
```

```
57      }
58
59      public String getAddress2() {
60          return Address2;
61      }
62      public void setAddress2(String Address2) {
63          this.Address2 = Address2;
64      }
65
66      public String getBookUpdates() {
67          return BookUpdates;
68      }
69      public void setBookUpdates(String BookUpdates) {
70          this.BookUpdates = BookUpdates;
71      }
72
73      public Integer getStateNo() {
74          return StateNo;
75      }
76      public void setStateNo(Integer StateNo) {
77          this.StateNo = StateNo;
78      }
79
80      public Integer getCountryNo() {
81          return CountryNo;
82      }
83      public void setCountryNo(Integer CountryNo) {
84          this.CountryNo = CountryNo;
85      }
86
87      public String getCity() {
88          return City;
89      }
90      public void setCity(String City) {
91          this.City = City;
92      }
93
94      public Integer getCustomerNo() {
95          return CustomerNo;
96      }
97      public void setCustomerNo(Integer CustomerNo) {
98          this.CustomerNo = CustomerNo;
99      }
100
101     public String getDob() {
102         return Dob;
103     }
104     public void setDob(String Dob) {
```

```
105        this.Dob = Dob;
106     }
107
108     public String getEmailAddress() {
109        return EmailAddress;
110     }
111     public void setEmailAddress(String EmailAddress) {
112        this.EmailAddress = EmailAddress;
113     }
114
115     public String getFirstName() {
116        return FirstName;
117     }
118     public void setFirstName(String FirstName) {
119        this.FirstName = FirstName;
120     }
121
122     public String getLastIP() {
123        return LastIP;
124     }
125     public void setLastIP(String LastIP) {
126        this.LastIP = LastIP;
127     }
128
129     public String getLastLogin() {
130        return LastLogin;
131     }
132     public void setLastLogin(String LastLogin) {
133        this.LastLogin = LastLogin;
134     }
135
136     public String getLastName() {
137        return LastName;
138     }
139     public void setLastName(String LastName) {
140        this.LastName = LastName;
141     }
142
143     public String getNewRelease() {
144        return NewRelease;
145     }
146     public void setNewRelease(String NewRelease) {
147        this.NewRelease = NewRelease;
148     }
149
150     public String getPassword() {
151        return Password;
152     }
```

```
153     public void setPassword(String Password) {
154         this.Password = Password;
155     }
156
157     public String getPincode() {
158         return Pincode;
159     }
160     public void setPincode(String Pincode) {
161         this.Pincode = Pincode;
162     }
163
164     public String getUsername() {
165         return Username;
166     }
167     public void setUsername(String Username) {
168         this.Username = Username;
169     }
170 }
```

SECTION V: BACKEND [ADMINISTRATION] SOFTWARE DESIGN DOCUMENTATION

Manage Users

This module allows performing the following operations:

- ❏ Adding new system users
- ❏ Editing existing system users
- ❏ Viewing existing system users
- ❏ Deleting existing system users

This module uses the bms.SystemUsers table to perform the above operations.

This module is made up of the following:

Type	Name	Description
JSP	manageUsers.jsp	The data entry form
Struts 2		
Action	SystemUsersAction.java	The action class that facilitates data operations.
Validation	SystemUsersAction-validation.xml	The XML based validation file.
DAO Class	SystemUsersDAO.java	The interfaces for the DAO layer.
	PaginationDAO.java	
	PopulateDdlbsDAO.java	
	SystemUsersDAOImpl.java	The implementation classes that performs the actual data operations.
	PaginationDAOImpl.java	
	PopulateDdlbsDAOImpl.java	
Utility Class	PopulateDdlbs.java	The class that populates the list objects.
Struts Configuration	struts-SystemUsers.xml	Struts configuration file.
Hibernate		
Mapping	hibernate.cfg.xml	The mapping file that holds Model class mapping.
Model Class	SystemUsers.java	The model class.

JSP [manageUsers.jsp]

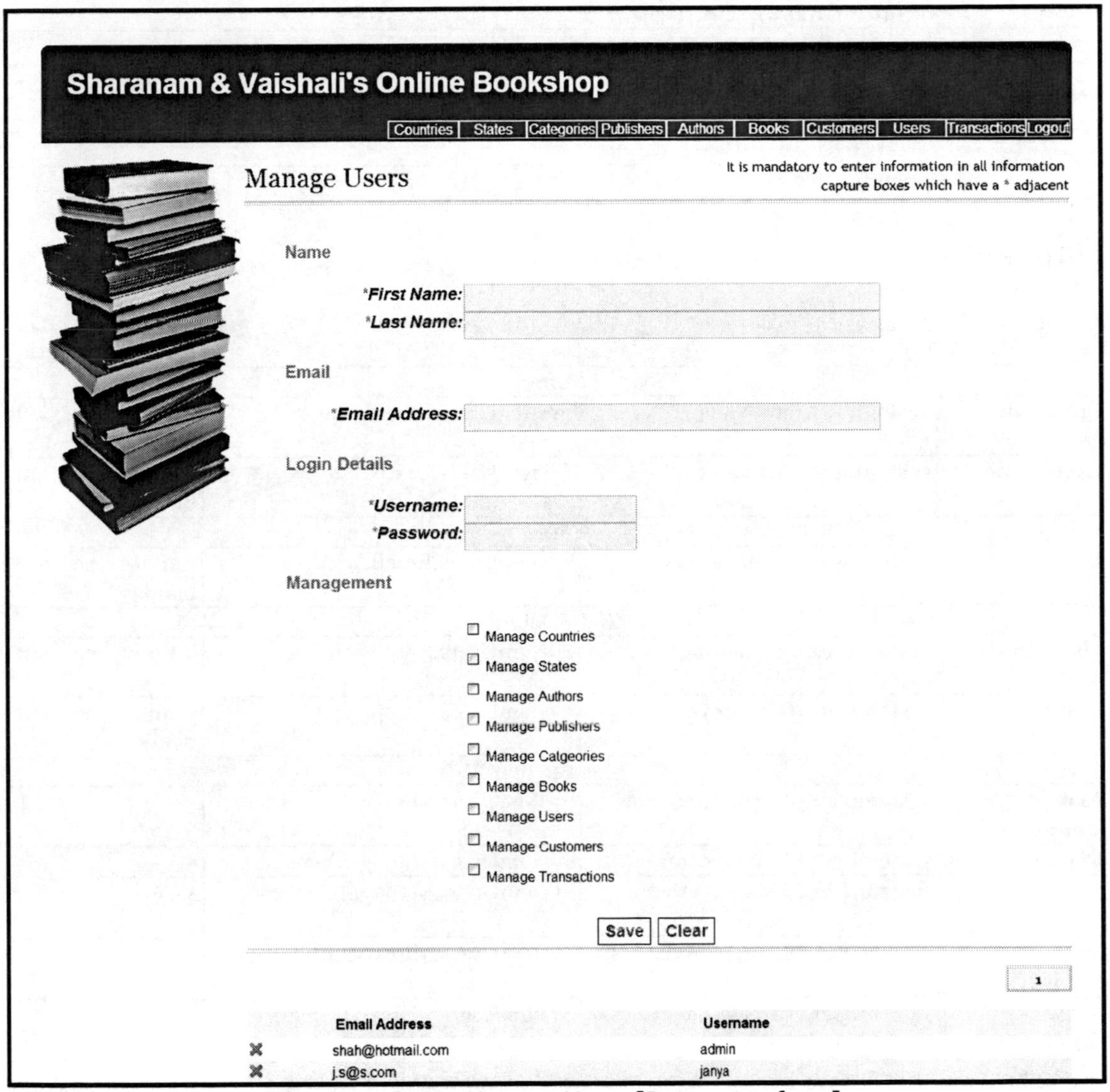

Sharanam & Vaishali's Online Bookshop

| Countries | States | Categories | Publishers | Authors | Books | Customers | Users | Transactions | Logout |

Manage Users

It is mandatory to enter information in all information
capture boxes which have a * adjacent

Name

First Name:
Last Name:

Email

Email Address:

Login Details

Username:
Password:

Management

☐ Manage Countries
☐ Manage States
☐ Manage Authors
☐ Manage Publishers
☐ Manage Catgeories
☐ Manage Books
☐ Manage Users
☐ Manage Customers
☐ Manage Transactions

Save   Clear

1

	Email Address	Username
✖	shah@hotmail.com	admin
✖	j.s@s.com	janya

Diagram 40.1: Manage Users [Data entry form]

This is a JSP which holds a data entry form, as shown in diagram 40.1. This form appears when the user clicks Users .

Form Specifications

File Name	manageUsers.jsp
Title	BookShop[Sharanam & Vaishali Shah] - Manage Users
Bound To Table	bms.SystemUsers
Form Name	frmUsers
Action	doInsertUser
Method	POST

Data Fields

Label	Name	Bound To	Validation Rules
Name			
First Name	systemuser.FirstName	SystemUsers.FirstName	Cannot be left blank
Last Name	systemuser.LastName	SystemUsers.LastName	Cannot be left blank
Email			
Email Address	systemuser.EmailAddress	SystemUsers.EmailAddress	Cannot be left blank
Login Details			
Username	systemuser.Username	SystemUsers.Photograph	Cannot be left blank
Password	systemuser.password	SystemUsers.Speciality	Cannot be left blank
Management			
Manage Countries	systemuser.ManageCountries	SystemUsers.ManageCountries	- -
Manage States	systemuser.ManageStates	SystemUsers.ManageStates	- -
Manage Authors	systemuser.ManageAuthors	SystemUsers.ManageAuthors	- -
Manage Publishers	systemuser.ManagePublishers	SystemUsers.ManagePublishers	- -
Manage Categories	systemuser.ManageCategories	SystemUsers.ManageCategories	- -
Manage Books	systemuser.ManageBooks	SystemUsers.ManageBooks	- -
Manage Users	systemuser.ManageUsers	SystemUsers.ManageUsers	
Manage Customers	systemuser.ManageCustomers	SystemUsers.ManageCustomers	
Manage Transactions	systemuser.ManageTransactions	SystemUsers.ManageTransactions	

Micro-Help For Form Fields

Form Field	Micro Help Statement
	Name
systemuser.FirstName	Enter the first name
systemuser.LastName	Enter the last name
	Email
systemuser.EmailAddress	Enter the email address
	Login Details
systemuser.Username	Enter the username
systemuser.password	Enter the password
	Management
systemuser.ManageCountries	Select to manage countries
systemuser.ManageStates	Select to manage states
systemuser.ManageAuthors	Select to manage authors
systemuser.ManagePublishers	Select to manage publishers
systemuser.ManageCategories	Select to manage categories
systemuser.ManageBooks	Select to manage books
systemuser.ManageUsers	Select to manage system users
systemuser.ManageCustomers	Select to manage customers
systemuser.ManageTransactions	Select to manage transactions

Data Controls

Object	Label	Name
s:submit	Save	btnSubmit
s:reset	Clear	btnReset

Code Spec

```
1  <%@page contentType="text/html" pageEncoding="UTF-8"%>
2  <%@ taglib prefix="s" uri="/struts-tags" %>
3  <!DOCTYPE HTML PUBLIC "-//W3C//DTD HTML 4.01 Transitional//EN"
4    "http://www.w3.org/TR/html4/loose.dtd">
5  <html xmlns="http://www.w3.org/1999/xhtml">
6    <head>
7      <title>BookShop [Sharanam & Vaishali Shah] - Manage Users</title>
8      <meta http-equiv="content-type" content="text/html; charset=iso-8859-1">
9      <link href="/BookShop/css/admin.css" type="text/css" rel="stylesheet">
10     <s:head/>
11   </head>
12   <body>
13     <s:include value="header.jsp" />
14     <br>
```

```
15    <s:form action="doInsertUser" method="post" name="frmUsers" id="frmUsers"
      validate="true">
16      <s:token/>
17      <s:hidden name="systemuser.UserNo" id="UserNo"/>
18      <table width="100%" border="0" align="center" cellpadding="0" cellspacing="0">
19        <tr>
20          <td valign="top" width="20%">
21            <img src="/BookShop/images/leftImg.jpg" height="350"/>
22          </td>
23          <td valign="top">
24            <table width="100%" border="0" align="center" cellpadding="0"
              cellspacing="0">
25              <tr>
26                <td>
27                  <table border="0" cellpadding="0" cellspacing="0"
                    width="100%">
28                    <tr>
29                      <td class="manageForms">Manage Users</td>
30                      <td class="information" valign="top" align="right">
31                        It is mandatory to enter information in all information
                          <br>capture boxes which have a <span
                          class="mandatory">*</span> adjacent
32                      </td>
33                    </tr>
34                  </table>
35                </td>
36              </tr>
37              <tr><td class="hrLine"> </td></tr>
38              <tr align="left" valign="top">
39                <td>
40                  <table width="90%" border="0" align="center" cellpadding="0"
                    cellspacing="0">
41                    <tr>
42                      <td>
43                        <table width="100%" border="0" cellpadding="0"
                          cellspacing="0">
44                          <tr>
45                            <td class="Arial16BlueB">
46                              <br />Name<br /><br />
47                            </td>
48                          </tr>
49                          <s:textfield required="true" requiredposition="left"
                            id="FirstName" label="First Name"
                            name="systemuser.FirstName" title="Enter the first
                            name" maxLength="25" size="55"/>
50                          <s:textfield required="true" requiredposition="left"
                            id="LastName" label="Last Name"
                            name="systemuser.LastName" title="Enter the last
                            name" maxLength="25" size="55"/>
51                          <s:actionerror/>
52                          <tr>
53                            <td class="Arial16BlueB">
54                              <br />Email<br /><br />
55                            </td>
```

```
56      </tr>
57      <s:textfield required="true" requiredposition="left"
        id="EmailAddress" label="Email Address"
        name="systemuser.EmailAddress" title="Enter the email
        address" maxLength="50" size="55"/>
58      <tr>
59        <td class="Arial16BlueB">
60          <br />Login Details<br /><br />
61        </td>
62      </tr>
63      <s:textfield required="true" requiredposition="left"
        maxLength="25" label="Username"
        name="systemuser.Username" title="Enter the
        username" />
64      <s:textfield required="true" requiredposition="left"
        maxLength="8" label="Password"
        name="systemuser.Password" title="Enter the
        password" />
65      <tr>
66        <td class="Arial16BlueB">
67          <br />Management<br /><br />
68        </td>
69      </tr>
70      <s:checkbox label="Manage Countries"
        id="ManageCountries"
        name="systemuser.ManageCountries" title="Select to
        manage countries"/>
71      <s:checkbox label="Manage States" id="ManageStates"
        name="systemuser.ManageStates" title="Select to
        manage states"/>
72      <s:checkbox label="Manage Authors"
        id="ManageAuthors"
        name="systemuser.ManageAuthors" title="Select to
        manage authors"/>
73      <s:checkbox label="Manage Publishers"
        id="ManagePublishers"
        name="systemuser.ManagePublishers" title="Select to
        manage publishers"/>
74      <s:checkbox label="Manage Catgeories"
        id="ManageCategories"
        name="systemuser.ManageCategories" title="Select to
        manage categories"/>
75      <s:checkbox label="Manage Books" id="ManageBooks"
        name="systemuser.ManageBooks" title="Select to
        manage books"/>
76      <s:checkbox label="Manage Users" id="ManageUsers"
        name="systemuser.ManageUsers" title="Select to
        manage system users"/>
77      <s:checkbox label="Manage Customers"
        id="ManageCustomers"
        name="systemuser.ManageCustomers" title="Select to
        manage customers"/>
78      <s:checkbox label="Manage Transactions"
        id="ManageTransactions"
```

```
                                    name="systemuser.ManageTransactions" title="Select to
                                    manage transactions"/>
79                                </table>
80                            </td>
81                        </tr>
82                        <tr>
83                            <td style="text-align: center;">
84                                <br /><br />
85                                <s:submit theme="simple" cssClass="groovybutton"
                                    name="btnSubmit" id="btnSubmit" value="Save" />
86                                <s:reset theme="simple" cssClass="groovybutton"
                                    name="btnReset" id="btnReset" value="Clear"
                                    onclick="javascript:document.location.href='showManageU
                                    sers.action'"/>
87                            </td>
88                        </tr>
89                    </table>
90                </td>
91            </tr>
92            <tr><td class="hrLine"> </td></tr>
93            <tr>
94                <td align="center">
95                    <table width="60px" border="0" align="right" cellpadding="3"
                        cellspacing="1" style="border:#c3bca4 1px solid">
96                        <tr>
97                            <s:bean name="org.apache.struts2.util.Counter"
                                id="counter">
98                                <s:param name="last" value="%{pageCount}" />
99                            </s:bean>
100                           <s:iterator value="#counter">
101                               <td align="center" width="2px" style="border:#c3bca4
                                    1px solid; background:#efebde; font-family:sans-serif;
                                    font-size:12px; font-weight:bolder; text-align:center;
                                    vertical-align:middle;">
102                                   <a href="<s:url
                                        action="iterateManageUsersPage"><s:param
                                        name="pageNo"><s:property
                                        /></s:param></s:url>"><s:property /></a>
103                               </td>
104                           </s:iterator>
105                       </tr>
106                   </table>
107               </td>
108           </tr>
109           <tr>
110               <td>
111                   <br>
112                   <table class="view" align="center" cellspacing="0"
                        cellpadding="0" width="100%">
113                       <tr>
114                           <th width="10%" align="center"> </th>
115                           <th width="45%" class="Arial13BrownB" align="left">Email
                                Address</th>
116                           <th width="45%" class="Arial13BrownB"
```

```
                                    align="left">Username</th>
117                                 </tr>
118                                 <s:iterator value="systemusers" id="systemusers"
                                    status="stat">
119                                     <tr title="Click to edit" class="<s:if test="#stat.odd ==
                                    true">odd</s:if><s:else>even</s:else>">
120                                         <td width="10%" valign="top">
121                                             <s:if test="Username=='admin'">
122                                                 <img src="/BookShop/images/TrashIcon.png"
                                                    border="0" alt="Cannot be deleted"/>
123                                             </s:if>
124                                             <s:else>
125                                                 <a href="<s:url action="doDeleteUser"><s:param
                                                    name="systemuser.UserNo" value="UserNo"
                                                    /></s:url>">
126                                                     <img src="/BookShop/images/TrashIcon.png"
                                                        border="0" alt="Delete" style="cursor:pointer;"/>
127                                                 </a>
128                                             </s:else>
129                                         </td>
130                                         <td width="45%" class="manageList"
                                            onclick="javascript:location.href='<s:url
                                            action='showEditUser'><s:param
                                            name='systemuser.UserNo' value='UserNo' /></s:url>'">
131                                             <s:property value="EmailAddress"/>
132                                         </td>
133                                         <td width="45%" class="manageList"
                                            onclick="javascript:location.href='<s:url
                                            action='showEditUser'><s:param
                                            name='systemuser.UserNo' value='UserNo' /></s:url>'">
134                                             <s:property value="Username"/>
135                                         </td>
136                                     </tr>
137                                 </s:iterator>
138                                 <s:if test="#systemusers==null">
139                                     <span class="emptyMessage">Currently there exists no users
                                        in the database. Please add a few users to begin managing
                                        them.</span>
140                                 </s:if>
141                             </table>
142                         </td>
143                     </tr>
144                 </table>
145             </td>
146         </tr>
147     </table>
148     </s:form>
149     <s:include value="adminFooter.jsp" />
150 </body>
151 </html>
```

Explanation:

This is a standard data entry form, which captures the system user details. By default, when the form loads, it is in the **INSERT** and **VIEW** mode. The form also has Delete and Edit options to delete and edit a particular system user record.

Action [SystemUsersAction.java]

This is an action class with the following specifications:

Class Name	SystemUsersAction
Package	com.sharanamvaishali.action
Extends	ActionSupport
Implements	- -

Objects		
Object Name	**Class Name**	**Object Type**
systemusersDAO	SystemUsersDAO	Data Access Layer
ddlb	PopulateDdlbs	Java Class
pg	PaginationDAO	Data Access Layer
systemuser	SystemUsers	Model

Properties			
Property Name	**Property Type**	**Methods**	
For the data entry form fields			
systemuser	SystemUsers	getSystemuser()	setSystemuser()
ddlb	PopulateDdlbs	getDdlb()	setDdlb()
For the data grid population			
systemusers	List<SystemUsers>	getSystemusers()	setSystemusers()
For pagination			
pageNo	int	getPageNo()	setPageNo()
pageCount	int	getPageCount()	setPageCount()

Methods	
Method Name	**Return Values**
saveSystemUser()	SUCCESS ERROR
view()	SUCCESS
removeSystemUser()	SUCCESS
editSystemUser()	SUCCESS
getPage()	SUCCESS

Code Spec

```
1  package com.sharanamvaishali.action;
2
3  import com.opensymphony.xwork2.ActionSupport;
```

```
 4  import com.sharanamvaishali.dao.PaginationDAO;
 5  import com.sharanamvaishali.dao.PaginationDAOImpl;
 6  import com.sharanamvaishali.dao.SystemUsersDAO;
 7  import com.sharanamvaishali.dao.SystemUsersDAOImpl;
 8  import com.sharanamvaishali.model.SystemUsers;
 9  import java.util.List;
10  import org.apache.struts2.interceptor.validation.SkipValidation;
11
12  public class SystemUsersAction extends ActionSupport{
13      private SystemUsersDAO systemusersDAO = new SystemUsersDAOImpl();
14
15      private PaginationDAO pg = new PaginationDAOImpl();
16
17      private SystemUsers systemuser;
18
19      private List<SystemUsers> systemusers;
20
21      private int pageNo, pageCount;
22
23      public int getPageNo() {
24          return pageNo;
25      }
26      public void setPageNo(int pageNo) {
27          this.pageNo = pageNo;
28      }
29
30      public int getPageCount() {
31          return pageCount;
32      }
33      public void setPageCount(int pageCount) {
34          this.pageCount = pageCount;
35      }
36
37      public SystemUsers getSystemuser() {
38          return systemuser;
39      }
40      public void setSystemuser(SystemUsers systemuser) {
41          this.systemuser = systemuser;
42      }
43
44      public List<SystemUsers> getSystemusers() {
45          return systemusers;
46      }
47      public void setSystemusers(List<SystemUsers> systemusers) {
48          this.systemusers = systemusers;
49      }
50
51      public String saveSystemUser() throws Exception{
```

```
52          try{
53             if(systemuser.getUserNo() != null) {
54                systemusersDAO.updateSystemUser(systemuser);
55             } else{
56                systemusersDAO.saveSystemUser(systemuser);
57             }
58          } catch(Exception e) {
59             addActionError(e.getCause().toString().split("[:]")[1]);
60             return ERROR;
61          }
62          return SUCCESS;
63       }
64
65       @SkipValidation
66       public String view() throws Exception{
67          pageNo = 1;
68          getPage();
69          return SUCCESS;
70       }
71
72       @SkipValidation
73       public String removeSystemUser() throws Exception{
74          systemusersDAO.deleteSystemUser(systemuser.getUserNo());
75          return SUCCESS;
76       }
77
78       @SkipValidation
79       public String editSystemUser() throws Exception{
80          systemuser =
             systemusersDAO.getSystemUserById(systemuser.getUserNo());
81          view();
82          return SUCCESS;
83       }
84
85       @SkipValidation
86       public String getPage() throws Exception{
87          pageCount = pg.getTotalPages("SystemUsers");
88          systemusers = pg.getPage(pageNo-1, "SystemUsers").getList();
89          return SUCCESS;
90       }
91 }
```

Explanation:

The following section describes the above code spec.

saveSystemUser()

saveSystemUser() is invoked when the user keys in the desired data and clicks **Save**.

saveSystemUser():

❑ Performs an update operation [using SystemUsersDAO's updateSystemUser()] if **systemuser.getUserNo()** returns a valid UserNo

❑ Performs an insert operation [using SystemUsersDAO's saveSystemUser()] if **systemuser.getUserNo()** returns empty

view()

view() is invoked every time Manage Users is served.

It invokes **getPage()** to populate the List object [systemusers] which is used in the JSP page's **<s:iterator>** to populate the data grid. This data grid displays existing records from the **SystemUsers** database table.

@SkipValidation is used to skip validation for this method.

removeSystemUser()

removeSystemUser() is invoked when the user clicks ✖ adjacent to the desired record [in the data grid] for deletion.

The delete operation is performed by invoking SystemUsersDAO's **deleteSystemUser()**.

deleteSystemUser() is passed **UserNo** which is made available by JSP using **<s:param>** on click of ✖.

@SkipValidation is used to skip validation for this method.

editSystemUser()

editSystemUser() is invoked when the user clicks a desired record from the data grid in Manage Users for updating it.

It populates the bean class object [systemuser] with the chosen record's data. The data is retrieved using SystemUsersDAO's **getSystemUserById()** which is passed UserNo which is made available by JSP's <s:param> on click of the record.

Struts 2 framework automatically transfers the values from the bean class object to the FORM fields thus making it available to the user for editing the same.

@SkipValidation is used to skip validation for this method.

getPage()

getPage() is invoked every time Manage Users is served or the user clicks a page number link from Manage Users using pagination.

It calculates the total number of pages for pagination purpose and stores the same in the property named **pageCount**.

It populates the List object [authors] which is used in the JSP page's <s:iterator> to form the data grid. This data grid displays existing records from the SystemUsers database table.

The data to be populated in the List object is retrieved using PaginationDAO's **getPage()** which returns the records belonging to the appropriate page number.

@SkipValidation is used to skip validation for this method.

DAO Class

Interface [SystemUsersDAO.java]

This is a Data Access Object interface with the following specifications:

Class Name	Package
SystemUsersDAO	com.sharanamvaishali.dao

Code Spec

```
1  package com.sharanamvaishali.dao;
2
3  import com.sharanamvaishali.model.SystemUsers;
4
5  public interface SystemUsersDAO {
6      public void saveSystemUser(SystemUsers systemUsers);
7      public void updateSystemUser(SystemUsers systemUsers);
8      public void deleteSystemUser(int UserNo);
9      public SystemUsers getSystemUserById(int UserNo);
10 }
```

REMINDER

PopulateDdlbsDAO.java is explained later in the *Section VII: Common Files Software Design Documentation* under the *Chapter 59: Populating Drop Down List Boxes.*

PaginationDAO.java is explained later in the *Section V: Backend [Administration] Software Design Documentation* under the *Chapter 42: Common Files.*

Implementation Class [SystemUsersDAOImpl.java]

This is a **Data Access Object** class with the following specifications:

Class Name	SystemUsersDAOImpl
Package	com.sharanamvaishali.dao
Implements	SystemUsersDAO

Objects	
Object Name	**Class Name**
session	Session
transaction	Transaction

Methods		
Method Name	**Arguments**	**Return Values**
saveSystemUser()	SystemUsers systemUsers	void
updateSystemUser()	SystemUsers systemUsers	void
deleteSystemUser()	Integer UserNo	void
getSystemUserById()	Integer UserNo	SystemUsers

Code Spec

```
1   package com.sharanamvaishali.dao;
2
3   import com.sharanamvaishali.model.SystemUsers;
4   import com.sharanamvaishali.utility.HibernateUtil;
5   import org.hibernate.Session;
6   import org.hibernate.Transaction;
7
8   public class SystemUsersDAOImpl implements SystemUsersDAO {
9       Session session = HibernateUtil.getSession();
10      Transaction transaction;
11
12      @Override
13      public void saveSystemUser(SystemUsers systemUsers) {
14          try {
15              transaction = session.beginTransaction();
16              session.save(systemUsers);
17              transaction.commit();
```

```
18        } catch (RuntimeException e) {
19            if(systemUsers != null) {
20                transaction.rollback();
21            }
22            throw e;
23        }
24    }
25
26    @Override
27    public void updateSystemUser(SystemUsers systemUsers) {
28        try {
29            transaction = session.beginTransaction();
30            session.update(systemUsers);
31            transaction.commit();
32        } catch (RuntimeException e) {
33            if(systemUsers != null) {
34                transaction.rollback();
35            }
36            throw e;
37        }
38    }
39
40    @Override
41    public void deleteSystemUser(int UserNo) {
42        Object SystemUsers = null;
43        try {
44            transaction = session.beginTransaction();
45            SystemUsers = session.load(SystemUsers.class, UserNo);
46            session.delete(SystemUsers);
47            transaction.commit();
48        } catch (RuntimeException e) {
49            if(SystemUsers != null) {
50                transaction.rollback();
51            }
52            throw e;
53        }
54    }
55
56    @Override
57    public SystemUsers getSystemUserById(int UserNo) {
58        return (SystemUsers) session.createQuery("FROM SystemUsers WHERE
          UserNo = :UserNo").setInteger("UserNo", UserNo).uniqueResult();
59    }
60 }
```

Explanation:

The following section describes the above code spec.

saveSystemUser()

saveSystemUser() does the actual saving of the system user in the SystemUsers database table.

saveSystemUser() uses **save()** of Session, which takes care of adding new system user details when the user has entered all the system user details and clicked | **Save** |.

After the save operation is performed, the transaction is committed to make the changes permanent.

Whilst performing the save operation, if a runtime exception occurs, than the transaction is **rolled back**.

updateSystemUser()

updateSystemUser() does the actual updation of the existing system user in the SystemUsers database table.

updateSystemUser() uses **update()** of Session, which takes care of updating an existing system user details when the user has made changes to the existing system user details and clicked | **Save** |.

After the update operation is performed, the transaction is committed to make the changes permanent.

Whilst performing the update operation, if a runtime exception occurs, than the transaction is **rolled back**.

deleteSystemUser()

deleteSystemUser() deletes the appropriate system user based on **UserNo** received as a reference.

This method uses:

❑ **load()** of Session, which retrieves the appropriate System User to be deleted using UserNo as a reference

❑ **delete()** of Session, which deletes the system user from the SystemUsers database table

After the delete operation is performed, the transaction is committed to make the changes permanent.

Whilst performing the delete operation, if a runtime exception occurs, than the transaction is rolled back.

getSystemUserById()

getSystemUserById() returns the appropriate system user's object from the SystemUsers database table using **UserNo** as the reference.

This method uses:

- **createQuery()** of Session, which creates a new instance of Query to retrieve the System User details using UserNo as reference

- **setInteger()** of Query, which states the parameter to be used as the WHERE clause criteria when querying the SystemUsers database table

- **uniqueResult()** of Query, which ensures that only unique record is retrieved from the SystemUsers database table and prevents any kinds of errors

REMINDER

PopulateDdlbsDAOImpl.java is explained later in the *Section VII: Common Files Software Design Documentation* under the *Chapter 59: Populating Drop Down List Boxes.*

PaginationDAOImpl.java is explained later in the *Section V: Backend [Administration] Software Design Documentation* under the *Chapter 42: Common Files.*

Validations [SystemUsersAction-validation.xml]

If the required **input** fields are kept empty whilst submitting the form, SystemUsersAction-validation.xml takes care of the validations.

Code Spec

```
1  <?xml version="1.0" encoding="UTF-8"?>
2  <!DOCTYPE validators PUBLIC '-//OpenSymphony Group//XWork Validator
   1.0.2//EN' 'http://www.opensymphony.com/xwork/xwork-validator-1.0.2.dtd'>
3  <validators>
4     <field name="systemuser.FirstName">
5        <field-validator type="requiredstring">
6           <message>Please enter the first name.</message>
7        </field-validator>
8     </field>
```

```
 9
10      <field name="systemuser.LastName">
11        <field-validator type="requiredstring">
12          <message>Please enter the last name.</message>
13        </field-validator>
14      </field>
15
16      <field name="systemuser.EmailAddress">
17        <field-validator type="requiredstring" short-circuit="true">
18          <message>Please enter the email address.</message>
19        </field-validator>
20        <field-validator type="email" short-circuit="true">
21          <message>Invalid email address.</message>
22        </field-validator>
23      </field>
24
25      <field name="systemuser.Username">
26        <field-validator type="requiredstring">
27          <message>Please enter the username.</message>
28        </field-validator>
29      </field>
30
31      <field name="systemuser.Password">
32        <field-validator type="requiredstring">
33          <message>Please enter the password.</message>
34        </field-validator>
35      </field>
36  </validators>
```

If any errors are detected the data entry form is re-served with appropriate error messages, as shown in diagram 40.2.

struts-SystemUsers.xml file holds a mapping to serve the data entry form:

```
17        <action name="doInsertUser" method="saveSystemUser"
          class="com.sharanamvaishali.action.SystemUsersAction">
18          <interceptor-ref name="defaultStack"/>
19          <interceptor-ref name="token"/>
20          <result name="success" type="redirectAction">doViewUsers</result>
21          <result name="input">/admin/manageUsers.jsp</result>
22          <result name="error">/admin/manageUsers.jsp</result>
23        </action>
```

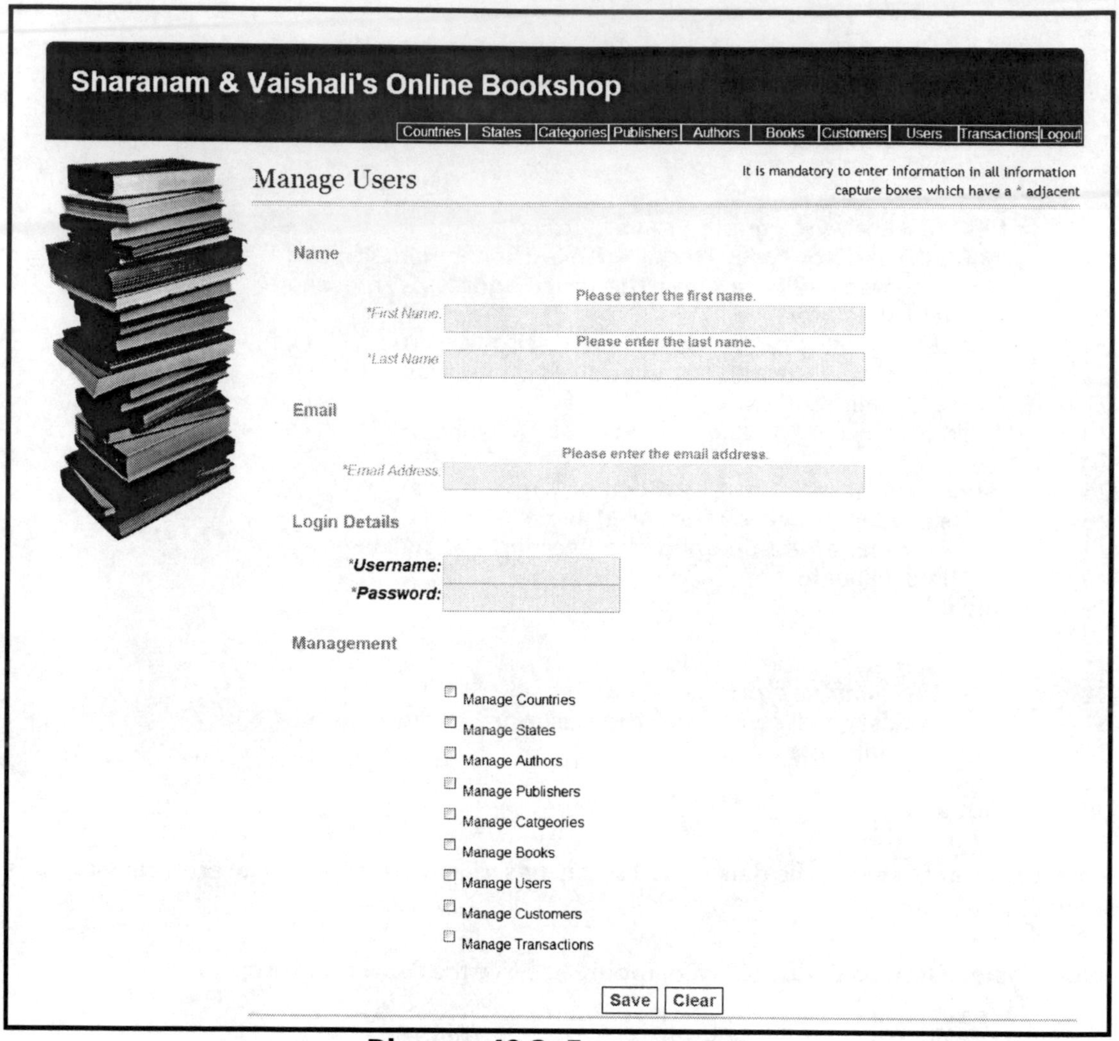

Sharanam & Vaishali's Online Bookshop

| Countries | States | Categories | Publishers | Authors | Books | Customers | Users | Transactions | Logout |

Manage Users

It is mandatory to enter information in all information capture boxes which have a * adjacent

Name

Please enter the first name.
*First Name:

Please enter the last name.
*Last Name:

Email

Please enter the email address.
*Email Address:

Login Details

*Username:

*Password:

Management

☐ Manage Countries
☐ Manage States
☐ Manage Authors
☐ Manage Publishers
☐ Manage Catgeories
☐ Manage Books
☐ Manage Users
☐ Manage Customers
☐ Manage Transactions

[Save] [Clear]

Diagram 40.2: Error messages

REMINDER

In the diagram 40.2, the error message for Username and Password are not displayed even though they are mandatory. The reason being that the previous validator i.e. Email Address is marked as short-circuit. The validators marked as short-circuit will prevent the evaluation of subsequent validators i.e. the validators of Username and Password.

Struts Configuration [struts-SystemUsers.xml]

This is the struts configuration file with the following specifications:

File Name	Package Name	Extends
Transactions	manageUsers	default

Actions	
Action Name	**Results**
showManageUsers	SUCCESS - manageUsers.jsp
iterateManageUsersPage	SUCCESS - manageUsers.jsp
doInsertUser	SUCCESS - doViewUsers
	INPUT - manageUsers.jsp
	ERROR - manageUsers.jsp
doViewUsers	SUCCESS - manageUsers.jsp
	ERROR - showManageUsers
doDeleteUser	SUCCESS - doViewUsers
showEditUser	SUCCESS - manageUsers.jsp

Code Spec

```xml
1   <?xml version="1.0" encoding="UTF-8"?>
2   <!DOCTYPE struts PUBLIC
3   "-//Apache Software Foundation//DTD Struts Configuration 2.0//EN"
4   "http://struts.apache.org/dtds/struts-2.0.dtd">
5   <struts>
6      <package name="manageUsers" extends="default">
7         <default-interceptor-ref name="chkSession"/>
8
9         <action name="showManageUsers" method="view"
        class="com.sharanamvaishali.action.SystemUsersAction">
10           <result>/admin/manageUsers.jsp</result>
11        </action>
12
13        <action name="iterateManageUsersPage" method="getPage"
        class="com.sharanamvaishali.action.SystemUsersAction">
14           <result>/admin/manageUsers.jsp</result>
15        </action>
16
17        <action name="doInsertUser" method="saveSystemUser"
        class="com.sharanamvaishali.action.SystemUsersAction">
18           <interceptor-ref name="defaultStack"/>
19           <interceptor-ref name="token"/>
20           <result name="success" type="redirectAction">doViewUsers</result>
21           <result name="input">/admin/manageUsers.jsp</result>
22           <result name="error">/admin/manageUsers.jsp</result>
23        </action>
```

```
24
25        <action name="doViewUsers" method="view"
          class="com.sharanamvaishali.action.SystemUsersAction">
26            <result name="success">/admin/manageUsers.jsp</result>
27            <result name="error" type="redirectAction">showManageUsers</result>
28        </action>
29
30        <action name="doDeleteUser" method="removeSystemUser"
          class="com.sharanamvaishali.action.SystemUsersAction">
31            <result name="success" type="redirectAction">doViewUsers</result>
32        </action>
33
34        <action name="showEditUser" method="editSystemUser"
          class="com.sharanamvaishali.action.SystemUsersAction">
35            <result name="success">/admin/manageUsers.jsp</result>
36        </action>
37    </package>
38 </struts>
```

Explanation:

The following section describes the above code spec.

showManageUsers.action

showManageUsers is an action to help viewing.

This means the data entry form and the list of system user details are displayed.

The list of system user details are retrieved by **SystemUsersAction**'s **view()**.

iterateManageUsersPage.action

iterateManageUsersPage is an action to help iterate.

This means displaying 10 records of system user details per page in the form of data grid.

This iterated data is retrieved by **SystemUsersAction**'s **getPage()**.

doInsertUser.action

doInsertUser is an action to help adding new system user details or updating existing system user details.

defaultStack interceptor is referenced, which a complete stack with all the common interceptors in place.

token interceptor is referenced, which checks for valid token presence in Action and prevents duplicate form submission.

doInsertUser.action:

❑ Calls **SystemUsersAction's saveSystemUser()** to add new system user details or update the existing system user details

❑ Ensures that the captured data is valid

❑ If the validation is successful then the data is saved and the result is redirected to **doViewUsers.action**

❑ If the validation fails then the Manage Users page along with error messages is displayed

doViewUsers.action

doViewUsers is an action to help viewing.

This means the list of system user details is displayed.

The list of author details are retrieved by **SystemUsersAction's view()**.

If there are no data available in the database then the error message is displayed in the Manage Users page by redirecting the page to **showManageUsers.action**.

doDeleteUser.action

In case, the user chooses to delete a system user and clicks ✖, **doDeleteUser.action** is the action to help delete a system user record from Manage Users.

doDeleteUser.action:

❑ Calls **SystemUsersAction's removeSystemUser()** to delete a system user record

❑ If the system user record is deleted successfully then the result is redirected to **doViewUsers.action**

showEditUser.action

showEditUser is an action to help the editing of existing system users.

In case, the user chooses to edit a system user and clicks that particular record, **showEditUser.action** helps fill up the Manage Users form with system user details.

showEditUser.action:

❑ Calls **SystemUsersAction's editSystemUser()** to retrieve the system user details

❑ Returns to the Manage Users page along with the data to be populated in the form

Domain Class [SystemUsers.java]

This is a domain class with the following specifications:

Class Name	Package	Implements
SystemUsers	com.sharanamvaishali.model	java.io.Serializable

Properties		
Property Name	**Property Type**	**Methods**
UserNo	Integer	getUserNo()	setUserNo()
Username	String	getUsername()	setUsername()
Password	String	getPassword()	setPassword()
EmailAddress	String	getEmailAddress()	setEmailAddress()
FirstName	String	getFirstName()	setFirstName()
LastName	String	getLastName()	setLastName()
ManageCountries	String	getManageCountries()	setManageCountries()
ManageStates	String	getManageStates()	setManageStates()
ManageAuthors	String	getManageAuthors()	setManageAuthors()
ManagePublishers	String	getManagePublishers()	setManagePublishers()
ManageCategories	String	getManageCategories()	setManageCategories()
ManageUsers	String	getManageUsers()	setManageUsers()
ManageBooks	String	getManageBooks()	setManageBooks()
ManageCustomers	String	getManageCustomers()	setManageCustomers()
ManageTransactions	String	getManageTransactions()	setManageTransactions()
LastLogin	String	getLastLogin()	setLastLogin()

Code Spec

```
1   package com.sharanamvaishali.model;
2
3   import javax.persistence.Column;
4   import javax.persistence.Entity;
5   import javax.persistence.GeneratedValue;
6   import javax.persistence.Id;
7   import javax.persistence.Table;
8
9   @Entity
10  @Table(name="SYSTEMUSERS")
```

```
11   public class SystemUsers implements java.io.Serializable {
12       @Id
13       @GeneratedValue
14       @Column(name="USERNO")
15       private Integer UserNo;
16       @Column(name="USERNAME")
17       private String Username;
18       @Column(name="PASSWORD")
19       private String Password;
20       @Column(name="EMAILADDRESS")
21       private String EmailAddress;
22       @Column(name="FIRSTNAME")
23       private String FirstName;
24       @Column(name="LASTNAME")
25       private String LastName;
26       @Column(name="MANAGECOUNTRIES")
27       private String ManageCountries;
28       @Column(name="MANAGESTATES")
29       private String ManageStates;
30       @Column(name="MANAGEAUTHORS")
31       private String ManageAuthors;
32       @Column(name="MANAGEPUBLISHERS")
33       private String ManagePublishers;
34       @Column(name="MANAGECATEGORIES")
35       private String ManageCategories;
36       @Column(name="MANAGEUSERS")
37       private String ManageUsers;
38       @Column(name="MANAGEBOOKS")
39       private String ManageBooks;
40       @Column(name="MANAGECUSTOMERS")
41       private String ManageCustomers;
42       @Column(name="MANAGETRANSACTIONS")
43       private String ManageTransactions;
44       @Column(name="LASTLOGIN")
45       private String LastLogin;
46
47       public SystemUsers() {
48       }
49
50       public String getEmailAddress() {
51           return EmailAddress;
52       }
53       public void setEmailAddress(String EmailAddress) {
54           this.EmailAddress = EmailAddress;
55       }
56
57       public String getFirstName() {
58           return FirstName;
```

```java
59      }
60      public void setFirstName(String FirstName) {
61          this.FirstName = FirstName;
62      }
63
64      public String getLastLogin() {
65          return LastLogin;
66      }
67      public void setLastLogin(String LastLogin) {
68          this.LastLogin = LastLogin;
69      }
70
71      public String getLastName() {
72          return LastName;
73      }
74      public void setLastName(String LastName) {
75          this.LastName = LastName;
76      }
77
78      public String getManageAuthors() {
79          return ManageAuthors;
80      }
81      public void setManageAuthors(String ManageAuthors) {
82          this.ManageAuthors = ManageAuthors;
83      }
84
85      public String getManageBooks() {
86          return ManageBooks;
87      }
88      public void setManageBooks(String ManageBooks) {
89          this.ManageBooks = ManageBooks;
90      }
91
92      public String getManageCategories() {
93          return ManageCategories;
94      }
95      public void setManageCategories(String ManageCategories) {
96          this.ManageCategories = ManageCategories;
97      }
98
99      public String getManageStates() {
100         return ManageStates;
101     }
102     public void setManageStates(String ManageStates) {
103         this.ManageStates = ManageStates;
104     }
105
106     public String getManageCountries() {
```

```
107          return ManageCountries;
108      }
109      public void setManageCountries(String ManageCountries) {
110          this.ManageCountries = ManageCountries;
111      }
112
113      public String getManageCustomers() {
114          return ManageCustomers;
115      }
116      public void setManageCustomers(String ManageCustomers) {
117          this.ManageCustomers = ManageCustomers;
118      }
119
120      public String getManagePublishers() {
121          return ManagePublishers;
122      }
123      public void setManagePublishers(String ManagePublishers) {
124          this.ManagePublishers = ManagePublishers;
125      }
126
127      public String getManageTransactions() {
128          return ManageTransactions;
129      }
130      public void setManageTransactions(String ManageTransactions) {
131          this.ManageTransactions = ManageTransactions;
132      }
133
134      public String getManageUsers() {
135          return ManageUsers;
136      }
137      public void setManageUsers(String ManageUsers) {
138          this.ManageUsers = ManageUsers;
139      }
140
141      public String getPassword() {
142          return Password;
143      }
144      public void setPassword(String Password) {
145          this.Password = Password;
146      }
147
148      public Integer getUserNo() {
149          return UserNo;
150      }
151      public void setUserNo(Integer UserNo) {
152          this.UserNo = UserNo;
153      }
154
```

```
155    public String getUsername() {
156        return Username;
157    }
158    public void setUsername(String Username) {
159        this.Username = Username;
160    }
161 }
```

SECTION V: BACKEND [ADMINISTRATION] SOFTWARE DESIGN DOCUMENTATION

Manage Transactions

This module allows performing the following operations:

❑ Selecting the username

❑ Viewing the transactions made by that user

This module uses the bms.Transactions and bms.Customers table to perform the above operations.

This module is made up of the following:

Type	Name	Description
JSP	manageTransactions.jsp	The data entry form

Struts 2		
Action	TransactionsAction.java	The action class that facilitates data operations.
Validation	TransactionsAction-validation.xml	The XML based validation file.
DAO Class	TransactionsDAO.java	The interface for the DAO layer.
	TransactionsDAOImpl.java	The implementation class that performs the actual data operations.
Struts Configuration	struts-Transactions.xml	Struts configuration file.
Hibernate		
Mapping	hibernate.cfg.xml	The mapping file that holds Model class mapping.
Model Class	Transactions.java	The model class.
	Customers.java	

JSP [manageTransactions.jsp]

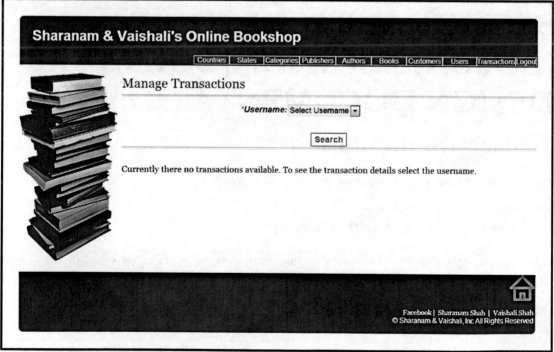

Diagram 41.1: Manage Transactions [Data entry form]

This is a JSP which holds a data entry form, as shown in diagram 41.1. This form appears when the user clicks Transactions .

Form Specifications

File Name	manageTransactions.jsp
Title	BookShop[Sharanam & Vaishali Shah] - Manage Transactions
Bound To Table	bms.Transactions
Form Name	frmTransactions
Action	doViewTransactions
Method	POST

Data Fields

Label	Name	Bound To	Validation Rules
Username	Username	Customers.Username	Cannot be left blank

Micro-Help For Form Fields

Form Field	Micro Help Statement
Username	Select Username

Data Controls

Object	Label	Name
s:submit	Search	btnSubmit

Code Spec

```
1   <%@page contentType="text/html" pageEncoding="UTF-8"%>
2   <%@ taglib prefix="s" uri="/struts-tags" %>
3   <!DOCTYPE HTML PUBLIC "-//W3C//DTD HTML 4.01 Transitional//EN"
4      "http://www.w3.org/TR/html4/loose.dtd">
5   <html xmlns="http://www.w3.org/1999/xhtml">
6     <head>
7       <title>BookShop [Sharanam & Vaishali Shah] - Manage Transactions</title>
8       <meta http-equiv="content-type" content="text/html; charset=iso-8859-1">
9       <link href="/BookShop/css/admin.css" type="text/css" rel="stylesheet">
10      <s:head/>
11    </head>
12    <body>
13      <s:include value="header.jsp" />
14      <br>
```

```
15    <s:form id="frmTransactions" name="frmTransactions" method="post"
      action="doViewTransactions" validate="true">
16      <s:token/>
17      <table width="100%" border="0" align="center" cellpadding="0" cellspacing="0">
18        <tr>
19          <td valign="top" width="20%">
20            <img src="/BookShop/images/leftImg.jpg" height="350"/>
21          </td>
22          <td valign="top">
23            <table border="0" cellpadding="0" cellspacing="0" align="center"
            width="100%">
24              <tr>
25                <td>
26                  <table border="0" cellpadding="0" cellspacing="0"
                  width="100%">
27                    <tr>
28                      <td class="manageForms">Manage Transactions</td>
29                      <td class="information" valign="top"
                      align="right"> </td>
30                    </tr>
31                  </table>
32                </td>
33              </tr>
34              <tr><td class="hrLine"> </td></tr>
35              <tr align="left" valign="top">
36                <td>
37                  <table width="90%" border="0" align="center" cellpadding="0"
                  cellspacing="0">
38                    <tr>
39                      <td>
40                        <table width="100%" border="0" cellpadding="0"
                        cellspacing="0">
41                          <s:select label="Username" name="Username"
                          id="Username" required="true" requiredposition="true"
                          list="ddlbUsernames" listKey="Username"
                          listValue="Username" headerKey=""
                          headerValue="Select Username"></s:select>
42                        </table>
43                      </td>
44                    </tr>
45                    <tr>
46                      <td style="text-align: center;">
47                        <br /><br />
48                        <s:submit theme="simple" cssClass="groovybutton"
                        name="btnSubmit" id="btnSubmit" value="Search" />
49                      </td>
50                    </tr>
51                  </table>
52                </td>
53              </tr>
54              <tr><td class="hrLine"> </td></tr>
55              <tr>
56                <td>
57                  <br />
```

```
58    <table class="view" align="center" cellspacing="0" cellpadding="0"
      width="100%">
59        <s:iterator value="transactions" id="transactions"
      status="stat">
60            <s:if test="#stat.index == 0">
61                <tr>
62                    <th width="8%" class="Arial13BrownB"
      align="left"> </th>
63                    <th width="10%" class="Arial13BrownB"
      align="left">Date</th>
64                    <th width="70%" class="Arial13BrownB"
      align="left">Book Name</th>
65                    <th width="12%" class="Arial13BrownB"
      align="left">Amount</th>
66                </tr>
67            </s:if>
68            <tr class="<s:if test="#stat.odd ==
      true">odd</s:if><s:else>even</s:else>">
69                <td width="8%" valign="top" align="left">
70                    <s:property value="TransactionNo"/>
71                </td>
72                <td width="10%" valign="top" align="left">
73                    <s:property value="TransactionDate"/>
74                </td>
75                <td width="70%" valign="top" align="left">
76                    <s:property value="BookName" />
77                </td>
78                <td width="12%" valign="top" align="left">
79                    <s:property value="Cost" />
80                </td>
81            </tr>
82        </s:iterator>
83        <s:if test="#transactions==null">
84            <span class="emptyMessage">Currently there no transactions
      available. To see the transaction details select the
      username.</span>
85        </s:if>
86    </table>
87    </td>
88    </tr>
89    </table>
90    </td>
91    </tr>
92    </table>
93    </s:form>
94    <s:include value="adminFooter.jsp" />
95    </body>
96 </html>
```

Explanation:

This is a standard data entry form, which captures the username to display the transactions made by that particular user.

Action [TransactionsAction.java]

This is an action class with the following specifications:

Class Name	TransactionsAction
Package	com.sharanamvaishali.action
Extends	ActionSupport
Implements	- -

Objects		
Object Name	**Class Name**	**Object Type**
transactionsDAO	TransactionsDAO	Data Access Layer

Properties		
Property Name	**Property Type**	**Methods**
For the data grid population		
transactions	List<Transactions>	getTransactions() setTransactions()
For drop down list box		
ddlbUsernames	List<Customers>	getDdlbUsernames() setDdlbUsernames()
Username	String	getUsername() setUsername()

Methods	
Method Name	**Return Values**
populateUsernames()	SUCCESS
view()	SUCCESS

Code Spec

```
1   package com.sharanamvaishali.action;
2
3   import com.opensymphony.xwork2.ActionSupport;
4   import com.sharanamvaishali.dao.TransactionsDAO;
5   import com.sharanamvaishali.dao.TransactionsDAOImpl;
6   import com.sharanamvaishali.model.Customers;
7   import com.sharanamvaishali.model.Transactions;
8   import java.util.List;
9   import org.apache.struts2.interceptor.validation.SkipValidation;
10
11  public class TransactionsAction extends ActionSupport{
12      private TransactionsDAO transactionsDAO = new TransactionsDAOImpl();
13
14      private List<Transactions> transactions;
15
16      private List<Customers> ddlbUsernames;
17
18      private String Username;
19
```

```
20      public List<Transactions> getTransactions() {
21          return transactions;
22      }
23      public void setTransactions(List<Transactions> transactions) {
24          this.transactions = transactions;
25      }
26
27      public List<Customers> getDdlbUsernames() {
28          return ddlbUsernames;
29      }
30      public void setDdlbUsernames(List<Customers> ddlbUsernames) {
31          this.ddlbUsernames = ddlbUsernames;
32      }
33
34      public String getUsername() {
35          return Username;
36      }
37      public void setUsername(String Username) {
38          this.Username = Username;
39      }
40
41      @SkipValidation
42      public String populateUsernames(){
43          ddlbUsernames = transactionsDAO.getUsernames();
44          return SUCCESS;
45      }
46
47      @SkipValidation
48      public String view() throws Exception{
49          populateUsernames();
50          transactions = transactionsDAO.getTransactions(Username);
51          return SUCCESS;
52      }
53  }
```

Explanation:

The following section describes the above code spec.

populateUsernames()

populateUsernames() is invoked every time the Manage Transactions page is served.

It invokes TransactionsDAO's getUsernames() which retrieves and returns a list of Usernames which is made available to the Manage Transactions page for displaying the same in the drop down list box.

view()

view() is invoked when the username is selected and Search is clicked.

It also invokes populateUsernames() to populate the List object [ddlbUsernames] which is used in the Manage Transactions page's **<s:select>** to populate the drop down list box. This dropdown list box displays existing records from the **Customers** database table.

Then it invokes TransactionsDAO's **getTransactions()** to populate the List object [transactions] which is used in the Manage Transactions page's **<s:iterator>** to populate the data grid. getTransactions() is passed the selected username. This data grid displays existing records from the **Transactions** database table.

@SkipValidation is used to skip validation for this method.

DAO Class

Interface [TransactionsDAO.java]

This is a Data Access Object interface with the following specifications:

Class Name	Package
TransactionsDAO	com.sharanamvaishali.dao

Code Spec

```
1  package com.sharanamvaishali.dao;
2
3  import com.sharanamvaishali.model.Transactions;
4  import java.util.List;
5
6  public interface TransactionsDAO {
7      public List getUsernames();
8      public List getTransactions(String username);
9  }
```

Implementation Class [TransactionsDAOImpl.java]

This is a Data Access Object class with the following specifications:

Class Name	TransactionsDAOImpl
Package	com.sharanamvaishali.dao
Implements	TransactionsDAO

Objects	
Object Name	**Class Name**
session	Session

Methods		
Method Name	**Arguments**	**Return Values**
getUsernames()	– –	List
getTransactions()	String username	List

Code Spec

```
1   package com.sharanamvaishali.dao;
2
3   import com.sharanamvaishali.model.Transactions;
4   import com.sharanamvaishali.utility.HibernateUtil;
5   import java.util.List;
6   import org.hibernate.Session;
7
8   public class TransactionsDAOImpl implements TransactionsDAO {
9       Session session = HibernateUtil.getSession();
10
11      @Override
12      public List getUsernames() {
13          try {
14              return session.createQuery("FROM Customers").list();
15          } catch(Exception e) {
16              System.out.print("Error while fetching" + e);
17              return null;
18          }
19      }
20
21      @Override
22      public List getTransactions(String username) {
23          try {
24              return session.createQuery("FROM Transactions WHERE Username =
                :Username").setString("Username", username).list();
25          } catch(Exception e) {
26              System.out.print("Error while fetching" + e);
27              return null;
28          }
29      }
30  }
```

Explanation:

The following section describes the above code spec.

getUsernames()

getUsernames() is invoked by **TransactionsAction**'s populateUsernames() every time the Manage Transactions page is served.

getUsernames() does the actual retrieval of all the registered usernames available in the **Customers** database table.

It retrieves [using createQuery()], populates the List object [ddlbUsernames] created in TransactionsAction and returns the same to **TransactionsAction**'s populateUsernames(). This List will be used in the Manage Transactions page's drop down list box. This drop down list box displays existing records from the **Customers** database table.

This method uses **list()** of Query, which returns the query results as a List

getTransactions()

getTransactions() is invoked by **TransactionsAction**'s view().

getTransactions() does the actual retrieval of all the transactions on a particular username from the **Transactions** database table.

It retrieves [using createQuery()], populates the List object [transactions] created in TransactionsAction and returns the same to **TransactionsAction**'s view(). This List will be used in the Manage Transactions page's <s:iterator> to form the data grid. This data grid displays existing records from the **Transactions** database table.

This method uses **setString()** of Query, which state the parameter to be used as the WHERE clause criteria when querying the Transactions database table

Validations [TransactionsAction-validation.xml]

If the required **input** fields are kept empty whilst submitting the form, TransactionsAction-validation.xml takes care of the validations.

Code Spec

```
1   <?xml version="1.0" encoding="UTF-8"?>
2   <!DOCTYPE validators PUBLIC '-//OpenSymphony Group//XWork Validator
    1.0.2//EN' 'http://www.opensymphony.com/xwork/xwork-validator-1.0.2.dtd'>
3   <validators>
4     <field name="Username">
```

```
5        <field-validator type="requiredstring">
6            <message>Please select the username.</message>
7        </field-validator>
8     </field>
9  </validators>
```

If any errors are detected the data entry form is re-served with appropriate error messages, as shown in diagram 41.2.

struts-Transactions.xml file holds a mapping to serve the data entry form:

```
13        <action name="doViewTransactions" method="view"
          class="com.sharanamvaishali.action.TransactionsAction">
14            <interceptor-ref name="defaultStack"/>
15            <interceptor-ref name="token"/>
16            <result name="success">/admin/manageTransactions.jsp</result>
17            <result name="error"
          type="redirectAction">showManageTransactions</result>
18        </action>
```

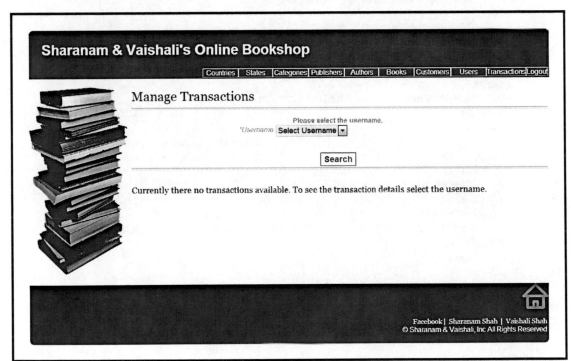

Diagram 41.2: Error messages

Struts Configuration [struts-Transactions.xml]

This is the struts configuration file with the following specifications:

File Name	Package Name	Extends
Transactions	manageTransactions	default

Actions	
Action Name	**Results**
showManageTransactions	SUCCESS - manageTransactions.jsp
doViewTransactions	SUCCESS - manageTransactions.jsp
	ERROR - showManageTransactions

Code Spec

```
1   <?xml version="1.0" encoding="UTF-8"?>
2   <!DOCTYPE struts PUBLIC
3   "-//Apache Software Foundation//DTD Struts Configuration 2.0//EN"
4   "http://struts.apache.org/dtds/struts-2.0.dtd">
5   <struts>
6     <package name="manageTransactions" extends="default">
7       <default-interceptor-ref name="chkSession"/>
8
9       <action name="showManageTransactions" method="populateUsernames"
        class="com.sharanamvaishali.action.TransactionsAction">
10        <result>/admin/manageTransactions.jsp</result>
11      </action>
12
13      <action name="doViewTransactions" method="view"
        class="com.sharanamvaishali.action.TransactionsAction">
14        <interceptor-ref name="defaultStack"/>
15        <interceptor-ref name="token"/>
16        <result name="success">/admin/manageTransactions.jsp</result>
17        <result name="error"
          type="redirectAction">showManageTransactions</result>
18      </action>
19    </package>
20  </struts>
```

Explanation:

The following section describes the above code spec.

showManageTransactions.action

showManageTransactions is an action to help viewing.

This means the data entry form is displayed.

The list of usernames are retrieved by **TransactionsAction's** **populateUsernames()**.

doViewTransactions.action

doViewTransactions is an action to help viewing.

This means the list of transaction details of a particular user is displayed.

defaultStack interceptor is referenced, which a complete stack with all the common interceptors in place.

token interceptor is referenced, which checks for valid token presence in Action and prevents duplicate form submission.

The list of transaction details are retrieved by **TransactionsAction's** **view()**.

If there are no data available in the database then the error message is displayed in the Manage Transaction page by redirecting the page to **showManageTransactions.action**.

Domain Class [Transactions.java]

This is a domain class with the following specifications:

Class Name	Package	Implements
Transactions	com.sharanamvaishali.model	java.io.Serializable

Properties		
Property Name	**Property Type**	**Methods**
transactionDetailNo	Integer	getTransactionDetailNo() setTransactionDetailNo()
transactionNo	Integer	getTransactionNo() setTransactionNo()
cost	Integer	getCost() setCost()
qty	Integer	getQty() setQty()
transactionDate	Date	getTransactionDate() setTransactionDate()
username	String	getUsername() setUsername()
bookName	String	getBookName() setBookName()

Code Spec

```
1  package com.sharanamvaishali.model;
2
3  import java.util.Date;
```

```
4  import javax.persistence.Column;
5  import javax.persistence.Entity;
6  import javax.persistence.GeneratedValue;
7  import javax.persistence.Id;
8  import javax.persistence.Table;
9
10 @Entity
11 @Table(name="TRANSACTIONS")
12 public class Transactions implements java.io.Serializable {
13     @Id
14     @GeneratedValue
15     @Column(name="TRANSACTIONDETAILNO")
16     private Integer transactionDetailNo;
17     @Column(name="TRANSACTIONNO")
18     private Integer transactionNo;
19     @Column(name="COST")
20     private Integer cost;
21     @Column(name="QTY")
22     private Integer qty;
23     @Column(name="TRANSACTIONDATE")
24     private Date transactionDate;
25     @Column(name="USERNAME")
26     private String username;
27     @Column(name="BOOKNAME")
28     private String bookName;
29
30     public Transactions() {
31     }
32
33     public Integer getTransactionDetailNo() {
34         return transactionDetailNo;
35     }
36     public void setTransactionDetailNo(Integer transactionDetailNo) {
37         this.transactionDetailNo = transactionDetailNo;
38     }
39
40     public Integer getTransactionNo() {
41         return this.transactionNo;
42     }
43     public void setTransactionNo(Integer transactionNo) {
44         this.transactionNo = transactionNo;
45     }
46
47     public Date getTransactionDate() {
48         return this.transactionDate;
49     }
50     public void setTransactionDate(Date transactionDate) {
51         this.transactionDate = transactionDate;
52     }
```

```
53
54     public String getUsername() {
55         return this.username;
56     }
57     public void setUsername(String username) {
58         this.username = username;
59     }
60
61     public String getBookName() {
62         return this.bookName;
63     }
64     public void setBookName(String bookName) {
65         this.bookName = bookName;
66     }
67
68     public Integer getCost() {
69         return this.cost;
70     }
71     public void setCost(Integer cost) {
72         this.cost = cost;
73     }
74
75     public Integer getQty() {
76         return this.qty;
77     }
78     public void setQty(Integer qty) {
79         this.qty = qty;
80     }
81 }
```

Chapter

42

SECTION V: BACKEND [ADMINISTRATION] SOFTWARE DESIGN DOCUMENTATION

Common Includes

Administration Header

This module is made up of the following:

Type	Name	Description
JSP	header.jsp	The header of the administration section.

JSP [header.jsp]

Sharanam & Vaishali's Online Bookshop

| Countries | States | Categories | Publishers | Authors | Books | Customers | Users | Transactions | Logout |

Diagram 42.1: Header of the Administration Section

This is a JSP which holds the header of the administration section, as shown in diagram 42.1.

This file is included in the beginning of the BODY section in all the Manage forms:

```
<body>
    <s:include value="header.jsp" />
```

Code Spec

```
1   <%@page contentType="text/html" pageEncoding="UTF-8"%>
2   <%@ taglib prefix="s" uri="/struts-tags" %>
3   <div id="headerDiv">
4      <table class="headerTable" border="0" width="100%">
5         <tr>
6            <td>
7               <h1>Sharanam & Vaishali's Online Bookshop</h1>
8            </td>
9         </tr>
10     </table>
11     <br/>
12     <table border="0" cellspacing="0" cellpadding="0" width="100%">
13        <tr>
14           <td width="37%"> </td>
15           <s:if test="#session.countries=='true'">
16              <td align="center" class="menuborder" width="7%">
17                 <s:a href="showManageCountries.action">Countries</s:a>
18              </td>
19           </s:if>
20           <s:if test="#session.states=='true'">
21              <td align="center" class="menuborder" width="7%">
22                 <s:a href="showManageStates.action">States</s:a>
23              </td>
24           </s:if>
25           <s:if test="#session.categories=='true'">
26              <td align="center" class="menuborder" width="7%">
27                 <s:a href="showManageCategories.action">Categories</s:a>
28              </td>
29           </s:if>
30           <s:if test="#session.publishers=='true'">
31              <td align="center" class="menuborder" width="7%">
32                 <s:a href="showManagePublishers.action">Publishers</s:a>
33              </td>
34           </s:if>
35           <s:if test="#session.authors=='true'">
36              <td align="center" class="menuborder" width="7%">
37                 <s:a href="showManageAuthors.action">Authors</s:a>
38              </td>
39           </s:if>
40           <s:if test="#session.books=='true'">
41              <td align="center" class="menuborder" width="7%">
42                 <s:a href="showManageBooks.action">Books</s:a>
43              </td>
```

```
44          </s:if>
45          <s:if test="#session.customers=='true'">
46             <td align="center" class="menuborder" width="7%">
47                <s:a href="showManageCustomers.action">Customers</s:a>
48             </td>
49          </s:if>
50          <s:if test="#session.users=='true'">
51             <td align="center" class="menuborder" width="7%">
52                <s:a href="showManageUsers.action">Users</s:a>
53             </td>
54          </s:if>
55          <s:if test="#session.transactions=='true'">
56             <td align="center" class="menuborder" width="7%">
57                <s:a href="showManageTransactions.action">Transactions</s:a>
58             </td>
59          </s:if>
60          <td align="center" class="menuborder" width="7%">
61             <a href="<s:url action="doLogout" />">Logout</a>
62          </td>
63       </tr>
64    </table>
65  </div>
```

Explanation:

This JSP is the header file of the administration section.

This JSP holds:

❑ The name of the Shop owner

❑ The links of all the Manage forms

❑ The link to logout i.e. return to the admin login page

Administration Footer

This module is made up of the following:

Type	Name	Description
JSP	adminFooter.jsp	The footer of the administration section.

JSP [adminFooter.jsp]

Diagram 42.2: Footer of the Administration Section

This is a JSP which holds the footer of the administration section, as shown in diagram 42.2.

This file is included at the end of the BODY section in all the Manage forms:

```
    <s:include value="adminFooter.jsp" />
</body>
```

Code Spec

```
1  <%@page contentType="text/html" pageEncoding="UTF-8"%>
2  <%@ taglib prefix="s" uri="/struts-tags" %>
3  <table id="footer" width="100%" border="0" cellpadding="0" cellspacing="0">
4     <tr>
5       <td class="footerIconAlgin">
6         <s:a href="showHomePage.action">
7           <img src="/BookShop/images/home.png" title="Home(End User)"/>
8         </s:a>
9       </td>
10    </tr>
11    <tr>
12      <td class="footerTextAlgin" width="25%">
13        <br/>
14        <span><a href="http://www.facebook.com/sharanamvaishali"
          target="_blank">Facebook</a> | </span>
15        <span><a href="http://www.sharanamshah.com" target="_blank">Sharanam
          Shah</a></span>
16         | 
17        <span><a href="http://www.vaishalishahonline.com" target="_blank">Vaishali
          Shah</a></span>
18        <br/>
19        <span>&copy; Sharanam & Vaishali, Inc All Rights Reserved </span>
20      </td>
21    </tr>
22 </table>
```

Explanation:

This JSP is the footer file of the administration section.

This JSP holds:

❑   The link to the home page of the application i.e. the customer facing home page

❑   The name of the creator of the application

Double Post

This module is made up of the following:

Type	Name	Description
JSP	doublePost.jsp	The double post error message page.

JSP [doublePost.jsp]

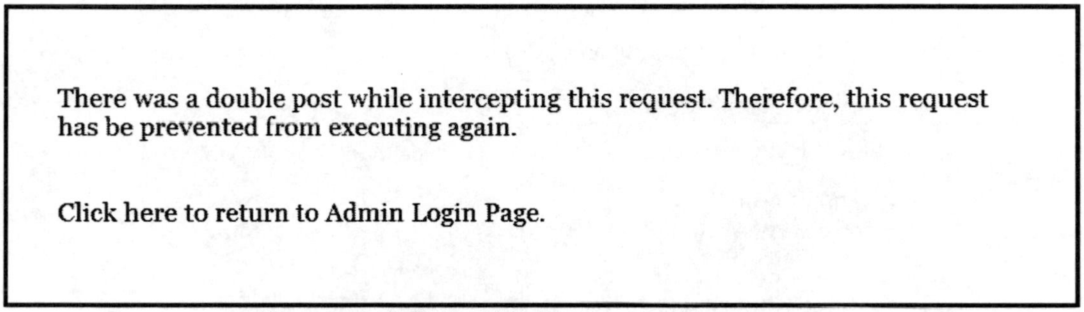

There was a double post while intercepting this request. Therefore, this request has be prevented from executing again.

Click here to return to Admin Login Page.

Diagram 42.3: Double Post error message page

This is a JSP which holds the error message when the user tries to post the data double time, as shown in diagram 42.3.

The double posting is taken care by <s:token> in the Manage Forms:

```
<s:form action="doInsertAuthor" method="post" name="frmAuthors" id="frmAuthors"
enctype="multipart/form-data" validate="true">
    <s:token/>
    <s:hidden name="author.AuthorNo" id="AuthorNo"/>
```

struts.xml holds the action for double posting:

```
<global-results>
    <result name="invalid.token">/doublePost.jsp</result>
```

All Struts configuration file for the Manage Forms also holds the reference for double posting:

```
<action name="doInsertAuthor" method="saveAuthor"
class="com.sharanamvaishali.action.AuthorsAction">
    <interceptor-ref name="defaultStack"/>
    <interceptor-ref name="token"/>
    <result name="success" type="redirectAction">doViewAuthors</result>
    <result name="input">/admin/manageAuthors.jsp</result>
</action>
```

Code Spec

```
1   <%@page contentType="text/html" pageEncoding="UTF-8"%>
2   <%@ taglib prefix="s" uri="/struts-tags" %>
3   <!DOCTYPE HTML PUBLIC "-//W3C//DTD HTML 4.01 Transitional//EN"
4     "http://www.w3.org/TR/html4/loose.dtd">
5   <html xmlns="http://www.w3.org/1999/xhtml">
6     <head>
7       <title>BookShop [Sharanam & Vaishali Shah] - Double Post Error</title>
8       <meta http-equiv="content-type" content="text/html; charset=iso-8859-1">
9       <link href="/BookShop/css/admin.css" type="text/css" rel="stylesheet">
10      <s:head />
11    </head>
12    <body>
13      <s:include value="header.jsp" />
14      <br>
15      <table width="100%" border="0" align="center" cellpadding="0" cellspacing="0">
16        <tr>
17          <td valign="top">
18            <table width="100%" border="0" align="center" cellpadding="0"
                 cellspacing="0">
19              <tr>
20                <td class="doublePost">
21                  There was a double post while intercepting this request. Therefore, this
                    request has be prevented from executing again.
22                </td>
23              </tr>
24              <tr>
25                <td class="doublePost">
26                  <br><br>Click here to return to <s:url id="back" value="/"/><s:a
                    href="admin.action">Admin Login Page</s:a>.
27                </td>
28              </tr>
29            </table>
30          </td>
31        </tr>
32      </table>
33      <s:include value="adminFooter.jsp" />
34    </body>
35  </html>
```

Explanation:

This JSP is the error message for double posting i.e. the user is not allowed to click Save
twice at the same time.

This JSP holds:

❑   The link to the administration login page

Stylesheet

This module is made up of the following:

Type	Name	Description
CSS	admin.css	The stylesheet for the administration section.

Code Spec

```
 1  a {
 2      text-decoration: none;
 3      color: #660000;
 4      font-family: Georgia, serif;
 5  }
 6
 7  a:hover {
 8      text-decoration: none;
 9      color: #FF0000;
10      font-family: Georgia, serif;
11  }
12
13  body {
14      font-family: helvetica, arial, sans-serif;
15      font-size: 13px;
16      color: #333;
17      text-decoration: none;
18      margin: 30px;
19      padding: 0;
20  }
21
22  img {
23      border: none;
24  }
25
26  .groovybutton {
27      font-size:15px;
28      font-weight:bold;
29      color:#CC0000;
30      background-color:#FFFFFF;
31      filter:progid:DXImageTransform.Microsoft.Gradient(GradientType=0,StartColorStr='#ffC
        C99FF',EndColorStr='#ffFFFFCC');
32      border-top-style:groove;
33      border-top-color:#FF0099;
34      border-bottom-style:groove;
35      border-bottom-color:#FF0099;
36      border-left-style:groove;
37      border-left-color:#FF0099;
38      border-right-style:groove;
39      border-right-color:#FF0099;
40      height: 25px;
```

```
41  }
42
43  INPUT, SELECT {
44      font: 14px/20px Arial, Helvetica, sans-serif;
45      color: #0b0b0b;
46      border: #c3bca4 1px solid;
47      height: 22px;
48      background-color: #efebde;
49  }
50
51  TEXTAREA {
52      font: 14px/20px Arial, Helvetica, sans-serif;
53      color: #0b0b0b;
54      border: #c3bca4 1px solid;
55      background-color: #efebde;
56  }
57
58  .hrLine {
59      height: 20px;
60      background: url('/BookShop/images/hr.jpg') repeat-x;
61  }
62
63  .information {
64      font-weight: normal;
65      font-size: 13px;
66      color: #333333;
67      font-family: "Trebuchet MS";
68      text-decoration: none;
69      text-align: right;
70      vertical-align: top;
71  }
72
73  .manageForms {
74      font: 24px Georgia;
75      color: #786e4e;
76      height: 37px;
77  }
78
79  .menuborder {
80      border: 1px solid #ffffff;
81      font-family: Geneva, Arial, Helvetica, sans-serif;
82      text-align: center;
83  }
84
85  .menuborder a {
86      font-family: Geneva, Arial, Helvetica, sans-serif;
87      text-align: center;
88      color: white;
89  }
90
91  .menuborder:hover {
92      font-family: Geneva, Arial, Helvetica, sans-serif;
93      background-color: #ffffff;
94      text-align: center;
```

```
 95  }
 96
 97  .menuborder:hover a{
 98     font-family: Geneva, Arial, Helvetica, sans-serif;
 99     color: #000000;
100     text-align: center;
101  }
102
103  .mandatory {
104     font-weight: bold;
105     font-size: 13px;
106     color: red;
107     font-family: "Trebuchet MS";
108  }
109
110  .error {
111     color: red;
112  }
113
114  .doublePost {
115     font: 16px/18px Georgia, serif;
116     color: #786e4e;
117     text-align: left;
118     vertical-align: top;
119  }
120
121  #headerDiv {
122     height:88px;
123     background-image: url('/BookShop/images/transparent-bg.png');
124     width:100%;
125     border: 2px solid #000;
126     -moz-border-radius: 8px;
127     border-radius: 8px;
128     -moz-border-bottom-left-radius: 0px;
129     -moz-border-bottom-right-radius: 0px;
130     border-bottom-left-radius: 0px;
131     border-bottom-right-radius: 0px;
132     color: white;
133  }
134
135  #footer {
136     color:white;
137     margin-top: 20px;
138     float:left;
139     position:relative;
140     width: 100%;
141     height:88px;
142     background-image: url('/BookShop/images/transparent-bg.png');
143     border-radius: 8px;
144     -moz-border-top-left-radius: 0px;
145     -moz-border-top-right-radius: 0px;
146     border-top-left-radius: 0px;
147     border-top-right-radius: 0px;
```

```
148       padding-bottom: 18px;
149    }
150
151    #footer a{
152       text-decoration: none;
153       color: #fff;
154    }
155
156    .footerTextAlgin {
157       text-align:right;
158       vertical-align: bottom;
159    }
160
161    .footerIconAlgin {
162       text-align:right;
163       vertical-align: bottom;
164    }
165
166    .headerTable {
167       float:left;
168       color:white;
169       padding-left: 20px;
170    }
171
172    .loginButtonAlign {
173       text-align: right;
174    }
175
176    .loginButton {
177       background: url('/BookShop/images/login.jpg') no-repeat;
178       border: 0;
179       cursor: pointer;
180       width: 68px;
181       height: 40px;
182    }
183
184    .Arial13BrownB {
185       font-family: "Arial", Times, serif;
186       font-size: 13px;
187       font-weight: bold;
188       color: #990000;
189    }
190
191    .emptyMessage {
192       font:16px/18px Georgia, serif;
193       width:300px;
194       color:#990000;
195       height:37px;
196    }
197
198    .manageList {
199       vertical-align: top;
200       text-align: left;
201       cursor: pointer;
```

```
202  }
203
204  .view {
205      border: 0px solid blue;
206      border-collapse: collapse;
207  }
208
209  .view th {
210      background-color: #EFEBDE;
211      color: #666;
212      text-align: left;
213      border: 1px solid white;
214      padding: 5px;
215  }
216
217  .view td {
218      padding: 3px;
219  }
220
221  .view tr.odd {
222      background-color: #fafbff;
223  }
224
225  .view tr.even {
226      background-color: #EFEBDE;
227  }
228
229  .Arial16BlueB {
230      font-family: "Arial", Times, serif;
231      font-size: 16px;
232      font-weight: bold;
233      color: blue;
234  }
235
236  .label {
237      font-family: "Arial", Times, serif;
238      font-size: 15px;
239      font-weight: bold;
240      color: #990000;
241  }
```

Page

This is a common Java module that brings the pagination functionality to this application's data grids.

It uses **Hibernate** to query and retrieve the appropriate page of the result set. It then returns the page [list of records] to the calling method [usually PaginationDAO's methods] to in turn return that page [list of records] to the action class to finally render the same in JSP's data grid.

This all begins when the user clicks the desired page number on a JSP with data grid to view the records of that page.

Page Class [Page.java]

This is a Java class with the following specifications:

Class Name	Package
Page	Com.sharanamvaishali.utility

Constructor	
Name	**Arguments**
Page()	Query query int page int pageSize

Methods	
Method Name	**Return Values**
isNextPage()	boolean
isPreviousPage()	boolean
getList()	List

Code Spec

```
1    package com.sharanamvaishali.utility;
2
3    import java.util.List;
4    import org.hibernate.Query;
5
6    public class Page {
7        private List results;
8        private int pageSize;
9        private int page;
10
11       public Page(Query query, int page, int pageSize) {
12           this.page = page;
13           this.pageSize = pageSize;
14           results = query.setFirstResult(page *
                 pageSize).setMaxResults(pageSize).list();
15       }
16
17       public boolean isNextPage() {
18           return results.size() > pageSize;
19       }
20
21       public boolean isPreviousPage() {
22           return page > 0;
23       }
```

```
24
25      public List getList() {
26          return isNextPage() ? results.subList(0, pageSize-1) : results;
27      }
28  }
```

Explanation:

The following section describes the above code spec.

Page()

Page() is a parameterized constructor of the Page class. It accepts the following:

❑ The query object that hold the query

❑ The page number to be retrieved

❑ The number of records on that page

Based on the parameters values, it returns the list of the records that fall under that page.

getPage() of PaginationDAO invokes this class's constructor to control pagination:

`return new Page(session.createQuery(query), page, 10);`

isNextPage()

isNextPage() when invoked returns true if there exists another page after the current page and false otherwise.

isPreviousPage()

isPreviousPage() when invoked returns true if there exists a page before the current page and false otherwise.

getList()

getList() when invoked returns the list created by the constructor of this class.

DAO Class

Interface [PaginationDAO.java]

This is a Data Access Object interface with the following specifications:

Class Name	Package
PaginationDAO	com.sharanamvaishali.dao

Code Spec

```
1   package com.sharanamvaishali.dao;
2
3   import com.sharanamvaishali.utility.Page;
4
5   public interface PaginationDAO {
6       public Page getPage(int page, String tableName);
7       public int getTotalPages(String tableName);
8   }
```

Implementation Class [PaginationDAOImpl.java]

This is a Data Access Object class with the following specifications:

Class Name	PaginationDAOImpl
Package	com.sharanamvaishali.dao
Implements	PaginationDAO

Objects	
Object Name	**Class Name**
session	Session

Methods		
Method Name	**Arguments**	**Return Values**
getPage()	int page String tableName	Page
getTotalPages()	String tableName	int

Code Spec

```
1   package com.sharanamvaishali.dao;
2
3   import com.sharanamvaishali.utility.HibernateUtil;
4   import com.sharanamvaishali.utility.Page;
5   import org.hibernate.Session;
6
7   public class PaginationDAOImpl implements PaginationDAO {
```

```
 8      Session session = HibernateUtil.getSession();
 9
10      @Override
11      public Page getPage(int page, String tableName) {
12         try {
13            String query = "FROM " + tableName;
14            return new Page(session.createQuery(query), page, 10);
15         } catch(Exception e) {
16            System.out.print("Error while fetching" + e);
17            return null;
18         }
19      }
20
21      @Override
22      public int getTotalPages(String tableName) {
23         try {
24            String total = session.createSQLQuery("SELECT COUNT(*) AS Total FROM "
                 + tableName).addScalar("Total").uniqueResult().toString();
25            return (int) Math.ceil(Double.parseDouble(total)/10);
26         } catch(Exception e) {
27            System.out.print("Error while fetching" + e);
28            return 0;
29         }
30      }
31   }
```

Explanation:

The following section describes the above code spec.

getPage()

getPage(), based on the table name and the page number, extracts the appropriate records belonging to the page number and returns the same in the form of Page object.

getPage() retrieves the records by calling the constructor of the Page class.

getPage() allows retrieving the page when a user clicks the page number from JSP.

getTotalPages()

getTotalPages() when invoked retrieves the total number of pages based on the number of records in the table and the maximum number of records on a page.

The value that getTotalPages() returns is used to form the pagination links in JSP.

Chapter

43

SECTION VI: FRONTEND [CUSTOMER FACING] SOFTWARE DESIGN DOCUMENTATION

Homepage

This is the entry point to this application.

This module allows performing the following operations:

❑ **Login as a customer**

❑ **Search Books**

❑ **View**

    o   New Releases

    o   Updated Books

    o   Top Titles

    o   Authors

    o   Publishers

- o   Popular Searches
- o   Categories
- o   Category wise books
- ❏ **Add books to cart**
- ❏ **Show Cart** [If the user is logged in]
- ❏ **Sign Up**
- ❏ **Logout** [If the user is logged in]

This module uses the following tables to perform the above operations:

- ❏   bms.Authors
- ❏   bms.Publishers
- ❏   bms.Books
- ❏   bms.PopularSearches
- ❏   bms.Customers
- ❏   bms.Categories

This module is made up of the following:

Type	Name	Description
JSP index.jsp		The Index page i.e. the starting point of the application.
	home.jsp	The home page.
	login.jsp	The Login form for the registered users.
	leftMenu.jsp	The list of New Releases, Updated Books, Our Authors, Our Publishers, Top Titles.
	categories.jsp	The list of categories and category wise books.
	popularSearches.jsp	The list of Popular Searches.
Struts 2		
Action HomePageAction.java		The action classes that facilitates data operations.
	CustomerLoginAction.java	
DAO Class BooksDAO.java		The interfaces for the DAO layer.
	AuthorsDAO.java	
	PublishersDAO.java	
	CategoriesDAO.java	
	PopularSearchesDAO.java	
	LoginDAO.java	

Type	Name	Description
Struts 2 [Continued]		
DAO Class	BooksDAOImpl.java	The implementation classes that perform the actual data operations.
	AuthorsDAOImpl.java	
	PublishersDAOImpl.java	
	CategoriesDAOImpl.java	
	PopularSearchesDAOImpl.java	
	LoginDAOImpl.java	
Struts Configuration	struts-HomePage.xml	The Struts configuration files.
	struts-CustomerLogin.xml	
Hibernate		
Mapping	hibernate.cfg.xml	The mapping file that holds Model class mapping.
Model Class	Books.java	The model classes.
	Authors.java	
	Publishers.java	
	Catgeories.java	
	PopularSearches.java	
	Customers.java	

JSP

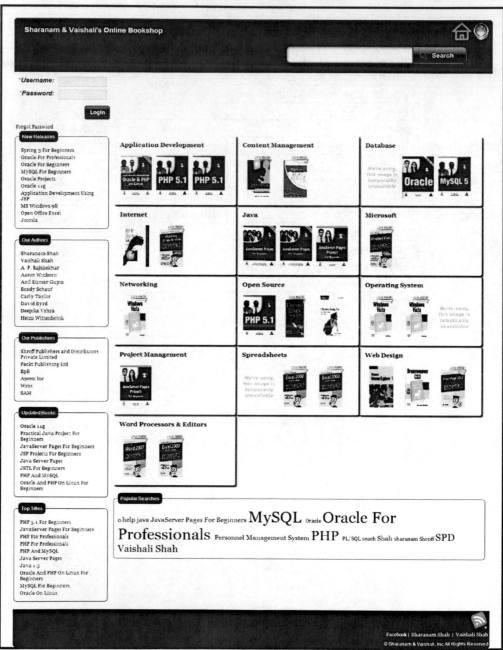

Diagram 43.1: Home page

index.jsp

Diagram 43.2: Index page [Loading application]

This is a JSP [the default page] which appears when the user invokes the application, as shown in diagram 43.2.

Form Specifications

File Name	index.jsp
Title	BookShop[Sharanam & Vaishali Shah]

Code Spec

```
1   <!DOCTYPE HTML PUBLIC "-//W3C//DTD HTML 4.01 Transitional//EN"
2   "http://www.w3.org/TR/html4/loose.dtd">
3   <html>
4     <head>
5       <meta http-equiv="Refresh" content="2;URL=showHomePage.action">
6       <title>BookShop [Sharanam & Vaishali Shah]</title>
7     </head>
8     <body>
9       <table height="500" border="0" cellpadding="25" align="center">
10        <tr>
11          <td valign="top">
```

```
12                <img src="/BookShop/images/BookShop.jpg" height="250"/>
13                <br/><br/>
14                <font color="#6b8e23" size="4">Loading Application</font>
15                <img id="WaitImage" src="/BookShop/images/progressbar_box.gif">
16            </td>
17          </tr>
18        </table>
19      </body>
20   </html>
```

Explanation:

This is the JSP file of the index page.

This is the startup point when the application is called.

home.jsp

This is a JSP which appears after the loading of the application takes place, as shown in diagram 43.1.

Form Specifications

File Name	home.jsp
Title	BookShop[Sharanam & Vaishali Shah] - Home Page

Code Spec

```
1  <%@page contentType="text/html" pageEncoding="UTF-8"%>
2  <%@ taglib prefix="s" uri="/struts-tags" %>
3  <%@ taglib prefix="sx" uri="/struts-dojo-tags" %>
4  <!DOCTYPE HTML PUBLIC "-//W3C//DTD HTML 4.01 Transitional//EN"
5    "http://www.w3.org/TR/html4/loose.dtd">
6  <html>
7    <head>
8      <title>BookShop[Sharanam & Vaishali Shah] - Home Page</title>
9      <meta http-equiv="content-type" content="text/html; charset=iso-8859-1">
10     <link href="/BookShop/css/frontend.css" type="text/css" rel="stylesheet">
11     <sx:head parseContent="true"/>
12    </head>
13    <body>
14      <div id="bodyDiv">
15        <s:include value="userHeader.jsp" />
16        <table border="0" width="100%" cellpadding="0" cellspacing="0">
17          <tr>
18            <td colspan="2" valign="top" align="left">
19              <s:include value="login.jsp" />
20            </td>
21          </tr>
```

```
22              </table>
23              <table width="100%" border="0" cellpadding="0" cellspacing="0">
24                <tr>
25                  <td width="20%" valign="top">
26                    <s:include value="leftMenu.jsp" />
27                  </td>
28                  <td width="80%" valign="top" align="center">
29                    <table width="100%" cellpadding="10" cellspacing="0">
30                      <tr>
31                        <td>
32                          <s:include value="categories.jsp" />
33                        </td>
34                      </tr>
35                      <tr>
36                        <td valign="top">
37                          <s:include value="popularSearches.jsp" />
38                        </td>
39                      </tr>
40                    </table>
41                  </td>
42                </tr>
43              </table>
44              <s:include value="footer.jsp" />
45          </div>
46        </body>
47  </html>
```

Explanation:

This is the JSP file of the home page. This JSP includes other JSP files such as the Login JSP, the Popular Searches JSP and so on.

leftMenu.jsp

This is a JSP, which includes the following sections, as shown in the diagram 43.3:

❑   New Releases

❑   Updated Books

❑   Our Authors

❑   Our Publishers

❑   Top Titles

This JSP is included in the home page.

New Releases

Spring 3 For Beginners
Oracle For Professionals
Oracle For Beginners
MySQL For Beginners
Oracle Projects
Oracle 11g
Application Development Using JSP
MS Windows 98
Open Office Excel
Joomla

Our Authors

Sharanam Shah
Vaishali Shah
A. P. Rajshekhar
Aaron Winborn
Anil Kumar Gupta
Brady Schauf
Carly Taylor
David Byrd
Deepika Vohra
Heinz Wittenbrink

Our Publishers

Shroff Publishers and Distributors Private Limited
Packt Publishing Ltd
BpB
Apress Inc
Wrox
SAM

Updated Books

Oracle 11g
Practical Java Project For Beginners
JavaServer Pages For Beginners
JSP Projects For Beginners
Java Server Pages
JSTL For Beginners
PHP And MySQL
Oracle And PHP On Linux For Beginners

Top Titles

PHP 5.1 For Beginners
JavaServer Pages For Beginners
PHP For Professionals
PHP For Professionals
PHP And MySQL
Java Server Pages
Java 1.5
Oracle And PHP On Linux For Beginners
MySQL For Beginners
Oracle On Linux

Diagram 43.3: Left Menu page

Code Spec

```
1   <%@page contentType="text/html" pageEncoding="UTF-8"%>
2   <%@ taglib prefix="s" uri="/struts-tags" %>
3   <!DOCTYPE HTML PUBLIC "-//W3C//DTD HTML 4.01 Transitional//EN"
4       "http://www.w3.org/TR/html4/loose.dtd">
5   <table width="100%" cellpadding="0" cellspacing="0">
6       <tr>
7           <td valign="top">
8               <fieldset>
9                   <legend>New Releases</legend>
10                  <table align="center" cellspacing="4" cellpadding="0" width="100%">
11                      <s:iterator value="newReleasesBooks" id="newReleasesBooks">
12                          <tr title="Click to view book details">
13                              <td align="left" style="cursor:pointer;">
14                                  <a href='<s:url action='showBookDetails'><s:param
                                    name='book.BookNo' value='BookNo' /></s:url>'>
15                                      <s:property value="BookName"/>
16                                  </a>
17                              </td>
18                          </tr>
19                      </s:iterator>
20                  </table>
21              </fieldset>
22          </td>
23      </tr>
24  </table>
25  <br>
26  <table width="100%" cellpadding="0" cellspacing="0">
27      <tr>
28          <td valign="top">
29              <fieldset>
30                  <legend>Our Authors</legend>
31                  <table align="center" cellspacing="4" cellpadding="0" width="100%">
32                      <s:iterator value="authors" id="authors">
33                          <tr title="Click to view author details">
34                              <td align="left" style="cursor:pointer;">
35                                  <a href='<s:url action='showAuthorDetails'><s:param
                                    name='author.AuthorNo' value='AuthorNo' /></s:url>'>
36                                      <s:property value="FirstName"/> <s:property
                                    value="LastName"/>
37                                  </a>
38                              </td>
39                          </tr>
40                      </s:iterator>
41                  </table>
42              </fieldset>
43          </td>
44      </tr>
45  </table>
46  <br>
47  <table width="100%" cellpadding="0" cellspacing="0">
48      <tr>
49          <td valign="top">
```

```
50              <fieldset>
51                <legend>Our Publishers</legend>
52                <table align="center" cellspacing="4" cellpadding="0" width="100%">
53                  <s:iterator value="publishers" id="publishers">
54                    <tr title="Click to view publisher details">
55                      <td align="left" style="cursor:pointer;">
56                        <a href='<s:url action='showPublisherDetails'><s:param
                            name='publisher.PublisherNo' value='PublisherNo' /></s:url>'>
57                          <s:property value="PublisherName"/>
58                        </a>
59                      </td>
60                    </tr>
61                  </s:iterator>
62                </table>
63              </fieldset>
64            </td>
65          </tr>
66  </table>
67  <br>
68  <table width="100%" cellpadding="0" cellspacing="0">
69      <tr>
70        <td valign="top">
71            <fieldset>
72              <legend>Updated Books</legend>
73                <table align="center" cellspacing="4" cellpadding="0" width="100%">
74                  <s:iterator value="updatedBooks" id="updatedBooks">
75                    <tr title="Click to view book details">
76                      <td align="left" style="cursor:pointer;">
77                        <a href='<s:url action='showBookDetails'><s:param
                            name='book.BookNo' value='BookNo' /></s:url>'>
78                          <s:property value="BookName"/>
79                        </a>
80                      </td>
81                    </tr>
82                  </s:iterator>
83                </table>
84            </fieldset>
85        </td>
86      </tr>
87  </table>
88  <br>
89  <table width="100%" cellpadding="0" cellspacing="0">
90      <tr>
91        <td valign="top">
92            <fieldset>
93              <legend>Top Titles</legend>
94                <table align="center" cellspacing="4" cellpadding="0" width="100%">
95                  <s:iterator value="topTitlesBooks" id="topTitlesBooks">
96                    <tr title="Click to view book details">
97                      <td align="left" style="cursor:pointer;">
98                        <a href='<s:url action='showBookDetails'><s:param
                            name='book.BookNo' value='BookNo' /></s:url>'>
99                          <s:property value="BookName"/>
100                       </a>
101                     </td>
```

```
102                    </tr>
103                 </s:iterator>
104              </table>
105            </fieldset>
106       </td>
107     </tr>
108  </table>
```

Explanation:

This is the JSP, which is included in the home page.

categories.jsp

This is a JSP, which includes the Categories section and the books available under each category, as shown in diagram 43.4.

This JSP is included in the home page.

Diagram 43.4: Categories page

Code Spec

```
1  <%@page contentType="text/html" pageEncoding="UTF-8"%>
2  <%@ taglib prefix="s" uri="/struts-tags" %>
3  <!DOCTYPE HTML PUBLIC "-//W3C//DTD HTML 4.01 Transitional//EN"
```

```
4     "http://www.w3.org/TR/html4/loose.dtd">
5   <s:iterator value="categories" id="categories" status="categoriesStatus">
6     <table id="portlets-content-main" align="center" border="0" cellspacing="4"
      cellpadding="2" width="33%" class="allCategoriesTable">
7        <tr>
8          <td align="left" class="categoriesNames" title="<s:property
           value="Description"/>">
9            <a href='<s:url action='showAllBooksForCat'><s:param
             name='category.CategoryNo' value='CategoryNo' /></s:url>'>
10             <s:property value="Category"/>
11           </a>
12           <br><br>
13           <s:action name="showBooksForThisCategory" executeResult="false"
             id="booksVal">
14             <s:param name="CategoryNo"><s:property
               value="CategoryNo"/></s:param>
15           </s:action>
16           <s:iterator value="#booksVal.books" id="books" status="booksStatus">
17             <table align="left" border="0" cellspacing="1" cellpadding="1" width="33%"
               class="allCategoriesTable">
18               <tr>
19                 <td title="<s:property value="Synopsis"/>">
20                   <a href='<s:url action='showBookDetails'><s:param
                     name='book.BookNo' value='BookNo' /></s:url>'>
21                     <img title="<s:property value="BookName"/>" alt="<s:property
                       value="BookName"/>"
                       src="getFile.action?columnName=CoverPage&tableName=Books&wh
                       ereClause=BookNo&whereClauseValue=<s:property value="BookNo"
                       />" height="110px" width="80px"/>
22                   </a>
23                 </td>
24               </tr>
25               <tr>
26                 <td title="Click here to add to shopping cart">
27                   <s:if test="#session.username!=null">
28                     <a href="<s:url action="addToCart"><s:param
                       name="BookNo"><s:property
                       value="BookNo"/></s:param><s:param
                       name="BookName"><s:property
                       value="BookName"/></s:param><s:param
                       name="Cost"><s:property value="Cost"/></s:param></s:url>">
29                       <img src="/BookShop/images/cart.jpg" style="cursor:pointer;"
                         border="0"/>
30                     </a>
31                   </s:if>
32                 </td>
33               </tr>
34             </table>
35           </s:iterator>
36         </td>
37       </tr>
38     </table>
39   </s:iterator>
```

Explanation:

This is the JSP, which is included in the home page.

login.jsp

This is a JSP, which includes the login form, as shown in diagram 43.5.

This JSP is included in the home page.

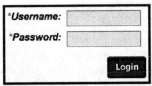

Diagram 43.5: Login page

Form Specifications

File Name	login.jsp
Form Name	frmMemberLogin
Bound To Table	bms.Customers
Action	doCustomerLogin
Method	POST

Data Fields

Label	Name	Bound To	Validation Rules
Username	customer.Username	Customers.Username	Cannot be left blank
Password	customer.Password	Customers.Password	Cannot be left blank

Micro-Help For Form Fields

Form Field	Micro Help Statement
customer.Username	Enter the username
customer.Password	Enter the password

Data Controls

Object	Label	Name
s:submit	Login	login

Code Spec

```
1  <%@page contentType="text/html" pageEncoding="UTF-8"%>
2  <%@ taglib prefix="s" uri="/struts-tags" %>
3  <!DOCTYPE HTML PUBLIC "-//W3C//DTD HTML 4.01 Transitional//EN"
4    "http://www.w3.org/TR/html4/loose.dtd">
5  <s:if test="#session.username==null">
6    <s:form action="doCustomerLogin" method="post" name="frmMemberLogin"
       id="frmMemberLogin">
7      <table align="lf" cellspacing="0" cellpadding="4" border="0" width="248px">
8        <tr>
9          <td colspan="2" align="left" class="error">
10           <s:property value="message" />
11         </td>
12       </tr>
13       <s:textfield required="true" requiredposition="left" maxLength="15" size="15"
           label="Username" name="customer.Username" title="Enter the username"/>
14       <s:password required="true" requiredposition="left" maxLength="8" size="15"
           label="Password" name="customer.Password" title="Enter the password"/>
15       <tr>
16         <td>
17           <s:submit cssClass="loginButton" name="login" value="" />
18         </td>
19       </tr>
20       <tr>
21         <td align="left" colspan="2">
22           <s:a href="showForgotPassword.action">Forgot Password</s:a>
23         </td>
24       </tr>
25     </table>
26   </s:form>
27 </s:if>
28 <s:else>
29   <table align="left" cellspacing="0" cellpadding="4" border="0" width="248px">
30     <tr>
31       <td align="left" valign="top">
32         <span style="font:20px/26px Georgia,serif; width:228px; color:#786e4e;
           height:37px;">Welcome <s:property value="#session.username" /></span>
33       </td>
34     </tr>
35   </table>
36 </s:else>
```

Explanation:

This is a simple JSP page which holds a HTML form to capture the login credentials. These credentials are passed to the Action class which takes care of authenticating the user credentials and if found valid takes the user in.

The login data entry form allows the registered users to login to the frontend application.

After a user logs in to the frontend application, the user is allowed to:

❑ Add books to the cart

❑ See a list of books added to the cart

❑ Make payments for the books added to the cart

❑ Download the TOC and Sample Chapter of the desired books

popularSearches.jsp

This is a JSP, which includes the popular searches, as shown in diagram 43.6.

This JSP is included in the home page.

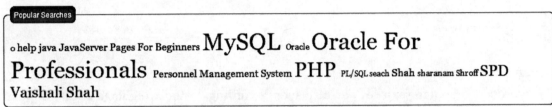

Diagram 43.6: Popular Searches page

Code Spec

```
1   <%@page contentType="text/html" pageEncoding="UTF-8"%>
2   <%@ taglib prefix="s" uri="/struts-tags" %>
3   <!DOCTYPE HTML PUBLIC "-//W3C//DTD HTML 4.01 Transitional//EN"
4     "http://www.w3.org/TR/html4/loose.dtd">
5   <fieldset>
6    <legend>Popular Searches</legend>
7    <s:iterator value="popularSearches" id="popularSearches">
8      <s:if test="#popularSearches[1]>=1 && #popularSearches[1]<5">
9        <a href="<s:url action='performSearch'><s:param name='SearchCriteria'
         value='#popularSearches[0]' /></s:url>" style="font-size:13px; cursor:pointer;"
         title="Click to search for <s:property value='#popularSearches[0]'/>">
10         <s:property value="#popularSearches[0]"/>
11       </a>
12     </s:if>
13     <s:if test="#popularSearches[1]>=5 && #popularSearches[1]<10">
14       <a href="<s:url action='performSearch'><s:param name='SearchCriteria'
         value='#popularSearches[0]' /></s:url>" style="font-size:17px; cursor:pointer;"
         title="Click to search for <s:property value='#popularSearches[0]'/>">
15         <s:property value="#popularSearches[0]"/>
16       </a>
17     </s:if>
18     <s:if test="#popularSearches[1]>=10 && #popularSearches[1]<15">
19       <a href="<s:url action='performSearch'><s:param name='SearchCriteria'
```

```
          value='#popularSearches[0]' /></s:url>" style="font-size:25px; cursor:pointer;"
          title="Click to search for <s:property value='#popularSearches[0]'/>">
20            <s:property value="#popularSearches[0]"/>
21        </a>
22    </s:if>
23    <s:if test="#popularSearches[1]>=15 && #popularSearches[1]<20">
24        <a href="<s:url action='performSearch'><s:param name='SearchCriteria'
          value='#popularSearches[0]' /></s:url>" style="font-size:35px; cursor:pointer;"
          title="Click to search for <s:property value='#popularSearches[0]'/>">
25            <s:property value="#popularSearches[0]"/>
26        </a>
27    </s:if>
28    <s:if test="#popularSearches[1]>=20">
29        <a href="<s:url action='performSearch'><s:param name='SearchCriteria'
          value='#popularSearches[0]' /></s:url>" style="font-size:40px; cursor:pointer;"
          title="Click to search for <s:property value='#popularSearches[0]'/>">
30            <s:property value="#popularSearches[0]"/>
31        </a>
32    </s:if>
33    </s:iterator>
34  </fieldset>
```

Explanation:

The words of popular searches are displayed according to the weightage of the popular search values. The more popular keywords are displayed bigger whereas the less popular words are displayed smaller.

Action Classes

HomePageAction.java

This is an action class with the following specifications:

Class Name	HomePageAction
Package	com.sharanamvaishali.action
Extends	ActionSupport
Implements	- -

Objects		
Object Name	**Class Name**	**Object Type**
popularSearchDAO	PopularSearchesDAO	Data Access Layer
bookDAO	BooksDAO	Data Access Layer
authorDAO	AuthorsDAO	Data Access Layer
publisherDAO	PublishersDAO	Data Access Layer
categoryDAO	CategoriesDAO	Data Access Layer

Properties			
Property Name	**Property Type**	**Methods**	
books	List<Books>	getBooks()	setBooks()
newReleasesBooks	List<Books>	getNewReleasesBooks()	setNewReleasesBooks()
updatedBooks	List<Books>	getUpdatedBooks()	setUpdatedBooks()
topTitlesBooks	List<Books>	getTopTitlesBooks()	setTopTitlesBooks()
authors	List<Authors>	getPageCount()	setPageCount()
publishers	List<Publishers>	getPublishers()	setPublishers()
categories	List<Categories>	getCategories()	setCategories()
popularSearches	List	getPopularSearches()	setPopularSearches()
categoryNo	int	getCategoryNo()	setCategoryNo()

Methods	
Method Name	**Return Values**
viewBooksByCategory()	SUCCESS
view()	SUCCESS

Code Spec

```
1   package com.sharanamvaishali.action;
2
3   import com.opensymphony.xwork2.ActionSupport;
4   import com.sharanamvaishali.dao.AuthorsDAO;
5   import com.sharanamvaishali.dao.AuthorsDAOImpl;
6   import com.sharanamvaishali.dao.BooksDAO;
7   import com.sharanamvaishali.dao.BooksDAOImpl;
8   import com.sharanamvaishali.dao.CategoriesDAO;
9   import com.sharanamvaishali.dao.CategoriesDAOImpl;
10  import com.sharanamvaishali.dao.PopularSearchesDAO;
11  import com.sharanamvaishali.dao.PopularSearchesDAOImpl;
12  import com.sharanamvaishali.dao.PublishersDAO;
13  import com.sharanamvaishali.dao.PublishersDAOImpl;
14  import com.sharanamvaishali.model.Authors;
15  import com.sharanamvaishali.model.Books;
16  import com.sharanamvaishali.model.Categories;
17  import com.sharanamvaishali.model.Publishers;
18  import java.util.List;
19
20  public class HomePageAction  extends ActionSupport{
21      private PopularSearchesDAO popularSearchDAO = new
        PopularSearchesDAOImpl();
22
23      private BooksDAO bookDAO = new BooksDAOImpl();
24
25      private AuthorsDAO authorDAO = new AuthorsDAOImpl();
26
27      private PublishersDAO publisherDAO = new PublishersDAOImpl();
28
```

```
29      private CategoriesDAO categoryDAO = new CategoriesDAOImpl();
30
31      private List<Books> books, newReleasesBooks, updatedBooks, topTitlesBooks;
32
33      private List<Authors> authors;
34
35      private List<Publishers> publishers;
36
37      private List<Categories> categories;
38
39      private List popularSearches;
40
41      private int CategoryNo;
42
43      public int getCategoryNo() {
44          return CategoryNo;
45      }
46      public void setCategoryNo(int CategoryNo) {
47          this.CategoryNo = CategoryNo;
48      }
49
50      public List getPopularSearches() {
51          return popularSearches;
52      }
53      public void setPopularSearches(List popularSearches) {
54          this.popularSearches = popularSearches;
55      }
56
57      public List<Books> getBooks() {
58          return books;
59      }
60      public void setBooks(List<Books> books) {
61          this.books = books;
62      }
63
64      public List<Books> getNewReleasesBooks() {
65          return newReleasesBooks;
66      }
67      public void setNewReleasesBooks(List<Books> newReleasesBooks) {
68          this.newReleasesBooks = newReleasesBooks;
69      }
70
71      public List<Books> getUpdatedBooks() {
72          return updatedBooks;
73      }
74      public void setUpdatedBooks(List<Books> updatedBooks) {
75          this.updatedBooks = updatedBooks;
76      }
77
```

```
78      public List<Books> getTopTitlesBooks() {
79          return topTitlesBooks;
80      }
81      public void setTopTitlesBooks(List<Books> topTitlesBooks) {
82          this.topTitlesBooks = topTitlesBooks;
83      }
84
85      public List<Authors> getAuthors() {
86          return authors;
87      }
88      public void setAuthors(List<Authors> authors) {
89          this.authors = authors;
90      }
91
92      public List<Publishers> getPublishers() {
93          return publishers;
94      }
95      public void setPublishers(List<Publishers> publishers) {
96          this.publishers = publishers;
97      }
98
99      public List<Categories> getCategories() {
100         return categories;
101     }
102     public void setCategories(List<Categories> categories) {
103         this.categories = categories;
104     }
105
106     public String viewBooksByCategory() throws Exception{
107         books = categoryDAO.listBooksByCategory(CategoryNo);
108         return SUCCESS;
109     }
110
111     public String view() throws Exception{
112         newReleasesBooks = bookDAO.listNewReleases();
113         authors = authorDAO.listOurAuthors();
114         publishers = publisherDAO.listOurPublishers();
115         updatedBooks = bookDAO.listUpdatedBooks();
116         topTitlesBooks = bookDAO.listTopTitles();
117         categories = categoryDAO.listCategories();
118         popularSearches = popularSearchDAO.listPopularSearches();
119         return SUCCESS;
120     }
121 }
```

Explanation:

The following section describes the above code spec.

viewBooksByCategory()

viewBooksByCategory() is invoked:
> → Every time the homepage is served
> > → For every category that is listed

It populates the List object [books] created earlier with the books belonging to a particular category. This object is used in categories.jsp to displays the three books under every category.

The data to be populated is retrieved using CategoriesDAO's listBooksByCategory().

view()

view() is invoked every time the homepage is served.

It populates the following List objects:
- newReleasesBooks
- authors
- publishers
- updatedBooks
- topTitlesBooks
- categories
- popularSearches

These List objects are populated using the methods of BooksDAO, AuthorsDAO, PublishersDAO, CategoriesDAO and PopularSearchesDAO.

These List objects are made available to leftMenu.jsp using the Getter/Setter methods.

leftMenu.jsp uses **<s:iterator>** to iterate through these objects, extract the required values and displays them using **<s:property>**.

CustomerLoginAction.java

This is an action class with the following specifications:

Class Name	CustomerLoginAction
Package	com.sharanamvaishali.action
Extends	ActionSupport

Implements	SessionAware
	ServletRequestAware

Objects		
Object Name	**Class Name**	**Object Type**
loginDAO	LoginDAO	Data Access Layer
customer	Customers	Model

Properties			
Property Name	**Property Type**	**Methods**	
customer	Customers	getCustomer()	setCustomer()
message	String	getMessage()	- -
session	Map	getSession()	setSession()
request	HttpServletRequest	getServletRequest()	setServletRequest()

Methods	
Method Name	**Return Values**
loginCustomer()	SUCCESS
	ERROR
logoffCustomer()	SUCCESS

Code Spec

```
1   package com.sharanamvaishali.action;
2
3   import com.opensymphony.xwork2.ActionContext;
4   import com.opensymphony.xwork2.ActionSupport;
5   import com.sharanamvaishali.dao.LoginDAO;
6   import com.sharanamvaishali.dao.LoginDAOImpl;
7   import com.sharanamvaishali.model.Customers;
8   import java.util.*;
9   import javax.servlet.http.HttpServletRequest;
10  import org.apache.struts2.interceptor.ServletRequestAware;
11  import org.apache.struts2.interceptor.SessionAware;
12
13  public class CustomerLoginAction extends ActionSupport implements
    SessionAware, ServletRequestAware{
14      private LoginDAO loginDAO = new LoginDAOImpl();
15
16      private Customers customer;
17
18      private String message;
19
20      private Map session;
21
22      private HttpServletRequest request;
23
24      public HttpServletRequest getServletRequest(){
```

```
25          return request;
26       }
27       @Override
28       public void setServletRequest(HttpServletRequest request){
29          this.request = request;
30       }
31
32       public Map getSession() {
33          return session;
34       }
35       @Override
36       public void setSession(Map session) {
37          this.session = session;
38       }
39
40       public String getMessage() {
41          return message;
42       }
43
44       public Customers getCustomer() {
45          return customer;
46       }
47       public void setCustomer(Customers customer) {
48          this.customer = customer;
49       }
50
51       public String loginCustomer() throws Exception {
52          Customers objCustomer = (Customers)
            loginDAO.validateCustomerLogin(customer.getUsername(),
            customer.getPassword(), request.getRemoteAddr());
53          if(objCustomer != null){
54             session = ActionContext.getContext().getSession();
55             session.put("username", customer.getUsername());
56             session.put("lastlogin", objCustomer.getLastLogin());
57             session.put("lastip", objCustomer.getLastIP());
58          } else {
59             message = "Invalid Username or Password. Please try again";
60             return ERROR;
61          }
62          return SUCCESS;
63       }
64
65       @SkipValidation
66       public String logoffCustomer() throws Exception{
67          session = ActionContext.getContext().getSession();
68          session.remove("username");
69          session.remove("lastlogin");
70          session.remove("lastip");
71          session.clear();
```

```
72      return SUCCESS;
73    }
74 }
```

Explanation:

The following section describes the above code spec.

loginCustomer()

loginCustomer() is invoked when the customer keys in the username and password and clicks Login .

loginCustomer() passes the captured login information to LoginDAO's **validateCustomerLogin()**, which validates and returns an object with the authenticated users data.

If the object holds user data then the same is added to the **SESSION**.

The following information is added to the SESSION:

❑ Username

❑ Last Login date and time stamp

❑ IP address from where the customer had last logged in

This information is displayed in the application's header:

If the object does not hold user data then an appropriate error message is send to login.jsp.

Invalid Username or Password. Please try again

Username: shah

Password:

Login

logoffCustomer()

logoffCustomer() is invoked when the customer clicks .

logoffCustomer() destroys the session.

DAO Classes

Interfaces

BooksDAO.java

This is a Data Access Object interface with the following specifications:

Class Name	Package
BooksDAO	com.sharanamvaishali.dao

Code Spec

```
1  package com.sharanamvaishali.dao;
2
3  import java.util.List;
4
5  public interface BooksDAO {
6     public List listNewReleases();
7     public List listUpdatedBooks();
8     public List listTopTitles();
9  }
```

AuthorsDAO.java

This is a Data Access Object interface with the following specifications:

Class Name	Package
AuthorsDAO	com.sharanamvaishali.dao

Code Spec

```
1  package com.sharanamvaishali.dao;
2
3  import java.util.List;
4
5  public interface AuthorsDAO {
6     public List listOurAuthors();
```

```
7 }
```

PublishersDAO.java

This is a Data Access Object interface with the following specifications:

Class Name	Package
PublishersDAO	com.sharanamvaishali.dao

Code Spec

```
1  package com.sharanamvaishali.dao;
2
3  import java.util.List;
4
5  public interface PublishersDAO {
6      public List listOurPublishers();
7  }
```

CategoriesDAO.java

This is a Data Access Object interface with the following specifications:

Class Name	Package
CategoriesDAO	com.sharanamvaishali.dao

Code Spec

```
1  package com.sharanamvaishali.dao;
2
3  import java.util.List;
4
5  public interface CategoriesDAO {
6      public List listCategories();
7      public List listBooksByCategory(int CategoryNo);
8  }
```

PopularSearchesDAO.java

This is a Data Access Object interface with the following specifications:

Class Name	Package
PopularSearchesDAO	com.sharanamvaishali.dao

Code Spec

```
1   package com.sharanamvaishali.dao;
2
3   import java.util.List;
4
5   public interface PopularSearchesDAO {
6       public List listPopularSearches();
7       public int getTotalPopularSearches();
8       public void deletePopularSearches();
9   }
```

LoginDAO.java

This is a Data Access Object interface with the following specifications:

Class Name	Package
LoginDAO	com.sharanamvaishali.dao

Code Spec

```
1   package com.sharanamvaishali.dao;
2
3   import com.sharanamvaishali.model.Customers;
4
5   public interface LoginDAO {
6       public Object validateCustomerLogin(String Username, String Password, String
        LastIP);
7       public void updateCustomerLastLoginDetails(Customers customers);
8   }
```

Implementation Classes

BooksDAOImpl.java

This is a Data Access Object class with the following specifications.

Class Name	BooksDAOImpl
Package	com.sharanamvaishali.dao
Implements	BooksDAO

Objects	
Object Name	**Class Name**
session	Session

Methods		
Method Name	Arguments	Return Values
listNewReleases()	– –	List
listUpdatedBooks()	– –	List
listTopTitles()	– –	List

Code Spec

```
1   package com.sharanamvaishali.dao;
2
3   import com.sharanamvaishali.utility.HibernateUtil;
4   import java.util.List;
5   import org.hibernate.Session;
6
7   public class BooksDAOImpl implements BooksDAO {
8       Session session = HibernateUtil.getSession();
9
10      @Override
11      public List listNewReleases() {
12          return session.createQuery("FROM Books ORDER BY Year
            DESC").setMaxResults(10).list();
13      }
14
15      @Override
16      public List listUpdatedBooks() {
17          return session.createQuery("FROM Books WHERE Edition <> 'First' ORDER
            BY Year DESC").setMaxResults(10).list();
18      }
19
20      @Override
21      public List listTopTitles() {
22          return session.createQuery("FROM Books ORDER BY Hits
            DESC").setMaxResults(10).list();
23      }
24  }
```

Explanation:

The following section describes the above code spec.

listNewReleases()

listNewReleases() does the actual retrieval of the available newly released books.

This method fires a SELECT query that attempts to retrieve the records from the Books database table.

All the records that the query retrieves are extracted and returned as a **List** object.

This List object is returned to the calling method i.e. HomePageAction's **view()**:

```
public String view() throws Exception{
    newReleasesBooks = bookDAO.listNewReleases();
}
```

Finally, HomePageAction returns this List object to the JSP which renders it.

The JSP i.e. leftMenu.jsp [a .jsp file included in home.jsp] on taking charge uses **<s:iterator>** to iterate over the contents of the List object **newReleasesBooks**.

```
<s:iterator value="newReleasesBooks" id="newReleasesBooks">
    <tr title="Click to view book details">
        <td align="left" style="cursor:pointer;">
            <a href='<s:url action='showBookDetails'><s:param
            name='book.BookNo' value='BookNo' /></s:url>'>
                <s:property value="BookName">
```

newReleasesBooks object holds all those records retrieved by the SQL query.

Each record's column values are extracted using **<s:property>**.

listUpdatedBooks()

listUpdatedBooks() does the actual retrieval of the available updated books.

This method fires a SELECT query that attempts to retrieve the records from the Books database table.

All the records that the query retrieves are extracted and returned as a **List** object.

This List object is returned to the calling method i.e. HomePageAction's **view()**:

```
public String view() throws Exception{
    updatedBooks = bookDAO.listUpdatedBooks();
}
```

Finally, HomePageAction returns this List object to the JSP which renders it.

The JSP i.e. leftMenu.jsp [a .jsp file included in home.jsp] on taking charge uses **<s:iterator>** to iterate over the contents of the List object **updatedBooks**.

```
<s:iterator value="updatedBooks" id="updatedBooks">
    <tr title="Click to view book details">
        <td align="left" style="cursor:pointer;">
            <a href='<s:url action='showBookDetails'><s:param
            name='book.BookNo' value='BookNo' /></s:url>'>
                <s:property value="BookName"/>
```

updatedBooks object holds all those records retrieved by the SQL query.

Each record's column values are extracted using **<s:property>**.

listTopTitles()

listTopTitles() does the actual retrieval of the available top titled books.

This method fires a SELECT query that attempts to retrieve the records from the Books database table.

All the records that the query retrieves are extracted and returned as a **List** object.

This List object is returned to the calling method i.e. HomePageAction's **view()**:

```
public String view() throws Exception{
    topTitlesBooks = bookDAO.listTopTitles();
}
```

Finally, HomePageAction returns this List object to the JSP which renders it.

The JSP i.e. leftMenu.jsp [a .jsp file included in home.jsp] on taking charge uses **<s:iterator>** to iterate over the contents of the List object **topTitlesBooks**.

```
<s:iterator value="topTitlesBooks" id="topTitlesBooks">
    <tr title="Click to view book details">
        <td align="left" style="cursor:pointer;">
            <a href='<s:url action='showBookDetails'><s:param
            name='book.BookNo' value='BookNo' /></s:url>'>
                <s:property value="BookName"/>
```

topTitlesBooks object holds all those records retrieved by the SQL query.

Each record's column values are extracted using **<s:property>**.

AuthorsDAOImpl.java

This is a Data Access Object class with the following specifications.

Class Name	AuthorsDAOImpl
Package	com.sharanamvaishali.dao
Implements	AuthorsDAO

Objects	
Object Name	**Class Name**
session	Session

Methods		
Method Name	**Arguments**	**Return Values**
listOurAuthors()	- -	List

Code Spec

```
1  package com.sharanamvaishali.dao;
2
3  import com.sharanamvaishali.utility.HibernateUtil;
4  import java.util.List;
5  import org.hibernate.Session;
6
7  public class AuthorsDAOImpl implements AuthorsDAO {
8      Session session = HibernateUtil.getSession();
9
10     @Override
11     public List listOurAuthors() {
12         return session.createQuery("FROM Authors").setMaxResults(10).list();
13     }
14 }
```

Explanation:

The following section describes the above code spec.

listOurAuthors()

listOurAuthors() does the actual retrieval of the available authors.

This method fires a SELECT query that attempts to retrieve the records from the Authors database table.

All the records that the query retrieves are extracted and returned as a **List** object.

This List object is returned to the calling method i.e. HomePageAction's **view()**:

```
public String view() throws Exception{
   authors = authorDAO.listOurAuthors();
}
```

Finally, HomePageAction returns this List object to the JSP which renders it.

The JSP i.e. leftMenu.jsp [a .jsp file included in home.jsp] on taking charge uses **<s:iterator>** to iterate over the contents of the List object **authors**.

```
<s:iterator value="authors" id="authors">
   <tr title="Click to view author details">
      <td align="left" style="cursor:pointer;">
         <a href='<s:url action='showAuthorDetails'><s:param
         name='author.AuthorNo' value='AuthorNo' /></s:url>'>
            <s:property value="FirstName"/> <s:property
            value="LastName"/>
```

authors object holds all those records retrieved by the SQL query.

Each record's column values are extracted using **<s:property>**.

PublishersDAOImpl.java

This is a **Data Access Object** class with the following specifications.

Class Name	PublishersDAOImpl
Package	com.sharanamvaishali.dao
Implements	PublishersDAO

Objects	
Object Name	**Class Name**
Session	Session

Methods		
Method Name	**Arguments**	**Return Values**
listOurPublishers()	- -	List

Code Spec

```
1  package com.sharanamvaishali.dao;
2
3  import com.sharanamvaishali.utility.HibernateUtil;
4  import java.util.List;
5  import org.hibernate.Session;
6
```

```
 7  public class PublishersDAOImpl implements PublishersDAO {
 8     Session session = HibernateUtil.getSession();
 9
10     @Override
11     public List listOurPublishers() {
12        return session.createQuery("FROM Publishers").setMaxResults(10).list();
13     }
14  }
```

Explanation:

The following section describes the above code spec.

listOurPublishers()

listOurPublishers() does the actual retrieval of the available publishers.

This method fires a SELECT query that attempts to retrieve the records from the Publishers database table.

All the records that the query retrieves are extracted and returned as a **List** object.

This List object is returned to the calling method i.e. HomePageAction's **view()**:

```
public String view() throws Exception{
    publishers = publisherDAO.listOurPublishers();
}
```

Finally, HomePageAction returns this List object to the JSP which renders it.

The JSP i.e. leftMenu.jsp [a .jsp file included in home.jsp] on taking charge uses **<s:iterator>** to iterate over the contents of the List object **publishers**.

```
<s:iterator value="publishers" id="publishers">
   <tr title="Click to view publisher details">
      <td align="left" style="cursor:pointer;">
         <a href='<s:url action='showPublisherDetails'><s:param
         name='publisher.PublisherNo' value='PublisherNo' /></s:url>'>
            <s:property value="PublisherName"/>
```

publishers object holds all those records retrieved by the SQL query.

Each record's column values are extracted using **<s:property>**.

CategoriesDAOImpl.java

This is a **Data Access Object** class with the following specifications.

Class Name	CategoriesDAOImpl
Package	com.sharanamvaishali.dao
Implements	CategoriesDAO

Objects	
Object Name	**Class Name**
Session	Session

Methods		
Method Name	**Arguments**	**Return Values**
listCategories()	- -	List
listBooksByCategory()	int CategoryNo	List

Code Spec

```
1   package com.sharanamvaishali.dao;
2
3   import com.sharanamvaishali.utility.HibernateUtil;
4   import java.util.List;
5   import org.hibernate.Session;
6
7   public class CategoriesDAOImpl implements CategoriesDAO {
8       Session session = HibernateUtil.getSession();
9
10      @Override
11      public List listCategories() {
12          return session.createQuery("FROM Categories ORDER BY Category").list();
13      }
14
15      @Override
16      public List listBooksByCategory(int CategoryNo) {
17          return session.createQuery("FROM Books WHERE CategoryNo =
            :CategoryNo").setInteger("CategoryNo",
            CategoryNo).setMaxResults(3).list();
18      }
19  }
```

Explanation:

The following section describes the above code spec.

listCategories()

listCategories() does the actual retrieval of the available categories.

This method fires a SELECT query that attempts to retrieve the records from the Categories database table.

All the records that the query retrieves are extracted and returned as a **List** object.

This List object is returned to the calling method i.e. HomePageAction's **view()**:

```
public String view() throws Exception{
    categories = categoryDAO.listCategories();
}
```

Finally, HomePageAction returns this List object to the JSP which renders it.

The JSP i.e. leftMenu.jsp [a .jsp file included in home.jsp] on taking charge uses **<s:iterator>** to iterate over the contents of the List object **categories**.

```
<s:iterator value="categories" id="categories" status="categoriesStatus">
    <table id="portlets-content-main" align="center" border="0" cellspacing="4"
    cellpadding="2" width="33%" class="allCategoriesTable">
      <tr>
        <td align="left" class="categoriesNames" title="<s:property
        value="Description"/>">
          <a href='<s:url action='showAllBooksForCat'><s:param
          name='category.CategoryNo' value='CategoryNo' /></s:url>'>
            <s:property value="Category"/>
          </a>
```

categories object holds all those records retrieved by the SQL query.

Each record's column values are extracted using **<s:property>**.

listBooksByCategories()

listBooksByCategories() does the actual retrieval of the available books category wise.

This method fires a SELECT query that attempts to retrieve the records from the Books database table.

All the records that the query retrieves are extracted and returned as a **List** object.

This List object is returned to the calling method i.e. HomePageAction's **viewBooksByCategory()**:

```
public String viewBooksByCategory() throws Exception{
    books = categoryDAO.listBooksByCategory(CategoryNo);
}
```

Finally, HomePageAction returns this List object to the JSP which renders it.

The JSP i.e. leftMenu.jsp [a .jsp file included in home.jsp] on taking charge uses **\<s:iterator>** to iterate over the contents of the List object **books**.

```
<s:iterator value="#booksVal.books" id="books" status="booksStatus">
   <table align="left" border="0" cellspacing="1" cellpadding="1" width="33%"
   class="allCategoriesTable">
      <tr>
        <td title="<s:property value="Synopsis"/>">
          <a href='<s:url action='showBookDetails'><s:param
          name='book.BookNo' value='BookNo' /></s:url>'>
            <img title="<s:property value="BookName"/>" alt="<s:property
            value="BookName"/>"
            src="getFile.action?columnName=CoverPage&tableName=Books&w
            ereClause=BookNo&whereClauseValue=<s:property value="BookNo"
            />" height="110px" width="80px"/>
```

books object holds all those records retrieved by the SQL query.

Each record's column values are extracted using **\<s:property>**.

PopularSearchesDAOImpl.java

This is a **Data Access Object** class with the following specifications.

Class Name	PopularSearchesDAOImpl
Package	com.sharanamvaishali.dao
Implements	PopularSearchesDAO

Objects	
Object Name	**Class Name**
Session	Session
transaction	Transaction

Methods		
Method Name	**Arguments**	**Return Values**
listPopularSearches()	– –	List
getTotalPopularSearches()	– –	int
deletePopularSearches()	– –	Void

Code Spec

```
1  package com.sharanamvaishali.dao;
2
3  import com.sharanamvaishali.model.PopularSearches;
4  import com.sharanamvaishali.utility.HibernateUtil;
```

```
 5  import java.util.Iterator;
 6  import java.util.List;
 7  import org.hibernate.Session;
 8  import org.hibernate.Transaction;
 9
10  public class PopularSearchesDAOImpl implements PopularSearchesDAO {
11      Session session = HibernateUtil.getSession();
12      Transaction transaction = null;
13
14      @Override
15      public List listPopularSearches() {
16          deletePopularSearches();
17          return session.createSQLQuery("SELECT Value, COUNT(*) AS Weight FROM
            PopularSearches GROUP BY Value").list();
18      }
19
20      @Override
21      public int getTotalPopularSearches(){
22          Object TransactionNo = session.createSQLQuery("SELECT COUNT(*) AS Total
            FROM PopularSearches").addScalar("Total").uniqueResult();
23          return Integer.parseInt(TransactionNo.toString());
24      }
25
26      @Override
27      public void deletePopularSearches() {
28          if(getTotalPopularSearches()>600) {
29              List<PopularSearches> ps = session.createQuery("FROM
                PopularSearches").setMaxResults(10).list();
30              for (Iterator i = ps.iterator(); i.hasNext();) {
31                  transaction = session.beginTransaction();
32                  Object objPs = i.next();
33                  session.delete(objPs);
34                  transaction.commit();
35              }
36          }
37      }
38  }
```

Explanation:

The following section describes the above code spec.

listPopularSearches()

listPopularSearches() does the actual retrieval of the available popular searches.

This method fires a SELECT query that attempts to retrieve the records from the PopularSearches database table.

All the records that the query retrieves are extracted and returned as a **List** object.

This List object is returned to the calling method i.e. HomePageAction's **view()**:

```
public String view() throws Exception{
    popularSearches = popularSearchDAO.listPopularSearches();
}
```

Finally, HomePageAction returns this List object to the JSP which renders it.

The JSP i.e. leftMenu.jsp [a .jsp file included in home.jsp] on taking charge uses **<s:iterator>** to iterate over the contents of the List object **popularSearches**.

```
<s:iterator value="popularSearches" id="popularSearches">
  <s:If test="#popularSearches[1]>=1 && #popularSearches[1]<5">
    <a href="<s:url action='performSearch'><s:param name='SearchCriteria'
    value='#popularSearches[0]' /></s:url>" style="font-size:13px; cursor:pointer;
    title="Click to search for <s:property value='#popularSearches[0]'/>">
      <s:property value="#popularSearches[0]"/>
  </a>
```

popularSearches object holds all those records retrieved by the SQL query.

Each record's column values are extracted using **<s:property>**.

getTotalPopularSearches()

getTotalPopularSearches() retrieves the total number of records available in the PopularSearches database table.

This method uses:

- ❑ **addScalar()** of Query, which declares a scalar query
- ❑ **uniqueResult()** of Query, which returns single instance of a persistence object. If no result are found, then it returns a null value

deletePopularSearches()

deletePopularSearch() deletes the PopularSearch entries, if the total records in the PopularSearch cross 600 entries.

This method uses **delete()** of Session, which deletes the 10 records from the PopularSearches database table.

LoginDAOImpl.java

This is a **Data Access Object** class with the following specifications.

Class Name	LoginDAOImpl
Package	com.sharanamvaishali.dao
Implements	LoginDAO

Objects	
Object Name	**Class Name**
Session	Session
Transaction	Transaction

Methods		
Method Name	**Arguments**	**Return Values**
validateCustomerLogin()	String username String Password String LastIP	Object
updateCustomerLastLoginDetails()	Customers customers	void

Code Spec

```
1   package com.sharanamvaishali.dao;
2
3   import com.sharanamvaishali.model.Customers;
4   import com.sharanamvaishali.utility.HibernateUtil;
5   import org.hibernate.Query;
6   import org.hibernate.Session;
7   import org.hibernate.Transaction;
8
9   public class LoginDAOImpl implements LoginDAO {
10      Session session = HibernateUtil.getSession();
11      Transaction transaction = null;
12
13      @Override
14      public Object validateCustomerLogin(String Username, String Password, String
        LastIP) {
15          Query query = session.createQuery("FROM Customers WHERE Username =
            :Username AND Password = :Password");
16          query.setString("Username", Username);
17          query.setString("Password", Password);
18          Customers customer = (Customers) query.uniqueResult();
19          if(customer != null) {
20              customer.setLastIP(LastIP);
21              customer.setLastLogin((new java.util.Date().toString()));
22              updateCustomerLastLoginDetails(customer);
23          }
24          return customer;
```

```
25      }
26
27      @Override
28      public void updateCustomerLastLoginDetails(Customers customers) {
29         try {
30            transaction = session.beginTransaction();
31            session.update(customers);
32            transaction.commit();
33         } catch (RuntimeException e) {
34            if(customers != null) {
35               transaction.rollback();
36            }
37            throw e;
38         }
39      }
40   }
```

Explanation:

The following section describes the above code spec.

validateCustomerLogin()

validateCustomerLogin() is invoked by **CustomerLoginAction's loginCustomer()** to authenticate Customers.

This method receives Username and Password which is used as the WHERE clause criteria. It queries the Customers database table using Hibernate Session's **createQuery()** to retrieve the chosen record's data to return to loginCustomer():

FROM Customers WHERE Username = :Username AND Password = :Password

If the query returns a record, then the Last Login details of that customer are updated using updateCustomerLastLoginDetails().

updateCustomerLastLoginDetails()

updateCustomerLastLoginDetails() is invoked by **validateCustomerLogin()**.

It receives an updated object of the Customers bean class.

This method uses Hibernate Session's **update()** to update the Customers database table.

After the update operation is complete the transaction is committed to make the changes permanent.

Struts Configuration

struts.xml

This is the main struts configuration file with the following specifications:

File Name	Package Name	Extends
struts.xml	default	struts-default

Actions	
Action Name	**Results**
showHomePage	SUCCESS - home.jsp

Code Spec

```
1  <!DOCTYPE struts PUBLIC
2  "-//Apache Software Foundation//DTD Struts Configuration 2.0//EN"
3  "http://struts.apache.org/dtds/struts-2.0.dtd">
4  <struts>
5     <package name="default" extends="struts-default">
6        <action name="showHomePage" method="view"
          class="com.sharanamvaishali.action.HomePageAction">
7           <result>/frontend/home.jsp</result>
8        </action>
9     </package>
10 </struts>
```

Explanation:

The following section describes the above code spec.

showHomePage.action

showHomePage is an action to help viewing.

This means the list of new releases, updated books, authors, top titles books, publishers and categories details are displayed.

The above list details are retrieved by **HomePageAction**'s **view()**.

REMINDER

Only the actions related to Home page are explained in this chapter. The remaining actions are explained later in the *Section VII: Common Files Software Design Documentation* under the *Chapter 61: Configuration Files*.

struts-HomePage.xml

This is the struts configuration file with the following specifications:

File Name	Package Name	Extends
HomePage	homePage	default

Actions	
Action Name	**Results**
showBooksForThisCategory	SUCCESS - home.jsp

Code Spec

```
1   <?xml version="1.0" encoding="UTF-8"?>
2   <!DOCTYPE struts PUBLIC
3   "-//Apache Software Foundation//DTD Struts Configuration 2.0//EN"
4   "http://struts.apache.org/dtds/struts-2.0.dtd">
5   <struts>
6     <package name="homePage" extends="default">
7       <action name="showBooksForThisCategory"
        method="viewBooksByCategory"
        class="com.sharanamvaishali.action.HomePageAction">
8         <result>/frontend/home.jsp</result>
9       </action>
10    </package>
11  </struts>
```

Explanation:

The following section describes the above code spec.

showBooksForThisCategory.action

showBooksForThisCategory is an action to help viewing.

This means the list of books based on categories details are displayed.

The list of books based on categories details are retrieved by **HomePageAction's** **viewBooksByCategory()**.

REMINDER

 Only the actions related to Home page are explained in this chapter. The remaining actions are explained later in the *Chapter 44: Book Details, Chapter 45: Author Details, Chapter 46: Publisher Details* and *Chapter 47: Category Details*.

struts-CustomerLogin.xml

This is the struts configuration file with the following specifications:

File Name	Package Name	Extends
CustomerLogin	frontendLogin	default

Actions	
Action Name	**Results**
doCustomerLogin	SUCCESS - showHomePage ERROR - home.jsp INPUT - home.jsp
doCustomerLogout	SUCCESS - showHomePage

Code Spec

```
1   <?xml version="1.0" encoding="UTF-8"?>
2   <!DOCTYPE struts PUBLIC
3   "-//Apache Software Foundation//DTD Struts Configuration 2.0//EN"
4   "http://struts.apache.org/dtds/struts-2.0.dtd">
5   <struts>
6     <package name="frontendLogin" extends="default">
7       <action name="doCustomerLogin" method="loginCustomer"
        class="com.sharanamvaishali.action.CustomerLoginAction">
8         <result name="success" type="redirectAction">showHomePage</result>
9         <result name="error">/frontend/home.jsp</result>
10        <result name="input">/frontend/home.jsp</result>
11      </action>
12
13      <action name="doCustomerLogout" method="logoffCustomer"
        class="com.sharanamvaishali.action.CustomerLoginAction">
14        <result name="success" type="redirectAction">showHomePage</result>
15      </action>
16    </package>
17  </struts>
```

Explanation:

The following section describes the above code spec.

doCustomerLogin.action

doCustomerLogin is an action to help validate customer's login credentials.

doCustomerLogin.action:

❑ Calls **CustomerLoginAction's loginCustomer()** to validate the customer's login credentials

❑ Ensures that the captured data is valid

❑ If the validation is successful then the customer's details like the username, last IP address and last login date is retrieved and the same is redirected to **showHomePage.action**

❑ If the validation fails then the Home page along with error message is displayed

doCustomerLogout.action

doCustomerLogout is an action to help customer logout.

doCustomerLogout.action:

❑ Calls **CustomerLoginAction's logoffCustomer()** to destroy the session

❑ Redirects the customer to showHomePage.action, which displays the login form

REMINDER

 Only the actions related to Home page are explained in this chapter. The remaining actions are explained later in the *Chapter 52: Forgot Password*.

Domain Class [PopularSearches.java]

This is a domain class with the following specifications:

Class Name	Package	Implements
PopularSearches	com.sharanamvaishali.model	java.io.Serializable

Properties			
Property Name	Property Type	Methods	
searchNo	Integer	getSearchNo()	setSearchNo()
value	String	getValue()	setValue()

Code Spec

```
1  package com.sharanamvaishali.model;
2
3  import javax.persistence.Column;
4  import javax.persistence.Entity;
5  import javax.persistence.GeneratedValue;
6  import javax.persistence.Id;
```

```
 7  import javax.persistence.Table;
 8
 9  @Entity
10  @Table(name="POPULARSEARCHES")
11  public class PopularSearches implements java.io.Serializable {
12      @Id
13      @GeneratedValue
14      @Column(name="SEARCHNO")
15       private Integer searchNo;
16      @Column(name="VALUE")
17       private String value;
18
19      public PopularSearches() {
20      }
21
22      public Integer getSearchNo() {
23          return this.searchNo;
24      }
25      public void setSearchNo(Integer searchNo) {
26          this.searchNo = searchNo;
27      }
28
29      public String getValue() {
30          return this.value;
31      }
32      public void setValue(String value) {
33          this.value = value;
34      }
35  }
```

REMINDER

 Customers.java [the model class] is explained in the *Chapter 39: Manage Customers*.

Books.java [the model class] is explained in the *Chapter 38: Manage Books*.

Publishers.java [the model class] is explained in the *Chapter 36: Manage Publishers*.

Categories.java [the model class] is explained in the *Chapter 35: Manage Categories*.

Authors.java [the model class] is explained in the *Chapter 37: Manage Authors*.

Chapter

44

SECTION VI: FRONTEND [CUSTOMER FACING] SOFTWARE DESIGN DOCUMENTATION

Book Details

This module allows viewing the details of the book. This page is invoked when a user clicks a book name or the book image from the frontend.

This module uses the bms.Books table to retrieve that particular book's data.

This module is made up of the following:

Type	Name	Description
JSP	showBookdetails.jsp	The details of a particular book.
Struts 2		
Action	ShowBookDetailsAction.java	The action class that facilitates data operations.
DAO Class	BooksDAO.java	The interface for the DAO layer.
	BooksDAOImpl.java	The implementation class that perform the actual data operations.

Type	Name	Description
Struts 2 [Continued]		
Struts Configuration	struts-HomePage.xml	The Struts configuration file.
Hibernate		
Mapping	hibernate.cfg.xml	The mapping file that holds Model class mapping.
Model Class	Books.java	The model class.

JSP [showBookDetails.jsp]

Book Details Without Logging In

A link identified by a book name in one of these sections when clicked, displays book details of the selected book, as shown in diagram 44.1.

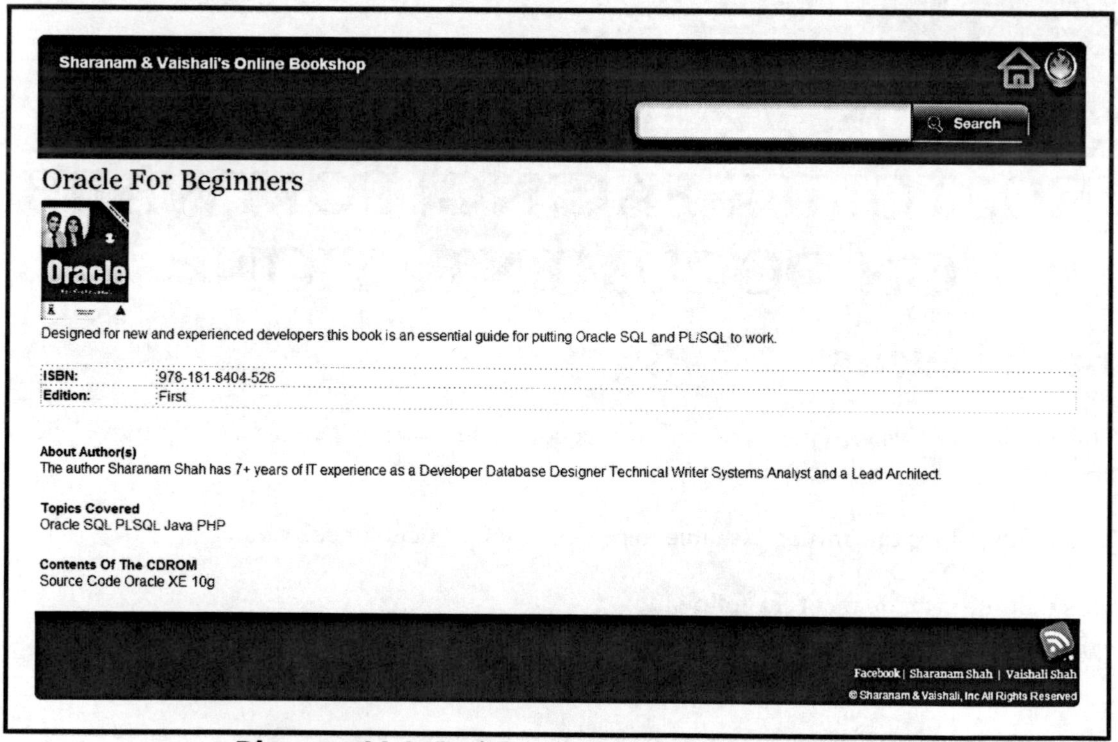

Diagram 44.1: Book Details page [without logged in]

Book Details After Logging In

If the customer has logged in and is viewing the book details page, then the page appears with additional options that allow adding the book to the cart, downloading sample chapters and TOC, as shown in diagram 44.2.

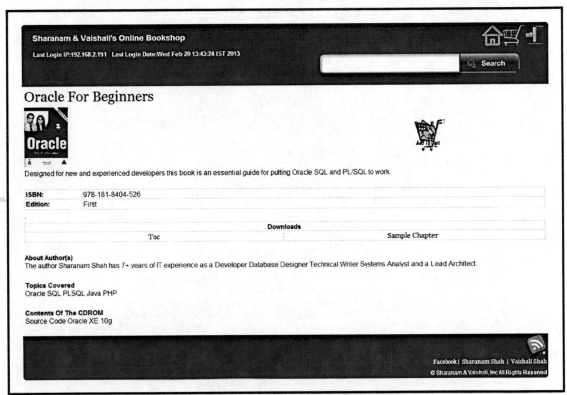

Diagram 41.2: Book Details page [after logging in]

Form Specifications

File Name	showBookDetails.jsp
Title	\<s:property value="book.BookName"/>
Bound To Table	bms.Books

Code Spec

```
1  <%@page contentType="text/html" pageEncoding="UTF-8"%>
2  <%@ taglib prefix="s" uri="/struts-tags" %>
```

```
3   <!DOCTYPE HTML PUBLIC "-//W3C//DTD HTML 4.01 Transitional//EN"
4       "http://www.w3.org/TR/html4/loose.dtd">
5   <html>
6     <head>
7        <meta http-equiv="Content-Type" content="text/html; charset=UTF-8">
8        <title><s:property value="book.BookName"/></title>
9        <link href="/BookShop/css/frontend.css" type="text/css" rel="stylesheet">
10       <s:head />
11     </head>
12     <body>
13       <div id="bodyDiv">
14         <s:include value="userHeader.jsp" />
15         <table border="0" width="100%" cellspacing="4" cellpadding="1">
16           <tr>
17             <td colspan="2" align="left" valign="top" class="spanShowDetails">
18                <s:property value="book.BookName"/>
19             </td>
20           </tr>
21           <tr>
22             <td align="left" valign="top">
23                <img
                   src="getFile.action?columnName=CoverPage&tableName=Books&whereClau
                   se=BookNo&whereClauseValue=<s:property value="book.BookNo" />"
                   width="100px"/>
24             </td>
25             <td align="center">
26                <s:if test="#session.username!=null">
27                   <a href="<s:url action="addToCart"><s:param
                      name="BookNo"><s:property
                      value="book.BookNo"/></s:param><s:param
                      name="BookName"><s:property
                      value="book.BookName"/></s:param><s:param
                      name="Cost"><s:property value="book.Cost"/></s:param></s:url>">
28                      <img src="/BookShop/images/addToCart.jpg" width="74px"
                         height="74px" style="cursor:pointer;" border="0"/>
29                   </a>
30                </s:if>
31             </td>
32           </tr>
33           <tr>
34             <td align="left" class="Arial16GrayN" colspan="2"><s:property
                 value="book.Synopsis" /></td>
35           </tr>
36           <tr><td colspan="2"> </td></tr>
37           <tr>
38             <td align="left" colspan="2">
39                <table border="0" cellspacing="2" cellpadding="0" width="100%"
                   style="border:1px dashed #0099ff;">
40                   <tr>
41                      <td class="Arial15BrownB" width="10%" align="left"
                         style="border-bottom:1px dashed #0099ff; border-right:1px dashed
                         #0099ff;">ISBN: </td>
42                      <td valign="top" class="Arial16GrayN" colspan="2" width="80%"
                         style="border-bottom:1px dashed #0099ff;"><s:property
```

```
             value="book.ISBN"/></td>
43          </tr>
44          <tr>
45             <td class="Arial15BrownB" width="10%" align="left"
               style="border-right:1px dashed #0099ff;">Edition: </td>
46             <td valign="top" class="Arial16GrayN" colspan="2"
               width="80%"><s:property value="book.Edition"/></td>
47          </tr>
48        </table>
49        <br>
50        <s:if test="#session.username!=null">`
51          <table border="0" cellspacing="2" cellpadding="0" width="100%"
               style="border:1px dashed #0099ff;">
52             <tr>
53                <td class="Arial15BrownB" colspan="3" width="20%"
                  align="center" style="border-bottom:1px dashed
                  #0099ff;">Downloads</td>
54             </tr>
55             <tr>
56                <td valign="top" colspan="2" class="Arial16GrayN" width="50%"
                  align="center" style="border-right:1px dashed #0099ff;">
57                   <a
                     href="getPDF.action?columnName=Toc&tableName=Books&wher
                     eClause=BookNo&whereClauseValue=<s:property
                     value="book.BookNo" />">Toc</a>
58                </td>
59                <td valign="top" class="Arial16GrayN" width="50%"
                  align="center">
60                   <a
                     href="getPDF.action?columnName=SampleChapter&tableName=
                     Books&whereClause=BookNo&whereClauseValue=<s:property
                     value="book.BookNo" />">Sample Chapter</a>
61                </td>
62             </tr>
63          </table>
64        </s:if>
65        </td>
66      </tr>
67      <tr><td colspan="2"> </td></tr>
68      <tr>
69        <td colspan="2">
70          <table width="100%" border="0" cellspacing="0" cellpadding="0"
               align="center">
71             <tr>
72                <td class="Arial15BrownB" align="left">About Author(s)</td>
73             </tr>
74             <tr>
75                <td class="Arial16GrayN" align="left"><s:property
                  value="book.AboutAuthors"/></td>
76             </tr>
77          </table>
78        </td>
79      </tr>
80      <tr><td colspan="2"> </td></tr>
```

```
81              <tr>
82                <td colspan="2">
83                  <table width="100%" border="0" cellspacing="0" cellpadding="0"
                     align="center">
84                    <tr>
85                      <td class="Arial15BrownB" align="left">Topics Covered</td>
86                    </tr>
87                    <tr>
88                      <td class="Arial16GrayN" align="left"><s:property
                         value="book.TopicsCovered"/></td>
89                    </tr>
90                  </table>
91                </td>
92              </tr>
93              <tr><td colspan="2"> </td></tr>
94              <tr>
95                <td colspan="2">
96                  <table width="100%" border="0" cellspacing="0" cellpadding="0"
                     align="center">
97                    <tr>
98                      <td class="Arial15BrownB" align="left">Contents Of The
                         CDROM</td>
99                    </tr>
100                   <tr>
101                     <td class="Arial16GrayN" align="left"><s:property
                         value="book.ContentsCDROM"/></td>
102                   </tr>
103                 </table>
104               </td>
105             </tr>
106           </table>
107           <s:include value="footer.jsp" />
108         </div>
109       </body>
110     </html>
```

Explanation:

The JSP displays the details of the book.

Whilst populating the book details in JSP, the system checks if the user has logged in. Only if the user has logged in, additional links to the following are displayed:

❏   Add To Cart

❏   TOC and Sample Chapter download

This check is performed by accessing the username from the SESSION object.

Action Class [ShowBookDetailsAction.java]

This is an action class with the following specifications:

Class Name	ShowBookDetailsAction
Package	com.sharanamvaishali.action
Extends	ActionSupport
Implements	- -

Objects		
Object Name	**Class Name**	**Object Type**
bookDAO	BooksDAO	Data Access Layer
book	Books	Model

Properties			
Property Name	**Property Type**	**Methods**	
For displaying the Book Details			
book	Books	getBook()	setBook()

Methods	
Method Name	**Return Values**
viewBooks()	SUCCESS

Code Spec

```
1   package com.sharanamvaishali.action;
2
3   import com.opensymphony.xwork2.ActionSupport;
4   import com.sharanamvaishali.dao.BooksDAO;
5   import com.sharanamvaishali.dao.BooksDAOImpl;
6   import com.sharanamvaishali.model.Books;
7
8   public class ShowBookDetailsAction extends ActionSupport{
9       private BooksDAO bookDAO = new BooksDAOImpl();
10
11      private Books book;
12
13      public Books getBook() {
14          return book;
15      }
16      public void setBook(Books book) {
17          this.book = book;
18      }
19
20      public String viewBooks() throws Exception{
21          book = bookDAO.getBookById(book.getBookNo());
22          bookDAO.updateHits(book);
23          return SUCCESS;
```

```
24    }
25 }
```

Explanation:

The following section describes the above code spec.

viewBooks()

viewBooks() is invoked for every book hyperlink in the following sections of **home.jsp:**

❑   New Releases

❑   Update Books

❑   Top Titles

❑   Books available under each Category

viewBooks():

❑   Retrieves the appropriate Book's details using **BookNo** as the reference. It calls BooksDAO's **getBookById()** which returns the details of the book as a Book object. BookNo is made available by JSP's <s:param> on click of the record. Struts 2 framework automatically transfers the values from Books bean class object to the JSP thus making it available to the user for viewing the same

❑   Updates the Books object's Hits column by calling BookDAO's **updateHits()**, based on which the Top Titles section on the homepage is served

DAO Class

Interface [BooksDAO.java]

This is a Data Access Object interface with the following specifications:

Class Name	Package
BooksDAO	com.sharanamvaishali.dao

Code Spec

```
1  package com.sharanamvaishali.dao;
2
3  import com.sharanamvaishali.model.Books;
4
5  public interface BooksDAO {
6      public Books getBookById(int BookNo);
```

```
7    public void updateHits(Books books);
8 }
```

Implementation Class [BooksDAOImpl.java]

This is a **Data Access Object** class with the following specifications.

Class Name	BooksDAOImpl
Package	com.sharanamvaishali.dao
Implements	BooksDAO

Objects	
Object Name	**Class Name**
session	Session
transaction	Transaction

Methods		
Method Name	**Arguments**	**Return Values**
getBooksById()	int BookNo	Books
updateHits()	Books books	void

Code Spec

```
1    package com.sharanamvaishali.dao;
2
3    import com.sharanamvaishali.model.Books;
4    import com.sharanamvaishali.utility.HibernateUtil;
5    import org.hibernate.Session;
6    import org.hibernate.Transaction;
7
8    public class BooksDAOImpl implements BooksDAO {
9        Session session = HibernateUtil.getSession();
10       Transaction transaction;
11
12       @Override
13       public Books getBookById(int BookNo) {
14           return (Books) session.createQuery("FROM Books WHERE BookNo =
               :BookNo").setInteger("BookNo", BookNo).uniqueResult();
15       }
16
17       @Override
18       public void updateHits(Books books) {
19           try {
20               transaction = session.beginTransaction();
21               books.setHits(books.getHits()+1);
22               session.update(books);
23               transaction.commit();
24           } catch (RuntimeException e) {
```

```
25          if(books != null) {
26              transaction.rollback();
27          }
28          throw e;
29      }
30  }
31 }
```

Explanation:

The following section describes the above code spec.

REMINDER

 BooksDAO's **getBookById()** is explained in the *Chapter 38: Manage Books*, which retrieves the book details based on BookNo.

updateHits()

updateHits() updates the Hits column of the appropriate Book's object from the Books database table using BookNo as the reference.

It performs an update operation [using update() of Session] to increment the hits counter [Hits column of the books table] for that book.

After the update operation is performed, the transaction is committed to make the changes permanent.

Whilst performing the update operation, if a runtime exception occurs, than the transaction is **rolled back**.

Struts Configuration [struts-HomePage.xml]

This is the struts configuration file with the following specifications:

File Name	Package Name	Extends
HomePage	homePage	default
Actions		

Action Name	Results
showBookDetails	SUCCESS - showBookDetails.jsp

Code Spec

```
1  <?xml version="1.0" encoding="UTF-8"?>
```

```
 2  <!DOCTYPE struts PUBLIC
 3  "-//Apache Software Foundation//DTD Struts Configuration 2.0//EN"
 4  "http://struts.apache.org/dtds/struts-2.0.dtd">
 5  <struts>
 6    <package name="homePage" extends="default">
 7      <action name="showBookDetails" method="viewBooks"
        class="com.sharanamvaishali.action.ShowBookDetailsAction">
 8        <result name="success">/frontend/showBookDetails.jsp</result>
 9      </action>
10    </package>
11  </struts>
```

Explanation:

The following section describes the above code spec.

showBookDetails.action

showBookDetails is an action to help viewing.

This means the details of a particular book are displayed.

The details of a particular book are retrieved by **ShowBookDetailsAction's viewBooks()**.

REMINDER

Only the actions related to Show Book Details are explained in this chapter. The remaining actions are explained later in the *Chapter 43: Homepage, Chapter 45: Author Details, Chapter 46: Publisher Details* and *Chapter 47: Category Details.*

REMINDER

Books.java [the model class] is explained in the *Chapter 38: Manage Books.*

Chapter

45

SECTION VI: FRONTEND [CUSTOMER FACING] SOFTWARE DESIGN DOCUMENTATION

Author Details

This module allows viewing the details of the author and the books written by that particular author along with its details. This page is invoked when a user clicks the author name from the frontend.

This module uses bms.Authors table to retrieve that particular author's data and bms.Books table to retrieve the books written by that author.

This module is made up of the following:

Type	Name	Description
JSP	showAuthordetails.jsp	The details of a particular author along with the book details written by that particular author.

Type	Name	Description
Struts 2		
Action	ShowAuthorDetailsAction.java	The action class that facilitates data operations.
DAO Class	AuthorsDAO.java	The interface for the DAO layer.
	AuthorsDAOImpl.java	The implementation class that perform the actual data operations.
Struts Configuration	struts-HomePage.xml	The Struts configuration file.
Hibernate		
Mapping	hibernate.cfg.xml	The mapping file that holds Model class mapping.
Model Class	Authors.java Books.java	The model classes.

JSP [showAuthorDetails.jsp]

Author Details Without Logging In

A link identified by an author name in the section **Our Authors** when clicked, displays author details of the selected author, as shown in diagram 45.1.

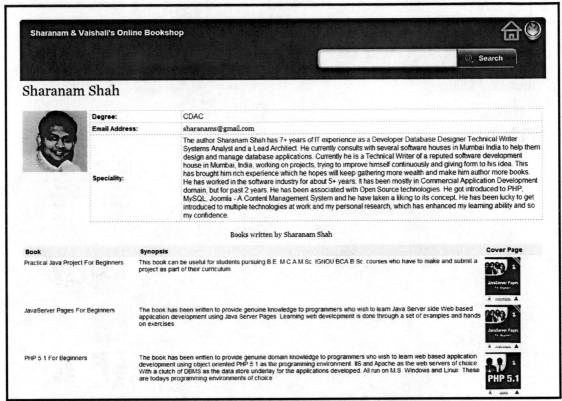

Diagram 45.1: Author Details page [without logged in]

Author Details After Logging In

This page shows the Add to cart link for every book written by that particular author, as shown in diagram 45.2, for the logged in users.

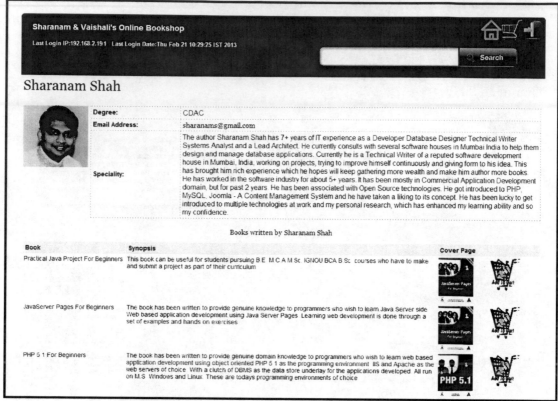

Diagram 45.2: Author Details page [after logging in]

Clicking an entry from the list displays that book's details [explained in the *Chapter 44: Book Details*].

Form Specifications

File Name	showAuthorDetails.jsp
Title	<s:property value="author.FirstName"/>
	<s:property value="author.LastName" />'s Profile
Bound To Table	bms.Authors
	bms.Books

Code Spec

```
1  <%@page contentType="text/html" pageEncoding="UTF-8"%>
2  <%@ taglib prefix="s" uri="/struts-tags" %>
3  <!DOCTYPE HTML PUBLIC "-//W3C//DTD HTML 4.01 Transitional//EN"
```

```
 4      "http://www.w3.org/TR/html4/loose.dtd">
 5    <html>
 6      <head>
 7        <meta http-equiv="Content-Type" content="text/html; charset=UTF-8">
 8        <title><s:property value="author.FirstName"/> <s:property value="author.LastName"
          />'s Profile</title>
 9        <link href="/BookShop/css/frontend.css" type="text/css" rel="stylesheet">
10        <s:head />
11      </head>
12      <body>
13        <div id="bodyDiv">
14          <s:include value="userHeader.jsp" />
15          <table width="100%" border="0" cellspacing="4" cellpadding="1">
16            <tr>
17              <td colspan="2" align="left" valign="top" class="spanShowDetails">
18                <s:property value="author.FirstName"/> <s:property
                  value="author.LastName" />
19              </td>
20            </tr>
21            <tr><td colspan="2"> </td></tr>
22            <tr>
23              <td align="left" valign="top">
24                <img
                  src="getFile.action?columnName=Photograph&tableName=Authors&whereCl
                  ause=AuthorNo&whereClauseValue=<s:property value="author.AuthorNo"
                  />" width="150px"/>
25              </td>
26              <td align="left" valign="top">
27                <table cellspacing="0" border="0" cellpadding="4" width="100%"
                  style="border:1px dashed #0099ff;">
28                  <tr>
29                    <td class="Arial15BrownB" width="20%" align="left"
                      style="border-right:1px dashed #0099ff; border-bottom:1px dashed
                      #0099ff;">
30                      Degree: 
31                    </td>
32                    <td class="Arial16GrayN" valign="top" width="80%"
                      style="border-bottom:1px dashed #0099ff;">
33                      <s:property value="author.Degree" />
34                    </td>
35                  </tr>
36                  <tr>
37                    <td class="Arial15BrownB" width="20%" align="left"
                      style="border-right:1px dashed #0099ff; border-bottom:1px dashed
                      #0099ff;">
38                      Email Address: 
39                    </td>
40                    <td class="Arial16GrayN" valign="top" width="80%"
                      style="border-bottom:1px dashed #0099ff;">
41                      <a href='mailto:<s:property value="author.EmailAddress"/>'>
42                        <s:property value="author.EmailAddress" />
43                      </a>
44                    </td>
45                  </tr>
```

```
46              <tr>
47                  <td class="Arial15BrownB" width="20%" align="left"
                    style="border-right:1px dashed #0099ff;">
48                      Speciality: 
49                  </td>
50                  <td class="Arial16GrayN" valign="top" width="80%">
51                      <s:property value="author.Speciality" />
52                  </td>
53              </tr>
54          </table>
55      </td>
56  </tr>
57  <tr>
58      <td colspan="2" align="center">
59          <br>
60          <span style="font:16px/18px Georgia, serif; width:300px; color:#990000;
            height:37px;">Books written by <s:property value="author.FirstName"/>
            <s:property value="author.LastName" /></span>
61          <br><br>
62          <table class="view" align="center" cellspacing="0" cellpadding="6"
            width="100%">
63              <tr>
64                  <th width="20%" style="font-family:Arial, Times, serif; font-size:
                    14px; font-weight: bold; color:#990000;" align="left">Book</th>
65                  <th width="60%" style="font-family:Arial, Times, serif; font-size:
                    14px; font-weight: bold; color:#990000;" align="left">Synopsis</th>
66                  <th width="10%" style="font-family:Arial, Times, serif; font-size:
                    14px; font-weight: bold; color:#990000;" align="left">Cover
                    Page</th>
67                  <s:if test="#session.username!=null">
68                      <th width="10%" align="left"> </th>
69                  </s:if>
70              </tr>
71          <s:iterator value="books">
72              <tr title="Click to view" class="Arial14GrayN">
73                  <td width="20%" class="showBookList"
                    onclick="javascript:location.href='<s:url
                    action='showBookDetails'><s:param name='book.BookNo'
                    value='BookNo' /></s:url>'">
74                      <s:property value="BookName"/>
75                  </td>
76                  <td width="60%" class="showBookList"
                    onclick="javascript:location.href='<s:url
                    action='showBookDetails'><s:param name='book.BookNo'
                    value='BookNo' /></s:url>'">
77                      <s:property value="Synopsis"/>
78                  </td>
79                  <td width="10%" class="showBookList"
                    onclick="javascript:location.href='<s:url
                    action='showBookDetails'><s:param name='book.BookNo'
                    value='BookNo' /></s:url>'">
80                      <img
                    src="getFile.action?columnName=CoverPage&tableName=Books&
                    whereClause=BookNo&whereClauseValue=<s:property
```

```
                                    value="BookNo" />" width="80px"/>
81                          </td>
82                          <s:if test="#session.username!=null">
83                              <td width="10%" class="showBookList">
84                                  <a href="<s:url action="addToCart"><s:param
                                    name="BookNo"><s:property
                                    value="BookNo"/></s:param><s:param
                                    name="BookName"><s:property
                                    value="BookName"/></s:param><s:param
                                    name="Cost"><s:property
                                    value="Cost"/></s:param></s:url>">
85                                      <img src="/BookShop/images/addToCart.jpg"
                                    width="74px" height="74px" style="cursor:pointer;"
                                    border="0"/>
86                                  </a>
87                              </td>
88                          </s:if>
89                      </tr>
90                  </s:iterator>
91              </table>
92          </td>
93      </tr>
94  </table>
95  <s:include value="footer.jsp" />
96  </div>
97  </body>
98  </html>
```

Explanation:

The JSP displays the details of the author and books written by that author.

Whilst populating these details in JSP, the system checks if the user has logged in. Only if the user has logged in, the additional link i.e. Add To Cart is displayed.

This check is performed by accessing the username from the SESSION object.

Action Class [ShowAuthorDetailsAction.java]

This is an action class with the following specifications:

Class Name	ShowAuthorDetailsAction
Package	com.sharanamvaishali.action
Extends	ActionSupport
Implements	- -

Objects		
Object Name	**Class Name**	**Object Type**
authorDAO	AuthorsDAO	Data Access Layer
author	Authors	Model

Properties			
Property Name	Property Type	Methods	
For displaying the Author Details			
author	Authors	getAuthor()	setAuthor()
books	List<Books>	getBooks()	setBooks()

Methods	
Method Name	Return Values
viewAuthorBooks()	SUCCESS

Code Spec

```
1   package com.sharanamvaishali.action;
2
3   import com.opensymphony.xwork2.ActionSupport;
4   import com.sharanamvaishali.dao.AuthorsDAO;
5   import com.sharanamvaishali.dao.AuthorsDAOImpl;
6   import com.sharanamvaishali.model.Authors;
7   import com.sharanamvaishali.model.Books;
8   import java.util.List;
9
10  public class ShowAuthorDetailsAction extends ActionSupport{
11      private AuthorsDAO authorDAO = new AuthorsDAOImpl();
12
13      private Authors author;
14
15      private List<Books> books;
16
17      public Authors getAuthor() {
18          return author;
19      }
20      public void setAuthor(Authors author) {
21          this.author = author;
22      }
23
24      public List<Books> getBooks() {
25          return books;
26      }
27      public void setBooks(List<Books> books) {
28          this.books = books;
29      }
30
31      public String viewAuthorBooks() throws Exception{
32          author = authorDAO.getAuthorById(author.getAuthorNo());
33          books = authorDAO.getBooksByAuthor(author.getAuthorNo());
34          return SUCCESS;
```

```
35    }
36  }
```

Explanation:

The following section describes the above code spec.

viewAuthorBooks()

viewAuthorBooks() is invoked for every author hyperlink in the **Our Authors** section of **home.jsp**.

viewAuthorBooks():

❑ Retrieves the appropriate Author's details using **AuthorNo** as the reference. It calls AuthorsDAO's **getAuthorById()** which returns the details of the author as a Author object. **AuthorNo** is made available by JSP's <s:param> on click of the record. Struts 2 framework automatically transfers the values from Authors bean class object to the JSP thus making it available to the user for viewing the same

❑ Retrieves the books using **AuthorNo** as the reference. It calls AuthorDAO's **getBooksByAuthor()** which returns the books for that particular author as a Book List object. **AuthorNo** is made available by JSP's <s:param> on click of the record. Struts 2 framework automatically transfers the values from Books bean class object to the JSP thus making it available to the user for viewing the same

DAO Class

Interface [AuthorsDAO.java]

This is a Data Access Object interface with the following specifications:

Class Name	Package
AuthorsDAO	com.sharanamvaishali.dao

Code Spec

```
1  package com.sharanamvaishali.dao;
2
3  import com.sharanamvaishali.model.Authors;
4  import java.util.List;
5
6  public interface AuthorsDAO {
7      public Authors getAuthorById(int AuthorNo);
8      public List getBooksByAuthor(int AuthorNo);
9  }
```

Implementation Class [AuthorsDAOImpl.java]

This is a **Data Access Object** class with the following specifications.

Class Name	AuthorsDAOImpl
Package	com.sharanamvaishali.dao
Implements	AuthorsDAO

Objects	
Object Name	**Class Name**
session	Session

Methods		
Method Name	**Arguments**	**Return Values**
getAuthorById()	int AuthorNo	Authors
getBooksByAuthor()	int AuthorNo	List

Code Spec

```
1   package com.sharanamvaishali.dao;
2
3   import com.sharanamvaishali.model.Authors;
4   import com.sharanamvaishali.utility.HibernateUtil;
5   import java.util.List;
6   import org.hibernate.Session;
7
8   public class AuthorsDAOImpl implements AuthorsDAO {
9       Session session = HibernateUtil.getSession();
10
11      @Override
12      public Authors getAuthorById(int AuthorNo) {
13          return (Authors) session.createQuery("FROM Authors WHERE AuthorNo =
            :AuthorNo").setInteger("AuthorNo", AuthorNo).uniqueResult();
14      }
15
16      @Override
17      public List getBooksByAuthor(int AuthorNo) {
18          try {
19              return session.createQuery("FROM Books WHERE Author1No = :AuthorNo
                OR Author2No = :AuthorNo OR Author3No = :AuthorNo OR Author4No =
                :AuthorNo").setInteger("AuthorNo", AuthorNo).list();
20          } catch(Exception e) {
21              System.out.print("Error while fetching" + e);
22              return null;
23          }
24      }
25  }
```

Explanation:

The following section describes the above code spec.

REMINDER

 AuthorsDAO's **getAuthorById()** is explained in the *Chapter 37: Manage Authors*, which retrieves the author details based on AuthorNo.

getBooksByAuthor()

getBooksByAuthor() returns the appropriate books List object from the Books database table using **AuthorNo** as the reference.

getBooksByAuthor() uses:

❑ **setInteger()** of Query, which states the parameter to be used as the WHERE clause criteria when querying the Books database table

❑ **list()** of Query, which returns the appropriate books from the Books database table belonging to a particular author

getBooksByAuthor() returns an error message in case there are no records found in the Books database table belonging to a particular author.

Struts Configuration [struts-HomePage.xml]

This is the struts configuration file with the following specifications:

File Name	Package Name	Extends
HomePage	homePage	default

Actions	
Action Name	**Results**
showAuthorDetails	SUCCESS - showAuthorDetails.jsp

Code Spec

```
1  <?xml version="1.0" encoding="UTF-8"?>
2  <!DOCTYPE struts PUBLIC
3  "-//Apache Software Foundation//DTD Struts Configuration 2.0//EN"
4  "http://struts.apache.org/dtds/struts-2.0.dtd">
5  <struts>
6    <package name="homePage" extends="default">
7      <action name="showAuthorDetails" method="viewAuthorBooks"
         class="com.sharanamvaishali.action.ShowAuthorDetailsAction">
```

```
8              <result name="success">/frontend/showAuthorDetails.jsp</result>
9          </action>
10     </package>
11  </struts>
```

Explanation:

The following section describes the above code spec.

showAuthorDetails.action

showAuthorDetails is an action to help viewing.

This means the details of a particular author and the books written by that particular author are displayed.

The details of a particular author and the books written by that particular author are retrieved by **ShowAuthorDetailsAction's viewAuthorBooks()**.

REMINDER

Only the actions related to Show Author Details are explained in this chapter. The remaining actions are explained later in the *Chapter 43: Homepage, Chapter 44: Book Details, Chapter 46: Publisher Details* and *Chapter 47: Category Details.*

REMINDER

Authors.java [the model class] is explained in the *Chapter 37: Manage Authors.*

Books.java [the model class] is explained in the *Chapter 38: Manage Books.*

Chapter

46

SECTION VI: FRONTEND [CUSTOMER FACING] SOFTWARE DESIGN DOCUMENTATION

Publisher Details

This module allows viewing the details of the publisher and the books published by that publisher along with its details. This page is invoked when a user clicks the publisher name from the frontend.

This module uses bms.Publishers table to retrieve that particular publisher's data and bms.Books to retrieve the books published by that publisher.

This module is made up of the following:

Type	Name	Description
JSP	showPublisherdetails.jsp	The details of a particular publisher along with the book details published by that particular publisher.

Type	Name	Description
Struts 2		
Action	ShowPublisherDetailsAction.java	The action class that facilitates data operations.
DAO Class	PublishersDAO.java	The interface for the DAO layer.
	PublishersDAOImpl.java	The implementation class that perform the actual data operations.
Struts Configuration	struts-HomePage.xml	The Struts configuration file.
Hibernate		
Mapping	hibernate.cfg.xml	The mapping file that holds Model class mapping.
Model Class	Publishers.java Books.java	The model classes.

JSP [showPublisherDetails.jsp]

Publisher Details Without Logging In

A link identified by a publisher name in the section **Our Publishers** when clicked, displays publisher details of the selected publisher, as shown in diagram 46.1.

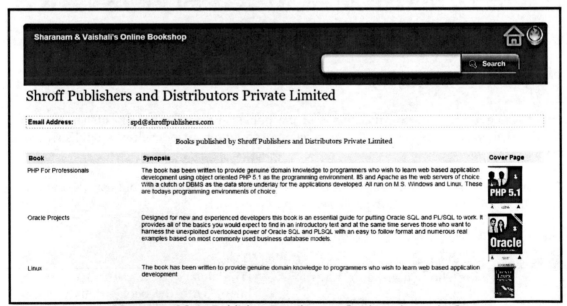

Diagram 46.1: Publisher Details page [without logged in]

Publisher Details After Logging In

This page shows the Add to cart link for every book published by that particular publisher, as shown in diagram 46.2, for the logged in users.

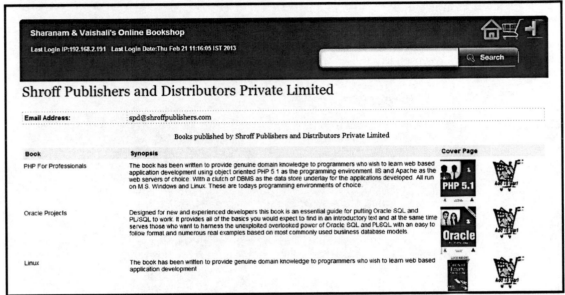

Diagram 46.2: Publisher Details page [after logging in]

Clicking an entry from the list displays that book's details [explained in the *Chapter 44: Book Details*].

Form Specifications

File Name	showPublisherDetails.jsp
Title	<s:property value="publisher.PublisherName"/>'s Profile
Bound To Table	bms.Publishers
	bms.Books

Code Spec

```
1  <%@page contentType="text/html" pageEncoding="UTF-8"%>
2  <%@ taglib prefix="s" uri="/struts-tags" %>
3  <!DOCTYPE HTML PUBLIC "-//W3C//DTD HTML 4.01 Transitional//EN"
4    "http://www.w3.org/TR/html4/loose.dtd">
5  <html>
6    <head>
```

```
7     <meta http-equiv="Content-Type" content="text/html; charset=UTF-8">
8     <title><s:property value="publisher.PublisherName"/>'s Profile</title>
9     <link href="/BookShop/css/frontend.css" type="text/css" rel="stylesheet">
10    <s:head />
11   </head>
12   <body>
13     <div id="bodyDiv">
14       <s:include value="userHeader.jsp" />
15       <table width="100%" border="0" cellspacing="4" cellpadding="1">
16         <tr>
17           <td align="left" valign="top" class="spanShowDetails">
18             <s:property value="publisher.PublisherName"/>
19           </td>
20         </tr>
21         <tr><td> </td></tr>
22         <tr>
23           <td align="left" valign="top">
24             <table cellspacing="0" border="0" cellpadding="4" width="100%"
                   style="border:1px dashed #0099ff;">
25               <tr>
26                 <td class="Arial15BrownB" width="20%" align="left"
                       style="border-right:1px dashed #0099ff;">
27                   Email Address: 
28                 </td>
29                 <td class="Arial16GrayN" valign="top" width="80%">
30                   <a href='mailto:<s:property value="publisher.EmailAddress"/>'>
31                     <s:property value="publisher.EmailAddress" />
32                   </a>
33                 </td>
34               </tr>
35             </table>
36           </td>
37         </tr>
38         <tr>
39           <td align="center">
40             <br>
41             <span style="font:16px/18px Georgia, serif; width:300px; color:#990000;
                   height:37px;">Books published by <s:property
                   value="publisher.PublisherName"/></span>
42             <br><br>
43             <table class="view" align="center" cellspacing="0" cellpadding="6"
                   width="100%">
44               <tr>
45                 <th width="20%" align="left" style="font-family:Arial, Times, serif;
                       font-size: 14px; font-weight: bold; color:#990000;">Book</th>
46                 <th width="60%" align="left" style="font-family:Arial, Times, serif;
                       font-size: 14px; font-weight: bold; color:#990000;">Synopsis</th>
47                 <th width="10%" align="left" style="font-family:Arial, Times, serif;
                       font-size: 14px; font-weight: bold; color:#990000;">Cover
                   Page</th>
48                 <s:if test="#session.username!=null">
49                   <th width="10%" align="left"> </th>
50                 </s:if>
51               </tr>
```

```
52              <s:iterator value="books">
53                  <tr title="Click to view" class="Arial14GrayN">
54                      <td width="20%" class="showBookList"
                        onclick="javascript:location.href='<s:url
                        action='showBookDetails'><s:param name='book.BookNo'
                        value='BookNo' /></s:url>'">
55                          <s:property value="BookName"/>
56                      </td>
57                      <td width="60%" class="showBookList"
                        onclick="javascript:location.href='<s:url
                        action='showBookDetails'><s:param name='book.BookNo'
                        value='BookNo' /></s:url>'">
58                          <s:property value="Synopsis"/>
59                      </td>
60                      <td width="10%" class="showBookList"
                        onclick="javascript:location.href='<s:url
                        action='showBookDetails'><s:param name='book.BookNo'
                        value='BookNo' /></s:url>'">
61                          <img
                        src="getFile.action?columnName=CoverPage&tableName=Books
                        &whereClause=BookNo&whereClauseValue=<s:property
                        value="BookNo" />" width="80px"/>
62                      </td>
63                      <s:if test="#session.username!=null">
64                          <td width="10%" class="showBookList">
65                              <a href="<s:url action="addToCart"><s:param
                        name="BookNo"><s:property
                        value="BookNo"/></s:param><s:param
                        name="BookName"><s:property
                        value="BookName"/></s:param><s:param
                        name="Cost"><s:property
                        value="Cost"/></s:param></s:url>">
66                                  <img src="/BookShop/images/addToCart.jpg"
                        width="74px" height="74px" style="cursor:pointer;"
                        border="0"/>
67                              </a>
68                          </td>
69                      </s:if>
70                  </tr>
71              </s:iterator>
72          </table>
73      </td>
74  </tr>
75  </table>
76  <s:include value="footer.jsp" />
77  </div>
78  </body>
79  </html>
```

Explanation:

The JSP displays the details of the publisher and books published by that publisher.

Whilst populating these details in JSP, the system checks if the user has logged in. Only if the user has logged in, an additional link i.e. Add To Cart is displayed.

This check is performed by accessing the username from the SESSION object.

Action Class [ShowPublisherDetailsAction.java]

This is an action class with the following specifications:

Class Name	ShowPublisherDetailsAction
Package	com.sharanamvaishali.action
Extends	ActionSupport
Implements	- -

Objects		
Object Name	**Class Name**	**Object Type**
publisherDAO	PublishersDAO	Data Access Layer
publisher	Publishers	Model

Properties		
Property Name	**Property Type**	**Methods**
For displaying the Author Details		
publisher	Publishers	getPublisher() setPublisher()
books	List<Books>	getBooks() setBooks()

Methods	
Method Name	**Return Values**
viewPublisherBooks()	SUCCESS

Code Spec

```
1   package com.sharanamvaishali.action;
2
3   import com.opensymphony.xwork2.ActionSupport;
4   import com.sharanamvaishali.dao.PublishersDAO;
5   import com.sharanamvaishali.dao.PublishersDAOImpl;
6   import com.sharanamvaishali.model.Books;
7   import com.sharanamvaishali.model.Publishers;
8   import java.util.List;
9
10  public class ShowPublisherDetailsAction extends ActionSupport{
11      private PublishersDAO publisherDAO = new PublishersDAOImpl();
12
13      private Publishers publisher;
14
15      private List<Books> books;
16
```

```
17      public Publishers getPublisher() {
18          return publisher;
19      }
20      public void setPublisher(Publishers publisher) {
21          this.publisher = publisher;
22      }
23
24      public List<Books> getBooks() {
25          return books;
26      }
27      public void setBooks(List<Books> books) {
28          this.books = books;
29      }
30
31      public String viewPublisherBooks() throws Exception{
32          publisher = publisherDAO.getPublisherById(publisher.getPublisherNo());
33          books = publisherDAO.getBookByPublisher(publisher.getPublisherNo());
34          return SUCCESS;
35      }
36 }
```

Explanation:

The following section describes the above code spec.

viewPublisherBooks()

viewPublisherBooks() is invoked for every publisher hyperlink in the **Our Publishers** section of **home.jsp**.

viewPublisherBooks():

❑ Retrieves the appropriate Publisher's details using **PublisherNo** as the reference. It calls PublishersDAO's **getPublisherById()** which returns the details of the publisher as a Publisher object. **PublisherNo** is made available by JSP's <s:param> on click of the record. Struts 2 framework automatically transfers the values from Publishers bean class object to the JSP thus making it available to the user for viewing the same

❑ Retrieves the books using **PublisherNo** as the reference. It calls PublisherDAO's **getBooksByPublisher()** which returns the books published by that particular publisher as a Book List object. **PublisherNo** is made available by JSP's <s:param> on click of the record. Struts 2 framework automatically transfers the values from Books bean class object to the JSP thus making it available to the user for viewing the same

DAO Class

Interface [PublishersDAO.java]

This is a Data Access Object interface with the following specifications:

Class Name	Package
PublishersDAO	com.sharanamvaishali.dao

Code Spec

```
1  package com.sharanamvaishali.dao;
2
3  import com.sharanamvaishali.model.Publishers;
4  import java.util.List;
5
6  public interface PublishersDAO {
7      public Publishers getPublisherById(int PublisherNo);
8      public List getBookByPublisher(int PublisherNo);
9  }
```

Implementation Class [PublishersDAOImpl.java]

This is a **Data Access Object** class with the following specifications.

Class Name	PublishersDAOImpl
Package	com.sharanamvaishali.dao
Implements	PublishersDAO

Objects	
Object Name	**Class Name**
session	Session

Methods		
Method Name	**Arguments**	**Return Values**
getPublisherById()	int PublisherNo	Publishers
getBooksByPublisher()	int PublisherNo	List

Code Spec

```
1  package com.sharanamvaishali.dao;
2
3  import com.sharanamvaishali.model.Publishers;
4  import com.sharanamvaishali.utility.HibernateUtil;
5  import java.util.List;
```

```
6   import org.hibernate.Session;
7
8   public class PublishersDAOImpl implements PublishersDAO {
9       Session session = HibernateUtil.getSession();
10
11      @Override
12      public Publishers getPublisherById(int PublisherNo) {
13          return (Publishers) session.createQuery("FROM Publishers WHERE
                PublisherNo = :PublisherNo").setInteger("PublisherNo",
                PublisherNo).uniqueResult();
14      }
15
16      @Override
17      public List getBookByPublisher(int PublisherNo) {
18          try {
19              return session.createQuery("FROM Books WHERE PublisherNo =
                    :PublisherNo").setInteger("PublisherNo", PublisherNo).list();
20          } catch(Exception e) {
21              System.out.print("Error while fetching" + e);
22              return null;
23          }
24      }
25  }
```

Explanation:

The following section describes the above code spec.

REMINDER

 PublishersDAO's **getPublisherById()** is explained in the *Chapter 36: Manage Publishers*, which retrieves the publisher details based on PublisherNo.

getBooksByPublisher()

getBooksByPublisher() returns the appropriate books List object from the Books database table using **PublisherNo** as the reference.

getBooksByPublisher() uses:

❑ **setInteger()** of Query, which states the parameter to be used as the WHERE clause criteria when querying the Books database table

❑ **list()** of Query, which returns the appropriate books from the Books database table published by a particular publisher

getBooksByPublisher() returns an error message in case there are no records found in the Books database table published by a particular publisher.

Struts Configuration [struts-HomePage.xml]

This is the struts configuration file with the following specifications:

File Name	Package Name	Extends
HomePage	homePage	default

Actions	
Action Name	**Results**
showPublisherDetails	SUCCESS - showPublisherDetails.jsp

Code Spec

```
1  <?xml version="1.0" encoding="UTF-8"?>
2  <!DOCTYPE struts PUBLIC
3  "-//Apache Software Foundation//DTD Struts Configuration 2.0//EN"
4  "http://struts.apache.org/dtds/struts-2.0.dtd">
5  <struts>
6    <package name="homePage" extends="default">
7      <action name="showPublisherDetails" method="viewPublisherBooks"
       class="com.sharanamvaishali.action.ShowPublisherDetailsAction">
8        <result name="success">/frontend/showPublisherDetails.jsp</result>
9      </action>
10   </package>
11 </struts>
```

Explanation:

The following section describes the above code spec.

showPublisherDetails.action

showPublisherDetails is an action to help viewing.

This means the details of a particular publisher and the books published by that particular publisher are displayed.

The details of a particular publisher and the books published by that particular publisher are retrieved by **ShowPublisherDetailsAction's viewPublisherBooks()**.

REMINDER

Only the actions related to Show Publisher Details are explained in this chapter. The remaining actions are explained later in the *Chapter 43: Homepage, Chapter 44: Book Details, Chapter 45: Author Details* and *Chapter 47: Category Details.*

REMINDER

  Publishers.java [the model class] is explained in the *Chapter 36: Manage Publishers*.

Books.java [the model class] is explained in the *Chapter 38: Manage Books*.

Chapter

47

SECTION VI: FRONTEND [CUSTOMER FACING] SOFTWARE DESIGN DOCUMENTATION

Category Details

This module allows viewing the details of the category and the books for that category along with its details. This page is invoked when a user clicks the category name from the frontend.

This module uses bms.Categories table to retrieve that particular category's data and bms.Books to retrieve the books for that category.

This module is made up of the following:

Type	Name	Description
JSP	showCategoryDetails.jsp	The details of a particular category along with the details of the books under that particular category.

Type	Name	Description
Struts 2		
Action	ShowCategoryDetailsAction.java	The action class that facilitates data operations.
DAO Class	CategoriesDAO.java	The interface for the DAO layer.
	CategoriesDAOImpl.java	The implementation class that perform the actual data operations.
Struts Configuration	struts-HomePage.xml	The Struts configuration file.
Hibernate		
Mapping	hibernate.cfg.xml	The mapping file that holds Model class mapping.
Model Class	Categories.java Books.java	The model classes.

JSP [showCategoryDetails.jsp]

Category Details Without Logging In

A link identified by a category name in the section **Categories** when clicked, displays category details of the selected category, as shown in diagram 47.1.

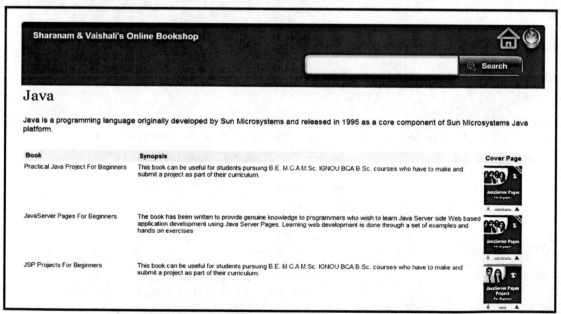

Diagram 47.1: Category Details page [without logged in]

Category Details After Logging In

This page shows the Add to cart link for every book categorized under that particular category, as shown in diagram 47.2, for the logged in users.

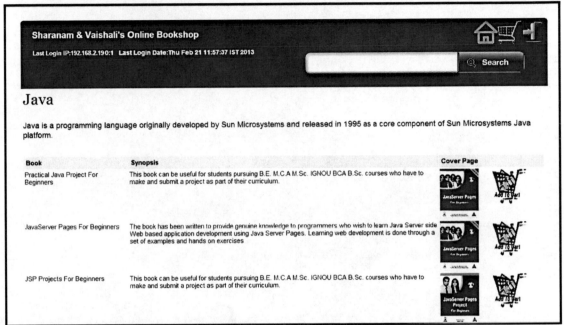

Diagram 47.2: Category Details page [after logging in]

Clicking an entry from the list displays that book's details [explained in the *Chapter 44: Book Details*].

Form Specifications

File Name	showCategoryDetails.jsp
Title	<s:property value="category.Category"/>
Bound To Table	bms.Categories bms.Books

Code Spec

```
1  <%@page contentType="text/html" pageEncoding="UTF-8"%>
2  <%@ taglib prefix="s" uri="/struts-tags" %>
3  <!DOCTYPE HTML PUBLIC "-//W3C//DTD HTML 4.01 Transitional//EN"
```

```
4        "http://www.w3.org/TR/html4/loose.dtd">
5    <html>
6      <head>
7          <meta http-equiv="Content-Type" content="text/html; charset=UTF-8">
8          <title><s:property value="category.Category"/></title>
9          <link href="/BookShop/css/frontend.css" type="text/css" rel="stylesheet">
10         <s:head />
11     </head>
12     <body>
13         <div id="bodyDiv">
14             <s:include value="userHeader.jsp" />
15             <table width="100%" border="0" cellspacing="4" cellpadding="1">
16                 <tr>
17                     <td align="left" valign="top" class="spanShowDetails">
18                         <s:property value="category.Category"/>
19                     </td>
20                 </tr>
21                 <tr><td> </td></tr>
22                 <tr>
23                     <td align="left" valign="top" class="Arial16GrayN">
24                         <s:property value="category.Description" />
25                     </td>
26                 </tr>
27                 <tr>
28                     <td>
29                         <br><br>
30                         <table class="view" align="center" cellspacing="0" cellpadding="6"
                           width="100%">
31                             <tr>
32                                 <th width="20%" style="font-family:Arial, Times, serif; font-size:
                               14px; font-weight: bold; color:#990000;" align="left">Book</th>
33                                 <th width="60%" style="font-family:Arial, Times, serif; font-size:
                               14px; font-weight: bold; color:#990000;"
                               align="left">Synopsis</th>
34                                 <th width="10%" style="font-family:Arial, Times, serif; font-size:
                               14px; font-weight: bold; color:#990000;" align="left">Cover
                               Page</th>
35                                 <s:if test="#session.username!=null">
36                                     <th width="10%" align="left"> </th>
37                                 </s:if>
38                             </tr>
39                             <s:iterator value="books">
40                                 <tr title="Click to view" class="Arial14GrayN">
41                                     <td width="20%" class="showBookList"
                                   onclick="javascript:location.href='<s:url
                                   action='showBookDetails'><s:param name='book.BookNo'
                                   value='BookNo' /></s:url>'">
42                                         <s:property value="BookName"/>
43                                     </td>
44                                     <td width="60%" class="showBookList"
                                   onclick="javascript:location.href='<s:url
                                   action='showBookDetails'><s:param name='book.BookNo'
                                   value='BookNo' /></s:url>'">
45                                         <s:property value="Synopsis"/>
```

```
46                         </td>
47                         <td width="10%" class="showBookList"
                           onclick="javascript:location.href='<s:url
                           action='showBookDetails'><s:param name='book.BookNo'
                           value='BookNo' /></s:url>'">
48                             <img
                               src="getFile.action?columnName=CoverPage&tableName=Books
                               &whereClause=BookNo&whereClauseValue=<s:property
                               value="BookNo" />" width="80px"/>
49                         </td>
50                         <s:if test="#session.username!=null">
51                             <td width="10%" class="showBookList">
52                                 <a href="<s:url action="addToCart"><s:param
                                   name="BookNo"><s:property
                                   value="BookNo"/></s:param><s:param
                                   name="BookName"><s:property
                                   value="BookName"/></s:param><s:param
                                   name="Cost"><s:property
                                   value="Cost"/></s:param></s:url>">
53                                     <img src="/BookShop/images/addToCart.jpg"
                                       width="74px" height="74px" style="cursor:pointer;"
                                       border="0"/>
54                                 </a>
55                             </td>
56                         </s:if>
57                     </tr>
58                 </s:iterator>
59             </table>
60         </td>
61     </tr>
62 </table>
63 <s:include value="footer.jsp" />
64     </div>
65 </body>
66 </html>
```

Explanation:

The JSP displays the details of the category and books available under that category.

Whilst populating these details in JSP, the system checks if the user has logged in. Only if the user has logged in, additional link of Add To Cart is displayed.

This check is performed by accessing the username from the SESSION object.

Action Class [ShowCategoryDetailsAction.java]

This is an action class with the following specifications:

Class Name	ShowCategoryDetailsAction
Package	com.sharanamvaishali.action

Extends	ActionSupport
Implements	- -

Objects		
Object Name	**Class Name**	**Object Type**
categoryDAO	CategoriesDAO	Data Access Layer
category	Categories	Model

Properties		
Property Name	**Property Type**	**Methods**
For displaying the Author Details		
category	Categories	getCategory()	setCategory()
books	List<Books>	getBooks()	setBooks()

Methods	
Method Name	**Return Values**
viewCategoryBooks()	SUCCESS

Code Spec

```
1   package com.sharanamvaishali.action;
2
3   import com.opensymphony.xwork2.ActionSupport;
4   import com.sharanamvaishali.dao.CategoriesDAO;
5   import com.sharanamvaishali.dao.CategoriesDAOImpl;
6   import com.sharanamvaishali.model.Books;
7   import com.sharanamvaishali.model.Categories;
8   import java.util.List;
9
10  public class ShowCategoryDetailsAction extends ActionSupport{
11      private CategoriesDAO categoryDAO = new CategoriesDAOImpl();
12
13      private Categories category;
14
15      private List<Books> books;
16
17      public Categories getCategory() {
18          return category;
19      }
20      public void setCategory(Categories category) {
21          this.category = category;
22      }
23
24      public List<Books> getBooks() {
25          return books;
26      }
27      public void setBooks(List<Books> books) {
28          this.books = books;
```

```
29     }
30
31     public String viewCategoryBooks() throws Exception{
32         category = categoryDAO.getCategoryById(category.getCategoryNo());
33         books = categoryDAO.getAllBooksByCategory(category.getCategoryNo());
34         return SUCCESS;
35     }
36 }
```

Explanation:

The following section describes the above code spec.

viewCategoryBooks()

viewCategoryBooks() is invoked for every publisher hyperlink in the **Category** section of **home.jsp**.

viewCategoryBooks():

❑   Retrieves the appropriate Category's details using **CategoryNo** as the reference. It calls CategoriesDAO's **getCategoryById()** which returns the details of the category as a Category object. **CategoryNo** is made available by JSP's <s:param> on click of the record. Struts 2 framework automatically transfers the values from Categories bean class object to the JSP thus making it available to the user for viewing the same

❑   Retrieves the books using **CategoryNo** as the reference. It calls CategoriesDAO's **getAllBooksByCategory()** which returns the books categorized under that particular category as a Book List object. **CategoryNo** is made available by JSP's <s:param> on click of the record. Struts 2 framework automatically transfers the values from Categories bean class object to the JSP thus making it available to the user for viewing the same

DAO Class

Interface [CategoriesDAO.java]

This is a Data Access Object interface with the following specifications:

Class Name	Package
CategoriesDAO	com.sharanamvaishali.dao

Code Spec

```
1   package com.sharanamvaishali.dao;
2
```

```
3   import com.sharanamvaishali.model.Categories;
4   import java.util.List;
5
6   public interface CategoriesDAO {
7       public Categories getCategoryById(int CategoryNo);
8       public List getAllBooksByCategory(int CategoryNo);
9   }
```

Implementation Class [CategoriesDAOImpl.java]

This is a **Data Access Object** class with the following specifications.

Class Name	CategoriesDAOImpl
Package	com.sharanamvaishali.dao
Implements	CategoriesDAO

Objects	
Object Name	**Class Name**
session	Session

Methods		
Method Name	**Arguments**	**Return Values**
getCategoryById()	int CategoryNo	Categories
getAllBooksByCategory()	int CategoryNo	List

Code Spec

```
1   package com.sharanamvaishali.dao;
2
3   import com.sharanamvaishali.model.Categories;
4   import com.sharanamvaishali.utility.HibernateUtil;
5   import java.util.List;
6   import org.hibernate.Session;
7
8   public class CategoriesDAOImpl implements CategoriesDAO {
9       Session session = HibernateUtil.getSession();
10
11      @Override
12      public Categories getCategoryById(int CategoryNo) {
13          return (Categories) session.createQuery("FROM Categories WHERE
            CategoryNo = :CategoryNo").setInteger("CategoryNo",
            CategoryNo).uniqueResult();
14      }
15
16      @Override
17      public List getAllBooksByCategory(int CategoryNo) {
18          try {
```

```
19              return session.createQuery("FROM Books WHERE CategoryNo =
                :CategoryNo").setInteger("CategoryNo", CategoryNo).list();
20          } catch(Exception e) {
21              System.out.print("Error while fetching" + e);
22              return null;
23          }
24      }
25  }
```

Explanation:

The following section describes the above code spec.

REMINDER

 CategoriesDAO's **getCategoryById()** is explained in the *Chapter 35: Manage Categories*, which retrieves the category details based on CategoryNo.

getAllBooksByCategory()

getAllBooksByCategory() returns the appropriate books List object from the Books database table using **CategoryNo** as the reference.

getAllBooksByCategory() uses:

❑ **setInteger()** of Query, which states the parameter to be used as the WHERE clause criteria when querying the Books database table

❑ **list()** of Query, which returns the appropriate books from the Books database table categorized under a particular category

getAllBooksByCategory() returns an error message in case there are no records found in the Books database table categorized under a particular category.

Struts Configuration [struts-HomePage.xml]

This is the struts configuration file with the following specifications:

File Name	Package Name	Extends
HomePage	homePage	default

Actions	
Action Name	**Results**
showCategoryDetails	SUCCESS - showCategoryDetails.jsp

Code Spec

```
1  <?xml version="1.0" encoding="UTF-8"?>
2  <!DOCTYPE struts PUBLIC
3  "-//Apache Software Foundation//DTD Struts Configuration 2.0//EN"
4  "http://struts.apache.org/dtds/struts-2.0.dtd">
5  <struts>
6    <package name="homePage" extends="default">
7      <action name="showCategoryDetails" method="viewCategoryBooks"
       class="com.sharanamvaishali.action.ShowCategoryDetailsAction">
8        <result name="success">/frontend/showCategoryDetails.jsp</result>
9      </action>
10   </package>
11 </struts>
```

Explanation:

The following section describes the above code spec.

showCategoryDetails.action

showCategoryDetails is an action to help viewing.

This means the details of a particular category and the books categorized under that particular category are displayed.

The details of a particular category and the books categorized under that particular category are retrieved by **ShowCategoryDetailsAction's viewCategoryBooks()**.

REMINDER

Only the actions related to Show Category Details are explained in this chapter. The remaining actions are explained later in the *Chapter 43: Homepage, Chapter 44: Book Details, Chapter 45: Author Details* and *Chapter 46: Publisher Details*.

REMINDER

Categories.java [the model class] is explained in the *Chapter 35: Manage Categories*.

Books.java [the model class] is explained in the *Chapter 38: Manage Books*.

Chapter

48

SECTION VI: FRONTEND [CUSTOMER FACING] SOFTWARE DESIGN DOCUMENTATION

Search Results

This module allows viewing the details of the search criteria such as the book name, ISBN and so on. This page is invoked when a user either clicks [Search] after entering the search criteria or directly clicks the words available under the Popular Searches section of the home page.

This module uses bms.Books, bms.Authors and bms.Publishers tables to retrieve the particular search criteria's data and bms.PopularSearches to add and delete the search criteria values.

This module is made up of the following:

Type	Name	Description
JSP	searchResults.jsp	The list of search criteria along with its details.

Type	Name	Description
Struts 2		
Action	SearchResultsAction.java	The action class that facilitates data operations.
DAO Class	SearchDAO.java	The interface for the DAO layer.
	SearchDAOImpl.java	The implementation class that perform the actual data operations.
Struts Configuration	struts-Search.xml	The Struts configuration file.
Hibernate		
Mapping	hibernate.cfg.xml	The mapping file that holds Model class mapping.
Model Class	PopularSearches.java Books.java	The model classes.

JSP [searchResults.jsp]

When 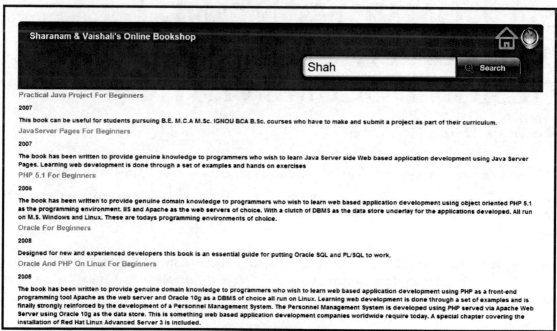 is clicked or when the Popular Searches word is clicked, the search result page appears, as shown in diagram 48.1.

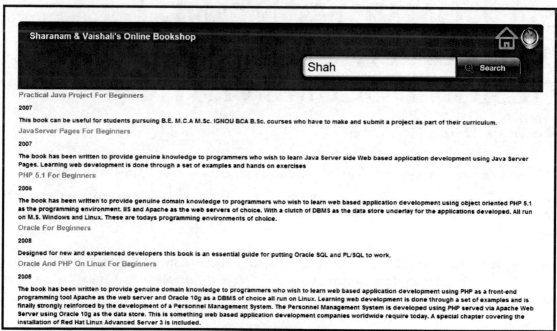

Diagram 48.1: The Search Results

Form Specifications

File Name	searchResults.jsp
Title	BookShop[Sharanam & Vaishali Shah] - Search Results
Bound To Table	bms.PopularSearches
	bms.Books
	bms.Author
	bms.Publishers

Code Spec

```
1   <%@page contentType="text/html" pageEncoding="UTF-8"%>
2   <%@ taglib prefix="s" uri="/struts-tags" %>
3   <%@ taglib prefix="sx" uri="/struts-dojo-tags" %>
4   <!DOCTYPE HTML PUBLIC "-//W3C//DTD HTML 4.01 Transitional//EN"
5     "http://www.w3.org/TR/html4/loose.dtd">
6   <html>
7     <head>
8       <title>BookShop [Sharanam & Vaishali Shah] - Search Results</title>
9       <meta http-equiv="content-type" content="text/html; charset=iso-8859-1">
10      <link href="/BookShop/css/frontend.css" type="text/css" rel="stylesheet">
11      <sx:head parseContent="true"/>
12    </head>
13    <body>
14      <div id="bodyDiv">
15        <s:include value="userHeader.jsp" />
16        <s:iterator value="search" id="search">
17          <table border="0" width="100%" cellpadding="0" cellspacing="2" align="left">
18            <tr>
19              <td class="searchName" valign="top"><s:property
                  value="#search[1]"/></td>
20            </tr>
21            <tr>
22              <td valign="top" class="searchYear"><s:property
                  value="#search[2]"/></td>
23            </tr>
24            <tr>
25              <td valign="top" class="searchSynopsis"><s:property
                  value="#search[3]"/></td>
26            </tr>
27          </table>
28        </s:iterator>
29        <s:if test="#search==null">
30          <span style="font:16px/18px Georgia, serif; width:300px; color:#990000;
            height:37px;">Currently there are no search results.<br><br>To search follow
            the suggestions like:<ul><li>make sure all words are spelled
            correctly</li><li>try different keywords</li><li>try more general
            keywords.</li></ul></span>
31        </s:if>
32        <s:include value="footer.jsp" />
```

```
33      </div>
34    </body>
35  </html>
```

Explanation:

The JSP displays the details of the book for the word searched for.

Action Class [SearchResultsAction.java]

This is an action class with the following specifications:

Class Name	SearchResultsAction
Package	com.sharanamvaishali.action
Extends	ActionSupport
Implements	- -

Objects		
Object Name	Class Name	Object Type
searchDAO	SearchDAO	Data Access Layer

Properties			
Property Name	Property Type	Methods	
search	List<Books>	getSearch()	setSearch()
SearchCriteria	String	getSearchCriteria()	setSearchCriteria()

Methods	
Method Name	Return Values
performSearch()	SUCCESS

Code Spec

```
1   package com.sharanamvaishali.action;
2
3   import com.opensymphony.xwork2.ActionSupport;
4   import com.sharanamvaishali.dao.SearchDAO;
5   import com.sharanamvaishali.dao.SearchDAOImpl;
6   import com.sharanamvaishali.model.Books;
7   import java.util.List;
8
9   public class SearchResultsAction extends ActionSupport{
10      private SearchDAO searchDAO = new SearchDAOImpl();
11
12      private String SearchCriteria;
13
14      private List<Books> search;
15
16      public List<Books> getSearch() {
```

```
17        return search;
18    }
19    public void setSearch(List<Books> search) {
20        this.search = search;
21    }
22
23    public String getSearchCriteria() {
24        return SearchCriteria;
25    }
26    public void setSearchCriteria(String SearchCriteria) {
27        this.SearchCriteria = SearchCriteria;
28    }
29
30    public String performSearch() throws Exception{
31        if(SearchCriteria != null) {
32            search = searchDAO.searchResults(SearchCriteria);
33        } else {
34            search = searchDAO.searchAllResults();
35        }
36        return SUCCESS;
37    }
38 }
```

Explanation:

The following section describes the above code spec.

performSearch()

performSearch() is invoked when:

- ☐   `Search` is clicked [with a search criteria] in the Search section of the header

- ☐   `Search` is clicked [without a search criteria] in the Search section of the header

- ☐   The desired hyperlink is clicked in the Popular Searches section of home.jsp

performSearch():

- ☐   Checks whether the search criteria or keyword is entered or clicked

- ☐   If the search criteria or keyword is entered or clicked, then SearchDAO's searchResults() is invoked, which retrieves the appropriate Book's details using SearchCriteria as the reference

- ☐   If `Search` is clicked [without a search criteria], then SearchDAO's searchAllResults() is invoked, which retrieves all the Book's details

DAO Class

Interface [SearchDAO.java]

This is a Data Access Object interface with the following specifications:

Class Name	Package
SearchDAO	com.sharanamvaishali.dao

Code Spec

```
1   package com.sharanamvaishali.dao;
2
3   import com.sharanamvaishali.model.PopularSearches;
4   import java.util.List;
5
6   public interface SearchDAO {
7       public List searchResults(String searchCriteria);
8       public List searchAllResults();
9       public void savePopularSearches(PopularSearches popularSearches);
10  }
```

Implementation Class [SearchDAOImpl.java]

This is a Data Access Object class with the following specifications.

Class Name	SearchDAOImpl
Package	com.sharanamvaishali.dao
Implements	SearchDAO

Objects	
Object Name	**Class Name**
session	Session
transaction	Transaction

Methods		
Method Name	**Arguments**	**Return Values**
searchResults()	String searchCriteria	List
searchAllResults()	- -	List
savePopularSearches()	PopularSearches popularSearches	void

Code Spec

```
1   package com.sharanamvaishali.dao;
2
```

```
3  import com.sharanamvaishali.model.PopularSearches;
4  import com.sharanamvaishali.utility.HibernateUtil;
5  import java.util.List;
6  import org.hibernate.Query;
7  import org.hibernate.Session;
8  import org.hibernate.Transaction;
9
10 public class SearchDAOImpl implements SearchDAO {
11     Session session = HibernateUtil.getSession();
12     Transaction transaction = null;
13
14     @Override
15     public List searchResults(String searchCriteria) {
16         Query query = session.createSQLQuery("SELECT DISTINCT BookNo,
           BookName, Year, Synopsis"
17                 + " FROM Books, Authors, Publishers "
18                 + "WHERE Authors.AuthorNo = Books.Author1No "
19                 + "OR Authors.AuthorNo = Books.Author2No "
20                 + "OR Authors.AuthorNo = Books.Author3No "
21                 + "OR Authors.AuthorNo = Books.Author4No "
22                 + "OR Publishers.PublisherNo = Books.PublisherNo "
23                 + "AND (BookName LIKE '%"+ searchCriteria + "%' "
24                 + "OR ISBN LIKE '%"+ searchCriteria + "%' "
25                 + "OR Edition LIKE '%"+ searchCriteria + "%' "
26                 + "OR Year LIKE '%"+ searchCriteria + "%' "
27                 + "OR Synopsis LIKE '%"+ searchCriteria + "%' "
28                 + "OR AboutAuthors LIKE '%"+ searchCriteria + "%' "
29                 + "OR TopicsCovered LIKE '%"+ searchCriteria + "%' "
30                 + "OR ContentsCDROM LIKE '%"+ searchCriteria + "%' "
31                 + "OR Cost LIKE '%"+ searchCriteria + "%' "
32                 + "OR FirstName LIKE '%"+ searchCriteria + "%' "
33                 + "OR LastName LIKE '%"+ searchCriteria + "%' "
34                 + "OR PublisherName LIKE '%"+ searchCriteria + "%')");
35         PopularSearches ps = new PopularSearches();
36         ps.setValue(searchCriteria);
37         savePopularSearches(ps);
38         return query.list();
39     }
40
41     @Override
42     public List searchAllResults() {
43         return session.createSQLQuery("SELECT DISTINCT BookNo, BookName, Year,
           Synopsis"
44                 + " FROM Books, Authors, Publishers "
45                 + "WHERE Authors.AuthorNo = Books.Author1No "
46                 + "OR Authors.AuthorNo = Books.Author2No "
47                 + "OR Authors.AuthorNo = Books.Author3No "
48                 + "OR Authors.AuthorNo = Books.Author4No "
```

```
49                   + "OR Publishers.PublisherNo = Books.PublisherNo")
50                   .list();
51      }
52
53      @Override
54      public void savePopularSearches(PopularSearches popularSearches) {
55         try {
56            transaction = session.beginTransaction();
57            session.save(popularSearches);
58            transaction.commit();
59         } catch (RuntimeException e) {
60            if(popularSearches != null) {
61               transaction.rollback();
62            }
63            throw e;
64         }
65      }
66  }
```

Explanation:

The following section describes the above code spec.

searchResults()

searchResults() returns the appropriate search results from the database table using **SearchCriteria** as the reference.

searchResults() uses:

❏ **createSQLQuery()** of Session, which returns the List of Object arrays with scalar values for each column in the Books, Authors and Publishers table

❏ **list()** of Query, which returns the appropriate search results from the Books table

❏ Creates an object of **PopularSearches** entity to set the search criteria

❏ Calls **savePopularSearches()**, which inserts the **SearchCriteria** into **PopularSearches**

searchAllResults()

searchAllResults() returns all the search results from the database table.

searchResults() uses:

❏ **createSQLQuery()** of Session, which returns the List of Object arrays with scalar values for each column in the Books, Authors and Publishers table

❏ **list()** of Query, which returns all the search results from the Books table *savePopularSearches()*

savePopularSearches() does the actual saving of the SearchCriteria in the PopularSearches database table.

savePopularSearches() uses **save()** of Session, which takes care of adding the SearchCriteria.

After the save operation is performed, the transaction is committed to make the changes permanent.

Whilst performing the save operation, if a runtime exception occurs, than the transaction is **rolled back**.

Struts Configuration [struts-Search.xml]

This is the struts configuration file with the following specifications:

File Name	Package Name	Extends
Search	search	default

Actions	
Action Name	**Results**
performSearch	SUCCESS - searchResults.jsp

Code Spec

```
1   <?xml version="1.0" encoding="UTF-8"?>
2   <!DOCTYPE struts PUBLIC
3   "-//Apache Software Foundation//DTD Struts Configuration 2.0//EN"
4   "http://struts.apache.org/dtds/struts-2.0.dtd">
5   <struts>
6     <package name="search" extends="default">
7       <action name="performSearch" method="performSearch"
          class="com.sharanamvaishali.action.SearchResultsAction">
8         <result name="success">/frontend/searchResults.jsp</result>
9       </action>
10    </package>
11  </struts>
```

Explanation:

The following section describes the above code spec.

performSearch.action

performSearch is an action to help viewing.

This means the details of search criteria or keyword entered or clicked are displayed.

The details of search criteria or keyword entered or clicked are retrieved by **SearchResultsAction's performSearch()**.

REMINDER

 PopularSearches.java [the model class] is explained in the *Chapter 43: Homepage*.

Chapter

49

SECTION VI: FRONTEND [CUSTOMER FACING] SOFTWARE DESIGN DOCUMENTATION

Cart

This module allows adding the books to the cart and then viewing the details of the books purchased along with the total amount to be paid.

When the user logs in:

appears in the home page in the Catgeories section

appears in the Show Book Details, ShowAuthor Details, Show Publisher Details and Show Category Details pages

To add a book to the cart, the user needs to log in and either click [icon] or [icon] .

The home page holds a link to the Shopping Cart. The link appears only if the user has logged in.

After the books are added using the **Add To Cart** link, the details about the books purchased are displayed in the **Show Cart** page.

Here, the user can view the cart details and if desired checkout. On checkout, this module with the help of **PerformTransactionAction**, makes appropriate entries in the Transactions database table and then transfers the book data [books in the cart] to the Google Wallet for allowing the user to make the online payment.

This module is made up of the following:

Type	Name	Description
JSP	showCart.jsp	The list of books in the cart with its details.
Struts 2		
Action	CartAction.java	The action class that facilitates data operations.
Struts Configuration	struts-Cart.xml	The Struts configuration file.
Hibernate		
Mapping	hibernate.cfg.xml	The mapping file that holds Model class mapping.
Model Class	CartItem.java	The model class.

JSP [showCart.jsp]

When the user clicks 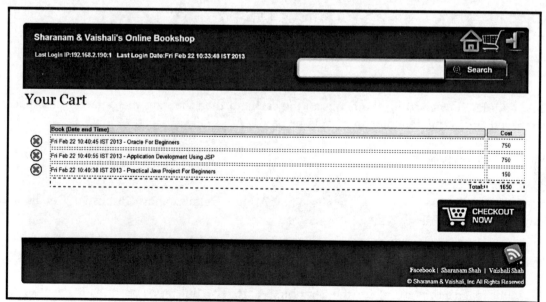, showCart.jsp is served, as shown in diagram 49.1.

Diagram 49.1: Show Cart

If the customer has not added any books to the cart it appears empty, as shown in diagram 49.2.

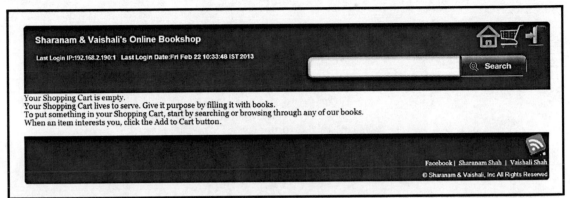

Diagram 49.2: The Empty Cart

Form Specifications

File Name	showCart.jsp
Title	BookShop[Sharanam & Vaishali Shah] - Your Cart
Action	removeFromCart.action
	performTransaction.action

Code Spec

```
1   <%@page contentType="text/html" pageEncoding="UTF-8"%>
2   <%@ taglib prefix="s" uri="/struts-tags" %>
3   <!DOCTYPE HTML PUBLIC "-//W3C//DTD HTML 4.01 Transitional//EN"
4     "http://www.w3.org/TR/html4/loose.dtd">
5   <html>
6     <head>
7       <title>BookShop [Sharanam & Vaishali Shah] - Your Cart</title>
8       <meta http-equiv="content-type" content="text/html; charset=iso-8859-1">
9       <link href="/BookShop/css/frontend.css" type="text/css" rel="stylesheet">
10      <sx:head parseContent="true"/>
11    </head>
12    <body>
13      <div id="bodyDiv">
14        <s:include value="userHeader.jsp" />
15        <s:if test="totalCost>0">
16        <table width="100%" border="0" cellspacing="4" cellpadding="1">
17          <tr>
18            <td colspan="2" align="left" valign="top" class="spanShowDetails">
19              Your Cart<br/><br/>
20            </td>
21          </tr>
```

```
22        <tr>
23          <td align="center" valign="top" width="5%"> </td>
24          <td align="left" class="showCartList">
25            <strong>Book (Date and Time)</strong>
26          </td>
27          <td align="center" class="showCartList">
28            <strong>Cost</strong>
29          </td>
30        </tr>
31        <s:iterator value="cartItems">
32          <tr>
33            <td align='center' valign='top'>
34              <a href="<s:url action="removeFromCart"><s:param
                 name="BookName"><s:property
                 value="BookName"/></s:param></s:url>">
35                <img src="/BookShop/images/delete.png" border="0" width="25px"
                   alt="Click to remove the Book from the cart">
36              </a>
37            </td>
38            <td align='left' style='border:1px dashed #990033;'>
39              <s:property value="BookName"/>
40            </td>
41            <td align='center' style='border:1px dashed #990033;'>
42              <s:property value="Cost"/>
43            </td>
44          </tr>
45        </s:iterator>
46        <tr>
47          <td align="center" valign="top" width="5%"> </td>
48          <td align="right" valign="top" style='border:2px dashed #990033;'>
49            <strong>Total:</strong>
50          </td>
51          <td align="center" valign="top" style='border:2px dashed #990033;'>
52            <strong><s:property value="totalCost"/></strong>
53          </td>
54        </tr>
55      </table>
56    </s:if>
57    <s:if test="totalCost<=0">
58      <span style="font:16px/18px Georgia, serif; width:300px; color:#990000;
         height:37px;">Your Shopping Cart is empty.<br>Your Shopping Cart lives to
         serve. Give it purpose by filling it with books.<br>To put something in your
         Shopping Cart, start by searching or browsing through any of our
         books.<br>When an item interests you, click the Add to Cart button.</span>
59    </s:if>
60    <s:else>
61      <table width="100%" border="0" cellspacing="0" cellpadding="0">
62        <tr>
63          <td align="right" valign="top">
64            <br/>
65            <s:i18n name="bookshop">
66              <s:if test="getText('googleMerchantID')!=''">
67                <a href="performTransaction.action">
68                  <img
```

```
                         src="/BookShop/images/checkout.gif?merchant_id=<s:text
                         name='googleMerchantID'/>&style=white&variant=text&loc=en_
                         US"/>
69                              </a>
70                          </s:if>
71                      </s:i18n>
72                  </td>
73              </tr>
74          </table>
75      </s:else>
76      <s:include value="footer.jsp" />
77   </div>
78  </body>
79 </html>
```

Explanation:

The JSP displays the details of the books added to the cart by the customer.

This JSP also allows the user to delete/remove a book from the cart using ⊗.

<s:i18n>

<s:i18n> gets a resource bundle and places it on the ValueStack. This allows the other tags to access messages from the bundle and not just the bundle associated with the current action.

<s:i18n name="bookshop">

Where, **name** is the name of the resource bundle. In this application, the resource bundle used is bookshop.properties, which holds the values such as merchant ID of the Google wallet, the email address, username and password of the BookShop Online.

Action Class [CartAction.java]

This is an action class with the following specifications:

Class Name	CartAction
Package	com.sharanamvaishali.action
Extends	ActionSupport
Implements	SessionAware

Properties			
Property Name	**Property Type**	**Methods**	
cartItems	List	getCartItems()	setCartItems()
BookNo	int	getBookNo()	setBookNo()
Cost	int	getCost()	setCost()
totalCost	int	getTotalCost()	setTotalCost()

Properties			
Property Name	**Property Type**	**Methods**	
BookName	String	getBookName()	setBookName()
session	Map	getSession()	setSession()

Methods	
Method Name	**Return Values**
showCart()	SUCCESS
addBook()	SUCCESS
removeBook()	SUCCESS

Code Spec

```
1   package com.sharanamvaishali.action;
2
3   import com.opensymphony.xwork2.ActionContext;
4   import com.opensymphony.xwork2.ActionSupport;
5   import com.sharanamvaishali.model.CartItem;
6   import java.util.ArrayList;
7   import java.util.Iterator;
8   import java.util.List;
9   import java.util.Map;
10  import org.apache.struts2.interceptor.SessionAware;
11
12  public class CartAction extends ActionSupport implements SessionAware{
13      private List cartItems;
14
15      private int BookNo, Cost, totalCost;
16
17      private String BookName;
18
19      private Map session;
20
21      public int getBookNo() {
22          return BookNo;
23      }
24      public void setBookNo(int BookNo) {
25          this.BookNo = BookNo;
26      }
27
28      public int getCost() {
29          return Cost;
30      }
31      public void setCost(int Cost) {
32          this.Cost = Cost;
33      }
34
```

```java
35      public int getTotalCost() {
36          return totalCost;
37      }
38      public void setTotalCost(int totalCost) {
39          this.totalCost = totalCost;
40      }
41
42      public String getBookName() {
43          return BookName;
44      }
45      public void setBookName(String BookName) {
46          this.BookName = BookName;
47      }
48
49      public Map getSession() {
50          return session;
51      }
52      @Override
53      public void setSession(Map session) {
54          this.session = session;
55      }
56
57      public List getCartItems() {
58          return cartItems;
59      }
60      public void setCartItems(List cartItems) {
61          this.cartItems = cartItems;
62      }
63
64      public String showCart() throws Exception{
65          cartItems = new ArrayList();
66          for (Iterator it = session.entrySet().iterator(); it.hasNext();) {
67              Map.Entry entry = (Map.Entry) it.next();
68              Object key = entry.getKey();
69              Object value = entry.getValue();
70              if(!(key.toString().equals("username") ||
                 key.toString().equals("lastlogin") || key.toString().equals("lastip"))) {
71                  CartItem cart = new CartItem();
72                  cart.setBookName(key.toString());
73                  cart.setCost(value.toString());
74                  totalCost += Integer.parseInt(value.toString());
75                  cartItems.add(cart);
76              }
77          }
78          return SUCCESS;
79      }
80
81      public String addBook() throws Exception{
```

```
82          String datetime = (new java.util.Date()).toString();
83          String book = datetime + " - " + BookName;
84          int cost = Cost;
85          session = ActionContext.getContext().getSession();
86          session.put(book, cost);
87          return SUCCESS;
88      }
89
90      public String removeBook() throws Exception{
91          session = ActionContext.getContext().getSession();
92          session.remove(BookName);
93          return SUCCESS;
94      }
95  }
```

Explanation:

The following section describes the above code spec.

showCart()

showCart() in invoked when the user clicks [cart icon] from the header to view the cart and the items it holds.

showCart() retrieves the session contents that are related to the cart and populates the same in the List object. This List object is then made available to showCart.jsp that displays the cart items to the user.

addBook()

addBook() in invoked when the user clicks [icon] from the Categories section or [icon] from the Show Book Details, Show Author Details, Show Publisher Details or Show Category details page to add the book details such as the date and time, the cost of the book.

The details of the books are added to the session.

removeBook()

removeBook() is invoked when the user chooses to delete a book from the cart using [icon].

removeBook() removes the selected book from the session.

Struts Configuration [struts-Cart.xml]

This is the struts configuration file with the following specifications:

File Name	Package Name	Extends
Cart	cart	default

Actions	
Action Name	**Results**
showCart	SUCCESS - showCart.jsp
addToCart	SUCCESS
removeFromCart	SUCCESS

Code Spec

```
1   <?xml version="1.0" encoding="UTF-8"?>
2   <!DOCTYPE struts PUBLIC
3   "-//Apache Software Foundation//DTD Struts Configuration 2.0//EN"
4   "http://struts.apache.org/dtds/struts-2.0.dtd">
5   <struts>
6      <package name="cart" extends="default">
7         <action name="showCart" method="showCart"
           class="com.sharanamvaishali.action.CartAction">
8            <result>/frontend/showCart.jsp</result>
9         </action>
10
11        <action name="addToCart" method="addBook"
           class="com.sharanamvaishali.action.CartAction">
12           <result type="redirect">
13             <param name="location">
14               ${#context.get(@org.apache.struts2.StrutsStatics@HTTP_REQUEST
                 ).getHeader("Referer")}
15             </param>
16           </result>
17        </action>
18
19        <action name="removeFromCart" method="removeBook"
           class="com.sharanamvaishali.action.CartAction">
20           <result type="redirectAction">showCart</result>
21        </action>
22     </package>
23  </struts>
```

Explanation:

The following section describes the above code spec.

showCart.action

showCart is an action to help viewing.

This means the details of book such as the book name, the date and time and the cost of the book are displayed.

The details of book are retrieved by **CartAction's showCart()**.

addToCart.action

addToCart is an action to help adding.

This means the details of book such as the book name, the date and time and the cost of the book are added to the session.

The details of book are added by **CartAction's addBook()**.

removeFromCart.action

removeFromCart is an action to help deleting.

This means the details of book such as the book name, the date and time and the cost of the book are deleted from the session.

The details of book are deleted by **CartAction's removeBook()**.

REMINDER

Only the actions related to Cart are explained in this chapter. The remaining actions are explained later in the *Chapter 50: Checkout*.

Domain Class [CartItem.java]

This is a domain class with the following specifications:

Class Name	Package	Implements
CartItem	com.sharanamvaishali.model	java.io.Serializable

Constructor	
Constructor Name	**Arguments**
CartItem()	- -
CartItem()	String BookName String Cost

Properties			
Property Name	**Property Type**	**Methods**	
BookName	String	getBookName()	setBookName()
Cost	String	getCost()	setCost()

Code Spec

```
1   package com.sharanamvaishali.model;
2
3   public class CartItem {
4       private String BookName, Cost;
5
6       public CartItem() {
7       }
8
9       public CartItem(String BookName, String Cost) {
10          this.BookName = BookName;
11          this.Cost = Cost;
12      }
13
14      public String getBookName() {
15          return BookName;
16      }
17      public void setBookName(String BookName) {
18          this.BookName = BookName;
19      }
20
21      public String getCost() {
22          return Cost;
23      }
24      public void setCost(String Cost) {
25          this.Cost = Cost;
26      }
27  }
```

Chapter

50

SECTION VI: FRONTEND [CUSTOMER FACING] SOFTWARE DESIGN DOCUMENTATION

Checkout

This module is invoked when a user clicks available in showCart.jsp.

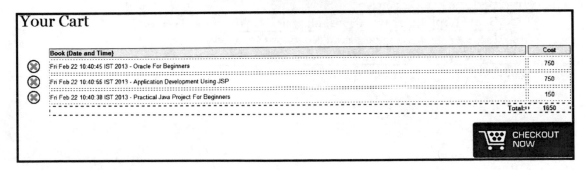

This sends the cart details to Google Wallet for further processing and payment.

This module uses the bms.Transactions table to make entries of the books purchased and then invokes Google Wallet [in sandbox mode for demonstration purpose only] where the user can make the payment of the purchases made.

This module is made up of the following:

Type	Name	Description
JSP	performTransaction.jsp	The page which redirects the user to Google Wallet page for payment.
Struts 2		
Action	PerformTransactionAction.java	The action class that facilitates data operations.
DAO Class	TransactionsDAO.java	The interface for the DAO layer.
	TransactionsDAOImpl.java	The implementation class that perform the actual data operations.
Struts Configuration	struts-Cart.xml	The Struts configuration file.
Hibernate		
Mapping	hibernate.cfg.xml	The mapping file that holds Model class mapping.
Model Class	CartItem.java Transactions.java	The model classes.

JSP [checkOut.jsp]

When the user clicks **CHECKOUT NOW**, the user is first directed to performTransaction.jsp which in turn re-directs to the Google Wallet.

Form Specifications

File Name	performTransaction.jsp
Title	BookShop[Sharanam & Vaishali Shah] - Performing Transaction - Please wait....
Action	https://sandbox.google.com/checkout/cws/v2/Merchant/<s:text name='googleMerchantID'/>/checkoutForm
Method	POST

Data Fields

Type	Name	Value
Hidden	item_name_<s:property value="#cartItemsStatus.index" />	<s:property value="BookName" />
Hidden	item_description_<s:property value="#cartItemsStatus.index" />	<s:property value="BookName" />
Hidden	item_quantity_<s:property value="#cartItemsStatus.index" />	1
Hidden	item_price_<s:property value="#cartItemsStatus.index" />	<s:property value="Cost" />
Hidden	checkout-flow-support.merchant-checkout-flow-support.continue-shopping-url	http://localhost:8080/BookShop/
Hidden	_charset_	- -

Code Spec

```
1   <%@page contentType="text/html" pageEncoding="UTF-8"%>
2   <%@ taglib prefix="s" uri="/struts-tags" %>
3   <%@ taglib prefix="sx" uri="/struts-dojo-tags" %>
4   <!DOCTYPE HTML PUBLIC "-//W3C//DTD HTML 4.01 Transitional//EN"
5    "http://www.w3.org/TR/html4/loose.dtd">
6   <html>
7     <head>
8       <title>BookShop [Sharanam & Vaishali Shah] - Performing Transaction - Please
        wait....</title>
9       <meta http-equiv="content-type" content="text/html; charset=iso-8859-1">
10      <link href="/BookShop/css/frontend.css" type="text/css" rel="stylesheet">
11      <sx:head parseContent="true"/>
12    </head>
13    <body>
14      <s:i18n name="bookshop">
15        <form method="POST"
          action="https://sandbox.google.com/checkout/cws/v2/Merchant/<s:text
          name='googleMerchantID'/>/checkoutForm" accept-charset="utf-8">
16          <s:iterator value="cartItems" status="cartItemsStatus">
17            <input type="hidden" name="item_name_<s:property
              value="#cartItemsStatus.index" />" value="<s:property value="BookName"
              />">
18            <input type="hidden" name="item_description_<s:property
              value="#cartItemsStatus.index" />" value="<s:property value="BookName"
              />">
19            <input type="hidden" name="item_quantity_<s:property
              value="#cartItemsStatus.index" />" value="1">
20            <input type="hidden" name="item_price_<s:property
              value="#cartItemsStatus.index" />" value="<s:property value="Cost" />">
21          </s:iterator>
22          <input type="hidden"
```

```
       name="checkout-flow-support.merchant-checkout-flow-support.continue-shoppin
       g-url" value="http://localhost:8080/BookShop/"/>
23       <input type="hidden" name="_charset_"/>
24     </form>
25   </s:i18n>
26   <script>
27     <!--
28       document.forms[0].submit();
29     -->
30   </script>
31   </body>
32 </html>
```

Explanation:

The JSP is invoked after the book data is added in the bms.Transactions table.

This JSP dynamically generates the **FORM** for submission to the Google Wallet.

```
<form method="POST"
action="https://sandbox.google.com/checkout/cws/v2/Merchant/<s:text
name='googleMerchantID'/>/checkoutForm" accept-charset="utf-8">
    <s:iterator value="cartItems" status="cartItemsStatus">
      <input type="hidden" name="item_name_<s:property
      value="#cartItemsStatus.index" />" value="<s:property value="BookName"
      />">
      <input type="hidden" name="item_description_<s:property
      value="#cartItemsStatus.index" />" value="<s:property value="BookName"
      />">
      <input type="hidden" name="item_quantity_<s:property
      value="#cartItemsStatus.index" />" value="1">
      <input type="hidden" name="item_price_<s:property
      value="#cartItemsStatus.index" />" value="<s:property value="Cost" />">
    </s:iterator>
    <input type="hidden"
name="checkout-flow-support.merchant-checkout-flow-support.continue-shoppin
g-url" value="http://localhost:8080/BookShop/"/>
    <input type="hidden" name="_charset_"/>
</form>
```

This helps sending all the books data from the cart to the Google Wallet for billing and calculation.

After the FORM is generated the same is automatically submitted to Google Wallet [sandbox] using:

```
<script>
  <!--
    document.forms[0].submit();
  -->
</script>
```

Action Class [PerformTransactionAction.java]

This is an action class with the following specifications:

Class Name	PerformTransactionAction
Package	com.sharanamvaishali.action
Extends	ActionSupport
Implements	SessionAware

Objects		
Object Name	**Class Name**	**Object Type**
transactionsDAO	TransactionsDAO	Data Access Object

Properties			
Property Name	**Property Type**	**Methods**	
cartItems	List	getCartItems()	setCartItems()
session	Map	getSession()	setSession()

Methods	
Method Name	**Return Values**
addTransactions()	SUCCESS

Code Spec

```
1   package com.sharanamvaishali.action;
2
3   import com.opensymphony.xwork2.ActionSupport;
4   import com.sharanamvaishali.dao.TransactionsDAO;
5   import com.sharanamvaishali.dao.TransactionsDAOImpl;
6   import com.sharanamvaishali.model.CartItem;
7   import com.sharanamvaishali.model.Transactions;
8   import java.util.ArrayList;
9   import java.util.Date;
10  import java.util.Iterator;
11  import java.util.List;
12  import java.util.Map;
13  import org.apache.struts2.interceptor.SessionAware;
14
15  public class PerformTransactionAction extends ActionSupport implements
    SessionAware{
16      private TransactionsDAO transactionsDAO = new TransactionsDAOImpl();
17
18      private List cartItems;
19
20      private Map session;
21
22      public List getCartItems() {
23          return cartItems;
```

```
24      }
25      public void setCartItems(List cartItems) {
26          this.cartItems = cartItems;
27      }
28
29      public Map getSession() {
30          return session;
31      }
32      @Override
33      public void setSession(Map session) {
34          this.session = session;
35      }
36
37      public String addTransactions() throws Exception{
38          cartItems = new ArrayList();
39          for (Iterator it = session.entrySet().iterator(); it.hasNext();) {
40              Map.Entry entry = (Map.Entry) it.next();
41              Object key = entry.getKey();
42              Object value = entry.getValue();
43              int transactionNo = transactionsDAO.getNextTransactionNo();
44              if(!(key.toString().equals("username") ||
                    key.toString().equals("lastlogin") || key.toString().equals("lastip"))) {
45                  Transactions transaction = new Transactions();
46                  transaction.setUsername(session.get("username").toString());
47                  transaction.setBookName(key.toString());
48                  transaction.setCost(Integer.parseInt(value.toString()));
49                  transaction.setQty(1);
50                  transaction.setTransactionDate(new Date());
51                  transaction.setTransactionNo(transactionNo);
52                  transactionsDAO.saveTransaction(transaction);
53                  CartItem cart = new CartItem();
54                  cart.setBookName(key.toString());
55                  cart.setCost(value.toString());
56                  cartItems.add(cart);
57              }
58          }
59          session.clear();
60          return SUCCESS;
61      }
62  }
```

Explanation:

The following section describes the above code spec.

addTransactions()

addTransactions() is invoked when the user clicks .

addTransactions() retrieves the session contents [related to the cart i.e. the **book name** and the **book cost**] and inserts them as transactions in the **Transactions** database table with the help of TransactionsDAO's **saveTransaction()**.

Finally, the extracted session contents [related to the cart items] are added to a list object which will be made available to performTransactions.jsp that generates the FORM for onward submission to Google Wallet's payment gateway.

DAO Class

Interface [TransactionsDAO.java]

This is a Data Access Object interface with the following specifications:

Class Name	Package
TransactionsDAO	com.sharanamvaishali.dao

Code Spec

```
1  package com.sharanamvaishali.dao;
2
3  import com.sharanamvaishali.model.Transactions;
4
5  public interface TransactionsDAO {
6      public void saveTransaction(Transactions transactions);
7      public int getNextTransactionNo();
8  }
```

Implementation Class [TransactionsDAOImpl.java]

This is a **Data Access Object** class with the following specifications.

Class Name	TransactionsDAOImpl
Package	com.sharanamvaishali.dao
Implements	TransactionsDAO

Objects	
Object Name	**Class Name**
session	Session
transaction	Transaction

Methods		
Method Name	**Arguments**	**Return Values**
saveTransaction()	Transactions transactions	void
getNextTransactionNo()	- -	int

Code Spec

```
1   package com.sharanamvaishali.dao;
2
3   import com.sharanamvaishali.model.Transactions;
4   import com.sharanamvaishali.utility.HibernateUtil;
5   import org.hibernate.Session;
6   import org.hibernate.Transaction;
7
8   public class TransactionsDAOImpl implements TransactionsDAO {
9       Session session = HibernateUtil.getSession();
10      Transaction transaction = null;
11
12      @Override
13      public void saveTransaction(Transactions transactions){
14          try {
15              transaction = session.beginTransaction();
16              session.save(transactions);
17              transaction.commit();
18          } catch (RuntimeException e) {
19              if(transactions != null) {
20                  transaction.rollback();
21              }
22              throw e;
23          }
24      }
25
26      @Override
27      public int getNextTransactionNo(){
28          try {
29              Object TransactionNo = session.createSQLQuery("SELECT
                    MAX(TransactionNo)+1 AS TransactionNo FROM
                    Transactions").addScalar("TransactionNo").uniqueResult();
30              return Integer.parseInt(TransactionNo.toString());
31          } catch(RuntimeException e){
32              return 1;
33          }
```

```
34    }
35  }
```

Explanation:

The following section describes the above code spec.

saveTransaction()

saveTransaction() is invoked by **PerformTransactionAction**'s **addTransactions()** when a user makes any purchases.

It performs an insert operation [using save() of Session]. The captured form data is passed to save() which is made available by addTransactions() as a method parameter.

After the insert operation is performed, the transaction is committed to make the changes permanent.

Whilst performing the insert operation, if a runtime exception occurs, than the transaction is **rolled back.**

getNextTransactionNo()

getNextTransactionNo() is invoked by **PerformTransactionAction**'s **addTransactions()** every time a record is added in the Transactions database table.

It retrieves [using createSQLQuery()] and returns the next TransactionNo to addTransactions().

getNextTransactionNo() uses:

❑ **addScalar()** of Session, which declares a scalar query based on TransactionNo

❑ **uniqueResult()** of Query, which ensures that only unique record is retrieved from the Transactions database table and prevents any kinds of errors

❑ **Integer** class, which wraps a value of the primitive type **int** in an TransactionNo object

❑ **parseInt()** of Integer, which parses the string argument as a signed decimal integer

Struts Configuration [struts-Cart.xml]

This is the struts configuration file with the following specifications:

File Name	Package Name	Extends
Cart	cart	default

Actions	
Action Name	**Results**
performTransaction	SUCCESS - performTransaction.jsp

Code Spec

```
1   <?xml version="1.0" encoding="UTF-8"?>
2   <!DOCTYPE struts PUBLIC
3   "-//Apache Software Foundation//DTD Struts Configuration 2.0//EN"
4   "http://struts.apache.org/dtds/struts-2.0.dtd">
5   <struts>
6     <package name="cart" extends="default">
7       <action name="performTransaction" method="addTransactions"
        class="com.sharanamvaishali.action.PerformTransactionAction">
8         <result>/frontend/performTransaction.jsp</result>
9       </action>
10    </package>
11  </struts>
```

Explanation:

The following section describes the above code spec.

showCart.action

showCart is an action to help viewing.

This means the details of book such as the book name, the date and time and the cost of the book are displayed.

The details of book are retrieved by **CartAction**'s **showCart()**.

REMINDER

Only the actions related to Checkout are explained in this chapter. The remaining actions are explained later in the *Chapter 49: Cart*.

REMINDER

Transactions.java [the model class] is explained in the *Chapter 41: Manage Transactions*.

Chapter

51

SECTION VI: FRONTEND [CUSTOMER FACING] SOFTWARE DESIGN DOCUMENTATION

Sign Up

This module allows registering the customers. After signing up, the customers can purchase books and download the TOC and the sample chapter.

This module uses the bms.Customers table to perform the above operations.

This module is made up of the following:

Type	Name	Description
JSP	registration.jsp	The data entry form.
	registrationThankYou.jsp	The thank you page of registration.
Struts 2		
Action	RegistrationAction.java	The action class that facilitates data operations.
Validation	RegistrationAction-validation.xml	The XML based validation file.

Type	Name	Description
Struts 2 [Continued]		
DAO Class	CustomerDAO.java	The interfaces for the DAO layer.
	PopulateDdlbsDAO.java	
	CustomersDAOImpl.java	The implementation classes that performs the
	PopulateDdlbsDAOImpl.java	actual data operations.
Utility Class	PopulateDdlbs.java	The class that populates the list objects.
Struts Configuration	struts-Registration.xml	The Struts configuration file.
Hibernate		
Mapping	hibernate.cfg.xml	The mapping file that holds Model class mapping.
Model Class	Customers.java	The model class.

JSP

registration.jsp

Visitors can sign up to the site using on the homepage.

when clicked delivers the Signup page, as shown in diagram 51.1.

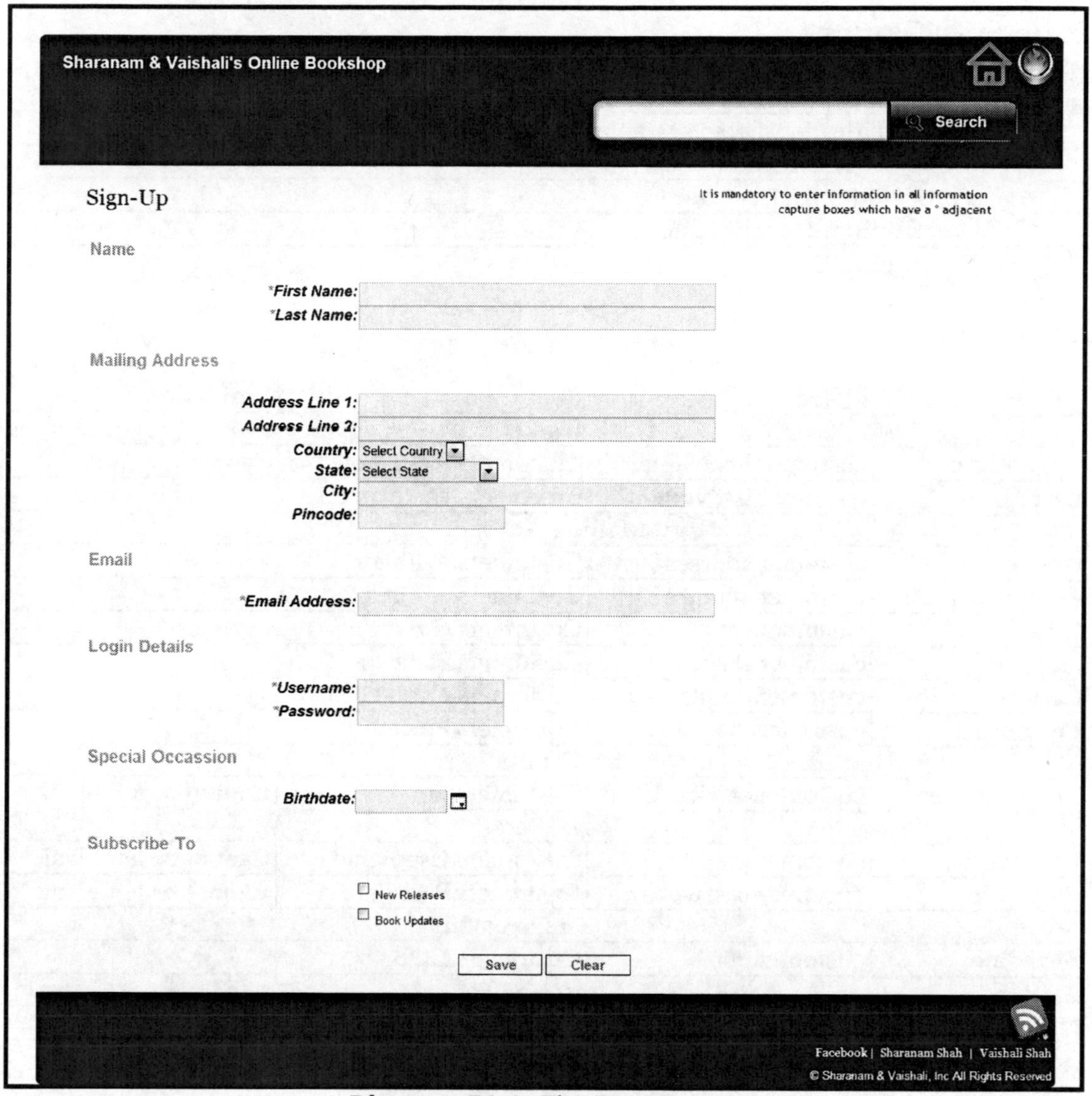

Diagram 51.1: The Signup page

This is a JSP which holds a data entry form, as shown in diagram 51.1.

Form Specifications

File Name	registration.jsp
Title	BookShop[Sharanam & Vaishali Shah] – Registration
Bound To Table	bms.Customers
Form Name	frmCustomers
Action	doInsertCustomer
Method	POST

Data Fields

Label	Name	Bound To	Validation Rules
Name			
First Name	customer.firstName	Customers.FirstName	Cannot be left blank
Last Name	customer.lastName	Customers.LastName	Cannot be left blank
Mailing Address			
Address Line 1	customer.address1	Customers.Address1	- -
Address Line 2	customer.address2	Customers.Address2	- -
City	customer.city	Customers.City	- -
State	customer.stateNo	Customers.StateNo	- -
Country	customer.countryNo	Customers.CountryNo	- -
Pincode	customer.pincode	Customers.Pincode	- -
Email			
Email Address	customer.emailAddress	Customers.EmailAddress	Cannot be left blank
Login Details			
Username	customer.userName	Customers.Username	Cannot be left blank
Password	customer.password	Customers.Password	Cannot be left blank
Special Occasion			
Birthdate	customer.dob	Customers.DOB	- -
Subscribe To			
New Releases	customer.newRelease	Customers.NewRelease	- -
Book Updates	customer.bookUpdates	Customers.BookUpdates	- -

Micro-Help For Form Fields

Form Field	Micro Help Statement
Name	
customer.firstName	Enter the first name
customer.lastName	Enter the last name

Form Field	Micro Help Statement
Mailing Address	
customer.address1	Enter the street address
customer.address2	Enter the street address
customer.city	Enter the city
customer.stateNo	Select the state
customer.countryNo	Select the country
customer.pincode	Enter the pincode
Email	
customer.emailAddress	Enter the email address
Login Details	
customer.userName	Enter the username
customer.password	Enter the password
Special Occasion	
customer.dob	Enter the birthdate
Subscribe To	
customer.newRelease	Select to new releases
customer.bookUpdates	Select to book updates

Data Controls

Object	Label	Name
s:submit	Save	btnSubmit
s:reset	Clear	btnReset

Code Spec

```
1   <%@page contentType="text/html" pageEncoding="UTF-8"%>
2   <%@ taglib prefix="s" uri="/struts-tags" %>
3   <%@ taglib prefix="sx" uri="/struts-dojo-tags" %>
4   <!DOCTYPE HTML PUBLIC "-//W3C//DTD HTML 4.01 Transitional//EN"
5     "http://www.w3.org/TR/html4/loose.dtd">
6   <html>
7     <head>
8       <title>BookShop [Sharanam & Vaishali Shah] - Registration</title>
9       <meta http-equiv="content-type" content="text/html; charset=iso-8859-1">
10      <link href="/BookShop/css/frontend.css" type="text/css" rel="stylesheet">
11      <sx:head parseContent="true"/>
12    </head>
13    <body>
14      <div id="bodyDiv">
15        <s:include value="userHeader.jsp" />
16        <s:form action="doInsertCustomer" method="post" name="frmCustomers"
          id="frmCustomers" validate="true">
17          <s:hidden name="customer.CustomerNo" id="CustomerNo"/>
```

```
18          <table width="100%" border="0" align="center" cellpadding="0"
         cellspacing="0">
19            <tr>
20              <td>
21                <table border="0" cellpadding="0" cellspacing="0" width="100%">
22                  <tr>
23                    <td valign="top" align="left" class="spanHeader">
24                      Sign-Up
25                    </td>
26                    <td class="information">
27                      It is mandatory to enter information in all information
                        <br>capture boxes which have a <span
                        class="mandatory">*</span> adjacent
28                    </td>
29                  </tr>
30                </table>
31              </td>
32            </tr>
33            <tr align="left" valign="top">
34              <td>
35                <table width="90%" border="0" align="center" cellpadding="0"
                   cellspacing="0">
36                  <tr>
37                    <td>
38                      <table width="100%" border="0" cellpadding="0"
                         cellspacing="0">
39                        <tr>
40                          <td class="headingLabel">
41                            <br />Name<br /><br />
42                          </td>
43                        </tr>
44                        <s:textfield required="true" requiredposition="left"
                           id="FirstName" label="First Name"
                           name="customer.FirstName" title="Enter the first name"
                           maxLength="25" size="55"/>
45                        <s:textfield required="true" requiredposition="left"
                           id="LastName" label="Last Name"
                           name="customer.LastName" title="Enter the last name"
                           maxLength="25" size="55"/>
46                        <tr>
47                          <td class="headingLabel">
48                            <br />Mailing Address<br /><br />
49                          </td>
50                        </tr>
51                        <s:textfield id="Address1" label="Address Line 1"
                           name="customer.Address1" title="Enter the street address"
                           maxLength="50" size="55"/>
52                        <s:textfield id="Address2" label="Address Line 2"
                           name="customer.Address2" title="Enter the street address"
                           maxLength="50" size="55"/>
53                        <s:select list="ddlb.ddlbCountries" listKey="CountryNo"
                           listValue="Country" headerKey="" headerValue="Select
                           Country" id="CountryNo" name="customer.CountryNo"
                           label="Country" title="Select the country"></s:select>
```

```
54      <s:select list="ddlb.ddlbStates" listKey="StateNo"
        listValue="State" headerKey="" headerValue="Select State"
        id="StateNo" name="customer.StateNo" label="State"
        title="Select the state"></s:select>
55      <s:textfield id="City" label="City" name="customer.City"
        title="Enter the city name" maxLength="50" size="50"/>
56      <s:textfield id="Pincode" label="Pincode"
        name="customer.Pincode" title="Enter the pincode"
        maxLength="15" size="20"/>
57      <s:actionerror/>
58      <tr>
59         <td class="headingLabel">
60            <br />Email<br /><br />
61         </td>
62      </tr>
63      <s:textfield required="true" requiredposition="left"
        id="EmailAddress" label="Email Address"
        name="customer.EmailAddress" title="Enter the email
        address" maxLength="50" size="55"/>
64      <tr>
65         <td class="headingLabel">
66            <br />Login Details<br /><br />
67         </td>
68      </tr>
69      <s:textfield required="true" requiredposition="left"
        maxLength="25" label="Username"
        name="customer.Username" title="Enter Username" />
70      <s:textfield required="true" requiredposition="left"
        maxLength="8" label="Password" name="customer.Password"
        title="Enter Password" />
71      <tr>
72         <td class="headingLabel">
73            <br />Special Occassion<br /><br />
74         </td>
75      </tr>
76      <sx:datetimepicker name="customer.Dob" label="Birthdate"
        displayFormat="yyyy-MM-dd"/>
77      <tr>
78         <td class="headingLabel">
79            <br />Subscribe To<br /><br />
80         </td>
81      </tr>
82      <s:checkbox label="New Releases" id="NewReleases"
        name="customer.NewRelease"/>
83      <s:checkbox label="Book Updates" id="BookUpdates"
        name="customer.BookUpdates"/>
84               </table>
85            </td>
86         </tr>
87         <tr>
88            <td align="center">
89               <br /><br />
90               <s:submit theme="simple" cssClass="groovybutton"
        name="btnSubmit" id="btnSubmit" value="Save" />
```

```
91                              <s:reset theme="simple" cssClass="groovybutton"
                                   name="btnReset" id="btnReset" value="Clear" />
92                          </td>
93                      </tr>
94                  </table>
95              </td>
96          </tr>
97      </table>
98          </s:form>
99          <s:include value="footer.jsp" />
100     </div>
101     </body>
102 </html>
```

Explanation:

This is a standard data entry form. By default when the form loads, it's in the **INSERT** mode.

After JSP loads, the user can simply key in the required data and click Save . After saving the data in the database, an email is sent to the user indicating a successful sign up and the user is taken to the Sign up Thank You page.

registrationThankYou.jsp

Once Save is clicked, after entering the correct data in the sign up form, the Signup Thank You page is delivered, as shown in diagram 51.2.

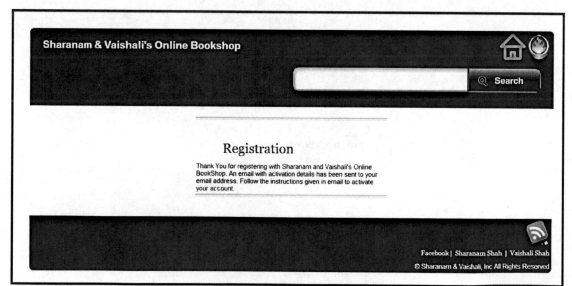

Diagram 51.2: The Signup Thank You page

This is a JSP which holds a thank you message indicating a successful sign up, as shown in diagram 51.2.

Form Specifications

File Name	registrationUpThankYou.jsp
Title	BookShop[Sharanam & Vaishali Shah] - Registration Thank You

Code Spec

```
1  <%@page contentType="text/html" pageEncoding="UTF-8"%>
2  <%@ taglib prefix="s" uri="/struts-tags" %>
3  <%@ taglib prefix="sx" uri="/struts-dojo-tags" %>
4  <!DOCTYPE HTML PUBLIC "-//W3C//DTD HTML 4.01 Transitional//EN"
5    "http://www.w3.org/TR/html4/loose.dtd">
6  <html>
7    <head>
8      <title>BookShop [Sharanam & Vaishali Shah] - Registration Thank You</title>
9      <meta http-equiv="Content-Type" content="text/html; charset=UTF-8">
10     <link href="/BookShop/css/frontend.css" type="text/css" rel="stylesheet">
11     <sx:head parseContent="true"/>
12   </head>
13   <body>
14     <div id="bodyDiv">
15       <s:include value="userHeader.jsp" />
16       <table border="0" cellspacing="0" cellpadding="2" align="center">
17         <tr><td> </td></tr>
18         <tr><td class="hrLine"> </td></tr>
19         <tr><td class="spanHeader">Registration</td></tr>
20         <tr>
21           <td class="thankYouContent">
22             Thank You for registering with Sharanam and Vaishali's Online BookShop. An
               email with activation details has been sent to your email address. Follow the
               instructions given in email to activate your account.
23           </td>
24         </tr>
25         <tr><td class="hrLine"> </td></tr>
26       </table>
27       <s:include value="footer.jsp" />
28     </div>
29   </body>
30 </html>
```

Explanation:

This is a thank you of the sign up form. This page appears once the user registers successfully.

Action Class [RegistrationAction.java]

This is an action class with the following specifications:

Class Name	RegistrationAction
Package	com.sharanamvaishali.action
Extends	ActionSupport
Implements	- -

Objects		
Object Name	**Class Name**	**Object Type**
customerDAO	CustomersDAO	Data Access Object
customer	Customers	Model

Properties			
Property Name	**Property Type**	**Methods**	
For the data entry form fields			
customer	Customers	getCustomer()	setCustomer()

Methods	
Method Name	**Return Values**
execute()	SUCCESS
saveCustomer()	SUCCESS
	ERROR
registrationThankYouMail()	SUCCESS

Code Spec

```
1   package com.sharanamvaishali.action;
2
3   import com.opensymphony.xwork2.ActionContext;
4   import com.opensymphony.xwork2.ActionSupport;
5   import com.sharanamvaishali.dao.CustomersDAO;
6   import com.sharanamvaishali.dao.CustomersDAOImpl;
7   import com.sharanamvaishali.model.Customers;
8   import com.sharanamvaishali.utility.PopulateDdlbs;
9   import com.sharanamvaishali.utility.SendMail;
10  import java.util.Locale;
11  import java.util.ResourceBundle;
12  import org.apache.struts2.interceptor.validation.SkipValidation;
13
14  public class RegistrationAction extends ActionSupport{
15      private CustomersDAO customerDAO = new CustomersDAOImpl();
16
17      private PopulateDdlbs ddlb = new PopulateDdlbs();
18
19      private Customers customer;
```

```
20
21      public PopulateDdlbs getDdlb() {
22          return ddlb;
23      }
24      public void setDdlb(PopulateDdlbs ddlb) {
25          this.ddlb = ddlb;
26      }
27
28      public Customers getCustomer() {
29          return customer;
30      }
31      public void setCustomer(Customers customer) {
32          this.customer = customer;
33      }
34
35      @SkipValidation
36      @Override
37      public String execute(){
38          return SUCCESS;
39      }
40
41      public String saveCustomer() throws Exception{
42          try{
43              customerDAO.saveCustomer(customer);
44              registrationThankYouMail();
45          } catch (Exception e){
46              addActionError(e.getCause().toString().split("[:]")[1]);
47              return ERROR;
48          }
49          return SUCCESS;
50      }
51
52      @SkipValidation
53      public String registrationThankYouMail() throws Exception{
54          Locale locale = ActionContext.getContext().getLocale();
55          ResourceBundle bundle = ResourceBundle.getBundle("bookshop", locale);
56          if(!bundle.getString("emailFrom").equals("") &&
             !bundle.getString("emailUser").equals("") &&
             !bundle.getString("emailFromPasswd").equals("")) {
57              String toEmailAddress = customer.getEmailAddress();
58              String emailSubject = "Sharanam & Vaishali's Online BookShop:
                Registration mail.";
59              String emailMessage = "<table width='500' border='0' align='center'
                cellpadding='15' cellspacing='0' style='font-family:Verdana, Arial,
                Helvetica, sans-serif; font-size:12pt; color:#5a5a5a;'><tr><td
                align='left'>Dear " + customer.getFirstName() + ",</td></tr><tr><td
                align='left'>Your login details are:<br/><br/>Username: " +
                customer.getUsername() + "<br />Password: " + customer.getPassword()
                + "<br /><br/>Thank you for using  this site.<br /><br/>Regards,<br
```

```
          />Sharanam & Vaishali's Online BookShop<br /><br /><br />THIS IS AN
          AUTOMATED MESSAGE; PLEASE DO NOT REPLY. </td></tr></table>";
60        SendMail.sendMail(bundle.getString("emailFrom"),
          bundle.getString("emailUser"), bundle.getString("emailFromPasswd"),
          toEmailAddress, emailSubject, emailMessage);
61      }
62      return SUCCESS;
63    }
64 }
```

Explanation:

The following section describes the above code spec.

execute()

execute() is invoked when the user clicks to register.

execute() makes available the drop down list box values to the Registration data entry form.

@SkipValidation is used to skip validation for this method.

saveCustomer()

saveCustomer() is invoked when the user keys in the desired data and clicks `Save`.

saveCustomer() performs an insert operation [using CustomersDAO's saveCustomer()].

The captured form data is passed as an object of the Customers bean class [**customer**] to CustomersDAO's methods.

registrationThankYouMail()

registrationThankYouMail() when invoked sends an email to the registered user.

registrationThankYouMail() is invoked by saveCustomer() after the user is registered.

@SkipValidation is used to skip validation for this method.

DAO Class

Interface [CustomersDAO.java]

This is a Data Access Object interface with the following specifications:

Class Name	Package
CustomersDAO	com.sharanamvaishali.dao

Code Spec

```
1  package com.sharanamvaishali.dao;
2
3  import com.sharanamvaishali.model.Customers;
4
5  public interface CustomersDAO {
6      public void saveCustomer(Customers customers);
7  }
```

REMINDER

 PopulateDdlbsDAO.java is explained later in the *Section VII: Common Files Software Design Documentation* under the *Chapter 59: Populating Drop Down List Boxes*.

Implementation Class [CustomersDAOImpl.java]

This is a Data Access Object class with the following specifications:

Class Name	CustomersDAOImpl
Package	com.sharanamvaishali.dao
Implements	CustomersDAO

Objects	
Object Name	**Class Name**
session	Session
transaction	Transaction

Methods		
Method Name	**Arguments**	**Return Values**
saveCustomer()	Customers customers	void

Code Spec

```
1  package com.sharanamvaishali.dao;
2
```

```
 3  import com.sharanamvaishali.model.Customers;
 4  import com.sharanamvaishali.utility.HibernateUtil;
 5  import org.hibernate.Session;
 6  import org.hibernate.Transaction;
 7
 8  public class CustomersDAOImpl implements CustomersDAO {
 9      Session session = HibernateUtil.getSession();
10      Transaction transaction;
11
12      @Override
13      public void saveCustomer(Customers customers) {
14          try {
15              transaction = session.beginTransaction();
16              session.save(customers);
17              transaction.commit();
18          } catch (RuntimeException e) {
19              if(customers != null) {
20                  transaction.rollback();
21              }
22              throw e;
23          }
24      }
25  }
```

Explanation:

The following section describes the above code spec.

saveCustomer()

saveCustomer() does the actual saving of the customer in the Customers database table.

saveCustomer() uses **save()** of Session, which takes care of adding new customer details when the user has entered all the customer details and clicked [**Save**].

After the save operation is performed, the transaction is committed to make the changes permanent.

Whilst performing the save operation, if a runtime exception occurs, the transaction is **rolled back**.

Validations [RegistrationAction-validation.xml]

If the required **input** fields are kept empty whilst submitting the form, RegistrationAction-validation.xml takes care of the validations.

Code Spec

```
1   <?xml version="1.0" encoding="UTF-8"?>
2   <!DOCTYPE validators PUBLIC '-//OpenSymphony Group//XWork Validator
    1.0.2//EN' 'http://www.opensymphony.com/xwork/xwork-validator-1.0.2.dtd'>
3   <validators>
4     <field name="customer.FirstName">
5       <field-validator type="requiredstring">
6         <message>Please enter the first name.</message>
7       </field-validator>
8     </field>
9
10    <field name="customer.LastName">
11      <field-validator type="requiredstring">
12        <message>Please enter the last name.</message>
13      </field-validator>
14    </field>
15
16    <field name="customer.EmailAddress">
17      <field-validator type="requiredstring" short-circuit="true">
18        <message>Please enter the email address.</message>
19      </field-validator>
20      <field-validator type="email" short-circuit="true">
21        <message>Invalid email address.</message>
22      </field-validator>
23    </field>
24
25    <field name="customer.Username">
26      <field-validator type="requiredstring">
27        <message>Please enter the username.</message>
28      </field-validator>
29    </field>
30
31    <field name="customer.Password">
32      <field-validator type="requiredstring">
33        <message>Please enter the password.</message>
34      </field-validator>
35    </field>
36  </validators>
```

If any Errors are detected the data entry form is re-served with appropriate error messages, as shown in diagram 51.3.

struts-Registration.xml file holds a mapping to serve the data entry form:

```
15    <action name="doInsertCustomer" method="saveCustomer"
      class="com.sharanamvaishali.action.RegistrationAction">
16      <result name="success"
```

```
           type="redirectAction">showRegistrationThankYouPage</result>
17         <result name="input">/frontend/registration.jsp</result>
18         <result name="error">/frontend/registration.jsp</result>
19     </action>
```

Sharanam & Vaishali's Online Bookshop

🔍 **Search**

Sign-Up

It is mandatory to enter information in all information capture boxes which have a * adjacent

Name

Please enter the first name.
*First Name:

Please enter the last name.
*Last Name:

Mailing Address

Address Line 1:
Address Line 2:
Country: Select Country ▾
State: Select State ▾
City:
Pincode:

Email

Please enter the email address.
*Email Address:

Login Details

*Username:
*Password:

Special Occassion

Birthdate: 📅

Subscribe To

☐ New Releases
☐ Book Updates

Save   Clear

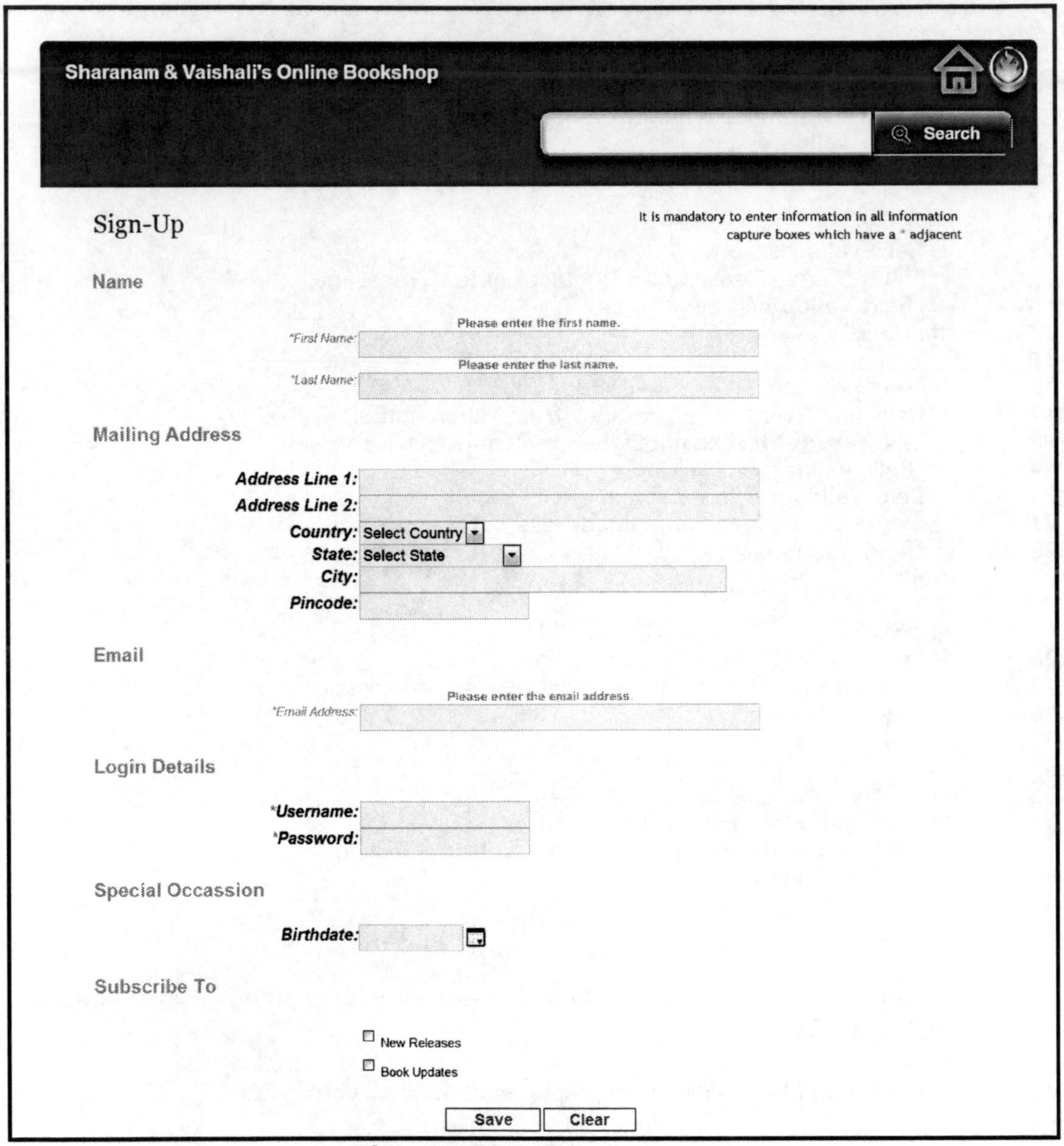

Diagram 51.3: Error messages

REMINDER

In the diagram 51.3, the error message for Username and Password are not displayed even though they are mandatory. The reason being that the previous validator i.e. Email Address is marked as short-circuit. The validators marked as short-circuit will prevent the evaluation of subsequent validators i.e. the validators of Username and Password.

Struts Configuration [struts-Registration.xml]

This is the struts configuration file with the following specifications:

File Name	Package Name	Extends
Registration	registration	default

Actions	
Action Name	**Results**
showRegistrationThankYouPage	SUCCESS - registrationThankYou.jsp
showRegistrationPage	SUCCESS - registration.jsp
doInsertCustomer	SUCCESS - showRegistrationThankYouPage INPUT - registration.jsp ERROR - registration.jsp

Code Spec

```
1   <?xml version="1.0" encoding="UTF-8"?>
2   <!DOCTYPE struts PUBLIC
3   "-//Apache Software Foundation//DTD Struts Configuration 2.0//EN"
4   "http://struts.apache.org/dtds/struts-2.0.dtd">
5   <struts>
6     <package name="registration" extends="default">
7       <action name="showRegistrationThankYouPage">
8         <result>/frontend/registrationThankYou.jsp</result>
9       </action>
10
11      <action name="showRegistrationPage"
        class="com.sharanamvaishali.action.RegistrationAction">
12        <result>/frontend/registration.jsp</result>
13      </action>
14
15      <action name="doInsertCustomer" method="saveCustomer"
        class="com.sharanamvaishali.action.RegistrationAction">
16        <result name="success"
          type="redirectAction">showRegistrationThankYouPage</result>
17        <result name="input">/frontend/registration.jsp</result>
18        <result name="error">/frontend/registration.jsp</result>
19      </action>
```

```
20   </package>
21  </struts>
```

Explanation:

The following section describes the above code spec.

showRegistrationThankYouPage.action

showRegistrationThankYouPage is an action to help viewing.

This means the registration thank you is displayed after successful registration.

showRegistrationPage.action

showRegistrationPage is an action to help initializing the data entry form.

This means the registration data entry form is displayed to the user to register.

doInsertCustomer.action

doInsertCustomer is an action to help adding new customer details.

doInsertCustomer.action:

❑ Calls **RegistrationAction's saveCustomer()** to add new customer details
❑ Ensures that the captured data is valid
❑ If the validation is successful then the data is saved and the result is redirected to **showRegistrationThankYouPage.action**
❑ If the validation fails then the Sign Up page along with error messages is displayed

REMINDER

Customers.java [the model class] is explained in the *Chapter 39: Manage Customers*.

SECTION VI: FRONTEND [CUSTOMER FACING] SOFTWARE DESIGN DOCUMENTATION

Forgot Password

Forgot Password is a data entry form which retrieves the password and sends the same via an email when the appropriate username is entered.

This module uses the bms.Customers table to perform the above operations.

This module is made up of the following:

Type	Name	Description
JSP	forogtPassword.jsp	The data entry form.
Struts 2		
Action	CustomerLoginAction.java	The action class that facilitates data operations.
DAO Class	LoginDAO.java	The interface for the DAO layer.
	LoginDAOImpl.java	The implementation class that performs the actual data operations.

Type	Name	Description
Struts 2 [Continued]		
Struts Configuration	struts-CustomerLogin.xml	The Struts configuration file.
Hibernate		
Mapping	hibernate.cfg.xml	The mapping file that holds Model class mapping.
Model Class	Customers.java	The model class.

JSP [forgotPassword.jsp]

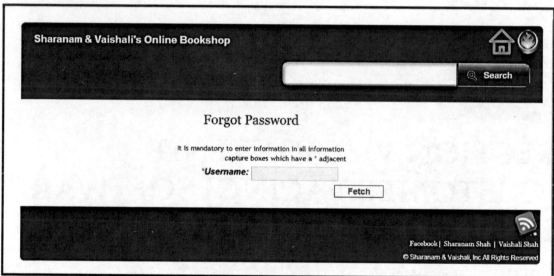

Diagram 52.1: The Forgot Password data entry form

This is a JSP which holds a data entry form, as shown in diagram 52.1. This form appears when the user clicks Forgot Password link available on the home page of the application.

Form Specifications

File Name	forgotPassword.jsp
Title	BookShop[Sharanam & Vaishali Shah] - Forgot Password
Bound To Table	bms.Customers
Form Name	frmForgotPassword
Action	doRetrievePassword
Method	POST

Data Fields

Label	Name	Bound To	Validation Rules
Username	customer.Username	Customers.Username	Cannot be left blank

Micro-Help For Form Fields

Form Field	Micro Help Statement
customer.Username	Enter the username

Data Controls

Object	Label	Name
s:submit	Fetch	SendPassword

Code Spec

```
1   <%@page contentType="text/html" pageEncoding="UTF-8"%>
2   <%@ taglib prefix="s" uri="/struts-tags" %>
3   <%@ taglib prefix="sx" uri="/struts-dojo-tags" %>
4   <!DOCTYPE HTML PUBLIC "-//W3C//DTD HTML 4.01 Transitional//EN"
5     "http://www.w3.org/TR/html4/loose.dtd">
6   <html>
7     <head>
8       <title>BookShop [Sharanam & Vaishali Shah] - Forgot Password</title>
9       <meta http-equiv="content-type" content="text/html; charset=iso-8859-1">
10      <link href="/BookShop/css/frontend.css" type="text/css" rel="stylesheet">
11      <sx:head parseContent="true"/>
12    </head>
13    <body>
14      <div id="bodyDiv">
15        <s:include value="userHeader.jsp" />
16        <s:form name="frmForgotPassword" method="post" action="doRetrievePassword">
17          <table border="0" cellspacing="0" cellpadding="2" align="center">
18            <tr>
19              <td colspan="2" class="spanHeader">
20                Forgot Password
21              </td>
22            </tr>
23            <tr>
24              <td colspan="2" class="information">
25                It is mandatory to enter information in all information <br>capture boxes
                  which have a <span class="mandatory">*</span> adjacent
26              </td>
27            </tr>
28            <tr>
29              <td colspan="2" class="error">
30                <s:property value="message" />
```

```
31                      </td>
32                    </tr>
33              <s:textfield required="true" requiredposition="left" maxLength="25"
                    label="Username" name="customer.Username" title="Enter the username"/>
34              <tr>
35                  <td colspan="2" valign="top" align="center">
36                      <s:submit cssClass="groovybutton" title="Retrieve Password"
                        name="SendPassword" value="Fetch" />
37                  </td>
38                </tr>
39              </table>
40          </s:form>
41          <s:include value="footer.jsp" />
42      </div>
43    </body>
44  </html>
```

Explanation:

The Forgot password data entry form retrieves the password for the customers who have forgotten their password.

The password of the customer is send via an email, if the user enters the correct username.

Action Class [CustomerLoginAction.java]

This is an action class with the following specifications:

Class Name	CustomerLoginAction
Package	com.sharanamvaishali.action
Extends	ActionSupport
Implements	- -

Objects		
Object Name	**Class Name**	**Object Type**
loginDAO	LoginDAO	Data Access Object
customer	Customers	Model

Properties		
Property Name	**Property Type**	**Methods**
For the data entry form fields		
customer	Customers	getCustomer()	setCustomer()
messge	String	getMessage()	- -

Methods	
Method Name	**Return Values**
retrieveCustomerPassword()	SUCCESS ERROR

Code Spec

```
1   package com.sharanamvaishali.action;
2
3   import com.opensymphony.xwork2.ActionContext;
4   import com.opensymphony.xwork2.ActionSupport;
5   import com.sharanamvaishali.dao.LoginDAO;
6   import com.sharanamvaishali.dao.LoginDAOImpl;
7   import com.sharanamvaishali.model.Customers;
8   import com.sharanamvaishali.utility.SendMail;
9   import java.util.*;
10
11  public class CustomerLoginAction extends ActionSupport {
12      private LoginDAO loginDAO = new LoginDAOImpl();
13
14      private Customers customer;
15
16      private String message;
17
18      public String getMessage() {
19          return message;
20      }
21
22      public Customers getCustomer() {
23          return customer;
24      }
25      public void setCustomer(Customers customer) {
26          this.customer = customer;
27      }
28
29      public String retrieveCustomerPassword() throws Exception {
30          Customers objCustomers = (Customers)
            loginDAO.getCustomerPassword(customer.getUsername());
31          if(objCustomers != null){
32              Locale locale = ActionContext.getContext().getLocale();
33              ResourceBundle bundle = ResourceBundle.getBundle("bookshop", locale);
34              if(!bundle.getString("emailFrom").equals("") &&
                !bundle.getString("emailUser").equals("") &&
                !bundle.getString("emailFromPasswd").equals("")) {
35                  String toEmailAddress = objCustomers.getEmailAddress();
36                  String emailSubject = "Sharanam & Vaishali's Online Bookshop: Forgot
                    Password mail";
37                  String emailMessage = "<table width='500' border='0' align='center'
                    cellpadding='15' cellspacing='0' style='font-family:Verdana, Arial,
                    Helvetica, sans-serif; font-size:12pt; color:#5a5a5a;'><tr><td
                    align='left'>Dear " + objCustomers.getFirstName() +
                    ",</td></tr><tr><td align='left'>As requested, please find your login
```

```
     details below:<br/><br/>Username: " + objCustomers.getUsername()
     + "<br />Password: " + objCustomers.getPassword() + "<br
     /><br/>Thank you for using  this site.<br /><br/>Regards,<br
     />Sharanam & Vaishali's Online BookShop<br /><br />THIS IS AN
     AUTOMATED MESSAGE; PLEASE DO NOT REPLY.</td></tr></table>";
38   SendMail.sendMail(bundle.getString("emailFrom"),
     bundle.getString("emailUser"), bundle.getString("emailFromPasswd"),
     toEmailAddress, emailSubject, emailMessage);
39        }
40      } else {
41        message = "Invalid Username or Email Address. Please try again";
42        return ERROR;
43      }
44      return SUCCESS;
45   }
46 }
```

Explanation:

The following section describes the above code spec.

retrieveCustomerPassword()

retrieveCustomerPassword() is invoked when the user keys in the username and clicks
Fetch using the Forgot Password data entry form.

retrieveCustomerPassword() retrieves the appropriate Customer's details using **Username** as
the reference. It calls LoginDAO's getCustomerPassword(), which returns the details of the
customer as a Customer Object.

Customer object then validates and returns an object with the authenticated customer's data.
If the object holds customer data then an email is sent to the customer's registered email
address with the login details. If the object does not hold user data then an appropriate error
message is send to the Forgot Password page.

Diagram 52.2: Forgot Password [Error message]

DAO Class

Interface [LoginDAO.java]

This is a Data Access Object interface with the following specifications:

Class Name	Package
LoginDAO	com.sharanamvaishali.dao

Code Spec

```
1  package com.sharanamvaishali.dao;
2
3  public interface LoginDAO {
4      public Object getCustomerPassword(String Username);
5  }
```

Implementation Class [LoginDAOImpl.java]

This is a Data Access Object class with the following specifications:

Class Name	LoginDAOImpl
Package	com.sharanamvaishali.dao

Implements	LoginDAO	
Objects		
Object Name		**Class Name**
session		Session
Methods		
Method Name	**Arguments**	**Return Values**
getCustomerPassword()	String Username	Object

Code Spec

```
1   package com.sharanamvaishali.dao;
2
3   import com.sharanamvaishali.utility.HibernateUtil;
4   import org.hibernate.Session;
5
6   public class LoginDAOImpl implements LoginDAO {
7       Session session = HibernateUtil.getSession();
8
9       @Override
10      public Object getCustomerPassword(String Username) {
11          return session.createQuery("FROM Customers WHERE Username =
            :Username").setString("Username", Username).uniqueResult();
12      }
13  }
```

Explanation:

The following section describes the above code spec.

getCustomerPassword()

getCustomerPassword() is invoked by CustomerLoginAction's **retrieveCustomerPassword()** to retrieve the forgotten password.

getCustomerPassword() receives Username which is used as the WHERE clause criteria. It queries the Customers database tables using Hibernate Session's **createQuery()** to retrieve the chosen record's data to return to retrieveCustomerPassword():

FROM Customers WHERE Username = :Username

getCustomerPassword() uses:

❑ **setString()** of Query, which states the parameter to be used as the WHERE clause criteria when querying the Customers database table

❑ **uniqueResult()** of Query, which ensures that only unique record is retrieved from the Customers database table and prevents any kinds of errors

Struts Configuration [struts-CustomerLogin.xml]

This is the struts configuration file with the following specifications:

File Name	Package Name	Extends
CustomerLogin	frontendLogin	default

Actions	
Action Name	**Results**
doRetrievePassword	SUCCESS - showHomePage ERROR - forgotPassword.jsp
showForgotPassword	SUCCESS - forgotPassword.jsp

Code Spec

```
1   <?xml version="1.0" encoding="UTF-8"?>
2   <!DOCTYPE struts PUBLIC
3   "-//Apache Software Foundation//DTD Struts Configuration 2.0//EN"
4   "http://struts.apache.org/dtds/struts-2.0.dtd">
5   <struts>
6     <package name="frontendLogin" extends="default">
7       <action name="doRetrievePassword" method="retrieveCustomerPassword"
        class="com.sharanamvaishali.action.CustomerLoginAction">
8         <result name="success" type="redirectAction">showHomePage</result>
9         <result name="error">/frontend/forgotPassword.jsp</result>
10      </action>
11
12      <action name="showForgotPassword">
13        <result>/frontend/forgotPassword.jsp</result>
14      </action>
15    </package>
16  </struts>
```

Explanation:

The following section describes the above code spec.

doRetrievePassword.action

doRetrievePassword is an action to help retrieve the customer's login details via an email.

doRetrievePassword.action:

❑ Calls **CustomerLoginAction's retrieveCustomerPassword()** to retrieve customer's login details

❑ Ensures that the captured data is valid

❑ If the validation is successful then the data is retrieved and the same is send via an email to the appropriate customer and the customer is redirected to **showHomePage.action**

❑ If the validation fails then the Forgot Password page along with error messages is displayed

showForgotPassword.action

showForgotPassword is an action to help initializing the data entry form.

This means the forgot password data entry form is displayed to the user to retrieve the forgotten password.

REMINDER

Only the actions related to Forgot Password are explained in this chapter. The remaining actions are explained earlier in the *Chapter 43: Homepage*.

REMINDER

Customers.java [the model class] is explained in the *Chapter 39: Manage Customers*.

Chapter

53

SECTION VI: FRONTEND [CUSTOMER FACING] SOFTWARE DESIGN DOCUMENTATION

Common Includes

Frontend Header

This module is made up of the following:

Type	Name	Description
JSP	userHeader.jsp	The header of the frontend [customer facing] section.

JSP [userHeader.jsp]

When the user is not logged in, the header appears, as shown in diagram 53.1.

Diagram 53.1: Header of the Frontend Section [User not logged in]

When the user is logged in, the header appears, as shown in diagram 53.2.

Diagram 53.2: Header of the Frontend Section [User logged in]

This file is included in the beginning of the BODY section in all the frontend files:

```
<body>
  <div id="bodyDiv">
    <s:include value="userHeader.jsp" />
```

Form Specifications

File Name	userHeader.jsp
Form Name	frmSearch
Method	POST

Data Fields

Label	Name	Bound To	Validation Rules
- -	SearchCriteria	- -	- -

Micro-Help For Form Fields

Form Field	Micro Help Statement
SearchCriteria	Enter the search criteria

Data Controls

Object	Label	Name	Action
s:submit	- -	Search	performSearch.action

Code Spec

```
1  <%@page contentType="text/html" pageEncoding="UTF-8"%>
2  <%@ taglib prefix="s" uri="/struts-tags" %>
3  <!DOCTYPE HTML PUBLIC "-//W3C//DTD HTML 4.01 Transitional//EN"
4    "http://www.w3.org/TR/html4/loose.dtd">
5  <div id="headerDiv">
6    <table border="0" cellpadding="0" cellspacing="0" width="100%">
7      <tr>
8        <td width="45%" class="topAlign" align="left">
9          <table id="welcome" border="0" width="100%">
10           <tr>
11             <td>
12               <h2>Sharanam & Vaishali's Online Bookshop</h2>
13             </td>
14           </tr>
15           <tr>
16             <td class="Arial13WhiteB">
17               <s:if test="#session.username==null"> </s:if>
18               <s:else>
19                 Last Login IP:<s:property value="#session.lastip" />  
20                 Last Login Date:<s:property value="#session.lastlogin" />
21               </s:else>
22             </td>
23           </tr>
24         </table>
25       </td>
26       <td width="55%">
27         <table border="0" width="100%">
28           <tr>
29             <td>
30               <s:if test="#session.username==null">
31                 <table border="0" valign="top" align="right" cellpadding="0"
                     cellspacing="0">
32                   .  <tr>
33                       <td>
34                         <s:a href="showHomePage.action">
35                           <img src="/BookShop/images/home.png" title="Home
                              (End User)"/>
36                         </s:a>
37                       </td>
38                       <td>
39                         <s:a href="showRegistrationPage.action">
40                           <img src="/BookShop/images/signup.png" title="Sign
                              Up"/>
41                         </s:a>
42                       </td>
43                     </tr>
44                 </table>
45               </s:if>
46               <s:else>
47                 <table border="0" valign="top" align="right" cellpadding="0"
                     cellspacing="0">
```

```
48                        <tr>
49                          <td>
50                            <s:a href="showHomePage.action">
51                              <img src="/BookShop/images/home.png" title="Home
                                (End User)"/>
52                            </s:a>
53                          </td>
54                          <td>
55                            <s:a href="showCart.action">
56                              <img src="/BookShop/images/showCart.png" title="Show
                                Cart"/>
57                            </s:a>
58                          </td>
59                          <td>
60                            <a href="<s:url action="doCustomerLogout" />">
61                              <img src="/BookShop/images/logout.png"
                                title="Logout"/>
62                            </a>
63                          </td>
64                        </tr>
65                      </table>
66                    </s:else>
67                  </td>
68                </tr>
69                <tr>
70                  <td align="right">
71                    <br/>
72                    <s:form name="frmSearch" id="frmSearch" method="post">
73                      <table border="0" cellspacing="0" cellpadding="0" width="100%">
74                        <tr>
75                          <td align="right">
76                            <table border="0" cellpadding="0" cellspacing="0">
77                              <s:textfield id="SearchCriteria" name="SearchCriteria"
                                cssClass="search-text" title="Enter the search criteria"/>
78                            </table>
79                          </td>
80                          <td align="left">
81                            <table border="0" width="100%" cellpadding="0"
                                cellspacing="0">
82                              <s:submit action="performSearch" theme="simple"
                                cssClass="search-button" name="Search" id="Search"
                                value="" />
83                            </table>
84                          </td>
85                        </tr>
86                      </table>
87                    </s:form>
88                  </td>
89                </tr>
90              </table>
91            </td>
92          </tr>
93        </table>
94    </div>
```

Explanation:

This is a JSP which holds the header of the frontend section. It also holds the search form, where the user can search for books.

When the user is logged in, the links Home, Show Cart and Logout are displayed along with the last login date and IP address of the user who has logged in, as shown in diagram 53.2.

When the user is not logged in, the links Home and Sign Up are displayed, as shown in diagram 53.1.

Frontend Footer

This module is made up of the following:

Type	Name	Description
JSP	footer.jsp	The footer of the frontend [customer facing] section.

JSP [footer.jsp]

Diagram 53.3: Footer of the Frontend [customer facing] Section

This is a JSP which holds the footer of the frontend section, as shown in diagram 50.3.

This file is included at the end of the BODY section in all the frontend files:

```
    <s:include value="footer.jsp" />
  </div>
</body>
```

Code Spec

```
1  <%@page contentType="text/html" pageEncoding="UTF-8"%>
2  <%@ taglib prefix="s" uri="/struts-tags" %>
3  <div class="frontendFooter" id="frontendFooter">
4      <div id="frontendFooterContainer">
5          <div id="copyright">
6                
7              <s:a href="admin.action"><img src="/BookShop/images/admin.png"
                 title="Administration"/></s:a>
8              <br/>
9              <span><a href="http://www.facebook.com/sharanamvaishali"
```

```
        target="_blank">Facebook</a> | </span>
10      <span><a href="http://www.sharanamshah.com" target="_blank">Sharanam
        Shah</a></span>
11       | 
12      <span><a href="http://www.vaishalishahonline.com" target="_blank">Vaishali
        Shah</a></span>
13      <br/>
14      <span>&copy; Sharanam & Vaishali, Inc All Rights Reserved </span>
15    </div>
16   </div>
17 </div>
```

Explanation:

This JSP is the footer file of the frontend section.

This JSP holds:

❑   The link to the administration section

❑   The name of the creator of the application

Stylesheet

This module is made up of the following:

Type	Name	Description
CSS	frontend.css	The stylesheet for the frontend [customer facing] section.

Code Spec

```
1  html {
2      overflow-y: scroll;
3      overflow-x: auto;
4      height:100%;
5  }
6
7  body {
8      width: 95%;
9      height:100%;
10     font-family: helvetica, arial, sans-serif;
11     font-size: 12px;
12     color: #333;
13     text-decoration: none;
14     margin: 30px;
15     padding: 0;
16     background: url('/BookShop/images/chess.jpg') no-repeat center center fixed;
17     -webkit-background-size: cover;
18     -moz-background-size: cover;
```

```
19      -o-background-size: cover;
20      background-size: cover;
21   }
22
23   img {
24      border: none;
25   }
26
27   fieldset {
28      padding: 10px 10px;
29      border: 1px solid #663366;
30      -moz-border-radius: 8px;
31      border-radius: 8px;
32   }
33
34   legend {
35      background: #663366;
36      color:#fff;
37      border: solid 1px black;
38      -webkit-border-radius: 8px;
39      -moz-border-radius: 8px;
40      border-radius: 8px;
41      padding: 6px;
42   }
43
44   #bodyDiv {
45      position: absolute;
46      background-image: url('/BookShop/images/mainbg.png');
47      background-repeat:repeat;
48      width:95%;
49   }
50
51   #headerDiv {
52      height:138px;
53      background-image: url(../images/transparent-bg.png);
54      width:100%;
55      border: 2px solid #000;
56      -moz-border-radius: 8px;
57      border-radius: 8px;
58      -moz-border-bottom-left-radius: 0px;
59      -moz-border-bottom-right-radius: 0px;
60      border-bottom-left-radius: 0px;
61      border-bottom-right-radius: 0px;
62   }
63
64   #welcome {
65      float:left;
66      color:white;
67      padding-left: 20px;
```

```
68  }
69
70  #portlets-head-main {
71      text-align: left;
72      font-size: 16px!important;
73      color: #333333;
74      background: #D8D8D8;
75      filter: progid:DXImageTransform.Microsoft.gradient(startColorstr='#ffffff',
            endColorstr='#D8D8D8');
76      background: -webkit-gradient(linear, left top, left bottom, from(#ffffff),
            to(#D8D8D8));
77      background: -moz-linear-gradient(top, #ffffff, #D8D8D8);
78      border: 1px solid #D8D8D8;
79      -moz-border-top-right-radius: 4px;
80      border-top-right-radius: 4px;
81      padding: 5px 0px 5px 5px;
82  }
83
84  #portlets-content-main {
85      padding: 10px 10px;
86      border: 2px;
87      -moz-box-shadow: 4px 4px 4px #663366;
88      -webkit-box-shadow: 4px 4px 4px #663366;
89      box-shadow: 4px 4px 4px #663366;
90      -moz-border-radius: 4px;
91      border-radius: 4px;
92  }
93
94  #searchBar {
95      text-align: right;
96      height: 50px;
97      width:100%;
98      line-height: 5px;
99  }
100
101 .search-text {
102     padding: 0 30px 0 10px;
103     margin: 0;
104     border: 0;
105     line-height:40px;
106     background: #ffffff;
107     height:43px;
108     background:url('/BookShop/images/text-input-bg.png') no-repeat;
109     font-family: sans-serif;
110     font-size: 25px;
111     color: #333333;
112 }
113
114 .search-button {
```

```
115    height: 28px;
116    padding: 0 30px 0 10px;
117    margin: 0;
118    border: 0;
119    width:135px;
120    height:43px;
121    font-family: sans-serif;
122    font-size: 14px;
123    color: #333333;
124    background: #ffffff;
125    line-height:28px;
126    vertical-align: top;
127    background:url('/BookShop/images/search-button.png') no-repeat center;
128 }
129
130 #frontendFooter {
131    color:white;
132    margin-top: 20px;
133    float:left;
134    position:relative;
135    width: 100%;
136    background-image: url('/BookShop/images/transparent-bg.png');
137    border-radius: 8px;
138    -moz-border-top-left-radius: 0px;
139    -moz-border-top-right-radius: 0px;
140    border-top-left-radius: 0px;
141    border-top-right-radius: 0px;
142 }
143
144 #frontendFooter a{
145    text-decoration: none;
146    color: #fff;
147 }
148
149 #copyright {
150    text-align:right;
151 }
152
153 #copyright span {
154    line-height:25px;
155 }
156
157 #footerContainer {
158    width:100%;
159    padding: 20px 0 20px 0;
160    margin-left:auto;
161    margin-right:auto;
162 }
163
```

```
164  a {
165     text-decoration: none;
166     color: #660000;
167     font-family: Georgia, serif;
168  }
169
170  a:hover {
171     text-decoration: none;
172     color: #FF0000;
173     font-family: Georgia, serif;
174  }
175
176  .label {
177     font-family: "Arial", Times, serif;
178     font-size: 16px;
179     font-weight: bold;
180     color: #990000;
181  }
182
183  .headingLabel {
184     font-family: "Arial", Times, serif;
185     font-size: 18px;
186     font-weight: bold;
187     color: #0099ff;
188  }
189
190  .categoriesNames {
191     font-family: Verdana,Arial,Helvetica,sans-serif;
192     font-size: 16px;
193     font-weight: bold;
194     color: #990000;
195     text-align: left;
196     vertical-align: top;
197  }
198
199  .groovybutton {
200     font-size:15px;
201     font-weight:bold;
202     color:#CC0000;
203     background-color:#FFFFFF;
204     filter:progid:DXImageTransform.Microsoft.Gradient(GradientType=0,StartColor
        Str='#ffCC99FF',EndColorStr='#ffFFFFCC');
205     border-top-style:groove;
206     border-top-color:#FF0099;
207     border-bottom-style:groove;
208     border-bottom-color:#FF0099;
209     border-left-style:groove;
210     border-left-color:#FF0099;
```

```
211     border-right-style:groove;
212     border-right-color:#FF0099;
213     width: 90px;
214  }
215
216  INPUT, SELECT {
217     font: 14px/20px Arial, Helvetica, sans-serif;
218     color: #0b0b0b;
219     border: #c3bca4 1px solid;
220     height: 22px;
221     background-color: #efebde;
222  }
223
224  .hrLine {
225     height: 20px;
226     background: url('/BookShop/images/hr.jpg') repeat-x;
227  }
228
229  .view {
230     border: 0px solid blue;
231     border-collapse: collapse;
232  }
233
234  .view th {
235     background-color: #EFEBDE;
236     color: #666;
237     text-align: left;
238     border: 1px solid white;
239     padding: 5px;
240  }
241
242  .view td {
243     padding: 3px;
244  }
245
246  .view tr.odd {
247     background-color: #fafbff;
248  }
249
250  .view tr.even {
251     background-color: #EFEBDE;
252  }
253
254  .spanHeader {
255     font: 24px/30px Georgia, serif;
256     width:300px;
257     color: #786e4e;
258     height:37px;
```

```
259      text-align: left;
260      vertical-align: top;
261      padding-top: 20px;
262      padding-left: 50px;
263  }
264
265  .thankYouContent {
266      vertical-align: top;
267      text-align: left;
268      width: 300px;
269  }
270
271  .information {
272      font-weight: normal;
273      font-size: 13px;
274      color: #333333;
275      font-family: "Trebuchet MS";
276      text-decoration: none;
277      text-align: right;
278      vertical-align: top;
279      padding-top: 20px;
280      padding-right: 70px;
281  }
282
283  .mandatory {
284      font-weight: bold;
285      font-size: 13px;
286      color: #0099ff;
287      font-family: "Trebuchet MS";
288  }
289
290  .error {
291      color: red;
292  }
293
294  .searchName {
295      font-family: "Arial", Times, serif;
296      font-size: 15px;
297      font-weight: bold;
298      color: blue;
299      line-height: 20px;
300  }
301
302  .searchYear {
303      font-family: "Arial", Times, serif;
304      font-size: 13px;
305      font-weight: bold;
306      color: green;
```

```
307        line-height: 30px;
308    }
309
310    .searchSynopsis {
311        font-family: "Arial", Times, serif;
312        font-size: 13px;
313        font-weight: bold;
314        color: #666666;
315        line-height: 18px;
316    }
317
318    .allCategoriesTable {
319        position: relative;
320        float: left;
321    }
322
323    .topAlign {
324        vertical-align: top;
325    }
326
327    .loginButton {
328        background: url('/BookShop/images/login.jpg') no-repeat;
329        border: 0;
330        cursor: pointer;
331        width: 68px;
332        height: 40px;
333        text-align: right;
334        vertical-align: top;
335    }
336
337    .spanShowDetails {
338        font: 32px/34px Georgia,serif;
339        width: 300px;
340        color: #990000;
341        height: 37px;
342    }
343
344    .showBookList {
345        vertical-align: top;
346        text-align: left;
347        cursor: pointer;
348    }
349
350    .showCartList {
351        vertical-align: top;
352        border: 1px solid #990033;
353        background-color: #FFFF99;
354    }
355
```

```
356   .Arial13WhiteB {
357       font-family: "Arial", Times, serif;
358       font-size: 13px;
359       font-weight: bold;
360       color: white;
361   }
362
363   .Arial15BrownB {
364       font-family: "Arial", Times, serif;
365       font-size: 15px;
366       font-weight: bold;
367       color: #990000;
368   }
369
370   .Arial16GrayN {
371       font-family: "Arial", Times, serif;
372       font-size: 16px;
373       font-weight: normal;
374       color: #666666;
375   }
376
377   .Arial14GrayN {
378       font-family: "Arial", Times, serif;
379       font-size: 14px;
380       font-weight: normal;
381       color: #666666;
382   }
```

Chapter

54

SECTION VII: COMMON FILES SOFTWARE DESIGN DOCUMENTATION

Common JavaServer Pages

Exception Error Message Page

This module is made up of the following:

Type	Name	Description
JSP	error.jsp	The error page for catching exception errors.

JSP [error.jsp]

This JSP displays the error messages related to **java.lang.Exception**.

Your are seeing the error page.

Click here to return to the site.

In order that the development team can address this error, please report what you were doing that caused this error.

The following information can help the development team find where the error happened and what can be done to prevent it from happening in the future.

```
        java.lang.NullPointerException
at com.sharanamvaishali.dao.BooksDAOImpl.updateHits(BooksDAOImpl.java:106)
at com.sharanamvaishali.action.ShowBookDetailsAction.viewBooks(ShowBookDetailsAction.java:44)
at sun.reflect.NativeMethodAccessorImpl.invoke0(Native Method)
```

Diagram 54.1: Exception related errors

This file is specified in web.xml:

```
24    <error-page>
25       <exception-type>java.lang.Exception</exception-type>
26       <location>/error.jsp</location>
27    </error-page>
```

Code Spec

```
1    <!DOCTYPE HTML PUBLIC "-//W3C//DTD HTML 4.0 Transitional//EN">
2    <%@ page isErrorPage="true" %>
3    <html>
4      <head>
5        <title>BookShop [Sharanam & Vaishali Shah] - Error Page</title>
6        <link href="/BookShop/css/frontend.css" type="text/css" rel="stylesheet">
7      </head>
8      <body>
9        <font size="4" color="red">Your are seeing the error page.</font>
10       <br><br>
11       <font size="2">Click<a href="showHomePage.action"> here </a>to return to the
         site.</font>
12       <br><br>
13       <p style="font-family:serif; font-size:small; text-align:justify;">
14          In order that the development team can address this error, please report what you
            were doing that caused this error.
15          <br/><br/>
16          The following information can help the development team find where the error
            happened and what can be done to prevent it from happening in the future.
17       </p>
18       <br/>
19       <%
20          if(null == exception) {
21             exception =
               (Throwable)request.getAttribute("org.apache.struts.action.EXCEPTION");
22          }
23       %>
24       <pre style="font-size:12px; text-align:left;">
25          <%
```

```
26              if(null == exception) {
27                  out.write("Source of error is unknown.");
28              } else {
29                  java.io.StringWriter sw = new java.io.StringWriter();
30                  java.io.PrintWriter pw = new java.io.PrintWriter(sw);
31                  exception.printStackTrace(pw);
32                  out.write(sw.getBuffer().toString());
33              }
34          %>
35      </pre>
36  </body>
37 </html>
```

Explanation:

This is a JSP which catches **java.lang.Exception** errors and displays the same to the user.

java.lang.Exception indicates conditions that a reasonable application might want to catch.

404 or Not Found Error Message Page

This module is made up of the following:

Type	Name	Description
JSP	pagenotfound.jsp	The error message page for 404 or page not found.

JSP [pagenotfound.jsp]

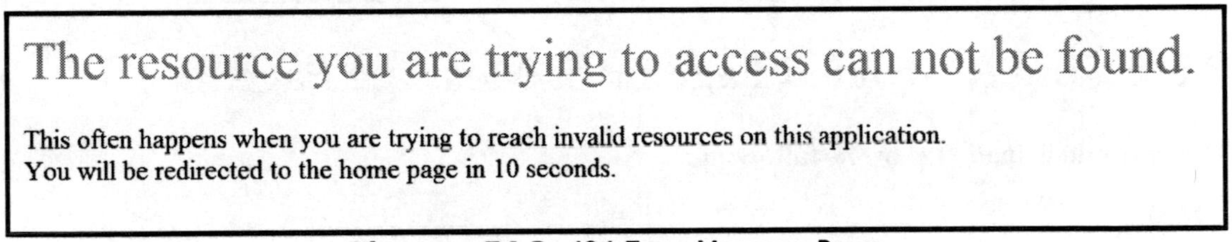

The resource you are trying to access can not be found.

This often happens when you are trying to reach invalid resources on this application.
You will be redirected to the home page in 10 seconds.

Diagram 54.2: 404 Error Message Page

This is a JSP which displays 404 or Not Found error message, as shown in diagram 54.2.

This file is specified in web.xml:

```
20      <error-page>
21          <error-code>404</error-code>
22          <location>/pagenotfound.jsp</location>
23      </error-page>
```

Code Spec

```
1   <!DOCTYPE HTML PUBLIC "-//W3C//DTD HTML 4.0 Transitional//EN">
2   <meta http-equiv="refresh" content="10;URL=showHomePage.action">
3   <html>
4     <head>
5       <title>BookShop [Sharanam & Vaishali Shah] - Page Not Found</title>
6     </head>
7     <body>
8       <p>
9         <font color="red" size="6">The resource you are trying to access can not be
            found.</font>
10        <br/><br/>
11        This often happens when you are trying to reach invalid resources on this
            application.<br/>
12        You will be redirected to the home page in 10 seconds.
13        <br/><br/>
14      </p>
15    </body>
16  </html>
```

Explanation:

This JSP is the page, which displays the 404 or page not found error message.

404 or Page Not Found error message is a HTTP standard response code indicating that the customer was able to communicate with the server, but the server could not find what was requested.

This JSP then redirects the customer to the homepage of the frontend section.

Accessing Restricted Page Error Message Page

This module is made up of the following:

Type	Name	Description
JSP	sessionnotfound.jsp	The error message page for accessing the restricted page.

JSP [sessionnotfound.jsp]

You are trying to access a restricted area.

This often happens when you are trying to reach resources without logging in to this application. You will be redirected to the home page in 10 seconds.

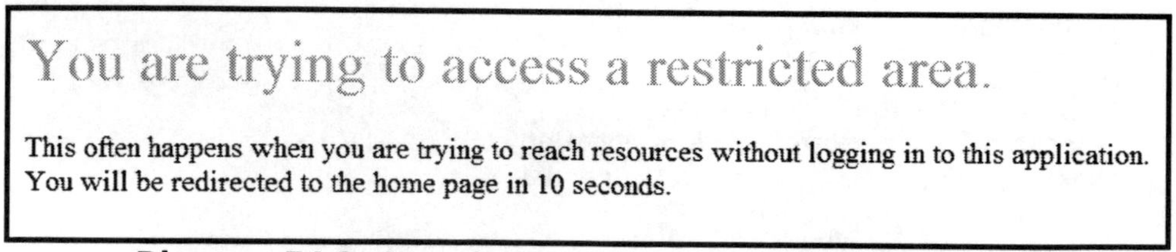

Diagram 54.3: Accessing Restricted Page Error Message Page

This is a JSP which displays error message for accessing restricted page, as shown in diagram 54.3.

This file is specified in struts.xml:

```
<result name="loginAction"
type="redirect">/sessionnotfound.jsp</result>
</global-results>
```

Code Spec

```
1   <!DOCTYPE HTML PUBLIC "-//W3C//DTD HTML 4.0 Transitional//EN">
2   <meta http-equiv="refresh" content="10;URL=showHomePage.action">
3   <html>
4     <head>
5       <title>BookShop [Sharanam & Vaishali Shah] - Please Login</title>
6     </head>
7     <body>
8       <font color="red" size="6">You are trying to access a restricted area.</font>
9       <br/><br/>
10      This often happens when you are trying to reach resources without logging in to this
        application.<br/>
11      You will be redirected to the home page in 10 seconds.
12      <br/><br/>
13    </body>
14  </html>
```

Explanation:

This JSP is the page, which displays the error message for trying to enter the page without login.

This JSP then redirects the customer to the homepage of the frontend section.

Chapter

55

SECTION VII: COMMON FILES SOFTWARE DESIGN DOCUMENTATION

Hibernate Session Factory

This is a common Java module that creates a Hibernate Session Factory based on the values available in the Hibernate's configuration file called hibernate.cfg.xml and provides a session to perform database operations.

Creating Session Factory

Session factory is automatically created when the application makes a request.

Every time a request is made, Struts 2 framework's configured filter [com.sharanamvaishali.utility.Struts2Dispatcher in web.xml] comes into picture which invokes this class's **configureSessionFactory()** to create and make the session factory available to this application.

web.xml

```
<filter>
   <filter-name>struts2</filter-name>
   <filter-class>com.sharanamvaishali.utility.Struts2Dispatcher</filter-class>
</filter>
```

Providing A Session To Work With

Every time the application [especially the DAO classes] requires performing a database operation, an object of Session is created and a session is retrieved using this class's getSession():

```
import com.sharanamvaishali.utility.HibernateUtil;
import org.hibernate.Session;
import org.hibernate.Transaction;

public class CountriesDAOImpl implements CountriesDAO {
  Session session = HibernateUtil.getSession();
  Transaction transaction;
```

After this session is available, it is used to perform database operations, for example:

```
transaction = session.beginTransaction();
```

```
session.save(countries);
```

```
session.update(countries);
```

```
Countries = session.load(Countries.class, CountryNo);
```

```
session.delete(Countries);
```

```
session.createQuery("FROM Countries");
```

Hibernate Utility Class [HibernateUtil.java]

This is a Java class with the following specifications:

Class Name	Package
HibernateUtil	Com.sharanamvaishali.utility
Properties	
Property Name	**Class Name**
sessionFactory	static SessionFactory
serviceRegistry	static ServiceRegistry

Methods		
Method Name	**Arguments**	**Return Values**
configureSessionFactory()	– –	static SessionFactory
getSession()	– –	static Session

Code Spec

```
1   package com.sharanamvaishali.utility;
2
3   import org.hibernate.HibernateException;
4   import org.hibernate.Session;
5   import org.hibernate.SessionFactory;
6   import org.hibernate.cfg.Configuration;
7   import org.hibernate.service.ServiceRegistry;
8   import org.hibernate.service.ServiceRegistryBuilder;
9
10  public class HibernateUtil {
11      private static SessionFactory sessionFactory;
12      private static ServiceRegistry serviceRegistry;
13
14      public static SessionFactory configureSessionFactory() throws
        HibernateException {
15          Configuration configuration = new Configuration();
16          configuration.configure();
17          serviceRegistry = new
            ServiceRegistryBuilder().applySettings(configuration.getProperties()).buildSe
            rviceRegistry();
18          sessionFactory = configuration.buildSessionFactory(serviceRegistry);
19          return sessionFactory;
20      }
21
22      public static Session getSession() {
23          return sessionFactory.openSession();
24      }
25  }
```

Explanation:

The following section describes the above code spec.

configureSessionFactory()

configureSessionFactory() is defined, which creates SessionFactory.

SessionFactory allows creating sessions. SessionFactory caches generate SQL statements and other mapping metadata that Hibernate uses at runtime.

An instance of **Configuration** is created.

Configuration is used to configure and bootstrap Hibernate. It is meant only as a initialization-time object. The application uses a Configuration instance to specify the location of mapping documents and Hibernate-specific properties and then create SessionFactory.

Using it's **configure()**, the session factory is built. This step indicates Hibernate to load **hibernate.cfg.xml**. Using **getProperties()**, all the properties are retrieved from hibernate.cfg.xml.

An instance of ServiceRegistryBuilder is created.

ServiceRegistryBuilder is the builder for standard ServiceRegistry instances.

ServiceRegistry is a registry of services.

Using it's applySettings(), groups of incoming setting values are to be applied.

buildServiceRegistry() of ServiceRegistryBuilder builds the service registry accounting for all settings and service initiators and services.

buildSessionFactory() of Configuration creates a SessionFactory using the properties and mappings in the current configuration. SessionFactory will be immutable, so changes made to Configuration after building SessionFactory will not affect it. buildSessionFactory() takes a parameter named ServiceRegistry, which is the registry of services to be used in creating the session factory.

configureSessionFactory() throws **HibernateException**, is the base Throwable type for Hibernate.

getSession()

getSession(), a getter method, when invoked, returns an instance of Session.

Session is the main runtime interface between a Java application and Hibernate. This is the central API class abstracting the notion of a persistence service. The main function of the Session is to offer create, read and delete operations for instances of mapped entity classes.

openSession() of SesisonFactory creates an instance of Session. This instance represents the primary interface to the Hibernate framework.

Chapter

56

SECTION VII: COMMON FILES SOFTWARE DESIGN DOCUMENTATION

Struts 2 Dispatcher

This is a common Java module that acts as Struts 2 filter.

To integrate this application with Hibernate, a custom Struts 2 dispatcher is created. This class extends StrutsPrepareAndExecuteFilter dispatcher.

Struts2Dispatcher:

❑ Executes the super classes's **init()**

❑ Overrides **init()** to create a session factory

This custom class enables the Hibernate support in the application.

Every time a request is made, this filter class [configured in web.xml] comes into picture which invokes **HibernateUtil's configureSessionFactory()** to create and make the session factory available to this application.

web.xml

```
<filter>
   <filter-name>struts2</filter-name>
   <filter-class>com.sharanamvaishali.utility.Struts2Dispatcher</filter-class>
</filter>
```

Struts2Dispatcher.java

This is the Filter class with the following specifications:

Class Name	Package
Struts2Dispatcher	Com.sharanamvaishali.utility

Methods		
Method Name	**Arguments**	**Return Values**
init()	FilterConfig filterConfig	void

Code Spec

```
1  package com.sharanamvaishali.utility;
2
3  import javax.servlet.*;
4  import org.apache.struts2.dispatcher.ng.filter.StrutsPrepareAndExecuteFilter;
5  import org.hibernate.HibernateException;
6
7
8  public class Struts2Dispatcher extends StrutsPrepareAndExecuteFilter {
9     @Override
10    public void init(FilterConfig filterConfig) throws ServletException {
11       super.init(filterConfig);
12       try {
13          HibernateUtil.configureSessionFactory();
14       } catch (HibernateException e) {
15          throw new ServletException(e);
16       }
17    }
18  }
```

Explanation:

The following section describes the above code spec.

Struts2Dispatcher extends **StrutsPrepareAndExecuteFilter**, which handles both the preparation and execution phases of Struts dispatching process. This filter is better to use when there are no another filter that needs access to action context information such as Sitemesh.

StrutsPrepareAndExecuteFilter is used instead of FilterDispatcher, since Struts 2.1.3 FilterDispatcher is deprecated.

init()

init() is invoked by the Servlet container once when the Servlet filter is placed into service. Filter Configuration passed to this method contains the initialized parameters of the Servlet filter.

FilterConfig is a filter configuration object used by a Servlet container to pass information to a filter during initialization.

In init(), super class's init() is invoked.

A Hibernate session is spawned using **configureSessionFactory()** of **HibernateUtil** created earlier.

init() catches **HibernateException**, which is any exception that occurs inside the persistence layer or JDBC driver.

init() throws **ServletException**, which defines a general exception a Servlet can throw when it encounters difficulty.

SECTION VII: COMMON FILES SOFTWARE DESIGN DOCUMENTATION

Authentication Interceptor

This is a common Java module that ensures that a user does not reach a restricted area without being authenticated.

This is an interceptor declared as:

```
<interceptor name="loginInterceptor"
class="com.sharanamvaishali.utility.AuthenticationInterceptor" />
```

This interceptor is invoked for every action that holds a reference as:

```
<interceptor-ref name="loginInterceptor" />
```

If the user who has not logged in, attempts to reach a restricted area, this interceptor returns loginAction. A Global result is available in struts.xml to take care of this returned value:

```
<global-results>
    <result name="invalid.token">/doublePost.jsp</result>
    <result name="loginAction" type="redirect">/sessionnotfound.jsp</result>
</global-results>
```

This result displays JSP, as shown in diagram 54.3, in the *Chapter 54: Common JavaServer Pages*.

Interceptor Class [AuthenticationInterceptor.java]

This is a Java class with the following specifications:

Class Name	AuthenticationInterceptor
Package	com.sharanamvaishali.utility
Extends	- -
Implements	Interceptor

Methods		
Method Name	**Arguments**	**Return Values**
intercept()	ActionInvocation actionInvocation	loginAction
destroy()	- -	SUCCESS
init()	- -	SUCCESS

Code Spec

```
1   package com.sharanamvaishali.utility;
2
3   import com.opensymphony.xwork2.ActionInvocation;
4   import com.opensymphony.xwork2.interceptor.Interceptor;
5   import java.util.Map;
6
7   public class AuthenticationInterceptor implements Interceptor {
8       @Override
9       public String intercept(ActionInvocation actionInvocation) throws Exception {
10          Map session = actionInvocation.getInvocationContext().getSession();
11          if (session.get("username") == null) {
12              return "loginAction";
13          } else {
14              return actionInvocation.invoke();
15          }
16      }
17
18      @Override
```

```
19      public void init() {
20      }
21
22      @Override
23      public void destroy() {
24      }
25  }
```

Explanation:

The following section describes the above code spec.

intercept()

intercept() allows Interceptor to do some processing on the request before and/or after the rest of the processing of the request by ActionInvocation or to short-circuit the processing and just return a String return code.

Here, intercept() is invoked when the user attempts to access a restricted area [without logging in]. Struts 2 framework invokes this method [the default method of this class] for all those actions who refer to it as:

<interceptor-ref name="loginInterceptor" />

intercept():

❑   Accesses the current session with the help of **getInvocationContext().getSession()**

❑   Determines if the current session holds a value for the key called **username**

    o   If it **does not hold** a value then returns loginAction to inform Struts 2 framework to serve sessionnotfound.jsp

    o   If it **holds** a value then informs Struts 2 framework to allow the action invocation that will allow the user to access what the user is attempting to

init()

init() is called after an interceptor is created, but any requests are processed using intercept(), giving Interceptor a chance to initialize any needed resources.

destroy()

destroy() is called to let an interceptor clean up any resources it has allocated.

Chapter

58

SECTION VII: COMMON FILES SOFTWARE DESIGN DOCUMENTATION

Retrieving Blob Values

This is an action class that allows retrieving the uploaded files [CoverPage, Photograph, TOC, SampleChapter].

It uses **Hibernate** to query and retrieve the appropriate column's data and streams the same to JSP that demanded it.

It all begins like this:

1. A JSP needs to display a file [image]. To achieve this:

```
<img src="getFile.action?columnName=CoverPage&tableName=Books&
whereClause=BookNo&whereClauseValue=<s:property value="book.BookNo" />"
width="100px"/>
```

OR

2.   A JSP needs to allow the user to download a file [PDF]. To achieve this:

```
<a href="getPDF.action?columnName=Toc&tableName=Books&whereClause=BookNo
&whereClauseValue=<s:property value="book.BookNo" />">
   Toc
</a>
```

3.   Since in either cases an action is invoked, **struts.xml** is consulted to determine the actual action class and the method:

```
<action name="getFile" class="com.sharanamvaishali.utility.GetFileAction">
   <result name="success" type = "stream">
      <param name="contentType">image/jpeg</param>
      <param name="inputName">iStream</param>
      <param name="contentDisposition">filename="file.jpg"</param>
      <param name="bufferSize">1024</param>
   </result>
</action>
```

4.   Based on this information, **GetFileAction**'s **execute()** is invoked

5.   execute():

   o   Uses Hibernate and queries the database table using the parameter values it receives:

      ▪   columnName

      ▪   tableName

      ▪   whereClause

      ▪   whereClauseValue

   o   Streams the retrieved column value using the **stream** result configured in struts.xml

Action Class [GetFileAction.java]

This is an Action class with the following specifications:

Class Name	GetFileAction
Package	com.sharanamvaishali.utility
Extends	ActionSupport
Implements	- -

Properties			
Property Name	**Property Type**	**Methods**	
columnName	String	getColumnName()	setColumnName()
tableName	String	getTableName()	setTableName()
whereClause	String	getWhereClause()	setWhereClause()
whereClauseValue	String	getWhereClauseValue()	setWhereClauseValue()
iStream	InputStream	getIStream()	setIStream()

Methods		
Method Name	**Arguments**	**Return Values**
execute()	- -	SUCCESS

Code Spec

```
1   package com.sharanamvaishali.utility;
2
3   import com.opensymphony.xwork2.ActionSupport;
4   import java.io.InputStream;
5   import java.sql.Blob;
6   import org.hibernate.Query;
7   import org.hibernate.Session;
8   import org.hibernate.type.StandardBasicTypes;
9
10  public class GetFileAction extends ActionSupport{
11      private String columnName, tableName, whereClause, whereClauseValue;
12
13      private InputStream iStream = null;
14
15      public GetFileAction() {
16      }
17
18      public String getColumnName() {
19          return columnName;
20      }
21      public void setColumnName(String columnName) {
22          this.columnName = columnName;
23      }
24
25      public String getWhereClause() {
26          return whereClause;
27      }
28      public void setWhereClause(String whereClause) {
29          this.whereClause = whereClause;
30      }
31
32      public String getWhereClauseValue() {
33          return whereClauseValue;
34      }
35      public void setWhereClauseValue(String whereClauseValue) {
36          this.whereClauseValue = whereClauseValue;
37      }
38
39      public String getTableName() {
40          return tableName;
41      }
```

```
42    public void setTableName(String tableName) {
43        this.tableName = tableName;
44    }
45
46    public InputStream getIStream() {
47        return iStream;                        .
48    }
49    public void setIStream(InputStream iStream) {
50        this.iStream = iStream;
51    }
52
53    @Override
54    public String execute() throws Exception {
55        Session session = HibernateUtil.getSession();
56        try {
57            String strQuery = "SELECT " + columnName + " FROM "+ tableName + "
              WHERE " + whereClause + " = " + whereClauseValue;
58            Query query = session.createSQLQuery(strQuery).addScalar(columnName,
              StandardBasicTypes.BLOB);
59            Blob blobFile = (Blob) query.uniqueResult();
60            iStream = blobFile.getBinaryStream();
61        } catch(Exception e) {
62            String strQuery = "SELECT Image FROM DefaultValues";
63            Query query = session.createSQLQuery(strQuery).addScalar("Image",
              StandardBasicTypes.BLOB);
64            Blob blobFile = (Blob) query.uniqueResult();
65            iStream = blobFile.getBinaryStream();
66        }
67        return SUCCESS;
68    }
69 }
```

Explanation:

The following section describes the above code spec.

execute()

execute() is invoked when a JSP attempts to access a BLOB column value to either display it as an image or allow download.

execute() is invoked every time the BLOB content [photograph or a PDF file] needs to be downloaded and viewed.

This method uses a native SQL query to retrieve the BLOB contents. This query is formed on the basis of **columnName, tableName, whereClause, whereClauseValue**.

Based on the values held in these action class variables, the SQL query retrieves only the **BLOB** content of a particular record. The content retrieved is assigned to an **InputStream** object which is streamed and made available to the calling JSP page by Struts 2 Framework.

If the content being asked for is not available in the database table, then the default photograph is retrieved from the **DefaultValues** database table and streamed instead.

Chapter

59

SECTION VII: COMMON FILES SOFTWARE DESIGN DOCUMENTATION

Populating Drop Down List Boxes

This is a Java class that provides List objects to populate the following drop down list boxes:

- ❑ ddlbCountries → Countries
- ❑ ddlbStates → States
- ❑ ddlbAuthors → Authors
- ❑ ddlbPublishers → Publishers
- ❑ ddlbCategories → Categories

It uses the methods of **PopulateDdlbsDAO** to retrieve the lists.

An object of this class is created in all those action class that require populating drop down list boxes:

```
private PopulateDdlbs ddlb = new PopulateDdlbs();
```

The **list** attribute of the drop down list box elements in JSP can simply refer to the List object properties to gain access to the list that holds the values:

```
<s:select list="ddlb.ddlbCountries" listKey="CountryNo" listValue="Country"
headerKey="" headerValue="Select Country" id="CountryNo" name="author.CountryNo"
label="Country" title="Select the country">
</s:select>
```

Java Class [PopulateDdlbs.java]

This is a Java class with the following specifications:

Class Name	PopulateDdlbs
Package	com.sharanamvaishali.utility
Extends	– –
Implements	– –

Objects		
Object Name	**Class Name**	**Object Type**
populateDdlbsDAO	PopulateDdlbsDAO	Data Access Object

Constructor	
Name	**Arguments**
PopulateDdlbs()	– –

Properties			
Property Name	**Property Type**	**Methods**	
ddlbCountries	List <Countries>	getDdlbCountries()	setDdlbCountries()
ddlbCitiesStates	List <CityState>	getDdlbCitiesStates()	setDdlbCitiesStates()
ddlbAuthors	List <Authors>	getDdlbAuthors()	setDdlbAuthors()
ddlbPublishers	List <Publishers>	getDdlbPublishers()	setDdlbPublishers()
ddlbCategoris	List <Categories>	getDdlbCategories()	setDdlbCategories()

Code Spec

```
1   package com.sharanamvaishali.utility;
2
3   import com.sharanamvaishali.dao.PopulateDdlbsDAO;
4   import com.sharanamvaishali.dao.PopulateDdlbsDAOImpl;
5   import com.sharanamvaishali.model.Authors;
6   import com.sharanamvaishali.model.Categories;
7   import com.sharanamvaishali.model.Countries;
8   import com.sharanamvaishali.model.Publishers;
9   import com.sharanamvaishali.model.States;
10  import java.util.List;
11
12  public class PopulateDdlbs {
13      private List<Countries> ddlbCountries;
14
```

```
15      private List<States> ddlbStates;
16
17      private List<Authors> ddlbAuthors;
18
19      private List<Publishers> ddlbPublishers;
20
21      private List<Categories> ddlbCategories;
22
23      private PopulateDdlbsDAO populateDdlbsDAO = new PopulateDdlbsDAOImpl();
24
25      public PopulateDdlbs() {
26         ddlbCountries = populateDdlbsDAO.getAllCountries();
27         ddlbStates = populateDdlbsDAO.getAllStates();
28         ddlbAuthors = populateDdlbsDAO.getAllAuthors();
29         ddlbPublishers = populateDdlbsDAO.getAllPublishers();
30         ddlbCategories = populateDdlbsDAO.getAllCategories();
31      }
32
33      public List<Countries> getDdlbCountries() {
34         return ddlbCountries;
35      }
36      public void setDdlbCountries(List<Countries> ddlbCountries) {
37         this.ddlbCountries = ddlbCountries;
38      }
39
40      public List<States> getDdlbStates() {
41         return ddlbStates;
42      }
43      public void setDdlbStates(List<States> ddlbStates) {
44         this.ddlbStates = ddlbStates;
45      }
46
47      public List<Authors> getDdlbAuthors() {
48         return ddlbAuthors;
49      }
50      public void setDdlbAuthors(List<Authors> ddlbAuthors) {
51         this.ddlbAuthors = ddlbAuthors;
52      }
53
54      public List<Categories> getDdlbCategories() {
55         return ddlbCategories;
56      }
57      public void setDdlbCategories(List<Categories> ddlbCategories) {
58         this.ddlbCategories = ddlbCategories;
59      }
60
61      public List<Publishers> getDdlbPublishers() {
62         return ddlbPublishers;
```

```
63    }
64    public void setDdlbPublishers(List<Publishers> ddlbPublishers) {
65        this.ddlbPublishers = ddlbPublishers;
66    }
67 }
```

Explanation:

The following section describes the above code spec.

PopulateDdlbs()

PopulateDdlbs() is the default constructor of this class that is invoked automatically when an action class creates an object of it.

This constructor populates the following List objects using the methods of PopulateDdlbsDAO:

❑   ddlbCountries → Countries

❑   ddlbStates → States

❑   ddlbAuthors → Authors

❑   ddlbPublishers → Publishers

❑   ddlbCategories → Categories

DAO Class

Interface [PopulateDdlbsDAO.java]

This is a Data Access Object interface with the following specifications:

Class Name	Package
PopulateDdlbsDAO	com.sharanamvaishali.dao

Code Spec

```
1    package com.sharanamvaishali.dao;
2
3    import java.util.List;
4
5    public interface PopulateDdlbsDAO {
6        public List getAllCountries();
7        public List getAllStates();
8        public List getAllAuthors();
```

```
9      public List getAllPublishers();
10     public List getAllCategories();
11   }
```

Implementation Class [PopulateDdlbsDAOImpl.java]

This is a **Data Access Object** class with the following specifications:

Class Name	PopulateDdlbsDAOImpl
Package	com.sharanamvaishali.dao
Implements	PopulateDdlbsDAO

Objects	
Object Name	**Class Name**
session	Session

Properties	
Property Name	**Class Name**
countries	List <Countries>
states	List <States>
authors	List <Authors>
publishers	List <Publishers>
categories	List <Categories>

Methods	
Method Name	**Return Values**
getAllCountries()	List
getAllStates()	List
getAllAuthors()	List
getAllPublishers()	List
getAllCategories()	List

Code Spec

```
1    package com.sharanamvaishali.dao;
2
3    import com.sharanamvaishali.model.Authors;
4    import com.sharanamvaishali.model.Categories;
5    import com.sharanamvaishali.model.Countries;
6    import com.sharanamvaishali.model.Publishers;
7    import com.sharanamvaishali.model.States;
8    import com.sharanamvaishali.utility.HibernateUtil;
9    import java.util.List;
10   import org.hibernate.Session;
11
12   public class PopulateDdlbsDAOImpl implements PopulateDdlbsDAO {
13       Session session = HibernateUtil.getSession();
14
```

```
15      private List<Countries> countries;
16
17      private List<States> states;
18
19      private List<Authors> authors;
20
21      private List<Publishers> publishers;
22
23      private List<Categories> categories;
24
25      @Override
26      public List getAllCountries() {
27        try {
28          countries = session.createQuery("FROM Countries").list();
29          return countries;
30        } catch(Exception e) {
31          System.out.print("Error while fetching" + e);
32          return null;
33        }
34      }
35
36      @Override
37      public List getAllStates() {
38        try {
39          states = session.createQuery("FROM States").list();
40          return states;
41        } catch(Exception e) {
42          System.out.print("Error while fetching" + e);
43          return null;
44        }
45      }
46
47      @Override
48      public List getAllAuthors() {
49        try {
50          authors = session.createQuery("FROM Authors").list();
51          return authors;
52        } catch(Exception e) {
53          System.out.print("Error while fetching" + e);
54          return null;
55        }
56      }
57
58      @Override
59      public List getAllPublishers() {
60        try {
61          publishers = session.createQuery("FROM Publishers").list();
62          return publishers;
```

```
63          } catch(Exception e) {
64              System.out.print("Error while fetching" + e);
65              return null;
66          }
67      }
68
69      @Override
70      public List getAllCategories() {
71          try {
72              categories = session.createQuery("FROM Categories").list();
73              return categories;
74          } catch(Exception e) {
75              System.out.print("Error while fetching" + e);
76              return null;
77          }
78      }
79  }
```

Explanation:

The following section describes the above code spec.

getAllCountries()

getAllCountries() does the actual retrieving of all the Country details.

getAllCountries() uses:

❑   **createQuery()** of Session, which creates a new instance of Query to retrieve the Country details

❑   **list()** of Query, which returns all the Country details from the Countries database table

getAllStates()

getAllStates() does the actual retrieving of all the State details.

getAllStates() uses:

❑   **createQuery()** of Session, which creates a new instance of Query to retrieve the State details

❑   **list()** of Query, which returns all the State details from the States database table

getAllAuthors()

getAllAuthors() does the actual retrieving of all the Author details.

getAllAuthors() uses:

❏ **createQuery()** of Session, which creates a new instance of Query to retrieve the Author details

❏ **list()** of Query, which returns all the Author details from the Authors database table

getAllPublishers()

getAllPublishers() does the actual retrieving of all the Publisher details.

getAllPublishers() uses:

❏ **createQuery()** of Session, which creates a new instance of Query to retrieve the Publisher details

❏ **list()** of Query, which returns all the Publisher details from the Publishers database table

getAllCategories()

getAllCategories() does the actual retrieving of all the Category details.

getAllCategories() uses:

❏ **createQuery()** of Session, which creates a new instance of Query to retrieve the Category details

❏ **list()** of Query, which returns all the Category details from the Categories database table

Chapter

60

SECTION VII: COMMON FILES SOFTWARE DESIGN DOCUMENTATION

Sending Mails

This is a Java class that holds a static method that accepts:

- ❑ The Email address of the Gmail account
- ❑ Username of the Gmail account
- ❑ Password of the Gmail account
- ❑ Email address of the recipient
- ❑ Subject of the mail
- ❑ The message of the mail

Based on these values, this class uses the free SMTP server provided by Gmail and dispatches the email. <u>This requires having a Gmail user account **pre-created** whose email address/password can be used to send emails to the desired recipients.</u>

Java Class [SendMail.java]

This is a Java class with the following specifications:

Class Name	SendMail
Package	com.sharanamvaishali.utility
Extends	- -
Implements	- -

Constructor	
Name	**Class Name**
sendMail()	String emailFrom
	String emailUser
	String emailFromPassword
	String emailID
	String subj
	String message

Code Spec

```
1   package com.sharanamvaishali.utility;
2
3   import java.util.*;
4   import javax.mail.*;
5   import javax.mail.internet.*;
6
7   public class SendMail {
8       public static void sendMail(String emailFrom, String emailUser, String
        emailFromPasswd, String emailID, String subj, String message) throws
        Exception {
9           String host = "smtp.gmail.com", user = emailUser, pass =
            emailFromPasswd;
10          String SSL_FACTORY = "javax.net.ssl.SSLSocketFactory";
11          String to = emailID;
12          String from = emailFrom;
13          String subject = subj;
14          String messageText = message;
15          boolean sessionDebug = true;
16
17          Properties props = System.getProperties();
18          props.put("mail.host", host);
19          props.put("mail.transport.protocol.", "smtp");
20          props.put("mail.smtp.auth", "true");
21          props.put("mail.smtp.", "true");
22          props.put("mail.smtp.port", "465");
23          props.put("mail.smtp.socketFactory.fallback", "false");
24          props.put("mail.smtp.socketFactory.class", SSL_FACTORY);
```

```
25
26            Session mailSession = Session.getDefaultInstance(props, null);
27            mailSession.setDebug(sessionDebug);
28
29            Message msg = new MimeMessage(mailSession);
30            msg.setFrom(new InternetAddress(from));
31            InternetAddress[] address = {new InternetAddress(to)};
32            msg.setRecipients(Message.RecipientType.TO, address);
33            msg.setSubject(subject);
34            msg.setContent(messageText, "text/html");
35
36            Transport transport = mailSession.getTransport("smtp");
37            transport.connect(host, user, pass);
38
39            try {
40                transport.sendMessage(msg, msg.getAllRecipients());
41            } catch (Exception e) {
42                System.out.println("Error" + e.getMessage());
43            }
44            transport.close();
45        }
46 }
```

Explanation:

The following section describes the above code spec.

sendMail()

This is a static method that is invoked by the action or DAO classes to send emails to the users on the following occasions:

❑ Successful Registration/Signup

❑ Book Updates

❑ New Books Added

❑ Forgotten Password successfully retrieved

Action or DAO class would hold the following code spec to invoke sendMail():

```
String toEmailAddress = objCustomer.getEmailAddress();
String emailSubject = "Sharanam & Vaishali's Online BookShop: " +
books.getBookName() + " has been added.";
String emailMessage =
"<html>
    <head>
        <meta http-equiv='Content-Type' content='text/html;
        charset=iso-8859-1'/>
```

```
        <title>" + books.getBookName() + " has been added.</title>
    </head>
    <body>
        <table width='500' border='0' align='center' cellpadding='15'
        cellspacing='0' style='font-family: Verdana, Arial, Helvetica, sans-serif;
        font-size: 12pt; color:#5a5a5a;'>
            <tr>
                <td align='left'>Dear " + objCustomer.getFirstName() + ",</td>
            </tr>
            <tr>
                <td align='left'>
                    <br/><br/>
                    ISBN: " + books.getISBN() + "<br />
                    Edition: " + books.getEdition() + "<br />
                    Synopsis: " + books.getSynopsis() + "<br />
                    Topics covered: " + books.getTopicsCovered() + "<br /><br/>
                    Thank you for using  this site.<br/><br/>
                    Regards,<br />Sharanam & Vaishali's Online Bookshop
                    <br /><br /><br />
                    THIS IS AN AUTOMATED MESSAGE; PLEASE DO NOT REPLY.
                </td>
            </tr>
        </table>
    </body>
</html>";
SendMail.sendMail(bundle.getString("emailFrom"),
                bundle.getString("emailUser"),
                bundle.getString("emailFromPasswd"),
                toEmailAddress, emailSubject, emailMessage);
```

The email that the user receives:

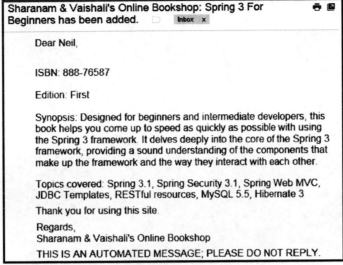

Diagram 60.1

Chapter

61

SECTION VII: COMMON FILES SOFTWARE DESIGN DOCUMENTATION

Configuration Files

Struts Configuration File [struts.xml]

This module is made up of the following:

Type	Name	Description
Struts Configuration	struts.xml	The main struts configuration file.
	struts.properties	The configuration settings i.e. constant values.

struts.xml

struts.xml holds the configuration information that is added/modified as actions are developed. This is the place where Struts 2 filter looks for configurations.

Code Spec

```
1   <!DOCTYPE struts PUBLIC
2   "-//Apache Software Foundation//DTD Struts Configuration 2.0//EN"
3   "http://struts.apache.org/dtds/struts-2.0.dtd">
4   <struts>
5     <package name="default" extends="struts-default">
6       <interceptors>
7         <interceptor name="loginInterceptor"
          class="com.sharanamvaishali.utility.AuthenticationInterceptor" />
8         <interceptor-stack name="chkSession">
9           <interceptor-ref name="defaultStack" />
10          <interceptor-ref name="loginInterceptor" />
11        </interceptor-stack>
12      </interceptors>
13
14      <global-results>
15        <result name="invalid.token">/doublePost.jsp</result>
16        <result name="loginAction"
          type="redirect">/sessionnotfound.jsp</result>
17      </global-results>
18
19      <action name="showHomePage" method="view"
        class="com.sharanamvaishali.action.HomePageAction">
20        <result>/frontend/home.jsp</result>
21      </action>
22
23      <action name="getPDF" class="com.sharanamvaishali.utility.GetFileAction">
24        <result name="success" type = "stream">
25          <param name="contentType">application/pdf</param>
26          <param name="inputName">iStream</param>
27          <param name="contentDisposition">filename="file.pdf"</param>
28          <param name="bufferSize">1024</param>
29        </result>
30      </action>
31
32      <action name="getFile" class="com.sharanamvaishali.utility.GetFileAction">
33        <result name="success" type = "stream">
34          <param name="contentType">image/jpeg</param>
35          <param name="inputName">iStream</param>
36          <param name="contentDisposition">filename="file.jpg"</param>
37          <param name="bufferSize">1024</param>
38        </result>
39      </action>
40    </package>
41
42    <include file="struts-AdminLogin.xml" />
43    <include file="struts-Countries.xml" />
```

```
44      <include file="struts-States.xml" />
45      <include file="struts-Authors.xml" />
46      <include file="struts-Publishers.xml" />
47      <include file="struts-Categories.xml" />
48      <include file="struts-SystemUsers.xml" />
49      <include file="struts-Books.xml" />
50      <include file="struts-Customers.xml" />
51      <include file="struts-Transactions.xml" />
52
53      <include file="struts-CustomerLogin.xml" />
54      <include file="struts-HomePage.xml" />
55      <include file="struts-Registration.xml" />
56      <include file="struts-Search.xml" />
57      <include file="struts-Cart.xml" />
58   </struts>
```

Explanation:

The following section describes the above code spec.

\<struts\>

This is the **outermost tag** that contains Struts 2 specific configuration. All other tags are held within this tag.

\<package\>

struts.xml is broken down into logical units called **packages**.

\<package\> is used to group together configurations that share common attributes such as interceptor stacks or URL namespaces.

Packages are meant to help group the application's components based on commonality of function or domain.

Packages group the following into a logical configuration unit:

❑   Actions

❑   Result types

❑   Interceptors

❑   Interceptor stacks

The name Attribute [name="default"]

Indicates the name of the package.

The extends Attribute [extends="struts-default"]

Indicates the name of the parent package to inherit from.

This attribute holds a package name whose components will be inherited by the current package that is being defined. <u>This is very similar to the **extends** keyword in Java.</u>

HINT

 The **struts-default** package declares a huge set of commonly needed Struts 2 components ranging from complete interceptor stacks to all the common result types. These can be inherited by simply extending it.

Extending the struts-default package helps a developer avoid a lot of manual labor. This is because extending this package brings a lot of components along with it. One such component is the default Interceptor Stack.

<interceptors>

To use an interceptor, it has to be registered by using <interceptors>. Interceptors defined in a package can be used by all actions in the package.

<interceptor>

Interceptors are declared in <interceptor>.

The name Attribute [name="loginInterceptor"]

Indicates the unique name of the interceptor.

The class Attribute [class="com.sharanamvaishali.utility.AuthenticationInterceptor"]

Indicates the class name of the interceptor.

\<interceptor-stack\>

With most Struts application having multiple action elements, repeating the list of interceptors for each action can be a daunting task. In order to alleviate this problem, Struts allows creating interceptor stacks that group required interceptors. Instead of referencing interceptors from within each action element, reference the interceptor stack instead.

\<interceptor-stack\> allows creating interceptor stacks.

\<interceptor-stack\> is a convenient way of referencing a sequenced chunk of interceptors by name.

The name Attribute [name="chkSession"]

Indicates the unique name of the interceptor stack.

HINT

The Interceptors are defined in a stack that specifies the execution order. In some cases, the order of the Interceptors on the stack can be very important.

\<interceptor-ref\>

To apply an interceptor to an action or interceptor stacks, \<interceptor-ref\> is used.

The name Attribute [name="defaultStack"]

Indicates the unique name of the interceptor to be applied.

In this application, two interceptors are often used in the following orders:
- defaultStack
- loginInterceptor

Rather than referencing them again and again in the action declarations, an interceptor stack is created by name **chkSession**.

\<global-results\>

A package element may contain \<global-results\> that contains results that act as general results. If an action cannot find a matching result under its action declaration, it will search \<global-results\>, if any.

In this application there two <global-results>:

❑   For double posting the same data

❑   For session expiration

<action>

The action maps an identifier to handle an action class. The action's name and framework use the mapping to determine how to process the request, when a request is matched.

The name Attribute [name="showHomePage"]

The action's **name** attribute indicates the name of the action within the Web application.

The action's name is concatenated with the package's namespace to come up with the URL of the request:
http://www.myserver.com/showHomePage.action

The method Attribute [method="view"]

This is an optional attribute. This indicates the method to be invoked on a Request.

REMINDER

 If this is un-specified, the filter assumes **execute()**.

The class Attribute [class="com.sharanamvaishali.action.HomePageAction"]

The **class** attribute indicates which Java class will be instantiated for the Request.

<result>

Each action element can have **one or more** result elements.

Each result is a possible view that the action can launch.

The name Attribute [name="success"]

This is an optional attribute, which indicates the result name.

REMINDER

 If this is un-specified, the filter assumes **success** as the name.

The type Attribute [type="stream"]

This is an optional attribute, which indicates the kind of result.

REMINDER

 If this is un-specified, the filter assumes dispatcher which forwards the Web browser to the View [JSP] specified.

<param>

<param> is nested within another element such as <action>, <result> or <interceptor> to pass a value to the enclosing object.

The name Attribute [name="contentType"]

Indicates the name of the parameter.

In this example, <param> is used to set the property of the result.

<include>

<include> can be used to modularize a Struts 2 application. This tag allows including other configuration files. It is always a child to **<struts>**.

The file Attribute [file="struts-AdminLogin.xml"]

This is the only attribute of <include>. It allows specifying the name of the file to be included. The file being included should have a structure identical to **struts.xml**.

struts.properties

struts.properties provides a mechanism to change the default behavior of the framework.

The values configured in this file will override the default values configured in default.properties which is contained in struts2-core-2.x.x.x.jar distribution.

Code Spec

```
1  struts.custom.i18n.resources=bookshop
2  struts.multipart.maxSize=53477376
```

Explanation:

The following section describes the above code spec.

struts.custom.i18n.resources

Specifies the name of the resource bundle to be used by default.

struts.multipart.maxSize

Specifies the maximum size to upload the photograph, cover page and PDFs of TOC and sample chapters.

Hibernate Configuration File

This module is made up of the following:

Type	Name	Description
Hibernate Configuration	hibernate.cfg.xml.jsp	The Hibernate Configuration file.

Hibernate.cfg.xml

Hibernate uses **hibernate.cfg.xml** to setup the required environment. This file is used to provide the information which is necessary for making database connections.

hibernate.cfg.xml configuration defines information such as:

❑ The database connection

❑ The transaction factory class

❑ Resource mappings

And so on.

Code Spec

```
1   <?xml version="1.0" encoding="UTF-8"?>
2   <!DOCTYPE hibernate-configuration PUBLIC "-//Hibernate/Hibernate Configuration
    DTD //EN" "http://www.hibernate.org/dtd/hibernate-configuration-3.0.dtd">
3   <hibernate-configuration>
4    <session-factory>
5     <property
      name="hibernate.dialect">org.hibernate.dialect.MySQLDialect</property>
6     <property
      name="hibernate.connection.driver_class">com.mysql.jdbc.Driver</property>
```

```
 7      <property
        name="hibernate.connection.url">jdbc:mysql://localhost:3306/bms</property>
 8      <property name="hibernate.connection.username">root</property>
 9      <property name="hibernate.connection.password">123456</property>
10      <property name="hibernate.default_catalog">bms</property>
11      <mapping class="com.sharanamvaishali.model.Countries"/>
12      <mapping class="com.sharanamvaishali.model.States"/>
13      <mapping class="com.sharanamvaishali.model.Authors"/>
14      <mapping class="com.sharanamvaishali.model.Categories"/>
15      <mapping class="com.sharanamvaishali.model.Publishers"/>
16      <mapping class="com.sharanamvaishali.model.SystemUsers"/>
17      <mapping class="com.sharanamvaishali.model.Customers"/>
18      <mapping class="com.sharanamvaishali.model.Books"/>
19      <mapping class="com.sharanamvaishali.model.Transactions"/>
20      <mapping class="com.sharanamvaishali.model.PopularSearches"/>
21    </session-factory>
22  </hibernate-configuration>
```

Explanation:

The configuration file requires the following properties:

hibernate.dialect

Is the name of the SQL dialect for the database. It informs Hibernate whether the given database supports identity columns, altering relational tables and unique indexes, among other database specific details.

HINT

 Hibernate ships with more than 20 SQL dialects supporting each of the major database vendors including Oracle, DB2, MySQL and PostgreSQL.

hibernate.connection.driver_class

Is the JDBC connection class for the specific database.

hibernate.connection.url

Is the full JDBC URL to the database.

hibernate.connection.username

Is the username used to connect to the database.

hibernate.connection.password

Is the password used to authenticate the username.

The connection properties are common to any Java developer who has worked with JDBC in the past.

REMINDER

 Since a connection pool is not specified, Hibernate uses its own rudimentary connection-pooling mechanism. The internal pool is fine for basic testing .

Mapping Class

Hibernate also needs to know the location and names of the mapping class describing the persistent classes.

<mapping> provides the name of each mapping class as well as its location relative to the application classpath.

The following mapping classes are included to the configuration file:
- Countries.java
- States.java
- Authors.java
- Categories.java
- Publishers.java
- SystemUsers.java
- Customers.java
- Books.java
- Transactions.java
- PopularSearches.java

Google Wallet Attributes

This module is made up of the following:

Type	Name	Description
Properties	bookshop.properties	The file holding Google Wallet attributes.

bookshop.properties

This is a Properties file, which holds the Google Wallet attributes.

Code Spec

```
1  googleMerchantID=<The Google Merchant ID>
2  emailFrom=<Username>@gmail.com
3  emailUser=<Username>
4  emailFromPasswd=<Password>
```

Explanation:

The properties [Resource Bundle] file that holds:

- googleMerchantID

- emailFrom

- emailUser

- emailFromPasswd

The keys and values defined in this properties file will be available to all the view pages that are rendered after executing an Action class.

Standard Deployment Descriptor

Deployment Descriptor refers to a configuration file for an artifact that is deployed to some container/engine.

In the Java Platform, EE, deployment descriptor describes how a component, module or application such as a web application. It directs a deployment tool to deploy a module or application with specific container options, security settings and describes specific configuration requirements.

XML is used for the syntax of these deployment descriptor files.

This module is made up of the following:

Type	Name	Description
Deployment Descriptor	web.xml	The configuration file that is deployed to a container/engine.

web.xml

web.xml provides configuration and deployment information for the Web components that comprise a Web application.

In Java, web applications use web.xml to determine how URLs map to Servlets, which URLs require authentication and other information.

web.xml resides in the app's WAR under **WEB-INF/** directory.

web.xml is part of the Servlet standard for web applications.

Code Spec

```
1   <?xml version="1.0" encoding="UTF-8"?>
2   <web-app version="2.5" xmlns="http://java.sun.com/xml/ns/javaee"
    xmlns:xsi="http://www.w3.org/2001/XMLSchema-instance"
    xsi:schemaLocation="http://java.sun.com/xml/ns/javaee
    http://java.sun.com/xml/ns/javaee/web-app_2_5.xsd">
3     <filter>
4        <filter-name>struts2</filter-name>
5        <filter-class>com.sharanamvaishali.utility.Struts2Dispatcher</filter-class>
6     </filter>
7     <filter-mapping>
8        <filter-name>struts2</filter-name>
9        <url-pattern>/*</url-pattern>
10    </filter-mapping>
11    <session-config>
12       <session-timeout>30</session-timeout>
13    </session-config>
14    <welcome-file-list>
15       <welcome-file>index.jsp</welcome-file>
16    </welcome-file-list>
17    <error-page>
18       <error-code>404</error-code>
19       <location>/pagenotfound.jsp</location>
20    </error-page>
21    <error-page>
22       <exception-type>java.lang.Exception</exception-type>
23       <location>/error.jsp</location>
24    </error-page>
25  </web-app>
```

Explanation:
The following section describes the above code spec.

Filter

struts2 filter is defined. **com.sharanamvaishali.utility.Struts2Dispatcher** is the fully-qualified class name of the **struts2** filter.

struts2 is the name of the filter to which a URL pattern is mapped. This name corresponds to the name assigned in <filter-name> under <filter>.

/* is a pattern used to resolve URLs. This URL must follow the rules specified in the Servlet 2.3 Specification.

Session

The session attributes for this web application is defined.

The session timeout is set, which is the number of minutes after which sessions in the web application will expire.

Default Welcome File

index.jsp is used as a default welcome file, which means when the application is run the server by default will display this file.

Error Page

<error-page> specifies a mapping between an error code or exception type to the path of a resource in the web application.

404 is mapped to **/pagenotfound.jsp**, which is the location of a resource to display in response to the error.

java.lang.Exception is a fully qualified class name of a Java exception type, which is mapped to **/error.jsp**, which is the location of a resource to display in response to the error.

Chapter

62

SECTION VIII: RUNNING THE PROJECT

Assembling And Deploying The Project Using NetBeans IDE

This chapter depicts the steps to assemble the code spec explained so far into a project called **BookShop** and then finally deploy the project using the NetBeans IDE.

Prerequisites

NetBeans IDE 7.2

Since the BookShop application is build using the NetBeans IDE, install the NetBeans IDE and then assemble and deploy the project. *The setup file is available in this book's accompanying CDROM.*

MySQL 5.5.28

This application uses MySQL as the data store, install it prior proceeding. *The setup file is available in this book's accompanying CDROM.*

An Important Note!!!

A completely ready to use project assembled in NetBeans IDE is available on this book's CDROM. This chapter only helps understanding the assembling steps.

If you want to learn to assemble a fresh copy of this project, follow the steps indicated hereafter.

You can skip the assembling section and choose to directly run the application that's available on this book's accompanying CDROM, in which case, **it is required**:

❏ To have the MySQL database engine up and running

❏ To have **bms** database loaded on the MySQL database engine. For more information on how to do this, refer to the *Loading The BMS Database In MySQL* topic of this chapter

❏ To fill up the values in the application's properties, hibernate configuration and standard deployment descriptor files for the application to run. For more information on how to do this, refer to the *Modifying Configuration Files* topic of this chapter

Creating A Web Application

To begin the assembling exercise, open NetBeans IDE. This book's accompanying CDROM holds the setup file for the NetBeans IDE 7.2.

Select **File → New Project**, to create a new **Web Application**. **New Project** dialog box appears, as shown in diagram 62.1.1.

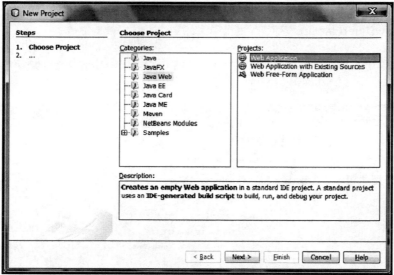

Diagram 62.1.1: New Project dialog box

Select **Java Web → Web Application**, as shown in diagram 62.1.1. Click Next >.

New Web Application dialog box appears, as shown in diagram 62.1.2.

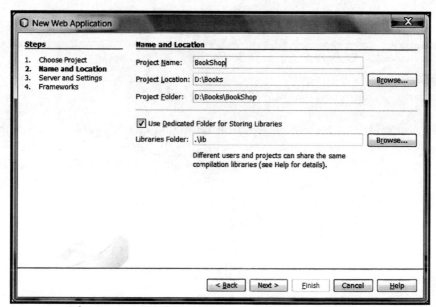

Diagram 62.1.2: New Web Application dialog box

Enter the name of the Web application as **BookShop** in the **Project Name** and keep the defaults, as shown in diagram 62.1.2. Click Next > .

Server and Settings section of the **New Web Application** dialog box appears, as shown in diagram 62.1.3.

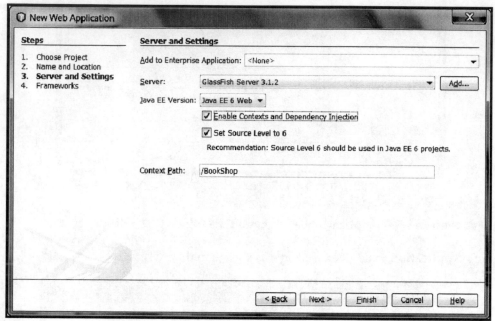

Diagram 62.1.3: Server and Settings section

Keep the defaults, as shown in diagram 62.1.3. Click Next > .

Frameworks section of the **New Web Application** dialog box appears, as shown in diagram 62.1.4.

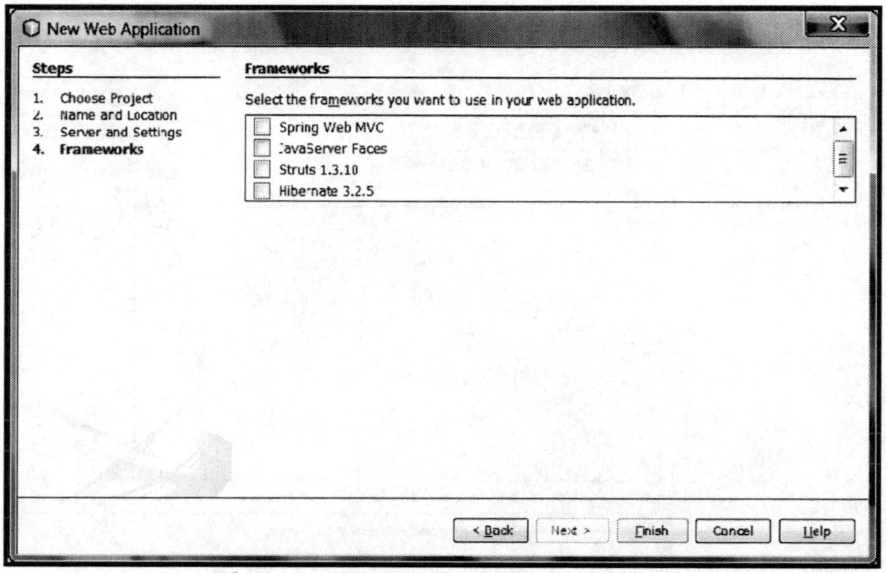

Diagram 62.1.4: Frameworks section

Do not select any frameworks, as shown in diagram 62.1.4. Click Finish .

BookShop application is created in the NetBeans IDE.

Adding The Libraries To The Project

Right-click on the **BookShop** application, select **Properties**.

Project Properties - BookShop dialog box appears, as shown in diagram 62.2.1.

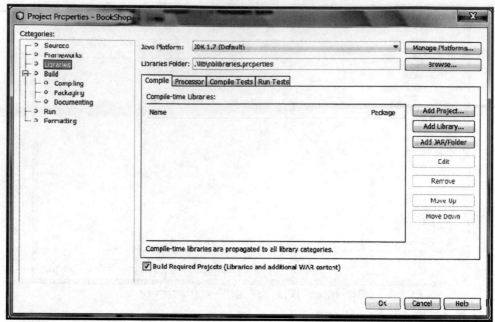

Diagram 62.2.1: Project Properties - BookShop dialog box

Select **Libraries** available in the **Categories** list, as shown in diagram 62.2.1.

Click [Add JAR/Folder]. This displays **Add JAR/Folder** dialog box that allows choosing the JAR files, as shown in diagram 62.2.2.

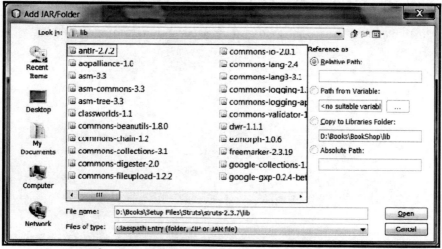

Diagram 62.2.2: Add JAR/Folder dialog box

Add the following library files:

1. **Struts Libraries:**
    a) From <Drive>:\struts-2.3.7\lib:
        o   asm-3.3.jar
        o   asm-commons-3.3.jar
        o   asm-tree-3.3.jar
        o   commons-beanutils-1.8.0.jar
        o   commons-collections-3.1.jar
        o   commons-fileupload-1.2.2.jar
        o   commons-io-2.0.1.jar
        o   commons-lang-2.4.jar
        o   commons-lang3-3.1.jar
        o   commons-logging-1.1.1.jar
        o   freemarker-2.3.19.jar
        o   ognl-3.0.5.jar
        o   struts2-convention-plugin-2.3.7.jar
        o   struts2-core-2.3.7.jar
        o   struts2-dojo-plugin-2.3.7.jar
        o   struts2-pell-multipart-plugin-2.3.7.jar
        o   xwork-core-2.3.7.jar

2. **Hibernate Libraries:**
    a) From <Drive>:\hibernate-release-4.1.9.Final\lib**required:**
        o   antlr-2.7.7.jar
        o   dom4j-1.6.1.jar
        o   hibernate-commons-annotations-4.0.1.FINAL.jar
        o   hibernate-core-4.1.9.FINAL.jar
        o   hibernate-jpa-2.0-api-1.0.1.FINAL.jar
        o   javassist-3.17.1-GA.jar
        o   jboss-logging-3.1.0.GA.jar
        o   jboss-transaction-api_1.1_spec-1.0.0.FINAL.jar

   b) From <Drive>:\hibernate-release-4.1.9.Final\lib**jpa:**

      o hibernate-entitymanager-4.1.9.FINAL.jar

3. **Additional Libraries:**

   a) From <Drive>:**mysql-connector-java-5.1.22:**

      o mysql-connector-java-5.1.22-bin.jar

   b) From <Drive>:**displaytag-1.2:**

      o displaytag-1.2.jar

      o displaytag-export-poi-1.2.jar

      o displaytag-portlet-1.2.jar

   c) Mails

      o javax.mail.jar

      o mail.jar

   d) From <Drive>:**slf4j-1.6.4:**

      o slf4j-api-1.6.4.jar

      o slf4j-simpl-1.6.4.jar

After adding all the JAR files, click [Open]. This adds all the libraries to the project.

Building The Code Spec

Create the following .java class files:

Model Classes

Countries.java

To create this class, right-click the **BookShop** project and select **New → Java Class…** as shown in diagram 62.3.1.

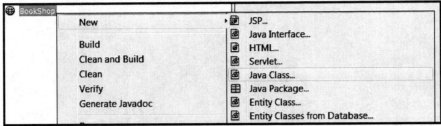

Diagram 62.3.1: Selecting Java Class...

New Java Class dialog box appears, as shown in diagram 62.3.2.

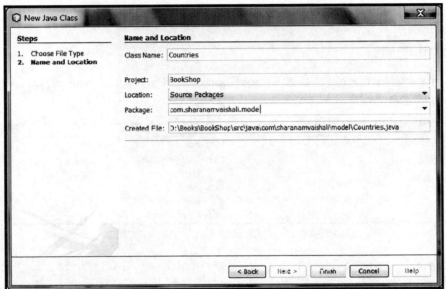

Diagram 62.3.2: New Java Class dialog box

Enter **Countries** as the **Class Name** and **com.sharanamvaishali.model** as the **Package**, as shown in diagram 62.3.2.

Click Finish. Countries.java is created in the NetBeans IDE. Key in the appropriate code.

Similarly create the following model classes:

❑ States.java

❑ Categories.java

❑ Publishers.java

❑ Authors.java

- ❑   Books.java
- ❑   Customers.java
- ❑   SystemUsers.java
- ❑   Transactions.java
- ❑   CartItem.java
- ❑   PopularSearches.java

Data Access Object [DAO] Layer

Interfaces

CountriesDAO.java

To create this interface, right-click the **BookShop** project and select **New → Java Interface…** as shown in diagram 62.4.1.

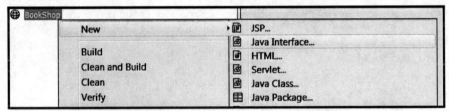

Diagram 62.4.1: Selecting Java Interface…

New Java Interface dialog box appears, as shown in diagram 62.4.2.

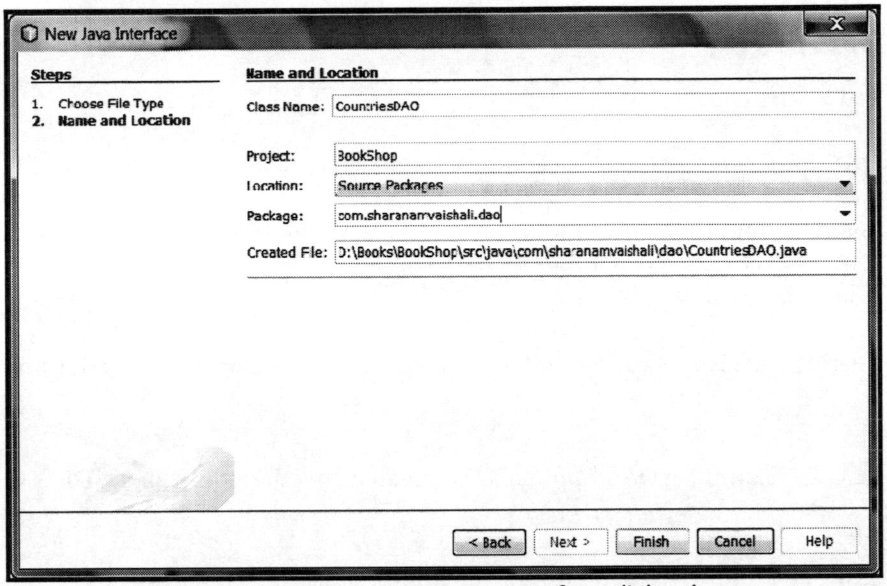

Diagram 62.4.2: New Java Interface dialog box

Enter **CountriesDAO** as the **Class Name** and **com.sharanamvaishali.dao** as the **Package**, as shown in diagram 62.4.2.

Click [Finish]. CountriesDAO.java is created in the NetBeans IDE. Key in the appropriate code.

Similarly create the following DAO interface:

❑ StatesDAO.java

❑ CategoriesDAO.java

❑ PublishersDAO.java

❑ AuthorsDAO.java

❑ BooksDAO.java

❑ CustomersDAO.java

❑ SystemUsersDAO.java

❑ TransactionsDAO.java

❑ LoginDAO.java

❑ PaginationDAO.java

❑ PopularSearchesDAO.java

❑ PopulateDdlbsDAO.java

❑   SearchDAO.java

Implementations

CountriesDAOImpl.java

To create this class, right-click the **BookShop** project and select **New → Java Class...**.

New Java Class dialog box appears.

Enter **CountriesDAOImpl** as the **Class Name** and **com.sharanamvaishali.dao** as the **Package**.

Click ⬛ Finish . CountriesDAOImpl.java is created in the NetBeans IDE. Key in the appropriate code.

Similarly create the following DAO implementation classes:

❑   StatesDAOImpl.java
❑   CategoriesDAOImpl.java
❑   PublishersDAOImpl.java
❑   AuthorsDAOImpl.java
❑   BooksDAOImpl.java
❑   CustomersDAOImpl.java
❑   SystemUsersDAOImpl.java
❑   TransactionsDAOImpl.java
❑   LoginDAOImpl.java
❑   PaginationDAOImpl.java
❑   PopularSearchesDAOImpl.java
❑   PopulateDdlbsDAOImpl.java
❑   SearchDAOImpl.java

Utility Classes

AuthenticationInterceptor.java

To create this class, right-click the **BookShop** project and select **New → Java Class...**.

New Java class dialog box appears.

Enter **AuthenticationInterceptor** as the **Class Name** and **com.sharanamvaishali.utility** as the **Package**.

Click [**Finish**]. AuthenticationInterceptor.java is created in the NetBeans IDE. Key in the appropriate code.

Similarly create the following Utility Classes:
- ❏ GetFileAction.java
- ❏ HibernateUtil.java
- ❏ Page.java
- ❏ PopulateDdlbs.java
- ❏ SendMail.java
- ❏ Struts2Dispatcher.java

Actions

CountriesAction.java

To create this class, right-click the **BookShop** project and select **New → Java Class....**

New Java class dialog box appears.

Enter **CountriesAction** as the **Class Name** and **com.sharanamvaishali.action** as the **Package**.

Click [**Finish**]. CountriesAction.java is created in the NetBeans IDE. Key in the appropriate code.

Similarly create the following Actions:
- ❏ StatesAction.java
- ❏ CategoriesAction.java
- ❏ PublishersAction.java
- ❏ AuthorsAction.java
- ❏ BooksAction.java
- ❏ CustomersAction.java
- ❏ SystemUsersAction.java

- ❏ TransactionsAction.java
- ❏ CartAction.java
- ❏ CustomerLoginAction.java
- ❏ HomePageAction.java
- ❏ PerformTransactionAction.java
- ❏ RegistrationAction.java
- ❏ SearchResultsAction.java
- ❏ ShowAuthorDetailsAction.java
- ❏ ShowBookDetailsAction.java
- ❏ ShowCategoryDetailsAction.java
- ❏ ShowPublisherDetailsAction.java
- ❏ SystemUsersLoginAction.java

Action Validations [XML]

CountriesAction-validation.xml

To create the validation file, right-click the **BookShop** application and select **New** →
Other..., as shown in diagram 62.5.1.

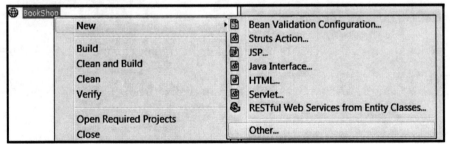

Diagram 62.5.1: Selecting Other...

New File dialog box appears, as shown in diagram 62.5.2.

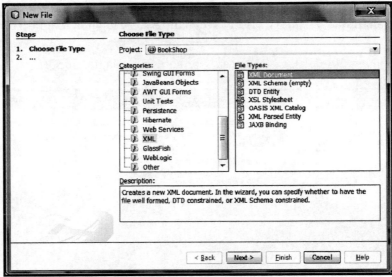

Diagram 62.5.2: New File dialog box

Select **XML** available under the **Categories** list and **XML Document** available under the **File types**, as shown in diagram 62.5.2.

Click [Next >]. **New XML Document** dialog box appears, as shown in diagram 62.5.3.

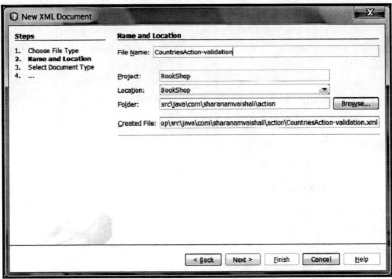

Diagram 62.5.3: New XML Document dialog box

Enter **CountriesAction-validation** as the **File Name** and **src\java\com\sharanamvaishali\action** as the **Folder**, as shown in diagram 62.5.3.

Click Next > . **New File** dialog box appears, as shown in diagram 62.5.4.

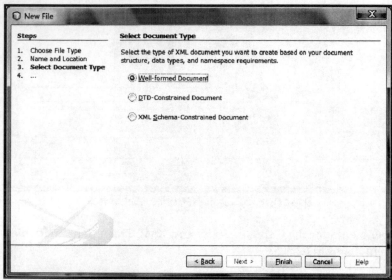

Diagram 62.5.4: New File dialog box

Keep the defaults.

Click Finish . The NetBeans IDE creates CountriesAction-validation.xml. Key in the appropriate code.

Similarly create the following Action Validations:

- StatesAction-validation.xml
- CategoriesAction-validation.xml
- PublishersAction-validation.xml
- AuthorsAction-validation.xml
- BooksAction-validation.xml
- CustomersAction-validation.xml
- SystemUsersAction-validation.xml
- TransactionsAction-validation.xml
- RegistrationAction-validation.xml

❑ SystemUsersLoginAction-validation.xml

Views [JSPs]

login.jsp

To create this JSP, right-click the **BookShop** project and select **New → JSP...**, as shown in diagram 62.6.1.

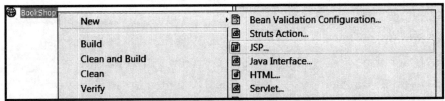

Diagram 62.6.1: Selecting JSP...

New JSP dialog box appears, as shown in diagram 62.6.2.

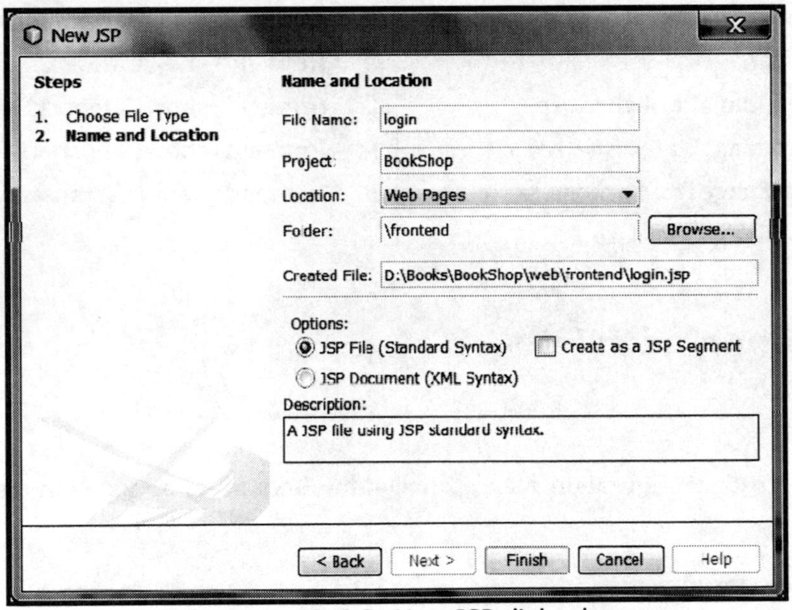

Diagram 62.6.2: New JSP dialog box

Enter **login** as the **File Name** and **\frontend** as the **Folder**, as shown in diagram 62.6.2.

Click [Finish]. login.jsp is created under the folder **\frontend** in the NetBeans IDE. Key in the appropriate code.

Similarly create the following views:

- doublePost.jsp
- error.jsp
- index.jsp
- pagenotfound.jsp
- sessionnotfound.jsp
- \admin\adminFooter.jsp
- \admin\header.jsp
- \admin\adminLogin.jsp
- \admin\manageAuthors.jsp
- \admin\manageBooks.jsp
- \admin\manageCategories.jsp
- \admin\manageCountries.jsp
- \admin\manageCustomers.jsp
- \admin\managePublishers.jsp
- \admin\manageStates.jsp
- \admin\manageTransactions.jsp
- \admin\manageUsers.jsp

- \frontend\registration.jsp
- \frontend\registrationThankYou.jsp
- \frontend\categories.jsp
- \frontend\footer.jsp
- \frontend\forgotPassword.jsp
- \frontend\userHeader.jsp
- \frontend\home.jsp
- \frontend\leftMenu.jsp
- \frontend\popularSearches.jsp
- \frontend\searchResults.jsp
- \frontend\showAuthorDetails.jsp
- \frontend\showBookDetails.jsp
- \frontend\showCart.jsp
- \frontend\showCategoryDetails.jsp
- \frontend\showPublisherDetails.jsp
- \frontend\performTransaction.jsp

Struts Configuration Files

struts.xml

To create the struts configuration file, right-click the **BookShop** application and select **New → Other...**.

New File dialog box appears.

Select **XML** available under the **Categories** list and **XML Document** available under the **File types**.

Click [Next >]. **New XML Document** dialog box appears.

Enter **struts** as the **File Name** and **src\java** as the **Folder**.

Click [Next >]. **New File** dialog box appears.

Keep the defaults.

Click [Finish]. The NetBeans IDE creates struts.xml. Key in the appropriate code.

Similarly create the following struts configurations:
- struts-AdminLogin.xml
- struts-Authors.xml
- struts-Books.xml
- struts-Cart.xml
- struts-Categories.xml
- struts-Countries.xml
- struts-CustomerLogin.xml
- struts-Customers.xml
- struts-HomePage.xml
- struts-Publishers.xml
- struts-Registration.xml
- struts-Search.xml
- struts-States.xml
- struts-SystemUsers.xml
- struts-Transactions.xml

Standard Deployment Descriptor [web.xml]

To create web.xml, right-click the **Bookshop** project and select **New → Other...**, as shown in diagram 62.7.1.

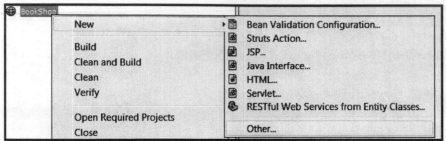

Diagram 62.7.1: Selecting Other...

New File dialog box appears, as shown in diagram 62.7.2.

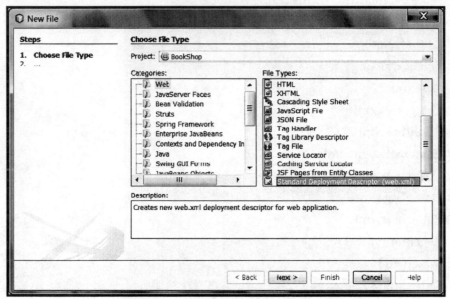

Diagram 62.7.2: New File dialog box

Select **Web** available under the **Categories** list and **Standard Deployment Descriptor (web.xml)** available under the **File Type** list, as shown in diagram 62.7.2.

Click **Next >** . The details of web.xml are shown in the dialog box, as shown in diagram 62.7.3, which is not editable.

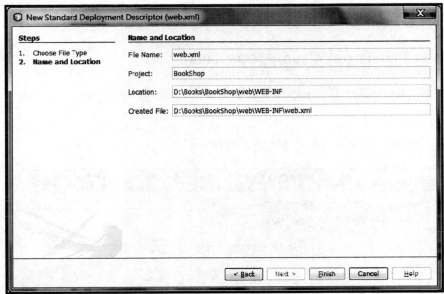

Diagram 55.7.3: New File dialog box

Click **Finish** . web.xml is created under the folder /WEB-INF in the NetBeans IDE. Key in the appropriate code.

Hibernate Configuration File [hibernate.cfg.xml]

To create the configuration file, right-click the **BookShop** application and select **New →
Other...**.

New File dialog box appears.

Select **XML** available under the **Categories** list and **XML Document** available under the **File
types**.

Click **Next >** . **New XML Document** dialog box appears.

Enter **hibernate.cfg** as the **File Name** and **src\java** as the **Folder**.

Click **Next >** . **New File** dialog box appears.

Keep the defaults.

Click [Finish]. The NetBeans IDE creates hibernate.cfg.xml. Key in the appropriate code.

Properties File [bookshop.properties]

To create the properties file, right-click the **BookShop** application and select **New** →
Other....

New File dialog box appears, as shown in diagram 62.8.1.

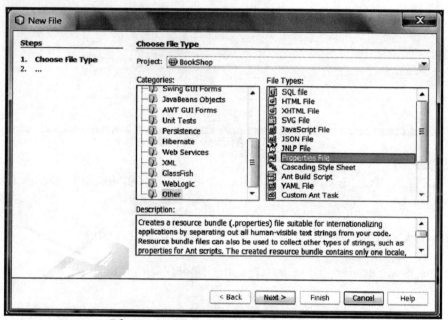

Diagram 62.8.1: New File dialog box

Select **Other** available under the **Categories** list and **Properties File** available under the **File
types,** as shown in diagram 62.8.1.

Click [Next >]. **New Properties File** dialog box appears, as shown in diagram 62.8.2.

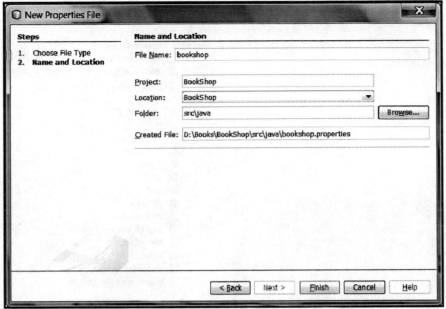

Diagram 62.8.2: New Properties File dialog box

Enter **bookshop** as the **File Name** and **src\java** as the **Folder**, as shown in diagram 62.8.2.

Click [**Finish**]. The NetBeans IDE creates bookshop.properties. Key in the appropriate code.

Similarly create the following properties file:

❑   struts.properties

Images And CSS

After the source packages, views and configuration files are in place, create the following images and CSS.

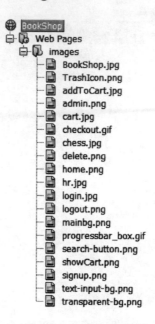

Modifying Configuration Files

After all the project files are in place, before compiling and running the application, modify the following configuration files.

bookshop.properties

This file holds the mail and the Google checkout attributes. Key in the appropriate details indicated by <>.

1 googleMerchantID=<The Google Merchant ID>
2 emailFrom=<Username>@gmail.com
3 emailUser=<Username>
4 emailFromPasswd=<Password>

hibernate.cfg.xml

This file holds the database connection details. Key in the appropriate username and password:

```
1   <?xml version="1.0" encoding="UTF-8"?>
2   <!DOCTYPE hibernate-configuration PUBLIC "-//Hibernate/Hibernate Configuration DTD //EN"
    "http://www.hibernate.org/dtd/hibernate-configuration-3.0.dtd">
3   <hibernate-configuration>
4    <session-factory>
5     <property name="hibernate.dialect">org.hibernate.dialect.MySQLDialect</property>
6     <property name="hibernate.connection.driver_class">com.mysql.jdbc.Driver</property>
7     <property name="hibernate.connection.url">jdbc:mysql://localhost:3306/bms</property>
8     <property name="hibernate.connection.username">root</property>
9     <property name="hibernate.connection.password">Password</property>
10    <property name="hibernate.default_catalog">bms</property>
11    <mapping class="com.sharanamvaishali.model.Countries"/>
12    <mapping class="com.sharanamvaishali.model.States"/>
13    <mapping class="com.sharanamvaishali.model.Authors"/>
14    <mapping class="com.sharanamvaishali.model.Categories"/>
15    <mapping class="com.sharanamvaishali.model.Publishers"/>
16    <mapping class="com.sharanamvaishali.model.SystemUsers"/>
17    <mapping class="com.sharanamvaishali.model.Customers"/>
18    <mapping class="com.sharanamvaishali.model.Books"/>
19    <mapping class="com.sharanamvaishali.model.Transactions"/>
20    <mapping class="com.sharanamvaishali.model.PopularSearches"/>
21   </session-factory>
22  </hibernate-configuration>
```

web.xml

This file holds some additional filters. Hence change the default web.xml [build by the NetBeans IDE] to look like the following:

```
1   <?xml version="1.0" encoding="UTF-8"?>
2   <web-app version="2.5" xmlns="http://java.sun.com/xml/ns/javaee"
    xmlns:xsi="http://www.w3.org/2001/XMLSchema-instance"
    xsi:schemaLocation="http://java.sun.com/xml/ns/javaee
    http://java.sun.com/xml/ns/javaee/web-app_2_5.xsd">
3      <filter>
4         <filter-name>struts2</filter-name>
5         <filter-class>com.sharanamvaishali.utility.Struts2Dispatcher</filter-class>
6      </filter>
7      <filter-mapping>
8         <filter-name>struts2</filter-name>
9         <url-pattern>/*</url-pattern>
10     </filter-mapping>
11     <session-config>
12        <session-timeout>30</session-timeout>
13     </session-config>
```

```
14      <welcome-file-list>
15         <welcome-file>index.jsp</welcome-file>
16      </welcome-file-list>
17      <error-page>
18         <error-code>404</error-code>
19         <location>/pagenotfound.jsp</location>
20      </error-page>
21      <error-page>
22         <exception-type>java.lang.Exception</exception-type>
23         <location>/error.jsp</location>
24      </error-page>
25   </web-app>
```

Loading The BMS Database In MySQL

Creating The MySQL Database

Assuming that the MySQL database is up and running, log into the database using the **MySQL Command Line Client** utility.

Create a database called **bms**.

Switch to that database.

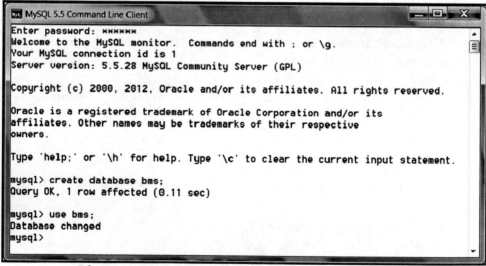

Diagram 62.9.1: MySQL Command Line Client window

Creating Tables With Sample Data

This book's accompanying CDROM [<CDROM Drive>:/Code/BookShop] holds a SQL script with the tables and sample data that can be used to quickly begin using this application.

To do so, copy the SQL script called **bms.sql** to the local hard disk drive and issue the source command, as shown in diagram 62.9.2.

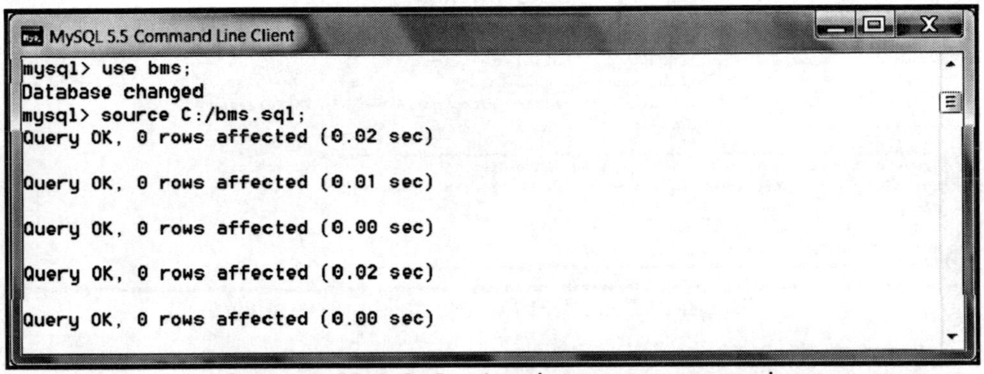

MySQL 5.5 Command Line Client
mysql> use bms;
Database changed
mysql> source C:/bms.sql;
Query OK, 0 rows affected (0.02 sec)
Query OK, 0 rows affected (0.01 sec)
Query OK, 0 rows affected (0.00 sec)
Query OK, 0 rows affected (0.02 sec)
Query OK, 0 rows affected (0.00 sec)

Diagram 62.9.2: Issuing the source command

This will import all the tables along with the sample data.

Building The Project

Now that the files, the database tables and the data is in place, **build** the project **BookShop** using the NetBeans IDE, as shown in diagram 62.10.1.

BookShop
Web P
Source
Librari
Config
New
Build
Clean and Build
Clean
Verify
Generate Javadoc

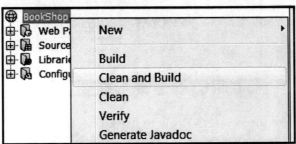

Diagram 62.10.1: Building the project

This compiles all the project files and the builds the WAR file, as shown in diagram 55.11.2.

```
Output - BookShop (clean,dist)

>>  Copying 1 file to D:\Books\NetBeansProject\BookShop\build\web\WEB-INF\lib
>>  Copying 1 file to D:\Books\NetBeansProject\BookShop\build\web\WEB-INF\lib
    Copying 1 file to D:\Books\NetBeansProject\BookShop\build\web\WEB-INF\lib
    Copying 1 file to D:\Books\NetBeansProject\BookShop\build\web\WEB-INF\lib
    Copying 1 file to D:\Books\NetBeansProject\BookShop\build\web\WEB-INF\lib
    Copying 1 file to D:\Books\NetBeansProject\BookShop\build\web\WEB-INF\lib
    Copying 1 file to D:\Books\NetBeansProject\BookShop\build\web\WEB-INF\lib
    Copying 1 file to D:\Books\NetBeansProject\BookShop\build\web\WEB-INF\lib
    Copying 1 file to D:\Books\NetBeansProject\BookShop\build\web\WEB-INF\lib
    library-inclusion-in-manifest:
    Created dir: D:\Books\NetBeansProject\BookShop\build\empty
    Created dir: D:\Books\NetBeansProject\BookShop\build\generated-sources\ap-source-output
    Compiling 66 source files to D:\Books\NetBeansProject\BookShop\build\web\WEB-INF\classes
    Note: Some input files use unchecked or unsafe operations.
    Note: Recompile with -Xlint:unchecked for details.
    Copying 30 files to D:\Books\NetBeansProject\BookShop\build\web\WEB-INF\classes
    compile:
    compile-jsps:
    Created dir: D:\Books\NetBeansProject\BookShop\dist
    Building jar: D:\Books\NetBeansProject\BookShop\dist\BookShop.war
    do-dist:
    dist:
    BUILD SUCCESSFUL (total time: 20 seconds)
```

Diagram 62.10.2: Project build successfully

Running The Project

After a successful build the project is ready to run.

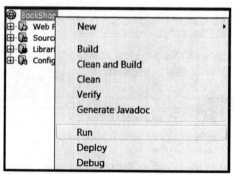

Diagram 62.11.1: Running the project

Clicking **Run** deploys the project's WAR file to the **Glassfish Server 3.1.2** [the one that was chosen when creating the BookShop project using the NetBeans IDE] and brings up the application's homepage in the system's default Web browser.

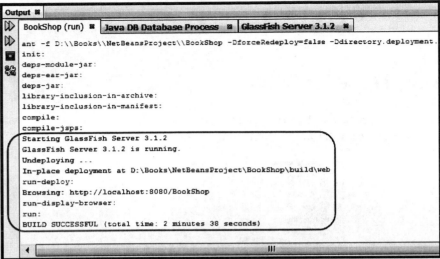

```
Output ⊠
  BookShop (run) ⊠   Java DB Database Process   ⊠   GlassFish Server 3.1.2   ⊠
  ant -f D:\\Books\\NetBeansProject\\BookShop -DforceRedeploy=false -Ddirectory.deployment.
  init:
  deps-module-jar:
  deps-ear-jar:
  deps-jar:
  library-inclusion-in-archive:
  library-inclusion-in-manifest:
  compile:
  compile-jsps:
  Starting GlassFish Server 3.1.2
  GlassFish Server 3.1.2 is running.
  Undeploying ...
  In-place deployment at D:\Books\NetBeansProject\BookShop\build\web
  run-deploy:
  Browsing: http://localhost:8080/BookShop
  run-display-browser:
  run:
  BUILD SUCCESSFUL (total time: 2 minutes 38 seconds)
```

Diagram 62.11.2: Deploying the application and browsing the BookShop index file

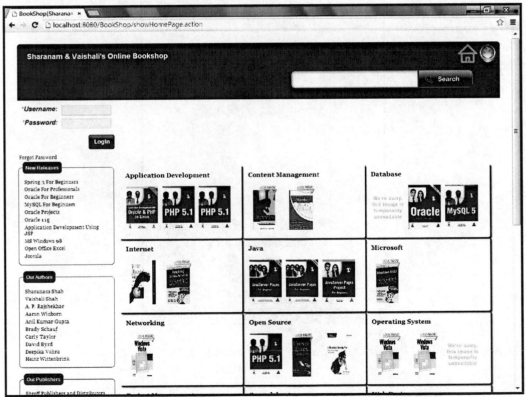

Diagram 62.11.3: The home page of the BookShop project

This chapter only shows how to assemble this application using the NetBeans IDE. This is useful for those who wish to learn the steps involved in creating such an application from scratch.

Switching The Web Server

This project can run on any web server of choice. To switch to a different Web server using NetBeans IDE, choose **BookShop → Properties**, as shown in diagram 62.12.1.

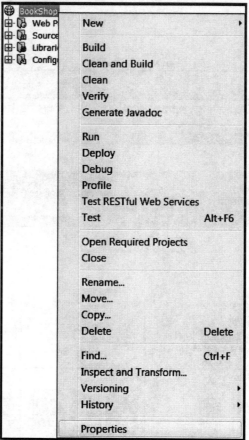

Diagram 62.12.1: Selecting Properties

Properties dialog box appears, as shown in diagram 62.12.2.

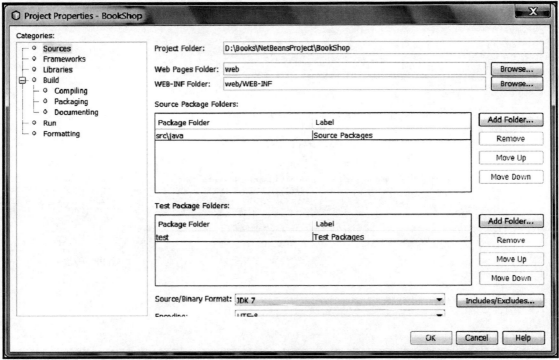

Diagram 62.12.2: Project Properties - BookShop dialog box

Go to **Run** and change the server to the desired one from the drop down list box, as shown in diagram 62.12.3.

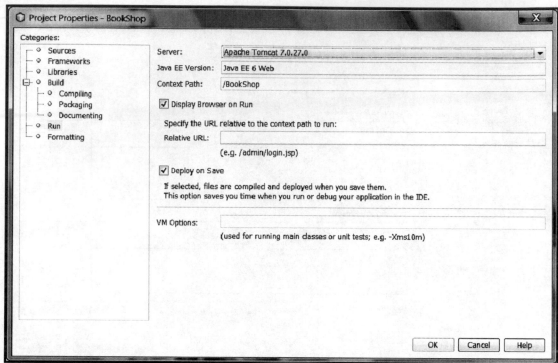

Diagram 62.12.3: Selecting the web server

Click [OK] when done.

Now, simply run the application using **BookShop → Run**. This will use the new web server to deploy and serve the application.

JavaDoc

Every module [.java file] in this project is well commented using JavaDoc complaint comments.

```
/**
 * A getter method for the country object of the Countries class created earlier.
 * @return The Countries object.
 */
```

This enables generating HTML based **Java Documentation** using the NetBeans IDE.

To generate JavaDoc, choose **BookShop → Generate Javadoc**, as shown in diagram 62.13.1.

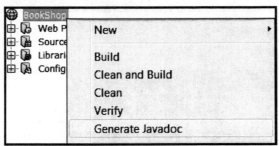

Diagram 62.13.1: Generating JavaDoc

Doing so compiles and generates the help files and serves the index page in the default Web browser as shown in diagram 62.13.2.

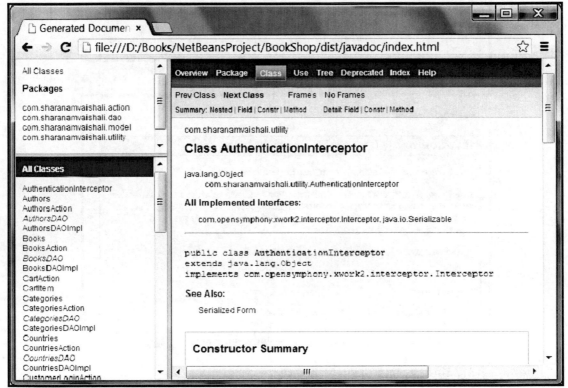

Diagram 62.13.2: The generated JavaDoc served

In this documentation, every method is well explained, as shown in diagram 62.13.3 and diagram 62.13.4.

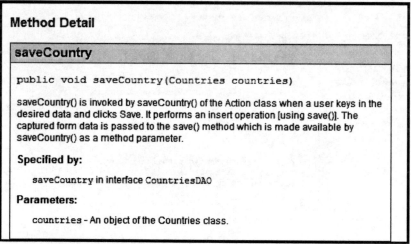

Method Summary

Modifier and Type	Method and Description
void	deleteCountry(int CountryNo) deleteCountry() is invoked by removeCountry() of the Action class when a user clicks X adjacent to the desired record from the data grid in the JSP page.
Countries	getCountryById(int CountryNo) getCountryById() is invoked by editCountry() of the Action class when a user chooses a record from the data grid in the JSP page for editing it.
void	saveCountry(Countries countries) saveCountry() is invoked by saveCountry() of the Action class when a user keys in the desired data and clicks Save.
void	updateCountry(Countries countries) updateCountry() is invoked by saveCountry() of the Action class when a user edits the desired data and clicks Save.

Diagram 62.13.3: Well explained methods [Summary]

Method Detail

saveCountry

```
public void saveCountry(Countries countries)
```

saveCountry() is invoked by saveCountry() of the Action class when a user keys in the desired data and clicks Save. It performs an insert operation [using save()]. The captured form data is passed to the save() method which is made available by saveCountry() as a method parameter.

Specified by:

saveCountry in interface CountriesDAO

Parameters:

countries - An object of the Countries class.

Diagram 62.13.4: Well explained methods [Detail]

In addition to this, information such as the implemented interfaces are depicted, as shown in diagram 62.13.5.

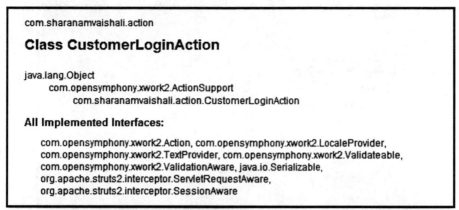

com.sharanamvaishali.action

Class CustomerLoginAction

java.lang.Object
    com.opensymphony.xwork2.ActionSupport
        com.sharanamvaishali.action.CustomerLoginAction

All Implemented Interfaces:

com.opensymphony.xwork2.Action, com.opensymphony.xwork2.LocaleProvider,
com.opensymphony.xwork2.TextProvider, com.opensymphony.xwork2.Validateable,
com.opensymphony.xwork2.ValidationAware, java.io.Serializable,
org.apache.struts2.interceptor.ServletRequestAware,
org.apache.struts2.interceptor.SessionAware

Diagram 62.13.5: Well detailed implemented interfaces

The JavaDoc feature will be very useful to the developers to get access to the explanation online whilst coding and going through this project, as shown in diagram 62.13.6.

```
public String saveCountry
    if(country.getCountryN         Navigate                          ▶
        countriesDAO.updat
    } else {                        Show Javadoc          Alt+F1
        countriesDAO.save(
    }                               Find Usages           Alt+F7
    return SUCCESS;
                                    Call Hierarchy
}
                                    Insert Code           Alt+Insert
```

Diagram 62.13.6: Accessing JavaDoc from within the code spec

The HTML files that Javadoc generates are available in the project's **dist** folder, as shown in diagram 62.13.7.

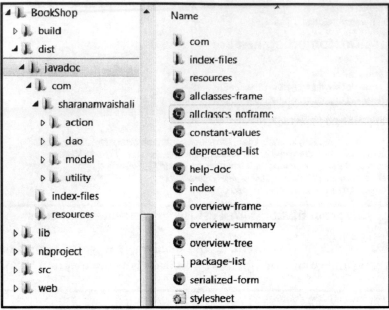

Diagram 62.13.7: JavaDoc in the **dist** folder

Chapter

63

SECTION IX: MIGRATION
Switching The Database [MySQL To Oracle]

Hibernate's portability across the relational databases is simply amazing.

It is literally a configuration change. The only change that is required is the configuration file property values.

All that is required is a Hibernate Dialect and a database connection driver to allow such change.

This portability is very useful especially in companies where deployment take place on a wide range of databases. Usually the development team is not even aware about which database the DBA manager would allocate depending on the license availability, for example, Oracle, Sybase or DB2.

The development team can simply begin and undergo the development phase using an open source database such as MySQL and then deploy the same on another database.

In this book, the project that is developed uses MySQL as the data store.

The client has decided to use Oracle Database 10g as the data store. Since Hibernate is used as the Object Mapping Framework, it's quite simple to switch the project to begin using Oracle Database 10g as the data store.

The following is what will be needed to switch from MySQL to Oracle:
Oracle Database 10g

1. Installing Oracle Database 10g

2. Creating a User / Schema with appropriate privileges

3. Creating an identical table structure

Application

1. Adding Oracle's JDBC driver [ojdbc6.jar] to the project's library files

2. Modifying the Hibernate configuration file [hibernate.cfg.xml] to begin using Oracle Database 11g as the database

That's it. Let's begin.

Installing Oracle Database 10g

The eXpress Edition of the Oracle Database 10g is available on this Book's accompany CDROM.

Simply double click the setup file located <Drive>:/OracleXEUniv.exe to run through the installation wizard.

Creating User / Schema With Appropriate Privileges

Login to the Oracle Database using its web interface, by selecting **Start → All Programs → Oracle Database 10g Express Edition → Go To Database Home Page**.

This brings up the login form, as shown in diagram 63.1.1. Login to Oracle using **System** as the username and the appropriate password [the one that was chosen whilst installing Oracle Database 10g XE].

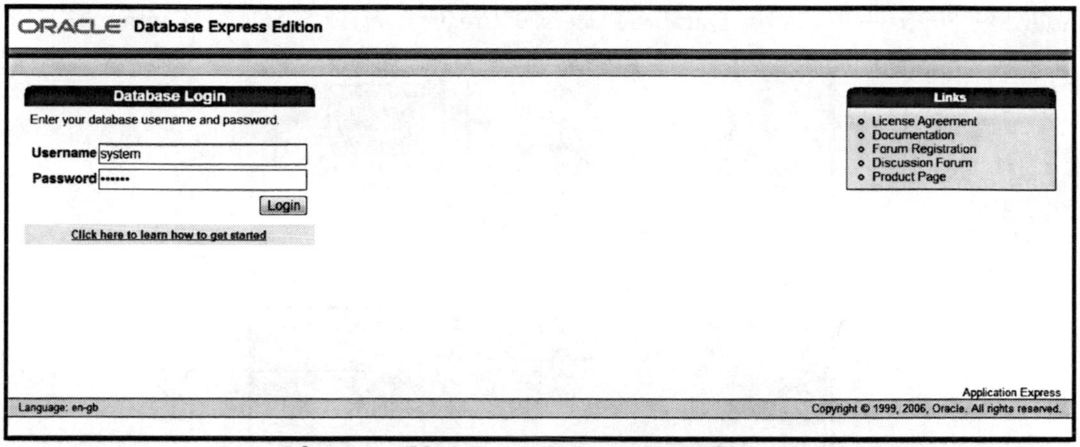

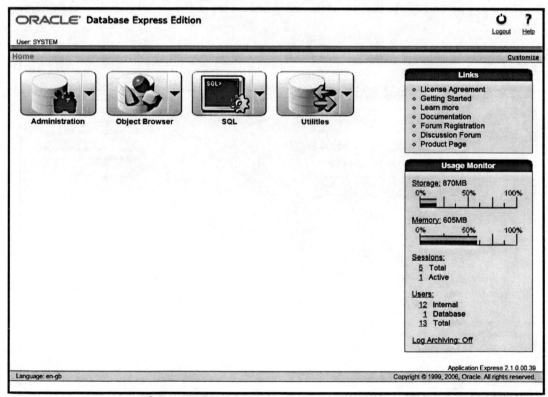

Diagram 63.1.1: Login in as SYSTEM user

Click Login . This displays the homepage of SYSTEM user, as shown in diagram 63.1.2.

Diagram 63.1.2: Homepage of SYSTEM user

Under **Administration** , choose **Database Users** → **Create User**, as shown in diagram 63.1.3.

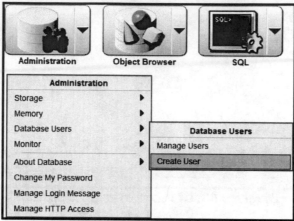

Diagram 63.1.3: Creating user

This displays **Create Database User** data entry form. Key in the details, as shown in diagram 63.1.4.

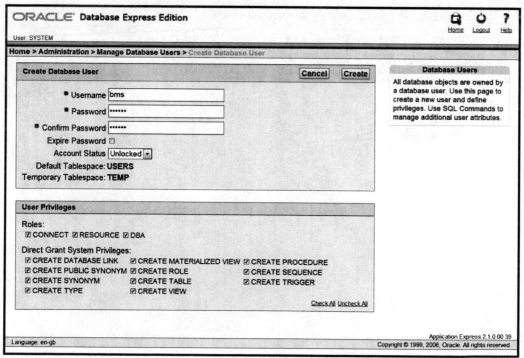

Diagram 64.1.5

The following are the details chosen for this user:

❏ **Username:** bms

❏ **Account Status:** Unlocked

❏ **Roles:** CONNECT, RESOURCE, DBA

❏ **Privileges:** CREATE DATABASE LINK, CREATE MATERIALIZED VIEW, CREATE PROCEDURE, CREATE PUBLIC SYNONYM, CREATE ROLE, CREATE SEQUENCE, CREATE SYNONYM, CREATE TABLE, CREATE TRIGGER, CREATE TYPE, CREATE VIEW

Click **Create** to create this user. This creates the user **bms**. Logout from there and close that window.

Creating Identical Table Structure

The following is the table structure to be created for holding the application data.

Countries

This table stores the country name captured using the Manage Countries d/e form.

Column Name	Data Type	Size	Null	Default	Constraints
CountryNo	Number	10	No	NULL	Primary key
Description	An identity number of the country					
Country	Varchar2	50	No	- -	Unique key
Description	The name of the country					

States

This table stores the state names captured using the Manage States d/e form.

Column Name	Data Type	Size	Null	Default	Constraints
StateNo	Number	10	No	NULL	Primary key
Description	An identity number of the state					
State	Varchar2	50	No	- -	- -
Description	The name of the state					

DefaultValues

This table stores the default image for all the not available images.

Column Name	Data Type	Size	Null	Default	Constraints
Image	LongBlob	- -	Yes	- -	- -
Description	The image displayed in case the author or book image is not uploaded while adding or updating.				

Authors

This table stores the author details captured using the Manage Authors d/e form.

Column Name	Data Type	Size	Null	Default	Constraints
AuthorNo	Number	10	No	- -	Primary Key
Description	An identity number of the author				
FirstName	Varchar2	30	No	- -	- -
Description	The first name of the author				
LastName	Varchar2	30	No	- -	- -
Description	The last name of the author				
Address1	Varchar2	50	Yes	NULL	- -
Description	The street address where the author resides				
Address2	Varchar2	50	Yes	NULL	- -
Description	The street address where the author resides				
StateNo	Number	10	Yes	NULL	States(StateNo)
Description	An identity number of the State				
City	Varchar2	50	Yes	NULL	- -
Description	The name of the City				
Pincode	Varchar2	20	Yes	NULL	- -
Description	The pincode of the city where the author resides				
CountryNo	Number	10	Yes	NULL	Country(CountryNo)
Description	An identity number of the country				
Degree	Varchar2	30	No	- -	- -
Description	The qualifications of the author				
EmailAddress	Varchar2	50	No	- -	Unique key
Description	The email address of the author				

Photograph	LongBlob	- -	Yes	NULL	- -
Description	The photograph of the author				

Speciality	Varchar2	4000	Yes	NULL	- -
Description	The speciality of the author				

DOB	Varchar2	15	Yes	NULL	- -
Description	The date of birth of the author				

Publishers

This table stores the publisher details captured using the Manage Publishers d/e form.

Column Name	Data Type	Size	Null	Default	Constraints
PublisherNo	Number	10	No	- -	Primary Key
Description	An identity number of the publisher				
PublisherName	Varchar2	50	No	- -	Unique key
Description	The name of the publisher				
Address1	Varchar2	50	Yes	NULL	- -
Description	The street address where the publisher resides				
Address2	Varchar2	50	Yes	NULL	- -
Description	The street address where the publisher resides				
CityStateNo	Number	10	Yes	NULL	States(StateNo)
Description	An identity number of the State				
City	Varchar2	50	Yes	NULL	- -
Description	The name of the City				
Pincode	Varchar2	20	Yes	NULL	- -
Description	The pincode of the city where the publisher resides				
CountryNo	Number	10	Yes	NULL	Country(CountryNo)
Description	An identity number of the country				
EmailAddress	Varchar2	50	No	- -	Unique key
Description	The email address of the publisher				

Categories

This table stores the category details captured using the Manage Categories d/e form.

Column Name	Data Type	Size	Null	Default	Constraints
CategoryNo	Number	10	No	- -	Primary key
Description	An identity number of the category				
Category	Varchar2	30	No	- -	Unique key
Description	The name of the category				
Description	Varchar2	4000	No	- -	- -
Description	The description of the category				

Books

This table stores the book details captured using the Manage Books d/e form.

Column Name	Data Type	Size	Null	Default	Constraints
BookNo	Number	10	No	- -	Primary Key
Description	An identity number of the book				
BookName	Varchar2	255	No	- -	- -
Description	The name of the book				
Author1No	Number	10	No	- -	Authors(AuthorNo)
Description	An identity number of the first author				
Author2No	Number	10	Yes	NULL	Authors(AuthorNo)
Description	An identity number of the second author				
Author3No	Number	10	Yes	NULL	Authors(AuthorNo)
Description	An identity number of the third author				
Author4No	Number	10	Yes	NULL	Authors(AuthorNo)
Description	An identity number of the fourth author				
PublisherNo	Number	10	No	- -	Publishers(PublisherNo)
Description	An identity number of the publisher				
CategoryNo	Number	10	No	- -	Categories(CategoryNo)
Description	An identity number of the category				
CoverPage	LongBlob	- -	Yes	NULL	- -
Description	The cover page image of the book				
ISBN	Varchar2	20	No	- -	Unique key
Description	The ISBN of the book				

Column Name	Data Type	Size	Null	Default	Constraints
Edition	Varchar2	20	No	- -	- -
Description	The edition of the book				
Year	Number	4	No	- -	- -
Description	The year when the book was published				
Cost	Number	12	No	- -	- -
Description	The cost of the book				
Synopsis	Varchar2	4000	No	- -	- -
Description	The synopsis of the book				
AboutAuthors	Varchar2	4000	No	- -	- -
Description	The information about the book authors				
TopicsCovered	Varchar2	4000	Yes	NULL	- -
Description	The topics covered in the book				
ContentsCDROM	Varchar2	4000	Yes	NULL	- -
Description	The contents of the CDROM of the book				
TOC	LongBlob	- -	Yes	NULL	- -
Description	The TOC of the book in PDF format				
SampleChapter	LongBlob	- -	Yes	NULL	- -
Description	The sample chapter of the book in PDF format				
Hits	Number	- -	Yes	0 [Zero]	- -
Description	The number of times the book was viewed				

Customers

This table stores the customer details captured while registering.

Column Name	Data Type	Size	Null	Default	Constraints
CustomerNo	Number	10	No	- -	Primary key
Description	An identity number of the customer				
Username	Varchar2	30	No	- -	Unique key
Description	The username of the customer				
Password	Varchar2	30	No	- -	- -
Description	The password of the customer				
EmailAddress	Varchar2	50	No	- -	Unique key
Description	The email address of the customer				
FirstName	Varchar2	30	No	- -	- -
Description	The first name of the customer				

Column Name	Data Type	Size	Null	Default	Constraints
LastName	Varchar2	30	No	- -	- -
Description	The last name of the customer				
Address1	Varchar2	50	Yes	NULL	- -
Description	The street address where the customer resides				
Address2	Varchar2	50	Yes	NULL	- -
Description	The street address where the customer resides				
StateNo	Number	10	Yes	NULL	States(StateNo)
Description	An identity number of the State				
City	Varchar2	50	Yes	NULL	- -
Description	The name of the City				
Pincode	Varchar2	20	Yes	NULL	- -
Description	The pincode of the city where the customer resides				
CountryNo	Number	10	Yes	NULL	Country(CountryNo)
Description	An identity number of the country				
DOB	Varchar2	15	Yes	NULL	- -
Description	The date of birth of the customer				
NewRelease	Varchar2	30	Yes	NULL	- -
Description	A flag to indicate if the customer has subscribed to New Releases				
BookUpdates	Varchar2	30	Yes	NULL	- -
Description	A flag to indicate if the customer has subscribed to Book Updates				
LastLogin	Varchar2	50	Yes	NULL	- -
Description	The last login date of the customer				
LastIP	Varchar2	25	Yes	NULL	- -
Description	The last IP address from where the customer had logged in				

PopularSearches

This table stores the search value of all the searches attempted by the user using the Search d/e form. These values are used to represent tag clouds under popular searches.

Column Name	Data Type	Size	Null	Default	Constraints
SearchNo	Number	10	No	- -	Primary key
Description	An identity number of the search				
Value	Varchar2	100	Yes	NULL	- -
Description	The value of the search				

SystemUsers

This table stores the system user details captured using the Manage Users d/e form.

Column Name	Data Type	Size	Null	Default	Constraints
UserNo	Number	10	No	- -	Primary key
Description	An identity number of the system user				
Username	Varchar2	30	No	- -	Unique key
Description	The username of the system user				
Password	Varchar2	30	No	- -	- -
Description	The password of the system user				
EmailAddress	Varchar2	50	No	- -	Unique key
Description	The email address of the system user				
FirstName	Varchar2	30	No	- -	- -
Description	The first name of the system user				
LastName	Varchar2	30	No	- -	- -
Description	The last name of the system user				
ManageCountries	Varchar2	10	Yes	NULL	- -
Description	A flag to indicate if the system user has permissions to Countries d/e form				
ManageStates	Varchar2	10	Yes	NULL	- -
Description	A flag to indicate if the system user has permissions to States d/e form				
ManageAuthors	Varchar	10	Yes	NULL	- -
Description	A flag to indicate if the system user has permissions to Authors d/e form				

Column Name	Data Type	Size	Null	Default	Constraints
ManagePublishers	Varchar2	10	Yes	NULL	- -
Description	A flag to indicate if the system user has permissions to Publishers d/e form				
ManageCategories	Varchar2	10	Yes	NULL	- -
Description	A flag to indicate if the system user has permissions to Categories d/e form				
ManageUsers	Varchar2	10	Yes	NULL	- -
Description	A flag to indicate if the system user has permissions to System Users d/e form				
ManageBooks	Varchar2	10	Yes	NULL	- -
Description	A flag to indicate if the system user has permissions to Books d/e form				
ManageCustomers	Varchar2	10	Yes	NULL	- -
Description	A flag to indicate if the system user has permissions to Customers d/e form				
ManageTransactions	Varchar2	10	Yes	NULL	- -
Description	A flag to indicate if the system user has permissions to Transactions d/e form				
LastLogin	Varchar2	25	Yes	NULL	- -
Description	The last login date of the system user				

Transactions

This table stores the entries of the transactions [purchases] performed by the users.

Column Name	Data Type	Size	Null	Default	Constraints
TransactionDetailNo	Number	15	No	- -	Primary key
Description	An identity number of the transaction details				
TransactionNo	Number	10	No	- -	- -
Description	An identity number of the transaction				
TransactionDate	Date	- -	No	- -	- -
Description	The date on which transaction is made				
Username	Varchar2	25	No	- -	Customers(Username)
Description	The username of the customer who made any purchases				
BookName	Varchar2	255	No	- -	- -
Description	The name of the book				

Column Name	Data Type	Size	Null	Default	Constraints
Cost	Number	12	No	- -	- -
Description	The cost of the book				
Qty	Number	5	No	- -	- -
Description	The quantity of the book				

Importing Oracle Dump File

To create this structure, use the Oracle dump file provided in this book's CDROM. This file is named as **bmsOracle.dat**.

Locate this file from the CDROM and copy it in a folder of choice.

Invoke the system command prompt located at <Drive>:\oraclexe\app\oracle\product\10.2.0\server\BIN\imp.exe. Import command prompt appears, as shown in diagram 63.2.1:

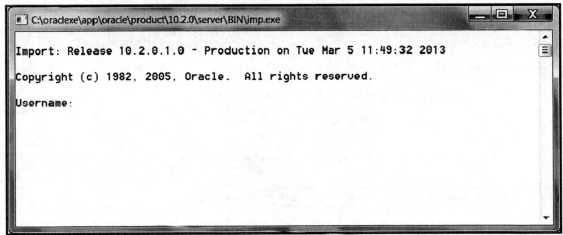

Diagram 63.2.1

Key in the username as **bms** [create earlier] and its associated password, as shown in diagram 63.2.2.

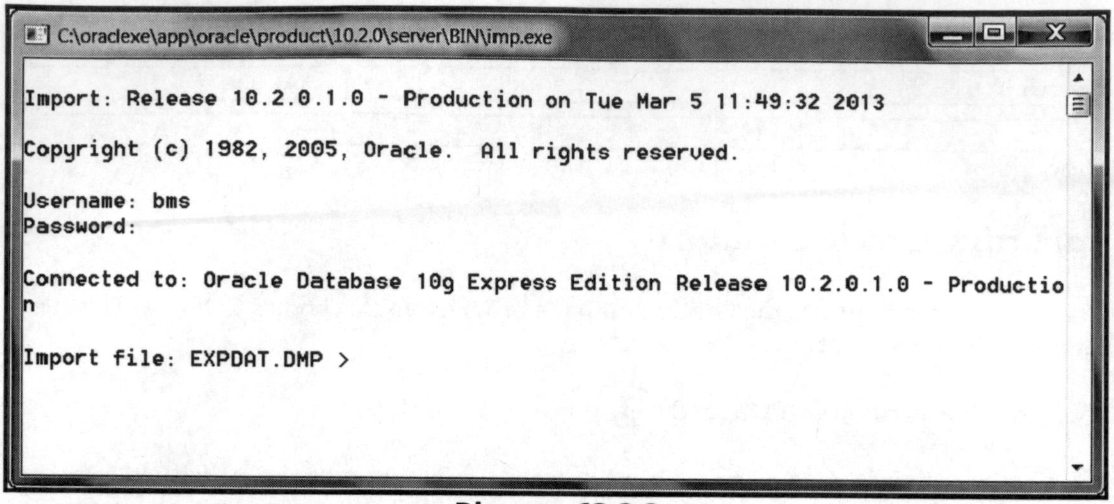

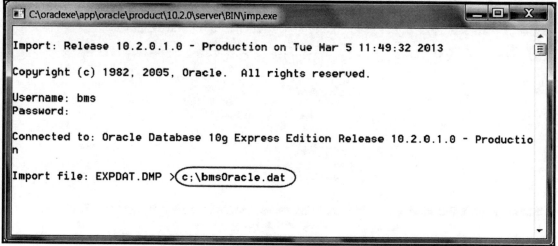

Diagram 63.2.2

Key in the path to the dump file [copied earlier], as shown in diagram 63.2.3.

Diagram 63.2.3

Press **Enter.**

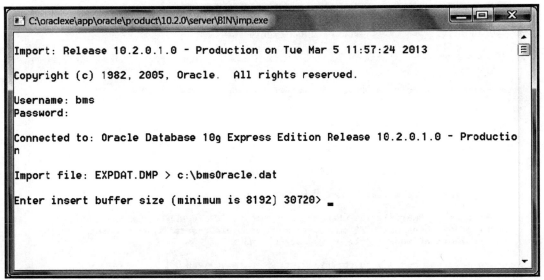

Diagram 63.2.4

Keep the default value and press **Enter**.

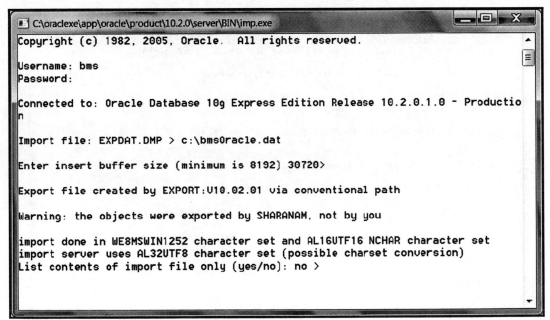

Diagram 63.2.5

Keep the default value and press **Enter**.

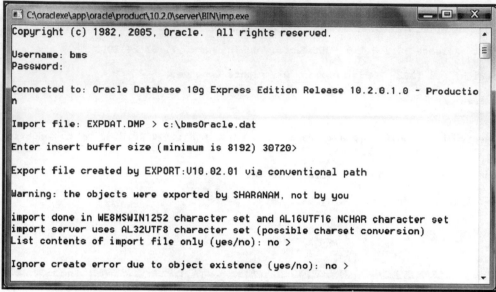

Diagram 63.2.6

Keep the default value and press **Enter**.

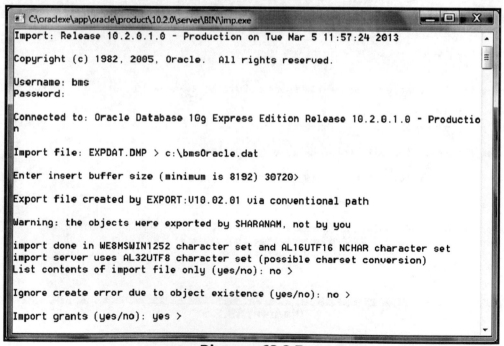

Diagram 63.2.7

Keep the default value and press **Enter**.

```
C:\oraclexe\app\oracle\product\10.2.0\server\BIN\imp.exe

Import: Release 10.2.0.1.0 - Production on Tue Mar 5 11:57:24 2013

Copyright (c) 1982, 2005, Oracle.  All rights reserved.

Username: bms
Password:

Connected to: Oracle Database 10g Express Edition Release 10.2.0.1.0 - Productio
n

Import file: EXPDAT.DMP > c:\bmsOracle.dat

Enter insert buffer size (minimum is 8192) 30720>

Export file created by EXPORT:V10.02.01 via conventional path

Warning: the objects were exported by SHARANAM, not by you

import done in WE8MSWIN1252 character set and AL16UTF16 NCHAR character set
import server uses AL32UTF8 character set (possible charset conversion)
List contents of import file only (yes/no): no >

Ignore create error due to object existence (yes/no): no >

Import grants (yes/no): yes >

Import table data (yes/no): yes >
```

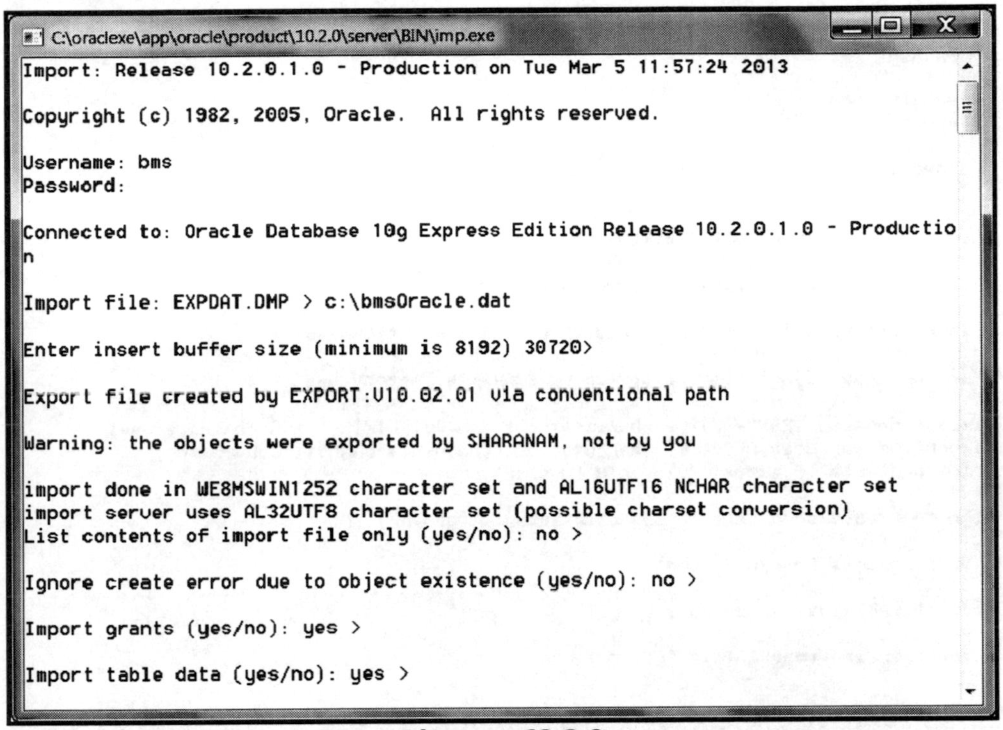

Diagram 63.2.8

Keep the default value and press **Enter**.

```
C:\oracle.exe\app\oracle\product\10.2.0\server\BIN\imp.exe                    [_][□][X]

Import: Release 10.2.0.1.0 - Production on Tue Mar 5 11:57:24 2013

Copyright (c) 1982, 2005, Oracle.  All rights reserved.

Username: bms
Password:

Connected to: Oracle Database 10g Express Edition Release 10.2.0.1.0 - Productio
n

Import file: EXPDAT.DMP > c:\bmsOracle.dat

Enter insert buffer size (minimum is 8192) 30720>

Export file created by EXPORT:V10.02.01 via conventional path

Warning: the objects were exported by SHARANAM, not by you

import done in WE8MSWIN1252 character set and AL16UTF16 NCHAR character set
import server uses AL32UTF8 character set (possible charset conversion)
List contents of import file only (yes/no): no >

Ignore create error due to object existence (yes/no): no >

Import grants (yes/no): yes >

Import table data (yes/no): yes >

Import entire export file (yes/no): no >
```

Diagram 63.2.9

Here, key in yes and press **Enter**.

This begins and completes the import process.

This makes all the tables with some sample data available for development purpose.

Adding Oracle's JDBC driver [ojdbc6.jar]

Now that the database with the appropriate user and tables is available, the project can be configured to begin talking to the Oracle Database.

Java provides a standard interface to connect to databases, which is known as JDBC [Java DataBase Connectivity].

Oracle provides an implementation library of this JDBC interface using which Java programs can connect to a running oracle database instance.

Oracle JDBC driver can be downloaded from:
http://www.oracle.com/technetwork/database/features/jdbc/index-091264.html

Since this application is using Oracle Database 10g and Java EE 6, download the latest version i.e. **ojdbc6.jar**.

Right-click on the **BookShop** application, select **Properties**.

Project Properties - BookShop dialog box appears.

Select **Libraries** available in the **Categories** list.

Click [**Add JAR/Folder**]. This displays **Add JAR/Folder** dialog box that allows choosing the JAR files.

Add **ojdbc6.jar** library file

This library file allows talking to Oracle Database on demand.

Modifying Hibernate's Configuration File [hibernate.cfg.xml]

Open hibernate.cfg.xml and add the following code spec to connect to Oracle Database 10g:

```
1   <?xml version="1.0" encoding="UTF-8"?>
2   <!DOCTYPE hibernate-configuration PUBLIC "-//Hibernate/Hibernate Configuration DTD
    //EN" "http://www.hibernate.org/dtd/hibernate-configuration-3.0.dtd">
3   <hibernate-configuration>
4    <session-factory>                                                    Add this
5   <!-- For Oracle - Schema bms, User bms -->
6      <property name="hibernate.dialect">org.hibernate.dialect.Oracle10gDialect</property>
7      <property
    name="hibernate.connection.driver_class">oracle.jdbc.OracleDriver</property>
8      <property
    name="hibernate.connection.url">jdbc:oracle:thin:@localhost:1521:XE</property>
9      <property name="hibernate.connection.username">bms</property>
10     <property name="hibernate.connection.password">123456</property>
11     <property name="hibernate.default_schema">bms</property>
12
13  <!-- For MySQL - Catalog bms, User root -->
14     <property name="hibernate.dialect">org.hibernate.dialect.MySQLDialect</property>
15     <property name="hibernate.connection.driver_class">com.mysql.jdbc.Driver</property>
16     <property
    name="hibernate.connection.url">jdbc:mysql://localhost:3306/bms</property>
17     <property name="hibernate.connection.username">root</property>     Delete this
18     <property name="hibernate.connection.password">123456</property>
```

```
19    <property name="hibernate.default_catalog">bms</property>
20
21      <mapping class="com.sharanamvaishali.model.Countries"/>
22      <mapping class="com.sharanamvaishali.model.States"/>
23      <mapping class="com.sharanamvaishali.model.Authors"/>
24      <mapping class="com.sharanamvaishali.model.Categories"/>
25      <mapping class="com.sharanamvaishali.model.Publishers"/>
26      <mapping class="com.sharanamvaishali.model.SystemUsers"/>
27      <mapping class="com.sharanamvaishali.model.Customers"/>
28      <mapping class="com.sharanamvaishali.model.Books"/>
29      <mapping class="com.sharanamvaishali.model.Transactions"/>
30      <mapping class="com.sharanamvaishali.model.PopularSearches"/>
31    </session-factory>
32  </hibernate-configuration>
```

Ensure that the username and password property is set to the appropriate username and password created in Oracle Database 10g Web Interface.

Modifying Oracle's System Processes

Since this application makes multiple database connections, the number of processes in Oracle needs to be increased to accommodate this.

Run the following command at the SQL prompt, as shown in diagram 63.3:

ALTER SYSTEM SET PROCESSES=150 SCOPE=SPFILE;

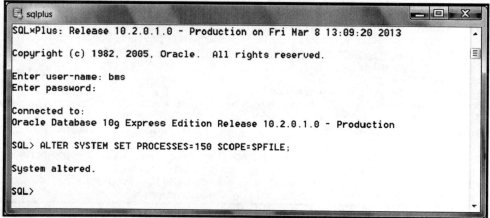

Diagram 63.3

Restart the Oracle Database 10g. That's it. Compile and run the project.

The home page should be served, as shown in diagram 63.4.

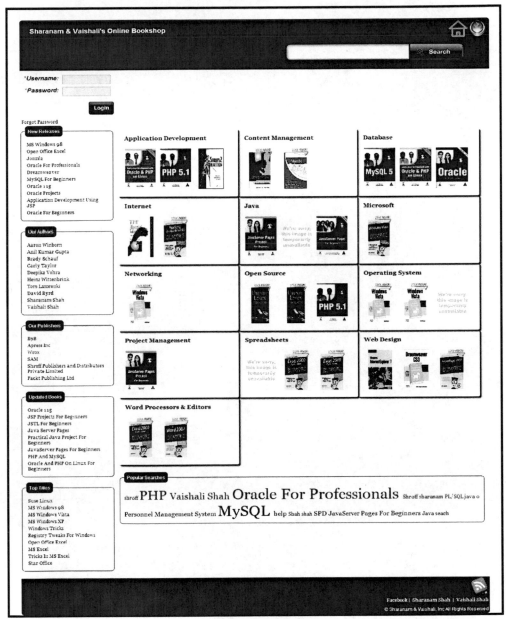

Diagram 63.4

In the very same manner, this hibernate based project can be switched to any other database of choice provided a **Hibernate Dialect** and the **Database Connection Driver** is available.

Appendix

A

SECTION X: APPENDIX
Understanding Google Wallet

Google Wallet is a fast, convenient checkout process that allows:

❑ Customers to buy products from the website with a single login

❑ Seller to process their orders and charge their credit or debit cards for free

In order to use the Google Wallet with the project, it is required to sign-up with Google as a merchant/seller.

Point the web browser to http://sandbox.google.com/checkout/seller/. This displays the homepage, as shown in diagram A.1.

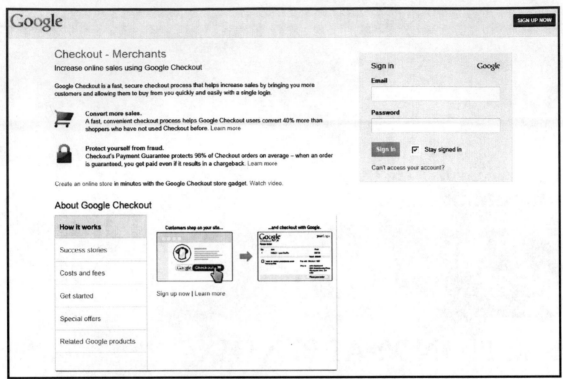

Diagram A.1: Checkout - Merchants

The seller holds the following email account with Google:
s.v.onlinebookshop@gmail.com

If an email account is not available, then create one with Google before proceeding.

Enter the email address and the password in the Sign in section and click **Sign in**. Google prompts for business information, as shown in diagram A.2.

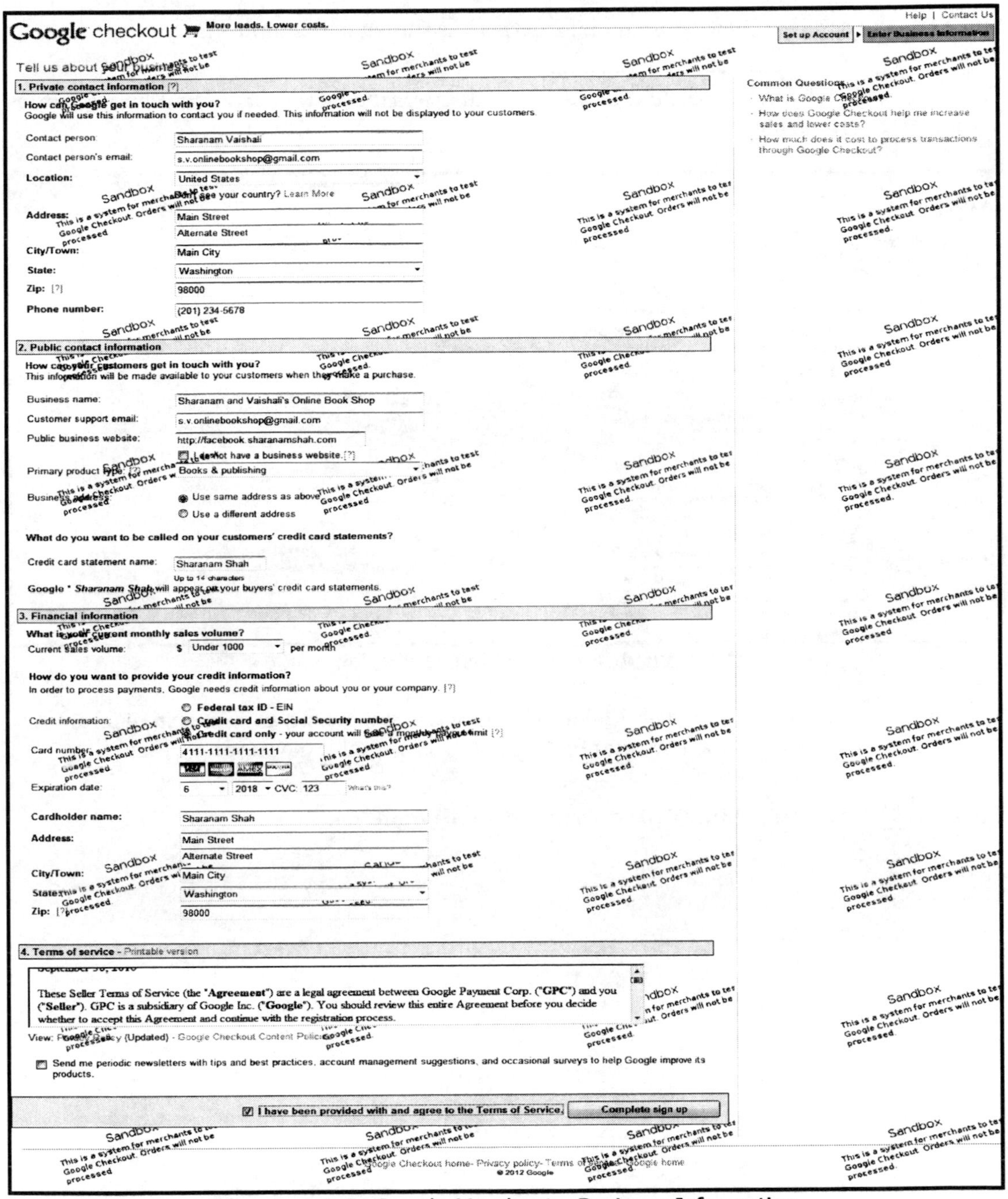

Diagram A.2: Google Merchant - Business Information

Since this is a sandbox, enter dummy information, as shown in diagram A.3.

Once done, click **Complete sign up**. This displays the merchant account homepage, as shown in diagram A.3.

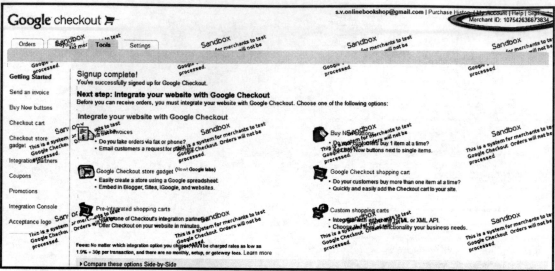

Diagram A.3: Google Merchant - Homepage

This completes the signup process. Make a note of the merchant ID, as shown in diagram A.9. This ID will be required when integrating Google checkout with the shopping cart.

Click **Settings**. This shows a page, as shown in diagram A.4.

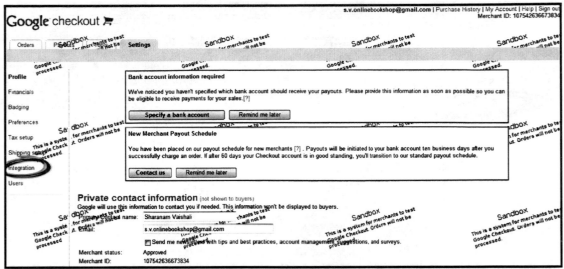

Diagram A.4: Settings

Click **Integration**. This brings up the Integration settings, as shown in diagram A.5.

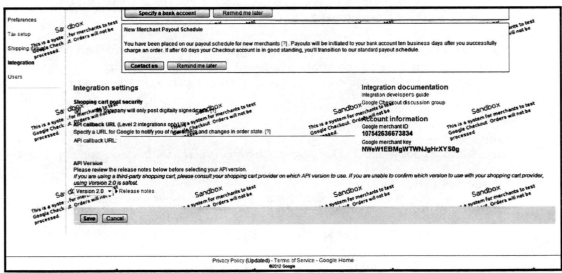

Diagram A.5: Integration settings

Change **Shopping cart post security** to accept unsigned carts by unchecking ☑ **My company will only post digitally signed carts**, as shown in diagram A.6.

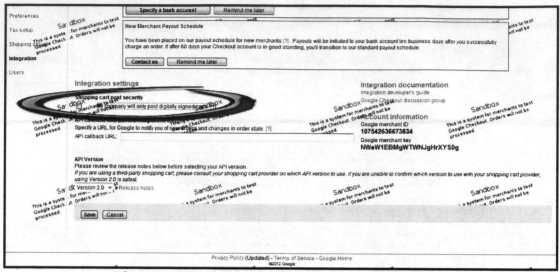

Diagram A.6: Changing the Shopping cart post security

Click .

The next step is to integrate this merchant account with the shopping cart.

In this project, the shopping cart holds the books in the session. This information needs to be collected/extracted from the session variables and sent to the following URL:
https://sandbox.google.com/checkout/cws/v2/Merchant/**<MerchantID>**/checkoutForm

REMINDER

Sandbox URL:
https://sandbox.google.com/checkout/cws/v2/Merchant/**<MerchantID>**/checkoutForm

Production URL:
https://checkout.google.com/api/checkout/v2/checkoutForm/Merchant/**<MerchantID>**

In this project, this is done in performTransactions.jsp, which is invoked when the user clicks

 from the **Show Cart** page, as shown in diagram A.7.

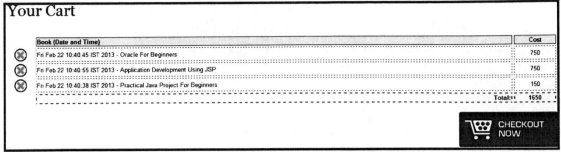

Diagram A.7: Show Cart

Clicking ![CHECKOUT NOW] submits the cart to performTransactions.jsp.

This script extracts the cart data from the session variables and holds it in a <FORM>.

Finally, the form is submitted to Google Wallet's sandbox URL along with the Merchant ID.

The code spec that extracts the cart details from the session and holds it using a set of pre-defined [by Google Wallet] hidden form fields in <FORM> is as follows:

```
<form method="POST"
action="https://sandbox.google.com/checkout/cws/v2/Merchant/<s:text
name='googleMerchantID'/>/checkoutForm" accept-charset="utf-8">
    <s:iterator value="cartItems" status="cartItemsStatus">
```

Explanation:

Traversing through the session variable's attributes.

Code spec:

```
<input type="hidden" name="item_name_<s:property
value="#cartItemsStatus.index" />" value="<s:property value="BookName"
/>">
```

Explanation:

Assigning book name to the Google pre-defined hidden form field named item_name_<No>. Here, for every book name being assigned in the **Iterator**, the hidden form field will be named as:

item_name_**1**

item_name_**2**

item_name_**3**

. . .

Code spec:

```
<input type="hidden" name="item_description_<s:property
value="#cartItemsStatus.index" />" value="<s:property value="BookName"
/>">
```

Explanation:

Assigning book synopsis to the Google pre-defined hidden form field named item_description_<No>. Here, for every book synopsis being assigned in the **Iterator**, the hidden form field will be named as:
item_description_1
item_ description _2
item_ description _3
. . .

Code spec:

```
<input type="hidden" name="item_quantity_<s:property
value="#cartItemsStatus.index" />" value="1">
```

Explanation:

Assigning book quantity to the Google pre-defined hidden form field named item_quantity_<No>. Here, for every book quantity being assigned in the **Iterator**, the hidden form field will be named as:
item_quantity_1
item_ quantity_2
item_ quantity_3
. . .

Since the cart does not support multiple quantities of the same product, 1 is hard coded.

Code spec:

```
<input type="hidden" name="item_price_<s:property
value="#cartItemsStatus.index" />" value="<s:property value="Cost" />">
```

Explanation:

Assigning book cost to the Google pre-defined hidden form field named item_price_<No>. Here, for every book cost being assigned in the **Iterator**, the hidden form field will be named as:
item_ price_1
item_ price_2
item_ price_3
. . .

Code spec:

```
<input type="hidden"
name="checkout-flow-support.merchant-checkout-flow-support.continue-shoppin
g-url" value="http://localhost:8080/BookShop/"/>
  <input type="hidden" name="_charset_"/>
</form>
```

Explanation:

Assigning the homepage URL to which the user can go by clicking Return to Sharanam & Vaishali's Online Bookshop » link on the Google Wallet's thank you page.

This completes the cart integration with Google Wallet.

WARNING

 For demonstration/learning purpose, the cart is integrated with the Google Wallet Sandbox URL.

The sandbox is a Google Wallet environment that allows testing the cart integration without affecting real transactions.

Points to keep in mind:

The sandbox sign-up process is identical to the production environment signup process. However, because the sandbox is a test system, it is not required to enter real credit card numbers, Social Security numbers or other information.

The only thing that is needed is to provide a valid email address, which becomes the username.

Creating an account for the sandbox environment does not create an account for the production environment and vice versa. It is required to sign up for each environment separately.

The sandbox account will have a different Merchant ID and Merchant Key compared to the production account.

The author Sharanam Shah [www.sharanamshah.com] has 9+ years of IT experience and is currently a technical writer for Saba Software Inc. He also consults with several software houses in Mumbai, India, to help them design and manage database application.

Vaishali Shah [www.vaishalishahonline.com], his wife, co-author, a technical writer and a freelance Web developer, has a rich experience of designing, developing and managing database systems. She specializes in the use of Java to design and build web based applications.

Struts 2

with Hibernate 4 Project

for Beginners

Accompanying CD of this Book can be downloaded from
http://www.shroffpublishers.com/support/9781619030053cd.zip